ped
26.6.07

An Introduction
to Language

An Introduction to Language

EIGHTH EDITION

Victoria Fromkin
Late, University of California, Los Angeles

Robert Rodman
North Carolina State University, Raleigh

Nina Hyams
University of California, Los Angeles

THOMSON

WADSWORTH

Australia • Brazil • Canada • Mexico • Singapore • Spain • United Kingdom • United States

An Introduction to Language
Eighth Edition
Victoria Fromkin, Robert Rodman, Nina Hyams

Publisher: *Michael Rosenberg*
Development Editor: *Helen Triller-Yambert*
Technology Project Manager: *Joe Gallagher*
Managing Marketing Manager: *Mandee Eckersley*
Associate Marketing Communications Manager:
  Patrick Rooney
Senior Project Manager, Editorial Production:
  Lianne Ames
Senior Print Buyer: *Mary Beth Hennebury*
Permissions Editor: *Sandra Lord*
Production Service: *Lachina Publishing Services*

Text Designer: *Brian Salisbury*
Cover Designer: *Irene Morris*
Compositor: *Lachina Publishing Services*
Cover Printer: *Phoenix Color Corp.*
Printer: *Maple Vail Book Manufacturing Group/York*
Cover Art: *© 2005 Artists Rights Society (ARS),*
  New York/ADAGP, Paris. Photo: CNAC/MNAM/
  Dist. Réunion des Musées Nationaux/Art
  Resource, NY. Kandinsky, Wassily (1866–1944)
  © ARS, NY

Library of Congress Control Number: 2006923334

ISBN 1-4130-1773-8

Thomson Higher Education
25 Thomson Place
Boston, MA 02210-1202
USA

For more information about our products,
contact us at:
Thomson Learning Academic Resource Center
1-800-423-0563

For permission to use material from this text or
product, submit a request online at
http://www.thomsonrights.com
Any additional questions about permissions can
be submitted by e-mail to
thomsonrights@thomson.com

In memory of Victoria Fromkin and Peter Ladefoged

Contents

PART 2
Grammatical Aspects of Language

PART 3
The Psychology of Language

PART 4
Language and Society

Preface

> Well, this bit which I am writing, called Introduction, is really the er-h'r'm of the book, and I have put it in, partly so as not to take you by surprise, and partly because I can't do without it now. There are some very clever writers who say that it is quite easy not to have an er-h'r'm, but I don't agree with them. I think it is much easier not to have all the rest of the book.
>
> **A. A. MILNE**
>
> The last thing we find in making a book is to know what we must put first.
>
> **BLAISE PASCAL**

The eighth edition of *An Introduction to Language* continues to be dedicated to the memory of our friend, colleague, mentor, and coauthor, Victoria Fromkin. Sadly, Vicki's own mentor and teacher, Peter Ladefoged, passed away this year. Both Vicki and Peter inspired your authors with their dedication to teaching and learning, and we are forever beholden to them.

Vicki loved language, and she loved to tell people about it. She found linguistics fun and fascinating, and she wanted every student and every teacher to think so, too. Though this edition has been completely rewritten for improved clarity and currency, we have nevertheless preserved Vicki's lighthearted, personal approach to a complex topic, including witty quotations from noted authors (A. A. Milne was one of Vicki's favorites). We hope we have kept the spirit of Vicki's love for teaching about language alive in the pages of this book.

The first seven editions of *An Introduction to Language* succeeded, with the help of dedicated teachers, in introducing the nature of human language to tens of thousands of students. This is a book that students enjoy and understand, and that professors find effective and thorough. Not only have majors in linguistics benefited from the book's easy-to-read yet comprehensive presentation, majors in fields as diverse as teaching English as a second language, foreign language studies, general education, psychology, sociology, and anthropology have enjoyed learning about language from this book.

This edition includes new developments in linguistics and related fields that will strengthen its appeal to a wider audience. Much of this information will enable students to gain insight and understanding about linguistic issues and debates appearing in the national media, and will help professors and students stay current with important linguistic research. We hope that it may also dispel certain common misconceptions that people have about language and language use.

Many more exercises (nearly 200 in toto) are now available in this edition for students to test their comprehension of the material in the text. For the first time, exercises are marked as "challenge" questions if they go beyond the scope of what is ordinarily expected in a first course in language study. An answer key is available to instructors to assist them in areas outside of their expertise.

Chapter 1 continues to be a concise introduction to the general study of language. It now includes a new section on "Language and Thought," which takes up the Sapir-Whorf hypothesis, in addition to expanded discussions of signed languages and animal "languages," all of which prove to be of high interest to students and motivate further investigation on their parts.

The second chapter, "Brain and Language," retains its forward placement in the book because we believe that one can learn about the brain through language, and about the nature of the human being through the brain. This chapter may be read and appreciated without technical knowledge of linguistics. When the centrality of language to human nature is appreciated, students will be motivated to learn more about human language, and about linguistics, because they will be learning more about themselves. As in the previous edition, highly detailed illustrations of MRI and PET scans of the brain are included, and this chapter highlights some of the new results and tremendous progress in the study of neurolinguistics over the past few years. The arguments for the autonomy of language in the human brain are carefully crafted so that the student sees how experimental evidence is applied to support scientific theories.

Chapters 3 and 4, on morphology and syntax, have been heavily revised to reflect current thinking on how words and sentences are structured and understood. In particular, the chapter on syntax now reflects the current views on binary branching, heads and complements, selection, and X-bar phrase structure, which we present to the student in clear, careful formulations.

Comparison of languages in these two chapters, and throughout the entire book, is intended to enhance the student's understanding of the differences among languages as well as the universal aspects of grammar. Nevertheless, the introductory spirit of these chapters is not sacrificed, and students gain a deep understanding of word and phrase structure with a minimum of formalisms and a maximum of insightful examples and explanations, supplemented as always by quotes, poetry, and humor.

Chapter 5, on semantics or meaning, has been rewritten and reorganized from the bottom up. Based on the theme of "What do you know about meaning when you know a language," the chapter first introduces students to truth-conditional semantics and the principle of compositionality. Following that are discussions of what happens when compositionality fails, as with idioms, metaphors, and anomalous sentences. Lexical semantics takes up various approaches to word meaning, including the concepts of reference and sense, semantic features, argument structure, and thematic roles. Finally, the chapter concludes with pragmatic considerations, including the distinction between linguistic and situational context in discourse, deixis, maxims of conversation, implicatures, and speech acts, all newly revised for currency and clarity.

Chapter 6, on phonetics, retains its former organization with one significant change: We have moved closer to IPA (International Phonetics Association) notation for English in keeping with current tendencies, but still retain /r/ for readability (versus /ɹ/). We continue to mention alternative notations that students may encounter in other publications.

Chapter 7, on phonology, has also been substantially revised and made far more concise by the removal of redundant material. This has permitted us to add a section on why phonological rules exist while still retaining the more succinct treatment. Material in this chapter continues to be presented with a greater emphasis on insights through linguistic data accompanied by small amounts of well-explicated formalisms, so that the student can appreciate the need for formal theories without experiencing the burdensome details.

The chapters comprising Part 3, "The Psychology of Language," have been both rewritten and restructured for clarity. Chapter 8, "Language Acquisition," is still rich in data from both English and other languages. Bilingualism and L2 acquisition are taken up in detail, and we include in this edition a thoroughly revised section on L2 teaching methods. The arguments for innateness and Universal Grammar that language acquisition provides are exploited to show the student how scientific theories of great import are discovered and supported through observation, experiment, and reason. As in most chapters, American Sign Language (ASL) is discussed, and its important role in understanding the biological foundations of language is emphasized.

In chapter 9, the section on psycholinguistics has been updated to conform to recent discoveries, and the section on computational linguistics reflects advances in machine translation, speech synthesis, speech recognition, and language understanding.

Part 4 is concerned with language in society, including sociolinguistics and historical linguistics. Chapter 10 has been totally revised, reorganized, and rewritten with far more emphasis on social dialects and the work of William Labov than in previous editions. A section on "genderlects"—the difference between men's and women's speech—has been added, as has a section on sociolinguistic analysis. The treatment of pidgins and creoles has been substantially revised over previous treatments to reflect the tremendous gains in understanding that have occurred since the seventh edition was published. Finally, there is now a section on "Language in Use" that takes up slang, profanity, racial epithets, euphemisms, and similar topics.

Attitudes toward language and how they reflect the views and mores of society are also included in this chapter. We establish the scientific basis for discussing such topics as Ebonics (a popular term for dialects of African American English), "accented" English as spoken by non-native speakers such as Hispanic immigrants, and so-called standard languages. Another section on language and sexism reflects a growing concern with this topic.

Chapter 11, on language change, includes a greatly expanded section on syntactic change and the reasons for it. The chapter has also been rewritten to improve clarity. In this chapter as well as in the chapters on morphology and phonology, "how to" sections on language analysis give students the opportunity for hands-on linguistic study. Exercises, many of them new, further increase the student's understanding of how language works.

Chapter 12, on writing systems, features additional discussions on written communication via the Internet, which has a flavor of its own. This chapter should be read by those interested in the teaching of reading, and offers some reasons as to "why Johnny can't read."

Terms that appear bold in the text are defined in the revised glossary at the end of the book. The glossary has been expanded and improved with nearly 50 more entries than in the seventh edition, providing students with a linguistic lexicon of more than 600 terms.

The order of presentation of chapters 3 through 7 was once thought to be nontraditional. Our experience, backed by previous editions of the book and the recommendations of colleagues throughout the world, has convinced us that it is easier for the novice to approach the structural aspects of language by first looking at morphology (the structure of the most familiar linguistic unit, the word). This is followed by syntax (the structure of sentences), which is also familiar to many students, as are numerous semantic concepts. We then proceed to the more novel (to students) phonetics and phonology, which students often find daunting. However, the book is written so that individual instructors can present material in the traditional order of phonetics, phonology, morphology, syntax, and semantics (chapters 6, 7, 3, 4, and 5) without confusion, if they wish.

As in previous editions, the primary concern has been with basic ideas rather than detailed expositions. This book assumes no previous knowledge on the part of the reader. An updated list of references at the end of each chapter is included to accommodate any reader who wishes to pursue a subject in more depth. Each chapter concludes with a summary and exercises to enhance the student's interest in and comprehension of the textual material.

We are deeply grateful to the individuals who have sent us suggestions, corrections, criticisms, cartoons, language data, and exercises, all of which we have tried to incorporate in this new edition. We received invaluable and detailed assistance from the following colleagues:

Adam Albright	MIT	Phonology
Donna Brinton	UCLA	L2 teaching
Daniel Bruhn	N.C. State University	General review
Ivano Caponigro	University of Milan	Semantics
Leonie Cornips	Meertens Institute	Sociolinguistics
Susie Curtiss	UCLA	Brain and language
Kyle Johnson	UMass, Amherst	Syntax
Nathan Klinedinst	UCLA	Syntax and semantics
Peter Ladefoged	UCLA	Phonetics
David Lightfoot	Georgetown University	History
Ian Roberts	Cambridge University	History
Philippe Schlenker	UCLA	Semantics
Carson Schütze	UCLA	Psycholinguistics
Bruce Sherwood	N.C. State University	General review
Neil Smith	University College London	General review
Donca Steriade	MIT	Phonology
Walt Wolfram	N.C. State University	Sociolinguistics

We benefited from email exchanges with Karol Boguszewski from Poland, Rabbi Robert Layman from Philadelphia, and Byungmin Lee from Korea, as well as personal communications with Deborah Grant, who seamlessly mixes yoga with linguistics.

We also are highly indebted to the following colleagues, whose insightful comments and recommendations after reviewing the seventh edition inspired many of the changes found in the eighth edition: Ralph S. Carlson, Azusa Pacific University; Robert Channon, Purdue University; Judy Cheatham, Greensboro College; Julie Damron, Brigham Young University; Rosalia Dutra, University of North Texas; Susan

Fiksdal, The Evergreen State College; Beverly Olson Flanigan and her teaching assistants, Ohio University; Jule Gomez de Garcia, California State University, San Marcos; Loretta Gray, Central Washington University; Helena Halmari, Sam Houston State University; Sharon Hargus, University of Washington; Benjamin H. Hary, Emory University; Tometro Hopkins, Florida International University; Dawn Ellen Jacobs, California Baptist University; Paul Justice, San Diego State University; Simin Karimi, University of Arizona; Robert D. King, University of Texas; Sharon M. Klein, California State University, Northridge; Elisabeth Kuhn, Virginia Commonwealth University; Mary Ann Larsen-Pusey, Fresno Pacific University; Harriet Luria, Hunter College, CUNY; Tracey McHenry, Eastern Washington University; Carol Neidle, Boston University; Anjali Pandey, Salisbury University; Vincent D. Puma, Flagler College; Natalie Schilling-Estes, Georgetown University; Dwan L. Shipley, Washington University; Muffy Siegel, Temple University; Willis Warren, Saint Edwards University; and Donald K. Watkins, University of Kansas.

Please forgive us if we have inadvertently omitted any names.

We continue to be grateful to Hanna and Antonio Damasio of the University of Iowa Medical School for information on their brain studies and the MRI and PET illustrations. We also thank the several authors of the excellent solutions manual available to instructors: Christina Esposito, Nathan Klinedinst, and Ingvar Lofstedt. These up-and-coming young linguists also helped formulate many of the exercises. Finally, we wish to thank the editorial and production team at Wadsworth. They have been superb and supportive in every way: Michael Rosenberg, publisher; Stephen Dalphin, acquisitions editor; Lianne Ames, senior production editor; Helen Triller-Yambert, developmental editor; Karen Judd, managing development editor; Ginjer Clarke, copy editor; Sandra Lord, permissions editor; Ronn Jost, project manager; Joan Shapiro, indexer; and Brian Salisbury, design.

Last but certainly not least, we acknowledge our debt to those we love and who love us and who inspire our work when nothing else will: Nina's son, Michael; Robert's wife, Helen; our parents; and our dearly beloved and still missed colleague, Vicki Fromkin.

The responsibility for errors in fact or judgment is, of course, ours alone. We continue to be indebted to the instructors who have used the earlier editions and to their students, without whom there would be no eighth edition.

Robert Rodman
Nina Hyams

About the Authors

Victoria Fromkin received her bachelor's degree in economics from the University of California, Berkeley, in 1944 and her M.A. and Ph.D. in linguistics from the University of California, Los Angeles, in 1963 and 1965, respectively. She was a member of the faculty of the UCLA Department of Linguistics from 1966 until her death in 2000, and served as its chair from 1972 to 1976. From 1979 to 1989 she served as the UCLA Graduate Dean and Vice Chancellor of Graduate Programs. She was a visiting professor at the Universities of Stockholm, Cambridge, and Oxford. Dr. Fromkin served as president of the Linguistics Society of America in 1985, president of the Association of Graduate Schools in 1988, and chair of the Board of Governors of the Academy of Aphasia. She received the UCLA Distinguished Teaching Award and the Professional Achievement Award, and served as the U.S. Delegate and a member of the Executive Committee of the International Permanent Committee of Linguistics (CIPL). She was an elected Fellow of the American Academy of Arts and Sciences, the American Association for the Advancement of Science, the New York Academy of Science, the American Psychological Society, and the Acoustical Society of America, and in 1996 was elected to membership in the National Academy of Sciences. She published more than one hundred books, monographs, and papers on topics concerned with phonetics, phonology, tone languages, African languages, speech errors, processing models, aphasia, and the brain/mind/language interface—all research areas in which she worked. Professor Fromkin passed away on January 19, 2000, at the age of 76.

Robert Rodman received his bachelor's degree in mathematics from UCLA in 1961, a master's degree in mathematics in 1965, a master's degree in linguistics in 1971, and his Ph.D. in linguistics in 1973. He has been on the faculties of the University of California at Santa Cruz, the University of North Carolina at Chapel Hill, Kyoto Industrial College in Japan, and North Carolina State University, where he is currently professor of computer science. His research areas are forensic linguistics and computer speech processing. Robert resides in Raleigh, North Carolina, with his wife, Helen, Blue the Labrador, and Gracie a rescued greyhound.

Nina Hyams received her bachelor's degree in journalism from Boston University in 1973 and her M.A. and Ph.D. degrees in linguistics from the Graduate Center of the City University of New York in 1981 and 1983, respectively. She joined the UCLA faculty in 1983, where she is currently professor of linguistics and codirector of the

UCLA Psycholinguistics Laboratory and the UCLA Infant Language Laboratory. Her main areas of research are childhood language development and syntax. She is author of the book *Language Acquisition and the Theory of Parameters* (D. Reidel Publishers, 1986), a milestone in language acquisition research. She has also published numerous articles on the development of syntax and morphology in children. She has been a visiting scholar at the University of Utrecht and the University of Leiden in the Netherlands and has given numerous lectures throughout Europe and Japan. Professor Hyams resides in Los Angeles with her son, Michael, and their two dogs, Pete and Max.

The Nature of Human Language

Reflecting on Noam Chomsky's ideas on the innateness of the fundamentals of grammar in the human mind, I saw that any innate features of the language capacity must be a set of biological structures, selected in the course of the evolution of the human brain.

S. E. LURIA, *A Slot Machine, A Broken Test Tube, An Autobiography*

The nervous systems of all animals have a number of basic functions in common, most notably the control of movement and the analysis of sensation. What distinguishes the human brain is the variety of more specialized activities it is capable of learning. The preeminent example is language.

NORMAN GESCHWIND, *1979*

Linguistics shares with other sciences a concern to be objective, systematic, consistent, and explicit in its account of language. Like other sciences, it aims to collect data, test hypotheses, devise models, and construct theories. Its subject matter, however, is unique: at one extreme it overlaps with such "hard" sciences as physics and anatomy; at the other, it involves such traditional "arts" subjects as philosophy and literary criticism. The field of linguistics includes both science and the humanities, and offers a breadth of coverage that, for many aspiring students of the subject, is the primary source of its appeal.

DAVID CRYSTAL, *1987*

What Is Language?

> When we study human language, we are approaching what some might call the "human essence," the distinctive qualities of mind that are, so far as we know, unique to man.
>
> **NOAM CHOMSKY**, Language and Mind

Whatever else people do when they come together—whether they play, fight, make love, or make automobiles—they talk. We live in a world of language. We talk to our friends, our associates, our wives and husbands, our lovers, our teachers, our parents, our rivals, and even our enemies. We talk to bus drivers and total strangers. We talk face-to-face and over the telephone, and everyone responds with more talk. Television and radio further swell this torrent of words. Hardly a moment of our waking lives is free from words, and even in our dreams we talk and are talked to. We also talk when there is no one to answer. Some of us talk aloud in our sleep. We talk to our pets and sometimes to ourselves.

The possession of language, perhaps more than any other attribute, distinguishes humans from other animals. To understand our humanity, one must understand the nature of language that makes us human. According to the philosophy expressed in the myths and religions of many peoples, language is the source of human life and power. To some people of Africa, a newborn child is a *kintu*, a "thing," not yet a *muntu*, a "person." Only by the act of learning language does the child become a human being. According to this tradition, then, we all become "human" because we all know at least one language. But what does it mean to "know" a language?

Linguistic Knowledge

When you know a language, you can speak and be understood by others who know that language. This means you have the capacity to produce sounds that signify certain meanings and to understand or interpret the sounds produced by others. But language is much more than speech. Deaf people produce and understand sign languages just as hearing persons produce and understand spoken languages. The languages of the deaf communities throughout the world are, except for their modality of expression, equivalent to spoken languages.

Most everyone knows at least one language. Five-year-old children are nearly as proficient at speaking and understanding as their parents. Yet the ability to carry out the simplest conversation requires profound knowledge that most speakers are unaware of. This is true for speakers of all languages, from Albanian to Zulu. A speaker of English can produce a sentence having two relative clauses without knowing what a relative clause is, such as

My goddaughter who was born in Sweden and who now lives in Iowa is named Disa, after a Viking queen.

In a parallel fashion, a child can walk without understanding or being able to explain the principles of balance and support, or the neurophysiological control mechanisms that permit one to do so. The fact that we may know something unconsciously is not unique to language.

What, then, do speakers of English or Quechua or French or Mohawk or Arabic know?

Knowledge of the Sound System

"B.C." © 1994 Creators Syndicate, Inc. Reprinted by permission of John L. Hart FLP and Creators Syndicate, Inc.

Part of knowing a language means knowing what sounds (or signs[1]) are in that language and what sounds are not. One way this unconscious knowledge is revealed is by the way speakers of one language pronounce words from another language. If you speak only English, for example, you may substitute an English sound for a non-English sound when pronouncing "foreign" words like French *ménage à trois*. If you pro-

---

[1] The sign languages of the deaf will be discussed throughout the book. A reference to "language" then, unless speech sounds or spoken languages are specifically mentioned, includes both spoken and signed languages.

nounce it as the French do, you are using sounds outside the English sound system.

French people speaking English often pronounce words like *this* and *that* as if they were spelled *zis* and *zat*. The English sound represented by the initial letters *th* in these words is not part of the French sound system, and the French mispronunciation reveals the speaker's unconscious knowledge of this fact.

Knowing the sound system of a language includes more than knowing the inventory of sounds. It includes knowing which sounds may start a word, end a word, and follow each other. The name of a former president of Ghana was *Nkrumah*, pronounced with an initial sound like the sound ending the English word *sink*. While this is an English sound, no word in English begins with the *nk* sound. Speakers of English who have occasion to pronounce this name often mispronounce it (by Ghanaian standards) by inserting a short vowel sound, like *Nekrumah* or *Enkrumah*. Children who learn English recognize that *nk* does not begin a word, just as Ghanaian children learn that words in their language may begin with the *nk* sound.

We will learn more about sounds and sound systems in chapters 6 and 7.

Knowledge of Words

Knowing the sounds and sound patterns in our language constitutes only one part of our linguistic knowledge. Knowing a language means also knowing that certain sequences of sounds signify certain concepts or **meanings**. Speakers of English know what *boy* means, and that it means something different from *toy* or *girl* or *pterodactyl*. When you know a language, you know words in that language, that is, the sound sequences that are related to specific meanings.

ARBITRARY RELATION OF FORM AND MEANING

> The minute I set eyes on an animal I know what it is. I don't have to reflect a moment; the right name comes out instantly. I seem to know just by the shape of the creature and the way it acts what animal it is. When the dodo came along he [Adam] thought it was a wildcat. But I saved him. I just spoke up in a quite natural way and said, "Well, I do declare if there isn't the dodo!"
>
> **MARK TWAIN,** Eve's Diary

If you do not know a language, the words (and sentences) of that language will be mainly incomprehensible, because the relationship between speech sounds and the meanings they represent is, for the most part, an **arbitrary** one. When you are acquiring a language, you have to learn that the sounds represented by the letters *house* signify the concept ; if you know French, this same meaning is represented by *maison*; if you know Twi, it is represented by *ɔdaŋ*; if you know Russian, by *dom*; if you know Spanish, by *casa*. Similarly, is represented by *hand* in English, *main* in French, *nsa* in Twi, *ruka* in Russian, and *mano* in Spanish.

The following are words in some different languages. How many of them can you understand?

    a. kyinii
    b. doakam
    c. odun
    d. asa

    e.   toowq
    f.   bolna
    g.   wartawan
    h.   inaminatu
    i.   yawwa

Speakers of the languages from which these words are taken know that they have the following meanings:

    a.   a large parasol (in Twi, a Ghanaian language)
    b.   living creature (in Tohono O'odham, an American Indian language)
    c.   wood (in Turkish)
    d.   morning (in Japanese)
    e.   is seeing (in Luiseño, a California Indian language)
    f.   to speak (in Hindi-Urdu); aching (in Russian)
    g.   reporter (in Indonesian)
    h.   teacher (in Warao, a Venezuelan Indian language)
    i.   right on! (in Hausa, a Nigerian language)

These examples show that the sounds of words are given meaning only by the language in which they occur, despite what Eve says in Mark Twain's satire *Eve's Diary*. A pterodactyl could have been called *ron, blick*, or *kerplunkity*.

As Juliet says in Shakespeare's *Romeo and Juliet*:

What's in a name? That which we call a rose
By any other name would smell as sweet.

This arbitrary relationship between **form** (sounds) and **meaning** (concept) of a word is also true in sign languages. If you see someone using a sign language you do not know, it is doubtful that you will understand the message from the signs alone. A person who knows Chinese Sign Language (CSL) would find it difficult to understand American Sign Language (ASL), and vice versa, as seen in Figure 1.1.

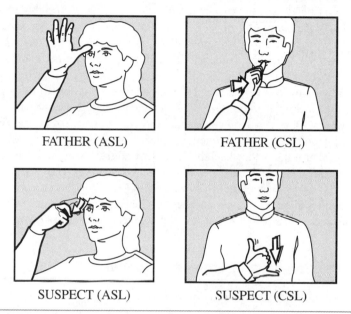

FATHER (ASL)   FATHER (CSL)

SUSPECT (ASL)   SUSPECT (CSL)

Figure 1.1 Arbitrary relation between gestures and meanings of the signs for *father* and *suspect* in ASL and CSL.[2]

Copyright © 1987 by MIT Press. Reproduced by permission of MIT Press.

Many signs were originally like miming, where the relationship between form and meaning was not arbitrary. Bringing the hand to the mouth to mean "eating," as in miming, would be nonarbitrary as a sign. Over time these signs may change, just as the pronunciation of words changes, and the miming effect is lost. These signs become **conventional**, so knowing the shape or movement of the hands does not reveal the meaning of the gestures in sign languages, as also shown in Figure 1.1.

There is some **sound symbolism** in language—that is, words whose pronunciation suggests the meaning. Most languages contain **onomatopoeic** words like *buzz* or *murmur* that imitate the sounds associated with the objects or actions they refer to. But even here, the sounds differ from language to language, reflecting the particular sound system of the language. In English *cock-a-doodle-doo* is an onomatopoeic word whose meaning is the crow of a rooster, whereas in Finnish the rooster's crow is

2 H. Poizner, E. S. Klima, and U. Bellugi. 1987. *What the Hands Reveal about the Brain.* Cambridge, MA: MIT Press.

kukkokiekuu. At the Internet address http://www.georgetown.edu/cball/animals/animals .html, you will find the onomatopoeic words in dozens of languages for the calls of dozens of animals. If you want to know the word for the sound that a turkey makes in Turkey, you can look it up. It's *glu-glu.*

Sometimes particular sound sequences seem to relate to a particular concept. In English many words beginning with *gl* relate to sight, such as *glare, glint, gleam, glitter, glossy, glaze, glance, glimmer, glimpse,* and *glisten.* However, such words are a very small part of any language, and *gl* may have nothing to do with "sight" in another language, or even in other words in English, such as *gladiator, glucose, glory, glutton, globe,* and so on.

English speakers know the *gl* words that relate to sight and those that do not; they know the onomatopoeic words and all the words in the basic vocabulary of the language. No speakers of English know all 472,000 entries in *Webster's Third New International Dictionary.* Even if someone did, that person would not know English. Imagine trying to learn a foreign language by buying a dictionary and memorizing words. No matter how many words you learned, you would not be able to form the simplest phrases or sentences in the language or understand a native speaker. No one speaks in isolated words. Of course, you could search in your traveler's dictionary for individual words to find out how to say something like "car—gas—where?" After many tries, a native speaker might understand this question and then point in the direction of a gas station. If the speaker answered you with a sentence, however, you probably would not understand what was said nor would you be able to look it up, because you would not know where one word ended and another began. Chapter 4 will explore how words are put together to form phrases and sentences, and chapter 5 will explore word and sentence meanings.

The Creativity of Linguistic Knowledge

> *Albert*: So are you saying that you were the best friend of the woman who was married to the man who represented your husband in divorce?
>
> *André*: In the history of speech, that sentence has never been uttered before.
>
> **NEIL SIMON,** The Dinner Party

Knowledge of a language enables you to combine sounds to form words, words to form phrases, and phrases to form sentences. You cannot buy a dictionary of any language with all the sentences of the language. No dictionary can list all the possible sentences, which are infinite. Knowing a language means being able to produce new sentences never spoken before and to understand sentences never heard before. The linguist Noam Chomsky, one of the people most responsible for the modern revolution in language and cognitive science, refers to this ability as part of the **creative aspect** of language use. Not every speaker of a language can create great literature, but you, and all persons who know a language, can and do create new sentences when you speak and understand new sentences created by others.

In pointing out the creative aspect of language, Chomsky made a powerful argument against the behaviorist view of language that prevailed in the first half of the twentieth century, which held that language is a set of learned responses to stimuli. While it is true that if someone steps on our toes we may automatically respond with a scream or a grunt, these sounds are not part of language. They are involuntary reactions to stimuli. After we reflexively cry out, we can then go on to say: "Thank you very much for stepping on my toes, because I was afraid I had elephantiasis and now that I can feel them hurt I know I don't," or any one of an infinite number of sentences, because the particular sentences we produce are not controlled by any stimulus.

Even some involuntary cries like "ouch" are constrained by our own language system, as are the filled pauses that are sprinkled throughout conversational speech, such as *er, uh,* and *you know* in English. They contain only the sounds found in the language. French speakers, for example, often fill their pauses with the vowel sound that starts with their word for egg—*oeuf*—a sound that does not occur in English.

Our creative ability is not only reflected in what we say but also includes our understanding of new or novel sentences. Consider the following sentence: "Daniel Boone decided to become a pioneer because he dreamed of pigeon-toed giraffes and cross-eyed elephants dancing in pink skirts and green berets on the wind-swept plains of the Midwest." You may not believe the sentence; you may question its logic; but you can understand it, although you probably never heard or read it before now.

Knowledge of a language, then, makes it possible to understand and produce new sentences. If you counted the number of sentences in this book that you have seen or heard before, the number would be small. Next time you write an essay or a letter, see how many of your sentences are new. Few sentences are stored in your brain, to be pulled out to fit some situation or matched with some sentence that you hear. Novel sentences never spoken or heard before cannot be stored in your memory.

Simple memorization of all the possible sentences in a language is impossible in principle. If for every sentence in the language a longer sentence can be formed, then there is no limit to the length of any sentence and therefore no limit to the number of sentences. In English you can say:

This is the house.

or

This is the house that Jack built.

or

This is the malt that lay in the house that Jack built.

or

This is the dog that worried the cat that killed the rat that ate the malt that lay in the house that Jack built.

And you need not stop there. How long, then, is the longest sentence? A speaker of English can say:

The old man came.

or

The old, old, old, old, old man came.

How many "olds" are too many? Seven? Twenty-three?

It is true that the longer these sentences become, the less likely we would be to hear or to say them. A sentence with 276 occurrences of "old" would be highly unlikely in either speech or writing, even to describe Methuselah, but such a sentence is theoretically possible. If you know English, you have the knowledge to add any number of adjectives as modifiers to a noun.

All human languages permit their speakers to form indefinitely long sentences; creativity is a universal property of human language.

Knowledge of Sentences and Nonsentences

To memorize and store an infinite set of sentences would require an infinite storage capacity. However, the brain is finite, and even if it were not, we could not store novel sentences. When you learn a language you must learn something finite—your vocabulary is finite (however large it may be)—and that can be stored. If putting one word after another in any order always formed sentences, then language could simply be a set of words. You can see that words are not enough by examining the following strings of words:

1. a. John kissed the little old lady who owned the shaggy dog.
   b. Who owned the shaggy dog John kissed the little old lady.
   c. John is difficult to love.
   d. It is difficult to love John.
   e. John is anxious to go.
   f. It is anxious to go John.
   g. John, who was a student, flunked his exams.
   h. Exams his flunked student a was who John.

If you were asked to put an asterisk or star before the examples that seemed ill formed or ungrammatical or "no good" to you, which ones would you mark? Our intuitive knowledge about what is or is not an allowable sentence in English leads us to star *b, f,* and *h.* Which ones did you star?

Would you agree with the following judgments?

2. a. What he did was climb a tree.
   b. *What he thought was want a sports car.[3]
   c. Drink your beer and go home!
   d. *What are drinking and go home?
   e. I expect them to arrive a week from next Thursday.
   f. *I expect a week from next Thursday to arrive them.
   g. Linus lost his security blanket.
   h. *Lost Linus security blanket his.

If you find the starred sentences unacceptable, as we do, you see that every string of words does not constitute a well-formed sentence in a language. Our knowledge of a language determines which strings of words are well-formed sentences and which are not. Therefore, in addition to knowing the words of the language, linguistic knowledge includes **rules** for forming sentences and making the kinds of judgments you made about the examples in (1) and (2). These rules must be finite in length and finite in number so that they can be stored in our finite brains. Yet, they must permit us to form and understand an infinite set of new sentences. They are not rules determined by a judge or a legislature, or even rules taught in a grammar class. They are unconscious rules that we acquire as young children as we develop language.

A language, then, consists of all the sounds, words, and infinitely many possible sentences. When you know a language, you know the sounds, the words, and the rules for their combination.

---

[3] The asterisk is used before examples that speakers find ungrammatical. This notation will be used throughout the book.

Linguistic Knowledge and Performance

"What's one and one and one and one and one and one and one and one and one and one?" "I don't know," said Alice. "I lost count." "She can't do Addition," the Red Queen interrupted.

LEWIS CARROLL, Through the Looking-Glass

Our linguistic knowledge permits us to form longer and longer sentences by joining sentences and phrases together or adding modifiers to a noun. Whether we stop at three, five, or eighteen adjectives, it is impossible to limit the number we could add if desired. Very long sentences are theoretically possible, but they are highly improbable. Evidently, there is a difference between having the knowledge necessary to produce sentences of a language and applying this knowledge. It is a difference between what we know, which is our **linguistic competence**, and how we use this knowledge in actual speech production and comprehension, which is our **linguistic performance**.

"The Born Loser" © Newspaper Enterprise Association, Inc.

Speakers of all languages have the knowledge to understand or produce sentences of any length. Here is an example from the ruling of a federal judge:

We invalidate the challenged lifetime ban because we hold as a matter of federal constitutional law that a state initiative measure cannot impose a severe limitation on the people's fundamental rights when the issue of whether to impose such a limitation on these rights is put to the voters in a measure that is ambiguous on its face and that fails to mention in its text, the proponent's ballot argument, or the state's official description, the severe limitation to be imposed."

However, physiological and psychological reasons limit the number of adjectives, adverbs, clauses, and so on. Speakers may run out of breath, lose track of what they have said, or die of old age before they are finished. Listeners my become confused, tired, bored, or disgusted.

When we speak, we usually wish to convey some message. At some stage in the act of producing speech, we must organize our thoughts into strings of words. Sometimes the message is garbled. We may stammer, or pause, or produce **slips of the tongue**. We may even sound like Tarzan in the cartoon, who illustrates the difference between linguistic knowledge and the way we use that knowledge in performance.

For the most part, linguistic knowledge is not conscious knowledge. The linguistic system—the sounds, structures, meanings, words, and rules for putting them all together—is acquired with no conscious awareness. Just as we may not be conscious of the principles that allow us to stand or walk, we are unaware of the rules of language. Our ability to speak and understand, and to make judgments about the grammaticality of sentences, reveals our knowledge of the rules of our language. This knowledge represents a complex cognitive system. The nature of this system is what this book is all about.

What Is Grammar?

> We use the term "grammar" with a systematic ambiguity. On the one hand, the term refers to the explicit theory constructed by the linguist and proposed as a description of the speaker's competence. On the other hand, it refers to this competence itself.
>
> **N. CHOMSKY AND M. HALLE,** The Sound Pattern of English

Descriptive Grammars

> There are no primitive languages. The great and abstract ideas of Christianity can be discussed even by the wretched Greenlanders.
>
> **JOHANN PETER SUESSMILCH,** 1756, in a paper delivered before the Prussian Academy

The way we are using the word *grammar* differs from most common usages. In our sense, the grammar includes the knowledge speakers have about the units and rules of their language—rules for combining sounds into words (called **phonology**), rules of word formation (called **morphology**), rules for combining words into phrases and phrases into sentences (called **syntax**), as well as the rules for assigning meaning (called **semantics**). The grammar, together with a mental dictionary that lists the words of the language, represents our linguistic competence. To understand the nature of language, we must understand the nature of grammar.

Every human being who speaks a language knows its grammar. When linguists wish to describe a language, they attempt to describe the rules (the grammar) of the language that exists in the minds of its speakers. Some differences will exist among speakers, but there must be shared knowledge too. The shared knowledge—the common parts of the grammar—makes it possible to communicate through language. To the extent that the linguist's description is a true model of the speakers' linguistic capacity, it is a successful description of the grammar and of the language. Such a model is called a **descriptive grammar**. It does not tell you how you should speak; it describes your basic linguistic knowledge. It explains how it is possible for you to speak and understand and make judgments about well-formedness, and it tells what you know about the sounds, words, phrases, and sentences of your language.

Linguists use the word *grammar* in two ways: the first refers to the **mental grammar** speakers have in their brains; the second to the model or description of this internalized grammar studied by linguists. Almost two thousand years ago the Greek grammarian Dionysius Thrax defined grammar as that which permits us either to speak a language or to speak about a language. From now on we will not differentiate these two meanings, because the linguist's descriptive grammar is an attempt at a formal statement (or theory) of the speaker's grammar.

When we say in later chapters that a sentence is **grammatical**, we mean that it conforms to the rules of the mental grammar (as described by the linguist); when we say that it is **ungrammatical**, we mean it deviates from the rules in some way. If, however, we posit a rule for English that does not agree with your intuitions as a speaker, then the grammar we are describing differs in some way from the mental grammar that represents your linguistic competence; that is, your language is not the one described. No language or variety of a language (called a **dialect**) is superior to any other in a linguistic sense. Every grammar is equally complex, logical, and capable of producing an infinite set of sentences to express any thought. If something can be expressed in one language or one dialect, it can be expressed in any other language or dialect. It might involve different means and different words, but it can be expressed. We will have more to say about dialects in chapter 10. This is true as well for languages of technologically underdeveloped cultures. The grammars of these languages are not primitive or ill formed in any way. They have all the richness and complexity of the grammars of languages spoken in technologically advanced cultures.

Prescriptive Grammars

It is certainly the business of a grammarian to find out, and not to make, the laws of a language.

JOHN FELL, Essay towards an English Grammar, *1784*

Any fool can make a rule
And every fool will mind it

HENRY DAVID THOREAU

The view that grammars are all equal is not shared by all grammarians now or in the past. From ancient times until the present, "purists" have believed that some versions of a language are better than others, that there are certain "correct" forms that all educated people should use in speaking and writing, and that language change is corruption. The Greek Alexandrians in the first century, the Arabic scholars at Basra in the eighth century, and numerous English grammarians of the eighteenth and nineteenth centuries held this view. They wished to *prescribe* rather than *describe* the rules of grammar, which gave rise to the writing of **prescriptive grammars**.

In the Renaissance a new middle class emerged who wanted their children to speak the dialect of the "upper" classes. This desire led to the publication of many prescriptive grammars. In 1762 Bishop Robert Lowth wrote *A Short Introduction to English Grammar with Critical Notes*. Lowth prescribed new rules for English, many of them influenced by his personal taste. Before the publication of his grammar, practically everyone—upper-class, middle-class, and lower-class—said *I don't have none, You was wrong about that*, and *Mathilda is fatter than me*. Lowth, however, decided that "two negatives make a positive" and therefore one should say *I don't have any*; that even when *you* is singular it should be followed by the plural *were*; and that *I* not *me, he* not *him, they* not *them*, and so forth should follow *than* in comparative constructions. Many of these prescriptive rules were based on Latin grammar, which had already given way to different rules in the languages that developed from Latin such as Italian and French. Because Lowth was influential and because the rising new class wanted to speak "properly," many of these new rules were legislated into English grammar, at least for the **prestige dialect**—that variety of the language spoken by people in positions of power.

The view that dialects that regularly use double negatives are inferior cannot be justified if one looks at the standard dialects of other languages in the world. Romance languages, for example, use double negatives, as the following examples from French and Italian show:

French:	Je	ne	veux	parler	avec	personne.
	I	not	want	to speak	with	no-one.

Italian:	Non	voglio	parlare	con	nessuno.
	not	I-want	to speak	with	no-one.

English translation: "I don't want to speak with anyone."

Prescriptive grammars such as Lowth's are different from the descriptive grammars we have been discussing. Their goal is not to describe the rules people know, but to tell them what rules they should follow. The great British Prime Minister Winston Churchill had this to say about the "rule" against ending a sentence with a preposition: "It is a rule up with which we should not put."

In 1908 the grammarian Thomas R. Lounsbury wrote: "There seems to have been in every period in the past, as there is now, a distinct apprehension in the minds of very many worthy persons that the English tongue is always in the condition approaching collapse and that arduous efforts must be put forth persistently to save it from destruction."

Today our bookstores are filled with books by language "purists" attempting to do just that. Edwin Newman, for example, in his books *Strictly Speaking* and *A Civil Tongue*, rails against those who use the word *hopefully* to mean "I hope," as in "Hopefully, it will not rain tomorrow," instead of using it "properly" to mean "with hope." What Newman fails to recognize is that language changes in the course of time and words change meaning. The meaning of *hopefully* has been broadened for most English speakers to include both usages. Other "saviors" of the English language blame television, the schools, and even the National Council of Teachers of English for failing to preserve the standard language, and they severely criticize anyone who suggests that African American English (AAE)[4] and other dialects are viable, complete languages.

In truth, human languages are without exception fully expressive, complete, and logical, as much so as they were two hundred or two thousand years ago. Hopefully, this book will convince you that all languages and dialects are rule governed, whether spoken by rich or poor, powerful or weak, learned or illiterate. Grammars and usages of particular groups in society may be dominant for social and political reasons, but from a linguistic (scientific) point of view, they are neither superior nor inferior to the grammars and usages of less prestigious segments of society.

Having said all this, it is undeniable that the **standard** dialect (defined in chapter 10) may be a better dialect for someone wishing to obtain a particular job or achieve a position of social prestige. In a society where "linguistic profiling" is used to discriminate against speakers of a minority dialect, it may behoove those speakers to learn

---

[4] AAE is also called African American Vernacular English (AAVE), Ebonics, and Black English (BE). It is spoken by some but by no means all African Americans. It is discussed in chapter 10.

the prestige dialect rather than wait for social change. But linguistically, prestige and standard dialects do not have superior grammars.

Finally, all of the preceding remarks apply to *spoken* language. Writing (see chapter 12) is not acquired naturally through simple exposure to others speaking the language (see chapter 8), but must be taught. Writing follows certain prescriptive rules of grammar, usage, and style that the spoken language does not, and is subject to little if any dialectal variation.

Teaching Grammars

I don't want to talk grammar. I want to talk like a lady.

G. B. SHAW, Pygmalion

"B.C." © 1986 Creators Syndicate, Inc. Reprinted by permission of John L. Hart FLP and Creators Syndicate, Inc.

The descriptive grammar of a language attempts to describe the rules internalized by a speaker of that language. It is different from a **teaching grammar**, which is used to learn another language or dialect. Teaching grammars are used in school to fulfill language requirements. They can be helpful to people who do not speak the standard or prestige dialect, but find it would be advantageous socially and economically to do so. Teaching grammars state explicitly the rules of the language, list the words and their pronunciations, and aid in learning a new language or dialect.

It is often difficult for adults to learn a second language without formal instruction, even when they have lived for an extended period in a country where the language is spoken. (Second language acquisition is discussed in more detail in chapter 8.) Teaching grammars assume that the student already knows one language and compares the grammar of the target language with the grammar of the native language. The meaning of a word is given by providing a **gloss**—the parallel word in the student's native language, such as *maison*, "house" in French. It is assumed that the student knows the meaning of the gloss "house," and so the meaning of the word *maison*.

Sounds of the target language that do not occur in the native language are often described by reference to known sounds. Thus the student might be aided in producing the French sound *u* in the word *tu* by instructions such as "Round your lips while producing the vowel sound in *tea*."

The rules on how to put words together to form grammatical sentences also refer to the learner's knowledge of his native language. For example, the teaching grammar *Learn Zulu* by Sibusiso Nyembezi states that "The difference between singular and plural is not at the end of the word but at the beginning of it," and warns that "Zulu does not have the indefinite and definite articles 'a' and 'the.'" Such statements assume that students know the rules of their own grammar, in this case English. Although such grammars might be considered prescriptive in the sense that they attempt to teach the student what is or is not a grammatical construction in the new language, their aim is different from grammars that attempt to change the rules or usage of a language that is already known by the speaker.

This book is not primarily concerned with either prescriptive or teaching grammars, which, however, are considered in chapter 10 in the discussion of standard and nonstandard dialects.

Language Universals

> In a grammar there are parts that pertain to all languages; these components form what is called the general grammar. In addition to these general (universal) parts, there are those that belong only to one particular language; and these constitute the particular grammars of each language.
>
> Du Marsais, c. 1750

There are rules of particular languages, such as English, Swahili, and Zulu, that form part of the individual grammars of these languages, and then there are rules that hold in all languages. Those rules representing the universal properties of all languages constitute a **Universal Grammar**. The linguist attempts to uncover the "laws" of particular languages and also the laws that pertain to all languages. The universal laws are of particular interest because they give us a window into the workings of the human mind in this cognitive domain.

About 1630, the German philosopher Alsted first used the term *general grammar* as distinct from *special grammar*. He believed that the function of a general grammar was to reveal those features "which relate to the method and etiology of grammatical concepts. They are common to all languages." Pointing out that "general grammar is the pattern 'norma' of every particular grammar whatsoever," he implored "eminent linguists to employ their insight in this matter." Three and a half centuries before Alsted, the scholar Robert Kilwardby held that linguists should be concerned with discovering the nature of language in general. So concerned was Kilwardby with Universal Grammar that he excluded considerations of the characteristics of particular languages, which he believed to be as "irrelevant to a science of grammar as the material of the measuring rod or the physical characteristics of objects were to geometry." Kilwardby was perhaps too much of a universalist. The particular properties of individual languages are relevant to the discovery of language universals, and they are of interest for their own sake.

People attempting to study Latin, Greek, French, or Swahili as a second language are so focused on learning those aspects of the second language that are different from their native language that they may be skeptical of the assertions that there are universal laws of language. Yet the more we investigate this question, the more evidence accumulates to support Chomsky's view that there is a Universal Grammar (UG) that is part of the human biologically endowed language faculty. We can think of UG as a system of rules and principles that characterize all grammars. The rules of

UG provide the basic blueprint that all languages follow. It specifies the different components of the grammar and their relations, how the different rules of these components are constructed, how they interact, and so on. It is a major aim of **linguistic theory** to discover the nature of UG. The linguist's goal is to reveal the "laws of human language" just as the physicist's goal is to reveal the "laws of the physical universe." The complexity of language—a product of the human brain—undoubtedly means this goal will never be fully achieved. All scientific theories are incomplete, and new hypotheses must be proposed to account for new data. Theories are continually changing as new discoveries are made. Just as physics was enlarged by Einstein's theories of relativity, so grows the linguistic theory of UG as discoveries shed new light on the nature of human language. The comparative study of many different languages is of central importance to this enterprise.

The Development of Grammar

> How comes it that human beings, whose contacts with the world are brief and personal and limited, are nevertheless able to know as much as they do know.
>
> BERTRAND RUSSELL

Linguistic theory is concerned not only with describing the knowledge that an adult speaker has of his or her language, but also with explaining how that knowledge is acquired. All normal children acquire (at least one) language in a relatively short period with apparent ease. They do this even though parents and other caregivers do not provide them with any specific language instruction. It is often remarked that children seem to "pick up" a language just from hearing it spoken around them. Children are language-learning virtuosos—whether a child is male or female, from a rich family or a disadvantaged one, whether she grows up on a farm or in the city, attends day care or is home all day—none of these factors fundamentally affect the way language develops. A child can acquire any language he is exposed to—English, Dutch, French, Swahili, Japanese—with comparable ease, and even though each of these languages has its own peculiar characteristics, children learn them all in very much the same way. For example, all children start out by using one word at a time. They then combine words into simple sentences. When they first begin to combine words into sentences, certain parts of the sentence may be missing. For example, the English-speaking two-year-old might say *Cathy build house* instead of *Cathy is building the house*. On the other side of the world, a Swahili-speaking child will say *mbuzi kula majani*, which translates as "goat eat grass," and which also lacks many required elements. They pass through other linguistic stages on their way to adultlike competence, and by about age five, children speak a language that is almost indistinguishable from the language of the adults around them.

In just a few short years, without the benefit of explicit guidance and regardless of personal circumstances, the young child—who may be unable to tie her shoes or do even the simplest arithmetic computation—masters the complex grammatical structures of her language and acquires a substantial **lexicon**. Just how children accomplish this remarkable cognitive achievement is a topic of intense interest to linguists. The child's success, as well as the uniformity of the acquisition process, point to a substantial innate component to language development. Chomsky, following the lead of the early rationalist philosophers, proposed that human beings are born with an innate blueprint for language, what we referred to earlier as Universal Grammar. Children are able to acquire language as quickly and effortlessly as they do because they do not have to figure out all the rules of their language, only those that are specific to their particular language. The universal properties—the laws of language—are part of their biological endowment. Linguistic theory aims to uncover those principles that characterize all human languages and to reveal the innate component of language that makes language acquisition possible. In chapter 8 we will discuss language acquisition in more detail.

Sign Languages: Evidence for the Innateness of Language

> It is not the want of organs that [prevents animals from making] . . . known their thoughts . . . for it is evident that magpies and parrots are able to utter words just like ourselves, and yet they cannot speak as we do, that is, so as to give evidence that they think of what they say. On the other hand, men who, being born deaf and mute . . . are destitute of the organs which serve the others for talking, are in the habit of themselves inventing certain signs by which they make themselves understood.
>
> RENÉ DESCARTES, Discourse on Method

The sign languages of deaf communities provide some of the best evidence to support the notion that humans are born with the ability to acquire language, and that these languages are governed by the same universal properties.

Because deaf children are unable to hear speech, they do not acquire spoken languages as hearing children do. However, deaf children who are exposed to sign language learn it in stages parallel to those of hearing children learning spoken languages. Sign languages are human languages that do not use sounds to express meanings. Instead, sign languages are visual-gestural systems that use hand, body, and facial gestures as the forms used to represent words. Sign languages are fully developed languages, and signers can create and comprehend unlimited numbers of new sentences, just as speakers of spoken languages do.

Current research on sign languages has been crucial in the attempt to understand the biological underpinnings of human language acquisition and use. Some understanding of sign languages is therefore essential.

About one in a thousand babies is born deaf or with a severe hearing deficiency. One major effect is the difficulty that deaf children have in learning a spoken language. It is nearly impossible for those who are unable to hear language to learn to speak naturally. Normal speech depends largely on auditory feedback. A deaf child will not learn to speak without extensive training in special schools or programs designed especially for deaf people.

Although deaf people can be taught to speak a language intelligibly, they can never understand speech as well as a hearing person. Seventy-five percent of spoken English words cannot be read on the lips accurately. The ability of many deaf individuals to comprehend spoken language is therefore remarkable; they combine lip reading with knowledge of the structure of language, the meaning redundancies that language has, and context.

If, however, human language is universal in the sense that all humans have the ability to learn a language, then it is not surprising that nonspoken languages have developed among nonhearing individuals. The more we learn about the human linguistic ability, the more it is clear that language acquisition and use are not dependent on the ability to produce and hear sounds, but on a much more abstract cognitive ability, biologically determined, that accounts for the similarities between spoken and sign languages.

AMERICAN SIGN LANGUAGE

The major language of the deaf community in the United States is **American Sign Language (ASL)**. ASL is an outgrowth of the sign language used in France and brought to the United States in 1817 by the great educator Thomas Hopkins Gallaudet.

Like all languages, ASL has its own grammar with a system of gestures, equivalent to the sound system of spoken languages, as well as morphological, syntactic, and semantic rules and a mental lexicon of signs.

In the United States, educators have created several signing systems in an attempt to represent spoken and/or written English. These artificial languages consist essentially in the replacement of each spoken English word (and grammatical elements such as the -*s* ending for plurals and the -*ed* ending for past tense) by a sign. The syntax and semantics of these manual codes for English are thus approximately the same as those of spoken English. The result is unnatural in that it is similar to trying to speak French by translating every English word or ending into its French counterpart. Problems result because there are not always corresponding forms in the two languages.

Signers sometimes need to represent a word or concept for which no sign exists. New coinages, foreign words, acronyms, certain proper nouns, technical vocabulary, or obsolete words as might be found in a signed interpretation of a play by Shakespeare are among some of these. For such cases ASL provides a series of hand shapes and movements that represent the letters of the English alphabet, permitting all such words and concepts to be expressed through finger spelling.

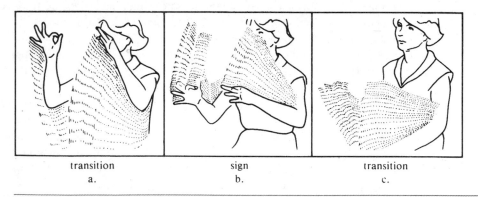

transition   sign   transition
a.   b.   c.

FIGURE 1.2 The ASL sign DECIDE: (a) and (c) show transitions from the sign; (b) illustrates the single downward movement of the sign. Reprinted from *The Signs of Language* by Edward Klima and Ursula Bellugi: Cambridge, Mass.: Harvard University Press.

Reprinted by permission of the publisher from *The Signs of Language* by Edward Klima and Ursula Bellugi, p. 62, copyright © 1979 by the President and Fellows of Harvard College.

Signs, however, are produced differently than finger-spelled words. As Klima and Bellugi observe, "The sign DECIDE cannot be analyzed as a sequence of distinct, separable configurations of the hand. Like all other lexical signs in ASL, but unlike the individual finger-spelled letters in D-E-C-I-D-E taken separately, the ASL sign DECIDE does have an essential movement but the hand shape occurs simultaneously with the movement. In appearance, the sign is a continuous whole."[5] This sign is shown in Figure 1.2.

Signers communicate ideas at a rate comparable to spoken communication. Moreover, language arts are not lost to the deaf community. Poetry is composed in sign language, and stage plays such as Sheridan's *The Critic* have been translated into sign language and acted by the National Theatre of the Deaf (NTD).

Deaf children acquire sign language much in the way that hearing children acquire a spoken language, going through the same linguistic stages, including the babbling stage. Deaf children babble on their hands, just as hearing children babble with their vocal tract. Deaf children often sign themselves to sleep just as hearing children talk themselves to sleep. Deaf children report that they dream in sign language as French-speaking children dream in French and Hopi children dream in Hopi. Deaf children sign to their dolls and stuffed animals. Slips of the hand occur similar to slips of the tongue; finger fumblers amuse signers as tongue twisters amuse speakers. Sign languages resemble spoken languages in all major aspects, showing that there truly are universals of language despite differences in the modality in which the language is performed. This universality is predictable because regardless of the modality in which it is expressed, language is a biologically based ability.

Animal "Languages"

> A dog cannot relate his autobiography; however eloquently he may bark, he cannot tell you that his parents were honest though poor.
>
> **BERTRAND RUSSELL**

Is language the exclusive property of the human species? The idea of talking animals is as old and as widespread among human societies as language itself. All cultures have legends in which some animal plays a speaking role. All over West Africa, children listen to folktales in which a "spider-man" is the hero. "Coyote" is a favorite figure in many Native American tales, and many an animal takes the stage in Aesop's famous fables. The fictional Doctor Doolittle's forte was communicating with all manner of animals, from giant snails to tiny sparrows.

If language is viewed only as a system of communication, then many species communicate. Humans also use systems other than language to relate to each other and to send and receive "messages," like so-called body language. The question is whether the communication systems used by other species are at all like human linguistic knowledge, which is acquired by children with no explicit instruction, and which is used creatively rather than in response to internal or external stimuli.

---

[5] Klima and Bellugi, *The Signs of Language,* pp. 38 and 62.

"Talking" Parrots

"Bizarro" © by Dan Piraro. Reprinted with permission of King Features Syndicate. All rights reserved.

Most humans who acquire language use speech sounds to express meanings, but such sounds are not a necessary aspect of language, as evidenced by the sign languages. The use of speech sounds is therefore not a basic part of what we have been calling language. The chirping of birds, the squeaking of dolphins, and the dancing of bees may potentially represent systems similar to human languages. If animal communication systems are not like human language, it will not be because of a lack of speech.

Conversely, when animals vocally imitate human utterances, it does not mean they possess language. Language is a system that relates sounds or gestures to meanings. Talking birds such as parrots and mynah birds are capable of faithfully reproducing words and phrases of human language that they have heard, but their utterances carry no meaning. They are speaking neither English nor their own language when they sound like us.

Talking birds do not dissect the sounds of their imitations into discrete units. *Polly* and *Molly* do not rhyme for a parrot. They are as different as *hello* and *goodbye*. One property of all human languages (which will be discussed further in chapter 6) is the discreteness of the speech or gestural units, which are ordered and reordered, combined and split apart. Generally, a parrot says what it is taught, or what it hears, and no more. If Polly learns "Polly wants a cracker" and "Polly wants a doughnut" and also learns to imitate the single words *whiskey* and *bagel*, she will not spontaneously produce, as children do, "Polly wants whiskey" or "Polly wants a bagel" or

"Polly wants whiskey and a bagel." If she learns *cat* and *cats*, and *dog* and *dogs*, and then learns the word *parrot*, she will be unable to form the plural *parrots* as children do by the age of three; nor can a parrot form an unlimited set of utterances from a finite set of units, nor understand utterances it has never heard before. Reports of an African grey parrot named Alex suggest that new methods of training animals may result in more learning than was previously believed possible. When the trainer uses words in context, Alex seems to relate some sounds with their meanings. This is more than simple imitation, but it is not how children acquire the complexities of the grammar of any language. It is more like a dog learning to associate certain sounds with meanings, such as *heel, sit, fetch*, and so on. A recent study in Germany reports on a nine-year-old border collie named Rico who has acquired a 200-word vocabulary (containing both German and English words). Rico did not require intensive training but was able to learn many of these words quite quickly.

However impressive these feats, the ability of a parrot to produce sounds similar to those used in human language, even if meanings are related to these sounds, and Rico's ability to understand sequences of sounds that correspond to specific objects, cannot be equated with the child's ability to acquire the complex grammar of a human language.

The Birds and the Bees

The birds and animals are all friendly to each other, and there are no disputes about anything. They all talk, and they all talk to me, but it must be a foreign language for I cannot make out a word they say.

MARK TWAIN, Eve's Diary

"Rose Is Rose" © United Feature Syndicate, Inc. Reprinted by permission.

Most animals possess some kind of "signaling" communication system. Among certain species of spiders there is a complex system for courtship. The male spider, before he approaches his ladylove, goes through an elaborate series of gestures to inform her that he is a spider and a suitable mate, and not a crumb or a fly to be eaten. These gestures are invariant. One never finds a creative spider changing or adding to the courtship ritual of his species.

A similar kind of gestural language is found among fiddler crabs. There are forty species, and each uses its own claw-waving movement to signal to another member of its "clan." The timing, movement, and posture of the body never change from one time to another or from one crab to another within the particular variety. Whatever the signal means, it is fixed. Only one meaning can be conveyed.

The imitative sounds of talking birds have little in common with human language, but the calls and songs of many species of birds do have a communicative function, and they resemble human languages in that there may be "dialects" within the same species. **Birdcalls** (consisting of one or more short notes) convey messages associated with the immediate environment, such as danger, feeding, nesting, flocking, and so on. **Bird songs** (more complex patterns of notes) are used to stake out territory and to attract mates. There is no evidence of any internal structure to these songs, nor can they be segmented into independently meaningful parts as words of human language can be. In a study of the territorial song of the European robin, it was discovered that the rival robins paid attention only to the alternation between high-pitched and low-pitched notes, and which came first did not matter. The message varies only to the extent of how strongly the robin feels about his possession and to what extent he is prepared to defend it and start a family in that territory. The different alternations therefore express intensity and nothing more. The robin is creative in his ability to sing the same thing in many ways, but not creative in his ability to use the same units of the system to express many different messages with different meanings.

Despite certain superficial similarities to human language, birdcalls and songs are fundamentally different kinds of communicative systems. The kinds of messages that can be conveyed are limited, and messages are stimulus controlled.

This distinction is also true of the system of communication used by honeybees. A forager bee is able to return to the hive and communicate to other bees where a source of food is located. It does so by performing a dance on a wall of the hive that reveals the location and quality of the food source. For one species of Italian honeybee, the dancing behavior may assume one of three possible patterns: *round* (which indicates locations near the hive, within 20 feet or so); *sickle* (which indicates locations at 20 to 60 feet from the hive); and *tail-wagging* (for distances that exceed 60 feet). The number of repetitions per minute of the basic pattern in the tail-wagging dance indicates the precise distance: the slower the repetition rate, the longer the distance.

The bees' dance is an effective system of communication for bees. It is capable, in principle, of infinitely many different messages, like human language; but unlike human language, the system is confined to a single subject—food source. An experimenter who forced a bee to walk to the food source showed the inflexibility. When the bee returned to the hive, it indicated a distance twenty-five times farther away than the food source actually was. The bee had no way of communicating the special circumstances in its message. This absence of creativity makes the bees' dance qualitatively different from human language.

In the seventeenth century, the philosopher and mathematician René Descartes pointed out that the communication systems of animals are qualitatively different from the language used by humans:

> It is a very remarkable fact that there are none so depraved and stupid, without even excepting idiots, that they cannot arrange different words together, forming of them a statement by which they make known their thoughts; while, on the other hand, there is no other animal, however perfect and fortunately circumstanced it may be, which can do the same.

Descartes goes on to state that one of the major differences between humans and animals is that human use of language is not just a response to external, or even internal, stimuli, as are the sounds and gestures of animals. He warns against confusing human use of language with "natural movements which betray passions and may be . . . manifested by animals."

To hold that animals communicate by systems qualitatively different from human language systems is not to claim human superiority. Humans are not inferior to the one-celled amoeba because they cannot reproduce by splitting in two; they are just different sexually. They are not inferior to hunting dogs, whose sense of smell is far better than that of human animals. As we will discuss in the next chapter, the human language ability is rooted in the human brain, just as the communication systems of other species are determined by their biological structure. All the studies of animal communication systems, including those of chimpanzees (discussed in chapter 8), provide evidence for Descartes's distinction between other animal communication systems and the linguistic creative ability possessed by the human animal.

Language and Thought

> It was intended that when Newspeak had been adopted once and for all and Oldspeak forgotten, a heretical thought—that is, a thought diverging from the principles of IngSoc—should be literally unthinkable, at least so far as thought is dependent on words.
>
> **GEORGE ORWELL,** *appendix to* 1984

Many people are fascinated by the question of how language relates to thought. It is natural to imagine that something as powerful and fundamental to human nature as language would influence how we think about or perceive the world around us. This is clearly reflected in the appendix of George Orwell's masterpiece *1984*, quoted above. Over the years, many claims have been made regarding the relationship between language and thought. The claim that the structure of a language influences how its speakers perceive the world around them is most closely associated with the linguist Edward Sapir and his student Benjamin Whorf, and is therefore referred to as the **Sapir-Whorf hypothesis**. In 1929 Sapir wrote:

> Human beings do not live in the objective world alone, nor in the world of social activity as ordinarily understood, but are very much at the mercy of the particular language which has become the medium of expression for their society . . . we see and hear and otherwise experience very largely as we do because the language habits of our community predispose certain choices of interpretation.[6]

Whorf made even stronger claims:

> The background linguistic system (in other words, the grammar) of each language is not merely the reproducing instrument for voicing ideas but rather is itself the shaper of ideas, the program and guide for the individual's mental activity, for his analysis of impressions, for his synthesis of his mental stock in trade. . . . We dissect nature along lines laid down by our native languages.[7]

---

[6] Edward Sapir. 1929. *Language*. New York: Harcourt, Brace & World, Inc., p. 207.

[7] J. B. Carroll (ed). 1956. *Language, Thought, and Reality; Selected Writings of Benjamin Lee Whorf*. Cambridge, MA: MIT Press.

The strongest form of the Sapir-Whorf hypothesis is called **linguistic determinism** because it holds that the language we speak *determines* how we perceive and think about the world. In this view, language acts like a filter on reality. One of Whorf's best-known claims in support of linguistic determinism was that the Hopi Indians do not perceive time in the same way as speakers of European languages because the Hopi language does not make the grammatical distinctions of tense that, for example, English does with words and word endings such as *did, will, shall, -s, -ed,* and *-ing.*

A weaker form of the hypothesis is **linguistic relativism**, which says that different languages encode different categories and that speakers of different languages therefore think about the world in different ways. For example, languages break up the color spectrum at different points. In Navaho, blue and green are one word. Russian has different words for dark blue and sky blue, while in English we need to use additional words *dark* and *sky* to express the difference. The American Indian language Zuni does not distinguish between the colors yellow and orange. Languages also differ in how they express locations. For example, in Italian you ride "in" a bicycle and you go "in" a country while in English you ride "on" a bicycle and you go "to" a country. In English we say that a ring is placed "on" a finger and a finger is placed "in" the ring. Korean, on the other hand, has one word for both situations, *kitta,* which expresses the idea of a tight-fitting relation between the two objects. Spanish has two different words for the inside of a corner (*esquina*) and the outside of a corner (*rincon*). The Whorfian claim that is perhaps most familiar is that the Arctic language Inuit has many more words than English for snow and that this affects the worldview of the Inuit people.

7-28
© 1999
Bil Keane, Inc.
Dist. by King Features Synd.

"At the store today, the computer wasn't ON line, we stood IN line, and Billy was OUT of line."

"Family Circus" © 1999 Bil Keane, Inc. Reprinted with permission of King Features Syndicate.

That languages show linguistic distinctions in their lexicons and grammar is certain, and we will see many examples of this in later chapters. The question is to what extent—if at all—such distinctions determine or influence the thoughts and perceptions of speakers. The Sapir-Whorf hypothesis is controversial, but it is clear that the strong form of this hypothesis is false. Peoples' thoughts and perceptions are not determined by the words and structures of their languages. We are not prisoners of our linguistic systems. If speakers were unable to think about something for which their language had no specific word, translations would be impossible, as would learning a second language. English may not have a special word for the inside of a corner as opposed to the outside of a corner, but we are perfectly able to express these concepts using more than one word. In fact, we just did. If we could not think about something for which we do not have words, how would infants ever learn their first word, much less a language?

Many of the specific claims of linguistic determinism have been shown to be incorrect. For example, the Hopi language may not have words and word endings for specific tenses, but the language has other expressions for time, including words for the days of the week, parts of the day, words for yesterday and tomorrow, lunar phases, seasons, and so on. The Hopi people use various kinds of calendars and various devices for time-keeping based on the sundial. Clearly, they have a sophisticated concept of time despite the lack of a tense system in the language.

Similarly, although languages differ in their color words, speakers can readily perceive colors that are not named in their language. Grand Valley Dani is a language spoken in New Guinea with only two color words, black and white (dark and light). In experimental studies, speakers of the language were able to learn to recognize the color red, and they did better with fire-engine red than off-red. This would not be possible if their color perceptions were fixed by their language. Our perception of color is determined by the structure of the human eye, not by the structure of language.

Anthropologists have shown that Inuit has no more words for snow than English does (around a dozen: *sleet, blizzard, slush, flurry*, etc.), but even if it did, this would not show that language conditions the Inuits' experience of the world, but rather that experience with a particular world creates the need for certain words. In this respect the Inuit speaker is no different from the computer programmer, who has a technical vocabulary for Internet protocols or the linguist who has many specialized words regarding language. In this book we will introduce you to many new words and linguistic concepts, and surely you will learn them! This would be impossible if your thoughts about language were determined by the linguistic vocabulary you now have.

In our understanding of the world, we are certainly not "at the mercy of whatever language we speak," as Sapir suggested. However, we may ask whether the language we speak *influences* our cognition in some way. In the domain of color categorization, for example, it has been shown that if a language lacks a word for red, say, then it's harder for speakers to re-identify red objects. In other words, having a label seems to make it easier to store or access information in memory.

The question has also been raised regarding the possible influence of grammatical gender on how people think about objects. Many languages (e.g., Spanish and German) classify nouns as masculine or feminine; in Spanish "key" is *la llave* (feminine) and "bridge" is *el puente* (masculine). Some psychologists have suggested that speakers of gender-marking languages think about objects as having gender, much like people or animals have. In one study, speakers of German and Spanish were asked to describe various objects using English adjectives (the speakers were proficient in English). In general they used more masculine adjectives—independently rated as such—to describe objects that are grammatically masculine in their language. For example, Spanish speakers described bridges (*el puente*) as *big, dangerous, long, strong,* and *sturdy*. In German the word for bridge is feminine (*die Brücke*), and German speakers used more feminine adjectives such as *beautiful, elegant, fragile, peaceful, pretty,* and *slender*. Interestingly, it has also been noted that English speakers, too, make consistent judgments about the gender of objects, even though English has no grammatical gender on common nouns. It may be, then, that regardless of the language spoken, humans have a tendency to anthropomorphize objects and this tendency is somehow enhanced if the language itself has grammatical gender. Though it is too early to come to any firm conclusions, the results of these and similar studies seem to support a weak version of linguistic relativism.

Politicians and marketers certainly believe that language can influence our thoughts and values. One political party may refer to an inheritance tax as the "estate tax," while an opposing party refers to it as the "death tax." One politician may refer to "tax breaks for the wealthy," while another refers to "tax relief." In the abortion debate, some refer to the "right to choose" and others to the "right to life." The terminology reflects different ideologies, but the choice of expressions is primarily intended to sway public opinion. Politically correct (PC) language also reflects the idea that language can influence thought. Many people believe that by changing the way we talk, we can change the way we think; that if we eliminate racist and sexist terms from our language, we will become a less racist and sexist society. As we will discuss in chapter 10, language itself is not sexist or racist, but people can be, and because of this, particular words take on negative meanings. In his book *The Language Instinct*, Stephen Pinker uses the expression the *euphemism treadmill* to describe how the euphemistic terms that are created to replace negative words often take on the negative associations of the words they were coined to replace. In these cases, changing language has not resulted in a new worldview of the speakers.

Prescient as Orwell was with respect to how language could be used for social control, he was more circumspect with regard to the relationship between language and thought. He was careful to qualify his notions with the phrase "*at least so far as thought is dependent on words*." Current research shows that language does not determine how we think about and perceive the world. Future research should show the extent to which language influences other aspects of cognition such as memory and categorization.

What We Know about Language

Much is unknown about the nature of human languages, their grammars, and their use. The science of linguistics is concerned with these questions. Investigations of linguists and the analyses of spoken languages date back at least to 1600 B.C.E. in Mesopotamia. We have learned a great deal since that time. A number of facts pertaining to all languages can be stated:

1. Wherever humans exist, language exists.
2. There are no "primitive" languages—all languages are equally complex and equally capable of expressing any idea. The vocabulary of any language can be expanded to include new words for new concepts.
3. All languages change through time.

4. The relationships between the sounds and meanings of spoken languages and between the gestures and meanings of sign languages are for the most part arbitrary.

5. All human languages use a finite set of discrete sounds or gestures that are combined to form meaningful elements or words, which may be combined to form an infinite set of possible sentences.

6. All grammars contain rules of a similar kind for the formation of words and sentences.

7. Every spoken language includes discrete sound segments, like *p*, *n*, or *a*, that can all be defined by a finite set of sound properties or features. Every spoken language has a class of vowels and a class of consonants.

8. Similar grammatical categories (e.g., noun, verb) are found in all languages.

9. Universal semantic properties like *entailment* (one sentence inferring the truth of another) are found in every language in the world.

10. Every language has a way of negating, forming questions, issuing commands, referring to past or future time, and so on.

11. Speakers of all languages are capable of producing and comprehending an infinite set of sentences. Syntactic universals reveal that every language has a way of forming sentences such as:

   Linguistics is an interesting subject.

   I know that linguistics is an interesting subject.

   You know that I know that linguistics is an interesting subject.

   Cecelia knows that you know that I know that linguistics is an interesting subject.

   Is it a fact that Cecelia knows that you know that I know that linguistics is an interesting subject?

12. The ability of human beings to acquire, know, and use language is a biologically based ability rooted in the structure of the human brain and expressed in different modalities (spoken or signed).

13. Any normal child, born anywhere in the world, of any racial, geographical, social, or economic heritage, is capable of learning any language to which he or she is exposed.

It seems that Alsted and Du Marsais (and we could add many other universalists from all ages) were not spinning idle thoughts. We all possess human language.

Summary

We are all intimately familiar with at least one language, our own. Yet few of us ever stop to consider what we know when we know a language. No book contains, or could possibly contain, the English or Russian or Zulu language. The words of a language can be listed in a dictionary, but not all the sentences can be; and a language consists of these sentences as well as words. Speakers use a finite set of rules to produce and understand an infinite set of possible sentences.

These rules are part of the **grammar** of a language, which develops when you acquire the language and includes the sound system (the **phonology**), the structure and properties of words (the **morphology** and **lexicon**), how words may be combined into phrases and sentences (the **syntax**), and the ways in which sounds and meanings are related (the **semantics**). The sounds and meanings of individual words are related in an **arbitrary** fashion. If you had never heard the word *syntax* you would not, by its sounds, know what it meant. The gestures used by signers are also arbitrarily related to their meanings. Language, then, is a system that relates sounds (or hand and body gestures) with meanings. When you know a language, you know this system.

This knowledge (**linguistic competence**) is different from behavior (**linguistic performance**). If you woke up one morning and decided to stop talking (as the Trappist monks did after they took a vow of silence), you would still have knowledge of your language. This ability or competence underlies linguistic behavior. If you do not know the language, you cannot speak it, but if you know the language, you may choose not to speak.

There are different kinds of "grammars." The **descriptive grammar** of a language represents the unconscious linguistic knowledge or capacity of its speakers. Such a grammar is a model of the **mental grammar** every speaker of the language knows. It does not teach the rules of the language; it describes the rules that are already known. A grammar that attempts to legislate what your grammar should be is called a **prescriptive grammar**. It prescribes; it does not describe, except incidentally. **Teaching grammars** are written to help people learn a foreign language or a dialect of their own language.

The more that linguists investigate the thousands of languages of the world and describe the ways in which they differ from each other, the more they discover that these differences are limited. Linguistic universals pertain to each of the parts of grammars, the ways in which these parts are related, and the forms of rules. These principles comprise **Universal Grammar**, which provides a blueprint for the grammars of all possible human languages. Universal Grammar constitutes the innate component of the human language faculty that makes normal language development possible.

Strong evidence for Universal Grammar is found in the way children acquire language—by exposure. They need not be deliberately taught, although parents may enjoy "teaching" their children to speak or sign. Children will learn any human language to which they are exposed, and they learn it in definable stages, beginning at a very early age. By four or five years of age, children have acquired nearly the entire adult grammar. This suggests that children are born with a genetically endowed faculty to learn and use human language, which is part of the Universal Grammar.

The fact that deaf children learn **sign language** shows that the ability to hear or produce sounds is not a prerequisite for language learning. All of the sign languages in the world, which differ as spoken languages do, are visual-gestural systems that are as fully developed and as structurally complex as spoken languages. The major sign language used in the United States is **American Sign Language (ASL)**.

If language is defined merely as a system of communication, or the ability to produce speech sounds, then language is not unique to humans; however, certain characteristics of human language are not found in the communication systems of any other species. A basic property of human language is its **creative aspect**—a speaker's ability to combine the basic linguistic units to form an infinite set of well-formed grammatical sentences, most of which are novel, never before produced or heard.

The **Sapir-Whorf hypothesis** holds that the particular language we speak determines or influences our thoughts and perceptions of the world. Much of the early evidence in support of this hypothesis has not stood the test of time. More recent experimental studies suggest that the words and grammar of a language may affect aspects of cognition such as memory and categorization.

References for Further Reading

Bickerton, D. 1990. *Language and Species*. Chicago: Chicago University Press.

Chomsky, N. 1986. *Knowledge of Language: Its Nature, Origin, and Use*. New York and London: Praeger.

_____. 1975. *Reflections on Language*. New York: Pantheon Books.

_____. 1972. *Language and Mind*. Enlarged Edition. New York: Harcourt Brace Jovanovich.

Crystal, D. 1997. *Cambridge Encyclopedia of the English Language*. Cambridge, England: Cambridge University Press.

Hall, R. A. 1950. *Leave Your Language Alone*. Ithaca, NY: Linguistica.

Gentner, D., and S. Goldin-Meadow. 2003. *Language in Mind*. Cambridge, MA: MIT Press.

Jackendoff, R. 1997. *The Architecture of the Language Faculty*. Cambridge, MA: The MIT Press.

_____. 1994. *Patterns in the Mind: Language and Human Nature*. New York: Basic Books.

Klima, E. S., and U. Bellugi. 1979. *The Signs of Language*. Cambridge, MA: Harvard University Press.

Lane, H. 1989. *When the Mind Hears: A History of the Deaf*. New York: Vintage Books (Random House).

Milroy, J., and L. Milroy. 1998. *Authority in Language: Investigating Standard English,* 3rd edition. New York: Routledge.

Napoli, D. J. 2003. *Language Matters: A Guide to Everyday Thinking about Language*. New York: Oxford University Press.

Pinker, S. 1999. *Words and Rules: The Ingredients of Language*. New York: HarperCollins.

_____. 1994. *The Language Instinct*. New York: William Morrow.

Sebeok, T. A., ed. 1977. *How Animals Communicate.* Bloomington, IN: Indiana University Press.

Stokoe, W. 1960. *Sign Language Structure: An Outline of the Visual Communication System of the American Deaf*. Silver Springs, MD: Linstok Press.

Exercises

1. An English speaker's knowledge includes the sound sequences of the language. When new products are put on the market, the manufacturers have to think up new names for them that conform to the allowable sound patterns. Suppose you were hired by a manufacturer of soap products to name five new products. What names might you come up with? List them.

   We are interested in how the names are pronounced. Therefore, describe in any way you can how to say the words you list. Suppose, for example, you named one detergent *Blick*. You could describe the sounds in any of the following ways:

bl as in *blood, i* as in *pit, ck* as in *stick*
bli as in *bliss, ck* as in *tick*
b as in *boy, lick* as in *lick*

2. Consider the following sentences. Put a star (*) after those that do not seem to conform to the rules of your grammar, that are ungrammatical for you. State, if you can, why you think the sentence is ungrammatical.

   a. Robin forced the sheriff go.

   b. Napoleon forced Josephine to go.

   c. The devil made Faust go.

   d. He passed by a large pile of money.

   e. He came by a large sum of money.

   f. He came a large sum of money by.

   g. Did in a corner little Jack Horner sit?

   h. Elizabeth is resembled by Charles.

   i. Nancy is eager to please.

   j. It is easy to frighten Emily.

   k. It is eager to love a kitten.

   l. That birds can fly amazes.

   m. The fact that you are late to class is surprising.

   n. Has the nurse slept the baby yet?

   o. I was surprised for you to get married.

   p. I wonder who and Mary went swimming.

   q. Myself bit John.

   r. What did Alice eat the toadstool with?

   s. What did Alice eat the toadstool and?

3. It was pointed out in this chapter that a small set of words in languages may be onomatopoeic; that is, their sounds "imitate" what they refer to. *Ding-dong, tick-tock, bang, zing, swish*, and *plop* are such words in English. Construct a list of ten new onomatopoeic words. Test them on at least five friends to see if they are truly nonarbitrary as to sound and meaning.

4. Although sounds and meanings of most words in all languages are arbitrarily related, there are some communication systems in which the "signs" unambiguously reveal their "meaning."

   a. Describe (or draw) five different signs that directly show what they mean. *Example*: a road sign indicating an S curve.

   b. Describe any other communication system that, like language, consists of arbitrary symbols. Example: traffic signals, where red means stop and green means go.

5. Consider these two statements: *I learned a new word today. I learned a new sentence today.* Do you think the two statements are equally probable, and if not, why not?

6. What do the barking of dogs, the meowing of cats, and the singing of birds have in common with human language? What are some of the basic differences?

7. A wolf is able to express subtle gradations of emotion by different positions of the ears, the lips, and the tail. There are eleven postures of the tail that express such emotions as self-confidence, confident threat, lack of tension, uncertain threat, depression, defensiveness, active submission, and complete submission. This system seems to be complex. Suppose that there were a thousand different emotions that the wolf could express in this way. Would you then say a wolf had a language similar to a human's? If not, why not?

8. Suppose you taught a dog to *heel, sit up, roll over, play dead, stay, jump*, and *bark* on command, using the italicized words as cues. Would you be teaching it language? Why or why not?

9. State some rule of grammar that you have learned is the correct way to say something, but that you do not generally use in speaking. For example, you may have heard that *It's me* is incorrect and that the correct form is *It's I*. Nevertheless, you always use *me* in such sentences; your friends do also, and in fact, *It's I* sounds odd to you.

   Write a short essay presenting arguments against someone who tells you that you are wrong. Discuss how this disagreement demonstrates the difference between descriptive and prescriptive grammars.

10. Think of song titles that are "bad" grammar, but that, if corrected, would lack effect. For example, the 1929 "Fats" Waller classic "Ain't Misbehavin'" is clearly superior to the bland "I am not misbehaving." Try to come up with five or ten such titles.

11. Linguists who attempt to write a descriptive grammar of linguistic competence are faced with a difficult task. They must understand a deep and complex system based on a set of sparse and often inaccurate data. (Children learning language face the same difficulty.) Albert Einstein and Leopold Infeld captured the essence of the difficulty in their book *The Evolution of Physics*, written in 1938:

    > In our endeavor to understand reality we are somewhat like a man trying to understand the mechanism of a closed watch. He sees the face and the moving hands, even hears its ticking, but he has no way of opening the case. If he is ingenious he may form some picture of a mechanism which could be responsible for all the things he observes, but he may never be quite sure his picture is the only one which could explain his observations. He will never be able to compare his picture with the real mechanism and he cannot even imagine the possibility of the meaning of such a comparison.

    Write a short essay that speculates on how a linguist might go about understanding the reality of a person's grammar (the closed watch) by observing what that person says and doesn't say (the face and moving hands). For example, a person might never say *the sixth sheik's sixth sheep is sick as a dog*, but the grammar should specify that it is a well-formed sentence, just as it should somehow indicate that *Came the messenger on time* is ill-formed.

12. View the motion picture *My Fair Lady* (drawn from the play *Pygmalion* by George Bernard Shaw). Note every attempt to teach grammar (pronunciation, word choice, and syntax) to the character of Eliza Doolittle. This is an illustration of "teaching grammar."

13. Many people are bilingual or multilingual, speaking two or more languages with very different structures.

    a. What implications does bilingualism have for the debate about language and thought?

    b. Many readers of this textbook have some knowledge of a second language. Think of a linguistic structure or word in one language that does not exist in the second language and discuss how this does or does not affect your thinking when you speak the different languages. (If you know only one language, ask this question of a bilingual person you know.)

    c. Can you find an example of an untranslatable word or structure in one of the languages you speak?

14. The South American indigenous language Pirahã is said to lack numbers beyond two and distinct words for colors. Research this language—Google would be a good start—with regard to whether Pirahã supports or fails to support linguistic determinism and/or linguistic relativism.

2

Brain and Language

The functional asymmetry of the human brain is unequivocal, and so is its anatomical asymmetry. The structural differences between the left and the right hemispheres are visible not only under the microscope but to the naked eye. The most striking asymmetries occur in language-related cortices. It is tempting to assume that such anatomical differences are an index of the neurobiological underpinnings of language.

ANTONIO AND HANNA DAMASIO, UNIVERSITY OF IOWA, SCHOOL OF MEDICINE, DEPARTMENT OF NEUROLOGY

Attempts to understand the complexities of human cognitive abilities and especially the acquisition and use of language are as old and as continuous as history itself. What is the nature of the brain? What is the nature of human language? And what is the relationship between the two? Philosophers and scientists have grappled with these questions and others over the centuries. The idea that the brain is the source of human language and cognition goes back more than two thousand years. In Assyrian and Babylonian cuneiform tablets, there is mention of disorders of language that may develop "when man's brain holds fire." Egyptian doctors in 1700 B.C.E. noted in their papyrus records that "the breath of an outside god" had entered their patients who became "silent in sadness." The philosophers of ancient Greece speculated about the brain/mind relationship, but neither Plato nor Aristotle recognized the brain's crucial function in cognition or language. Aristotle's wisdom failed him when he suggested that the brain is a cold sponge whose function is to cool the blood. However, others who wrote during the same period showed greater insight, as illustrated in the following quote from the Hippocratic Treatises on the Sacred Disease, written c. 377 B.C.E.:

> [The brain is] the messenger of the understanding [and the organ whereby] in an especial manner we acquire wisdom and knowledge.

The study of language has been crucial to understanding the brain/mind relationship. Conversely, research on the brain in humans and other primates is helping to answer questions concerning the neurological basis for language. The study of the biological and neural foundations of language is called **neurolinguistics**.

The Human Brain

> "Rabbit's clever," said Pooh thoughtfully.
> "Yes," said Piglet, "Rabbit's clever."
> "And he has Brain."
> "Yes," said Piglet, "Rabbit has Brain."
> There was a long silence.
> "I suppose," said Pooh, "that that's why he never understands anything."
>
> **A. A. MILNE,** The House at Pooh Corner

The brain is the most complex organ of the body. It lies under the skull and consists of approximately 10 billion nerve cells (neurons) and billions of fibers that interconnect them. The surface of the brain is the **cortex**, often called "gray matter," consisting of billions of neurons. The cortex is the decision-making organ of the body. It receives messages from all of the sensory organs, initiates all voluntary actions, and is the storehouse of our memories. Somewhere in this gray matter resides the grammar that represents our knowledge of language.

The brain is composed of **cerebral hemispheres**, one on the right and one on the left, joined by the **corpus callosum**, a network of two million fibers (see Figure 2.1). The corpus callosum allows the two hemispheres of the brain to communicate with each other. Without this system of connections, the two hemispheres would operate

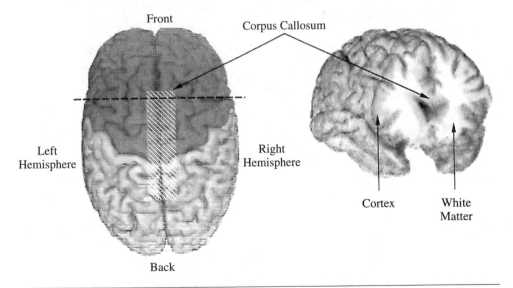

FIGURE 2.1 Three-dimensional reconstruction of the normal living human brain. The images were obtained from magnetic resonance data using the Brainvox technique. *Left panel* = view from top. *Right panel* = view from the front following virtual coronal section at the level of the dashed line.
Courtesy of Hanna Damasio.

independently. In general, the left hemisphere controls the right side of the body, and the right hemisphere controls the left side. If you point with your right hand, the left hemisphere is responsible for your action. Similarly, sensory information from the right side of the body (e.g., right ear, right hand, right visual field) is received by the left hemisphere of the brain, and sensory input to the left side of the body is received by the right hemisphere. This is referred to as **contralateral** brain function.

The Localization of Language in the Brain

"Peanuts" copyright © 1984 United Feature Syndicate, Inc. Reprinted by permission.

An issue of central concern has been to determine which parts of the brain are responsible for human linguistic abilities. In the early nineteenth century, Franz Joseph Gall proposed the theory of **localization**, which is the idea that different human cognitive abilities and behaviors are localized in specific parts of the brain. In light of our current knowledge about the brain, some of Gall's particular views are amusing. For example, he proposed that language is located in the frontal lobes of the brain because as a young man he had noticed that the most articulate and intelligent of his fellow students had protruding eyes, which he believed reflected overdeveloped brain material. He also put forth a pseudoscientific theory called "organology" that later came to be known as **phrenology**, which is the practice of determining personality traits, intellectual capacities, and other matters by examining the "bumps" on the skull. A disciple of Gall's, Johann Spurzheim, introduced phrenology to America, constructing elaborate maps and skull models such as the one shown in Figure 2.2, in which language is located directly under the eye.

Gall was a pioneer and a courageous scientist in arguing against the prevailing view that the brain was an unstructured organ. Although phrenology was long ago discarded as a scientific theory, Gall's view that the brain is not a uniform mass, and that linguistic and other cognitive capacities are functions of localized brain areas, has been upheld by scientific investigation of aphasia and other disorders, and more recently by functional brain imaging.

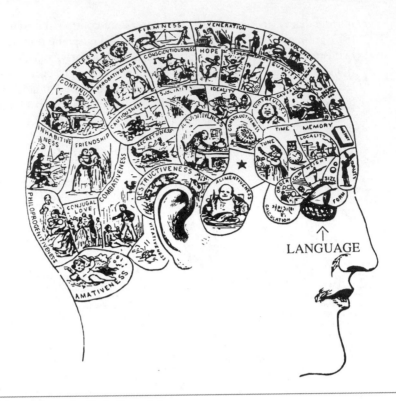

FIGURE 2.2 Phrenology skull model.

APHASIA

The study of **aphasia** has been an important area of research in understanding the relationship between brain and language. Aphasia is the neurological term for any language disorder that results from brain damage caused by disease or trauma. In the second half of the nineteenth century, significant scientific advances were made in localizing language in the brain based on the study of people with aphasia. In 1864 the French surgeon Paul Broca proposed that language is localized to the left hemisphere of the brain, and more specifically to the front part of the left hemisphere (now called **Broca's area**). At a scientific meeting in Paris, he claimed that we speak with the left hemisphere. Broca's finding was based on a study of his patients who suffered language deficits after brain injury. After these patients died, he performed autopsies, which revealed that damage to the left frontal lobe resulted in aphasia, whereas damage to the right side did not. In 1874, thirteen years after Broca's discovery, Carl Wernicke, a German neurologist, described another variety of aphasia that occurred in patients with lesions in the more posterior portions of the left hemisphere, now known as **Wernicke's area**. Language, then, is lateralized to the left hemisphere. **Lateralization** is the term used to refer to any cognitive function that is localized primarily on one side of the brain or the other.

Figure 2.3 is a view of the left side of the brain that shows Broca's and Wernicke's areas.

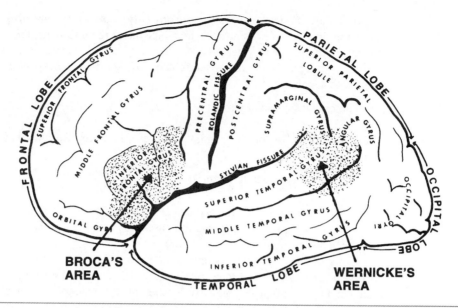

FIGURE **2.3** Lateral (*external*) view of the left hemisphere of the human brain, showing the position of Broca's and Wernicke's areas—two key areas of the cortex related to language processing.

The Linguistic Characterization of Aphasic Syndromes   Many aphasics do not show total language loss. Rather, different aspects of language are selectively impaired, and the kind of impairment is generally related to the location of the brain damage. Because of this damage-deficit correlation, research on patients with aphasia has provided a great deal of information about how language is organized in the brain.

Patients with injuries to Broca's area may have **Broca's aphasia,** as it is called today. Broca's aphasia is characterized by labored speech and certain kinds of word-finding difficulties, but it's primarily a disorder that affects the person's ability to form sentences with the rules of syntax. One of the most notable characteristics of Broca's aphasia is that the language is often **agrammatic,** meaning that it frequently lacks articles, prepositions, pronouns, and auxiliary verbs, which we will call "function words" for now. Broca's aphasics also typically omit inflections such as the past tense suffix *-ed* or the third person singular verb ending *-s.* Here is an excerpt of a conversation between a patient with Broca's aphasia and a doctor:

Doctor: Could you tell me what you have been doing in the hospital?

Patient: Yes, sure. Me go, er, uh, P.T. [physical therapy] none o'cot, speech . . . two times . . . read . . . r . . . ripe . . . rike . . . uh write . . . practice . . . get . . . ting . . . better.

Doctor: And have you been going home on weekends?

Patient: Why, yes . . . Thursday uh . . . uh . . . uh . . . no . . . Friday . . . Bar . . . ba . . . ra . . . wife . . . and oh car . . . drive . . . purpike . . . you know . . . rest . . . and TV.

Broca's aphasics (also called **agrammatic aphasics**) may also have difficulty understanding complex sentences in which comprehension depends exclusively on syntactic structure and where they cannot rely on their real-world knowledge. For example, an agrammatic aphasic might be confused as to who is chasing whom in passive sentences such as:

The cat was chased by the dog.

where it is plausible for either animal to chase the other. But they have less difficulty with

The car was chased by the dog.

where the meaning of the sentence can be provided by nonlinguistic knowledge. They know that it is implausible for cars to chase dogs and can use that knowledge to interpret the sentence.

Unlike Broca's patients, people with **Wernicke's aphasia** produce fluent speech with good intonation, and they may largely adhere to the rules of syntax. However, their language is often semantically incoherent. For example, one patient replied to a question about his health with:

I felt worse because I can no longer keep in mind from the mind of the minds to keep me from mind and up to the ear which can be to find among ourselves.

Another patient described a fork as "a need for a schedule" and another, when asked about his poor vision, replied, "My wires don't hire right."

People with damage to Wernicke's area have difficulty naming objects presented to them and also in choosing words in spontaneous speech. They may make numerous lexical errors (word substitutions), often producing **jargon** and **nonsense words**, as in the following example:

The only thing that I can say again is madder or modder fish sudden fishing sewed into the accident to miss in the purdles.

Another example is from a patient who was a physician before his aphasia. When asked if he was a doctor, he replied:

Me? Yes sir. I'm a male demaploze on my own. I still know my tubaboys what for I have that's gone hell and some of them go.

Severe Wernicke's aphasia is often referred to as **jargon aphasia**. The linguistic deficits exhibited by people with Broca's and Wernicke's aphasia point to a **modular** organization of language in the brain. We find that damage to different parts of the brain results in different kinds of linguistic impairment (e.g., syntactic versus semantic). This supports the hypothesis that the mental grammar, like the brain itself, is not an undifferentiated system, but rather consists of distinct components or modules with different functions.

The kind of word substitutions that aphasic patients produce also tell us about how words are organized in the mental lexicon. Sometimes the substituted words are similar to the intended words in their sounds. For example, *pool* might be substituted for *tool, sable* for *table*, or *crucial* for *crucible*. Sometimes they are similar in meaning (e.g., *table* for *chair* or *boy* for *girl*). These errors resemble the speech errors that anyone might make, but they occur far more frequently in people with Wernicke's aphasia. The substitution of semantically or phonetically related words tells us that neural connections exist among semantically related words and among words that sound alike. Words are not mentally represented in a simple list but rather in an organized network of connections.

Similar observations pertain to reading. Many word substitutions are made by aphasics who become dyslexic after brain damage. They are called *acquired dyslexics* because before their brain lesions they were normal readers (unlike developmental dyslexics who have difficulty learning to read). One group of these patients, when reading words printed on cards aloud, produced the kinds of substitutions shown in the following examples.

Stimulus	Response 1	Response 2
act	*play*	*play*
applaud	*laugh*	*cheers*
example	*answer*	*sum*
heal	*pain*	*medicine*
south	*west*	*east*

Similarly, the omission of function words by agrammatic aphasics shows that this class of words is mentally distinct from content words like nouns. The patient who produced the semantic substitutions cited previously was also agrammatic and was not able to read function words at all. When presented with words like *which* or *would*, he just said, "No" or "I hate those little words." However, he could read homophonous nouns and verbs, though with many semantic mistakes, as shown in the following:

Stimulus	Response	Stimulus	Response
witch	*witch*	which	*no!*
hour	*time*	our	*no!*
eye	*eyes*	I	*no!*
hymn	*bible*	him	*no!*
wood	*wood*	would	*no!*

In **acquired dyslexia**, which commonly accompanies agrammatism, there is a parallel between the elements that the patient mis-selects and those he cannot read.

These errors suggest that the mental dictionary in our brains is compartmentalized with content words and function words in different compartments. Furthermore, they provide evidence that these two classes of words are processed in different brain areas or by different neural mechanisms, further supporting the view that both the brain and language are structured in a complex, modular fashion.

Most of us have experienced word-finding difficulties in speaking if not in reading, as Alice did in "Wonderland" when she said:

> "And now, who am I? I will remember, if I can. I'm determined to do it!" But being determined didn't help her much, and all she could say, after a great deal of puzzling, was "L, I know it begins with L."

This **"tip-of-the-tongue" phenomenon** (often referred to as **TOT**) is not uncommon. But if you could *rarely* find the word you wanted, imagine how frustrated you would be. This is the fate of many aphasics whose impairment involves severe **anomia**—the inability to find the word you wish to speak.

It is important to note that the language difficulties suffered by aphasics are not caused by any general cognitive or intellectual impairment or loss of motor or sensory controls of the nerves and muscles of the speech organs or hearing apparatus. Aphasics can produce and hear sounds. Whatever loss they suffer has to do only with the language faculty (or specific parts of it).

Deaf signers with damage to the left hemisphere show aphasia for sign language similar to the language breakdown in hearing aphasics, even though sign language is a visual-spatial language. Deaf patients with lesions in Broca's area show language deficits like those found in hearing patients, namely severely dysfluent, agrammatic sign production, and those with damage to Wernicke's area have fluent but often semantically incoherent sign language, filled with made-up signs. Although deaf aphasic patients show marked sign language deficits, they have no difficulty in processing nonlinguistic visual spatial relationships, just as hearing aphasics have no problem with processing nonlinguistic auditory stimuli. This result is important because it shows that the left hemisphere is lateralized for language—an abstract system of symbols and rules—and not simply for hearing or speech. Language can be realized in different modalities, spoken or signed.

The kind of selective impairment that we find in people with aphasia has provided important information about the organization of different cognitive abilities, especially grammar and the lexicon. It tells us that language is a separate cognitive module—so aphasics can be otherwise cognitively normal—and also that within language, separate components can be differentially affected by damage to different regions of the brain.

Historical Descriptions of Aphasia   The interest in aphasia did not start with Broca. Long before Broca, Greek Hippocratic physicians reported that loss of speech often occurred simultaneously with paralysis of the right side of the body, but Broca's name is most closely associated with the left lateralization of language.

In the New Testament, St. Luke reports that Zacharias could not speak but could write, showing early recognition of the autonomy of different aspects of linguistic knowledge. In Psalm 137 of the Bible, we find the following: "If I forget thee, Oh Jerusalem, may my right hand lose its cunning and my tongue cleave to the roof of my mouth." Written sometime between 300 and 200 B.C.E., this passage also shows that a link between loss of speech and paralysis of the right side was recognized.

In 30 B.C.E., the Roman writer Valerius Maximus describes an Athenian who was unable to remember his "letters" after being hit in the head with a stone. Pliny the Elder (C.E. 23–79) refers to this same Athenian, noting that "with the stroke of a stone, he fell presently to forget his letters only, and could read no more; otherwise, his memory served him well enough."

Numerous clinical descriptions of patients with language deficits, but intact nonlinguistic cognitive systems, were published between the fifteenth and eighteenth centuries. Johannes Gesner in 1770 did not attribute these language difficulties to either general intellectual deficits or loss of memory, but to a specific impairment to language memory. He wrote: "Just as some verbal powers can become weakened without injury to others, memory also can be specifically impaired to a greater or lesser degree with respect to only certain classes of ideas."

Other reports describe patients suffering from acquired dyslexia who nevertheless preserved their ability to write, and patients who could write to dictation but could not read back what they had written.

Carl Linnaeus in 1745 published a case study of a man suffering from jargon aphasia, who spoke "as if it were a foreign language, having his own names for all words." An important observation regarding word substitution errors was made by Ryklof Michel von Goens in 1789 in his reference to a patient whom he described as follows:

> After an illness, she was suddenly afflicted with a forgetting, or, rather, an incapacity or confusion of speech. . . . If she desired a *chair*, she would ask for a *table*. . . . Sometimes she herself perceived that she misnamed objects; at other times, she was annoyed when a *fan*, which she had asked for, was brought to her, instead of the *bonnet*, which she thought she had requested.

The description of these and similarly afflicted patients reveals that they substituted words that were semantically or phonologically similar to the intended ones, producing errors similar to the normal word substitution errors that unafflicted persons might produce.

Physicians of the day described other kinds of linguistic breakdown in detail. Gesner observed and wrote about bilingual asymmetry in which, for example, an abbot retained his ability following brain damage to read Latin but not German.

The historical descriptions of language loss following brain damage, together with the later controlled scientific studies of aphasia, provide substantial evidence that language is predominantly and most frequently a left-hemisphere function. In most cases, lesions to the left hemisphere result in aphasia but injuries to the right do not (although such lesions result in deficits in facial recognition, pattern recognition, and other cognitive abilities).

BRAIN IMAGING TECHNOLOGY

The historical descriptions of aphasia illustrate that people have long been fascinated by the brain-language connection. Today we no longer need to rely on surgery or autopsy to locate brain lesions or to identify the language regions of the brain. Modern noninvasive brain recording technologies such as computed tomography (CT) scans and **magnetic resonance imaging (MRI)** can reveal lesions in the living brain shortly after the damage occurs. In addition, **positron emission tomography (PET)** and functional MRI (fMRI) scans provide images of the brain in action; it is now possible to detect changes in brain activity and to relate these changes to localized brain damage and cognitive tasks.

Figures 2.4 and 2.5 show MRI scans of the brains of a Broca's aphasic and a Wernicke's aphasic patient. The black areas show the sites of the lesions. Each diagram represents a slice of the left side of the brain.

PET and fMRI scans permit us to measure metabolic activity to particular areas of the brain. Areas of greater activity are those most involved in the mental processes at the moment of the scan. Supplemented by magnetic encephalography (MEG), which measures magnetic fields in the living brain, these techniques can show us how the healthy brain reacts to particular linguistic stimuli. In scientifically controlled studies, normal adults are asked to read word lists, read and understand entire phrases, and distinguish between grammatical and ungrammatical sentences. The results of these studies reaffirm the earlier findings that language resides in specific areas of the left hemisphere.

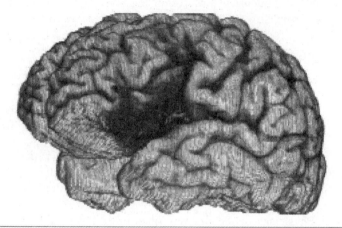

FIGURE 2.4 Three-dimensional reconstruction of the brain of a living patient with Broca's aphasia. Note area of damage in left frontal region (*dark gray*), which was caused by a stroke.
Courtesy of Hanna Damasio.

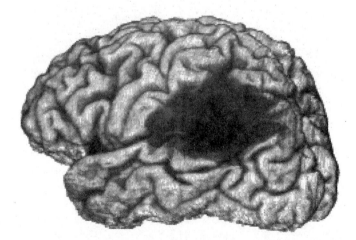

FIGURE 2.5 Three-dimensional reconstruction of the brain of a living patient with Wernicke's aphasia. Note area of damage in left posterior temporal and lower parietal region (*dark gray*), which was caused by a stroke.
Courtesy of Hanna Damasio.

For example, PET scans were used to locate and measure cortical activity of people who were asked to produce the past tense forms of regular and irregular verbs. Very different amounts and areas of cortical activation were found between the regular and irregular tasks. Nevertheless, all cortical activity was in the left hemisphere. These experiments support both the modular nature of the grammar and the left lateralization of language.

Dramatic evidence for a differentiated and structured brain is also provided by studies of both normal individuals and patients with lesions in regions of the brain other than Broca's and Wernicke's areas. Some patients have difficulty speaking a person's name; others have problems naming animals; and still others cannot name tools. fMRI studies revealed the shape and location of the brain lesions in each of these types of patient. The patients in each group had brain lesions in distinct, nonoverlapping regions of the left temporal lobe. In a follow-up PET scan study, *normal* subjects were asked to name persons, animals, or tools. Experimenters found that there was differential activation in the normal brains in just those sites that were damaged in the aphasics who were unable to name persons, animals, or tools.

Further evidence for the separation of cognitive systems is provided by the neurological and behavioral findings that follow brain damage. Some patients lose the ability to recognize sounds or colors or familiar faces while retaining all other functions. A patient may not be able to recognize his wife when she walks into the room until she starts to talk. This suggests the differentiation of many aspects of visual and auditory processing. There is now a consensus that higher mental functions are highly lateralized.

BRAIN PLASTICITY AND LATERALIZATION IN EARLY LIFE

It takes only one hemisphere to have a mind.

A. W. WIGAN, *1844*

Lateralization of language to the left hemisphere is a process that begins early in life. Wernicke's area is visibly distinctive in the left hemisphere of the fetus by the twenty-sixth gestational week. Infants as young as one week old show a greater electrical response in the left hemisphere to language and in the right hemisphere to music. Recent work with deaf and hearing babies between the ages of five and twelve months shows that there is left hemisphere dominance for babbling, an early linguistic function.

Whereas the left hemisphere is innately predisposed to specialize for language, there is also evidence of considerable *plasticity* (i.e., flexibility) in the system during the early stages of language development. This means that under certain circumstances, the right hemisphere can take over many of the language functions that would normally reside in the left hemisphere. An impressive illustration of plasticity is provided by children who have undergone a procedure known as **hemispherectomy**, in which a hemisphere of the brain is surgically removed. This procedure is used to treat otherwise intractable cases of epilepsy. In cases of left hemispherectomy after language acquisition has begun, children experience an initial period of aphasia and then reacquire a linguistic system that is virtually indistinguishable from that of normal children. They also show many of the development patterns of normal language acquisition. UCLA professor Susan Curtiss and colleagues have studied many of these children. They hypothesize that the latent linguistic ability of the right hemisphere is "freed" by the removal of the diseased left hemisphere, which may have had a strong inhibitory effect before the surgery.

In adults, however, surgical removal of the left hemisphere inevitably results in severe loss of the language function (and so is done only in life-threatening circumstances), whereas adults (and children) who have had their right hemispheres removed retain their language abilities, although other cognitive losses may result, such as those typically lateralized to the right hemisphere. The plasticity of the brain decreases with age and with the increasing specialization of the different hemispheres and regions of the brain.

Despite strong evidence that the left hemisphere is predetermined to be the language hemisphere in most humans, some evidence suggests that the right hemisphere plays a role at the earliest stages of language acquisition. Children with prenatal, perinatal, or childhood brain lesions in the right hemisphere can show delays and impairments in babbling and vocabulary learning, whereas children with early left hemisphere lesions demonstrate impairments in their ability to form phrases and sentences. Also, many children who undergo right hemispherectomy do not develop language, even though they still have a left hemisphere.

Various findings converge to show that the human brain is essentially designed to specialize for language in the left hemisphere but that the right hemisphere is involved in early language development. They also show that, under the right circumstances, the brain is remarkably resilient and that if brain damage or surgery occurs early in life, normal left hemisphere functions can be taken over by the right hemisphere.

SPLIT BRAINS

Persons suffering from intractable epilepsy may be treated by severing communication between their two hemispheres. Surgeons cut through the corpus callosum (see Figure 2.1), the fibrous network that connects the two halves. When this pathway is severed, there is no communication between the "two brains." Such **split-brain** patients also provide evidence for language lateralization and for understanding contralateral brain functions.

The psychologist Michael Gazzaniga states:

> With [the corpus callosum] intact, the two halves of the body have no secrets from one another. With it sectioned, the two halves become two different conscious mental spheres, each with its own experience base and control system for behavioral operations. . . . Unbelievable as this may seem, this is the flavor of a long series of experimental studies first carried out in the cat and monkey.[1]

When the brain is surgically split, certain information from the left side of the body is received only by the right side of the brain, and vice versa. To illustrate, suppose that a monkey is trained to respond with both its hands to a certain visual stimulus, such as a flashing light. After the training is complete, the brain is surgically split. The stimulus is then shown only to the left visual field (the right hemisphere). Because the right hemisphere controls the left side of the body, the monkey will perform only with the left hand.

---

[1] M. Gazzaniga. 1970. *The Bisected Brain.* New York: Appleton-Century-Crofts.

"ROGER DOESN'T USE THE LEFT SIDE OF THE BRAIN OR THE RIGHT SIDE. HE JUST USES THE MIDDLE."

Similarly, studies of humans who have undergone split-brain operations reveal that, as in the monkey brain, the two hemispheres of the human brain are distinct, and messages sent to the two sides of the brain result in different responses, depending on which side receives the message. If an object, for example, a pencil, is placed in the left hand of a split-brain person whose eyes are closed, the person can use the pencil appropriately but cannot name it. The right brain senses the pencil and distinguishes it from other objects (i.e., knows that it is a pencil), but the information cannot be relayed to the left brain for linguistic naming because the connections between the two halves have been severed. By contrast, if the pencil is placed in the right hand, the subject is immediately able to name it as well as to describe it because the sensory information from the right hand goes directly into the left hemisphere, where the language areas are also located.

Various experiments of this sort have provided information on the different capabilities of the two hemispheres. The right brain does better than the left in pattern-matching tasks, in recognizing faces, and in spatial orientation. The left hemisphere is superior for language, rhythmic perception, temporal-order judgments, and mathematical thinking. According to Gazzaniga, "the right hemisphere as well as the left hemisphere can emote and while the left can tell you why, the right cannot."

Studies of human split-brain patients have also shown that when the interhemispheric visual connections are severed, visual information from the right and left visual fields becomes confined to the left and right hemispheres, respectively. Because of the crucial endowment of the left hemisphere for language, written material delivered to the right hemisphere cannot be read if the brain is split, because the information cannot be transferred to the left hemisphere. An image or picture that is flashed to the right visual field of a split-brain patient (and therefore processed by the left hemisphere) can be named. However, when the picture is flashed in the left visual field and therefore "lands" in the right hemisphere, it cannot be named.

OTHER EXPERIMENTAL EVIDENCE OF BRAIN ORGANIZATION

Dichotic listening is an experimental technique that uses auditory signals to observe the behavior of the individual hemispheres of the human brain and provides strong evidence of lateralization. Subjects hear two different sound signals simultaneously through earphones. They may hear *curl* in one ear and *girl* in the other, or a cough in one ear and a laugh in the other. When asked to state what they heard in each ear, subjects are more frequently correct in reporting linguistic stimuli (words, nonsense syllables, and so on) delivered directly to the right ear, but are more frequently correct in reporting nonverbal stimuli (musical chords, environmental sounds, and so on) delivered to the left ear.

Both hemispheres receive signals from both ears, but the contralateral stimuli prevail over the **ipsilateral** (same-side) stimuli because they are processed more robustly. Their pathways are anatomically thicker (think of a four-lane highway versus a two-lane road) and are not delayed by the need to cross the corpus callosum. The accuracy with which subjects report what they hear is evidence that the left hemisphere is superior for linguistic processing, and the right hemisphere is superior for nonverbal information.

These experiments are important because they show not only that language is lateralized, but also that the left hemisphere is not superior for processing all sounds; it is only better for those sounds that are linguistic. The left side of the brain is specialized for language, not sound, as we also noted in connection with sign language research discussed earlier.

Other experimental techniques are also being used to map the brain and to investigate the independence of different aspects of language and the extent of the independence of language from other cognitive systems. Even before the advances in imaging technology of the 1980s and more recently, researchers were taping electrodes to different areas of the skull and investigating the electrical activity of the brain related to perceptual and cognitive information. In such experiments, scientists measure **event-related brain potentials (ERPs)**, which are the electrical signals emitted from the brain in response to different stimuli (events).

For example, ERP differences result when the subject hears speech sounds versus nonspeech sounds (with a greater response from the left hemisphere to speech). ERP experiments also show variations in timing, pattern, and area of response when subjects hear sentences that are meaningless, such as

The man admired Don's headache of the landscape.

as opposed to meaningful sentences such as

The man admired Don's sketch of the landscape.

showing greater left hemisphere than right hemisphere sensitivity to ungrammaticality.

Such experiments show that neuronal activity varies in location within the brain according to whether the stimulus is language or nonlanguage. The intensity of activity over time also varies according to different stages in processing the stimulus. Thus, ERP studies again show a left hemisphere specialization for grammar. Moreover, because ERPs provide detailed information about the timing of neuronal activity as the brain processes language, they can provide important information about the mechanisms that allow the brain to process language quickly and efficiently, on the scale of hundreds of milliseconds.

Additional evidence is provided by the patterns of neuronal activity in people reading different kinds of writing. For example, the Japanese language has two writing systems. One system, *kana*, is based on the sound system of the language; each symbol corresponds to a syllable. The other system, *kanji*, is ideographic; each symbol corresponds to a word. (More about this in chapter 12 on writing systems.) *Kanji* is not based on the sounds of the language. Japanese people with left-hemisphere damage are impaired in their ability to read *kana*, whereas people with right hemisphere damage are impaired in their ability to read *kanji*. Also, experiments with normal Japanese speakers show that the right hemisphere is better and faster than the left hemisphere at reading *kanji*, and vice versa.

The results of these neurolinguistic studies, which use different techniques and different subject populations, both normal and brain damaged, are converging to provide the information we seek on the relationship between the brain and various language and nonlanguage cognitive systems. However, as pointed out by Professors Colin Phillips and Kuniyoshi Sakai,

> . . . knowing where language is supported in the human brain is just one step on the path to finding what are the special properties of those brain regions that make language possible. . . . An important challenge for coming years will be to find whether the brain areas implicated in language studies turn out to have distinctive properties at the neuronal level that allow them to explain the special properties of human language.[2]

The Autonomy of Language

In addition to brain-damaged individuals who have lost their language ability, there are cases of children without brain lesions who nevertheless have difficulties in acquiring language or are much slower than the average child. They show no other

---

[2] C. Phillips and K. L. Sakai. 2005. "Language and the brain," in *Yearbook of Science and Technology 2005.* Boston: McGraw-Hill Publishers.

cognitive deficits, they are not autistic or retarded, and they have no perceptual problems. Such children are suffering from **specific language impairment (SLI)**. Only their linguistic ability is affected, and often only specific aspects of grammar are impaired.

Children with SLI have particular problems with the use of function words such as articles, prepositions, and auxiliary verbs. They also have difficulties with inflectional suffixes on nouns and verbs such as markers of tense and agreement. Several examples from a four-year-old boy with SLI illustrate the matter:

Meowmeow chase mice.
Show me knife.
It not long one.

An experimental study of several SLI children showed that they produced the past tense marker on the verb (as in *danc**ed***) about 27 percent of the time as compared to 95 percent by the normal control group. Similarly, the SLI children produced the plural marker -*s* (as in *boy**s***) only 9 percent of the time as compared to normal children, who produced it 95 percent of the time.

SLI children show that language may be impaired while general intelligence stays intact, supporting the view of a grammatical faculty that is separate from other cognitive systems. But is it possible for language to develop normally when general intelligence is impaired? If such individuals can be found, it argues strongly for the view that language does not derive from some general cognitive ability.

Other Dissociations of Language and Cognition

> . . . the human mind is not an unstructured entity but consists of components which can be distinguished by their functional properties.
> **NEIL SMITH AND IANTHI-MARIA TSIMPLI,** The Mind of a Savant: Language Learning and Modularity

There are numerous cases of intellectually handicapped individuals who, despite their disabilities in certain spheres, show remarkable talents in others. There are superb musicians and artists who lack the simple abilities required to take care of themselves. Such people are referred to as **savants**. Some of the most famous savants are human calculators who can perform arithmetic computations at phenomenal speed, or calendrical calculators who can tell you without pause on which day of the week falls any date in the last or next century.

Until recently, most such savants have been reported to be linguistically handicapped. They may be good mimics who can repeat speech like parrots, but they show meager creative language ability. Nevertheless, the literature reports cases of language savants who have acquired the highly complex grammar of their language (as well as other languages in some cases) but who lack nonlinguistic abilities of equal complexity. Laura and Christopher are two such cases.

LAURA

Laura was a retarded young woman with a nonverbal IQ of 41 to 44. She lacked almost all number concepts, including basic counting principles, and could draw only at a preschool level. She had an auditory memory span limited to three units. Yet, when at the age of sixteen she was asked to name some fruits, she responded with *pears, apples*, and *pomegranates*. In this same period she produced syntactically complex sentences like *He was saying that I lost my battery-powered watch that I loved* and *Last year at school when I first went there, three tickets were gave out by a police last year.*

Laura could not add 2 + 2. She was not sure of when "last year" was or whether it was before or after "last week" or "an hour ago," nor did she know how many tickets were "gave out," nor whether three was larger or smaller than two. Nevertheless, Laura produced complex sentences with multiple phrases. She used and understood passive sentences, and she was able to inflect verbs for number and person to agree with the subject of the sentence. She formed past tenses in accord with adverbs that referred to past time. She could do all this and more, but she could neither read nor write nor tell time. She did not know who the president of the United States was or what country she lived in or even her own age. Her drawings of humans resembled potatoes with stick arms and legs. Yet, in a sentence imitation task, she both detected and corrected grammatical errors.

Laura is but one of many examples of children who display well-developed grammatical abilities, less-developed abilities to associate linguistic expressions with the objects they refer to, and severe deficits in nonlinguistic cognition.

In addition, any notion that linguistic competence results simply from communicative abilities, or develops to serve communication functions, is belied by studies of children with good linguistic skills, but nearly no or severely limited communicative skills, such as high-functioning autistic children. The acquisition and use of language seem to depend on cognitive skills different from the ability to communicate in a social setting.

CHRISTOPHER

Christopher has a nonverbal IQ between 60 and 70 and must live in an institution because he is unable to take care of himself. The tasks of buttoning a shirt, cutting his fingernails, or vacuuming the carpet are too difficult for him. However, linguists find that his linguistic competence is as rich and as sophisticated as that of any native speaker. Furthermore, when given written texts in some fifteen to twenty languages, he translates them quickly, with few errors, into English. The languages include Germanic languages such as Danish, Dutch, and German; Romance languages such as French, Italian, Portuguese, and Spanish; as well as Polish, Finnish, Greek, Hindi, Turkish, and Welsh. He learned these languages from speakers who used them in his presence, or from grammar books. Christopher loves to study and learn languages. Little else is of interest to him. His situation strongly suggests that his linguistic ability is independent of his general intellectual ability.

The question as to whether the language faculty is a separate cognitive system or whether it is derivative of more general cognitive mechanisms is controversial and has received much attention and debate among linguists, psychologists, and neuropsychologists. Cases such as Laura and Christopher argue against the view that linguistic ability derives from general intelligence, because these two individuals (and others like them) developed language despite other intellectual deficits. A growing body of evidence supports the view that the human animal is biologically equipped from birth with an autonomous language faculty that is highly specific and that does not derive from general human intellectual ability.

Genetic Basis of Language

Studies of genetic disorders also reveal that one cognitive domain can develop normally along with abnormal development in other domains, and they also underscore the strong biological basis of language. Children with Turner's syndrome (a chromosomal anomaly) have normal language and advanced reading skills along with serious nonlinguistic (visual and spatial) cognitive deficits. Similarly, studies of the language of children and adolescents with Williams syndrome reveal a unique behavioral profile in which linguistic functions seem to be relatively preserved in the face of visual and spatial cognitive deficits and moderate retardation. In addition, developmental dyslexia and at least some types of SLI also appear to have a genetic basis.

Epidemiological studies show that SLI runs in families. A large multigenerational family, half of whom are language impaired, has been studied in detail. All of the people in the study are adult native speakers of English. The impaired members of this family have a very specific grammatical problem. They do not reliably indicate the tense of the verb. They routinely produce sentences such as the following:

She remembered when she hurts herself the other day.
He did it then he fall.
The boy climb up the tree and frightened the bird away.

These results point to SLI as a heritable disorder. Studies also show that monozygotic (identical) twins are more likely to both suffer from SLI than are dizygotic (fraternal) twins. Thus, evidence from aphasia, SLI, and other genetic disorders, along with the asymmetry of abilities in linguistic savants, strongly supports the view that the grammatical aspect of the language faculty is an autonomous, genetically determined module of the brain.

Language and Brain Development

"Jump Start" copyright © United Feature Syndicate. Reprinted with permission.

Language and the brain are intimately connected. Specific areas of the brain are devoted to language, and injury to these areas disrupts language. In the young child, injury to or removal of the left hemisphere has severe consequences for language development. Conversely, increasing evidence shows that normal brain development depends on early and regular exposure to language.

The Critical Period

Under normal circumstances, a child is introduced to language virtually at the moment of birth. Adults talk to him and to each other in his presence. Children do not require explicit language instruction, but they do need exposure to language in order to develop normally. Children who do not receive linguistic input during their formative years do not achieve native-like grammatical competence. Moreover, behavioral tests and brain imaging studies show that late exposure to language alters the fundamental organization of the brain for language.

The **critical-age hypothesis** assumes that language is biologically based and states that the ability to learn a native language develops within a fixed period, from birth to middle childhood. During this **critical period**, language acquisition proceeds easily, swiftly, and without external intervention. After this period, the acquisition of grammar is difficult and for most individuals never fully achieved. Children deprived of language during this critical period show atypical patterns of brain lateralization.

The notion of a critical period is true of many species and seems to pertain to species-specific, biologically triggered behaviors. Ducklings, for example, during the period from nine to twenty-one hours after hatching, will follow the first moving object they see, whether or not it looks or waddles like a duck. Such behavior is not the result of conscious decision, external teaching, or intensive practice. It unfolds according to what appears to be a maturationally determined schedule that is universal across the species. Similarly, as discussed in a later section, certain species of birds develop their bird song during a biologically determined window of time.

Instances of children reared in environments of extreme social isolation constitute "experiments in nature" for testing the critical-age hypothesis. Such reported cases go back at least to the eighteenth century. In 1758 Carl Linnaeus first included *Homo ferus* (wild or feral man) as a subdivision of *Homo sapiens*. According to Linnaeus, a defining characteristic of *Homo ferus* was his lack of speech or observable language of any kind.

The most dramatic cases of children raised in isolation are those described as "wild" or "feral" children, who have reportedly been reared with wild animals or have lived alone in the wilderness. In 1920 two feral children, Amala and Kamala, were found in India, supposedly having been reared by wolves. A celebrated case, documented in François Truffaut's film *The Wild Child*, is that of Victor, "the wild boy of Aveyron," who was found in 1798. It was ascertained that he had been left in the woods when very young and had somehow survived.

Other children have been isolated because of deliberate efforts to keep them from normal social intercourse. In 1970 a child called Genie in the scientific reports was discovered. She had been confined to a small room under conditions of physical restraint and had received only minimal human contact from the age of eighteen months until almost fourteen years. None of these children, regardless of the cause of isolation, was able to speak or knew any language at the time they were reintroduced into society.

This linguistic inability could simply be caused by the fact that these children received no linguistic input, showing that language acquisition, though an innate, neurologically based ability, must be triggered by input from the environment. In the documented cases of Victor and Genie, however, these children were unable to acquire language even after years of exposure, and in the case of Victor, despite deliberate and painstaking language training.

Genie did begin to acquire some language, but while she was able to learn a large vocabulary, including colors, shapes, objects, natural categories, and abstract as well as concrete terms, her syntax and morphology never fully developed. The UCLA linguist Susan Curtiss, who worked with Genie for several years, reported that Genie's utterances were, for the most part, "the stringing together of content words, often with rich and clear meaning, but with little grammatical structure." Many utterances produced by Genie at the age of fifteen and older, several years after her emergence from isolation, are like those of two-year-old children, and not unlike utterances of Broca's aphasia patients and people with SLI, such as the following:

Man motorcycle have.
Genie full stomach.
Genie bad cold live father house.
Want Curtiss play piano.
Open door key.

Genie's utterances lacked auxiliary verbs, articles, the third-person singular agreement marker, the past-tense marker, and most pronouns. She had no ability to form more complex types of sentences, such as the inversion of subject and verb needed to form questions (e.g., *Are you hungry*?). Genie started learning language after the critical period, and was therefore never able to fully acquire the grammatical rules of English.

Tests of lateralization (dichotic listening and ERP experiments) showed that Genie's language was lateralized to the *right* hemisphere. Her test performance was similar to that found in split-brain and left hemispherectomy patients, yet Genie was not brain damaged. Curtiss speculates that after the critical period, the usual language areas functionally atrophy because of inadequate linguistic stimulation. Genie's case also demonstrates that language is not the same as communication, because Genie was a powerful nonverbal communicator, despite her limited ability to acquire language.

Chelsea is a woman whose situation also supports the critical-age hypothesis. She was born deaf but was wrongly diagnosed as retarded. When she was thirty-one, her deafness was finally diagnosed and she was fitted with hearing aids. For years she has received extensive language training and therapy and has acquired a large vocabulary. However, like Genie, Chelsea has not been able to develop a grammar. ERP studies of the localization of language in Chelsea's brain have revealed an equal response to language in both hemispheres. In other words, Chelsea also does not show the normal asymmetric organization for language.

More than 90 percent of children who are born deaf or become deaf before they have acquired language are born to hearing parents. These children have also provided information about the critical age for language acquisition. Because most of their parents do not know sign language at the time these children are born, most receive delayed language exposure. Several studies have investigated the acquisition of American Sign Language (ASL) among deaf signers exposed to the language at different ages. Early learners who received ASL input from birth and up to six years of age did much better in the production and comprehension of complex signs and sign sentences than late learners who were not exposed to ASL until after the age of twelve, even though all of the subjects in these studies had used sign for more than twenty years. There was little difference, however, in vocabulary or knowledge of word order.

Another study compared patterns of lateralization in the brains of adult native speakers of English, adult native signers, and deaf adults who had not been exposed to sign language. The nonsigning deaf adults did not show the same cerebral asymmetries as either the hearing adults or the deaf signers.

The cases of Genie and other isolated children, as well as deaf late learners of ASL, show that children cannot fully acquire language unless they are exposed to it within the critical period—a biologically determined window of opportunity during which time the brain is prepared to develop language. Moreover, the critical period is linked to brain lateralization. The human brain is primed to develop language in specific areas of the left hemisphere, but the normal process of brain specialization depends on early and systematic experience with language.

Beyond the critical period, the human brain seems unable to acquire the grammatical aspects of language, even with substantial linguistic training or many years of exposure. However, it is possible to acquire words and various conversational skills after this point. This evidence suggests that the critical period holds for the acquisition of grammatical abilities, but not necessarily for all aspects of language.

The selective acquisition of certain components of language that occurs beyond the critical period is reminiscent of the selective impairment that occurs in various language disorders, where specific linguistic abilities are disrupted. This selectivity in both acquisition and impairment points to a strongly modularized language faculty. Language is separate from other cognitive systems and autonomous, and is itself a complex system with various components. In the chapters that follow, we will explore these different language components.

A Critical Period for Bird Song

That's the wise thrush; he sings each song twice over
Lest you should think he never could recapture
The first fine careless rapture!

ROBERT BROWNING, Home-thoughts from Abroad

4-20
© 2004 Bil Keane, Inc.
Dist. by King Features Synd.
www.familycircus.com

"How long do little birds hafta practice before they learn their song?"

"Family Circus" © Bil Keane, Inc. Reprinted with permission of King Features Syndicate.

Bird song lacks certain fundamental characteristics of human language, such as discrete sounds and creativity. However, certain species of birds show a critical period for acquiring their "language" similar to the critical period for human language acquisition.

Calls and songs of the chaffinch vary depending on the geographic area that the bird inhabits. The message is the same, but the form or "pronunciation" is different. Usually, a young bird sings a simplified version of the song shortly after hatching. Later, it undergoes further learning in acquiring the fully complex version. Because birds from the same brood acquire different chaffinch songs depending on the area in which they finally settle, part of the song must be learned. On the other hand, because the fledging chaffinch sings the song of its species in a simple degraded form, even if it has never heard it sung, some aspect of it is biologically determined, that is, innate.

The chaffinch acquires its fully developed song in several stages, just as human children acquire language. There is also a critical period in the song learning of chaffinches as well as white-crowned sparrows, zebra finches, and many other species. If these birds are not exposed to the songs of their species during certain fixed periods after their birth—the period differs from species to species—song acquisition does not occur. The chaffinch is unable to learn new song elements after ten months of age. If it is isolated from other birds before attaining the full complexity of its song and is then exposed again after ten months, its song will not develop further. If white-crowned sparrows lose their hearing during a critical period after they have learned to sing, they produce a song that differs from other white crowns. They need to hear themselves sing in order to produce particular whistles and other song features. If, however, the deafness occurs after the critical period, their songs are normal.

On the other hand, some bird species show no critical period. The cuckoo sings a fully developed song even if it never hears another cuckoo sing. These communicative messages are entirely innate. For other species, songs appear to be at least partially learned, and the learning may occur throughout the bird's lifetime. The bullfinch, for example, will learn elements of songs it is exposed to, even those of another species, and incorporate those elements into its own quiet warble. In a more recent example of unconstrained song learning, Danish ornithologists report that birds have begun to copy the ringing tones of cellular phones.

From the point of view of human language research, the relationship between the innate and learned aspects of bird song is significant. Apparently, the basic nature of the songs of some species is present from birth, which means that it is biologically and genetically determined. The same holds true for human language: its basic nature is innate. The details of bird song, and of human language, are acquired through experience that must occur within a critical period.

The Evolution of Language

As the voice was used more and more, the vocal organs would have been strengthened and perfected through the principle of the inherited effects of use; and this would have reacted on the power of speech. But the relation between the continued use of language and the development of the brain has no doubt been far more important. The mental powers in some early progenitor of man must have been more highly developed than in any existing ape, before even the most imperfect form of speech could have come into use.

CHARLES DARWIN, The Descent of Man

If the human brain is structured and wired for the acquisition and use of language, how and when did this development occur? Two scholarly societies, the American Anthropological Association and the New York Academy of Sciences, held forums in 1974 and 1976 to review research on this question. It is not a new question, and it seems to have arisen with the origin of the species.

In the Beginning: The Origin of Language

> Nothing, no doubt, would be more interesting than to know from historical documents the exact process by which the first man began to lisp his first words, and thus to be rid forever of all the theories on the origin of speech.
>
> **M. MULLER,** *1871*

All religions and mythologies contain stories of language origin. Philosophers through the ages have argued the question. Scholarly works have been written on the subject. Prizes have been awarded for the "best answer" to this eternally perplexing problem. Theories of divine origin, evolutionary development, and language as a human invention have all been suggested.

The difficulties inherent in answering this question are immense. Anthropologists believe that the species has existed for at least one million years, and perhaps for as long as five or six million years. Linguistic history suggests that spoken languages of the kind that exist today have been around for tens of thousands of years at the very least, but the earliest deciphered written records are barely six thousand years old. (The origin of writing is discussed in chapter 12.) These records appear so late in the history of the development of language that they provide no clue to its origin.

For these reasons, scholars in the latter part of the nineteenth century, who were only interested in "hard science," ridiculed, ignored, and even banned discussions of language origin. In 1886 the Linguistic Society of Paris passed a resolution to ignore papers concerned with this subject.

Despite the difficulty of finding scientific evidence, speculations on language origin have provided valuable insights into the nature and development of language, which prompted the great Danish linguist Otto Jespersen to state that "linguistic science cannot refrain forever from asking about the whence (and about the whither) of linguistic evolution." A brief look at some of these speculative notions will reveal this point.

GOD'S GIFT TO MANKIND?

> And out of the ground the Lord God formed every beast of the field, and every fowl of the air, and brought them unto Adam to see what he would call them; and whatsoever Adam called every living creature, that was the name thereof.
>
> GENESIS 2:19

According to Judeo-Christian beliefs, God gave Adam the power to name all things. Similar beliefs are found throughout the world. According to the Egyptians, the creator of speech was the god Thoth. Babylonians believed that the language giver was the god Nabu, and the Hindus attributed our unique language ability to a female god: Brahma was the creator of the universe, but his wife Sarasvati gave language to us.

Belief in the divine origin of language is intertwined with the supernatural properties that have been associated with the spoken word. Children in all cultures utter "magic" words like *abracadabra* to ward off evil or bring good luck. Harry Potter novels introduce the reader to a large vocabulary of magical words used to bring about magical ends such as *reparo* for fixing broken objects. Despite the childish jingle "Sticks and stones may break my bones, but names will never hurt me," name-calling is insulting, cause for legal punishment, and feared. In some cultures, when certain words are used, one is required to counter them by "knocking on wood," or some such ritualistic action.

In many religions, only special languages may be used in prayers and rituals. The Hindu priests of the fifth century B.C.E. believed that the original pronunciation of Vedic Sanskrit was sacred and must be preserved. This led to important linguistic study because their language had already changed greatly since the hymns of the Vedas had been written. The first linguist known to us is Panini, who wrote a descriptive grammar of Sanskrit in the fourth century B.C.E. that revealed the earlier pronunciation, which could then be used in religious worship. (For this monumental achievement, the Indian government issued a postage stamp in his honor in 2004.)

Although myths, customs, and superstitions do not tell us very much about language origin, they do tell us about the importance ascribed to language. There is no way to prove or disprove the divine origin of language, just as one cannot argue scientifically for or against the existence of God.

THE FIRST LANGUAGE

> Imagine the Lord talking French! Aside from a few odd words in Hebrew, I took it completely for granted that God had never spoken anything but the most dignified English.
>
> CLARENCE DAY, Life with Father

Among the proponents of the divine origin theory, a great interest arose in the language used by God, Adam, and Eve. For millennia, "scientific" experiments have reportedly been devised to verify particular theories of the first language. The Greek historian Herodotus reported that the Egyptian pharaoh Psammetichus (664–610 B.C.E.) sought to determine the most primitive language by experimental methods. The monarch was said to have placed two infants in an isolated mountain hut, to be cared for by a mute servant. The pharaoh believed that without linguistic input, the children would develop their own language and would thus reveal the original tongue of man. The Egyptian waited patiently for the children to become old enough to talk. According to the story, the first word uttered was *bekos*, the word for "bread" in Phrygian, a language once spoken in what is now Turkey. Based on this "experiment," this ancient language, which has long since died out, was thought to be the original language.

History is replete with other proposals. In the thirteenth century, the Holy Roman Emperor Frederick II of Hohenstaufen was said to have carried out a similar test, but the children died before they uttered a single word. James IV of Scotland (1473–1513), however, supposedly succeeded in replicating the experiment with the surprising results, according to legend, that the Scottish children "spak very guid Ebrew," providing "scientific evidence" that Hebrew was the language used in the Garden of Eden.

J. G. Becanus argued in the sixteenth century that German must have been the primeval language, because God would have used the "most perfect language." In 1830 the lexicographer Noah Webster asserted that the protolanguage must have been Chaldee (Aramaic), the language spoken in Jerusalem during the Roman occupation. In 1887 Joseph Elkins maintained that "there is no other language which can be more reasonably assumed to be the speech first used in the world's gray morning than can Chinese."

The belief that all languages originated from a single source—**the monogenetic theory of language origin**—is found not only in the Tower of Babel story in Genesis, but also in a similar legend of the Toltecs, early inhabitants of Mexico, and in the myths of other peoples as well.

We are no closer today to discovering the original language (or languages) than was Psammetichus, given the obscurities of prehistory. A more detailed discussion of the history of human languages is found in chapter 11.

HUMAN INVENTION OR THE CRIES OF NATURE?

> Language was born in the courting days of mankind; the first utterances of speech I fancy to myself like something between the nightly love lyrics of puss upon the tiles and the melodious love songs of the nightingale.
>
> **OTTO JESPERSEN,** Language, Its Nature, Development and Origin

The Greeks speculated about nearly everything in the universe, including language. The earliest surviving linguistic treatise that deals with the origin and nature of language is Plato's *Cratylus*. A common view among the classical Greeks, expressed by Socrates in this dialogue, was that at some ancient time, a "legislator" gave the correct, natural name to everything, and that words echoed the essence of their meanings.

Despite all evidence to the contrary, the idea that the earliest form of language was imitative, or echoic, was proposed up to the twentieth century. Called the bow-wow "theory," although hardly deserving that appellation, it claimed that a dog would be designated by the word *bow-wow* because of the sounds of his bark.

A parallel view states that language at first consisted of emotional ejaculations of pain, fear, surprise, pleasure, anger, and so on. French philosopher Jean-Jacques Rousseau proposed that the earliest manifestations of language were "cries of nature."

Another hypothesis suggests that language arose out of the rhythmical grunts of men and women working together. Jespersen suggested a more charming view when he proposed that language derived from song as an expressive rather than a communicative need. To Jespersen, love was the great stimulus for language development. Just as with the beliefs in a divine origin of language, these proposed origins are not verifiable by scientific means.

The Development of Language in the Species

There is much interest today among biologists as well as linguists in the relationship between the development of language and the evolutionary development of the human species. Some view language ability as a difference in degree between humans and other primates—a continuity view—and others see the onset of language ability as a qualitative leap—the discontinuity view. Some people on both sides of the discontinuity view believe that language is species specific.

In trying to understand the development of language, scholars past and present have debated the role played by the vocal tract and the ear. For example, it has been suggested that speech could not have developed in nonhuman primates because their vocal tracts were anatomically incapable of producing a large enough inventory of speech sounds. According to this hypothesis, the development of language is linked to the evolutionary development of the speech production and perception apparatus. This, of course, would be accompanied by changes in the brain and the nervous system toward greater complexity. Such a view implies that the languages of our human ancestors of millions of years ago may have been syntactically and phonologically simpler than any language known to us today. The notion "simpler" is left undefined, although it has been suggested that this primeval language had a smaller inventory of sounds.

One evolutionary step must have resulted in the development of a vocal tract capable of producing the wide variety of sounds of human language, as well as the mechanism for perceiving and distinguishing them. However, the existence of mynah birds and parrots is evidence that this step is insufficient to explain the origin of language, because these creatures have the ability to imitate human speech, but not the ability to acquire language.

More important, we know from the study of humans who are born deaf and learn sign languages that are used around them that the ability to hear speech sounds is not a necessary condition for the acquisition and use of language. In addition, the lateralization evidence from ERP and imaging studies of people using sign language, as well as evidence from sign language aphasia, show that sign language is organized in the brain like spoken language. Certain auditory locations within the cortex are activated during signing even though no sound is involved, supporting the contention that the brain is neurologically equipped to learn language rather than speech. The ability to produce and hear a wide variety of sounds therefore appears to be neither necessary nor sufficient for the development of language in the human species.

A major step in the development of language most probably relates to evolutionary changes in the brain. The linguist Noam Chomsky expresses this view:

It could be that when the brain reached a certain level of complexity it simply automatically had certain properties because that's what happens when you pack 10^{10} neurons into something the size of a basketball.[3]

The biologist Stephen Jay Gould expresses a similar view:

The Darwinist model would say that language, like other complex organic systems, evolved step by step, each step being an adaptive solution. Yet language is such an integrated "all or none" system, it is hard to imagine it evolving that way. Perhaps the brain grew in size and became capable of all kinds of things which were not part of the original properties.[4]

Other linguists, however, support a more Darwinian natural selection development of what is sometimes called "the language instinct":

All the evidence suggests that it is the precise wiring of the brain's microcircuitry that makes language happen, not gross size, shape, or neuron packing.[5]

The attempt to resolve this controversy clearly requires more research. Another point that is not yet clear is what role, if any, hemispheric lateralization played in language evolution. Lateralization certainly makes greater specialization possible. Research conducted with birds and monkeys, however, shows that lateralization is not unique to the human brain. Thus, while it may constitute a necessary step in the evolution of language, it is not a sufficient one.

We do not yet have definitive answers to the origin of language in the human brain. The search for these answers goes on and provides new insights into the nature of language and the nature of the human brain.

Summary

The attempt to understand what makes language acquisition and use possible has led to research on the brain-mind-language relationship. **Neurolinguistics** studies the brain mechanisms and anatomical structures that underlie linguistic competence and performance and how they developed over time.

The brain is the most complicated organ of the body, controlling motor and sensory activities and thought processes. Research conducted for over a century reveals that different parts of the brain control different body functions. The nerve cells that form the surface of the brain are called the **cortex**, which serves as the intellectual decision maker, receiving messages from the sensory organs and initiating all voluntary actions. The brain of all higher animals is divided into two parts called the **cerebral hemispheres**, which are connected by the **corpus callosum**, a network that permits the left and right hemispheres to communicate.

Each hemisphere exhibits **contralateral** control of functions. The left hemisphere controls the right side of the body, and the right hemisphere controls the left side.

---

[3] N. Chomsky. 1994. Video. *The Human Language Series*. Program Three. By G. Searchinger.
[4] S. J. Gould. 1994. Video. *The Human Language Series*. Program Three. By G. Searchinger.
[5] S. Pinker. 1995. *The Language Instinct*. New York: Morrow.

Despite the general symmetry of the human body, much evidence suggests that the brain is asymmetric, with the left and right hemispheres lateralized for different functions.

Neurolinguists have many tools for studying the brain, among them **dichotic listening** experiments and scans of various types such as computed tomography (CT), **magnetic resonance imaging (MRI)**, functional magnetic resonance imaging (fMRI), **positron emission tomography (PET)**, and magnetic encephalography (MEG). Additionally, **event-related brain potential (ERP)** measurements reveal activity in specific parts of the brain in response to specific stimuli. These techniques permit the study of the living brain as it processes language and reveals the **lateralization** or *asymmetry of function* of the two hemispheres, with the left hemisphere specialized for language. Furthermore, by applying these techniques to the study of persons who have had parts of the brain surgically removed, to **split-brain** patients, and to persons with **aphasia** (language dysfunction as a result of brain damage), localized areas of the brain can be associated with particular language functions. For example, lesions in the part of the brain called **Broca's area** may suffer from **Broca's aphasia**, which results in impaired syntax and **agrammatism**. Damage to **Wernicke's area** may result in **Wernicke's aphasia**, in which fluent speakers produce semantically anomalous utterances, or even worse, **jargon aphasia**, in which speakers produce nonsense forms that make their utterance uninterpretable. Damage to yet different areas can produce **anomia**, a form of aphasia in which the patient has word-finding difficulties.

Deaf signers with damage to the left hemisphere show aphasia for sign language similar to the language breakdown in hearing aphasics, even though sign language is a visual-spatial language.

Other evidence supports the lateralization of language. Children with early brain lesions in the left hemisphere, which result in **hemispherectomy**—the surgical removal of part or all of the left brain—show specific linguistic deficits, whereas other cognitive abilities remain intact. If the right brain is damaged or removed, however, language is unimpaired, but other cognitive disorders may result.

The language faculty is **modular**. It is independent from other cognitive systems with which it interacts. Evidence for modularity is found in studies of aphasia, of children with **specific language impairment (SLI)**, of **savants**, and of children who learn language past the **critical period**. Children with SLI suffer from language deficits, but are normal in other regards. Language savants are individuals with extraordinary language skills, but who are deficient in general intelligence. Their existence suggests that linguistic ability is not derived from some general cognitive ability but exists independently.

The genetic basis for an independent language module is supported by studies of SLI in families and twins and by studies of genetic anomalies associated with language disorders. The **critical-age hypothesis** states that there is a window of opportunity between birth and middle childhood for learning a first language. The imperfect language learning of persons exposed to language after this period supports the hypothesis. Some songbirds also appear to have a critical period for the acquisition of their calls and songs.

The origin of language in the species has been a topic for much speculation throughout history. The idea that language was God's gift to humanity is present in religions around the world. The continuing belief in the miraculous powers of language is tied to this notion. The assumption of the divine origin of language stimulated interest in discovering the first primeval language. There are legendary experiments in which children were isolated in the belief that their first words would reveal the original language.

Other views suggest that language is a human invention, stemming from "cries of nature," early gestures, **onomatopoeic** words, or even from songs to express love. The ancient Greeks believed that a "legislator" gave the true names to all things.

Language most likely evolved with the human species, possibly in stages, possibly in one giant leap. Research by linguists, evolutionary biologists, and neurologists support this view and the view that from the outset the human animal was genetically equipped to learn language. Studies of the evolutionary development of the brain provide some evidence for physiological and anatomic preconditions for language development.

References for Further Reading

Caplan, D. 1987. *Neurolinguistics and Linguistic Aphasiology*. Cambridge, England: Cambridge University Press.

———. 1992. *Language: Structure, Processing, and Disorders*. Cambridge, MA: MIT Press.

———. 2001. "Neurolinguistics." *The Handbook of Linguistics,* M. Aronoff and J. Rees-Miller (eds.). London: Blackwell Publishers.

Coltheart, M., K. Patterson, and J. C. Marshall, eds. 1980. *Deep Dyslexia*. London, England: Routledge & Kegan Paul.

Curtiss, S. 1977. *Genie: A Linguistic Study of a Modern-Day "Wild Child."* New York: Academic Press.

Damasio, H. 1981. "Cerebral Localization of the Aphasias," in *Acquired Aphasia*, M. Taylor Sarno (ed.). New York: Academic Press, pp. 27–65.

Gardner, H. 1978. "What We Know (and Don't Know) about the Two Halves of the Brain." *Harvard Magazine* 80: 24–27.

Gazzaniga, M. S. 1970. *The Bisected Brain*. New York: Appleton-Century-Crofts.

Geschwind, N. 1979. "Specializations of the Human Brain." *Scientific American* 206 (Sept.): 180–199.

Lenneberg, E. H. 1967. *Biological Foundations of Language*. New York: Wiley.

Obler, L. K., and K. Gjerlow. 1999. *Language and Brain*. Cambridge, England: Cambridge University Press.

Patterson, K. E., J. C. Marshall, and M. Coltheart (eds.). 1986. *Surface Dyslexia*. Hillsdale, NJ: Lawrence Erlbaum.

Pinker, S. 1994. *The Language Instinct*. New York: William Morrow.

Poizner, H., E. S. Klima, and U. Bellugi. 1987. *What the Hands Reveal about the Brain*. Cambridge, MA: MIT Press.

Searchinger, G. 1994. *The Human Language Series: 1, 2, 3*. New York: Equinox Film/Ways of Knowing, Inc.

Smith, N. V. 1998. "Jackdaws, sex and language acquisition." *Glot International.* Available online at www.linguistlistplus.com/glot/PDF/vol3/glot3-7.pdf.

Smith, N. V., and I-M. Tsimpli. 1995. *The Mind of a Savant: Language Learning and Modularity*. Oxford, England: Blackwell.

Springer, S. P., and G. Deutsch. 1997. *Left Brain, Right Brain,* 5th edition. New York: W. H. Freeman and Company.

Stam, J. 1976. *Inquiries into the Origin of Language: The Fate of a Question*. New York: Harper & Row.

Stromswold, K., D. Caplan, N. Alpert, and S. Rauch. 1996. "Localization of syntactic comprehension by positron emission tomography." *Brain and Language* 52: 452–473.

Stromswold, K. 2001. "The heretability of language." *Language* 77(4): 647–721.

Yamada, J. 1990. *Laura: A Case for the Modularity of Language*. Cambridge, MA: MIT Press.

Exercises

1. The Nobel Prize laureate Roger Sperry has argued that split-brain patients have two minds:

> Everything we have seen so far indicates that the surgery has left these people with two separate minds, that is, two separate spheres of consciousness. What is experienced in the right hemisphere seems to lie entirely outside the realm of experience of the left hemisphere.

Another Nobel Prize winner in physiology, Sir John Eccles, disagrees. He does not think the right hemisphere can think; he distinguishes between "mere consciousness," which animals possess as well as humans, and language, thought, and other purely human cognitive abilities. In fact, according to him, human nature is all in the left hemisphere.

Write a short essay discussing these two opposing points of view, stating your opinion on how to define "the mind."

2. a. Some aphasic patients, when asked to read a list of words, substitute other words for those printed. In many cases, the printed words and the substituted words are similar. The following data are from actual aphasic patients. In each case, state what the two words have in common and how they differ:

Printed Word	Word Spoken by Aphasic
i. liberty	freedom
canary	parrot
abroad	overseas
large	long
short	small
tall	long
ii. decide	decision
conceal	concealment
portray	portrait
bathe	bath
speak	discussion
remember	memory

b. What do the words in groups (i) and (ii) reveal about how words are likely to be stored in the brain?

3. The following sentences spoken by aphasic patients were collected and analyzed by Dr. Harry Whitaker. In each case, state how the sentence deviates from normal nonaphasic language.

    a. There is under a horse a new sidesaddle.

    b. In girls we see many happy days.

    c. I'll challenge a new bike.

    d. I surprise no new glamour.

    e. Is there three chairs in this room?

    f. Mike and Peter is happy.

    g. Bill and John likes hot dogs.

    h. Proliferate is a complete time about a word that is correct.

    i. Went came in better than it did before.

4. The investigation of individuals with brain damage has been a major source of information regarding the neural basis of language and other cognitive systems. One might suggest that this is like trying to understand how an automobile engine works by looking at a damaged engine. Is this a good analogy? If so, why? If not, why not? In your answer, discuss how a damaged system can or cannot provide information about the normal system.

5. What are the arguments and evidence that have been put forth to support the notion that there are two separate parts of the brain?

6. Discuss the statement by A. W. Wigan that "It only takes one hemisphere to have a mind."

7. In this chapter, dichotic listening tests in which subjects hear different kinds of stimuli in each ear were discussed. These tests showed that there were fewer errors made in reporting linguistic stimuli such as the syllables *pa, ta, ka* when heard through an earphone on the right ear; other nonlinguistic sounds such as a police car siren were processed with fewer mistakes if heard by the left ear. This is a result of the contralateral control of the brain. There is also a technique that permits visual stimuli to be received either by the right visual field, that is, the right eye alone (going directly to the left hemisphere), or the left visual field (going directly to the right hemisphere). What are some visual stimuli that could be used in an experiment to further test the lateralization of language?

8. The following utterances were made either by Broca's aphasics or Wernicke's aphasics. Indicate which is which by writing a "B" or "W" next to the utterance.

    a. Goodnight and in the pansy I can't say but into a flipdoor you can see it.

    b. Well . . . sunset . . . uh . . . horses nine, no, uh, two, tails want swish.

    c. Oh, . . . if I could I would, and a sick old man disflined a sinter, minter.

    d. Words . . . words . . . words . . . two, four, six, eight, . . . blaze am he.

9. Shakespeare's Hamlet surely had problems. Some say he was obsessed with being overweight because the first lines he speaks in the play when alone on the stage in Act II, Scene 2, are:

        O! that this too too solid flesh would melt,

        Thaw, and resolve itself into a dew;

Others argue that he may have had Wernicke's aphasia, as evidenced by the following passage from Act II, Scene 2:

> Slanders, sir: for the satirical rogue says here
>
> that old men have grey beards, that their faces are
>
> wrinkled, their eyes purging thick amber and
>
> plum-tree gum and that they have a plentiful lack of
>
> wit, together with most weak hams: all which, sir,
>
> though I most powerfully and potently believe, yet
>
> I hold it not honesty to have it thus set down, for you
>
> yourself, sir, should be old as I am, if like a crab
>
> you could go backward.

Take up the argument. Is Hamlet aphasic? Argue either case.

10. **Mini-research project**: Recently, it's been said that persons born with "perfect pitch" nonetheless need to exercise that ability at a young age or it goes away by adulthood. Find out what you can about this topic and write a one-page (or more) paper describing your investigation. Begin with defining "perfect pitch." Relate your discoveries to the *critical-age hypothesis* discussed in this chapter.

11. **Mini-article review project**: Read, summarize, and critically review the following article that appeared in *Science,* Volume 298, November 22, 2002, by Marc D. Hauser, Noam Chomsky, and W. Tecumseh Fitch, entitled "The Faculty of Language: What Is It, Who Has It, and How Did It Evolve?"

12. As discussed in the chapter, agrammatic aphasics may have difficulty reading function words, which are words that have little descriptive content, but they can read more contentful words such as nouns, verbs, and adjectives.

    a. Which of the following words would you predict to be difficult for such a person?

ore	bee	can (be able to)	but
not	knot	May	be
may	can (metal container)	butt	or
will (future)	might (possibility)	will (willingness)	might (strength)

    b. Discuss three sources of evidence that function words and content words are stored or processed differently in the brain.

13. The traditional writing system of the Chinese languages (e.g., Mandarin, Cantonese) is ideographic (i.e., each concept or word is represented by a distinct character). More recently, the Chinese government has adoped a spelling system called *pinyin*, which is based on the Roman alphabet, and in which each symbol represents a sound. Following are several Chinese words in their character and *pinyin* forms. (The digit following the Roman letters in *pinyin* is a tone indicator and may be ignored.)

木	mu4	tree
花	hua1	flower
人	ren2	man
家	jia1	home
狗	gou3	dog

Based on the information provided in this chapter, would the location of neural activity be the same or different when Chinese speakers read in these two systems? Explain.

14. **Research project**: Dame Margaret Thatcher, a former prime minister of the United Kingdom, has been (famously) quoted as saying: "If you want something said, ask a man . . . if you want something done, ask a woman." This suggests, perhaps, that men and women process information differently. This exercise asks you to take up the controversial question: *Are there gender differences in the brain having to do with how men and women process and use language?* You might begin your research by seeking answers (try the Internet) to questions about the incidence of SLI, dyslexia, and language development differences in boys versus girls.

PART 2

Grammatical Aspects of Language

The theory of grammar is concerned with the question: What is the nature of a person's knowledge of his language, the knowledge that enables him to make use of language in the normal, creative fashion? A person who knows a language has mastered a system of rules that assigns sound and meaning in a definite way for an infinite class of possible sentences.

N. CHOMSKY, Language and Mind

3

Morphology: The Words of Language

A word is dead
When it is said,
Some say.
I say it just
Begins to live
That day.

EMILY DICKINSON, *"A Word Is Dead"*

Every speaker of every language knows tens of thousands of words. *Webster's Third International Dictionary of the English Language* has more than 450,000 entries. Most speakers don't know all of these words. It has been estimated that a child of six knows as many as 13,000 words and the average high school graduate about 60,000. A college graduate presumably knows many more than that, but whatever our level of education, we learn new words throughout our lives, such as many words in this book that you will learn for the first time.

Words are an important part of linguistic knowledge and constitute a component of our mental grammars, but one can learn thousands of words in a language and still not know the language. Anyone who has tried to communicate in a foreign country by merely using a dictionary knows this is true. On the other hand, without words we would be unable to convey our thoughts through language or understand the thoughts of others.

Someone who doesn't know English would not know where one word begins or ends in an utterance like *Thecatsatonthemat*. We separate written words by spaces, but in the spoken language there are no pauses between most words. Without knowledge of the language, one can't tell how many words are in an utterance. Knowing a word means knowing that a particular sequence of sounds is associated with a particular meaning. A speaker of English has no difficulty in segmenting the stream of sounds into six individual words: *the, cat, sat, on, the,* and *mat* because each of these words is listed in his mental dictionary, or **lexicon** (the Greek word for *dictionary*), which is part of a speaker's linguistic knowledge. Similarly, a speaker of the American Indian language Potawatomi knows that *kwapmuknanuk* (which means "they see us") is just one word because this word, with its associated meaning and pronunciation, is part of his lexicon.

The lack of pauses between words in speech has provided humorists with much material. The comical hosts of the show *CarTalk*, aired on National Public Radio, close the show by reading a list of credits that includes the following cast of characters:

Copyeditor	Adeline Moore	(Add a line more)
Accounts payable	Ineeda Czech	(I need a check)
Pollution Control	Maury Missions	(More emissions)
Purchasing	Lois Bidder	(Lowest bidder)
Statistician	Marge Innovera	(Margin of error)
Russian chauffeur	Picov Andropov	(Pick up and drop off)
Legal firm	Dewey, Cheetham, and Howe[1]	(Do we cheat 'em, and how)

In all these instances, you would have to have knowledge of English words to make sense of and find humor in such plays on words.

The fact that the same sound sequences (Lois Bidder—lowest bidder) can be interpreted differently, even between languages, gave birth to an entertaining book. The title, *Mots D'Heures: Gousses, Rames*,[2] was derived from the fact that *Mother Goose Rhymes*, spoken in English, sounds to a French speaker a little like the French words meaning "Words of the Hours: Root and Branch." The first rhyme in French starts:

Un petit d'un petit
S'étonne aux Halles.

When interpreted as if it were English it would sound like:

Humpty Dumpty
Sat on a wall.

These examples show that the relation between sound and meaning is an arbitrary pairing, as discussed in chapter 1. *Un petit d'un petit* in French means "a little one of a little one," but in English the sounds resemble the name *Humpty Dumpty*.

When you know a word, you know its sound (pronunciation) and its meaning. Because the sound-meaning relation is arbitrary, it is possible to have words with the same sound and different meanings (*bear* and *bare)*, and words with the same meaning and different sounds (*sofa* and *couch*).

Some facts about words are not part of our linguistic knowledge of a language, such as their etymology (historical development: *algebra* from Arabic *al-jabr*), or information about the longest or shortest word in the language. Children do not learn such facts the way they learn the sound-meaning correspondences of the words of their language. Both children and adults have to be told that *pneumonoultramicroscopicsilicovolcanoconiosis*—a disease of the lungs—is (reputedly) the longest English word. As we shall see in chapter 8, children don't have to conduct such research acquiring their language. They learn words like *elephant, disappear, mother*, and all the other words they know without being taught them explicitly or looking them up in a dictionary.

---

[1] "Car Talk" from National Public Radio.™ Dewey, Cheetham & Howe, 2006, all rights reserved.
[2] L. d'Antin Van Routen, ed. and annotator. 1993. *Mots d'Heures: Gousses Rames. The d'Antin Manuscript*. London: Grafton.

Because each word is a sound-meaning unit, each word stored in our mental lexicon must be listed with its unique phonological representation, which determines its pronunciation, and with a meaning. For literate speakers, the spelling, or **orthography**, of most of the words we know is included.

Each word in your mental lexicon includes other information as well, such as whether it is a noun, a pronoun, a verb, an adjective, an adverb, a preposition, or a conjunction. That is, the mental lexicon also specifies the **grammatical category** or **syntactic class** of the word. You may not consciously know that a form like *love* is listed as both a verb and a noun, but a speaker has such knowledge, as shown by the phrases *I love you* and *You are the love of my life*. If such information were not in the mental lexicon, we would not know how to form grammatical sentences, nor would we be able to distinguish grammatical from ungrammatical sentences. In later chapters we will discuss the different classes of words—the syntactic categories such as nouns, verbs, adjectives, and so on; the phonological properties of words that specify their pronunciation; and the semantic properties of words, which determine their meanings.

Dictionaries

Dictionary, n. A malevolent literary device for cramping the growth of a language and making it hard and inelastic.

AMBROSE BIERCE, The Devil's Dictionary

The dictionaries that one buys in a bookstore contain some of the information found in our mental dictionaries. The first dictionary to be printed in England was the Latin-English *Promptuorium parvulorum* in 1499; another Latin-English dictionary by Sir Thomas Elyot was published in 1538. Noah Webster (1758–1843) published *An American Dictionary of the English Language* in two volumes in 1828. It contained about 70,000 entries.

One of the best efforts at **lexicography**—the editing or making of a dictionary—was the *Dictionary of the English Language* by Dr. Samuel Johnson, published in 1755 in two volumes.

The aim of most early **lexicographers**, whom Dr. Johnson called "harmless drudges," was to *prescribe* rather than *describe* the words of a language. They strove to be, as stated in Webster's dictionaries, the "supreme authority" of the "correct" pronunciation and meaning of a word. To Johnson's credit, he stated in his preface that he could not construct the language but could only "register" it.

All dictionaries, from *The Oxford English Dictionary* (often referred to as the *OED* and called the greatest lexicographic work ever produced), to the more commonly used collegiate dictionaries, provide the following information about each word: (1) spelling, (2) the "standard" pronunciation, (3) definitions to represent the word's one or more meanings, and (4) parts of speech (e.g., noun, verb, preposition). Other information may include the etymology or history of the word, whether the word is nonstandard (such as *ain't*) or slang, vulgar, or obsolete. Many dictionaries provide quotations from published literature to illustrate the given definitions, as was first done by Johnson.

In recent years, perhaps because of the increasing specialization in science and the arts, or the growing fragmentation of the populace, we see the proliferation of hundreds of specialty and subspecialty dictionaries. A reference librarian at UCLA's Engineering and Mathematical Sciences Library estimates that her library has more than six hundred such books.

Dictionaries of slang and jargon (see chapter 10) have existed for many years; so have multilingual dictionaries. In addition to these, the shelves of bookstores and libraries are now filled with dictionaries written specifically for biologists, engineers, agriculturists, economists, artists, architects, printers, gays and lesbians, transvestites, athletes, tennis players, and almost any group that has its own set of words to describe what they think and what they do. Our own mental dictionaries probably include only a small set of the entries in all of these dictionaries, but each word is in someone's lexicon.

Content Words and Function Words

"... and even ... the patriotic archbishop of Canterbury found it advisable—"

"Found what?" said the Duck.

"Found it," the Mouse replied rather crossly; "of course you know what 'it' means."

"I know what 'it' means well enough, when I find a thing," said the Duck; "it's generally a frog or a worm. The question is, what did the archbishop find?"

LEWIS CARROLL, Alice's Adventures in Wonderland

Languages make an important distinction between two kinds of words—content words and function words. Nouns, verbs, adjectives, and adverbs are the **content words**. These words denote concepts such as objects, actions, attributes, and ideas that we can think about like *children, anarchism, soar*, and *purple*. Content words are sometimes called the **open class** words because we can and regularly do add new words to these classes. A new word, *steganography*, which is the art of hiding information in electronic text, entered English with the Internet revolution. Verbs like *dis* have come into the language quite recently, as have nouns like *blog* and adverbs like *24/7*, pronounced "twenty-four seven."

Different languages may express the same concept using words of different grammatical classes. For example, Akan, which is spoken in Ghana, contains only a handful of adjectives. Most concepts that would be expressed with adjectives in English are expressed by verbs in Akan. Instead of saying "The sun is bright today," an Akan speaker will say "The sun 'brights' today."

Other classes of words do not have clear lexical meaning or obvious concepts associated with them, including conjunctions such as *and, or*, and *but*; prepositions such as *in* and *of*; the articles *the, a/an*, and pronouns such as *it* and *he* or *she*. These kinds of words are called **function words** because they specify grammatical relations and have little or no semantic content. For example, the articles indicate whether a noun is definite or indefinite—*the* boy or *a* boy. The preposition *of* indicates possession, as in "the book of yours," but this word indicates many other kinds of relations too. The *it* in *it's raining*, or *the archbishop found it advisable* are further examples of words whose function is purely grammatical—they are required by the rules of syntax, and as the cartoon suggests, we can hardly do without them.

Function words are sometimes called **closed class** words. It is difficult to think of any new conjunctions, prepositions, or pronouns that have recently entered the language. The small set of personal pronouns such as *I, me, mine, he, she*, and so on are part of this class. With the growth of the feminist movement, some proposals have been made for adding a neutral singular pronoun that would be neither masculine nor feminine and that could be used as the general, or **generic**, form. If such a pronoun existed, it might have prevented the department chairperson in a large university from making the incongruous statement: "We will hire the best person for the job regardless of his sex." Various proposals have been made to introduce a new gender-neutral pronoun into the language such as "e," pronounced like the letter name, but this is unlikely to happen because the closed classes are particularly unreceptive to new membership. Rather, speakers prefer to recruit already existing pronouns such as *they* and *their* for this job, as in "Anyone can do it if *they* try hard enough" or "Everyone should do *their* best." The use of the various forms of *they* is standard on the BBC (British Broadcasting System) as pronoun replacements for *anyone* and *everyone*, which may be regarded as singular or plural.

The difference between content and function words is illustrated by the following test that circulated recently over the Internet:

Please count the number of F's in the following text without reading further:

FINISHED FILES ARE THE
RESULT OF YEARS OF SCIENTIFIC
STUDY COMBINED WITH THE
EXPERIENCE OF YEARS.

If you are like most people, your answer will be three. That answer is wrong. The correct answer is six. Count again. This time pay attention to the function word OF.

This little test illustrates that the brain treats content and function words differently. A great deal of psychological and neurological evidence supports this claim. For example, the effect that we just illustrated with the OF test is much more pronounced in brain-damaged people. As discussed in chapter 2, some brain-damaged patients and people with specific language impairment have greater difficulty in using, understanding, or reading function words than they do with content words. Some aphasics are unable to read function words like *in* or *which* but can read the lexical content words *inn* and *witch*. The two classes of words also seem to function differently in **slips of the tongue** produced by normal individuals. For example, a speaker may inadvertently switch words producing "the journal of the editor" instead of "the editor of the journal," but the switching or exchanging of function words has not been observed. There is also evidence for this distinction from language acquisition (discussed in chapter 8). In the early stages of development, children often omit function words from their speech, for example, "doggie barking."

The linguistic evidence suggests that content words and function words play different roles in language. Content words bear the brunt of the meaning, whereas function words connect the content words to the larger grammatical context in ways that will be discussed later in this chapter and in subsequent chapters.

Morphemes: The Minimal Units of Meaning

"They gave it me," Humpty Dumpty continued, "for an un-birthday present."

"I beg your pardon?" Alice said with a puzzled air.

"I'm not offended," said Humpty Dumpty.

"I mean, what is an un-birthday present?"

"A present given when it isn't your birthday, of course."

LEWIS CARROLL, Through the Looking-Glass

In the foregoing dialogue, Humpty Dumpty is well aware that the prefix un- means "not," as further shown in the following pairs of words:

A	B
desirable	undesirable
likely	unlikely
inspired	uninspired
happy	unhappy
developed	undeveloped
sophisticated	unsophisticated

Webster's Third New International Dictionary lists about 2,700 adjectives beginning with *un-*. If we assume that the most basic unit of meaning is the word, what do we say about parts of words like *un-*, which has a fixed meaning? In all the words in the B column, *un-* means the same thing—"not." *Undesirable* means "not desirable," *unlikely* means "not likely," and so on. All the words in column B consist of at least two meaningful units: *un + desirable, un + likely, un + inspired*, and so on.

Just as *un-* occurs with the same meaning in the previous list of words, so does *phon-* in the following words. (You may not know the meaning of some of them, but you will when you finish this book.)

phone	phonology	phoneme
phonetic	phonologist	phonemic
phonetics	phonological	allophone
phonetician	telephone	euphonious
phonic	telephonic	symphony

Phon- is a minimal form in that it can't be decomposed. *Ph* doesn't mean anything; *pho*, though it may be pronounced like *foe*, has no relation in meaning to it;

and *on* is not the preposition spelled *o-n*. In all the words on the list, *phon* has the identical meaning, "pertaining to sound."

Words have internal structure, which is rule-governed. *Uneaten, unadmired*, and *ungrammatical* are words in English, but **eatenun, *admiredun*, and **grammaticalun* (to mean "not eaten," "not admired," "not grammatical") are not, because we do not form a negative meaning of a word by suffixing *un-* but by prefixing it.

When Samuel Goldwyn, the pioneer moviemaker, announced: "In two words: im-possible," he was reflecting the common view that words are the basic meaningful elements of a language. We have seen that this cannot be so, because some words contain several distinct units of meaning. The linguistic term for the most elemental unit of grammatical form is **morpheme**. The word is derived from the Greek word *morphe*, meaning "form." If Goldwyn had taken a linguistics course, he would have said, more correctly, "In two morphemes: im-possible."

The study of the internal structure of words, and of the rules by which words are formed, is **morphology**. This word itself consists of two morphemes, *morph + ology*. The suffix *-ology* means "science of" or "branch of knowledge concerning." Thus, the meaning of *morphology* is "the science of word forms."

Morphology is part of our grammatical knowledge of a language. Like most linguistic knowledge, this is generally unconscious knowledge.

A single word may be composed of one or more morphemes:

one morpheme	boy
	desire
two morphemes	boy + ish
	desire + able
three morphemes	boy + ish + ness
	desire + able + ity
four morphemes	gentle + man + li + ness
	un + desire + able + ity
more than four	un + gentle + man + li + ness
	anti + dis + establish + ment + ari + an + ism

A morpheme may be represented by a single sound, such as the morpheme *a* meaning "without" as in *amoral* or *asexual*, or by a single syllable, such as *child* and *ish* in *child + ish*. A morpheme may also consist of more than one syllable: by two syllables, as in *camel, lady,* and *water*; or by three syllables, as in *Hackensack* or *crocodile*; or by four or more syllables, as in *hallucinate, apothecary,* and *onomatopoeia*.

A morpheme—the minimal linguistic unit—is thus an arbitrary union of a sound and a meaning that cannot be further analyzed. This may be too simple a definition, but it will serve our purposes for now. Every word in every language is composed of one or more morphemes.

The decomposition of words into morphemes illustrates one of the fundamental properties of human language—**discreteness**. In all languages, discrete linguistic units combine in rule-governed ways to form larger units. Sound units combine to form morphemes, morphemes combine to form words, and words combine to form larger units—phrases and sentences.

Discreteness is one of the properties that distinguish human languages from the communication systems of other species. Our knowledge of these discrete units and the rules for combining them accounts for the creativity of human language. In Chapter 1, we defined linguistic creativity as a person's ability to produce and understand an infinite range of sentences, but linguistic creativity is also demonstrated by our knowledge of morphology.

With respect to words, linguistic creativity means that not only can we understand words that we have never heard before, but we can also create new words. We can decompose a word into its component parts, and if we know the meaning of those parts, we have a good guess at the meaning of the whole. We can also combine morphemes in novel ways to create new words whose meaning will be apparent to other speakers of the language. If you know that "to write" to a disk or a CD means to put information on it, you automatically understand that a *writable* CD is one that can take information; a *rewritable* CD is one where the original information can be written over; and an *unrewritable* CD is one that does not allow the user to write over the original information. You know the meanings of all these words by virtue of your knowledge of the individual morphemes *write, re-, -able,* and *un-* and the rules for their combination.

Bound and Free Morphemes

PREFIXES AND SUFFIXES

"LOOKS LIKE WE SPEND MOST OF OUR TIME INGING...
YOU KNOW, LIKE SLEEPING, EATING, RUNNING, CLIMBING..."

"Dennis the Menace" © Hank Ketcham. Reprinted with permission of North America Syndicate.

Our morphological knowledge has two components: knowledge of the individual morphemes and knowledge of the rules that combine them. One of the things we know about particular morphemes is whether they can stand alone or whether they must be attached to a base morpheme.

Some morphemes like *boy, desire, gentle,* and *man* may constitute words by themselves. These are **free morphemes**. Other morphemes like *-ish, -ness, -ly, dis-, trans-,* and *un-* are never words by themselves but are always parts of words. These **affixes** are **bound morphemes**. We know whether each affix precedes or follows other morphemes. Thus, *un-, pre-* (*premeditate, prejudge*), and *bi-* (*bipolar, bisexual*) are **prefixes**. They occur before other morphemes. Some morphemes occur only as **suffixes**, following other morphemes. English examples of suffix morphemes are *-ing* (e.g., *sleeping, eating, running, climbing*), *-er* (e.g., *singer, performer, reader,* and *beautifier*), *-ist* (e.g., *typist, copyist, pianist, novelist, collaborationist,* and *linguist*), and *-ly* (e.g., *manly, sickly, spectacularly,* and *friendly*), to mention only a few. *Linguist* is an interesting example because when we remove the suffix *-ist* we are left with the nonword *ling(u).* We return to this issue in a following section.

Morphemes are the minimal **linguistic signs** in all languages, and many languages have prefixes and suffixes, but languages may differ in how they deploy their morphemes. A morpheme that is a prefix in one language may be a suffix in another and vice versa. In English the plural morpheme *-s* is a suffix (e.g., *boys, machines, diskettes*). In Isthmus Zapotec, spoken in Mexico, the plural morpheme *ka-* is a prefix:

zigi	"chin"	kazigi	"chins"
zike	"shoulder"	kazike	"shoulders"
diaga	"ear"	kadiaga	"ears"

Languages may also differ in what meanings they express through affixation. In English we do not add an affix to derive a noun from a verb. We have the verb *dance* as in "I like to dance," and we have the noun *dance* as in "The salsa is a Latin dance." The form is the same in both cases. In Turkish, you derive a noun from a verb with the suffix *-ak,* as in the following examples:

dur	"to stop"	dur + ak	"stopping place"
bat	"to sink"	bat + ak	"sinking place" or "marsh/swamp"

To express reciprocal action in English we use the phrase *each other,* as in *understand each other, love each other.* In Turkish a morpheme is added to the verb:

anla	"understand"	anla + sh	"understand each other"
sev	"love"	sev + ish	"love each other"

The reciprocal suffix in these examples is pronounced as *sh* after a vowel and as *ish* after a consonant. This is similar to the process in English, in which we use *a* as the indefinite article morpheme before a noun beginning with a consonant, as in *a dog,* and *an* before a noun beginning with a vowel, as in *an apple.* We will discuss the various pronunciations of morphemes in chapter 7.

In Piro, an Arawakan language spoken in Peru, a single morpheme, *-kaka,* can be added to a verb to express the meaning "cause to":

cokoruha	"to harpoon"	cokoruha + kaka	"cause to harpoon"
salwa	"to visit"	salwa + kaka	"cause to visit"

In Karuk, a Native American language spoken in the Pacific Northwest, adding *-ak* to a noun forms the locative adverbial meaning "in."

| ikrivaam | "house" | ikrivaamak | "in a house" |

It is accidental that both Turkish and Karuk have a suffix *-ak*. Despite the similarity in form, the two meanings are different. Similarly, the reciprocal suffix *-ish* in Turkish is similar in form to the English suffix *-ish* as in *greenish*. Also in Karuk, the suffix *-ara* has the same meaning as the English *-y*, that is, "characterized by" (*hairy* means "characterized by hair").

| aptiik | "branch" | aptikara | "branchy" |

These examples illustrate again the arbitrary nature of the sound-meaning relationship.

In Russian the suffix *-shchik* added to a noun is similar in meaning to the English suffix *-er* in words like *reader, teenager, Londoner, racer,* and *first grader,* which may be affixed to words of different categories. The Russian suffix, however, is added to nouns only, as shown in the following examples:

Russian		**Russian**	
atom	"atom"	atomshchik	"atom-warmonger"
baraban	"drum"	barabanshchik	"drummer"
kalambur	"pun"	kalamburshchik	"punner"
beton	"concrete"	betonshchik	"concrete worker"
lom	"scrap"	lomshchik	"salvage collector"

These examples from different languages also illustrate free morphemes like *boy* in English, *dur* in Turkish, *salwa* in Piro, and *lom* in Russian, versus bound morphemes such as *-ish* in English, *-ak* in Karuk, *-shchik* in Russian, and so on.

INFIXES

Some languages also have **infixes**, morphemes that are inserted into other morphemes. Bontoc, spoken in the Philippines, is such a language, as illustrated by the following:

Nouns/Adjectives		**Verbs**	
fikas	"strong"	fumikas	"to be strong"
kilad	"red"	kumilad	"to be red"
fusul	"enemy"	fumusul	"to be an enemy"

In this language, the infix *-um-* is inserted after the first consonant of the noun or adjective. Thus, a speaker of Bontoc, who learns that *pusi* means "poor," would understand the meaning of *pumusi*, "to be poor," on hearing the word for the first time, just as an English speaker who learns the verb *sneet* would know that *sneeter* is "one who sneets." A Bontoc speaker who knows that *ngumitad* means "to be dark" would know that the adjective "dark" must be *ngitad*.

English infixing has been the subject of the Linguist List, a discussion group on the Internet. The interest in infixes in English is due to the fact that one can only infix full-word obscenities into another word, usually into adjectives or adverbs. The most common infix in America is the word *fuckin'* and all the euphemisms for it, such as *friggin, freakin, flippin*, and *fuggin* as in *in-fuggin-credible, un-fuckin-believable*, or *Kalama-flippin-zoo,* based on the city in Michigan. In Britain, a common infix is *bloody*, an obscene term in British English, and its euphemisms, such as *bloomin*. In the movie and stage musical *My Fair Lady*, the word *abso + bloomin + lutely* occurs in one of the songs sung by Eliza Doolittle.

CIRCUMFIXES

Some languages have **circumfixes**, morphemes that are attached to a base morpheme both initially and finally. These are sometimes called **discontinuous morphemes**. In Chickasaw, a Muskogean language spoken in Oklahoma, the negative is formed with both a prefix *ik-* and the suffix *-o*. The final vowel of the affirmative is dropped before the negative suffix is added. Examples of this circumfixing are:

Affirmative		Negative	
chokma	"he is good"	ik + chokm + o	"he isn't good"
lakna	"it is yellow"	ik + lakn + o	"it isn't yellow"
palli	"it is hot"	ik + pall + o	"it isn't hot"
tiwwi	"he opens (it)"	ik + tiww + o	"he doesn't open (it)"

An example of a more familiar circumfixing language is German. The past participle of regular verbs is formed by adding the prefix *ge-* and the suffix *-t* to the verb root. This circumfix added to the verb root *lieb* "love" produces *geliebt*, "loved" (or "beloved," when used as an adjective).

ROOTS AND STEMS

Morphologically complex words consist of a **root** and one or more affixes. A root is a lexical content morpheme that cannot be analyzed into smaller parts. Some examples of English roots are *paint* in *painter, read* in *reread, ceive* in *conceive,* and *ling* in *linguist*. A root may or may not stand alone as a word (*paint* and *read* do; *ceive* and *ling* don't). In languages that have circumfixes, the root is the form around which the circumfix attaches, for example, the Chickasaw root *chokm* in *ik-chokm-o* ("he isn't good"). In infixing languages the root is the form into which the infix is inserted, for example *fikas* in the Bontoc word *f-um-ikas* ("to be strong").

Semitic languages like Hebrew and Arabic have a unique morphological system. Nouns and verbs are built on a foundation of three consonants, and one derives related words by varying the pattern of vowels and syllables. For example, the root for "write" in Egyptian Arabic is *ktb*, from which the following words (among others) are formed:

katab	"he wrote"
kaatib	"writer"
kitáab	"book"
kútub	"books"

When a root morpheme is combined with an affix, it forms a **stem**, which may or may not be a word (*painter* is both a word and a stem; *-ceive + er* is only a stem). Other affixes can be added to a stem to form a more complex stem, as shown in the following:

root	Chomsky	(proper) noun
stem	Chomsky + ite	noun + suffix
word	Chomsky + ite + s	noun + suffix + suffix

root	believe	verb
stem	believe + able	verb + suffix
word	un + believe + able	prefix + verb + suffix
root	system	noun
stem	system + atic	noun + suffix
stem	un + system + atic	prefix + noun + suffix
stem	un + system + atic + al	prefix + noun + suffix + suffix
word	un + system + atic + al + ly	prefix + noun + suffix + suffix + suffix

With the addition of each new affix, a new stem and a new word are formed. Linguists sometimes use the word **base** to mean any root or stem to which an affix is attached. In the preceding example, *system, systematic, unsystematic,* and *unsystematical* would all be considered bases.

Huckles and Ceives

A morpheme was defined as the basic element of meaning, a phonological form that is arbitrarily united with a particular meaning and that cannot be analyzed into simpler elements. Although it holds for most of the morphemes in a language, this definition has presented problems for linguistic analysis for many years. Consider words like *cranberry, huckleberry,* and *boysenberry.* The *berry* part is no problem, but *huckle* and *boysen* occur only with *berry,* as did *cran* until *cranapple* juice came on the market, and other morphologically complex words using *cran-* followed. The *boysen-* part of *boysenberry* was named after Mr. Boysen, who developed it as a hybrid from the blackberry and raspberry. But few people are aware of this fact, and it is a bound stem morpheme that occurs only in this word. *Lukewarm* is another word with two stem morphemes, with *luke* occurring only in this word, because it is not the same morpheme as the name *Luke.*

Bound forms like *huckle-, boysen-,* and *luke-* require a redefinition of the concept of morpheme. Some morphemes have no meaning in isolation but acquire meaning only in combination with other specific morphemes. Thus the morpheme *huckle,* when joined with *berry,* has the meaning of a special kind of berry that is small, round, and purplish blue; *luke* when combined with *warm* has the meaning "sort of" or "somewhat," and so on.

The previous morphemes occur only in a single word of the language (combined with another morpheme). Other morphemes occur in many words, but they seem to lack a constant meaning from one word to another. Many words of Latin origin that entered the English language after the Norman Conquest of England in 1066 have this property. For example, the words *receive, conceive, perceive,* and *deceive* share a common root, *-ceive;* and the words *remit, permit, commit, submit, transmit,* and *admit* share the root *-mit.* For the original Latin speakers, the morphemes corresponding to *ceive* and *mit* had clear meanings, the latter from the verb *mittere,* "to send," and the former from the verb *capere,* "to seize." But for modern English speakers, Latinate morphemes such as *-ceive* and *-mit* have no independent meaning. Their meaning depends on the entire word in which they occur.

Other words seem to be composed of prefix + root morphemes in which the roots, like *cran-* or *-ceive,* never occur alone, but always with a specific prefix. We find *inept,* but *no *ept; ungainly,* but no *gainly; discern,* but no *cern; nonplussed,* but no *plussed.*

Similarly, the stems of *upholster, downhearted,* and *outlandish* do not occur by themselves: **holster* and **hearted* (with these meanings), and **landish* are not free morphemes. In addition, *downholster, uphearted,* and *inlandish,* their "opposites," are not words.

To complicate things a little further, there are words like *strawberry* in which the *straw* has no relationship to any other kind of *straw*; *gooseberry,* which is unrelated to *goose*; and *blackberry,* which may be blue or red. Some of these words may have historical origins, but there is no present meaningful connection. *The Oxford English Dictionary* entry for the word *strawberry* states that

> The reason for the name has been variously conjectured. One explanation refers the first element to Straw . . . a particle of straw or chaff, a mote describing the appearance of the achenes scattered over the surface of the strawberry.

That may be true of the word's origin, but today, the *straw-* in *strawberry* is not the same morpheme as that found in *straw hat* or *straw-colored.*

The meaning of a morpheme must be constant. The agentive morpheme *-er* means "one who does" in words like *singer, painter, lover,* and *worker,* but the same sounds represent the comparative morpheme, meaning "more," in *nicer, prettier,* and *taller.* Thus, two different morphemes may be pronounced identically. The identical form represents two morphemes because of the different meanings. The same sounds may occur in another word and not represent a separate morpheme. The final syllable in *father, -er,* is not a separate morpheme, because a father is not "one who faths." Similarly, in *water* the *-er* is not a distinct morpheme ending; *father* and *water* are single morphemes, or **monomorphemic** words. This follows from the concept of the morpheme as a sound-meaning unit.

Rules of Word Formation

> "I never heard of 'Uglification,'" Alice ventured to say. "What is it?" The Gryphon lifted up both its paws in surprise. "Never heard of uglifying!" it exclaimed. "You know what to beautify is, I suppose?" "Yes," said Alice doubtfully: "it means—to make—anything—prettier." "Well, then," the Gryphon went on, "if you don't know what to uglify is, you are a simpleton."
>
> **LEWIS CARROLL,** Alice's Adventures in Wonderland

When the Mock Turtle listed the branches of Arithmetic for Alice as "Ambition, Distraction, Uglification, and Derision," Alice was very confused. She wasn't really a simpleton, since *uglification* was not a common word in English until Lewis Carroll used it. Still, most English speakers would immediately know the meaning of *uglification* even if we had never heard or used the word before because we know the meaning of its individual parts—the root *ugly* and the affixes *-ify* and *-cation.*

We said earlier that knowledge of morphology includes knowledge of individual morphemes, their pronunciation, and their meaning, and knowledge of the rules for combining morphemes into complex words. The Mock Turtle added *-ify* to the adjective *ugly* and formed a verb. Many verbs in English have been formed in this way: *purify, amplify, simplify, falsify.* The suffix *-ify* conjoined with nouns also forms verbs: *objectify, glorify, personify.* Notice that the Mock Turtle went even further; he added the suffix *-cation* to *uglify* and formed a noun, *uglification*, as in *glorification, simplification, falsification, and purification*. By using the **morphological rules** of English, he created a new word. The rules that he used are as follows:

Adjective + ify   →   Verb   "to make Adjective"
Verb + (c)ation   →   Noun   "the process of making Adjective"

Derivational Morphology

Bound morphemes like *-ify* and *-cation* are called **derivational morphemes**. When they are added to a base, a new word with a new meaning is derived. The addition of *-ify* to *pure—purify*—means "to make pure" and the addition of *-cation—purification*—means "the process of making pure." If we invent an adjective, *pouzy*, to describe the effect of static electricity on hair, you will immediately understand the sentences "Walking on that carpet really pouzified my hair" and "The best method of pouzification is to rub a balloon on your head." This means that we must have a list of the derivational morphemes in our mental dictionaries as well as the rules that determine how they are added to a root or stem. The form that results from the addition of a derivational morpheme is called a **derived word**.

The Hierarchical Structure of Words

We saw earlier that morphemes are added in a fixed order. This order reflects the **hierarchical structure** of the word. A word is not a simple sequence of morphemes. It has an internal structure. For example, the word *unsystematic* is composed of three morphemes: *un-, system*, and *-atic*. The root is *system*, a noun, to which we add the suffix *-atic* resulting in an adjective, *systematic*. To this adjective, we add the prefix *un-* forming a new adjective, *unsystematic*.

In order to represent the hierarchical organization of words (and sentences), linguists use **tree diagrams**. The tree diagram for *unsystematic* is as follows:

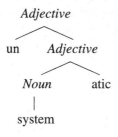

This tree represents the application of two morphological rules:

1. Noun + atic   →   Adjective
2. Un + Adjective   →   Adjective

Rule 1 attaches the derivational suffix *-atic* to the root noun, forming an adjective. Rule 2 takes the adjective formed by rule 1 and attaches the derivational prefix *un-*. The diagram shows that the entire word—*unsystematic*—is an adjective that is composed of an adjective—*systematic*—plus *un*. The adjective is itself composed of a noun—*system*—plus the suffix *-atic*.

Like the property of discreteness discussed earlier, hierarchical structure is an essential property of human language. Words (and sentences) have component parts, which relate to each other in specific, rule-governed ways. Although at first glance it may seem that, aside from order, the morphemes *un-* and *-atic* each relate to the root *system* in the same way, this is not the case. The root *system* is "closer" to *-atic* than it is to *un-*, and *un-* is actually connected to the adjective *systematic*, and not directly to *system*. Indeed, **unsystem* is not a word.

Further morphological rules can be applied to the given structure. For example, English has a derivational suffix *-al*, as in *egotistical, fantastical,* and *astronomical.* In these cases, *-al* is added to an adjective—*egotistic, fantastic, astronomic*—to form a new adjective. The rule for *-al* is as follows:

3. Adjective + al   →   Adjective

Another affix is *-ly*, which is added to adjectives—*happy, lazy, hopeful*—to form adverbs *happily, lazily, hopefully*. Following is the rule for *-ly*:

4. Adjective + ly   →   Adverb

Applying these two rules to the derived form *unsystematic*, we get the following tree for *unsystematically*:

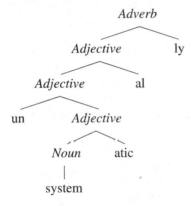

This is a rather complex word. Despite its complexity, it is well-formed because it follows the morphological rules of the language. On the other hand, a very simple word can be ungrammatical. Suppose in the above example we first added *un-* to the root *system*. That would have resulted in the nonword, **unsystem*.

*Unsystem is not a possible word because there is no rule of English that allows *un-* to be added to nouns. The large soft-drink company whose ad campaign promoted the *Uncola* successfully flouted this linguistic rule to capture people's attention. Part of our linguistic competence includes the ability to recognize possible versus impossible

words, like *unsystem* and *Uncola*. Possible words are those that conform to the rules; impossible words are those that do not.

Tree diagrams make explicit the way speakers represent the internal structure of the morphologically complex words in their language. In speaking and writing, we appear to string morphemes together sequentially as in *un + system + atic*. However, our mental representation of words is hierarchical as well as linear, and this is shown by tree diagrams.

The hierarchical organization of words is most clearly shown by structurally ambiguous words, words that have more than one meaning by virtue of having more than one structure. Consider the word *unlockable*. Imagine you are inside a room and you want some privacy. You would be unhappy to find the door is *unlockable*—"not able to be locked." Now imagine you are inside a locked room trying to get out. You would be very relieved to find that the door is *unlockable*—"able to be unlocked." These two meanings correspond to two different structures, as follows:

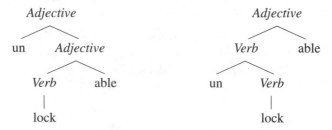

In the first structure the verb *lock* combines with the suffix *-able* to form an adjective *lockable* ("able to be locked"). Then the prefix *un-*, meaning "not," combines with the derived adjective to form a new adjective *unlockable* ("not able to be locked"). In the second case, the prefix *un-* combines with the verb *lock* to form a derived verb *unlock*. Then the derived verb combines with the suffix *-able* to form *unlockable*, "able to be unlocked."

An entire class of words in English follows this pattern: *unbuttonable, unzippable,* and *unlatchable*, among others. The ambiguity arises because the prefix *un-* can combine with an adjective, as illustrated in rule 2, or it can combine with a verb, as in *undo, unstaple, unearth,* and *unloosen*.

If words were only strings of morphemes without any internal organization, we could not explain the ambiguity of words like *unlockable*. These words also illustrate another important point, which is that structure is important to determining meaning. The same three morphemes occur in both versions of *unlockable*, yet there are two distinct meanings. The different meanings arise because of the two different structures.

More about Derivational Morphemes

Derivational morphemes have clear semantic content. In this sense they are like content words, except that they are not words. As we have seen, when a derivational morpheme is added to a base, it adds meaning. The derived word may also be of a different grammatical class than the original word, as shown by suffixes such as *-able* and *-ly*. When a verb is suffixed with *-able*, the result is an adjective, as in *desire + able, adore + able*. When the suffix *-en* is added to an adjective, a verb is derived, as in *dark + en*. One may form a noun from an adjective, as in *sweet + ie*. Other examples are:

Noun to Adjective	**Verb to Noun**	**Adjective to Adverb**
boy + ish	acquitt + al	exact + ly
virtu + ous	clear + ance	quiet + ly
Elizabeth + an	accus + ation	
pictur + esque	confer + ence	
affection + ate	sing + er	
health + ful	conform + ist	
alcohol + ic	predict + ion	
life + like	free + dom	

Noun to Verb	**Adjective to Noun**	**Verb to Adjective**
moral + ize	tall + ness	read + able
vaccin + ate	specific + ity	creat + ive
brand + ish	feudal + ism	migrat + ory
haste + n	abstract + ion	run + (n)y

Not all derivational morphemes cause a change in grammatical class.

Noun to Noun	**Verb to Verb**	**Adjective to Adjective**
friend + ship	un + do	pink + ish
human + ity	re + cover	in + flammable

Many prefixes fall into this category:

a + moral	mono + theism
auto + biography	re + print
ex + wife	semi + annual
super + human	sub + minimal

There are also suffixes of this type:

vicar + age	New Jersey + ite
old + ish	fadd + ist
Paul + ine	music + ian
America + n	pun + ster
veget + arian	humanit + arian

When a new word enters the lexicon by the application of morphological rules, other complex derivations may be **blocked**. For example, when *Commun + ist* entered the language, words such as *Commun + ite* (as in *Trotsky + ite*) or *Commun + ian* (as in *grammar + ian*) were not needed; their formation was blocked. Sometimes, however, alternative forms do coexist: for example, *Chomskyan* and *Chomskyist* and perhaps even *Chomskyite* (all meaning "follower of Chomsky's views of linguistics"). *Semanticist* and *semantician* are both used, but the possible word *semantite* is not.

Finally, derivational affixes appear to come in two classes. In one class, the addition of a suffix triggers subtle changes in pronunciation. For example, when we affix *-ity* to *specific* (pronounced "specifi*k*" with a k-sound), we get specificity (pronounced "specifisity" with an s-sound). When deriving *Elizabeth+an* from *Elizabeth*, the fourth vowel sound changes from the vowel in *Beth* to the vowel in *Pete*. Other suffixes such as *-y, -ive,* and *-ize* may induce similar changes: *sane/sanity, deduce/deductive, critic/criticize.*

On the other hand, suffixes such as *-er, -ful, -ish, -less, -ly,* and *-ness* may be tacked onto a base word without affecting the pronunciation, as in *baker, wishful, boyish, needless, sanely,* and *fullness.* Moreover, affixes from the first class cannot be attached to a base containing an affix from the second class: **need+less+ity, *moral+ize+ive;* but affixes from the second class may attach to bases with either kind of affix: *moral+iz(e)+er, need+less+ness.*

Lexical Gaps

"Peanuts" copyright © United Feature Syndicate. Reprinted by permission.

The redundancy of alternative forms such as *Chomskyan/Chomskyite*, all of which conform to the regular rules of word formation, may explain some of the **accidental gaps** (also called **lexical gaps**) in the lexicon. Accidental gaps are well-formed but nonexisting words. The actual words in the language constitute only a subset of the possible words. Speakers of a language may know tens of thousands of words. Dictionaries, as we noted, include hundreds of thousands of words, all of which are known by some speakers of the language. But no dictionary can list all **possible words** because it is possible to add to the vocabulary of a language in many ways. (Some of these will be discussed here and some in chapter 11 on language change.) There are always gaps in the lexicon—words not present but that could be added. Some of the gaps are due to the fact that a permissible sound sequence has no meaning attached to it (like *blick*, or *slarm*, or *krobe*). Note that the sequence of sounds must be in keeping with the constraints of the language. *bnick* is not a "gap" because no word in English can begin with a *bn*. We will discuss such constraints in chapter 7.

Other gaps result when possible combinations of morphemes never come into use. Speakers can distinguish between impossible words such as *unsystem* and *needlessity*, and possible, but nonexisting words, such as *disobvious, linguisticism,* and *antiquify*. The ability to make this distinction is further evidence that the morphological component of our mental grammar consists of not just a lexicon—a list of existing words—but also of rules that enable us to create and understand new words, and to recognize possible and impossible words.

Rule Productivity

Some morphological rules are **productive**, meaning that they can be used freely to form new words from the list of free and bound morphemes. The suffix *-able* appears to be a morpheme that can be conjoined with any verb to derive an adjective with the meaning of the verb and the meaning of *-able*, which is something like "able to be" as in *accept + able, laugh + able, pass + able, change + able, breathe + able, adapt + able*, and so on. The meaning of *-able* has also been given as "fit for doing" or "fit for being done." The productivity of this rule is illustrated by the fact that we find *-able* affixed to new verbs such as *downloadable* and *faxable*.

We have already noted that there is a morpheme in English meaning "not" that has the form *un-* and that, when combined with adjectives like *afraid, fit, free, smooth, American,* and *British*, forms the **antonyms**, or *negatives*, of these adjectives, such as *unafraid, unfit, un-American,* and so on. Note that unlike *-able*, *un-* does not change the grammatical category of the stem it attaches to.

We also saw that the prefix *un-* can be added to derived adjectives that have been formed by morphological rules:

un + believe + able

un + accept + able

un + speak + able

un + lock + able

We can also add *un-* to morphologically complex verbs that consist of a verb plus a particle like *up* or *off*, plus *-able* such as:

pick + up + able

turn + around + able

chop + off + able

talk + about + able

Un- prefixation derives the following words:

un + pick + up + able

un + chop + off + able

un + talk + about + able

Yet *un-* is not fully productive. We find *happy* and *unhappy*, *cowardly* and *uncowardly*, but not *sad* and *unsad, *brave* and **unbrave,* or *obvious* and *unobvious. The starred forms that follow may be merely accidental gaps in the lexicon. If someone refers to a person as being *unsad, we would know that the person referred to was "not sad," and an *unbrave person would not be brave. But, as the linguist Sandra Thompson points out, it may be the case that the "un-Rule" is most productive for adjectives that are derived from verbs, such as *unenlightened, unsimplified, uncharacterized, unauthorized, undistinguished*, and so on. It also appears that most acceptable *un-* words have polysyllabic bases, and while we have *unfit, uncool*, and *unclean*, many of the unacceptable *-un* forms have monosyllabic stems such as *unbig, ungreat, unred, unsad, unsmall, untall*.

Morphological rules may be more or less productive. The rule that adds an *-er* to verbs in English to produce a noun meaning "one who performs an action (once or habitually)" is a very productive morphological rule. Most English verbs accept this suffix: *examiner, exam-taker, analyzer, lover, hunter, predictor*, and so forth (*-or* and *-er* have the same pronunciation and are the same morpheme even though they are spelled differently). Now consider the following:

sincerity	from	*sincere*
warmth	from	*warm*
moisten	from	*moist*

The suffix *-ity* is found in many other words in English, like *chastity, scarcity*, and *curiosity*; and *-th* occurs in *health, wealth, depth, width*, and *growth*. We find *-en* in *sadden, ripen, redden, weaken,* and *deepen*. Still, the phrase "*The fiercity of the lion" sounds somewhat strange, as does the sentence "*I'm going to thinnen the sauce." Someone may use the word *coolth*, but, as Thompson points out, when words such as *fiercity, thinnen, fullen*, and *coolth* are used, usually it is either an error or an attempt at humor. It is possible that in such cases a morphological rule that was once productive (as shown by the existence of related pairs like *scarce/scarcity*) is no longer so. Our knowledge of the related pairs, however, may permit us to use these examples in forming new words, by analogy with the existing lexical items. Other derivational morphemes in English are not very productive, such as the diminutive suffixes in the words *pig + let* and *sap + ling*.

In the morphologically complex words that we have seen so far, we can easily predict the meaning based on the meaning of the morphemes that make up the word. *Unhappy* means "not happy" and *acceptable* means "fit to be accepted." However, one cannot always know the meaning of the words derived from free and derivational morphemes by knowing the morphemes themselves. The following *un-* forms have unpredictable meanings:

unloosen	"loosen, let loose"
unrip	"rip, undo by ripping"
undo	"reverse doing"

untread	"go back through in the same steps"
unearth	"dig up"
unfrock	"deprive (a cleric) of ecclesiastic rank"
unnerve	"fluster"

Morphologically complex words whose meanings are not predictable must be listed individually in our mental lexicons. However, the morphological rules must also be in the grammar, revealing the relation between words and providing the means for forming new words.

"Pullet Surprises"

Our knowledge of the morphemes and morphological rules of our language is often revealed by the "errors" we make. We may guess the meaning of a word we do not know. Sometimes we guess wrong, but our wrong guesses are nevertheless "intelligent."

Amsel Greene collected errors made by her students in vocabulary-building classes and published them in a book called *Pullet Surprises*.[3] The title is taken from a sentence written by one of her high school students: "In 1957 Eugene O'Neill won a Pullet Surprise." What is most interesting about these errors is how much they reveal about the students' knowledge of English morphology. The creativity of these students is illustrated in the following examples:

Word	**Student's Definition**
deciduous	"able to make up one's mind"
longevity	"being very tall"
fortuitous	"well protected"
gubernatorial	"to do with peanuts"
bibliography	"holy geography"
adamant	"pertaining to original sin"
diatribe	"food for the whole clan"
polyglot	"more than one glot"
gullible	"to do with sea birds"
homogeneous	"devoted to home life"

The student who used the word *indefatigable* in the sentence

She tried many reducing diets, but remained indefatigable.

clearly shows morphological knowledge: *in* meaning "not" as in *ineffective*; *de* meaning "off" as in *decapitate; fat* as in "fat"; *able* as in *able*; and combined meaning, "not able to take the fat off."

Sign Language Morphology

Sign languages are rich in morphology. Like spoken languages, they have root and affix morphemes, free and bound morphemes, lexical content and grammatical morphemes, derivational and inflectional morphemes, and morphological rules for their combination to form morphologically complex signs.

---

[3] A. Greene. 1969. *Pullet Surprises.* Glenview, IL: Scott, Foresman.

Figure 3.1 illustrates the derivational process in ASL that is equivalent to the formation of the nouns *comparison* and *measuring* from the verbs *compare* and *measure* in English. Everything about the root morpheme remains the same except for the movement of the hands.

Inflection of sign roots also occurs in ASL and all other sign languages, which characteristically modify the movement of the hands and the spatial contours of the area near the body in which the signs are articulated.

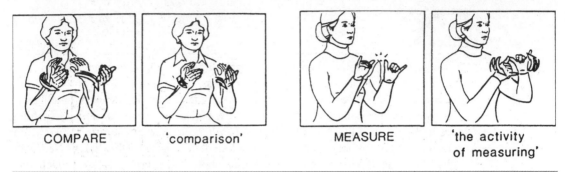

COMPARE   'comparison'   MEASURE   'the activity
                                                  of measuring'

FIGURE 3.1 Derivationally related sign in ASL.
Copyright © 1987 MIT Press. Reprinted by permission of the MIT Press.[4]

Word Coinage

We have seen that new words may be added to the vocabulary of a language by derivational processes. New words also enter a language in a variety of other ways. Some are created outright to fit some purpose—**coinage**. The advertising industry has added many words to English, such *as Kodak, nylon, Orlon*, and *Dacron*. Specific brand names such as *Xerox, Kleenex, Jell-O, Brillo*, and *Vaseline* are now sometimes used as the generic name for different brands of these types of products. Notice that some of these words were created from existing words (e.g., *Kleenex* from the word *clean* and *Jell-O* from *gel*).

In computer speech processing, the new words *cepstrum* and *cepstral* were purposely formed by reordering the letters of *spectrum* and *spectral*. Speakers do not agree on the pronunciation of these two words. Some say "sepstrum" with an *s*-sound, since the *c* precedes an *e*. Others say "kepstrum" since the *c* is pronounced as a *k* in the source word *spectrum*. Greek roots borrowed into English have also provided a means for coining new words. *Thermos* "hot" plus *metron* "measure" gives us *thermometer*. From *akros* "topmost" and *phobia* "fear," we get *acrophobia*, "dread of heights." To avoid going out on Friday the thirteenth, you may say that you have *triskaidekaphobia,* a profound fear of the number 13. An ingenious cartoonist, Robert Osborn, has "invented" some phobias, to each of which he gives an appropriate name:[5]

---

[4] H. Poizner, E. Klima, and U. Bellugi. 1987. *What the Hands Reveal about the Brain.* Cambridge, MA: MIT Press.
[5] From *An Osborn Festival of Phobias* by Robert Osborn and Eve Wengler. Copyright © 1971 Robert Osborn. Text copyright © 1971 Eve Wengler. Used by permission of Liveright Publishing Corporation.

logizomechanophobia	"fear of reckoning machines" from Greek *logizomai* "to reckon or compute" + *mekhane* "device" + *phobia*
ellipsosyllabophobia	"fear of words with a missing syllable" from Greek *elleipsis* "a falling short" + *syllabē* "syllable" + *phobia*
pornophobia	"fear of prostitutes" from Greek *porne* "harlot" + *phobia*

Latin, like Greek, has also provided prefixes and suffixes that are used productively with both native and nonnative roots. The prefix *ex-* comes from Latin:

ex-husband ex-wife ex-sister-in-law

The suffix *-able/-ible* that was discussed earlier is also Latin, borrowed via French, and can be attached to almost any English verb, as we noted, and as further illustrated in:

writable readable answerable movable

Words from Names

Eponyms are words that are coined from proper names and are another of the many creative ways that the vocabulary of a language expands. Here are some examples:

sandwich   Named for the fourth Earl of Sandwich, who put his food between two slices of bread so that he could eat while he gambled.

robot	After the mechanical creatures in the Czech writer Karel Capek's play *R.U.R.*, the initials standing for "Rossum's Universal Robots."
gargantuan	Named for Gargantua, the creature with a huge appetite created by Rabelais.
jumbo	After an elephant brought to the United States by P. T. Barnum. ("Jumbo olives" need not be as big as an elephant, however.)

We admit to ignorance of the Susan, an unknown servant from whom the compound *lazy susan* is derived; or the Betty or Charlotte or Chuck from whom we got *brown betty, charlotte russe*, or *chuck wagon*. We can point out, however, that *denim* was named for the material used for overalls and carpeting, which originally was imported "de Nîmes" ("from Nîmes") in France, and *argyle* from the kind of socks worn by the chiefs of Argyll of the Campbell clan in Scotland.

The word *paparazzo,* "a freelance photographer who doggedly pursues celebrities," was a little-known word until the death of Diana, Princess of Wales, in 1997, who was hounded by paparazzi (plural) before her fatal automobile accident. This eponym comes from the news photographer character Signor Paparazzo in the motion picture *La Dolce Vita.*

Back-Formations

> It had been a rough day, so when I walked into the party I was very chalant, despite my efforts to appear gruntled and consolate. I was furling my wieldy umbrella . . . when I saw her. . . . She was a descript person. . . . Her hair was kempt, her clothing shevelled, and she moved in a gainly way.
>
> **"HOW I MET MY WIFE," BY JACK WINTER.** The New Yorker, *July 25, 1994*[6]

Ignorance sometimes can be creative. A new word may enter the language because of an incorrect morphological analysis. For example, *peddle* was derived from *peddler* on the mistaken assumption that the *-er* was the agentive suffix. Such words are called **back-formations**. The verbs *hawk, stoke, swindle,* and *edit* all came into the language as back-formations—of *hawker, stoker, swindler*, and *editor. Pea* was derived from a singular word, *pease*, by speakers who thought *pease* was a plural.

Some word coinage comes from deliberately miscast back-formations. The word *bikini* is a monomorphemic eponym from the Bikini atoll of the Marshall Islands. Because the first syllable *bi-* is a morpheme meaning "two" in words like *bicycle*, some clever person called a topless bathing suit a *monokini*. Historically, a number of new words have entered the English lexicon in this way. Based on analogy with such pairs as *act/action, exempt/exemption,* and *revise/revision*, new words *resurrect, preempt,* and *televise* were formed from the existing words *resurrection, preemption*, and *television.*

Language purists sometimes rail against back-formations and cite *enthuse* and *liaise* (from *enthusiasm* and *liaison*) as examples of language corruption. However, language is not corrupt; it is adaptable and changeable, and even since 1994, the date of the epigraph that heads this section, *kempt* has entered the language as a back-formation meaning "neat and trim."

---

[6] The full version of this piece appears in *The Answer to Everything*, a comic memoir by Jack Winter.

Compounds

> . . . the Houynhnms have no Word in their Language to express any thing that is evil, except what they borrow from the Deformities or ill Qualities of the Yahoos. Thus they denote the Folly of a Servant, an Omission of a Child, a Stone that cuts their feet, a Continuance of foul or unseasonable Weather, and the like, by adding to each the Epithet of Yahoo. For instance, Hnhm Yahoo, Whnaholm Yahoo, Ynlhmnawihlma Yahoo, and an ill contrived House, Ynholmhnmrohlnw Yahoo.
>
> **JONATHAN SWIFT,** Gulliver's Travels

Two or more words may be joined to form new, **compound** words. The kinds of combinations that occur in English are nearly limitless, as the following table of compounds shows. Each entry in the table represents dozens of similar combinations.

	Adjective	Noun	Verb
Adjective	bittersweet	poorhouse	whitewash
Noun	headstrong	homework	spoonfeed
Verb	—	pickpocket	sleepwalk

Some compounds that have been introduced very recently into English are *carjack*, *mall rat*, *road rage*, *palm pilot*, and *slow-speed chase*. (Compounds are variously spelled with dashes, spaces, or nothing between the individual words.)

When the two words are in the same grammatical category, the compound will be in this category: noun + noun—*girlfriend, fighter-bomber, paper clip, elevator-operator, landlord, mailman*; adjective + adjective—*icy-cold, red-hot*, and *worldly-wise*. In English, the rightmost word in a compound is the **head** of the compound. The head is the part of a word or phrase that determines its broad meaning and grammatical category. Thus, when the two words fall into different categories, the class of the second or final word will be the grammatical category of the compound: noun + adjective = adjective—*headstrong, watertight, lifelong*; verb + noun = noun—*pickpocket, pinchpenny, daredevil, sawbones*. On the other hand, compounds formed with a preposition are in the category of the nonprepositional part of the compound; *overtake, hanger-on, undertake, sundown, afterbirth, downfall, uplift*. This is further evidence that prepositions form a closed-class category that does not readily admit new members.

Although two-word compounds are the most common in English, it would be difficult to state an upper limit: Consider *three-time loser, four-dimensional space-time, sergeant-at-arms, mother-of-pearl, man about town, master of ceremonies*, and *daughter-in-law*. Dr. Seuss uses the rules of compounding when he explains "when tweetle beetles battle with paddles in a puddle, they call it a *tweetle beetle puddle paddle battle*."[7]

Spelling does not tell us what sequence of words constitutes a compound; whether a compound is spelled with a space between the two words, with a hyphen, or with no separation at all depends on the idiosyncrasies of the particular compound, as shown, for example, in *blackbird, gold-tail*, and *smoke screen*.

---

[7] From *Fox in Socks* by Dr. Seuss, copyright ™ & copyright © by Dr. Seuss Enterprises, L.P. 1965, renewed 1993. Used by permission of Random House Children's Books, a division of Random House, Inc.

Like derived words, compounds have internal structure. This is clear from the ambiguity of a compound like *top + hat + rack*, which can mean "a rack for top hats" corresponding to the structure in tree diagram (1), or "the highest hat rack," corresponding to the structure in (2).

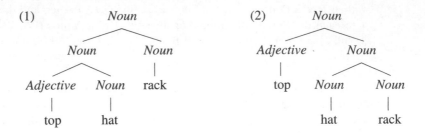

MEANING OF COMPOUNDS

The meaning of a compound is not always the sum of the meanings of its parts; a *blackboard* may be green or white. Everyone who wears a red coat is not a *Redcoat* (slang for British soldier during the American Revolutionary War). The difference between the sentences "She has a red coat in her closet" and "She has a Redcoat in her closet" would have been highly significant in America in 1776.

Other compounds reveal other meaning relations between the parts, which are not entirely consistent because many compounds are idiomatic (idioms are discussed in chapter 5). A *boathouse* is a house for boats, but a *cathouse* is not a house for cats. (It is slang for a house of prostitution or whorehouse.) A *jumping bean* is a bean that jumps, a *falling star* is a star that falls, and a *magnifying glass* is a glass that magnifies; but a *looking glass* is not a glass that looks, nor is an *eating apple* an apple that eats, and *laughing gas* does not laugh. *Peanut oil* and *olive oil* are oils made from something, but what about *baby oil*? And is this a contradiction: horse meat is dog meat? Not at all, since the first is meat *from* horses and the other is meat *for* dogs.

In the examples so far, the meaning of each compound includes at least to some extent the meanings of the individual parts. However, many compounds do not seem to relate to the meanings of the individual parts at all. A *jack-in-a-box* is a tropical tree, and a *turncoat* is a traitor. A *highbrow* does not necessarily have a high brow, nor does a *bigwig* have a big wig, nor does an *egghead* have an egg-shaped head.

Like certain words with the prefix *un-*, the meaning of many compounds must be learned as if they were individual whole words. Some of the meanings may be figured out, but not all. If you had never heard the word *hunchback*, it might be possible to infer the meaning; but if you had never heard the word *flatfoot*, it is doubtful you would know it means "detective" or "policeman," even though the origin of the word, once you know the meaning, can be figured out.

The pronunciation of English compounds differs from the way we pronounce the sequence of two words that are not compounded. In an actual compound, the first word is usually stressed (pronounced somewhat louder and higher in pitch), and in a noncompound phrase the second word is stressed. Thus we stress *Red* in *Redcoat* but *coat* in *red coat*. (Stress, pitch, and other "prosodic" features are discussed in chapters 6 and 7.)

Other languages have rules for conjoining words to form compounds, as seen by French *cure-dent*, "toothpick"; German *Panzerkraftwagen*, "armored car"; Russian *cetyrexetaznyi*, "four-storied"; Spanish *tocadiscos*, "record player." In the Native American language Tohono O'odham, the word meaning "thing" is *haʔichu*, and it combines with *doakam*, "living creatures," to form the compound *haʔichu doakam*, "animal life."

In Twi, by combining the word meaning "son" or "child," *ɔba*, with the word meaning "chief," *ɔhene*, one derives the compound *ɔheneba*, meaning "prince." By adding the word "house," *ofi*, to *ɔhene*, the word meaning "palace," *ahemfi* is derived. The other changes that occur in the Twi compounds are due to phonological and morphological rules in the language.

In Thai, the word "cat" is *mɛɛw*, the word for "watch" (in the sense of "to watch over") is *fâw*, and the word for "house" is *bâan*. The word for "watch cat" (like a watchdog) is the compound *mɛɛwfâwbâan*—literally, "catwatchhouse."

Compounding is a common and frequent process for enlarging the vocabulary of all languages.

Blends

Blends are similar to compounds in that they are produced by combining two words, but parts of the words that are combined are deleted. *Smog*, from *smoke* + *fog*; *brunch* from *breakfast* and *lunch*; *motel*, from *motor* + *hotel*; *infomercial* from *info* + *commercial*; and *urinalysis*, from *urine* + *analysis* are examples of blends that have attained full lexical status in English. *Podcast* (*podcasting, podcaster*) is a new word meaning "Internet audio broadcast" and recently joined the English language as a blend of *iPOD* and *broadcast*. Lewis Carroll's *chortle*, from *chuckle* + *snort,* has achieved limited acceptance in English. Carroll is famous for both coining and blending words. In *Through the Looking-Glass*, he describes the "meanings" of the made-up words in "Jabberwocky" as follows:

> . . . "Brillig" means four o' clock in the afternoon—the time when you begin broiling things for dinner . . . "Slithy" means "lithe and slimy". . . You see it's like a portmanteau—there are two meanings packed up into one word. . . . "Toves" are something like badgers—they're something like lizards—and they're something like corkscrews . . . also they make their nests under sundials—also they live on cheese . . . To "gyre" is to go round and round like a gyroscope. To "gimble" is to make holes like a gimlet. And "the wabe" is the grass-plot round a sun-dial . . . It's called "wabe" . . . because it goes a long way before it and a long way behind it . . . "Mimsy" is "flimsy and miserable" (there's another portmanteau . . . for you).

Carroll's "portmanteaus" are what we have called blends, and such words can become part of the regular lexicon.

Blending is even done by children. The blend *crocogator* from *crocodile* + *alligator* is attributed to three-year-old Elijah Peregrine. Grandmothers are not to be left out, and a Jewish one of African descent that we know came up with *shugeleh*, "darling," which we think is a blend of *sugar* + *bubeleh*, and which we confess we don't know how to spell. (*Bubeleh* is a Yiddish term of endearment.)

Reduced Words

Speakers tend to abbreviate words in various ways to shorten the messages they convey. This is seen dramatically in the creativity used on messages typed into cell phones in instant messaging and similar communication technologies. However, we will concern ourselves with *spoken* language and observe three reduction phenomena: *clipping, acronyms*, and *alphabetic abbreviations*.

Clipping is the abbreviation of longer words into shorter ones, such as *fax* for *facsimile, telly*, the British word for *television, prof* for *professor, piano* for *pianoforte*, and *gym* for *gymnasium*. Once considered slang, these words have now become lexicalized, that is, full words in their own right. These are only a few examples of such clipped forms that are now used as whole words. Other examples are *ad, bike, math, gas, phone, bus*, and *van* (from *advertisement, bicycle, mathematics, gasoline, telephone, omnibus*, and *caravan*). More recently, *dis* and *rad* (from *disrespect* and *radical*) have entered the language, and *dis* has come to be used as a verb meaning "to show disrespect."

Acronyms are words derived from the initials of several words. Such words are pronounced as the spelling indicates: *NASA* from *National Aeronautics and Space Administration, UNESCO* from *United Nations Educational, Scientific, and Cultural Organization*, and *UNICEF* from *United Nations International Children's Emergency Fund. Radar* from "*radio detecting and ranging,*" *laser* from "*light amplification by stimulated emission of radiation,*" *scuba* from "*self-contained underwater breathing apparatus,*" and *RAM* from "*random access memory,*" show the creative efforts of word coiners, as does *snafu*, which was coined by soldiers in World War II and is rendered in polite circles as "*situation normal, all fouled up.*" Recently coined additions are *AIDS* (1980s), from the initials of *acquired immune deficiency syndrome*, and *SARS* (2000s), from *severe acute respiratory syndrome*.

When the string of letters is not easily pronounced as a word, the "acronym" is produced by sounding out each letter, as in *NFL* for *National Football League, UCLA* for *University of California, Los Angeles*, and *MRI* for *magnetic resonance imaging*. These special kinds of acronyms are sometimes called **alphabetic abbreviations**.

Acronyms and alphabetic abbreviations are being added to the vocabulary daily with the proliferation of computers and widespread use of the Internet, including *blog* (*web log*), *jpeg* (*joint photographics expert group*), *GUI*, pronounced "*gooey,*" for *graphical user interface, PDA* (*personal digital assistant*), and *MP3* for *MPEG layer 3*, where *MPEG* itself is the acronym for *moving picture experts group*.

Inflectional Morphemes

Function words like *to, it*, and *be* are free morphemes. Many languages, including English, also have bound morphemes that have a strictly grammatical function. They mark properties such as tense, number, gender, case, and so forth. Such bound morphemes are called **inflectional morphemes**. They never change the syntactic category

"Zits" © Zits Partnership. Reprinted with permission of King Features Syndicate.

of the words or morphemes to which they are attached. Consider the forms of the verb in the following sentences:

1. I sail the ocean blue.
2. He sails the ocean blue.
3. John sailed the ocean blue.
4. John has sailed the ocean blue.
5. John is sailing the ocean blue.

In sentence (2) the *-s* at the end of the verb is an agreement marker; it signifies that the subject of the verb is third person, is singular, and that the verb is in the present tense. It doesn't add lexical meaning. The suffix *-ed* indicates past tense, and is also required by the syntactic rules of the language when verbs are used with *have*, just as *-ing* is required when verbs are used with forms of *be*.

English is no longer a highly inflected language, but we do have other inflectional endings such as the plural suffix, which is attached to certain singular nouns, as in *boy/boys* and *cat/cats*. At the present stage of English history, there are a total of eight bound inflectional affixes:

English Inflectional Morphemes		Examples
-s	third-person singular present	She wait-**s** at home.
-ed	past tense	She wait-**ed** at home.
-ing	progressive	She is eat-**ing** the donut.
-en	past participle	Mary has eat-**en** the donuts.
-s	plural	She ate the donut-**s**.
-'s	possessive	Disa**'s** hair is short.
-er	comparative	Disa has short-**er** hair than Karin.
-est	superlative	Disa has the short-**est** hair.

Inflectional morphemes in English typically come after the derivational morphemes in a word. Thus, to the derivationally complex word *commit + ment* one can add a plural ending to form *commit + ment + s*, but the order of affixes may not be reversed to derive the impossible *commit + s + ment = *commitsment*. However, with compounds the situation is complicated. Thus, for many speakers, the plural of *mother-in-law* is *mothers-in-law*, whereas the possessive form is *mother-in-law's*; the plural of *court-martial* is *courts-martial* and the plural *of attorney general* is *attorneys general* in a legal setting, but for most of the rest of us it's *attorney generals*.

Compared to many languages of the world, English has relatively little inflectional morphology. Some languages are highly inflected. In Swahili, which is widely spoken in eastern Africa, verbs can be inflected with multiple morphemes, as in *nimepiga* (ni+me+pig+a) meaning "he has hit something." Here the verb root *pig* meaning "hit" has two inflectional prefixes: *ni* meaning "I," and *me* meaning "completed action," and an inflectional suffix *a*, which is an object agreement morpheme.

Even the more familiar European languages have many more inflectional endings than English. In the Romance languages (languages descended from Latin), the verb has different inflectional endings depending on the subject of the sentence. The verb is inflected to agree in person and number with the subject, as illustrated by the Italian verb *parlare* meaning "to speak":

Io parl**o**	"I speak"	Noi parl**iamo**	"We speak"
Tu parl**i**	"You (singular) speak"	Voi parl**ate**	"You (plural) speak"
Lui/Lei parl**a**	"He/she speaks"	Loro parl**ano**	"They speak"

Some languages can also add content morphemes to the verb. Many North American languages are of this type. For example, in Mohawk the word *wahonwatia'tawitsherahetkenhten* means "she made the thing that one puts on one's body ugly for him." In such languages one word may be translated as an entire sentence. As the linguist Mark Baker notes, languages like Mohawk "use a different division of labor from languages like English, with more burden on morphology and less on syntax to express complex relations."

Students often ask for definitions of derivational morphemes as opposed to inflectional morphemes. There is no easy answer to this request. Perhaps the simplest answer is that derivational morphemes are affixes that are not inflectional. Inflectional morphemes signal grammatical relations and are required by the rules of sentence formation. Derivational morphemes, when affixed to roots and stems, may change the grammatical word class and/or the basic meaning of the word, which may then be inflected as to number (singular or plural), tense (present, past, future), and so on.

Exceptions and Suppletions

"Peanuts" copyright © United Feature Syndicate. Reprinted by permission.

The regular rule that forms plurals from singular nouns does not apply to words like *child, man, foot*, and *mouse*. These words are exceptions to the English inflectional rule of plural formation. Similarly, verbs like *go, sing, bring, run*, and *know* are exceptions to the regular past tense rule in English.

When children are learning English, they first learn the regular rules, which they apply to all forms. Thus, we often hear them say *mans* and *goed*. Later in the acquisition process, they specifically learn irregular plurals like *men* and *mice*, and irregular past tense forms like *came* and *went*. These children's errors are actually evidence that the regular rules exist.

Irregular, or **suppletive**, forms are treated separately in the grammar. That is, one cannot use the regular rules of inflectional morphology to add affixes to words that are exceptions like *child/children*, but must replace the noninflected form with another word. It is possible that for regular words, only the singular form need be specifically stored in the lexicon because we can use the inflectional rules to form plurals. But this can't be so with suppletive exceptions.

When a new word enters the language, the regular inflectional rules generally apply. The plural of *geek*, when it was a new word in English, was *geeks*, not *geeken*, although we are advised that some geeks wanted the plural of *fax* to be *faxen*, like *oxen*, when *fax* entered the language as a clip of *facsimile*. Never fear: its plural is *faxes*. The exception to this may be a loan word, a word borrowed from a foreign language. For example, the plural of Latin *datum* has always been *data*, never *datums*, though nowadays *data*, the one-time plural, is treated by many as a singular word like *information*. The past tense of the verb *hit*, as in the sentence "Yesterday you hit the ball," and the plural of the noun *sheep*, as in "The sheep are in the meadow," show that some morphemes seem to have no phonological shape at all. We know that *hit* in the above sentence is *hit + past* because of the time adverb *yesterday*, and we know that *sheep* is the phonetic form of *sheep + plural* because of the plural verb form *are*.

When a verb is derived from a noun, even if it is homophonous with an irregular verb, the regular rules apply to it. Thus *ring*, when used in the sense of encircle, is derived from the noun *ring*, and as a verb it is regular. We say *the police ringed the bank with armed men*, not *rang the bank with armed men*.

Similarly, when a noun is used in a compound in which its meaning is lost, such as *flatfoot*, meaning "cop," its plural follows the regular rule, so one says *two flatfoots* to refer to a pair of cops slangily, not *two flatfeet*. It's as if the noun is saying: "If you don't get your meaning from me, you don't get my special plural form."

Morphology and Syntax

"Curiouser and curiouser!" cried Alice (she was so much surprised, that for the moment she quite forgot how to speak good English).

Lewis Carroll, Alice's Adventures in Wonderland

Some grammatical relations can be expressed either inflectionally (morphologically) or syntactically (as part of the sentence structure). We can see this in the following sentences:

England's queen is Elizabeth II.	The Queen of England is Elizabeth II.
He loves books.	He is a lover of books.
The planes which fly are red.	The flying planes are red.
He is hungrier than she.	He is more hungry than she.

Some of you may form the comparative of *beastly* only by adding *-er*. *Beastlier* is often used interchangeably with *more beastly*. There are speakers who say both. We know when either form of the comparative can be used, as with *beastly*, or when just one can be used, as with *curious,* as pointed out by Lewis Carroll in the epigraph.

What one language signals with inflectional affixes, another does with word order, and another with function words. For example, in English, the sentence *Maxim defends Victor* means something different from *Victor defends Maxim*. The word order is critical. In Russian, all of the following sentences mean "Maxim defends Victor": (The *č* is pronounced like the *ch* in *cheese*; the *š* like the *sh* in *shoe*; the *j* like the *y* in *yet*.)

Maksim zaščiščajet Viktora.

Maksim Viktora zaščiščajet.

Viktora Maksim zaščiščajet.

Viktora zaščiščajet Maksim.

The inflectional suffix *-a* added to the name *Viktor* to derive *Viktora* shows that Victor, not Maxim, is defended.

Like many languages, Russian has **case** markers, which are grammatical morphemes added to nouns to indicate whether the noun is a subject, object, possessor, or some other grammatical role. As shown in the preceding examples, *-a* is an accusative (object) case marker, and it can also mark genitive (possession) as in *mjech' Viktor+a* means "Viktor's sword." *Viktor+u* is a dative form meaning "to Viktor," *Viktor+om* means "by Viktor," and *Viktor+je* means "about Viktor." Many of the grammatical relations that Russian expresses with case morphology, English expresses with prepositions.[8]

In English, to convey the future meaning of a verb, we must use a function word *will*, as in "John will come Monday." In French, the verb is inflected with a future tense morpheme. Notice the difference between "John is coming Monday," *Jean* vient *lundi*, and "John will come Monday," *Jean* viendra *lundi*. Similarly, where English uses the grammatical markers *have* to form a perfective (completed action) sentence and *be* to form a passive sentence, other languages use affixing to achieve the same meanings, as illustrated with Swahili. In Swahili the morpheme *-me* is a completed action marker and the morpheme *-w* is a passive marker:

*ni+**me**+pig+a m+pira*	*ni**me**piga mpira*	"I have hit a ball"
*m+pira i+li+pig+**w**+a*	*mpira ilipig**w**a*	"A ball was hit"

The meaning of the individual morphemes may not always indicate the meaning of a morphologically complex word (for example, *lowlife* to mean "disreputable person"). This problem is not true of inflectional morphology. If we know the meaning of the word *linguist*, we also know the meaning of the plural form *linguists*; if we know the meaning of the verb *analyze*, we know the meaning of *analyzed*, *analyzes*, and *analyzing*. This reveals another difference between derivational and inflectional morphology.

---

[8] These Russian examples were provided by Stella de Bode.

Figure 3.2 shows the way one may classify English morphemes.

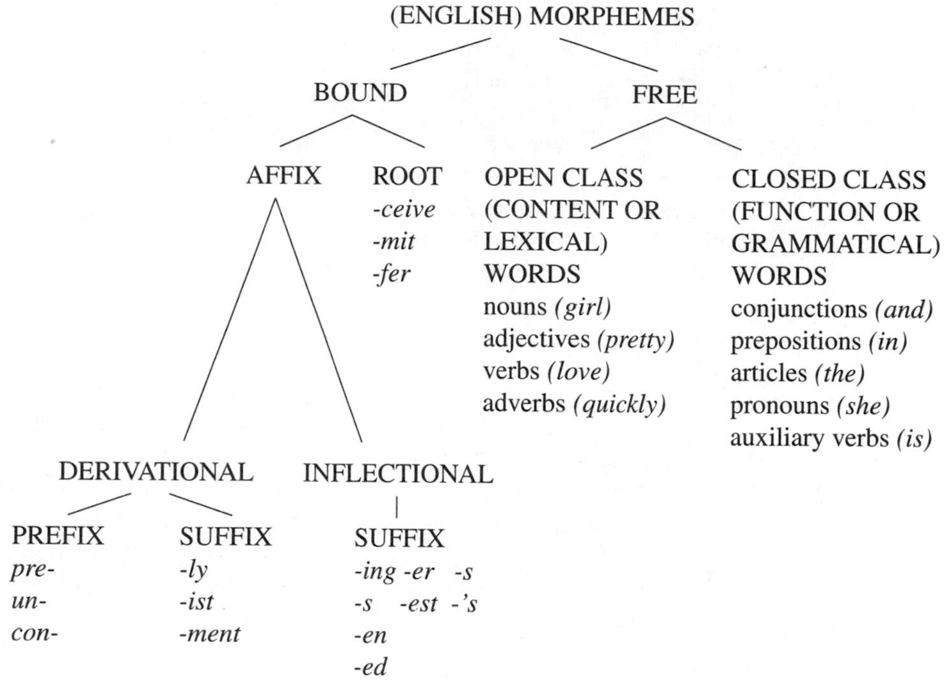

(ENGLISH) MORPHEMES

BOUND   FREE

AFFIX   ROOT   OPEN CLASS   CLOSED CLASS
         -ceive   (CONTENT OR   (FUNCTION OR
         -mit   LEXICAL)   GRAMMATICAL)
         -fer   WORDS   WORDS
                 nouns *(girl)*   conjunctions *(and)*
                 adjectives *(pretty)*   prepositions *(in)*
                 verbs *(love)*   articles *(the)*
                 adverbs *(quickly)*   pronouns *(she)*
                                        auxiliary verbs *(is)*

DERIVATIONAL   INFLECTIONAL

PREFIX   SUFFIX   SUFFIX
pre-   *-ly*   *-ing -er -s*
un-   *-ist*   *-s   -est -'s*
con-   *-ment*   *-en*
                      -ed

FIGURE 3.2 Classification of English Morphemes.

The mental grammar internalized by the language learner includes a lexicon listing all of the morphemes, as well as the derived words with unpredictable meanings. The morphological rules of the grammar permit speakers to use and understand the morphemes and words in forming and understanding new words.

Morphological Analysis: Identifying Morphemes

Speakers of a language have knowledge of the internal structure of a word since their mental grammars include a mental lexicon of morphemes and the morphological rules for their combination. Of course, mistakes are made while learning, but these are quickly remedied. (See chapter 8 for details of how children learn their language.)

Suppose you didn't know English and were a linguist from the planet Mars wishing to analyze the language. How would you discover the morphemes of English? How would you determine whether a word in that language had one, two, or more morphemes?

The first thing to do would be to ask native speakers how they say various words. (It would help to have a Martian-English interpreter along; otherwise, copious gesturing is in order.) Assume you are talented in miming and manage to collect the following sets or *paradigms* of forms:

Adjective	Meaning
ugly	"very unattractive"
uglier	"more ugly"
ugliest	"most ugly"
pretty	"nice looking"
prettier	"more nice looking"
prettiest	"most nice looking"
tall	"large in height"
taller	"more tall"
tallest	"most tall"

To determine what the morphemes are in such a list, the first thing a field linguist would do is to see if some forms mean the same thing in different words, that is, to look for *recurring* forms. We find them: *ugly* occurs in *ugly, uglier,* and *ugliest,* all of which include the meaning "very unattractive." We also find that *-er* occurs in *prettier* and *taller,* adding the meaning "more" to the adjectives to which it is attached. Similarly, *-est* adds the meaning "most." Furthermore, by asking additional questions of our English speaker, we find that *-er* and *-est* do not occur in isolation with the meanings of "more" and "most." We can therefore conclude that the following morphemes occur in English:

ugly	root morpheme
pretty	root morpheme
tall	root morpheme
-er	bound morpheme "comparative"
-est	bound morpheme "superlative"

As we proceed we find other words that end with *-er* (e.g., *singer, lover, bomber, writer, teacher*) in which the *-er* ending does not mean "comparative" but, when attached to a verb, changes it to a noun who "verbs," (e.g., *sings, loves, bombs, writes, teaches*). So we conclude that this is a different morpheme, even though it is pronounced the same as the comparative. We go on and find words like *number, somber, umber, butter, member,* and many others in which the *-er* has no separate meaning at all—a *somber* is not "one who sombs" and a *member* does not *memb*— and therefore these words must be monomorphemic.

Once you have practiced on the morphology of English, you might want to go on to describe another language. Paku was invented by a linguist for an old 1970s TV series called *Land of the Lost.* This was the language used by the monkey people called Pakuni. Suppose you found yourself in this strange land and attempted to find out what the morphemes of Paku were. Again, you would collect your data from a native Paku speaker and proceed as the Martian did with English. Consider the following data from Paku:

me	"I"	meni	"we"
ye	"you (singular)"	yeni	"you (plural)"
we	"he"	weni	"they (masculine)"
wa	"she"	wani	"they (feminine)"

abuma	"girl"	abumani	"girls"
adusa	"boy"	adusani	"boys"
abu	"child"	abuni	"children"
Paku	"one Paku"	Pakuni	"more than one Paku"

By examining these words you find that the plural forms end in *-ni* and the singular forms do not. You therefore conclude that *-ni* is a separate morpheme meaning "plural" that is attached as a suffix to a noun.

By following the analytical principles just discussed, you should be able to solve some of the more complex morphological puzzles that appear in the exercises.

Summary

Knowing a language means knowing the **morphemes** of that language, which are the elemental units that comprise words. Thus, *moralizers* is an English word composed of four morphemes: *moral + ize + er + s*. When you know a word or morpheme, you know both its **form** (sound) and its **meaning**; these are inseparable parts of the **linguistic sign**. The relationship between the form and meaning is **arbitrary**. There is no inherent connection between them (i.e., the words and morphemes of any language must be learned).

Morphemes may be **roots** (*girl, love, in, -ceive*); **derivational** (*un-, re-, -ly, -ness*); or **inflectional** (*-ing, -s, -ed*). Each morpheme is stored in your mental **lexicon** with information on its pronunciation (phonological representation), its meaning or function (semantic properties), and its syntactic category. Also contained in the lexicon are morphologically complex words whose meanings are unpredictable (e.g., *flatfoot, lowlife*).

The study of word formation and the internal structure of words is called **morphology**. Part of our linguistic competence includes knowledge of the rules of how morphemes combine. For example, inflectional morphemes in English are suffixes; in Swahili they may also be prefixes. Words are formed from root morphemes and may have affix morphemes attached. The **base** to which an affix is attached is called the **stem**, which itself may be a word. For example, *system* is a root, and the base to which *-atic* may be attached to form *systematic*, which is the base and stem to which *-al* may be affixed to form *systematical*, which is also the base and stem for affixing *-ly* to form the word *systematically*.

Some morphemes are **bound** in that they must be joined to other morphemes, are always parts of words, and are never words by themselves. Most morphemes are **free** in that they need not be attached to other morphemes; *free, king, serf,* and *bore* are free morphemes; *-dom*, as in *freedom, kingdom, serfdom,* and *boredom*, is a bound morpheme. **Affixes**, that is, **prefixes**, **suffixes**, **infixes**, and **circumfixes**, are bound morphemes. Prefixes occur before, suffixes after, infixes in the middle of, and circumfixes around stems or roots.

Some morphemes, like *huckle* in *huckleberry* and *-ceive* in *perceive* and *receive*, have constant phonological form but meanings determined only by the words in which they occur. They are instances of bound morphemes that are also roots.

Free morphemes consist of **open class** categories (**lexical categories**) such as noun and verb, which are easily expanded; and **closed class** categories (**functional categories**) such as articles and conjunctions, which rarely if ever admit new members.

Most bound morphemes are either derivational or inflectional affixes. Derivational affixes, when added to a root or stem, may change the syntactic word class and/or the meaning of the word. For example, adding *-ish* to the noun *boy* derives an adjective, and prefixing *un-* to *pleasant* changes the meaning by adding a negative element. Inflectional morphemes are determined by the rules of syntax. They are added to complete words and follow any derivational morphemes that happen to be present (in English!), for example *moral+ize+ed*, not **moral+ed+ize*.

The grammars of sign languages also include a morphological component consisting of root, derivational and inflectional sign morphemes, and the rules for their combination.

Grammars also include ways of adding words and morphemes to the lexicon. Words can be created through **coinage**, limited only by the coiner's imagination and the phonetic constraints of word formation. **Compounds** are also a source of new words. Morphological rules combine two or more words to form complex combinations like *rocking chair, deep-sea diver*, and *laptop*. Frequently, the meaning of compounds cannot be predicted from the meanings of their individual morphemes (*cathouse* meaning "bordello"). **Blends** are similar to compounds but usually combine shortened forms of two or more morphemes or words. *Brunch*, a late-morning meal, is a blend of *breakfast* and *lunch*.

Acronyms are words derived from the initials of several words—like *NASA* (*N*ational *A*eronautics and *S*pace *A*dministration)—which can be pronounced as a word; **alphabetic abbreviations** are also derived from initial letters but the letters are pronounced individually, like STD (ess tee dee—*s*exually *t*ransmitted *d*isease).

Eponyms (words taken from proper names such as *john* for "toilet"), **backformations** (*enthuse* from *enthusiasm*), and **clippings** (*fan* from fanatic) also add to the given stock of words.

A continuum of languages is determined by how much they rely on morphology to express linguistic relations. English has relatively little reliance on morphology compared to Mohawk, in which a single, morphologically complex word may contain all of the information of a complete sentence. Between English and Mohawk are languages like Swahili and Italian, which use affixation for some but not all grammatical information. While the particular morphemes and the particular morphological rules are language-dependent, the same general processes occur in all languages.

References for Further Reading

Anderson, S. R. 1992. *A-Morphous Morphology*. Cambridge, England: Cambridge University Press.

Aronoff, M. 1976. *Word Formation in Generative Grammar*. Cambridge, MA: MIT Press.

Bauer, L. 1983. *English Word-formation*. Cambridge, England: Cambridge University Press.

_____. 2003. *Introducing Linguistic Morphology,* 2nd edition. Washington, DC: Georgetown University Press.

Espy, W. R. 1978. *O Thou Improper, Thou Uncommon Noun: An Etymology of Words That Once Were Names*. New York: Clarkson N. Potter.

Jensen, J. T. 1990. *Morphology: Word Structure in Generative Grammar*. Amsterdam/Philadelphia: John Benjamins Publishing.

Katamba, F. 1993. *Morphology*. New York: Bedford/St. Martins.

Matthews, P. H. 1991. *Morphology: An Introduction to the Theory of Word Structure*, 2nd edition. Cambridge, England: Cambridge University Press.

Spencer, A. 1991. *Morphological Theory: An Introduction to Word Structure in Generative Grammar*. London: Basil Blackwell.

Stockwell, R., and D. Minkova. 2001. *English Words: History and Structure.* New York: Cambridge University Press.

Winchester, S. 1999. *The Professor and the Madman.* New York: HarperCollins.

Yoo, D. 1994. "The World of Abbreviations and Acronyms," *Verbatim: The Language Quarterly* (summer): 4–5.

Exercises

....

1. Here is how to estimate the number of words in your mental lexicon. Consult any standard dictionary.

   a. Count the number of entries on a typical page. They are usually bold-faced.

   b. Multiply the number of words per page by the number of pages in the dictionary.

   c. Pick four pages in the dictionary at random, say, pages 50, 75, 125, 303. Count the number of words on these pages.

   d. How many of these words do you know?

   e. What percentage of the words on the four pages do you know?

   f. Multiply the words in the dictionary by the percentage you arrived at in (e). You know approximately that many English words.

2. Divide the following words by placing a + between their morphemes. (Some of the words may be monomorphemic and therefore indivisible.)
   Example: replaces re + place + s

   a. retroactive

   b. befriended

   c. televise

   d. margin

   e. endearment

   f. psychology

   g. unpalatable

   h. holiday

   i. grandmother

   j. morphemic

   k. mistreatment

   l. deactivation

   m. saltpeter

   n. airsickness

3. Match each expression under A with the one statement under B that characterizes it.

A	B
a. noisy crow	1. compound noun
b. scarecrow	2. root morpheme plus derivational prefix
c. the crow	3. phrase consisting of adjective plus noun
d. crowlike	4. root morpheme plus inflectional affix
e. crows	5. root morpheme plus derivational suffix
	6. grammatical morpheme followed by lexical morpheme

4. Write the one proper description from the list under B for the italicized part of each word in A.

A	B
a. terroriz*ed*	1. free root
b. un*civil*ized	2. bound root
c. terror*ize*	3. inflectional suffix
d. *luke*warm	4. derivational suffix
e. *im*possible	5. inflectional prefix
	6. derivational prefix
	7. inflectional infix
	8. derivational infix

5. **A.** Consider the following nouns in Zulu and proceed to look for the recurring forms. Note that the ordering of morphemes is not identical across languages. Thus, what is a prefix in one language may be a suffix or an infix in another.

umfazi	"married woman"	abafazi	"married women"
umfani	"boy"	abafani	"boys"
umzali	"parent"	abazali	"parents"
umfundisi	"teacher"	abafundisi	"teachers"
umbazi	"carver"	ababazi	"carvers"
umlimi	"farmer"	abalimi	"farmers"
umdlali	"player"	abadlali	"players"
umfundi	"reader"	abafundi	"readers"

   a. What is the morpheme meaning "singular" in Zulu?

   b. What is the morpheme meaning "plural" in Zulu?

   c. List the Zulu stems to which the singular and plural morphemes are attached, and give their meanings.

   B. The following Zulu verbs are derived from noun stems by adding a verbal suffix.

fundisa	"to teach"	funda	"to read"
lima	"to cultivate"	baza	"to carve"

   d. Compare these words to the words in section A that are related in meaning, for example, umfundisi "teacher," abafundisi "teachers," fundisa "to teach." What is the derivational suffix that specifies the category verb?

   e. What is the nominal suffix (i.e., the suffix that forms nouns)?

   f. State the morphological noun formation rule in Zulu.

   g. What is the stem morpheme meaning "read"?

   h. What is the stem morpheme meaning "carve"?

6. Examine the following words from Michoacan Aztec.

nokali	"my house"	mopelo	"your dog"
nokalimes	"my houses"	mopelomes	"your dogs"
mokali	"your house"	ipelo	"his dog"
ikali	"his house"	nokwahmili	"my cornfield"
kalimes	"houses"	mokwahmili	"your cornfield"
		ikwahmili	"his cornfield"

a. The morpheme meaning "house" is:

(1) kal   (2) kali   (3) kalim   (4) ikal   (5) ka

b. The word meaning "cornfields" is:

(1) kwahmilimes   (2) nokwahmilimes   (3) nokwahmili   (4) kwahmili
(5) ikwahmilimes

c. The word meaning "his dogs" is:

(1) pelos   (2) ipelomes   (3) ipelos   (4) mopelo   (5) pelomes

d. If the word meaning "friend" is *mahkwa*, then the word meaning "my friends" is:

(1) momahkwa (2) imahkwas (3) momahkwames (4) momahkwaes
(5) nomahkwames

e. The word meaning "dog" is:

(1) pelo   (2) perro   (3) peli   (4) pel   (5) mopel

7. The following infinitive and past participle verb forms are found in Dutch.

Root	Infinitive	Past Participle	
wandel	wandelen	gewandeld	"walk"
duw	duwen	geduwd	"push"
stofzuig	stofzuigen	gestofzuigd	"vacuum-clean"

With reference to the morphological processes of prefixing, suffixing, infixing, and circumfixing discussed in this chapter and the specific morphemes involved:

a. State the morphological rule for forming an infinitive in Dutch.

b. State the morphological rule for forming the Dutch past participle form.

8. Below are some sentences in Swahili:

mtoto	amefika	"The child has arrived."
mtoto	anafika	"The child is arriving."
mtoto	atafika	"The child will arrive."
watoto	wamefika	"The children have arrived."
watoto	wanafika	"The children are arriving."
watoto	watafika	"The children will arrive."
mtu	amelala	"The person has slept."
mtu	analala	"The person is sleeping."
mtu	atalala	"The person will sleep."
watu	wamelala	"The persons have slept."
watu	wanalala	"The persons are sleeping."
watu	watalala	"The persons will sleep."
kisu	kimeanguka	"The knife has fallen."
kisu	kinaanguka	"The knife is falling."
kisu	kitaanguka	"The knife will fall."

visu	vimeanguka	"The knives have fallen."
visu	vinaanguka	"The knives are falling."
visu	vitaanguka	"The knives will fall."
kikapu	kimeanguka	"The basket has fallen."
kikapu	kinaanguka	"The basket is falling."
kikapu	kitaanguka	"The basket will fall."
vikapu	vimeanguka	"The baskets have fallen."
vikapu	vinaanguka	"The baskets are falling."
vikapu	vitaanguka	"The baskets will fall."

One of the characteristic features of Swahili (and Bantu languages in general) is the existence of noun classes. Specific singular and plural prefixes occur with the nouns in each class. These prefixes are also used for purposes of agreement between the subject noun and the verb. In the sentences given, two of these classes are included (there are many more in the language).

a. Identify all the morphemes you can detect, and give their meanings.

> *Example*: -toto "child"
> *m*- noun prefix attached to singular nouns of Class I
> *-a*- prefix attached to verbs when the subject is a singular noun of Class I

Be sure to look for the other noun and verb markers, including tense markers.

b. How is the verb constructed? That is, what kinds of morphemes are strung together and in what order?

c. How would you say in Swahili:
(1) The child is falling.
(2) The baskets have arrived.
(3) The person will fall.

9. One morphological process not discussed in this chapter is reduplication—the formation of new words through the repetition of part or all of a word—which occurs in many languages. The following examples from Samoan illustrate this kind of morphological rule.

manao	"he wishes"	mananao	"they wish"
matua	"he is old"	matutua	"they are old"
malosi	"he is strong"	malolosi	"they are strong"
punou	"he bends"	punonou	"they bend"
atamaki	"he is wise"	atamamaki	"they are wise"
savali	"he travels"	pepese	"they sing"
laga	"he weaves"		

a. What is the Samoan for:
(1) they weave
(2) they travel
(3) he sings

b. Formulate a general statement (a morphological rule) that states how to form the plural verb form from the singular verb form.

10. Following are listed some words followed by incorrect (humorous?) definitions:

Word	Definition
stalemate	"husband or wife no longer interested"
effusive	"able to be merged"
tenet	"a group of ten singers"
dermatology	"a study of derms"
ingenious	"not very smart"
finesse	"a female fish"
amphibious	"able to lie on both sea and land"
deceptionist	"secretary who covers up for his boss"
mathemagician	"Enron's accountant"
sexcedrin	"medicine for mate who says, 'sorry, I have a headache.'"
testostoroni	"hormonal supplement administered as pasta"
aesthetominophen	"medicine to make you look beautiful"
histalavista	"say goodbye to those allergies"
aquapella	"singing in the shower"

Give some possible reasons for the source of these silly "definitions." Illustrate your answers by reference to other words or morphemes. For example, *stalemate* comes from *stale* meaning "having lost freshness" and *mate* meaning "marriage partner." When mates appear to have lost their freshness, they are no longer as desirable as they once were.

11. a. List five acronyms and five alphabetic abbreviations currently in use in English. Do not use the ones given in the text.

b. Invent five acronyms and five alphabetic abbreviations (listing the words as well as the initials).

12. There are many asymmetries in English in which a root morpheme combined with a prefix constitutes a word but without the prefix is a nonword. A number of these are given in this chapter.

a. Following is a list of such nonword roots. Add a prefix to each root to form an existing English word.

Words	Nonwords
_____	*descript
_____	*cognito
_____	*beknownst
_____	*peccable
_____	*promptu
_____	*plussed
_____	*domitable
_____	*nomer

b. There are many more such multimorphemic words for which the root morphemes do not constitute words by themselves. See how many you can think of.

13. We have seen that the meaning of compounds is often not revealed by the meaning of its composite words. Crossword puzzles and riddles often make use of this by providing the meaning of two parts of a compound and asking for the resulting word. For example, infielder = diminutive/cease. Read this as asking for a word that means "infielder" by combining a word that means "diminutive" with a word which means "cease." The answer is *shortstop*. See if you can figure out the following:

a. sci-fi TV series = headliner/journey

b. campaign = farm building/tempest

c. at-home wear = tub of water/court attire

d. kind of pen = formal dance/sharp end

e. conservative = correct/part of an airplane

14. a. Consider the cartoon:

"Drabble" © Kevin Fagan. Dist. by United Feature Syndicate, Inc.

The humor is based on the ambiguity of the compound *ten-page book report*. Draw two trees similar to those in the text for *top hat rack* on page 96 to reveal the ambiguity.

b. Draw a tree to show the internal morpheme structure of *indecipherability*. (*Hint*: there are five morphemes.)

15. One of the characteristics of Italian is that articles and adjectives have inflectional endings that mark agreement in gender (and number) with the noun they modify. Based on this information, answer the questions that follow the list of Italian phrases.

un uomo	"a man"
un uomo robusto	"a robust man"
un uomo robustissimo	"a very robust man"
una donna robusta	"a robust woman"
un vino rosso	"a red wine"
una faccia	"a face"
un vento secco	"a dry wind"

a. What is the root morpheme meaning "robust"?

b. What is the morpheme meaning "very"?

    c. What is the Italian for:
      (1) "a robust wine"
      (2) "a very red face"
      (3) "a very dry wine"

16. Following is a list of words from Turkish. In Turkish, articles and morphemes indicating location are affixed to the noun.

deniz	"an ocean"	evden	"from a house"
denize	"to an ocean"	evimden	"from my house"
denizin	"of an ocean"	denizimde	"in my ocean"
eve	"to a house"	elde	"in a hand"

    a. What is the Turkish morpheme meaning "to"?

    b. What kind of affixes in Turkish correspond to English prepositions (e.g., prefixes, suffixes, infixes, free morphemes)?

    c. What would the Turkish word for "from an ocean" be?

    d. How many morphemes are there in the Turkish word *denizimde?*

17. The following are some verb forms in Chickasaw, a member of the Muskogean family of languages spoken in south-central Oklahoma.[9] Chickasaw is an endangered language. Currently, there are only about 100 speakers of Chickasaw, most of whom are over 70 years old.

Sachaaha	"I am tall"
Chaaha	"He/she is tall"
Chichaaha	"you are tall"
Hoochaaha	"they are tall"
Satikahbi	"I am tired"
Chitikahbitok	"you were tired"
Chichchokwa	"you are cold"
Hopobatok	"he was hungry"
Hoohopobatok	"they were hungry"
Sahopoba	"I am hungry"

    a. What is the root morpheme for the following verbs?
      (1) "to be tall"
      (2) "to be hungry"

    b. What is the morpheme meaning:
      (1) past tense
      (2) "I"
      (3) "You"
      (4) "He/she"

    c. If the Chickasaw root for "to be old" is *sipokni*, how would you say:
      (1) "You are old"
      (2) "He was old"
      (3) "They are old"

---

[9] The Chickasaw examples are provided by Pamela Munro.

18. The language Little-End Egglish, whose source is revealed in exercise 13, chapter 11, exhibits the following data:

a. kul "omelet"   zkulego "my omelet"   zkulivo "your omelet"

b. vet "yoke (of egg)"   zvetego "my yoke"   zvetivo "your yoke"

c. rok "egg"   zrokego "my egg"   zrokivo "your egg"

d. ver "egg shell"   zverego "my egg shell"   zverivo "your egg shell"

e. gup "soufflé"   zgupego "my soufflé"   zgupivo "your soufflé"

    i. Isolate the morphemes that indicate possession, first person singular, and second person (we don't know whether singular, plural, or both). Indicate whether the affixes are prefixes or suffixes.

    ii. Given that *vel* means egg white, how would a Little-End Egglisher say "my egg white"?

    iii. Given that *zpeivo* means "your hard-boiled egg," what is the word meaning "hard-boiled egg"?

    iv. If you knew that *zvetgogo* meant "our egg yoke," what would be likely to be the morpheme meaning "our"?

    v. If you knew that *borokego* meant "for my egg," what would be likely to be the morpheme bearing the benefactive meaning "for"?

4

Syntax: The Sentence Patterns of Language

To grammar even kings bow.

J. B. MOLIÈRE, Les Femmes Savantes, *II, 1672*

It is an astonishing fact that any speaker of any human language can produce and understand an infinite number of sentences. We can show this quite easily through examples such as the following:

The kind-hearted boy had many girlfriends.
The kindhearted, intelligent boy had many girlfriends.
The kindhearted, intelligent, handsome boy had many girlfriends.
.
.
.

John found a book in the library.
John found a book in the library in the stacks.
John found a book in the library in the stacks on the fourth floor.
.
.
.

The cat chased the mouse.
The cat chased the mouse that ate the cheese.
The cat chased the mouse that ate the cheese that came from the cow.
The cat chased the mouse that ate the cheese that came from the cow that grazed in the field.

In each case the speaker could continue creating sentences by adding another adjective, prepositional phrase, or relative clause. In principle, this could go on forever. All languages have mechanisms of this sort that make the number of sentences limitless. Given this fact, the sentences of a language cannot be stored in a dictionary format in our heads. Rather, sentences are composed of discrete units that are combined by rules. This system of rules explains how speakers can store infinite knowledge in a finite space—our brains.

The part of grammar that represents a speaker's knowledge of sentences and their structures is called **syntax**. The aim of this chapter is to show you what syntactic structure is and what the rules that determine syntactic structure are like. Most of the examples will be from the syntax of English, but the principles that account for syntactic structures are universal.

What the Syntax Rules Do

"Blondie" © 1990 King Features Syndicate. Reprinted with permission of King Features Syndicate.

The rules of syntax combine words into phrases and phrases into sentences. Among other things, the rules specify the correct word order for a language. For example, English is a Subject–Verb–Object (SVO) language. The English sentence in (1) is grammatical because the words occur in the right order; the sentence in (2) is ungrammatical because the word order is incorrect for English. (Recall that the asterisk or star preceding a sentence is the linguistic convention for indicating that the sentence is ungrammatical or ill-formed according to the rules of the grammar.)

1. The President nominated a new Supreme Court justice.
2. *President the new Supreme justice Court a nominated.

A second important role of the syntax is to describe the relationship between the meaning of a particular group of words and the arrangement of those words. For example, the "Rose Is Rose" cartoon illustrates that the word order of a sentence contributes significantly to its meaning. The sentences in (3) and (4) contain the same words, but the meanings are quite different.

3. He burps what he means.
4. He means what he burps.

"Rose Is Rose" © United Feature Syndicate, Inc.

The rules of the syntax also specify the **grammatical relations** of a sentence, such as **subject** and **direct object**. In other words, they provide the information that permits the hearer to know who is doing what to whom. This information is crucial to understanding the meaning of a sentence. For example, the grammatical relations in (5) and (6) are reversed, so the otherwise identical sentences have very different meanings.

5. Your dog chased my cat.
6. My cat chased your dog.

The rules of syntax also specify other constraints that sentences must adhere to. Consider, for example, the sentences in (7). As an exercise you can first read through them and place a star before those sentences that *you* consider to be ungrammatical.

7. (a) The boy found.
　　(b) The boy found quickly.
　　(c) The boy found in the house.
　　(d) The boy found the ball.

We predict that you will find the sentence in (7d) grammatical and the ones in (7a-c) ungrammatical. This is because the syntax rules specify that a verb like *found* must be followed by something, and that something cannot be an expression like *quickly* or *in the house* but must be like *the ball*.

Similarly, we expect you will find the sentence in (8b) grammatical while the sentence in (8a) is not.

8. (a) Disa slept the baby.
　　(b) Disa slept soundly.

The verb *sleep* patterns differently than *find* in that it may be followed solely by a word like *soundly* but not by other kinds of phrases such as *the baby*.

We also predict that you'll find that the sentences in (9a, d, e, f) are grammatical while (9b, c) are not. The examples in (9) show that specific verbs, such as *believe*, *try,* and *want*, behave differently with respect to the patterns of words that may follow them.

9. (a) Zack believes Robert to be a gentleman.
(b) Zack believes to be a gentleman.
(c) Zack tries Robert to be a gentleman.
(d) Zack tries to be a gentleman.
(e) Zack wants to be a gentleman.
(f) Zack wants Robert to be a gentleman.

The fact that all native speakers have the same judgments about the sentences in (7) to (9) tells us that grammatical judgments are neither idiosyncratic nor capricious, but are determined by rules that are shared by the speakers of a language.

In (10) we see that the phrase *ran up the hill* behaves differently from the phrase *ran up the bill,* even though the two phrases are superficially quite similar. For the expression *ran up the hill*, the rules of the syntax allow the word orders in (10a) and (10c), but not (10b). In *ran up the bill*, in contrast, the rules allow the order in (10d) and (10e), but not (10f).

10. (a) Jack and Jill ran up the hill.
(b) Jack and Jill ran the hill up.
(c) Up the hill ran Jack and Jill.
(d) Jack and Jill ran up the bill.
(e) Jack and Jill ran the bill up.
(f) Up the bill ran Jack and Jill.

The pattern shown in (10) illustrates that sentences are not simply strings of words with no further organization. If they were, there would be no reason to expect *ran up the hill* to behave differently from *ran up the bill*. These phrases act differently because they have different syntactic structures associated with them. In *ran up the hill*, the words *up the hill* form a unit, as follows:

He ran [up the hill]

(We use square brackets to indicate that a group of words forms a syntactic unit or *constituent.* We will have much more to say about syntactic constituents shortly.) The whole unit can be moved to the beginning of the sentence, as in (10c), but we cannot rearrange its subparts, as shown in (10b). On the other hand, in *ran up the bill*, the words *up the bill* do not form a natural unit, so they cannot be moved, and (10f) is ungrammatical.

"Tumbleweeds" © Tom K. Ryan. Reprinted with permission of King Features Syndicate.

Our syntactic knowledge crucially includes knowledge of how words form groups in a sentence, or how they are *hierarchically* arranged with respect to one another. Consider the "Tumbleweeds" cartoon. The humor depends on the ambiguity of the phrase *synthetic buffalo hides*, which can mean "buffalo hides that are synthetic" or "hides of synthetic buffalo." This example again illustrates that within a phrase or sentence, certain words are grouped together. The words in the phrase *synthetic buffalo hides* can be grouped in two ways. If the words are grouped as follows, we get the first meaning:

synthetic [buffalo hides]

When we group them like this,

[synthetic buffalo] hides

we get the second meaning.

The rules of syntax allow both of these groupings, which is why the expression is ambiguous. The following hierarchical diagrams illustrate the two structures:

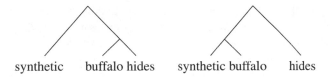

This is similar to what we find in morphology for words such as *unlockable*, which have two structures, corresponding to two meanings, as discussed in chapter 3.

Many sentences exhibit such ambiguities, often leading to humorous results. Consider the following two sentences, which appeared in classified ads:

For sale: an antique desk suitable for lady with thick legs and large drawers.
We will oil your sewing machine and adjust tension in your home for $10.00.

In the first ad, the humorous reading comes from the grouping [*a desk*] [*for lady with thick legs and large drawers*] as opposed to the intended [*a desk for lady*] [*with thick legs and large drawers*], where the legs and drawers belong to the desk. The second case is similar.

Because these ambiguities are a result of different structures, they are instances of **structural ambiguity**.

Contrast these sentences with:

This will make you smart.

The two interpretations of this sentence are due to the two meanings of *smart*— "clever" or "burning sensation." Such lexical or word-meaning ambiguities, as opposed to structural ambiguities, will be discussed in chapter 5.

The rules of syntax reveal the grammatical relations among the words of a sentence as well as their order and hierarchical organization. They also explain how the grouping of words relates to its meaning, such as when a sentence or phrase is ambiguous. In addition, the syntactic rules permit speakers to produce and understand a limitless number of sentences never produced or heard before—*the creative aspect of linguistic knowledge.* A major goal of linguistics is to show clearly and explicitly how syntactic rules account for this knowledge. A theory of grammar must provide a complete characterization of what speakers implicitly know about their language.

What Grammaticality Is Not Based On

> *Colorless green ideas sleep furiously.* This is a very interesting sentence, because it shows that syntax can be separated from semantics—that form can be separated from meaning. The sentence doesn't seem to mean anything coherent, but it sounds like an English sentence.
>
> **Howard Lasnik,** The Human Language: Part One

Importantly, a person's ability to make grammaticality judgments does not depend on having heard the sentence before. You may never have heard or read the sentence

Enormous crickets in pink socks danced at the prom.

but your syntactic knowledge tells you that it is grammatical. As we showed at the beginning of this chapter, people are able to understand, produce, and make judgments about an infinite range of sentences, most of which they have never heard before. This ability illustrates that our knowledge of language is creative—not creative in the sense that we are all poets, which we are not, but creative in that none of us is limited to a fixed repertoire of expressions. Rather, we can exploit the resources of our language and grammar to produce and understand a limitless number of sentences embodying a limitless range of ideas and emotions.

We showed that the structure of a sentence contributes to its meaning. However, grammaticality and meaningfulness are not the same thing, as shown by the following sentences:

Colorless green ideas sleep furiously.
A verb crumpled the milk.

Although these sentences do not make much sense, they are syntactically well formed. They sound funny, but their funniness is different from what we find in the following strings of words:

*Furiously sleep ideas green colorless.
*Milk the crumpled verb a.

There are also sentences that we understand even though they are not well formed according to the rules of the syntax. For example, most English speakers could interpret

*The boy quickly in the house the ball found.

although they know that the word order is incorrect. Similarly, we could probably assign a meaning to sentence (8a) (*Disa slept the baby*) in the previous section. If asked to fix it up, we would probably come up with something like "Disa put the baby to sleep," but we also know that as it stands, (8a) is not a possible sentence of English. To be a sentence, words must conform to specific patterns determined by the syntactic rules of the language.

Some sentences are grammatical even though they are difficult to interpret because they include nonsense words, that is, words with no agreed-on meaning. This is illustrated by the following lines from the poem "Jabberwocky" by Lewis Carroll:

'Twas brillig, and the slithy toves
Did gyre and gimble in the wabe;

These lines are grammatical in the linguistic sense that they obey the word order and other constraints of English. Such nonsense poetry is amusing precisely because the sentences comply with syntactic rules and sound like good English. Ungrammatical strings of nonsense words are not entertaining:

*Toves slithy the and brillig 'twas
wabe the in gimble and gyre did

Grammaticality also does not depend on the truth of sentences. If it did, lying would be impossible. Nor does it depend on whether real objects are being discussed or on whether something is possible. Untrue sentences can be grammatical, sentences discussing unicorns can be grammatical, and sentences referring to pregnant fathers can be grammatical.

The syntactic rules that permit us to produce, understand, and make grammaticality judgments are unconscious rules. The grammar is a mental grammar, different from the prescriptive grammar rules that we are taught in school. We develop the mental rules of grammar long before we attend school, as we shall see in chapter 8.

Sentence Structure

I really do not know that anything has ever been more exciting than diagramming sentences.

GERTRUDE STEIN

Suppose we wanted to write a template that described the structure of an English sentence, and more specifically, a template that gave the correct word order for English. We might come up with something like the following:

Det - N - V - Det - N

This template says that a determiner (an article) is followed by a noun, which is followed by a verb, and so on. It would describe English sentences such as the following:

The child found a puppy.
The professor wrote a book.
That runner won the race.

The implication of such a template would be that sentences are strings of words belonging to particular grammatical categories ("parts of speech") with no internal organization. We know, however, that such "flat" structures are incorrect. As noted earlier, sentences have a hierarchical organization; that is, the words are grouped into natural units. The words in the sentence

The child found a puppy.

may be grouped into [*the child*] and [*found a puppy*], corresponding to the subject and predicate of the sentence. A further division gives [*the child*] and then [[found] [*a puppy*]], and finally the individual words: [[the] [child]] [[found] [[a] [puppy]]]. It's sometimes easier to see the parts and subparts of the sentence in a **tree diagram**:

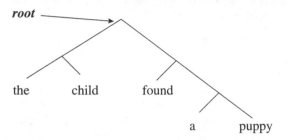

The "tree" is upside down with its "root" encompassing the entire sentence, "The child found a puppy," and its "leaves" being the individual words, *the, child, found, a, puppy*. The tree conveys the same information as the nested square brackets. The hierarchical organization of the tree reflects the groupings and subgroupings of the words of the sentence.

The tree diagram shows, among other things, that the phrase *found a puppy* divides naturally into two branches, one for the verb *found* and the other for the direct object *a puppy*. A different division, say, *found a* and *puppy*, is unnatural.

Constituents and Constituency Tests

The natural groupings of a sentence are called **constituents**. Various linguistic tests reveal the constituents of a sentence. The first test is the "stand alone" test. If a group of words can stand alone, they form a constituent. For example, the set of words that can be used to answer a question is a constituent. So in answer to the question "what did you find?" a speaker might answer, *a puppy*, but not *found a*. *A puppy* can stand alone while *found a* cannot.

The second test is "replacement by a pronoun." Pronouns can substitute for natural groups. In answer to the question "where did you find *a puppy*?" a speaker can say, "I found *him* in the park." Words such as *do* can also take the place of the entire predicate *found a puppy*, as in "John found a puppy and Bill *did* too." If a group of words can be replaced by a pronoun or a word like *do*, they form a constituent.

A third test of constituency is the "move as a unit" test. If a group of words can be moved, they form a constituent. For example, if we compare the following sentences to the sentence "the child found a puppy," we see that certain elements have moved:

It was *a puppy* that the child found.
A puppy was found by *the child*.

In the first example, the constituent *a puppy* has moved from its position following *found*; in the second example, the positions of *a puppy* and *the child* have been changed. In all such rearrangements the constituents *a puppy* and *the child* remain intact. *Found a* does not remain intact, because it is not a constituent.

In the sentence "the child found a puppy," the natural groupings or constituents are the subject *the child*, the predicate *found a puppy*, and the direct object *a puppy*.

Some sentences have a prepositional phrase in the predicate. Consider

The puppy played in the garden.

We can use our tests to show that *in the garden* is also a constituent, as follows:

Where did the puppy play? *In the garden* (stand alone)

The puppy played *there*. (replacement by a pronoun-like word)

In the garden is where the puppy played. (move as a unit)

It was *in the garden* that the puppy played.

As before, our knowledge of the **constituent structure** of a sentence may be graphically represented by a tree diagram. The tree diagram for the sentence "The puppy played in the garden" is as follows:

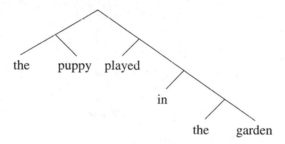

In addition to the syntactic tests just described, experimental evidence has shown that speakers do not represent sentences as strings of words but rather in terms of constituents. In these experiments, subjects listen to sentences that have clicking noises inserted into them at random points. In some cases the click occurs at a constituent boundary, and in other sentences, the click is inserted in the middle of a constituent. The subjects are then asked to report where the click occurred. There were two important results: (1) subjects noticed the click and recalled its location best when it occurred at a major constituent boundary (e.g., between the subject and predicate); and (2) clicks that occurred inside the constituent were reported to have occurred between constituents. In other words, subjects displaced the clicks and put them at constituent boundaries. These results show that speakers perceive sentences in chunks corresponding to grammatical constituents.

Every sentence in a language is associated with one or more constituent structures. If a sentence has more than one constituent structure, it is ambiguous, and each tree will correspond to one of the possible meanings. For example, the sentence "I bought an antique desk suitable for a lady with thick legs and large drawers" has two phrase structure trees associated with it. In one structure the phrase [*a lady with thick legs and large drawers*] forms a constituent. For example, it could stand alone in answer to a question *who did you buy an antique desk for?* In its second meaning, the phrase *with thick legs and large drawers* modifies the phrase *a desk for a lady*, and thus the structure is [[a desk for a lady][*with thick legs and large drawers*]].

Syntactic Categories

" I MISS THE GOOD OLD DAYS WHEN ALL WE HAD TO WORRY ABOUT WAS NOUNS AND VERBS."

© ScienceCartoonsPlus.com.

Might, could, would—they are contemptible auxiliaries.

GEORGE ELIOT (MARY ANN EVANS), Middlemarch

Each grouping in the tree diagrams of "The child found a puppy" and "The boy ran up the hill" is a member of a large family of similar expressions. For example, *the child* belongs to a family that includes *the police officer, your neighbor, this yellow cat, he, John,* and countless others. We can substitute any member of this family for *the child* without affecting the grammaticality of the sentence, although the meaning of course would change.

A police officer found a puppy.
Your neighbor found a puppy.
This yellow cat found a puppy.

A family of expressions that can substitute for one another without loss of grammaticality is called a **syntactic category**.

The child, a police officer, and so on belong to the syntactic category **noun phrase (NP)**, one of several syntactic categories in English and every other language in the world. NPs may function as the subject or as an object in a sentence. NPs often contain a *determiner* (like *a* or *the*) and a noun, but they may also consist of a proper name, a pronoun, a noun without a determiner, or even a clause or a sentence. Even though a proper noun like *John* and pronouns such as *he* and *him* are single words, they are technically NPs, because they pattern like NPs in being able to fill a subject or object or other NP slot.

John found the puppy.
He found the puppy.
Boys love puppies.
The puppy loved him.
The puppy loved John.

NPs can be more complex as illustrated by the sentence:

The girl that Paris loved married the man of her dreams.

The NP subject of this sentence is *the girl that Paris loved,* and the NP object is *the man of her dreams.*

Part of a speaker's knowledge of syntax is the specification of the syntactic categories. That is, speakers of English know that only items (a), (b), (e), (f), and (g) in the following list are NPs even if they have never heard the term *noun phrase* before.

1. (a) a bird
   (b) the red banjo
   (c) have a nice day
   (d) with a balloon
   (c) the woman who was laughing
   (f) it
   (g) John
   (h) went

You can test this claim by inserting each expression into three contexts: *Who found* _____, _____ *was seen by everyone*, and *What/who I heard was* _____. For example, **Who found have a nice day* is ungrammatical, as opposed to *Who found it?* or *John was seen by everyone.* Only NPs fit into these contexts because only NPs can function as subjects and objects.

There are other syntactic categories. The expression *found a puppy* is a **verb phrase (VP)**. A verb phrase always contains a **verb (V)**, and it may contain other categories, such as a noun phrase or **prepositional phrase (PP)**, which is a preposition followed by an NP. In (2) the VPs are those phrases that can complete the sentence "The child _____."

2. (a) saw a clown
   (b) a bird
   (c) slept
   (d) smart

(e) ate the cake

(f) found the cake in the cupboard

(g) realized that the earth was round

Inserting (a), (c), (e), (f), and (g) will produce grammatical sentences, whereas the insertion of (b) or (d) would result in an ungrammatical sentence. Thus, (a), (c), (e), (f), and (g) are verb phrases.

Syntactic categories include both phrasal categories such as NP, VP, AdjP (adjective phrase), PP (prepositional phrase), and AdvP (adverbial phrase), as well as lexical categories such as noun (N), verb (V), preposition (P), adjective (Adj), and adverb (Adv). Each lexical category has a corresponding phrasal category. Following is a list of lexical categories with some examples of each type:

Lexical categories

Noun (N)	*puppy, boy, soup, happiness, fork, kiss, pillow, cake, cupboard*
Verb (V)	*find, run, sleep, throw, realize, see, try, want, believe*
Preposition (P)	*up, down, across, into, from, by, with*
Adjective (Adj)	*red, big, candid, hopeless, fair, idiotic, lucky*
Adverb (Adv)	*again, carefully, luckily, never, very, fairly*

Many of these categories may already be familiar to you. Some of them, as mentioned earlier, are traditionally referred to as *parts of speech*. Other categories may be less familiar, for example, the category **determiner (Det)**, which includes the articles *a* and *the*, as well as **demonstratives** such as *this, that, these,* and *those*, and "counting words" such as *each* and *every*. Another less familiar category is **auxiliary (Aux)**, which includes the verbs *have, had, be, was, were,* and the **modals** *may, might, can, could, must, shall, should, will, would*. Aux and Det are **functional categories**, so called because their members have a grammatical function rather than a descriptive meaning. For example, determiners specify whether a noun is indefinite or definite (*a boy* vs. *the boy*), or the relation of the noun to the context (*this boy* vs. *that boy*). Auxiliaries provide the verb with a time frame, whether ongoing (*John **is** dancing*), completed in the past (*John **has** danced*), or occurring in the future (*John **will** dance*). Auxiliaries may also express notions such as possibility (*John **may** dance*) or necessity (*John **must** dance*) and so on.

Lexical categories typically have particular kinds of meanings associated with them. For example, verbs usually refer to actions, events, and states (*kick, marry, love*); adjectives to qualities or properties (*lucky, old*); common nouns to general entities (*dog, elephant, house*); proper nouns to particular individuals (*Noam Chomsky*) or places (*Dodger Stadium*) or other things that people give names to such as commercial products (*Coca-Cola, Viagra*). But the relationship between grammatical categories and meaning is more complex than these few examples suggest. Thus nouns such as *marriage* and *destruction* refer to events and others refer to states (*happiness, loneliness*). We can use abstract nouns such as *honor* and *beauty*, rather than adjectives, to refer to properties and qualities. In the sentence "Seeing is believing," *seeing* and *believing* are nouns but are not entities. Prepositions are usually used to express relationship between two entities involving a location (e.g., *the boy is in the room, the cat is under the bed*), but this is not always the case; the prepositions *of, by, about,* and *with* are not locational. Because of the difficulties involved in specifying the precise meaning of lexical categories, we do not usually define categories in terms of their meanings, but rather on the basis of their syntactic distribution (where they occur in a sentence) and morphological characteristics. For example, we define a noun as a word that can occur with a determiner (*the boy*) and that can take a plural marker (*boys*) among other properties.

All languages have syntactic categories such as N, V, and NP. Speakers know the syntactic categories of their language, even if they do not know the technical terms. Our knowledge of the syntactic classes is revealed when we substitute equivalent phrases, as we just did in examples (1) and (2), and when we use the various syntactic tests that we have discussed.

Phrase Structure Trees and Rules

Who climbs the Grammar-Tree distinctly knows
Where Noun and Verb and Participle grows.

John Dryden, *"The Sixth Satyr of Juvenal"*

Now that you know something about constituent structure and grammatical categories, you are ready to learn how the sentences of a language are constructed. We will begin by building trees for simple sentences and then proceed to slightly more complex structures. The trees that we will build here are more detailed than those we saw in the previous sections, because the branches of the tree will have category labels identifying each constituent. In this section we will also introduce the syntactic rules that describe the different kinds of structures represented by the trees.

The following tree diagram provides labels for each of the constituents of the sentence "The child found a puppy." These labels show that the entire sentence belongs to the syntactic category of S (because the S-node encompasses all the words). It also reveals that *the child* and *a puppy* belong to the category NP, that is, they are noun phrases, and that *found a puppy* belongs to the category VP or is a verb phrase, consisting of a verb and an NP. It also reveals the syntactic category of each of the words in the sentence.

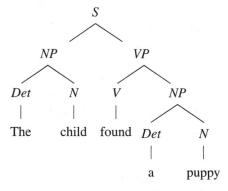

A tree diagram with syntactic category information is called a **phrase structure tree** or a **constituent structure tree**. This tree shows that a sentence is both a linear string of words and a hierarchical structure with phrases nested in phrases. Phrase structure trees (PS trees, for short) are explicit graphic representations of a speaker's knowledge of the structure of the sentences of his language.

PS trees represent three aspects of a speaker's syntactic knowledge:

1. The linear order of the words in the sentence
2. The identification of the syntactic categories of words and groups of words
3. The hierarchical structure of the syntactic categories (e.g., an S is composed of an NP followed by a VP, a VP is composed of a V that may be followed by an NP, and so on)

In chapter 3 we discussed the fact that the syntactic category of each word is listed in our mental dictionaries. We now see how this information is used by the syntax of the language. Words appear in trees under labels that correspond to their syntactic category. Nouns are under *N*, determiners under *Det*, verbs under *V*, and so on.

The larger syntactic categories, such as *VP*, consist of all the syntactic categories and words below that point, or **node**, in the tree. The *VP* in the above PS tree consists of syntactic category nodes *V* and *NP* and the words *found, a*, and *puppy*. Because *a puppy* can be traced up the tree to the node *NP*, this constituent is a noun phrase. Because *found* and *a puppy* can be traced up to the node *VP*, this constituent is a verb phrase. The PS tree reflects the speaker's intuitions about the natural groupings of words in a sentence. The PS tree also states implicitly what combinations of words are not syntactic categories. For example, because there is no node above the words *found* and *a* to connect them, the two words do not constitute a syntactic category, reflecting our earlier judgments.

In discussing trees, every higher node is said to **dominate** all the categories beneath it. VP dominates V, NP, and also dominates Det and N. A node is said to **immediately dominate** the categories one level below it. VP immediately dominates V and NP, the categories of which it is composed. Categories that are immediately dominated by the same node are **sisters**. V and NP are sisters in the phrase structure tree of "the child found a puppy."

A PS tree is a formal device for representing the speaker's knowledge of the structure of sentences in his language, as revealed by our linguistic intuitions. When we speak, we are not aware that we are producing sentences with such structures, but controlled experiments show that we use them in speech production and comprehension, as we will see in chapter 9.

The information represented in a PS tree can also be represented by another formal device: phrase structure (PS) rules. PS rules capture the knowledge that speakers have about the possible structures of a language. Just as a speaker cannot have an infinite list of sentences in her head, so she cannot have an infinite set of PS trees in her head. Rather, a speaker's knowledge of the permissible and impermissible structures must exist as a finite set of rules that "generate" (a favorite word of linguists) or specify a tree for any sentence in the language. To express the structure given above, we need the following PS rules:

1. S → NP VP
2. NP → Det N
3. VP → V NP

Phrase structure rules specify the well-formed structures of a language precisely and concisely. They express the regularities of the language and make explicit a speaker's knowledge of the order of words and the grouping of words into syntactic categories. For example, in English an NP may contain a determiner followed by a noun. This is represented by rule 2. This rule conveys two facts:

A noun phrase can contain a determiner followed by a noun in that order.

A determiner followed by a noun is a noun phrase.

You can think of PS rules as templates that a tree must match to be grammatical. To the left of the arrow is the dominating category, in this case NP, and the categories that it immediately dominates—that comprise it—appear on the right side, in this case Det and N. The right side of the arrow also shows the linear order of these components. Thus, the subtree for the English NP looks like this:

Rule 1 says that a sentence (S) contains (immediately dominates) an NP and a VP in that order. Rule 3 says that a verb phrase consists of a verb (V) followed by an NP. These rules are general statements and do not refer to any specific VP, V, or NP. The subtrees represented by rules 1 and 3 are as follows:

A VP need not contain an NP object, however. It may include a verb alone, as in the following sentences:

The woman laughed.
The man danced.
The horse galloped.

These sentences have the structure:

Thus a tree may have a VP that immediately dominates V, which would be permitted by rule 4, which must therefore be added to the grammar:

4. VP $\rightarrow$ V

The following sentences contain prepositional phrases following the Verb:

The puppy played in the garden.
The boat sailed up the river.
A girl laughed at the monkey.
The sheepdog rolled in the mud.

The PS tree for such sentences is

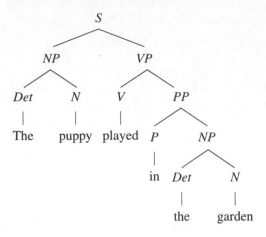

To permit structures of this type, we need two additional PS rules, as in 5 and 6.

5. VP → V PP
6. PP → P NP

Another option open to the VP is to contain or *embed* a sentence. For example, the sentence "The professor said that the student passed the exam" contains the sentence "the student passed the exam." Preceding the **embedded sentence** is the word *that*, which is a **complementizer (C)**. C is a functional category, like Aux and Det. Here is the structure of such sentence types:

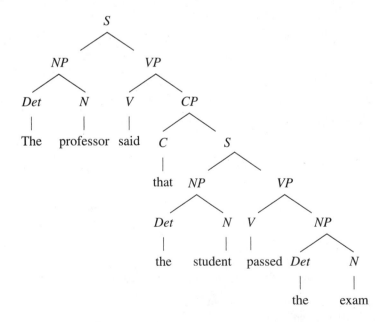

To allow such embedded sentences, we need to add these two new rules to our set of phrase structure rules.

7. VP → V CP
8. CP → C S

CP stands for complementizer phrase. Rule 8 says that CP contains a complementizer such as *that* followed by the embedded sentence. Other complementizers are *if* and *whether* in sentences like

> I don't know <u>whether</u> I should talk about this.
> The teacher asked <u>if</u> the students understood the syntax lesson.

which have structures similar to the one above.

Here are the PS rules we have discussed so far. A few other rules will be considered later.

1. S   → NP VP
2. NP → Det N
3. VP → V NP
4. VP → V
5. VP → V PP
6. PP → P NP
7. VP → V CP
8. CP → C S

Some Conventions for Building Phrase Structure Trees

> Everyone who is master of the language he speaks . . . may form new . . .
> phrases, provided they coincide with the genius of the language.
> **MICHAELIS,** Dissertation *(1769)*

One can use the phrase structure rules as a guide for building trees that follow the structural constraints of the language. In so doing, certain conventions are followed. The S occurs at the top or "root" of the tree (it's upside down). Another convention specifies how the rules are applied: First, find the rule with S on the left side of the arrow, and put the categories on the right side below the S, as shown here:

Once started, continue by matching any syntactic category at the bottom of the partially constructed tree to a category on the left side of a rule, then expand the tree with the categories on the right side. For example, we may expand the tree by applying the NP rule to produce:

The categories at the bottom are Det, N, and VP, but only VP occurs to the left of an arrow in the set of rules and so needs to be expanded using one of the VP rules. Any one of the rules will work. The order in which the rules appear in the list of rules is irrelevant. (We could have begun by expanding the VP rather than the NP.) Suppose we use rule 4 next. Then the tree has grown to look like this:

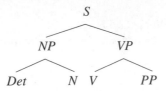

Convention dictates that we continue in this way until none of the categories at the bottom of the tree appears on the left side of any rule (i.e., no phrasal categories may remain unexpanded). The PP must expand into a P and an NP (rule 6), and the NP into a Det and an N. We can use a rule as many times as it can apply. In this tree, we used the NP rule twice. After we have applied all the rules that can apply, the tree looks like this:

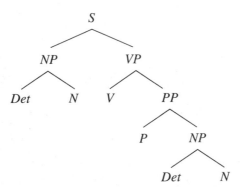

By following these conventions, we generate only trees specified by the PS rules, and hence only trees that conform to the syntax of the language. By implication, any tree not so specified will be ungrammatical, that is, not permitted by the syntax. At any point during the construction of a tree, any rule may be used as long as its left-side category occurs somewhere at the bottom of the tree. By choosing different VP rules, we could specify different structures corresponding to sentences such as:

The boys left. (VP → V)
The wind blew the kite. (VP → V NP)
The senator hopes that the bill passes. (VP → V CP)

Because the number of possible sentences in every language is infinite, there is also an infinite number of trees. However, all trees are built out of the finite set of substructures allowed by the grammar of the language, and these substructures are specified by the finite set of phrase structure rules.

The Infinity of Language

So, naturalists observe, a flea
Hath smaller fleas that on him prey;
And these have smaller still to bite 'em,
And so proceed ad infinitum.

JONATHAN SWIFT, *"On Poetry, A Rhapsody"*

"Cathy" copyright © 2000 Cathy Guisewite. Reprinted with permission of Universal Press Syndicate.
All rights reserved.

We noted at the beginning of the chapter that the number of sentences in a language is infinite and that languages have various means of creating longer and longer sentences, such as adding an adjective or a prepositional phrase, or as in the "Cathy" cartoon, including sentences within sentences. Even children know how to produce and understand very long sentences and know how to make them even longer, as illustrated by the children's rhyme about the house that Jack built.

This is the farmer sowing the corn,
that kept the cock that crowed in the morn,
that waked the priest all shaven and shorn,
that married the man all tattered and torn,
that kissed the maiden all forlorn,
that milked the cow with the crumpled horn,
that tossed the dog,
that worried the cat,
that killed the rat,
that ate the malt,
that lay in the house that Jack built.

The child begins the rhyme with *This is the house that Jack built*, continues by lengthening it to *This is the malt that lay in the house that Jack built*, and so on.

You can add any of the following to the beginning of the rhyme and still have a grammatical sentence:

I think that . . .
What is the name of the unicorn that noticed that . . .
Ask someone if . . .
Do you know whether . . .

Up to this point we haven't really needed phrase structure rules. They are a convenient and precise way of specifying syntactic structures, but we could have achieved the same result by merely specifying the finitely many legal tree structures in the grammar, with all other structures implicitly disallowed. However, once we acknowledge the unboundedness of sentences, we need a formal device to capture that crucial aspect of speakers' syntactic knowledge. It is no longer possible to specify each legal structure; there are infinitely many.

To see how this works, let us first look at the case of multiple prepositional phrases such as [*The girl walked* [*down the street*] [*over the hill*] [*through the woods*]] . . . VP substructures currently allow only one PP per sentence (VP → V PP — rule 5). We can rectify this problem by revising rule 5:

5. VP → VP PP

Rule 5 is different from the previous rules because it repeats its own category (VP) inside itself. This is an instance of a **recursive rule**. Recursive rules are of critical importance because they allow the grammar to generate an infinite set of sentences. Reapplying rule 5 shows how the syntax permits structures with multiple PPs, such as in the sentence "The girl walked down the street with a gun toward the bank."

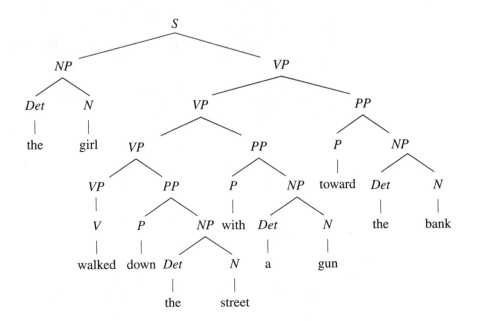

In this structure the VP rule 5 has applied three times and so there are three PPs [*down the street*] [*with a gun*] [*toward the bank*]. It is easy to see, however, that the rule could have applied four, five, six, or any number of times, and that would capture the knowledge that, for example, the PP *for no good purpose* could be tacked on at the end, and so on.

NPs can also contain PPs recursively. An example of this is shown by the phrase *the man with the telescope in a box*.

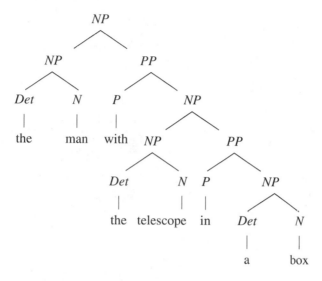

To show that speakers permit recursive NP structures of this sort, we need to include the following PS rule, which is parallel to the recursive VP rule 5.

9. NP → NP PP

The PS rules define the allowable structures of the language, and in so doing make predictions about structures that we may not have considered when formulating each rule individually. These predictions can be tested, and if they are not validated, the rules must be reformulated since they specify all and only the allowable structures. For example, rule 7 (VP → V CP) in combination with rules 8 (CP → C S) and 1 (S → NP VP) form a recursive set. (The recursiveness comes from the fact that S and VP occur on both the left and right side of the rules.) Those rules allow S to contain VP, which in turn contains CP, which in turn contains S, which in turn again contains VP and so on, potentially without end, as illustrated on the following page. These rules, formulated for different purposes, correctly predict the limitlessness of language in which sentences are embedded inside larger sentences, such as "The children hope that the teacher says that the principal decides that the school closes for the day."

Now we consider the case of multiple adjectives illustrated at the beginning of the chapter with sentences such as "The kind-hearted, intelligent, handsome boy had many girlfriends." In English, adjectives occur before the noun. As a first approximation we might follow the system we have adopted thus far and introduce a recursive NP rule with a prenominal adjective:

NP → Adj NP.

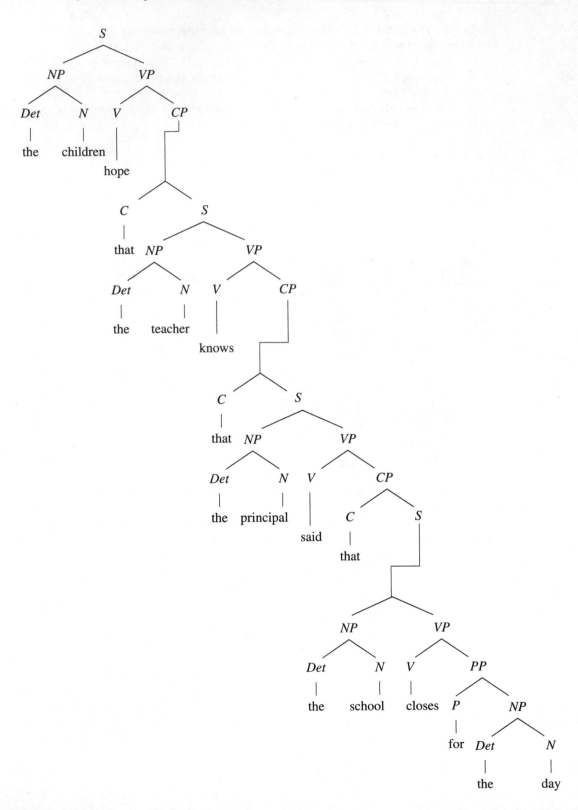

Repeated application of this rule would generate trees with multiple adjective positions, as desired.

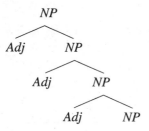

But there is something wrong, which is made apparent when we expand the lowest NP. The adjective can appear before the determiner, and this is not a possible word order in English NPs.

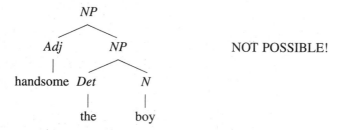

The problem is that although determiners and adjectives are both modifiers of the noun, they have a different status. First, an NP will never have more than one determiner in it, while it may contain many adjectives. Also, an adjective directly modifies the noun, while a determiner modifies the whole adjective(s) + noun complex. The expression "the big dog" refers to some specific dog that is big, and not just some dog of any size. In general, modification occurs between sisters. (We discuss modification further in Chapter 5.) If the adjective modifies the noun, then it is sister to the noun. If the determiner modifies the adjective + noun complex, then the determiner is sister to this complex. We can represent these two sisterhood relations by introducing an additional level of structure between NP and N. We refer to this level as N-bar (written as N').

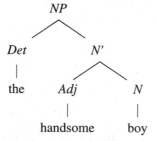

This structure provides the desired sisterhood relations, the adjective *handsome* is sister to the noun *boy*, which it therefore modifies, and the determiner is sister to the N' *handsome boy*. We must revise our NP rules to reflect this new structure, and add two rules for N'. Not all NPs have adjectives, of course. This is reflected in the second N' rule in which N' dominates only N.

NP →   Det N' (revised version of NP   →   Det N)
N' →   Adj N'
N' →   N

Let us now see how these revised rules generate NPs with multiple (potentially infinitely many) adjectives.

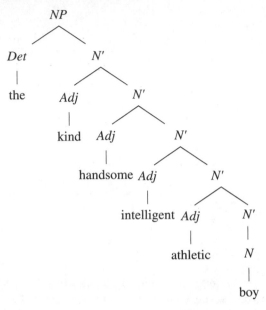

Thus far all the NPs we have looked at are common nouns with a simple definite or indefinite determiner (e.g., *the cat, a boy*), but NPs can consist of a simple pronoun (e.g., *he, she, we, they*) or a proper name (e.g., *Robert, California, Prozac*). To reflect determiner-less NP structures, we will need the rule

NP →   N'.

But that's not all. We have possessive noun phrases such as *Melissa's garden, the girl's shoes,* and *the man with the telescope's hat.* In these structures a possessive NP is written as NP's, the apostrophe not to be confused with the "bar" of N-bar, which is also denoted with an apostrophe. In each of the following trees the NP's is a left sister of the N', which it modifies.

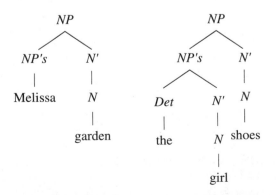

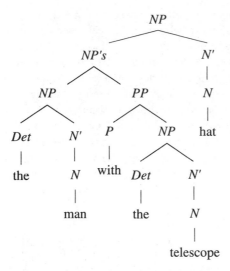

The embedding of categories within categories is common to all languages. Our brain capacity is finite, able to store only a finite number of categories and rules for their combination. Yet, these finite means place an infinite set of sentences at our disposal. This linguistic property also illustrates the difference between competence and performance, discussed in chapter 1. All speakers of English (and other languages) have as part of their linguistic competence—their mental grammars—the ability to embed phrases and sentences within each other ad infinitum. However, as the structures grow longer, they become increasingly more difficult to produce and understand. This could be due to short-term memory limitations, muscular fatigue, breathlessness, boredom, or any number of performance factors. (We will discuss performance factors more fully in chapter 9.) Nevertheless, these very long sentences would be well-formed according to the rules of the grammar.

Heads and Complements

"Mother Goose & Grimm" © Grimmy, Inc. Reprinted with permission of King Features Syndicate.

Phrase structure trees also show relationships among elements in a sentence. For example, the *subject* and *direct object* of the sentence can be structurally defined. The subject is the NP that is closest to, or immediately dominated by, the root S. The direct object is the NP that is closest to, or immediately dominated by, VP.

Another kind of relationship is that between the **head** of a phrase and its sisters. The head of a phrase is the word whose lexical category defines the type of phrase: the noun in a noun phrase, the verb in a verb phrase, and so on. Reviewing the PS rules in the previous section, we saw that every VP contains a verb, which is its head. The VP may also contain other categories, such as an NP or CP. Those sister categories are **complements**; they complete the meaning of the phrase. Loosely speaking, the entire phrase refers to whatever the head verb refers to. For example, the VP *find a puppy* refers to an event of "finding." The NP object in the VP that completes its meaning is a complement. The underscored CP (complementizer phrase) in the sentence "I thought <u>that the child found the puppy</u>" is also a complement. (Please do not confuse the terms *complementizer* and *complement*.)

Every phrasal category, then, has a head of its same syntactic type. NPs are headed by nouns, PPs are headed by prepositions, CPs by complementizers, and so on; and every phrasal head can have a complement, which provides further information about the head. In the sentence "The death of Lincoln shocked the nation," the PP *of Lincoln* is the complement to the head noun *death*. Other examples of complements are illustrated in the following examples, with the head in italics and the complement underlined:

an *argument* <u>over jelly beans</u> (noun complement — PP)

his *belief* <u>that justice will prevail</u> (noun complement — CP)

happy <u>to be here</u> (adjective complement — infinitive)

about <u>the war in Iraq</u> (preposition complement — NP)

wrote <u>a long letter to his only sister</u> (verb complement — NP PP)

tell <u>John that his mother is coming to dinner</u> (verb complement — NP CP)

Each of these examples is a phrase (NP, AdjP, PP, VP) that contains a head (N, Adj, P, V) followed by a complement of varying composition such as CP in the case of *belief,* or NP PP in the case of *write,* and so on. The head-complement relation is universal. All languages have phrases that are headed and that contain complements.

However, the order of the head and complement may differ in different languages. In English, for example, we see that the head comes first, followed by the complement. In Japanese, complements precede the head, as shown in the following examples:

Taro-ga	inu-o	mitsuketa
Taro-subject marker	dog-object marker	found	(Taro found a dog)

Inu-ga	niwa-de	asonde	iru
dog-subject marker	garden-in	playing	is	(The dog is playing in the garden)

In the first sentence, the complement *dog* precedes the head verb *found*. In the second, the PP complement *niwa-de* "in the garden" also precedes its head. We also note that English is a VO language, meaning that the verb ordinarily precedes its object. Japanese is an OV language, and this difference is also reflected in the head/complement word order.

SELECTION

Whether a verb takes a complement or not depends on the properties of the verb. For example, the verb *find* is a **transitive verb**. A transitive verb requires an NP complement (direct object), as in *The boy found the ball,* but not **The boy found,* or **The* *boy found in the house.* Some verbs like *eat* are optionally transitive. *John ate* and *John ate a sandwich* are both grammatical.

Verbs select different kinds of complements. For example, verbs like *put* and *give* take both an NP and a PP complement, but cannot occur with either alone:

> Sam put the milk in the refrigerator.
> *Sam put the milk.
> Gary gave the contract to his client.
> *Gary gave to his client.

Sleep is an **intransitive verb**; it cannot take an NP complement.

> Michael slept.
> *Michael slept a fish.

Some verbs, such as *think*, select a sentence complement, as in "I think that Sam won the race." Other verbs, like *tell*, select an NP and a sentence, as in "I told Sam that Michael was on his bicycle"; yet other verbs like *feel* select either an AdjP or a sentential complement. (Complements are italicized.)

> They felt *strong as oxen*.
> They feel *that they can win*.

As we will discuss later, sentences that are complements must often be preceded by a complementizer *that*.

Other categories besides verbs also select their complements. For example, the noun *belief* selects either a PP or a CP, while the noun *sympathy* selects a PP, but not a CP, as shown by the following examples:

> the belief *in freedom of speech*
> the belief *that freedom of speech is a basic right*
>
> their sympathy *for the victims*
> *their sympathy *that the victims are so poor*

Adjectives can also have complements. For example, the adjectives *tired* and *proud* select PPs:

> tired *of stale sandwiches*
> proud *of her children*

With noun selection, the complement is often optional. Thus sentences like "He respected their belief," "We appreciated their sympathy," "Elimelech was tired," and "All the mothers were proud" are syntactically well-formed with the meaning that might be conveyed by an explicit complement understood from context. Verb selection is often not optional, however, so that *He put the milk* is ungrammatical even if it is clear from context where the milk was put.

The information about the complement types selected by particular verbs and other lexical items is called **C-selection** (C stands for categorial) or **subcategorization,** and is included in the lexical entry of the item in our mental lexicon.

Verbs also include in their lexical entry a specification of certain intrinsic semantic properties of their subjects and complements, just as they select for syntactic categories.

This kind of selection is called **S-selection** (S for semantic). For example, the verb *murder* requires its subject and object to be human, while the verb *drink* requires its subject to be animate and its object liquid. Verbs such as *like, hate,* and so on select animate subjects. The following sentences violate S-selection and can only be used in a metaphorical sense. (We will use the symbol "!" to indicate a semantic anomaly.)

!The rock murdered the man.
!The beer drank the student.
!The tree liked the boy.

The famous sentence *Colorless green ideas sleep furiously,* discussed earlier in this chapter, is anomalous because (among other things) S-selection is violated (e.g., the verb *sleep* requires an animate subject). In chapter 5 we will discuss the semantic relationships between a verb and its subject and objects in far more detail.

The well-formedness of a phrase depends then on at least two factors: whether the phrase conforms to the structural constraints of the language as expressed in the PS rules, and whether it obeys the selectional requirements of the head, both syntactic (C-selection) and semantic (S-selection).

WHAT HEADS THE SENTENCE

We said earlier that all phrases have heads. One category that we have not yet discussed in this regard is sentence (S). For uniformity's sake, we want all the categories to be headed, but what would the head of S be? To answer this question, let us consider sentences such as the following:

Sam will kick the ball.
Sam has kicked the ball.
Sam is kicking the ball.
Sam may kick the ball.

As noted earlier, words like *will, has, is,* and *may* are auxiliary verbs, belonging to the category Aux, which also includes the modals such as *might, would, could, can,* and several others. They occur in structures such as in (1).

1.

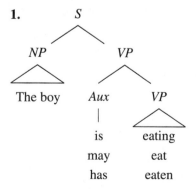

From now on we will adopt the convention of using a triangle under a node when the content of a category is not crucial to the point under discussion.

Auxiliary verbs specify a time frame for the sentence, whether the situation described by the sentence will take place, already took place, or is taking place now. A modal such as *may* contains "possibility" as part of its meaning, and says it is possible that the situation will occur at some future time. The category Aux is a natural category to head S. Just as the VP is about the event described by the verb—*eat ice cream* is about "eating"—so a sentence is about a situation or state of affairs that occurs at some point in time.

The parallel with other categories extends further. In the PS tree in (1), VP is the complement to Aux. The selectional relationship between Aux and VP is demonstrated by the fact that particular auxiliaries go with particular kinds of VPs. For example, the auxiliary *be* takes a progressive (-ing) form of the verb,

The boy **is** danc**ing**.

while the auxiliary *have* selects a past participle (-en) form of the verb,

The girl **has** eat**en**.

and the modals select the infinitival form of the verb (no affixes),

The child **must sleep**
The boy **may eat**.

To have a uniform notation, many linguists use the symbols **T (=tense)** and **TP (= tense phrase)** instead of Aux and S. Furthermore, just as the NP required the intermediate N-bar (N') category, the TP also has the intermediate T-bar (T') category, as in the phrase structure tree in (2):

2.

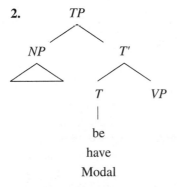

be
have
Modal

Indeed, many linguists assume that all XPs (i.e., NPs, PPs, VPs, TPs, AdjPs) can be broken down into three levels. This is referred to as **X-bar theory**. The basic X-bar schema is as follows:

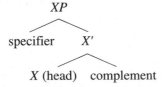

The schema says that an XP consists of a **specifier**, which is basically a modifier (and which is generally an optional constituent), and an X'. For example, an NP specifier is a determiner; a VP specifier is an adverb such as *never* or *often;* an AdjP specifier is a degree word such as *very* or *quite*. Any X' consists of a head X and a complement, which may be a phrasal category, thus giving rise to recursion. X-bar structure is thought to be universal, occurring in all the world's languages, though the order of the elements inside XP and X' may be reversed, as we saw in Japanese.

We will not adopt X-bar conventions in our description of syntax except on the few occasions where the notation provides an insight into the syntax of the language. For sentences we will generally use the more intuitive symbols S and AUX instead of TP and T, but you should think of Aux and S as having the same relationship to each other as V and VP, N and NP, and so on. To achieve this more straightforward approach, we will also ignore the T' category until it is needed later on in the description of the syntax of the main verb *be*.

Without the use of TP, T', and T, we need an additional PS rule to characterize structures containing Aux:

VP → Aux VP

Like the other recursive VP rules, this rule will allow multiple Aux positions.

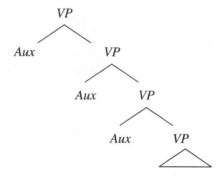

This is a desired consequence because English allows sentences with multiple auxiliaries like

The child may be sleeping.   (modal, be)
The dog has been barking all night.   (have, be)
The bird must have been flying home.   (modal, have, be)

The introduction of Aux into the system raises a question. Not all sentences seem to have auxiliaries. For example, the sentence "Sam kicked the ball" has no modal, *have* or *be*. There is, however, a time reference for this sentence, namely, the past tense on the verb *kicked*. In sentences without auxiliaries, the tense of the sentence is its head. Instead of having a word under the category Aux (or T), there is a tense specification, *present* or *past*, as in the following tree:

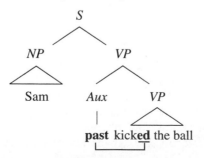

The inflection on the verb must agree with the tense in Aux. For example, if the tense of the sentence is *past*, then the verb must have an *-ed* affix (or must be an irregular past tense verb such as *ate*).

A property of English and many languages is that the head of S may contain only an abstract tense specification and no actual word, as just illustrated. In the English future tense, the word *will* occurs in Aux. The word *do* is a tense-bearing word that is found in negative sentences such as *John did not go* and questions such as *Where did John go?* In these sentences *did* means "past tense."

In addition to specifying the time reference of the sentence, Aux specifies the agreement features of the subject. For example, if the subject is *we*, Aux contains the features first-person plural; if the subject is *he* or *she*, Aux contains the features third-person singular. Thus, another function of the syntactic rules is to use Aux as a "matchmaker" between the subject and the verb. When the subject and the verb bear the same features, Aux makes a match; when they have incompatible features, Aux cannot make a match and the sentence is ungrammatical. This matchmaker function of syntactic rules is more obvious in languages such as Italian, which have many different agreement morphemes, as discussed in chapter 3. Consider the Italian sentence for "I go to school."

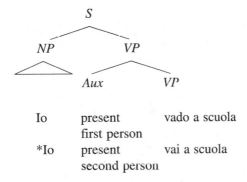

| Io | present
first person | vado a scuola |
| *Io | present
second person | vai a scuola |

The verb *vado*, "go," in the first sentence bears the first-person singular morpheme, *-o*, which matches the agreement feature in Aux, which in turn matches the subject *Io*, "I." Hence, the sentence is grammatical. In the second sentence, there is a mismatch between the first-person subject and the second-person features in Aux (and on the verb), and so the sentence is ungrammatical.

Structural Ambiguities

The structure of every sentence is a lesson in logic.

JOHN STUART MILL, *Inaugural address at St. Andres*

As mentioned earlier, certain kinds of ambiguous sentences have more than one phrase structure tree, each corresponding to a different meaning. The sentence *The boy saw the man with the telescope* is structurally ambiguous. Its two meanings correspond to the following two phrase structure trees. (For simplicity we omit Aux in these structures and we return to the non-X-bar notation.)

1.

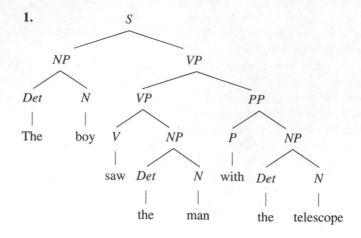

2.

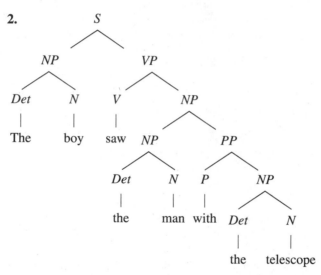

One meaning of this sentence is "the boy used a telescope to see the man." The first phrase structure tree represents this meaning. The key element is the position of the PP directly under the VP. Notice that although the PP is under VP, it is not a complement because phrasal categories don't take complements, and because it is not selected by the verb. The verb *see* selects an NP only. In this sentence, the PP has an adverbial function and modifies the verb.

In its other meaning, "the boy saw a man who had a telescope," the PP *with the telescope* occurs under the direct object NP, where it modifies the noun *man*. In this second meaning, the complement of the verb *see* is the entire NP—*the man with the telescope*.

The PP in the first structure is generated by the rule

VP → VP PP

In the second structure the PP is generated by the rule

NP → NP PP

Two interpretations are possible because the rules of syntax permit different structures for the same linear order of words.

Following is the set of PS rules that we have presented so far in the chapter. The rules have been renumbered.

1. S	→	NP VP
2. NP	→	Det N'
3. NP	→	N'
4. NP	→	NP's N'
5. NP	→	NP PP
6. N'	→	Adj N'
7. N'	→	N
8. VP	→	V
9. VP	→	V NP
10. VP	→	V CP
11. VP	→	Aux VP
12. VP	→	VP PP
13. PP	→	P NP
14. CP	→	C S

This is not the complete set of PS rules for the language. Various structures in English cannot be generated with these rules, some of which we will talk about later. But even this mini phrase structure grammar generates an infinite set of possible sentences because the rules are recursive. These PS rules specify the word order for English. As noted earlier, languages can differ with respect to the linear order of their constituents. For example, in Japanese, the object comes before the verb. Linear order aside, the hierarchical organization illustrated by the rules given previously is largely true for all languages, as expressed by X-bar schema.

More Structures

Normal human minds are such that . . . without the help of anybody, they will produce 1000 (sentences) they never heard spoke of . . . inventing and saying such things as they never heard from their masters, nor any mouth.

HUARTE DE SAN JUAN, *c. 1530–1592*

Many English sentence types are not accounted for by the phrase structure rules given so far, including:

1. The dog completely destroyed the shoe.
2. The cat and the dog were friends.
3. The cat is coy.

The sentence in (1) contains the adverb (Adv) *completely*. Adverbs are modifiers that can specify how an event happens (*quickly, slowly, completely*) or when it happens (*yesterday, tomorrow, often*). As modifiers, adverbs are sisters to phrasal (XP) categories.

In sentence (1) the adverb is a sister to VP, as illustrated in the following structure: (We ignore Aux in this structure.)

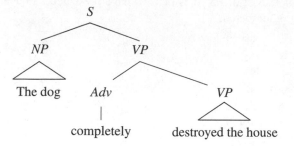

Some adverbs, such as *temporal adverbs* like *yesterday, today, last week,* and *manner adverbs* such as *quietly, violently, suddenly, carefully,* also occur to the right of VP as follows:

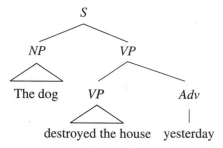

Adverbs also occur as sisters to S (which, recall, is also a phrasal category, TP).

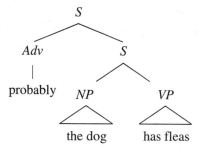

At this point you should be able to write the three PS rules that will account for the position of these adverbs.[1]

Sentence 2 contains a **coordinate structure** *The cat and the dog.* A coordinate structure results when two constituents of the same category (in this case, two NPs) are joined with a conjunction such as *and* or *or.* The coordinate NP has the following structure:

---

[1] Answer: S → Adv S   VP → Adv VP   VP → VP Adv

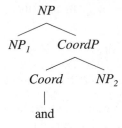

Though this may seem counterintuitive, in a coordinate structure the second member of the coordination (NP$_2$) forms a constituent with the conjunction *and*. We can show this by means of the "move as a unit" constituency test. In sentence (5) the words *and a CD* move together to the end of the sentence, whereas in (6) the constituent is broken, resulting in ungrammaticality.

4. Caley bought a book and a CD yesterday.
5. Caley bought a book yesterday and a CD.
6. *Caley bought a book and yesterday a CD.

Once again, we encourage you to write the two PS rules that generate this structure.[2]

You can also construct trees for other kinds of coordinate structures, such as VP or PP coordination, which follow the same pattern.

Michael writes poetry and surfs. (VP *and* VP)
Sam rode his bicycle to school and to the pool. (PP *and* PP)

Sentence (3) contains the main verb *be* followed by an adjective. The structure of *be* sentences is best illustrated using T′ notation. The main verb *be* acts like the modals and the auxiliaries *be* and *have*. For example, it is moved to the beginning of the sentence in questions (*Is the cat coy?*). For this reason we assume that the main verb *be* occurs under T and takes an XP complement. The XP may be AdjP, as shown in the tree structure for (3):

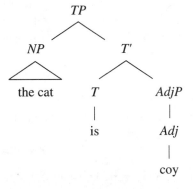

or an NP or PP as would occur in *The cat is a feline* or *The cat is in the tree*.

As before we will leave it as an exercise for you to construct the PS rules for these sentence types and the tree structures they generate.[3] (You might try drawing the tree structures; they should look very much like the one above.)

---

[2] Answer: NP → NP CoordP,   CoordP → Coord NP
[3] Answer: TP → NP T′,   T′ → T XP (where XP = AdjP, PP, NP)

There are also forms of embedded sentences other than those that we have discussed, for example:

Hilary is waiting *for you to sing* (Cf. You sing.)
The host wants *the president to leave early*. (Cf. The president leaves early.)
The host believes *the president to be punctual*. (Cf. The president is punctual.)

Although the detailed structure of these different embedded sentences is beyond the scope of this introduction, you should note that an embedded sentence may be an **infinitive**. An infinitive sentence does not have a tense. The embedded sentences *for you to sing, the president to leave early, and the president to be punctual* are infinitives. Such verbs as *want* and *believe*, among many others, can take an infinitive complement. This information, like other selectional properties, belongs to the lexical entry of the selecting verb (the higher verb in the tree).

Sentence Relatedness

I put the words down and push them a bit.

EVELYN WAUGH

Another aspect of our syntactic competence is the knowledge that certain sentences are related, such as the following pair:

The boy is sleeping.   Is the boy sleeping?

These sentences are related in the sense that they describe the same situation. The sentence in the first column asserts that a particular situation exists, a boy-sleeping situation. Such sentences are called **declarative** sentences. The sentence in the second column asks whether such a boy-sleeping situation holds. Sentences of the second sort are called **yes-no questions**. The only actual difference in meaning between these sentences is that one asserts a situation and the other asks for confirmation of a situation. This element of meaning is indicated by the different word orders. Thus this sentence pair illustrates that two sentences may have structural differences that correspond *in a systematic way* to meaning differences. This is a fact about language that the grammar must describe.

Transformational Rules

Method consists entirely in properly ordering and arranging the things to which we should pay attention.

RENÉ DESCARTES, *Oeuvres, Vol. X*

Phrase structure rules account for much syntactic knowledge, but they do not account for the fact that certain sentence types in the language relate systematically to other sentence types. The standard way of describing these relationships is to say that the related sentences come from a common underlying structure. Yes-no questions are a case in point, and they bring us back to a discussion of auxiliaries. Auxiliaries are central to the formation of yes-no questions as well as certain other types of sentences in English. In yes-no questions, the auxiliary appears in the position preceding the subject. Here are a few more examples:

The boy is sleeping.   Is the boy sleeping?
The boy has slept.   Has the boy slept?
The boy can sleep.   Can the boy sleep?
The boy will sleep.   Will the boy sleep?

A way to capture the relationship between a declarative and a yes-no question is to allow the PS rules to generate a structure corresponding to the declarative sentence. Another formal device, called a **transformational rule**, then moves the auxiliary before the subject. The rule "Move Aux" is formulated as follows:

Move the highest Aux to adjoin to (the root) S.

That is, Move Aux applies to structures like:

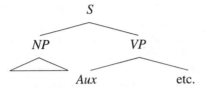

to give structures like:

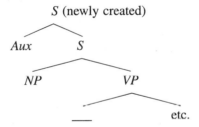

For example:

The boy is sleeping → Is the boy ___ sleeping

The rule takes the basic (NP-Aux) structure generated by the phrase structure rules and derives a second tree (the dash represents the position from which a constituent has been moved). The Aux is attached to the tree by **adjunction**. Adjunction is an operation that copies an existing node (in this case S) and creates a new level to which the moved category (in this case Aux) is appended.

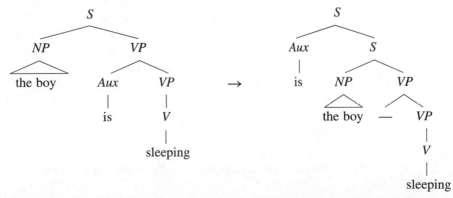

Questions are thus generated in two steps.

1. The phrase structure rules generate a basic structure.
2. Aux movement applies to produce the derived structure.

The basic structures of sentences, also called **deep structures** or **d-structures**, conform to the phrase structure rules. Variants on the basic sentence structures are derived via transformations. By generating questions in two steps, we are claiming that for speakers a relationship exists between a question and its corresponding statement. Intuitively, we know that such sentences are related. The transformational rule is a formal way of representing this knowledge.

The derived structures—the ones that follow the application of transformational rules—are called **surface structures** or **s-structures**. The phonological rules of the language—the ones that determine pronunciation—apply to s-structures. If no transformations apply, then d-structure and s-structure are the same. If transformations apply, then s-structure is the result after all transformations have had their effect. Much syntactic knowledge that is not expressed by phrase structure rules is accounted for by transformations, which can alter phrase structure trees by moving, adding, or deleting elements.

Other sentence types that are transformationally related are:

active-passive

The cat chased the mouse. → The mouse was chased by the cat.

there **sentences**

There was a man on the roof. → A man was on the roof.

PP preposing

The astronomer saw the quasar with the telescope. → With the telescope, the astronomer saw the quasar.

Structure-Dependent Rules

Transformations act on structures without regard to the particular words that they contain. They are **structure dependent**. The transformational rule of PP preposing moves any PP as long as it is immediately under the VP, as in *in the house, the puppy found the ball*; or *with the telescope, the boy saw the man*; and so on.

Evidence that transformations are structure dependent is provided by the fact that the sentence *With a telescope, the boy saw the man* is not ambiguous. It has only the meaning "the boy used a telescope to see the man," the meaning corresponding to phrase structure (1) on page 146 in which the PP is immediately dominated by the VP. In the structure corresponding to the other meaning, "the boy saw a man who had a telescope," the PP is in the NP as in (2) on page 146. The PP preposing transformation applies to the VP–PP structure and not to the NP–PP structure.

Another rule allows the complementizer *that* to be omitted when it precedes an embedded sentence but not a sentence that occurs in subject position, as illustrated by these pairs:

I know that you know.   I know you know.
That you know bothers me.   *You know bothers me.

This is a further demonstration that rules are structure dependent.

Agreement rules are also structure dependent. In many languages, including English, the verb must agree with the subject. The verb is marked with an -*s* when the subject is third-person singular.

> This guy seems kind of cute.
> These guys seem kind of cute.

Now consider these sentences:

> The *guy* we met at the party next door *seems* kind of cute.
> The *guys* we met at the party next door *seem* kind of cute.

The verb *seem* must agree with the subject, *guy* or *guys*. Even though there are various words between the head noun and the verb, the verb always agrees with the head noun. Moreover, there is no limit to how many words may intervene, or whether they are singular or plural, as the following sentence illustrates:

> The *guys* (*guy*) we met at the party next door that lasted until 3 A.M. and was finally broken up by the cops who were called by the neighbors *seem* (*seems*) kind of cute.

The phrase structure tree of such a sentence explains this aspect of linguistic competence:

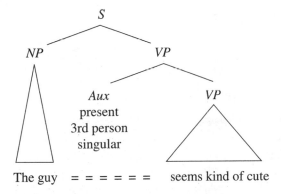

In the tree, "= = = = = =" represents the intervening structure, which may, in principle, be indefinitely long and complex. But speakers of English know that agreement depends on sentence structure, not the linear order of words. Agreement is between the subject and the main verb, where the subject is structurally defined as the NP immediately dominated by S. The agreement relation is mediated by Aux, which contains the tense and agreement features that match up the subject and verb. Other material can be ignored as far as the rule of agreement is concerned, although in actual performance, if the distance is too great, the speaker may forget what the head noun was.

A final illustration of structure dependency is found in the declarative-question pairs discussed previously. Consider the following sets of sentences:

> The boy who is sleeping was dreaming.
> Was the boy who is sleeping dreaming?

*Is the boy who sleeping was dreaming?
The boy who can sleep will dream.
Will the boy who can sleep dream?
*Can the boy who sleep will dream?

The ungrammatical sentences show that to form a question, the Aux of the topmost S, that is, the one following the entire first NP, moves to the position before the subject, not simply the *first* auxiliary in the sentence. We can see this in the following simplified phrase structure trees. There are two auxiliaries, one in the subject relative clause and the other in the main clause. The rule affects the auxiliary in the higher main clause.

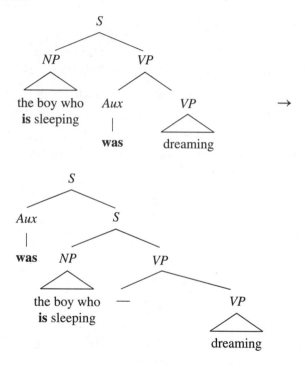

If the rule picked out the *first* Aux, we would have the ungrammatical sentence *Is the boy who__ sleeping was dreaming*. To derive the correct s-structures, transformations such as Move Aux must refer to phrase structure and not to the linear order of elements.

Structure dependency is a principle of Universal Grammar, and is found in all languages. For example, in languages that have subject-verb agreement, the dependency is between the verb and the head noun, and never some other noun such as the closest one, as shown in the following examples from Italian, German, Swahili, and English, respectively (the third-person singular agreement morpheme is in boldface and relates to the doubly underlined head noun, not the underlined noun even though the latter is nearest the main verb):

La <u>madre</u> con tanti <u>figli</u> lavor**a** molto.
Die <u>Mutter</u> mit den vielen <u>Kindern</u> arbeite**t** viel.
<u>Mama</u> anao <u>watoto</u> wengi **a**najitahidi.
The <u>mother</u> with many <u>children</u> work**s** a lot.

Syntactic Dependencies

Sentences are organized according to two basic principles: constituent structure and syntactic dependencies. As we have discussed, constituent structure refers to the hierarchical organization of the subparts of a sentence. The second important property is the dependencies among elements in the sentence. In other words, the presence of a particular word or morpheme can depend on the presence of some other word or morpheme in a sentence. We have already seen at least two examples of syntactic dependencies. Selection is one kind of dependency. Whether there is a direct object in a sentence depends on whether the verb is transitive or intransitive. More generally, complements depend on the properties of the head of their phrase. Agreement is another kind of dependency. The features in Aux (and on the verb) must match the features of the subject.

WH QUESTIONS

Whom are you? said he, for he had been to night school.

GEORGE ADE, Bang! Bang!: The Steel Box

The following **wh questions** illustrate another kind of dependency:

1. (a) What will Max chase?
   (b) Where has Pete put his bone?
   (c) Which dog do you think loves balls?

There are several points of interest in these sentences. First, the verb *chase* in sentence (a) is transitive, yet there is no direct object following it. There is a gap where the direct object should be. The verb *put* in sentence (b) selects a direct object and a prepositional phrase, yet there is no PP following *his bone*. Finally, the embedded verb *loves* in sentence (c) bears the third-person *-s* morpheme, yet there is no obvious subject to trigger this agreement. If we remove the *wh* phrases, the remaining sentences would be ungrammatical.

2. (a) *will Max chase ____?
   (b) *has Pete put his bone ____?
   (c) *do you think ____ loves balls?

The grammaticality of a sentence with a gap depends on there being a *wh* phrase at the beginning of the sentence. The sentences in (1) are grammatical because the *wh* phrase is acting like the object in (a), the prepositional phrase object in (b), and the embedded subject in (c).

We can explain the dependency between the *wh* phrase and the missing constituent if we assume that in each case the *wh* phrase originated in the position of the gap in a sentence with the corresponding declarative structure:

3. (a) Max will chase *what*?
   (b) Pete has put his bone *where*?
   (c) You think (that) *which dog* loves balls?

The *wh* phrase is then moved to the beginning of the sentence by a transformational rule: Move *wh*. Since embedded *wh* phrases (*I wonder* who Mary likes) are known to be complementizer phrases (CPs), we may deduce that main clause questions (*Who does Mary like*) are also CPs, like this:

Then the *wh* phrase can move to the empty Comp position at the left periphery of the sentence.

Thus, *wh* questions are generated in three steps:

1. The phrase structure rules generate the CP d-structure with the *wh* phrase occupying an NP position within the S: direct object in (3a); prepositional object in (3b); and subject in (3c).
2. Move Aux adjoins the auxiliary to S.
3. Move *wh* moves the *wh* phrase to Comp.

The following tree shows the d-structure of the sentence *What will Max chase?*

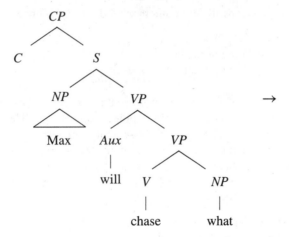

The s-structure representation of this sentence is:

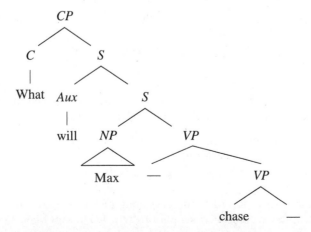

In question (1c), there is an auxiliary "do." Unlike the other auxiliaries (e.g., *can, have, be*), *do* is not part of the d-structure of the question. The d-structure of the question *Which dog did Michael feed?* is "Michael fed which dog?" Because Move Aux is structure dependent (like all rules), it ignores the content of the category. It will therefore move Aux even when Aux contains only a tense feature such as *past*. In this case, another transformational rule, called "*do* support," inserts *do* into the structure to carry the tense:

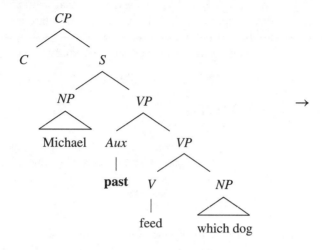

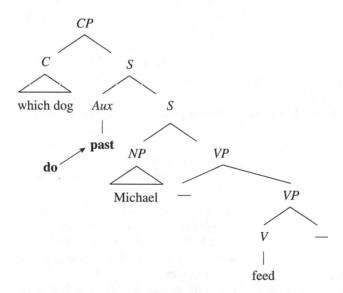

The first tree represents the d-structure to which the Aux and *wh* movement rules apply. The second tree shows the output of those transformations and the insertion of "do." "Do" combines with *past* to yield "did."

Unlike the other rules we have seen, which operate inside a phrase or clause, Move *wh* can move the *wh* phrase outside of its own clause. There is no limit to the distance that a *wh* phrase can move, as illustrated by the following sentences. The dashes indicate the position from which the *wh* phrase has been moved.

Who did Helen say the senator wanted to hire ____?
Who did Helen say the senator wanted the congressional representative to try to
hire ____?
Who did Helen say the senator wanted the congressional representative to try to
convince the Speaker of the House to get the Vice President to hire ____?

Long-distance dependencies created by *wh* movement are a fundamental part of
human language. They provide still further evidence that sentences are not simply
strings of words but are supported by a rich scaffolding of phrase structure trees. These
trees express the underlying structure of a sentence as well as its relation to other sentences in the language, and as always are reflective of your knowledge of syntax.

UG Principles and Parameters

Whenever the literary German dives into a sentence, that is the last you are
going to see of him till he emerges on the other side of the Atlantic with his
Verb in his mouth.

MARK TWAIN, A Connecticut Yankee in King Arthur's Court

In this chapter we have largely focused on English syntax, but much of the grammatical structure we have described for English also holds in other languages. This is
because Universal Grammar (UG) provides the basic design for all human languages,
and individual languages are simply variations on this basic design. Imagine a new
housing development. All of the houses have the same floor plan, but the occupants
have some choices to make. They can have carpet or hardwood floors, curtains or
blinds; they can choose their kitchen cabinets and the countertops, the bathroom tiles,
and so on. This is more or less how the syntax operates. Languages conform to a
basic design, and then there are choice points or points of variation.

All languages have phrase structure rules that specify the allowable d-structures.
In all languages, phrases consist of heads and complements, and sentences are headed
by Aux (or T), which is specified for information such as tense, agreement, and
modality. However, languages may have different word orders within the phrases and
sentences. The word order differences between English and Japanese, discussed earlier, illustrate the interaction of general and language-specific properties. UG specifies
the structure of a phrase. It must have a head and may take one or more complement
types (the X-bar schema discussed earlier). However, each language defines for itself
the relative order of these constituents: English is head initial, Japanese is head final.
We call the points of variation **parameters**.

All languages seem to have movement rules. Move Aux is a version of a more
general rule that exists in languages such as Dutch, in which the auxiliary moves, if
there is one, as in (1) and otherwise, the main verb moves, as in (2):

1. Zal Femke fietsen?
   will Femke bicycle ride   (Will Femke ride her bicycle?)
2. Leest Meindert veel boeken?
   reads Meindert many books   (Does Meindert read many books?)

In English, main verbs other than *be* do not move. Instead, English has "do" support to carry the tense and agreement features. All languages have expressions for requesting information about *who, when, where, what,* and *how.* Even if the question words do not always begin with "wh," we will refer to such questions as *wh* questions. In some languages, such as Japanese and Swahili, the *wh* phrase does not move. It remains in its original d-structure position. In Japanese the sentence is marked with a question morpheme, *no*:

Taro-ga	nani-o	mitsuketa-no?
Taro	what	found ?

Recall that Japanese word order is SOV, so the *wh* phrase *nani* ("what") is an object and occurs before the verb.

In Swahili the *wh* phrase—*nani* by pure coincidence—also stays in its base position:

Ulipatia	nani	kitabu
you gave	who	a book

However, in all languages with *wh* movement (i.e., movement of the question phrase), the moved element goes to Comp. The "landing site" of the moved phrase is determined by UG. Among the *wh* movement languages, there is some variation. In the Romance languages, such as Italian, the *wh* phrase moves as in English, but when the *wh* phrase questions the object of a preposition, the preposition must move together with the *wh* phrase. In English, by contrast, the preposition can be "stranded" (i.e., left behind in its original position):

A chi hai dato il libro?
To whom (did) you give the book?

*Chi hai dato il libro a?
Who(m) did you give the book to?

In some dialects of German, long-distance *wh* movement leaves a trail of *wh* phrases in the Comp position of the embedded sentence:

Mit	wem	glaubst	du	mit	wem	Hans	spricht?
With	whom	think	you	with	whom	Hans	talks

(Whom do you think Hans talks to?)

Wen	willst	du	wen	Hans	anruft?
Whom	want	you	whom	Hans	call

(Whom do you want Hans to call?)

In Czech the question phrase "how much" can be moved, leaving behind the NP it modifies:

Jak	velké	Václav	koupil	auto?
how	big	Václav	bought	car

(How big a car did Václav buy?)

Despite these variations, *wh* movement adheres to certain constraints. Although *wh* phrases such as *what, who,* and *which boy* can be inserted into any NP position, and are then free in principle to move to Comp, there are specific instances in which *wh* movement is blocked. For example, a *wh* phrase cannot move out of a relative clause like "... *the senator that wanted to hire who*, as in (1b). It also cannot move out of a clause beginning with *whether* or *if*, as in (2c) and (d). (Remember that the position from which the *wh* phrases have been moved is indicated with _____.)

1. (a) Emily paid a visit to the senator that wants to hire who?
   (b) *Who did Emily pay a visit to the senator that wants to hire _____?
2. (a) Miss Marple asked Sherlock whether Poirot had solved the crime.
   (b) Who did Miss Marple ask _____ whether Poirot had solved the crime?
   (c) *Who did Miss Marple ask Sherlock whether _____ had solved the crime?
   (d) *What did Miss Marple ask Sherlock whether Poirot had solved _____?

The only difference between the grammatical (2b) and the ungrammatical (2c) and (d) is that in the grammatical case the *wh* phrase originates in the higher clause, whereas in the ungrammatical ones the *wh* phrase comes from inside the *whether* clause. This illustrates that the constraint against movement depends on structure and not on the length of the sentence.

Some sentences can be very short and still not allow *wh* movement:

3. (a) Sam Spade insulted the fat man's henchman.
   (b) Who did Sam Spade insult?
   (c) Whose henchman did Sam Spade insult?
   (d) *Whose did Sam Spade insult henchman?
4. (a) John ate bologna and cheese.
   (b) John ate bologna with cheese.
   (c) *What did John eat bologna and?
   (d) What did John eat bologna with?

The sentences in (3) show that a *wh* phrase cannot be extracted from inside a possessive NP. In (3b) it is okay to question the whole direct object. In (3c) it is even okay to question a piece of the possessive NP, providing the entire *wh* phrase is moved, but (3d) shows that moving the *wh* word alone out of the possessive NP is illicit.

Sentence (4a) is a coordinate structure and has approximately the same meaning as (4b), which is not a coordinate structure. In (4c) moving a *wh* phrase out of the coordinate structure results in ungrammaticality, whereas in 4(d), it is okay to move the *wh* phrase out of the PP. The ungrammaticality of 4(c), then, is related to its structure and not to its meaning.

The constraints on *wh* movement are not specific to English. Such constraints operate in all languages that have *wh* movement. Like the principle of structure dependency and the principles governing the organization of phrases, the constraints on *wh* movement are part of UG. These aspects of grammar need not be learned. This blueprint for language is innate knowledge that the child brings to the task of acquiring a language. What children must learn are the language-specific aspects of grammar. Where there are parameters of variation, children must determine the correct choice for their language. The Japanese child must determine that the verb comes after the object in the VP, and the English-speaking child acquires the VO order. The Dutch-speaking child acquires a rule that moves the verb, while the English-speaking child must restrict his rule to auxiliaries. Italian, English, and Czech children learn that to form a question, the *wh* phrase moves, whereas Japanese and Swahili children determine that there is no movement. As far as we can tell, children fix these parameters very quickly. We will have more to say about how children do this in chapter 8.

Sign Language Syntax

All languages have rules of syntax similar in kind, if not in detail, to those of English, and sign languages are no exception. Signed languages have phrase structure rules that provide hierarchical structure and order constituents. A signer distinguishes *The dog chased the cat* from *The cat chased the dog* through the order of signing. The basic order of ASL is SVO. Unlike English, however, adjectives follow the head noun in ASL.

ASL has a category Aux, which expresses notions such as tense, agreement, modality, and so on. In Thai, to show that an action is continuous, the auxiliary verb *kamlang* is inserted before the verb. Thus *kin* means "eat" and *kamlang kin* means "is eating." In English a form of *be* is inserted and the main verb is changed to an *-ing* form. In ASL the sign for a verb such as *eat* may be articulated with a sweeping, repetitive movement to achieve the same effect. The sweeping, repetitive motion is a kind of auxiliary.

Many languages, including English, have a transformation that moves a direct object to the beginning of the sentence to draw particular attention to it, as in:

Many greyhounds, my wife has rescued.

The transformation is called **topicalization** because an object to which attention is drawn is generally the topic of the sentence or conversation. (The d-structure underlying this sentence is *My wife has rescued many greyhounds.*)

In ASL a similar reordering of signs accompanied by raising the eyebrows and tilting the head upward accomplishes the same effect. The head motion and facial expressions of a signer function as markers of the special word order, much as intonation does in English, or the attachment of prefixes or suffixes might in other languages.

There are constraints on topicalization similar to those on *wh* movement illustrated in a previous section. In English the following strings are ungrammatical:

*Henchman, Sam Spade insulted the fat man's.
*This film, John asked Mary whether she liked.
*Cheese, John ate bologna and for lunch.

Compare this with the grammatical:

The fat man's henchman, Sam Spade insulted.
This film, John asked Mary to see with her.
Bologna and cheese, John ate for lunch.

Sign languages exhibit similar constraints. The signed sequence *Henchman, Sam Spade insulted the fat man's* or the other starred examples are ungrammatical in ASL as in spoken languages.

ASL has *wh* phrases. The *wh* phrase in ASL may move or it may remain in its d-structure position as in Japanese and Swahili. The ASL equivalents of *Who did Bill see yesterday?* and *Bill saw who yesterday?* are both grammatical. As in topicalization, *wh* questions are accompanied by a nonmanual marker. For questions, this marker is a facial expression with furrowed brows and the head tilted back.

ASL and other sign languages show an interaction of universal and language-specific properties, just as spoken languages do. The rules of sign languages are structure dependent, and movement rules are constrained in various ways, as illustrated earlier. Other aspects are particular to sign languages, such as the facial gestures, which are an integral part of the grammar of sign languages but not of spoken languages. The fact that the principles and parameters of UG hold in both the spoken and manual modalities shows that the human brain is designed to acquire and use language, not simply speech.

Summary

Speakers of a language recognize the grammatical sentences of their language and know how the words in a sentence must be ordered and grouped to convey a certain meaning. All speakers are capable of producing and understanding an unlimited number of new sentences that have never before been spoken or heard. They also recognize ambiguities, know when different sentences mean the same thing, and correctly perceive the grammatical relations in a sentence, such as **subject** and **direct object**. This kind of knowledge comes from their knowledge of the **rules of syntax**.

Sentences have structure that can be represented by **phrase structure trees** containing **syntactic categories**. Phrase structure trees reflect the speaker's mental representation of sentences. Ambiguous sentences may have more than one phrase structure tree.

Phrase structure trees reveal the linear order of words and the constituency of each syntactic category. There are different kinds of syntactic categories: **phrasal categories**, such as NP and VP, are composed of other syntactic categories; **lexical categories**, such as Noun and Verb, and **functional categories**, such as Det, Aux, and Comp, are not decomposable and often correspond to individual words. The internal structure of the phrasal categories is universal. It consists of a **head** and its **complements**. The particular order of elements within the phrase is accounted for by the **phrase structure rules** of each language. NPs, VPs, and so on are headed by nouns, verbs, and the like. The sentence (S or TP) is headed by Aux (or T), which carries such information as tense, agreement, and modality.

A grammar is a formally stated, explicit description of the mental grammar or speaker's linguistic competence. Phrase structure rules characterize the basic phrase structure trees of the language, the **d-structures**.

Some PS rules allow the same syntactic category to appear repeatedly in a phrase structure tree, such as a sentence embedded in another sentence. These rules are **recursive** and reflect a speaker's ability to produce countless sentences of unrestricted length.

The **lexicon** represents the knowledge that speakers have about the vocabulary of their language. This knowledge includes the syntactic category of words and what elements may occur together, expressed as **c-selection** or **subcategorization**. The lexicon also contains semantic information including the kinds of NPs that can function as semantically coherent subjects and objects, **s-selection**.

Transformational rules account for relationships between sentences such as declarative and interrogative pairs including *wh* questions. Transformations can move constituents or insert function words such as *do* into a sentence. Much of the meaning of a sentence is interpreted from its d-structure. The output of the transformational rules is the **s-structure** of a sentence, the structure to which the phonological rules of the language apply.

The basic design of language is universal. Universal Grammar specifies that syntactic rules are **structure dependent** and that movement rules may not move phrases out of certain structures such as coordinate structures. These constraints exist in all languages—spoken and signed—and need not be learned. UG also contains parameters of variation, such as the order of heads and complements, and the variations on movement rules. A child acquiring a language must fix the parameters of UG for that language.

References for Further Reading

Baker, M.C. 2001. *The Atoms of Language: The Mind's Hidden Rules of Grammar*. New York: Basic Books.

Chomsky, N. 1995. *The Minimalist Program*. Cambridge, MA: MIT Press.

———. 1972. *Language and Mind*, rev. ed. New York: Harcourt Brace Jovanovich.

———. 1965. *Aspects of the Theory of Syntax*. Cambridge, MA: MIT Press.

Haegeman, L. 1991. *Introduction to Government and Binding Theory*. Oxford, England: Basil Blackwell.

Jackendoff, R. S. 1994. *Patterns in the Mind: Language and Human Nature*. New York: Basic Books.

Pinker, S. 1999. *Words and Rules: The Ingredients of Language*. New York: HarperCollins.

Radford, A. 1997. *Syntax: A Minimalist Introduction*. New York: Cambridge University Press.

Exercises

1. Besides distinguishing grammatical from ungrammatical sentences, the rules of syntax account for other kinds of linguistic knowledge, such as

   a. when a sentence is structurally ambiguous. (Cf. *The boy saw the man with a telescope.*)

   b. when two sentences with different structures mean the same thing. (Cf. *The father wept silently* and *The father silently wept.*)

   c. systematic relationships of form and meaning between two sentences, like declarative sentences and their corresponding interrogative form. (Cf. *The boy can sleep* and *Can the boy sleep?*)

   Draw on your linguistic knowledge of English to come up with an example illustrating each of these cases. (Use examples that are different from the ones in the chapter.) Explain why your example illustrates the point. If you know a language other than English, provide examples in that language, if possible.

2. Consider the following sentences:

   a. I hate war.

    b. You know that I hate war.

    c. He knows that you know that I hate war.

       A. Write another sentence that includes sentence (c).

       B. What does this set of sentences reveal about the nature of language?

       C. How is this characteristic of human language related to the difference between linguistic competence and performance? (*Hint*: Review these concepts in chapter 1.)

3. Paraphrase each of the following sentences in two ways to show that you understand the ambiguity involved:

    Example: Smoking grass can be nauseating.

    i. Putting grass in a pipe and smoking it can make you sick.

    ii. Fumes from smoldering grass can make you sick.

    a. Dick finally decided on the boat.

    b. The professor's appointment was shocking.

    c. The design has big squares and circles.

    d. That sheepdog is too hairy to eat.

    e. Could this be the invisible man's hair tonic?

    f. The governor is a dirty street fighter.

    g. I cannot recommend him too highly.

    h. Terry loves his wife and so do I.

    i. They said she would go yesterday.

    j. No smoking section available.

4. Draw two phrase structure trees representing the two meanings of the sentence "The magician touched the child with the wand." Be sure you indicate which meaning goes with which tree.

5. Draw the subtrees for the italicized NPs in the following sentences:

    a. *Every child's mother* hopes he will be happy.

    b. *The big dog's bone* is buried in the garden.

    c. *Angry men in dark glasses* roamed the streets.

    d. *My aunt and uncle's trip* to Alaska was wonderful.

    e. Challenge exercise: *Whose dirty underwear* is this?

6. In all languages, sentences can occur within sentences. For example, in exercise 2, sentence (b) contains sentence (a), and sentence (c) contains sentence (b). Put another way, sentence (a) is embedded in sentence (b), and sentence (b) is embedded in sentence (c). Sometimes embedded sentences appear slightly changed from their normal form, but you should be able to recognize and underline the embedded sentences in the following examples. Underline in the non-English sentences, when given, not in the translations. (The first one is done as an example.):

    a. Yesterday I noticed <u>my accountant repairing the toilet</u>.

    b. Becky said that Jake would play the piano.

   c. I deplore the fact that bats have wings.

   d. That Guinevere loves Lorian is known to all my friends.

   e. Who promised the teacher that Maxine wouldn't be absent?

   f. It's ridiculous that he washes his own Rolls-Royce.

   g. The woman likes for the waiter to bring water when she sits down.

   h. The person who answers this question will win $100.

   i. The idea of Romeo marrying a 13-year-old is upsetting.

   j. I gave my hat to the nurse who helped me cut my hair.

   k. For your children to spend all your royalty payments on recreational drugs is a shame.

   l. Give this fork to the person I'm getting the pie for.

   m. khǎw chyâ   wǎa khruu   maa. (Thai)

      He   believe that teacher come

      He believes that the teacher is coming.

   n. Je me demande quand il partira. (French)

      I   me ask   when he will leave

      I wonder when he'll leave.

   o. Jan zei   dat Piet dit boek niet heeft gelezen. (Dutch)

      Jan said that Piet this book not has   read

      Jan said that Piet has not read this book.

7. Following the patterns of the various tree examples in the text, draw phrase structure trees for the following sentences. (*Hint*: You may omit the N' level whenever N' dominates a single N, so that, for example, *the puppy* has the structure NP [Det N].)

   a. The puppy found the child.

   b. A frightened passenger landed the crippled airliner.

   c. The house on the hill collapsed in the wind.

   d. The ice melted.

   e. The hot sun melted the ice.

   f. A fast car with twin cams sped by the children on the grassy lane.

   g. The old tree swayed in the wind.

   h. **Challenge exercise**: The children put the toy in the box.

   i. The reporter realized that the senator lied.

   j. Broken ice melts in the sun.

   k. My guitar gently weeps.

   l. A stranger cleverly observed that a dangerous spy from the CIA lurks in the alley by the old tenement. (*Hint*: see footnote 1, page 148.)

8. Use the rules on page 147 to create five phrase structure trees of 6, 7, 8, 9, and 10 words. Use your mental lexicon to fill in the bottom of the tree.

9. We stated that the rules of syntax specify all and only the grammatical sentences of the language. Why is it important to say "only"? What would be wrong with a grammar that specified as grammatical sentences all of the truly grammatical ones plus a few that were not grammatical?

10. In this chapter we introduced X-bar theory, according to which each phrase has three levels of structure.

   Draw the subtree corresponding to each phrasal category, NP, AdjP, VP, PP, as it would look according to X-bar notation.

   Challenge exercise: What would the structure of CP be according to X-bar notation?

   Further challenge: Give a sample phrase structure for each tree that fully exploits its entire structure—e.g., *the father of the bride* for the NP.

11. Using one or more of the constituency tests (i.e., stand alone, move as a unit, replacement by a pronoun) discussed in the chapter, determine which boldfaced portions in the sentences are constituents. Provide the grammatical category of the constituents.

   a. Martha found **a lovely pillow** for the couch.

   b. The **light in this room** is terrible.

   c. I wonder **if Bonnie has finished packing her books**.

   d. Melissa slept **in her class**.

   e. **Pete and Max** are fighting over **the bone**.

   f. I gave a bone to Pete **and to Max** yesterday.

   g. I gave a bone to **Pete and** to Max yesterday.

12. The two sentences below contain a **verbal particle**:

      i.   He ran *up* the bill.

      ii.   He ran the bill *up*.

   The verbal particle *up* and the verb *run* depend on each other for the unique idiosyncratic meaning of the phrasal verb *run up*. (*Running up a bill* involves neither running nor the location up.) We showed earlier that in such cases the particle and *object* do not form a constituent, hence they cannot move as a unit:

      iii.   *Up the bill, John ran   (compare this to *Up the hill John ran.*)

   a. Using adverbs such as *completely,* show that the particle forms a constituent with the *verb* in [*run up*] *the bill*, while in *run* [*up the hill*], the preposition and NP object form a constituent.

   b. Now consider the following data:

      i.   Michael ran up the hill and over the bridge.

      ii.   *Michael ran up the bill and off his mouth.

      iii.   Michael ran up the bill and ran off his mouth.

   Use the data to argue that expressions like *up the bill* and *off his mouth* are not constituents.

13. In terms of c-selection restrictions, explain why the following are ungrammatical:

   a. *The man located.

   b. *Jesus wept the apostles.

   c. *Robert is hopeful of his children.

   d. *Robert is fond that his children love animals.

   e. *The children laughed the man.

14. In the chapter, we looked at transitive verbs that select a single NP direct object like *chase*. English also has **ditransitive verbs**, ones that may be followed by two NPs, such as *give*:

The emperor gave the vassal a castle.

Think of three other ditransitive verbs in English and give example sentences.

15. For each verb, list the different types of complements it selects and provide an example of each type:

   a. want

   b. force

   c. try

   d. believe

   e. say

16. All *wh* phrases can move to the left periphery of the sentence.

   a. Invent three sentences beginning with *what, which,* and *where*, in which the *wh* word is not in its d-structure position in the sentence. Give both versions of your sentence. Here is an example with the *wh* word *when*: *When could Marcy catch a flight out of here?* from *Marcy could catch a flight out of here when?*

   b. Draw the phrase structure tree for one of these sentences using the phrase structure and movement rules provided in the chapter.

      Challenge exercise: How could you reformulate the movement rules used to derive a *wh* question such as *What has Mary done with her life?* using an X-bar CP structure (see question 10)?

17. There are many systematic, structure-dependent relationships among sentences similar to the one discussed in the chapter between declarative and interrogative sentences. Here is another example based on ditransitive verbs (see exercise 14):

The boy wrote the senator a letter.
The boy wrote a letter to the senator.
A philanthropist gave the animal rights movement $1 million.
A philanthropist gave $1 million to the animal rights movement.

   a. Describe the relationship between the first and second members of the pairs of sentences.

   b. State why a transformation deriving one of these structures from the other is plausible.

18. State at least three differences between English and the following languages, using just the sentence(s) given. Ignore lexical differences (i.e., the different vocabulary). Here is an example:

Thai:	dèg	khon	níi	kamlang	kin.
	boy	*classifier*	this	*progressive*	eat

"This boy is eating."

	măa	tua	nán	kin	khâaw.
	dog	*classifier*	that	eat	rice

"That dog ate rice."

Three differences are (1) Thai has "classifiers." They have no English equivalent. (2) The words (determiners, actually) "this" and "that" follow the noun in Thai, but precede the noun in English. (3) The "progressive" is expressed by a separate word in Thai. The verb does not change form. In English, the progressive is indicated by the presence of the verb *to be* and the adding of *-ing* to the verb.

a. French

cet	homme	intelligent	comprendra	la question.
this	man	intelligent	will understand	the question

"This intelligent man will understand the question."

ces	hommes	intelligents	comprendront	les questions.
these	men	intelligent	will understand	the questions

"These intelligent men will understand the questions."

b. Japanese

watashi	ga	sakana	o	tabete	iru.
I	*subject marker*	fish	*object marker*	eat (*ing*)	am

"I am eating fish."

c. Swahili

mtoto			alivunja			kikombe.	
m-		toto	a-	li-	vunja	ki-	kombe
class marker		child	he	*past*	break	*class marker*	cup

"The child broke the cup."

watoto		wanavunja				vikombe.	
wa-		toto	wa-	na-	vunja	vi-	kombe
class marker		child	they	*present*	break	*class marker*	cup

"The children break the cups."

d. Korean

kɨ	sonyɔn-iee		wɨyu-lɨl		masi-ass-ta.		
kɨ	sonyɔn-	iee	wɨyu-	lɨl	masi-	ass-	ta
the	boy	*subject marker*	milk	*object marker*	drink	*past*	*assertion*

"The boy drank milk."

ki-nin   muɔs-il   mɔk-ass-ninya.
ki-   nin   muɔs-   il   mɔk-   ass-   ninya
he   *subject* what *object* eat   *past*   *question*
     marker   *marker*

"What did he eat?"

e. Tagalog

nakita   ni   Pedro-ng   puno   na   ang   bus.
nakita   ni   Pedro   -ng   puno   na   ang   bus.
saw   *article*   Pedro   that   full   already *topic* bus
                                                     marker

"Pedro saw that the bus was already full."

19. Transformations may delete elements. For example, the s-structure of the ambiguous sentence "George wants the presidency more than Martha" may be derived from two possible d-structures:

a. George wants the presidency more than he wants Martha.

b. George wants the presidency more than Martha wants the presidency.

A deletion transformation either deletes *he wants* from the structure of example (a), or *wants the presidency* from the structure of example (b). This is a case of **transformationally induced ambiguity**: two different d-structures with different semantic interpretations are transformed into a single s-structure.

Explain the role of a deletion transformation similar to the ones just discussed in the following cartoon:

"Hagar the Horrible" copyright © King Features Syndicate, Inc. Reprinted with special permission.

20. Advanced: Compare the following French and English sentences:

French	English
Jean boit toujours du vin.	John always drinks some wine.
Jean drinks always some wine	*John drinks always some wine
(*Jean toujours boit du vin)	
Marie lit jamais le journal.	Mary never reads the newspaper.
Marie reads never the newspaper	*Mary reads never the newspaper.

(*Marie jamais lit le journal)
Pierre lave souvent ses chiens.   Peter often washes his dogs.
Pierre washes often his dogs   *Peter washes often his dogs.
(*Pierre souvent lave ses chiens.)

a. Based on the above data, what would you hypothesize concerning the position of adverbs in French and English?

b. Now suppose that UG specifies that in *all languages* adverbs of frequency (e.g., *always, never, often, sometimes*) immediately precede the VP, as in the following tree. What rule would you need to hypothesize to derive the correct surface word order for French? (*Hint*: adverbs are not allowed to move.)

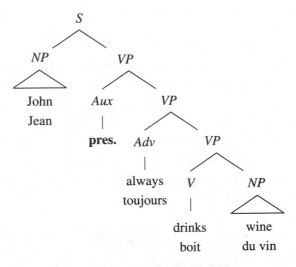

c. Do any verbs in English follow the same pattern as the French verbs?

21. Give the tree corresponding to the underlined portion of the sentence *The hole should have been being filled* by the workcrew.

22. Show that an embedded CP is a constituent by applying the constituency tests: stand alone, move as a unit, and replace with a pronoun. Consider the following sentences in formulating your answer, and provide further examples if you can. (The boldfaced words are the CP.)

Sam asked **if he could play soccer**.
I wonder **whether Michael walked the dog**.
Cher believes **that the students know the answer**.
It is a problem **that Sam broke his arm**.

23. **Challenge exercise**:

a. Give the d-structure tree for *Which dog does Michael think loves bones?* (*Hint*: the complementizer *that* must be present.)

b. Give the d-structure tree for *What does Michael think that his dog loves?*

c. Consider these data:

i. *Which dog does Michael think that loves bones?

ii. What does Michael think his dog loves?

In (ii) a complementizer deletion rule has deleted *that*. The rule is optional in that the sentence is grammatical with or without *that*. In (i), however, the complementizer must be deleted to prevent the ungrammatical sentence from being generated. What factor governs the optionality of the rule?

5

The Meaning of Language

> Language without meaning is meaningless.
>
> **ROMAN JAKOBSON**
>
> Surely all this is not without meaning.
>
> **HERMAN MELVILLE,** Moby Dick

For thousands of years philosophers have pondered the **meaning** of *meaning*, yet speakers of a language can easily understand what is said to them and can produce strings of words that are meaningful to other speakers. We use language to convey information to others (*My new bike is pink*), ask questions (*Who left the party early?*), give commands (*Stop lying!*), and express wishes (*May there be peace on earth*).

What do you know about meaning when you know a language? The answer is: an awful lot! To begin with, you know when a "word" is meaningful (*flick*) or meaningless (*blick*), and you know when a "sentence" is meaningful (*Jack swims*) or meaningless (*swims metaphorical every*). You know when a word is ambiguous (*bear*) and when a sentence is ambiguous (*Jack saw a man with a telescope*). You know when two words have essentially the same meaning, are synonymous (*sofa* and *couch*), and when two sentences are synonymous (*Jack put off the meeting, Jack put the meeting off*). And you know when words or sentences have opposite meanings (*alive/dead; Jack swims/Jack doesn't swim*).

If you are properly informed, you know the object that words refer to, for example, *the prime minister of France*; and even if the words do not have reference, such as *the present king of France,* or *a unicorn*, you still have a sense of what they mean, and if the particular objects happened to exist, you would have the knowledge to identify them.

You know, or have the capacity to discover, when sentences are true or false. That is, if you know the meaning of a sentence, you know its truth conditions. In some cases it's obvious, or redundant (*all kings are male* [true], *all bachelors are married* [false]); in other cases you need some further, nonlinguistic knowledge (*Molybdenum conducts electricity*), but by knowing the meaning, you know the kind of world knowledge that is needed. Often, if you know that a sentence is true (*Nina bathed her dogs*), you can infer that another sentence must also be true (*Nina's dogs got wet*), that is, the first sentence **entails** the second sentence.

All of this knowledge about meaning extends to an unlimited set of sentences, just like your syntactic knowledge, and is part of the grammar of the language. The job of the linguist is to reveal and make explicit this knowledge about meaning that every speaker has.

The study of the linguistic meaning of morphemes, words, phrases, and sentences is called **semantics**. Subfields of semantics are **lexical semantics**, which is concerned with the meanings of words, and the meaning relationships among words; and **phrasal** or **sentential semantics**, which is concerned with the meaning of syntactic units larger than the word. The study of how context affects meaning—for example, how the sentence *It's cold in here* comes to be interpreted as "close the windows" in certain situations—is called **pragmatics**.

What Speakers Know about Sentence Meaning

"Then you should say what you mean," the March Hare went on.

"I do," Alice hastily replied, "at least—I mean what I say—that's the same thing, you know."

"Not the same thing a bit!" said the Hatter. "You might just as well say that 'I see what I eat' is the same thing as 'I eat what I see'!"

"You might just as well say," added the March Hare, "that 'I like what I get' is the same thing as 'I get what I like'!"

"You might just as well say," added the Dormouse . . . "that 'I breathe when I sleep' is the same thing as 'I sleep when I breathe'!"

"It is the same thing with you," said the Hatter.

LEWIS CARROLL, Alice's Adventures in Wonderland

In this section we discuss the linguistic knowledge you have that permits you to determine the truth of sentences, when one sentence entails another, and whether a sentence is ambiguous. We will show you one attempt to account for this knowledge in the grammar by formulating semantic rules that build the meaning of a sentence from the meaning of its words and the way they combine syntactically. This is often called **truth-conditional semantics** because it takes the semantic knowledge of truth as basic. It is also called **compositional semantics** because it calculates the truth value of a sentence by composing, or putting together, the meaning of smaller units. We will limit our discussion to declarative sentences like *Jack swims* or *Jack kissed Laura*, because we can judge these kinds of sentences as either true or false. At least part of their meaning, then, will be their **truth value**.

Truth

> . . . Having Occasion to talk of Lying and false Representation, it was with much Difficulty that he comprehended what I meant. . . . For he argued thus: That the Use of Speech was to make us understand one another and to receive Information of Facts; now if any one said the Thing which was not, these Ends were defeated; because I cannot properly be said to understand him. . . . And these were all the Notions he had concerning that Faculty of Lying, so perfectly well understood, and so universally practiced among human Creatures.
>
> JONATHAN SWIFT, Gulliver's Travels

Let us begin by returning to Jack, who is swimming in the pool. If you are poolside and you hear the sentence *Jack swims*, and you know the meaning of that sentence, then you will judge the sentence to be true. On the other hand, if you are indoors and you happen to know that Jack never learned to swim, then when you hear the very same sentence *Jack swims*, you will judge the sentence to be false and you will think the speaker is misinformed or lying. More generally, if you know the meaning of a sentence, then you can determine under what conditions it is true or false.

Note that you do not need to actually know whether a sentence is true or false to know its meaning. Knowing the meaning informs you as to how to determine the truth value. The sentence *Molybdenum conducts electricity* has meaning and is perfectly understood precisely because we know how to determine whether it's true or false.

Knowing the meaning of a sentence, then, means knowing its **truth conditions**. Reducing the question of meaning to the question of truth conditions has proved to be very fruitful in understanding the various semantic properties of language.

For most sentences it does not make sense to say that they are true or false in general. Rather, they are true or false in a given situation, as we previously saw with *Jack swims*. But a restricted number of sentences are always true, no matter which situation you utter them in. They are called **tautologies**. (The term **analytic** is also used for such sentences.) Examples of tautologies are sentences like *Circles are round* or *A person who is single is not married*. Their truth is guaranteed by the meaning of their parts and the way they are put together, irrespective of circumstances.

Similarly, some sentences are always false. These are called **contradictions**. Examples of contradictions are sentences like *Circles are square* or *A bachelor is married*.

Finally, for a very small set of sentences, called **paradoxes**, it is impossible to ascribe a truth value. A well-known paradox is the sentence *This sentence is false*. It cannot be true, else it's false; it cannot be false, else it's true. Therefore it has no truth value, though it certainly has meaning. This is one indication that truth-conditional semantics, while informative, is incomplete.

Entailment and Related Notions

> "Take some more tea," the March Hare said to Alice, very earnestly.
>
> "I've had nothing yet," Alice replied in an offended tone, "so I can't take more."
>
> "You mean you can't take *less*," said the Hatter: "It's very easy to take *more* than nothing."
>
> LEWIS CARROLL, Alice's Adventures in Wonderland

If you know that the sentence *Jack swims beautifully* is true, then you also know that the sentence *Jack swims* must be true as well. This meaning relation is called **entailment**. We say that *Jack swims beautifully* entails *Jack swims*. More generally, one sentence entails another if whenever the first sentence is true the second one is also true, in all conceivable circumstances.

Generally, entailment goes in only one direction. So while the sentence *Jack swims beautifully* entails *Jack swims*, the reverse is not true. Knowing merely that *Jack swims* is true does not necessitate the truth of *Jack swims beautifully*; Jack could be a poor swimmer.

The notion of entailment can be used to reveal knowledge that we have about other meaning relations. For example, omitting tautologies and contradictions, two sentences are **synonymous** (or **paraphrases**) if they are both true or both false with respect to the same situations. Sentences like *Jack put off the meeting* and *Jack postponed the meeting* are synonymous, because when one is true the other must be true; and when one is false the other must also be false. We can describe this pattern in a more concise way by using the notion of entailment:

Two sentences are *synonymous* if they entail each other.

Thus if sentence A entails sentence B and vice versa, then whenever A is true B is true, and vice versa. Although entailment says nothing specifically about false sentences, it's clear that if sentence A entails sentence B, then whenever B is false, A must be false. (If A were true, B would have to be true.) And if B also entails A, then whenever A is false, B would have to be false. Thus mutual entailment guarantees identical truth values in all situations. When sentences are synonymous, we also say they are **paraphrases** of each other.

Two sentences are **contradictory** if, whenever one is true, the other is false or, equivalently, there is no situation in which they are both true or both false. For example, the sentences *Jack is alive* and *Jack is dead* are contradictory because if the sentence *Jack is alive* is true, then the sentence *Jack is dead* is false, and vice versa. In other words, *Jack is alive* and *Jack is dead* have opposite truth values. Like synonymy, contradiction can be reduced to a special case of entailment.

Two sentences are *contradictory* if one entails the negation of the other.

For instance, *Jack is alive* entails the negation of *Jack is dead*, namely *Jack is not dead*. Similarly, *Jack is dead* entails the negation of *Jack is alive*, namely *Jack is not alive*.

The notions of *contradiction* (always false) and *contradictory* (opposite in truth value) are related in that if two sentences are contradictory, their conjunction with *and* is a contradiction. Thus *Jack is alive and Jack is dead* is a contradiction; it cannot be true under any circumstances.

Ambiguity

Our semantic knowledge tells us when words or phrases (including sentences) have more than one meaning, that is, when they are ambiguous. In Chapter 4 we saw that the sentence *The boy saw the man with a telescope* was an instance of structural ambiguity. It is ambiguous because it can mean that the boy saw the man by using a

telescope or that the boy saw the man who was holding a telescope. The sentence is structurally ambiguous because it is associated with two different phrase structures, each corresponding to a different meaning. Here are the two structures:

(1)

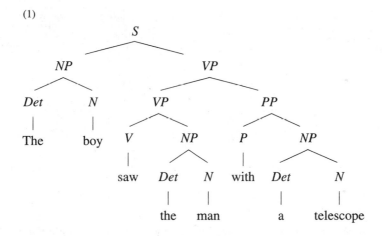

(2)

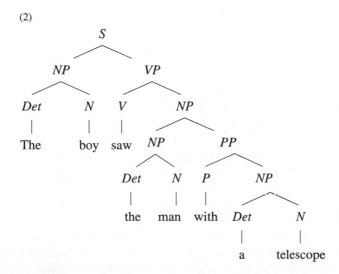

In (1) the PP *with a telescope* modifies the VP, and the interpretation is that the action of seeing occurred by use of a telescope. In (2) the PP *with a telescope* modifies the NP *the man*, and the interpretation is that the man has the telescope.

Lexical ambiguity arises when at least one word in a phrase has more than one meaning. For instance the sentence *This will make you smart* is ambiguous because of the two meanings of the word *smart*: "clever" or "burning sensation."

Our knowledge of lexical and structural ambiguities reveals that the meaning of a linguistic expression is built both on the words it contains and its syntactic structure. The notion that the meaning of an expression is composed of the meanings of its parts and how they are combined structurally is referred to as the **Principle of Compositionality**. In the next section we discuss the rules by which the meaning of a phrase or sentence is computed based on its composition.

Compositional Semantics

We have seen that the syntactic rules express speakers' knowledge about grammaticality, constituent structure, relations between sentences, and so on. Similarly, the semantic rules of the grammar must account for the semantic knowledge we have just discussed, including truth, reference, entailment, and ambiguity. A central property that our syntax must account for is the creativity of linguistic knowledge, that is, the fact that we can speak, produce, and make grammaticality judgments about an infinite set of sentences. In order to account for this creative aspect of language, we concluded in chapter 4 that our grammar builds sentences according to recursive syntactic rules that combine words into phrases and phrases into sentences.

The same creativity exists with respect to our semantic knowledge. You know the meaning of, and therefore how to determine the truth value of, an infinite number of sentences, most of which you have never heard before. Moreover, you know the entailments and ambiguities of these sentences. Because our semantic knowledge holds for an infinite set of sentences, we must conclude that our grammar contains general semantic rules that combine the meanings of words into meaningful phrases and sentences.

Semantic Rules

In the sentence *Jack swims*, we have the knowledge that the word *Jack*, which is usually called a **proper name**, refers to a precise object in the world, which is its **reference**. For instance, in the scenario given earlier, the referential meaning of *Jack* is the guy who is your friend and who is swimming happily in the pool right now. Based on this, we conclude that the meaning of the name *Jack* is the individual it refers to. (We will learn more about proper names and reference in the section on lexical semantics.)

Our semantic rules must be sensitive to the meaning of individual words and the structure in which they occur. So, taking as an example our simple sentence *Jack swims*, let us see how the semantic rules compute the meaning of this sentence. We start with the meaning of each word. We already saw that our knowledge regarding proper names tells us that the name *Jack* refers to an individual. What about the meaning of the verb *swim*? Part of its meaning is the group or set of individuals (human beings and animals) that swim. You will see in a moment how this aspect of the meaning of *swim* helps us understand sentences in a way that accords with our semantic knowledge. The meanings of the individual words are summarized as follows:

Word Meanings

Jack   refers to (or means) the individual Jack

swims   refers to (or means) the set of individuals that swim

The phrase structure tree for our sentence is as follows:

Syntactic Structure

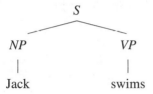

The tree tells us that syntactically the NP *Jack* and the VP *swims* combine to form a sentence. We want to mirror that combination at the semantic level: in other words, we want to combine the meaning of the NP *Jack* (an individual) and the meaning of the VP *swims* (a set of individuals) to obtain the meaning of the S *Jack swims*. This is done by means of semantic rule I.

SEMANTIC RULE I

The meaning of [$_S$ NP VP] is the following truth condition:

If the meaning of NP (an individual) is a member of the meaning of VP (a set of individuals), then S is TRUE, otherwise it is FALSE.

Rule I states that a sentence that is made up of a subject NP and a VP is true if the subject NP refers to an individual who is among the members of the set that constitute the meaning of the VP. Notice that this rule is completely general; it does not refer to any particular sentence, individuals, or verbs. It works equally well for sentences like *Ellen sings* or *Max barks*. Thus the meaning of *Max barks* is the truth condition (i.e., the "if-sentence") that states that the sentence is true if the individual meant by *Max* is among the set of individuals meant by *barks*, and so on.

Let us now try a slightly more complex case: the sentence *Jack kissed Laura*. The main syntactic difference between this example and the previous one is that we now have a transitive verb that requires an extra NP in object position; otherwise our semantic rules will derive the meaning using the same mechanical procedure as in the first example. We again start with the word meaning and syntactic structure:

Word Meanings

Jack	refers to (or means) the individual Jack
Laura	refers to (or means) the individual Laura
kissed	refers to (or means) the set of pairs of individuals X and Y such that X kissed Y.

Syntactic Structure

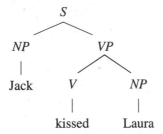

The meaning of the transitive verb kiss is still a set, but this time a set of pairs of individuals. The meaning of the VP, however, is still a set of individuals, namely those individuals who kissed Laura. This may be expressed formally in Semantic Rule II.

SEMANTIC RULE II

The meaning of [$_{VP}$ V NP] is the set of individuals X such that X is the first member of any pair in the meaning of V whose second member is the meaning of NP.

The meaning of the sentence is derived by first applying Semantic Rule II, which establishes the meaning of the VP as a certain set of individuals, namely those who kissed Laura. Now Semantic Rule I applies without further ado and gives the meaning of the sentence as the truth condition that determines S to be true whenever the meaning of *Jack* is a member of the set that is the meaning of the VP *kissed Laura.* In other words, S is true if Jack kissed Laura and false otherwise. These two semantic rules handle an essentially infinite number of intransitive and transitive sentences.

One last example will illustrate how the semantic knowledge of entailment may be represented in the grammar. Consider *Jack swims beautifully*, and consider further the meaning of the adverb *beautifully.* Its meaning is clearly not an individual or a set of individuals. Rather, the meaning of *beautifully* is an operation that reduces the size of the sets that are the meanings of verb phrases. When applied to the meaning of *swims*, it reduces the set of individuals who swim to the smaller set of those who swim beautifully. We won't express this rule formally, but it is now easy to see one source of entailment. The truth conditions that make *Jack swims beautifully* true are narrower than the truth conditions that make *Jack swims* true by virtue of the fact that among the individuals who swim, fewer of them swim beautifully. Therefore, any truth condition that causes *Jack swims beautifully* to be true necessarily causes *Jack swims* to be true, hence *Jack swims beautifully* entails *Jack swims.*

These rules, and many more like them, account for our knowledge about the truth value of sentences by taking the meanings of words and combining them according to the syntactic structure of the sentence. It is easy to see from these examples how ambiguous meanings arise. Because the meaning of a sentence is computed based on its hierarchical organization, different trees will have different meanings—structural ambiguity—even when the words are the same, as in the example *The boy saw the man with a telescope.* The occurrence of an ambiguous word—lexical ambiguity—when it combines with the other elements of a sentence, can make the entire sentence ambiguous, as in *She can't bear children.*

The semantic theory of sentence meaning that we just sketched is not the only possible one, but compositional truth-conditional semantics has proven to be an extremely powerful and useful tool for investigating the semantic properties of natural languages.

When Compositionality Goes Awry

The meaning of an expression is not always obvious, even to a native speaker of the language. Meanings may be obscured in many ways, or at least may require some imagination or special knowledge to be apprehended. Poets, pundits, and yes, even professors, can be difficult to understand.

In the previous sections we saw that semantic rules compute sentence meaning compositionally based on the meanings of words and the syntactic structure that contains them. There are, however, interesting cases in which compositionality breaks down, either because there is a problem with words or with the semantic rules. If one or more words in a sentence do not have a meaning, then obviously we will not be able to compute a meaning for the entire sentence. Moreover, even if the individual words have meaning but cannot be combined together as the syntactic structure and related semantic rules require, we will also not get to a meaning. We refer to these situations as semantic **anomaly**. Alternatively, it might require a lot of creativity and imagination to derive a meaning. This is what happens in **metaphors**. Finally, some expressions—called **idioms**—have a fixed meaning, that is, a meaning that is not compositional. Applying compositional rules to idioms gives rise to funny or inappropriate meanings.

ANOMALY

> Don't tell me of a man's being able to talk sense; everyone can talk sense. Can he talk nonsense?
>
> **WILLIAM PITT**

> There is no greater mistake in the world than the looking upon every sort of nonsense as want of sense.
>
> **LEIGH HUNT**

The semantic properties of words determine what other words they can be combined with. A sentence widely used by linguists that we encountered in chapter 4 illustrates this fact:

Colorless green ideas sleep furiously.

The sentence obeys all the syntactic rules of English. The subject is *colorless green ideas* and the predicate is *sleep furiously.* It has the same syntactic structure as the sentence

Dark green leaves rustle furiously.

but there is obviously something semantically wrong with the sentence. The meaning of *colorless* includes the semantic feature "without color," but it is combined with the adjective *green*, which has the feature "green in color." How can something be both "without color" and "green in color"? Other semantic violations occur in the sentence. Such sentences are *semantically anomalous*.

Other English "sentences" make no sense at all because they include "words" that have no meaning; they are **uninterpretable**. They can be interpreted only if some meaning for each nonsense word can be dreamt up. Lewis Carroll's "Jabberwocky" is probably the most famous poem in which most of the content words have no meaning—they do not exist in the lexicon of the grammar. Still, all the sentences sound as if they should be or could be English sentences:

> 'Twas brillig, and the slithy toves
> Did gyre and gimble in the wabe;
> All mimsy were the borogoves,
> And the mome raths outgrabe.
>
> . . .
>
> He took his vorpal sword in hand:
> Long time the manxome foe he sought—
> So rested he by the Tumtum tree,
> And stood awhile in thought.

Without knowing what *vorpal* means, you nevertheless know that

> He took his vorpal sword in hand

means the same thing as

> He took his sword, which was vorpal, in hand.
> It was in his hand that he took his vorpal sword.

Knowing the language, and assuming that *vorpal* means the same thing in the three sentences (because the same sounds are used), you can decide that the sense—the truth conditions—of the three sentences are identical. In other words, you are able to decide that two things mean the same thing even though you do not know what either one means. You decide by assuming that the semantic properties of *vorpal* are the same whenever it is used.

We now see why Alice commented, when she had read "Jabberwocky":

> "It seems very pretty, but it's *rather* hard to understand!" (You see she didn't like to confess, even to herself, that she couldn't make it out at all.) "Somehow it seems to fill my head with ideas—only I don't exactly know what they are! However, *somebody* killed *something*: that's clear, at any rate—"

Semantic violations in poetry may form strange but interesting aesthetic images, as in Dylan Thomas's phrase *a grief ago*. *Ago* is ordinarily used with words specified by some temporal semantic feature:

a week ago		*a table ago
an hour ago	but not	*a dream ago
a month ago		*a mother ago
a century ago		

When Thomas used the word *grief* with *ago*, he was adding a durational feature to grief for poetic effect, so while the noun phrase is anomalous, it evokes certain feelings.

In the poetry of e. e. cummings, there are phrases like

the six subjunctive crumbs twitch.
a man . . . wearing a round jeer for a hat.
children building this rainman out of snow.

Though all of these phrases violate some semantic rules, we can understand them; breaking the rules creates the imagery desired. The fact that we are able to understand, or at least interpret, anomalous expressions, and at the same time recognize their anomalous nature, demonstrates our knowledge of the semantic system and semantic properties of the language.

METAPHOR

Our doubts are traitors.

SHAKESPEARE

Walls have ears.

CERVANTES

The night has a thousand eyes and the day but one.

FRANCES WILLIAM BOURDILLON

When what appears to be an anomaly is nevertheless understood in terms of a meaningful concept, the expression becomes a metaphor. There is no strict line between anomalous and metaphorical expressions. Technically, metaphors are anomalous, but the nature of the anomaly creates the salient meanings that metaphors usually have. The anomalous *A grief ago* might come to be interpreted by speakers of English as "the unhappy time following a sad event" and therefore become a metaphor.

Metaphors may have a literal meaning as well as their metaphorical meaning, so in some sense they are ambiguous. However, when the semantic rules are applied to *Walls have ears*, for example, the literal meaning is so unlikely that listeners use their imagination for another interpretation. The Principle of Compositionality is very "rubbery," and when it fails to produce an acceptable literal meaning, listeners try to accommodate and stretch the meaning. This accommodation is based on semantic properties that are inferred or that provide some kind of resemblance or comparison that can end up as a meaningful concept.

This works only up to a certain point, however. It's not clear what the literal meaning of *Our doubts are traitors* might be, though the conceptual meaning that the act of doubting a precious belief is self-betrayal seems plausible. To interpret metaphors we need to understand at least the meaning of the words that comprise it, if not the literal meaning of the whole, and, significantly, facts about the world. To understand the metaphor

Time is money

it is necessary to know that in our society we are often paid according to the number of hours or days worked. In fact, "time," which is an abstract concept, is the subject of multiple metaphors. We "save time," "waste time," "manage time," push things "back in time," live on "borrowed time," and suffer the "ravages of time" as the "sands of time" drift away. In effect, the metaphors take the abstract concept of time and treat it as a concrete object of value.

Metaphor has a strong cultural component. Shakespeare uses metaphors that are lost on many of today's playgoers. "I am a man whom Fortune hath cruelly scratched," is most effective as a metaphor in a society like Shakespeare's that commonly depicts "Fortune" as a woman. On the other hand *There's a bug in my program* would make little sense in a culture without computers, even if the idea of having bugs in anything is indicative of a problem.

Many expressions now taken literally may have originated as metaphors, such as "the fall of the dollar," meaning its decline in value on the world market. Many people wouldn't bat an eyelash (another metaphor) at the literal interpretation of saving or wasting time. Metaphor is one of the factors in language change (see chapter 11). Metaphorical use of language is language creativity at its highest. Nevertheless, the basis of metaphorical use is very much the ordinary linguistic knowledge about words, their semantic properties, and their combining powers that all speakers possess.

IDIOMS

"Bizarro" © by Dan Piraro. Reprinted with permission of King Features Syndicate. All rights reserved.

Knowing a language includes knowing the morphemes, simple words, compound words, and their meanings. In addition, it means knowing fixed phrases, consisting of more than one word, with meanings that cannot be inferred from the meanings of the individual words. Here is where the Principle of Compositionality is superseded by expressions that act very much like individual morphemes in that they are not decomposable, but have a fixed meaning that must be learned. The usual semantic rules for combining meanings do not apply. All languages contain many such expressions, called *idioms*, or **idiomatic phrases**, as in these English examples:

sell down the river
rake over the coals
eat my hat
let their hair down
put his foot in his mouth
throw her weight around
snap out of it
cut it out
hit it off
get it off
bite your tongue
give a piece of your mind

Idioms are similar in structure to ordinary phrases except that they tend to be frozen in form and do not readily enter into other combinations or allow the word order to change. Thus,

1. She put her foot in her mouth.

has the same structure as

2. She put her bracelet in her drawer.

but

The drawer in which she put her bracelet was hers.
Her bracelet was put in her drawer.

are sentences related to sentence (2).

The mouth in which she put her foot was hers.
Her foot was put in her mouth.

do not have the idiomatic sense of sentence (1), except, perhaps, humorously.

On the other hand, the words of some idioms can be moved without affecting the idiomatic sense:

The FBI kept tabs on radicals.
Tabs were kept on radicals by the FBI.
Radicals were kept tabs on by the FBI.

Like metaphors, idioms can break the rules on combining semantic properties. The object of *eat* must usually be something with the semantic feature "edible," but in

He ate his hat.
Eat your heart out.

this restriction is violated.

Idioms often lead to humor:

What did the doctor tell the vegetarian about his surgically implanted heart valve from a pig?

That it was okay as long as he didn't "eat his heart out."

Idioms, grammatically as well as semantically, have special characteristics. They must be entered into the lexicon or mental dictionary as single items with their meanings specified, and speakers must learn the special restrictions on their use in sentences.

Most idioms originate as metaphorical expressions that establish themselves in the language and become frozen in their form and meaning.

Lexical Semantics (Word Meanings)

"There's glory for you!"

"I don't know what you mean by 'glory,'" Alice said.

Humpty Dumpty smiled contemptuously.

"Of course you don't—till I tell you. I meant 'there's a nice knock-down argument for you!'"

"But 'glory' doesn't mean 'a nice knock-down argument,'" Alice objected.

"When I use a word," Humpty Dumpty said, in rather a scornful tone, "it means just what I choose it to mean—neither more nor less."

"The question is," said Alice, "whether you can make words mean so many different things."

LEWIS CARROLL, Through the Looking-Glass

As just discussed, the meaning of a phrase or sentence is partially a function of the meanings of the words it contains. Similarly, the meaning of many words is a function of the morphemes that compose it, as we saw in chapter 3. However, there is a fundamental difference between word meaning—or *lexical semantics*—and sentence meaning. The meaning of most words and all morphemes is conventional; that is, speakers of a language implicitly agree on their meaning, and children acquiring the language must simply learn those meanings outright. On the other hand, the meaning of most sentences must be constructed by the application of semantic rules. In this section we will talk about the meaning relationships that exist between words and morphemes.

Although the agreed-upon meaning of a word may shift over time within a language community, as we shall see in chapter 11, we are not free as individuals to change the meanings of words at will; if we did we would be unable to communicate with each other. As we see from the quotation, Humpty Dumpty was unwilling to accept this convention. Fortunately, there are few Humpty Dumptys. All the speakers of a language share a basic vocabulary—the sounds and meanings of morphemes and words. Each of us knows the meanings of thousands of words. This knowledge permits us to use words to express our thoughts and to understand the thoughts of others. The meaning of words is part of linguistic knowledge. Your mental storehouse of information about words and morphemes is what we have been calling the *lexicon*.

Dictionaries such as the Oxford English Dictionary (OED) or Webster's Collegiate Dictionary are filled with words and their meanings. Dictionaries give the meaning of words using other words rather than in terms of some more basic vocabulary. In this sense a dictionary really provides *paraphrases* rather than meanings. It relies on our knowledge of the language to understand the definitions. The meanings associated with words in our mental lexicon are probably not like what we find in the OED or Webster's, although it is admittedly very difficult to specify precisely how word meanings are represented in the mind of speakers.

Theories of Word Meaning

It is natural . . . to think of there being connected with a sign . . . besides . . . the reference of the sign, also what I should like to call the sense of the sign. . . .

GOTTLOB FREGE, On Sense and Reference

If the meaning of a word is not like a dictionary entry, what is it? This question has been debated by philosophers and linguists for centuries. One proposal is that the meaning of a word is its **referent**, which is the thing or things in the real world that it refers to.

REFERENCE

"There's nothing here under 'Superman'—is it possible you made the reservation under another name?"

We have already determined that the meaning of proper names like *Jack* is the individual referred to, or its reference. Proper names are noun phrases (NPs); you can substitute a proper name in any NP position in a sentence and preserve grammaticality. There are other NPs that refer to individuals as well. For instance, NPs like *the happy swimmer, my friend, that guy* can all be used to refer to Jack in the situation where you've observed Jack swimming. The same is true for pronouns such as *I, you, him*, which also function as NPs. In all these cases, the reference of the NP—the individual it singles out under the circumstances in which it is used—is part of the meaning of the NP—its reference.

On the other hand, not every NP refers to an individual. For instance, the sentence *No baby swims* contains the NP *no baby*, but your linguistic knowledge tells you that this NP does not refer to any specific individual. If *no baby* has no reference, but is not meaningless, then something about meaning beyond reference must be present.

Also in support of that "extra something" is our knowledge that, while under certain circumstances *the happy swimmer* and *Jack* may have the same reference, the former has some further meaning, for we know that *the happy swimmer is happy* is a tautology—true in every conceivable situation, but *Jack is happy* is not a tautology, for there are circumstances under which that sentence might be false.

SENSE

If meaning were reference alone, then the meaning of words and expressions would be the objects pointed out in the real world. For example, the meaning of *dog* would be the set of canine objects. This theory of word meaning is attractive because it underscores the idea that meaning is a connection between language on the one hand, and objects and events in the world on the other.

An obvious problem for such a theory, however, is that speakers know many words that have no real-world referents (e.g., *hobbits, unicorns,* and *Harry Potter*). Yet speakers do know the meanings of these expressions. Similarly, what real-world entities would function words like *of* and *by*, or modal verbs such as *will* or *may* refer to?

A further problem is that two expressions may refer to the same individual but not have the same meaning. For example, *George W. Bush* and *the President* currently refer to the same individual, but the meaning of the NP *the President* is something like "the head of state," that is, an element of meaning is separate from its *reference* and is more enduring. This element of meaning is often termed **sense**. It is the extra something referred to earlier. *Unicorns, hobbits,* and *Harry Potter* have sense but no reference (in the real world). Conversely, proper names typically have only reference. A name like Chris Jones may point out a certain person, its referent, but has little linguistic meaning beyond that. Sometimes two different proper names have the same referent, such as Mark Twain and Samuel Langhorne Clemens, or Unabomber and Theodore Kaczinski. It is a hotly debated question in the philosophy of language as to whether two such expressions have the same or different senses.

Another proposal is that the meaning of a word is the mental image it conjures up in the mind of speakers. This solves the problem of unicorns, hobbits, and Harry Potter; we may have a clear image of these entities from books, movies, and so on, although they have no actual reference. However, many meaningful expressions are not associated with any clear, unique image agreed to by most speakers of the language. For example, what image is evoked by the expressions *very, if, 306*? It's difficult to say, yet these expressions are certainly meaningful. What is the image of oxygen as distinct from nitrogen—both are clear gases, yet they mean very different things. What mental image would we have of *dog* that is general enough to include Yorkshire Terriers and Great Danes and yet excludes foxes and wolves? Astronauts will likely have a very different mental image of the expression *space capsule* than the average person, yet people and astronauts do communicate with one another if they speak the same language.

Although the idea that the meaning of a word corresponds to a mental image is intuitive (because many words do provoke imagery), it is clearly inadequate as a general explanation of what people know about word meanings.

Lexical Relations

Does he wear a turban, a fez or a hat?
Does he sleep on a mattress, a bed or a mat, or a Cot,
The Akond of Swat?
Can he write a letter concisely clear,
Without a speck or a smudge or smear or Blot,
The Akond of Swat?

Edward Lear, The Akond of Swat

Although no theory of word meaning is complete, we know that speakers have considerable knowledge about the meaning relationships among different words in their mental lexicons, and any theory must take that knowledge into account.

Words are semantically related to one another in a variety of ways. The words that describe these relations often end in the bound morpheme *-nym*. The best-known lexical relations are synonyms, illustrated in the poem by Edward Lear, and antonyms or opposites. **Synonyms** are words or expressions that have the same meaning in some or all contexts. There are dictionaries of synonyms that contain many hundreds of entries, such as:

apathetic/phlegmatic/passive/sluggish/indifferent

pedigree/ancestry/genealogy/descent/lineage

A sign in the San Diego Zoo Wild Animal Park states:

Please do not *annoy, torment, pester, plague, molest, worry, badger, harry, harass, heckle, persecute, irk, bullyrag, vex, disquiet, grate, beset, bother, tease, nettle, tantalize,* or *ruffle* the animals.

It has been said that there are no perfect synonyms—that is, no two words ever have *exactly* the same meaning. Still, the following two sentences have very similar meanings:

He's sitting on the sofa. / He's sitting on the couch.

As discussed in Chapter 11, during the Norman occupation of England, many French words were imported into English. As a result, English contains many synonymous pairs consisting of a word with a Germanic root and another with a Latin root such as:

manly	virile
heal	recuperate
send	transmit
go down	descend

Words that are opposite in meaning are **antonyms**. There are several kinds of antonymy. There are complementary pairs:

alive/dead   present/absent   awake/asleep

They are complementary in that *alive = not dead* and *dead = not alive*, and so on.
There are **gradable pairs** of antonyms:

big/small   hot/cold   fast/slow   happy/sad

The meaning of adjectives in gradable pairs is related to the object they modify. The words do not provide an absolute scale. For example, we know that "a small elephant" is much bigger than "a large mouse." *Fast* is faster when applied to an airplane than to a car.

Another characteristic of certain pairs of gradable antonyms is that one is **marked** and the other **unmarked**. The unmarked member is the one used in questions of degree. We ask, ordinarily, "How *high* is the mountain?" (not "How low is it?"). We answer "Ten thousand feet high" but never "Ten thousand feet low," except humorously or ironically. Thus *high* is the unmarked member of *high/low*. Similarly, *tall* is the unmarked member of *tall/short*, *fast* the unmarked member of *fast/slow*, and so on.

Another kind of opposite involves pairs like

give/receive   buy/sell   teacher/pupil

They are called **relational opposites**, and they display symmetry in their meaning. If X *gives* Y to Z, then Z *receives* Y from X. If X is Y's *teacher*, then Y is X's *pupil*. Pairs of words ending in -*er* and -*ee* are usually relational opposites. If Mary is Bill's *employer*, then Bill is Mary's *employee*.

Some words are their own antonyms. These "autoantonyms" are words such as *cleave* "to split apart" or "to cling together" and *dust* "to remove something" or "to spread something," as in dusting furniture or dusting crops. Antonymic pairs that are pronounced the same but spelled differently are similar to autoantonyms: *raise* and *raze* are one such pair.

In English there are several ways to form antonyms. You can add the prefix *un*-:

likely/unlikely   able/unable   fortunate/unfortunate

or you can add *non*-:

entity/nonentity   conformist/nonconformist

or you can add *in*-:

tolerant/intolerant   discreet/indiscreet   decent/indecent

These strategies occasionally backfire, however. *Loosen* and *unloosen; flammable* and *inflammable*; *valuable* and *invaluable*, and a few other antiautonyms actually have the same or nearly the same meaning.

Other lexical relations include homonyms, polysemy, and hyponyms.

Words like *bear* and *bare* are **homonyms** (also called **homophones**). Homonyms are words that have different meanings but are pronounced the same, and may or may not be spelled the same. *To, too,* and *two* are homonyms despite their spelling differences. The three uses of *trunk(s)* illustrated in the cartoon are also homonyms.

Homonyms can create ambiguity. The sentence:

I'll meet you by the bank.

may mean "I'll meet you by the financial institution" or "I'll meet you by the riverside."

Homonyms are good candidates for humor as well as for confusion, as illustrated in the following passages from *Alice Adventures in Wonderland.*

"How is bread made?"

"I know *that!*" Alice cried eagerly.

"You take some flour—"

"Where do you pick the flower?" the White Queen asked. "In a garden, or in the hedges?"

"Well, it isn't *picked* at all," Alice explained; "it's ground—"

"How many acres of ground?" said the White Queen.

Or the following:

> "Mine is a long and sad tale!" said the Mouse, turning to Alice and sighing.
>
> "It is a long tail, certainly," said Alice, looking with wonder at the Mouse's tail, "but why do you call it sad?"

The humor of these passages is based on the different sets of homonyms: *flower* and *flour* and the two meanings of *ground*. Alice means *ground* as the past tense of *grind*, whereas the White Queen is interpreting *ground* to mean "earth." In the second passage the homonyms *tale* and *tail* create the confusion.

When a word has multiple meanings that are related conceptually or historically, it is said to be **polysemous** (polly-seamus). For example, the word *diamond* referring to a geometric shape and also to a baseball field that has that shape is polysemous. Open a dictionary of English to any page and you will find words with more than one definition (e.g., *guard, finger, and overture*). Each of these words is polysemous because each has several related meanings.

Speakers of English know that the words *red, white*, and *blue* are color words. Similarly, *lion, tiger, leopard,* and *lynx* are all felines. Such sets of words are called **hyponyms**. The relationship of *hyponymy* is between the more general term such as *color* and the more specific instances of it such as *red*. Thus *red* is a hyponym of *color*, and *lion* is a hyponym of *feline*; or equivalently, *color* has the hyponym *red* and *feline* has the hyponym *lion*.

A **metonym** is a word that substitutes for an object the name of an attribute or concept associated with that object. The use of *crown* for *king*, or for the government ruled by a king, is an example of metonymy. So is the use of *brass* to refer to military leaders. Metonyms are often employed by the news services. Sportswriters are especially adept, using *gridiron* to refer to football; *diamond* for baseball; *ice* for hockey; *turf* for horseracing; and so on. Metonyms for governments such as *Kremlin, Whitehall, Washington,* and *Baghdad* are commonplace. Metonyms need not be a single word. *Madison Avenue* is a metonym referring to the advertising industry; *Scotland Yard* refers to the Criminal Investigation Department in the United Kingdom. The association is that the Metropolitan Police were once housed in an area of London called Great Scotland Yard.

Semantic Features

In the previous sections we discussed word meaning in relation to objects in the world, and this permitted us to develop a truth-based semantics. We also explored the meaning of words in relation to other words. But it is also possible to look for a more basic set of **semantic features** or properties that are part of word meanings and that reflect our intuitions about what words mean.

Decomposing the meanings of words into semantic features can clarify how certain words relate to other words. For example, the basic property of antonyms is that they share all but one semantic feature. We know that *big* and *red* are not antonyms because they have too few semantic features in common. They are both adjectives, but *big* has a semantic feature "about size," whereas *red* has a semantic feature "about color." On the other hand, *buy/sell* are relational opposites because both contain a semantic feature like "change in location or possession," differing only in the direction of the change.

Semantic features are thought to be the conceptual elements by which a person understands the meanings of words and sentence. Consider, for example, the sentence:

The assassin killed Thwacklehurst.

If the word *assassin* is in your mental dictionary, you know that it was some *person* who murdered some *important person* named Thwacklehurst. Your knowledge of the meaning of *assassin* tells you that an animal did not do the killing, and that Thwacklehurst was not a little old man who owned a tobacco shop. Knowledge of *assassin* includes knowing that the individual to whom that word refers is human, is a murderer, and is a killer of important people. These pieces of information, then, are some of the semantic features of the word on which speakers of the language agree. The meaning of all nouns, verbs, adjectives, and adverbs—the content words—and even some of the function words such as *with* and *over* can at least partially be specified by such properties.

EVIDENCE FOR SEMANTIC FEATURES

Semantic properties are not directly observable. Their existence must be inferred from linguistic evidence. One source of such evidence is the speech errors, or "slips of the tongue," that we all produce. Consider the following unintentional word substitutions that some speakers have actually spoken.

Intended Utterance	Actual Utterance (Error)
bridge of the nose	bridge of the neck
when my gums bled	when my tongues bled
he came too late	he came too early
Mary was young	Mary was early
the lady with the dachshund	the lady with the Volkswagen
that's a horse of another color	that's a horse of another race
he has to pay her alimony	he has to pay her rent

These errors and thousands of others that have been collected and catalogued reveal that the incorrectly substituted words are not random substitutions but share some semantic feature with the intended words. *Nose, neck, gums*, and *tongues* are all "body parts" or "parts of the head." *Young, early*, and *late* are related to "time." *Dachshund* and *Volkswagen* are both "German" and "small." The common semantic features of *color* and *race* and of *alimony* and *rent* are rather obvious.

The semantic properties that describe the linguistic meaning of a word should not be confused with other nonlinguistic properties, such as physical properties. Scientists know that water is composed of hydrogen and oxygen, but such knowledge is not part of a word's meaning. We know that water is an essential ingredient of lemonade and baths. We don't need to know any of these things, though, to know what the word *water* means, and to be able to use and understand this word in a sentence.

SEMANTIC FEATURES AND GRAMMAR

Further evidence that words are composed of smaller bits of meaning is that semantic features interact with different aspects of grammar, such as the morphology or syntax. These effects show up in both nouns and verbs.

"Tumbleweeds" © Tom K. Ryan. Reprinted with permission of North America Syndicate.

Semantic Features of Nouns The same semantic feature may be shared by many words. "Female" is a semantic feature, sometimes indicated by the bound suffix *-ess,* that makes up part of the meaning of nouns such as:

tigress	hen	aunt	maiden
doe	mare	debutante	widow
ewe	vixen	girl	woman

The words in the last two columns are also distinguished by the semantic feature "human," which is also found in:

doctor	dean	professor	teenager
bachelor	parent	baby	child

Another part of the meaning of the words *baby* and *child* is that they are "young." (We will continue to indicate words by using *italics* and semantic features by double quotes.) The word *father* has the properties "male" and "adult" as do *uncle* and *bachelor*.

In some languages, though not English, nouns occur with **classifiers**, grammatical morphemes that mark their semantic class. In Swahili, for example, a noun that has the semantic feature "human" is marked with a prefix *m-* if singular and *wa-* if plural, as in *mtoto* "child" and *watoto* "children." On the other hand, a noun that has the feature "human artifact," such as *bed, chair*, or *knife*, is marked with the classifiers *ki* if singular and *vi* if plural, for example, *kiti* "chair" and *viti* "chairs."

Semantic properties may have syntactic effects. For example, the kinds of determiners that a noun may occur with are controlled by whether it is a "count" noun or a "mass" noun.

Consider these data:

I have two dogs.	*I have two rice(s).
I have a dog.	*I have a rice.
*I have dog.	I have rice.
He has many dogs.	*He has many rice(s).
*He has much dogs.	He has much rice.

Count nouns can be enumerated and pluralized—*one potato, two potatoes*. They may be preceded by the indefinite determiner *a*, and by the quantifier *many* as in *many potatoes*, but not by *much*, **much potato*. They must also occur with a determiner of some kind. Nouns such as *rice, water,* and *milk*, which cannot be enumerated or pluralized, are **mass nouns**. They cannot be preceded by *a* or *many*, and they can occur with the quantifier *much* or without any determiner at all. The count/mass distinction captures the fact that speakers have judgments about the grammaticality of different determiner types with different nouns. Without it we could not describe these differences.

Generally, the count/mass distinction corresponds to the difference between discrete objects and homogeneous substances. But it would be incorrect to say that this distinction is grounded in human perception, because different languages may treat the same object differently. For example, in English the words *hair, furniture,* and *spaghetti* are mass counts. We say *Some hair is curly, Much furniture is poorly made, John loves spaghetti.* In Italian, however, these words are count nouns, as illustrated in the following sentences:

Ivano ha mangiato molti spaghetti ieri sera.
Ivano ate many spaghettis last evening.
Piero ha comprato un mobile.
Piero bought a furniture.
Luisella ha pettinato i suoi capelli.
Luisella combed her hairs.

We would have to assume a radical form of linguistic determinism (remember the Sapir-Whorf hypothesis from chapter 1) to say that Italian and English speakers have different perceptions of hair, furniture, and spaghetti. It is more reasonable to assume that languages can differ to some extent in the semantic features they assign to words with the same referent, somewhat independently of the way they conceptualize that referent. Even within a particular language we can have different words—count and mass—to describe the same object or substance. For example, in English we have *shoes* (count) and *footwear* (mass), *coins* (count) and *change* (mass).

Semantic Features of Verbs Verbs can also be broken down into semantic features. For example, "cause" is a feature of verbs such as *darken, kill, uglify,* and so on.

darken	cause to become dark
kill	cause to die
uglify	cause to become ugly

"B.C." reprinted by permission of John L. Hart FLP and Creators Syndicate, Inc.

"Go" is a feature of verbs that mean a change in location or possession, such as *swim, crawl, throw, fly, give,* or *buy*:

Jack swims.
The baby crawled under the table.
The boy threw the ball over the fence.
John gave Mary a beautiful engagement ring.

Words like *swim* have an additional feature like "in liquid," while *crawl* is "close to a surface."

"Become" is a feature expressing the end state of the action of certain verbs. For example, the verb *break* can be broken down into the following components of meaning: "cause" to "become" broken.

The humor of the cartoon at the head of this section is that the verb *roll over* has a specific semantic feature, something like "activity about the longest axis." The snake's attempt to roll about its shortest axis indicates trouble with semantic features.

Verbal features, like features on nouns, may have syntactic consequences. For example, verbs can either describe **events**, such as *John kissed Mary/John ate oysters,* or **states**, such as *John knows Mary/John likes oysters.* The eventive/stative difference is mirrored in the syntax. Eventive sentences sound natural when passivized, when expressed progressively, when used imperatively, and with certain adverbs:

Eventives

Mary was kissed by John.	Oysters were eaten by John.
John is kissing Mary.	John is eating oysters.
Kiss Mary!	Eat oysters!
John deliberately kissed Mary.	John deliberately ate oysters.

The stative sentences seem peculiar, if not ungrammatical or anomalous, when cast in the same form. (The preceding "?" indicates the strangeness.)

Statives

?Mary is known by John.	?Oysters are liked by John.
?John is knowing Mary.	?John is liking oysters.
?Know Mary!	?Like oysters!
?John deliberately knows Mary.	?John deliberately likes oysters.

Negation is a particularly interesting component of the meaning of some verbs. Expressions such as *ever, anymore, budge an inch,* and many more are ungrammatical in certain simple affirmative sentences, but grammatical in corresponding negative ones. Such expressions are called **negative polarity items** because a negative feature elsewhere in the sentence allows them to appear. Consider these data:

*John thinks that he'll ever fly a plane anymore.
John doesn't think that he'll ever fly a plane anymore.
*John hopes that he'll ever fly a plane anymore.
John doubts that he'll ever fly a plane anymore.
John despairs that he'll ever fly a plane anymore.

This suggests that verbs such as *doubt* and *despair* have negation as a component of their meaning, for example "think that not" for *doubt,* and "has no hope" for *despair.*

The negative feature in the verb allows the negative polarity item to occur grammatically in this case without the overt presence of *not*.

Argument Structure

Verbs differ in terms of the number and types of NPs they can take as complements. As we noted in Chapter 4, transitive verbs such as *find, hit, chase*, and so on take, or c-select, a direct object complement, whereas intransitive verbs like *dance* or *sleep* do not take a complement at all. Ditransitive verbs such as *give* or *throw* take two object complements as in *John threw Mary a ball*. In addition, most verbs take a subject. The various NPs that occur with a verb are its **arguments**. Thus intransitive verbs have one argument: the subject; transitive verbs have two arguments: the subject and direct object; ditransitive verbs have three arguments: the subject, direct object, and indirect object. The **argument structure** of a verb is part of its meaning and is included in its lexical entry.

The verb not only determines the number of arguments in a sentence, but it also limits the semantic properties of both its subject and its complements. For example, *find* and *sleep* require (s-select) animate subjects. Thus the famous example of *colorless green ideas sleep furiously* is semantically anomalous because ideas (colorless or not) are not animate. Components of a verb's meaning can also be relevant to the choice of complements it can take. For example, the verbs in (1) and (3) can take two objects while those in (2) and (4) cannot.

1. John threw/tossed/kicked/flung the boy the ball.
2. *John pushed/pulled/lifted/hauled the boy the ball.
3. Mary faxed/radioed/emailed/phoned Helen the news.
4. *Mary murmured/mumbled/muttered/shrieked Helen the news.

Although all the verbs in (1) and (2) are verbs of motion, they differ in how the force of the motion is applied: the verbs in (1) involve a single quick motion whereas those in (2) involve an extended use of force. Similarly, the verbs in (3) and (4) are all verbs of communication, but their meanings differ in the means by which the message is communicated; those in (3) involve an external apparatus whereas the meaning of the verbs in (4) includes the type of voice used. Finally, ditransitive verbs have "transfer direct object to indirect object" in their meaning, which amplifies the "go" feature. In (1) the ball is transferred to the boy. In (3) the news is transferred, or leastwise transmitted, to Helen. The ditransitive verbs *give, write, send, throw*, and so on all have this property. Even when the transference is not overt, it may be inferred. Thus in *John baked Mary a cake*, there is an inferred transfer of the cake from John to Mary. These subtle aspects of meaning not only affect the argument structure of the verbs, but reveal some relationships between syntax and semantics.

THEMATIC ROLES

The NP subject of a sentence and the arguments in the VP are semantically related in various ways to the verb. The relations depend on the meaning of the particular verb. For example, the NP *the boy* in the sentence:

1. The boy rolled   a red ball.
      agent   theme

"B.C." © 1986 Creators Syndicate, Inc. Reprinted by permission of John L. Hart FLP and Creators Syndicate, Inc.

is the "doer" of the rolling action also called the **agent**. The NP *a red ball* is the **theme** or the "undergoer" of the rolling action. Relations such as agent and theme and others we will mention shortly are called **thematic roles**. Thematic roles express the kind of relation that holds between the arguments of the verb and the type of situation that the verb describes.

A further example is the sentence:

2. The boy threw the red ball to the girl.
    agent   theme   goal

The subject of *throw* is also an agent, so that in *The boy threw the red ball to the girl* "the boy" performs the action. *The red ball* is the theme and *the girl* bears the thematic role of **goal**, that is, the endpoint of a change in location or possession. The verb phrase is interpreted to mean that the theme of *throw* ends up in the position of the goal. Other thematic roles are **source**, where the action originates; **instrument**, the means used to accomplish the action; and **experiencer**, one receiving sensory input.

The particular thematic roles assigned by a verb can be traced back to components of the verb's meaning. For example, we noted earlier that verbs such as *throw, buy, fly* contain a feature "go" expressing a change in location or possession. The feature "go" is thus linked to the presence of the thematic roles of theme, source, and goal.

Thematic role assignment is also connected to syntactic structure. In the sentence in (2) the role of theme is assigned to the direct object *the ball* and the role of goal to the indirect object *the girl*. Verb pairs such as *sell* and *buy* both involve the feature "go." They are therefore linked to a thematic role of theme, which is assigned to the direct object, as in the following sentences:

3. John sold the book to Mary.
    agent   theme   goal

4. Mary bought the book from John.
    agent   theme   source

In addition, *sell* is linked to the presence of a goal (the recipient or endpoint of the transfer), and *buy* to the presence of a source (the initiator of the transfer). Thus, *buy/sell* are relational opposites because both contain the semantic feature "go" (the transfer of goods or services) and they differ only in the direction of transfer, that is, whether the indirect object is a source or goal. Thematic roles are not assigned to arguments randomly. There is a connection between the meaning of a verb and the syntactic structure of sentences containing the verb.

Our knowledge of verbs includes their syntactic category, which arguments they select, and the thematic roles they assign to their arguments.

Thematic roles are the same in sentences that are paraphrases.

1. The dog bit the stick. / The stick was bitten by the dog.
2. The trainer gave the dog a treat. / The trainer gave a treat to the dog.

In (1) *the dog* is the agent and *the stick* is the theme. In (2) *the treat* is the theme and *the dog* is the goal.

Thematic roles may remain the same in sentences that are *not* paraphrases, as in the following instances:

The boy opened the door with the key.
The key opened the door.
The door opened.

In all three of these sentences, *the door* is the theme, the object that is opened. In the first two sentences, *the key*, despite its different structural positions, retains the thematic role of instrument. The semantics of the three sentences, which speakers of English know, is determined by the meaning of the verb *open*.

Pragmatics

"Shoe" by Gary Brookins/Chris Cassatt. Copyright 1991 Tribune Media Services. Reprinted with permission.

Pragmatics is concerned with the interpretation of linguistic meaning in context. Two kinds of contexts are relevant. The first is *linguistic* context—the **discourse** that precedes the phrase or sentence to be interpreted; the second is *situational* context—virtually everything nonlinguistic in the environment of the speaker.

Speakers know how to combine words and phrases to form sentences, and they also know how to combine sentences into a larger discourse to express complex thoughts and ideas. **Discourse analysis** is concerned with the broad speech units comprising multiple sentences. It involves questions of style, appropriateness, cohesiveness, rhetorical force, topic/subtopic structure, differences between written and spoken discourse, as well as grammatical properties.

Within a discourse, preceding sentences affect the meaning of sentences that follow them in various ways. For example, the reference or meaning of pronouns often depends on prior discourse. As well, prior discourse often disambiguates words like *bank* in that the discussion may be about rafting on a river or interest rates.

Situational context, on the other hand, is the nonlinguistic environment in which a sentence or discourse happens. It is the context that allows speakers to seamlessly, even unknowingly, interpret questions like *Can you pass the salt?* as requests to carry out a certain action. Situational context includes the speaker, hearer, and any third parties present, along with their beliefs and their beliefs about what the others believe. It includes the physical environment, the subject of conversation, the time of day, and so on, ad infinitum. Almost any imaginable extralinguistic factor may, under appropriate circumstances, influence the way language is interpreted.

Pronouns provide a good way to illustrate the two kinds of contexts—linguistic and situational—that affect meaning.

Pronouns

Pronouns are lexical items that get their meaning from other NPs in the sentence or in the larger discourse. In other words, pronouns are sensitive to syntax and context for their interpretation. We'll take up syntactic matters first.

PRONOUNS AND SYNTAX

"Hi and Lois" © King Features Syndicate. Reprinted with permission of King Features Syndicate.

There are different types of pronouns. **Reflexive pronouns** are pronouns such as *himself* and *themselves*. In English, reflexive pronouns always get their meaning by referring back to an NP antecedent in the same clause, as illustrated in the following examples: (The underlining indicates that the reflexive refers back to the NP.)

1. *Jane* bit herself.
2. *Jane* said that Bill bit herself.
3. *Herself left.

In (1) the NP *Jane* and *herself* are in the same S; in (2) *herself* is in the embedded sentence *Bill bit herself* and hence too far from the antecedent *Jane*. In (3) *herself* has no antecedent at all, hence nothing to get its meaning from. The flouting of the rule that requires reflexives to have antecedents gives rise to the humor in the cartoon.

Languages also have pronouns that are not reflexive, such as *he, she, us, him, her, you*, and so on, which we will simply refer to as pronouns. Pronouns also depend on other elements for their meaning, but the syntactic conditions on pronouns are different from those on reflexives. Pronouns cannot refer to an antecedent in the same clause, but they are free to refer to an NP outside this clause, as illustrated in the following sentences: (Again, the underlining indicates the interpretation in which the pronoun refers back to the NP.)

4. *John believes him.
5. John believes that he is a genius.

The sentence in (4) is ungrammatical relative to the interpretation because *him* cannot take *John* as it antecedent. In (5), however, the pronoun *he* can be interpreted as *John*. Notice that in both sentences it is possible for the pronouns to refer to some other person not mentioned in the sentence (e.g., Pete or Harry). In this case the pronoun gets it reference from the larger discourse or nonlinguistic context.

PRONOUNS AND DISCOURSE

The 911 operator, trying to get a description of the gunman, asked, "What kind of clothes does he have on?"

Mr. Morawski, thinking the question pertained to Mr. McClure [the victim, who lay dying of a gunshot wound], answered, "He has a bloody shirt with blue jeans, purple striped shirt."

The 911 operator then gave police that description [the victim's] of a gunman.

THE NEWS AND OBSERVER, *Raleigh, North Carolina, 1/21/89*

Pronouns may be used in place of noun phrases from prior discourse or may be used to refer to entities presumably known to the participants of a discourse. When that presumption fails, miscommunication such as the one at the head of this section may result.

In a discourse, prior linguistic context plays a primary role in pronoun interpretation. In the following discourse:

It seems that the man loves the woman.
Many people think he loves her.

the most natural interpretation of *her* is "the woman" referred to in the first sentence, whoever she happens to be. But it is also possible for *her* to refer to a different person, perhaps one indicated with a gesture. In such a case *her* would be spoken with added emphasis:

Many people think he loves *her!*

Similar remarks apply to the reference of *he*, which is ordinarily coreferential with *the man*, but not necessarily so. Again, intonation and emphasis would provide clues.

When semantic rules and contextual interpretation determine that a pronoun is coreferential with an NP, we say that the pronoun is **bound** to that noun phrase antecedent. If *her* in the previous example refers to "the woman," it would be a bound pronoun. Reflexive pronouns are always bound. When a pronoun refers to some object not explicitly mentioned in the discourse, it is said to be **free** or **unbound**. The reference of a free pronoun must ultimately be determined by the situational context.

First- and second-person nonreflexive (*I/we, you*) pronouns are bound to the speaker and hearer, respectively. They therefore depend on the situational context, namely, who is doing the talking and who is being addressed. With third-person pronouns, as in the preceding example, semantic rules permit *her* either to be bound to *the woman*, or to be a free pronoun, referring to some person not explicitly mentioned. The ultimate interpretation is context-dependent.

Referring to the previous discourse, strictly speaking, it would not be ungrammatical if the discourse went this way:

It seems that the man loves the woman.
Many people think the man loves the woman.

However, most people would find that the discourse sounds stilted. Often in discourse, the use of pronouns is a stylistic decision, which is part of pragmatics.

Deixis

"Dennis the Menace" © Hank Ketcham. Reprinted with permission of North America Syndicate.

In all languages, the reference of certain words and expressions relies entirely on the situational context of the utterance, and can only be understood in light of these circumstances. This aspect of pragmatics is called **deixis** (pronounced "dike-sis"). As discussed earlier, the first- and second-person pronouns *I, me, my, mine, we, us, our, you, your, yours* are always deictic because their reference is entirely dependent on context. You must know who the speaker and listener are to interpret them.

Third-person pronouns are deictic if they are *free*. If they are *bound*, their reference is known from linguistic context.

Expressions such as

this person

that man

these women

those children

are also deictic, for they require situational information in order for the listener to make a referential connection and understand what is meant. These examples illustrate **person deixis**. They also show that the **demonstrative articles** like *this* and *that* are deictic.

There is also **time deixis** and **place deixis**. The following examples are all deictic expressions of time:

now	then	tomorrow
this time	that time	seven days ago
two weeks from now	last week	next April

To understand what specific times such expressions refer to, we need to know when the utterance was said. Clearly, *next week* has a different reference when uttered today than a month from today. If you found an undated notice announcing a "BIG SALE NEXT WEEK," you would not know whether the sale had already taken place.

Expressions of place deixis require contextual information about the place of the utterance, as shown by the following examples:

here	there	this place
that place	this ranch	those towers over there
this city	these parks	yonder mountains

The "Dennis the Menace" cartoon at the beginning of this section illustrates the confusion that may result if deictic expressions are misinterpreted.

Directional terms such as

| before/behind | left/right | front/back |

are deictic insofar as you need to know the orientation in space of the conversational participants to know their reference. In Japanese the verb *kuru* "come" can only be used for motion toward the place of utterance. A Japanese speaker cannot call up a friend and ask

May I *kuru* to your house?

as you might, in English, ask "May I come to your house?" The correct verb is *iku*, "go," which indicates motion away from the place of utterance. In Japanese these verbs thus have a deictic aspect to their meaning.

Deixis abounds in language use and marks one of the boundaries of semantics and pragmatics. Deictic expressions such as *I, an hour from now, behind me* have meaning to the extent that their referents are determined in a regular way as a function of the situation of use. (*I*, for example, picks out the speaker.) To complete their meaning, to determine their *reference*, it is necessary to know the situational context.

More on Situational Context

> Depending on inflection, *ah bon* [in French] can express shock, disbelief, indifference, irritation, or joy.
>
> PETER MAYLE, Toujours Provence

Much discourse is telegraphic. Verb phrases are not specifically mentioned, entire clauses are left out, direct objects disappear, pronouns abound. Yet, people still understand one another, and part of the reason is that rules of grammar and rules of discourse combine with contextual knowledge to fill in what's missing and make the discourse cohere. Much of the contextual knowledge is knowledge of who is speaking, who is listening, what objects are being discussed, and general facts about the world we live in—what we have been calling **situational context**.

Often what we say is not literally what we mean. When we ask at the dinner table if someone "can pass the salt" we are not querying their ability to do so, we are requesting that they do so. If I say "you're standing on my foot," I am not making idle conversation; I am asking you to stand somewhere else. We say "it's cold in here" to convey "shut the window," or "turn up the heat," or "let's leave," or a dozen other things that depend on the real-world situation at the time of speaking.

In the following sections, we will look at several ways that real-world context influences and interacts with meaning.

MAXIMS OF CONVERSATION

> Though this be madness, yet there is method in't.
>
> WILLIAM SHAKESPEARE, Hamlet

Speakers recognize when a series of sentences "hangs together" or when it is disjointed. The following discourse (*Hamlet,* Act II, Scene II), which gave rise to Polonius's aforementioned remark, does not seem quite right—it is not coherent.

Polonius: What do you read, my lord?

Hamlet: Words, words, words.

Polonius: What is the matter, my lord?

Hamlet: Between who?

Polonius: I mean, the matter that you read, my lord.

Hamlet: Slanders, sir: for the satirical rogue says here that old men have gray beards, that their faces are wrinkled, their eyes purging thick amber and plum-tree gum, and that they have a plentiful lack of wit, together with most weak hams: all which, sir, though I most powerfully and potently believe, yet I hold it not honesty to have it thus set down; for yourself, sir, should grow old as I am, if like a crab you could go backward.

Hamlet, who is feigning insanity, refuses to answer Polonius's questions "in good faith." He has violated certain conversational conventions, or **maxims of conversation**. These maxims were first discussed by the British philosopher H. Paul Grice and are therefore sometimes called Gricean Maxims. One such maxim, the **maxim of**

quantity, states that a speaker's contribution to the discourse should be as informative as is required—neither more nor less. Hamlet has violated this maxim in both directions. In answering "Words, words, words" to the question of what he is reading, he is providing too little information. His final remark goes to the other extreme in providing too much information.

He also violates the **maxim of relevance** when he "misinterprets" the question about the reading matter as a matter between two individuals.

The run-on nature of Hamlet's final remark, a violation of the **maxim of manner**, is another source of incoherence. This effect is increased in the final sentence by the somewhat bizarre metaphor that compares growing younger with walking backward, a violation of the **maxim of quality**, which requires sincerity and truthfulness.

Here is a summary of the four conversational maxims, parts of the broad **Cooperative Principle**.

Name of Maxim	Description of Maxim
Quantity	Say neither more nor less than the discourse requires.
Relevance	Be relevant.
Manner	Be brief and orderly; avoid ambiguity and obscurity.
Quality	Do not lie; do not make unsupported claims.

Unless speakers (like Hamlet) are being deliberately uncooperative, they adhere to these maxims and to other conversational principles, and assume others do too.

Bereft of context, if one man says (truthfully) to another "I have never slept with your wife," that would be grounds for provocation because that very topic of conversation should be unnecessary, a violation of the maxim of quantity.

Asking an able-bodied person at the dinner table, "Can you pass the salt?" if answered literally, would force the responder into stating the obvious, also a violation of the maxim of quantity. To avoid this, the person asked seeks a reason for the question, and deduces that the asker would like to have the salt shaker.

The maxim of relevance explains how saying "It's cold in here" to a person standing by an open, drafty window might be interpreted as a request to close it, or else why make the remark to that particular person in the first place?

Conversational conventions such as these allow the various sentence meanings to be sensibly combined into discourse meaning and integrated with context, much as rules of sentence grammar allow word meanings to be sensibly (and grammatically) combined into sentence meaning.

IMPLICATURES

> What does "yet" mean, after all? "I haven't seen *Reservoir Dogs* yet." What does that mean? It means you're going to go, doesn't it?
>
> **NICK HORNBY,** High Fidelity

In conversation we sometimes infer or conclude based not only on what was said, but also on assumptions about what the speaker is trying to achieve. In the examples just discussed—*It's cold in here, Can you please pass the salt,* and *I have never slept with your wife*—the person spoken to derives a meaning that is not the literal meaning of the sentences. In the first case he assumes that he is being asked to close the window;

in the second case he knows he's not being questioned but rather asked to pass the salt; and in the third case he will understand exactly the opposite of what is said, namely that the speaker has slept with his wife.

Such inferences are known as **implicatures**. Implicatures are deductions that are not made strictly on the basis of the content expressed in the discourse. Rather, they are made in accordance with the conversational maxims, taking into account both the linguistic meaning of the utterance as well as the particular circumstances in which the utterance is made.

Consider the following conversation:

Speaker A: Smith doesn't have any girlfriends these days.
Speaker B: He has been going to Dallas a lot lately.

The implicature is that Smith has a girlfriend in Dallas. The reasoning is that B's answer would be irrelevant unless it contributed information related to A's question. We assume speakers try to be cooperative. So it is fair to conclude that B uttered the second sentence because the reason that A goes to Dallas is that he has a girlfriend there.

Because implicatures are derived on the basis of assumptions about the speaker that might turn out to be wrong, they can be easily canceled. For this reason A could have responded as follows:

Speaker A: He goes to Dallas to visit his mother who is ill.

Although B's utterance implies that the reason Smith goes to Dallas is to visit his girlfriend, A's response cancels this implicature.

Earlier we spoke about entailment. Recall that a sentence entails another if whenever the first is true, the second is necessarily true. So the sentence *Jack swims beautifully* entails that *Jack swims*. That is, *Jack swims beautifully and Jack doesn't swim* is a contradiction. Unlike implicatures, entailments cannot be canceled. In the previous example, it is an entailment of A's first utterance that Mary is not Smith's girlfriend, because *Smith doesn't have any girlfriends these days and Mary is his girlfriend* is a contradiction. Compare that to *He has been going to Dallas a lot lately and he doesn't have a girlfriend in Dallas,* which is not a contradiction in any situation.

SPEECH ACTS

"Zits" © Zits Partnership. Reprinted with permission of King Features Syndicate.

You can use language to do things. You can use language to make promises, lay bets, issue warnings, christen boats, place names in nomination, offer congratulations, or swear testimony. The theory of **speech acts** describes how this is done.

By saying *I warn you that there is a sheepdog in the closet*, you not only say something, you *warn* someone. Verbs like *bet, promise, warn*, and so on are **performative verbs**. Using them in a sentence (in the first person, present tense) adds something extra over and above the statement.

There are hundreds of performative verbs in every language. The following sentences illustrate their usage:

> I *bet* you five dollars the Yankees win.
> I *challenge* you to a match.
> I *dare* you to step over this line.
> I *fine* you $100 for possession of oregano.
> I *move* that we adjourn.
> I *nominate* Batman for mayor of Gotham City.
> I *promise* to improve.
> I *resign!*
> I *pronounce* you husband and wife.

In all of these sentences, the speaker is the subject (i.e., the sentences are in first person), who by uttering the sentence is accomplishing some additional action, such as daring, nominating, or resigning. In addition, all of these sentences are affirmative, declarative, and in the present tense. They are typical **performative sentences**.

An informal test to see whether a sentence contains a performative verb is to begin it with the words *I hereby. . . .* Only performative sentences sound right when begun this way. Compare *I hereby apologize to you* with the somewhat strange *I hereby know you*. The first is generally taken as an act of apologizing. In all of the examples given, insertion of *hereby* would be acceptable. Snoopy in the following cartoon knows that *hereby* is used in performative sentences. The humor comes when he uses it for the nonperformative verb *despise*.

"Peanuts" © United Feature Syndicate, Inc. Reprinted with permission.

In studying speech acts, the importance of context is evident. In some situations *Band practice, my house, 6 to 8* is a reminder, but the same sentence may be a warning in a different context. We call this underlying purpose or the speaker's intention—be it a reminder, a warning, a promise, a threat, or whatever—the **illocutionary force** of a speech act. Because the illocutionary force of a speech act depends on the context of the utterance, speech act theory is a part of pragmatics.

Summary

Knowing a language means to know how to produce and understand the meaning of infinitely many sentences. The study of linguistic meaning is called **semantics**. **Lexical semantics** is concerned with the meanings of morphemes and words; **compositional semantics** with phrases and sentences. The study of how context affects meaning is called **pragmatics**.

Speakers' knowledge of sentence meaning includes knowing the **truth conditions** of declarative sentences; knowing when one sentence **entails** another sentence; knowing when two sentences are **paraphrases** or **contradictory**; knowing when a sentence is a **tautology**, **contradiction**, or **paradox**; and knowing when sentences are ambiguous, among other things. **Compositional semantics** is the building up of phrasal or sentence meaning from the meaning of smaller units by means of **semantic rules**.

There are cases when the meaning of larger units does not follow from the meaning of its parts. **Anomaly** is when the pieces do not fit sensibly together, as in *colorless green ideas sleep furiously;* **metaphors** are sentences that appear to be anomalous, but to which a meaningful concept can be attached, such as *time is money*; **idioms** are fixed expressions whose meaning is not compositional but rather must be learned as a whole unit, such as *kick the bucket* meaning "to die."

The meaning of words may be in part the objects referred to by the word, or its **reference**, but often there is more to a word than the object it denotes, and that part of meaning is called **sense**. The reference (today) of *the president* is George W. Bush, but the sense of the expression is "highest executive office." Some expressions have reference but little sense such as proper names, and some have sense but no reference such as *the present king of France.*

Words are related in various ways. They may be **synonyms**, various kinds of **antonyms** such as **gradable pairs** and **relational opposites**, or **homonyms**, words pronounced the same but with different meanings such as *bare* and *bear.*

Part of the meaning of words may be described by **semantic features** such as "female," "young," "cause," or "go." Nouns may have the feature "count," wherein they may be enumerated (one potato, two potatoes), or "mass," in which enumeration may require contextual interpretation (*one milk, *two milks, perhaps meaning "one glass or quart or portion of milk"). Some verbs have the feature of being "eventive" while others are "stative." The semantic feature of negation is found in many words and is evidenced by the occurrence of **negative polarity** items (e.g., *John doubts that Mary gives a hoot*, but **John thinks that Mary gives a hoot*).

Verbs have various **argument structures**, which describe the NPs that may occur with particular verbs. For example, intransitive verbs take only an NP subject, whereas **ditransitive** verbs take an NP subject, an NP direct object, and an NP indirect object. **Thematic roles** describe the semantic relations between a verb and its NP arguments. Some thematic roles are **agent**: the doer of an action; **theme**: the recipient of an action; and **goal**, **source**, **instrument**, and **experiencer**.

The general study of how context affects linguistic interpretation is *pragmatics.* Context may be *linguistic*—what was previously spoken or written—or *knowledge of the world,* including the speech situation, what we've called **situational context**.

Discourse consists of several sentences, including exchanges between speakers. Pragmatics is important when interpreting discourse, for example, in determining whether a pronoun in one sentence has the same referent as a noun phrase in another sentence.

Deictic terms such as *you, there, now, the other side* require knowledge of the situation (person spoken to, place, time, spatial orientation) of the utterance to be interpreted referentially.

Speakers of all languages adhere to various **cooperative principles** for communicating sincerely called **maxims of conversation**. Such maxims as "be relevant" or "say neither more nor less than the discourse requires" permit speakers to make indirect interpretations of such sentences as "It's cold in here" to infer "shut the windows" or "turn up the thermostat." The inferences that accompany an utterance in a situation where the maxims of conversation are being observed, such as inferring "pass the salt!" from "Can you pass the salt?" are known as **implicatures**. Implicatures are like entailments in that their truth follows from sentences of the discourse, but unlike entailments, which are necessarily true, implicatures may be cancelled by information added later.

The theory of **speech acts** tells us that people use language to do things such as lay bets, issue warnings, or nominate candidates. By using the words "I nominate Bill Smith," you may accomplish an act of nomination that allows Bill Smith to run for office. Verbs that "do things" are called **performative verbs**. The speaker's intent in making an utterance is known as **illocutionary force**. In the case of performative verbs, the illocutionary force is mentioned overtly. In other cases it must be determined from context.

References for Further Reading

Austin, J. L. 1962. *How to Do Things with Words*. Cambridge, MA: Harvard University Press.

Brown, G., and G. Yule. 1983. *Discourse Analysis*. Cambridge, England: Cambridge University Press.

Chierchia, G., and S. McConnell-Ginet. 2000. *Meaning and Grammar*, 2nd edition. Cambridge, MA: MIT Press.

Davidson, D., and G. Harman, eds. 1972. *Semantics of Natural Languages*. Dordrecht, The Netherlands: Reidel.

Fraser, B. 1995. *An Introduction to Pragmatics*. Oxford: Blackwell Publishers.

Green, G. M. 1989. *Pragmatics and Natural Language Understanding*. Hillsdale, NJ: Lawrence Erlbaum Associates.

Grice, H. P. 1989. "Logic and Conversation." Reprinted in *Studies in the Way of Words*. Cambridge, MA: Harvard University Press.

Jackendoff, R. 1993. *Patterns in the Mind*. New York: HarperCollins.

_____. 1983. *Semantics and Cognition*. Cambridge, MA: MIT Press.

Lakoff, G. 1987. *Women, Fire, and Dangerous Things: What Categories Reveal about the Mind*. Chicago: University of Chicago Press.

Lakoff, G., and M. Johnson. 1980. *Metaphors We Live By*. Chicago: University of Chicago Press.

Larson, R., and G. Segal. 1995. *Knowledge of Meaning*. Cambridge, MA: MIT Press.

Levinson, S. C. 1983. *Pragmatics*. Cambridge, England: Cambridge University Press.

Lyons, J. 1995. *Linguistic Semantics: An Introduction*. Cambridge, England: Cambridge University Press.

Mey, J. L. 2001. *Pragmatics: An Introduction,* 2nd edition. Oxford, England: Blackwell Publishers.

Saeed, J. 2003. *Semantics*, 2nd edition. Oxford, England: Blackwell Publishing.

Searle, J. R. 1969. *Speech Acts: An Essay in the Philosophy of Language*. Cambridge, England: Cambridge University Press.

Exercises

1. (This exercise requires knowledge of elementary set theory.)

   A. Suppose that the reference (meaning) of *swims* is the set of individuals consisting of Anna, Lu, Paul, and Benjamin. For which of the following sentences are the truth conditions produced by Semantic Rule I met?

      a. Anna swims.

      b. Jack swims.

      c. Benjamin swims.

   B. Suppose the reference (meaning) of *loves* is the set consisting of the following pairs of individuals: <Anna, Paul>, <Paul, Benjamin>, <Benjamin, Benjamin>, <Paul, Anna>. According to Semantic Rule II, what is the meaning of the verb phrase:

      a. loves Paul

      b. loves Benjamin

      c. loves Jack

   C. Given the information in (B), for which of the following sentences are the truth conditions produced by Semantic Rule I met?

      a. Paul loves Anna.

      b. Benjamin loves Paul.

      c. Benjamin loves himself.

      d. Anna loves Jack.

   D. **Challenge exercise**: Consider the sentence *Jack kissed Laura*. How would the actions of semantic rules (I) and (II) determine that the sentence is false if it were true that:

      a. Nobody kissed Laura.

      How about if it were true that:

      b. Jack did not kiss Laura, although other men did.

2. The following sentences are either tautologies (analytic), contradictions, or situationally true or false. Write *T* by the tautologies; *C* by the contradictions; and *S* by the other sentences.

   a. Queens are monarchs.

   b. Kings are female.

   c. Kings are poor.

   d. Queens are ugly.

   e. Queens are mothers.

   f. Kings are mothers.

   g. Dogs are four-legged.

   h. Cats are felines.

   i. Cats are stupid.

   j. Dogs are carnivores.

   k. George Washington is George Washington.

   l. George Washington is the first president.

   m. George Washington is male.

   n. Uncles are male.

   o. My aunt is a man.

   p. Witches are wicked.

   q. My brother is a witch.

   r. My sister is an only child.

   s. The evening star isn't the evening star.

   t. The evening star isn't Venus.

   u. Babies are adults.

   v. Babies can lift one ton.

   w. Puppies are human.

   x. My bachelor friends are all married.

   y. My bachelor friends are all lonely.

   z. Colorless ideas are green.

3. You are in a village in which every man must be shaved, and in which the lone (male) barber shaves all and only the men who do not shave themselves. Formulate a paradox based on this situation.

4. Should the semantic component of the grammar account for whatever a speaker means when uttering any meaningful expression? Defend your viewpoint.

5. A. The following sentences may be lexically or structurally ambiguous, or both. Provide paraphrases showing you comprehend all the meanings.

   Example: I saw him walking by the bank.

   Meaning 1: I saw him and he was walking by the bank of the river.
   Meaning 2: I saw him and he was walking by the financial institution.
   Meaning 3: I was walking by the bank of the river when I saw him.
   Meaning 4: I was walking by the financial institution when I saw him.

   a. We laughed at the colorful ball.

   b. He was knocked over by the punch.

   c. The police were urged to stop drinking by the fifth.

   d. I said I would file it on Thursday.

   e. I cannot recommend visiting professors too highly.

   f. The license fee for pets owned by senior citizens who have not been altered is $1.50. (Actual notice)

   g. What looks better on a handsome man than a tux? Nothing! (Attributed to Mae West)

    h. Wanted: Man to take care of cow that does not smoke or drink. (Actual notice)

    i. For Sale: Several old dresses from grandmother in beautiful condition. (Actual notice)

    j. Time flies like an arrow. (*Hint*: There are at least four paraphrases, but some of them require imagination.)

B. Do the same thing for the following newspaper headlines:

    k. POLICE BEGIN CAMPAIGN TO RUN DOWN JAYWALKERS

    l. DRUNK GETS NINE MONTHS IN VIOLIN CASE

    m. FARMER BILL DIES IN HOUSE

    n. STUD TIRES OUT

    o. SQUAD HELPS DOG BITE VICTIM

    p. LACK OF BRAINS HINDERS RESEARCH

    q. MINERS REFUSE TO WORK AFTER DEATH

    r. EYE DROPS OFF SHELF

    s. JUVENILE COURT TO TRY SHOOTING DEFENDANT

    t. QUEEN MARY HAVING BOTTOM SCRAPED

6. Explain the semantic ambiguity of the following sentences by providing two or more sentences that paraphrase the multiple meanings. *Example*: "She can't bear children" can mean either "She can't give birth to children" or "She can't tolerate children."

    a. He waited by the bank.

    b. Is he really that kind?

    c. The proprietor of the fish store was the sole owner.

    d. The long drill was boring.

    e. When he got the clear title to the land, it was a good deed.

    f. It takes a good ruler to make a straight line.

    g. He saw that gasoline can explode.

    h. You should see her shop.

    i. Every man loves a woman.

    j. **Challenge exercise**: Bill wants to marry a Norwegian woman.

7. Go on an idiom hunt. In the course of some hours in which you converse or overhear conversations, write down all the idioms that are used. If you prefer, watch the "soaps" or something similar for an hour or two and write down the idioms. Show your parents (or whomever) this book when they find you watching TV and you claim you're doing homework.

8. For each group of words given as follows, state what semantic feature or features distinguish between the classes of (a) words and (b) words. If asked, also indicate a semantic feature that the (a) words and the (b) words share.

Example: (a) widow, mother, sister, aunt, maid

(b) widower, father, brother, uncle, valet
The (a) and (b) words are "human."
The (a) words are "female" and the (b) words are "male."

A. (a) bachelor, man, son, paperboy, pope, chief

(b) bull, rooster, drake, ram
The (a) and (b) words are _____
The (a) words are _____
The (b) words are _____

B. (a) table, stone, pencil, cup, house, ship, car

(b) milk, alcohol, rice, soup, mud
The (a) words are _____
The (b) words are _____

C. (a) book, temple, mountain, road, tractor

(b) idea, love, charity, sincerity, bravery, fear
The (a) words are _____
The (b) words are _____

D. (a) pine, elm, ash, weeping willow, sycamore

(b) rose, dandelion, aster, tulip, daisy
The (a) and (b) words are _____
The (a) words are _____
The (b) words are _____

E. (a) book, letter, encyclopedia, novel, notebook, dictionary

(b) typewriter, pencil, pen, crayon, quill, charcoal, chalk
The (a) words are _____
The (b) words are _____

F. (a) walk, run, skip, jump, hop, swim

(b) fly, skate, ski, ride, cycle, canoe, hang-glide
The (a) and (b) words are _____
The (a) words are _____
The (b) words are _____

G. (a) ask, tell, say, talk, converse

(b) shout, whisper, mutter, drawl, holler
The (a) and (b) words are _____
The (a) words are _____
The (b) words are _____

H. (a) absent – present, alive – dead, asleep – awake, married – single

(b) big – small, cold – hot, sad – happy, slow – fast
The (a) and (b) words are _____
The (a) words are _____
The (b) words are _____

I. (a) alleged, counterfeit, false, putative, accused

(b) red, large, cheerful, pretty, stupid

(*Hint*: Is an alleged murderer always a murderer? Is a pretty girl always a girl?)

The (a) words are _____

The (b) words are _____

9. There are many *-nym* words that describe semantic relations and facts about words and word classes. We mentioned a few in this chapter such as synonyms, antonyms, homonyms, hyponyms, and metonyms. How many more *-nym* words and their meaning can you come up with? Try for five. Ten would be great. Fifteen is possible. (*Hint*: One such *-nym* word was the winning word in the 1997 National Spelling Bee.)

10. There are several kinds of antonymy. By writing a *c, g,* or *r* in column *C*, indicate whether the pairs in columns *A* and *B* are complementary, gradable, or relational opposites.

A	B	C
good	bad	_____
expensive	cheap	_____
parent	offspring	_____
beautiful	ugly	_____
false	true	_____
lessor	lessee	_____
pass	fail	_____
hot	cold	_____
legal	illegal	_____
larger	smaller	_____
poor	rich	_____
fast	slow	_____
asleep	awake	_____
husband	wife	_____
rude	polite	_____

11. For each definition, write in the first blank the word that has that meaning and in the second (and third if present) a differently spelled homonym that has a different meaning.

Example: "A pair": t(*wo*) t(*oo*) t(*o*)

a. "Naked": b _____ b _____
b. "Base metal": l _____ l _____
c. "Worships": p _____ p _____ p _____
d. "Eight bits": b _____ b _____ b _____
e. "One of five senses": s _____ s _____ c _____
f. "Several couples": p _____ p _____ p _____
g. "Not pretty": p _____ p _____
h. "Purity of gold unit": k _____ c _____
i. "A horse's coiffure": m _____ m _____ M _____
j. "Sets loose": f _____ f _____ f _____

12. Here are some proper names of U.S. restaurants. Can you figure out the basis for the name? (This is for fun—don't let yourself be graded.)

   a. Mustard's Last Stand

   b. Aunt Chilada's

   c. Lion on the Beach

   d. Pizza Paul and Mary

   e. Franks for the Memories

   f. Weiner Take All

   g. Dressed to Grill

   h. Deli Beloved

   i. Gone with the Wings

   j. Aunt Chovy's Pizza

   k. Polly Esther's

   l. Dewey, Cheatham & Howe
     (*Hint*: This is also the name of a made-up law firm.)

   m. Thai Me Up Café (truly—it's in L.A.)

   n. Romancing the Cone

13. The following sentences consist of a verb, its noun phrase subject, and various complements and prepositional phrases. Identify the thematic role of each NP by writing the letter *a, t, i, s, g, e* above the noun, standing for *agent, theme, instrument, source, goal, experiencer.*

          a   *t*   *s*   *i*
   Example: The boy took the books from the cupboard with a handcart.

   a. Mary found a ball.

   b. The children ran from the playground to the wading pool.

   c. One of the men unlocked all the doors with a paper clip.

   d. John melted the ice with a blowtorch.

   e. Helen looked for a cockroach.

   f. Helen saw a cockroach.

   g. Helen screamed.

   h. The ice melted.

   i. With a telescope, the boy saw the man.

   j. The farmer loaded hay onto the truck.

   k. The farmer loaded the hay with a pitchfork.

   l. The hay was loaded on the truck by the farmer.

14. Find a complete version of "The Jabberwocky" from *Through the Looking-Glass* by Lewis Carroll. Look up all the nonsense words in a good dictionary and see how many of them are lexical items in English. Note their meaning.

15. In sports and games, many expressions are "performative." By shouting *You're out*, the first base umpire performs an act. Think up a half-dozen or so similar examples and explain their use.

16. A criterion of a performative utterance is whether you can begin it with "I hereby." Notice that if you say sentence (a) aloud, it sounds like a genuine apology, but to say sentence (b) aloud sounds funny because you cannot perform an act of knowing:

    a. I hereby apologize to you.

    b. I hereby know you.

    Determine which of the following sentences are performative sentences by inserting "hereby" and seeing whether they sound right.

    c. I testify that she met the agent.

    d. I know that she met the agent.

    e. I suppose the Yankees will win.

    f. He bet her $2500 that Bush would win.

    g. I dismiss the class.

    h. I teach the class.

    i. We promise to leave early.

    j. I owe the IRS $1 million.

    k. I bequeath $1,000,000 to the IRS.

    l. I swore I didn't do it.

    m. I swear I didn't do it.

17. Consider the following "facts" and then answer the questions:

    Part A illustrates your ability to interpret meanings when syntactic rules have deleted parts of the sentence; Part B illustrates your knowledge of semantic features and entailment.

    A. Roses are red and bralkions are too.

       Booth shot Lincoln and Czolgosz, McKinley.

       Casca stabbed Caesar and so did Cinna.

       Frodo was exhausted as was Sam.

       (a) What color are bralkions?

       (b) What did Czolgosz do to McKinley?

       (c) What did Cinna do to Caesar?

       (d) What state was Sam in?

    B. Now consider these facts and answer the questions:
       Black Beauty was a stallion.
       Mary is a widow.
       John pretended to send Mary a birthday card.
       John didn't remember to send Jane a birthday card.
       Flipper is walking.

       (T = true; F = false)

       (e) Black Beauty was male?   T _____   F _____
       (f) Mary was never married? T _____   F _____

    (g) John sent Mary a card?   T _____   F _____

    (h) John sent Jane a card?   T _____   F _____

    (i) Flipper has legs?   T _____   F _____

18. The following sentences, when true, have certain entailments even if the situation is not completely known. What are some of them?

Example: The minors promised the police to stop drinking.

Entailments: The minors were drinking; the minors communicated with the police.

    a. We went to the ballpark again.

    b. Valerie regretted not receiving a new T-bird for Labor Day.

    c. That her pet turtle ran away made Emily very sad.

    d. The administration forgot that the professors support the students.

    e. It is an atrocity that the World Trade Center was attacked on September 11, 2001.

    f. It isn't tolerable that the World Trade Center was attacked on September 11, 2001.

    g. Disa wants more popcorn.

    h. Mary drank one more beer before leaving.

    i. Jack knows who discovered Pluto in 1930.

    j. Mary pretended to be asleep.

19. Circle any deictic expression in the following sentences. (*Hint*: Proper names and noun phrases that contain the definite article *the* are not considered deictic expressions.)

    a. I saw her standing there.

    b. Dogs are animals.

    c. Yesterday, all my troubles seemed so far away.

    d. The name of this rock band is "The Beatles."

    e. The Declaration of Independence was signed in 1776.

    f. The Declaration of Independence was signed last year.

    g. Copper conducts electricity.

    h. The treasure chest is to your right.

    i. These are the times that try men's souls.

    j. There is a tide in the affairs of men which taken at the flood leads on to fortune.

20. State for each pronoun in the following sentences whether it is free, bound, or either bound or free. Consider each sentence independently.

Example: John finds himself in love with her.
           himself—bound; her—free

Example: John said that he loved her.
           he—bound or free; her—free

    a. Louise said to herself in the mirror: "She's so ugly."

    b. The fact that he considers her pretty pleases Maria.

    c. Whenever she sees it, she thinks of herself.

    d. John discovered that a picture of himself was hanging in the post office, and that fact bugged him, but it pleased her.

    e. It seems that she and he will never stop arguing with them.

    f. Persons are prohibited from picking flowers from any but their own graves. (On a sign in a cemetery.)

21. Each of the following single statements has at least one implicature in the situation described. What is it?

    a. Statement: You make a better door than a window.
    Situation: Someone is blocking your view.

    b. Statement: It's getting late.
    Situation: You're at a party and it's 4 a.m.

    c. Statement: The restaurants are open until midnight.
    Situation: It's 10 o'clock and you haven't eaten dinner.

    d. Statement: If you'd diet, this wouldn't hurt so badly.
    Situation: Someone is standing on your toe.

    e. Statement: I thought I saw a fan in the closet.
    Situation: It's sweltering in the room.

    f. Statement: Mr. Smith dresses neatly, is well-groomed, and is always on time to class.
    Situation: The summary statement in a letter of recommendation to graduate school.

    g. Statement: Most of the food is gone.
    Situation: You arrived late at a cocktail party.

    h. Statement: John or Mary made a mistake.
    Situation: You're looking over some work done by John and Mary.

22. In each of the following dialogues between Jack and Laura, there is a conversational implicature. What is it?

    a. Jack: Did you make a doctor's appointment?
    Laura: Their line was busy.

    b. Jack: Do you have the play tickets?
    Laura: Didn't I give them to you?

    c. Jack: Does your grandmother have a live-in boyfriend?
    Laura: She's very traditional.

    d. Jack: How did you like the string quartet?
    Laura: I thought the violist was swell.

    e. Laura: What are Boston's chances of winning the World Series?
    Jack: Do bowling balls float?

    f. Laura: Do you own a cat?
    Jack: I'm allergic to everything.

g. Laura: Did you mow the grass and wash the car like I told you to?
Jack: I mowed the grass.

h. Laura: Do you want dessert?
Jack: Is the Pope Catholic?

23. **A.** Think of ten negative polarity items such as *give a hoot* or *have a red cent*.

   B. Challenge exercise: Can you think of other contexts without overt negation that "license" their use? (*Hint*: One answer is discussed in the text, but there are others.)

24. **Challenge exercise**: Suppose that, contrary to what was argued in the text, the noun phrase *no baby* does refer to some individual just like *the baby* does. It needn't be an actual baby but some abstract "empty" object that we'll call ∅. Show that this approach to the semantics of *no baby*, when applying Semantic Rule 1 and taking the restricting nature of adverbs into account (everyone who swims beautifully also swims), predicts that *No baby sleeps soundly* entails *No baby sleeps*, and explain why this is wrong.

6

Phonetics: The Sounds of Language

I gradually came to see that Phonetics had an important bearing on human relations—that when people of different nations pronounce each other's languages really well (even if vocabulary & grammar not perfect), it has an astonishing effect of bringing them together, it puts people on terms of equality, a good understanding between them immediately springs up.

FROM THE JOURNAL OF DANIEL JONES

When you know a language you know the *sounds* of that language, and you know how to combine those sounds into words. When you know English you know the sounds represented by the letters *b, s,* and *u,* and you are able to combine them to form the words *bus* or *sub.*

Although languages may contain different sounds, the sounds of all the languages of the world together constitute a class of sounds that the human vocal tract is designed to make. This chapter will discuss these speech sounds, how they are produced, and how they may be classified.

Sound Segments

"Keep out! Keep out! K-E-E-P O-U-T."

The study of speech sounds is called **phonetics.** To describe speech sounds, it is necessary to know what an individual sound is, and how each sound differs from all others. This is not as easy as it may seem, for when we speak, the sounds seem to run together and it isn't at all obvious where one sound ends and the next begins. However, when we know the language we hear the individual sounds in our "mind's ear," and avoid the confusion of the sign painter in the cartoon.

A speaker of English knows that there are three sounds in the word *bus.* Yet, physically the word is just one continuous sound. You can **segment** that one sound into parts because you know English. And you recognize those parts when they occur elsewhere as *b* does in *bet* or *rob,* and as *u* does in *up,* and as *s* does in *sister.*

It is not possible to segment the sound of someone clearing her throat into a sequence of discrete units. This is not because throat-clearing is one continuous sound. It is because such sounds are not speech and are therefore incapable of being segmented into the sounds of speech.

Speakers of English can separate *keepout* into the two words *keep* and *out* because they know the language. We do not generally pause between words (except to take a breath), even though we may think we do. Children learning a language reveal this fact. A two-year-old child going down stairs heard his mother say, "hold on." He replied, "I'm holing don, I'm holing don," not knowing where the break between words occurred. In fact, word boundary misperceptions have changed the form of words historically. At an earlier stage of English, the word *apron* was *napron.* However, the phrase *a napron* was so often misperceived as *an apron* that the word lost its initial *n.*

Some phrases and sentences that are clearly distinct when printed may be ambiguous when spoken. Read the following pairs aloud and see why we might misinterpret what we hear:

grade A	gray day
I scream	Ice cream
The sun's rays meet	The sons raise meat

The lack of breaks between spoken words and individual sounds often makes us think that speakers of foreign languages run their words together, unaware that we also do. X-ray motion pictures of someone speaking make this lack of breaks in speech very clear. One can see the tongue, jaw, and lips in continuous motion as the individual sounds are produced.

Yet, if you know a language you have no difficulty segmenting the continuous sounds. It doesn't matter if the language is written or not, or if the listener can read and write. Everyone who knows a language knows how to segment sentences into words, and words into sounds.

Identity of Speech Sounds

> By infinitesimal movements of the tongue countless different vowels can be produced, all of them in use among speakers of English who utter the same vowels no oftener than they make the same fingerprints.
>
> GEORGE BERNARD SHAW

It is truly amazing, given the continuity of the speech signal, that we are able to understand the individual words in an utterance. This ability is more surprising because no two speakers ever say the same word identically. The speech signal produced when one speaker says *cat* is not the same as that of another speaker's *cat*. Even two utterances of *cat* by the same speaker will differ to some degree.

Our knowledge of a language determines when we judge physically different sounds to be the same. We know which aspects of pronunciation are linguistically important and which are not. For example, if someone coughs in the middle of saying "How (cough) are you?" a listener will ignore the cough and interpret this simply as "How are you?" People speak at different pitch levels, at different rates of speed, and even with their heads encased in a helmet, like Darth Vader. However, such personal differences are not linguistically significant.

Our linguistic knowledge makes it possible to ignore nonlinguistic differences in speech. Furthermore, we are capable of making sounds that we know are not speech sounds in our language. Many English speakers can make a clicking sound of disapproval that writers sometimes represent as *tsk*. This sound never occurs as part of an English word. It is even difficult for many English speakers to combine this clicking sound with other sounds. Yet clicks are speech sounds in Xhosa, Zulu, Sosotho, and Khoikhoi—languages spoken in southern Africa—just like the *k* or *t* in English. Speakers of those languages have no difficulty producing them as parts of words. Thus, *tsk* is a speech sound in Xhosa but not in English. The sound represented by the letters *th* in the word *think* is a speech sound in English but not in French. In general, languages differ to a greater or lesser degree in the inventory of speech sounds out of which words are built.

The science of phonetics attempts to describe all of the sounds used in all languages of the world. **Acoustic phonetics** focuses on the physical properties of sounds; **auditory phonetics** is concerned with how listeners perceive these sounds; and **articulatory phonetics**—the primary concern of this chapter—is the study of how the vocal tract produces the sounds of language.

The Phonetic Alphabet

> The English have no respect for their language, and will not teach their children to speak it. They cannot spell it because they have nothing to spell it with but an old foreign alphabet of which only the consonants—and not all of them— have any agreed speech value.
>
> GEORGE BERNARD SHAW, *Preface to* Pygmalion

Orthography, or alphabetic spelling, does not represent the sounds of a language in a consistent way. To be scientific—and phonetics *is* a science—we must devise a way for the same sound to be spelled with the same letter every time, and for any letter to stand for the same sound every time.

To see that ordinary spelling with our Roman alphabet is woefully inadequate for the task, consider sentences such as:

Did h**e** bel**ie**ve that C**ae**sar could s**ee** the p**eo**ple s**ei**ze the s**ea**s?
The sill**y** am**oe**ba stole the k**ey** to the machine.

The same sound is represented variously by **e**, **ie**, **ae**, **ee**, **eo**, **ei**, **ea**, **y**, **oe**, **ey**, and **i**.

On the other hand, consider:

My father wanted many **a** village dame badly.

Here the letter **a** represents the various sounds in *father, wanted, many,* and so on.

Making the spelling waters yet muddier, we find that a combination of letters may represent a single sound:

*sh*oot	*ch*aracter	*Th*omas	*ph*ysics
ei*th*er	d*ea*l	rou*gh*	na*ti*on
c*oa*t	gla*ci*al	*th*eater	pl*ai*n

Or, conversely, the single letter **x,** when not pronounced as **z,** usually stands for the *two* sounds **ks** as in sex (you may have to speak aloud to hear that *sex* is pronounced seks).

Some letters have no sound in certain words (so-called *silent* letters):

*m*nemonic	autum*n*	resi*g*n	*gh*ost
*p*terodactyl	*w*rite	hol*e*	cor*p*s
*p*sychology	s*w*ord	de*b*t	*g*naw
bou*gh*	lam*b*	is*l*and	*k*not

Or, conversely, there may be no letter to represent sounds that occur. In many words, the letter *u* represents a *y* sound followed by a *u* sound:

c*u*te	(sounds like k**y**ute; compare: c*oo*t)
f*u*me	(sounds like f**y**ume; compare: f*oo*l)
*u*se	(sounds like **y**use; compare: *U*zbekistan)

Throughout several centuries English scholars have advocated spelling reform. George Bernard Shaw complained that spelling was so inconsistent that *fish* could be spelled *ghoti*—gh as in *tough,* o as in *women,* and ti as in *nation.* Nonetheless, spelling reformers failed to change our spelling habits, and it took phoneticians to invent an alphabet that absolutely guaranteed a one sound–one symbol correspondence. There could be no other way to study the sounds of all human languages scientifically.

In 1888 members of the International Phonetic Association developed a **phonetic alphabet** to symbolize the sounds of all languages. They utilized both ordinary letters and invented symbols. Each character of the alphabet had exactly one value across all of the world's languages. Someone who knew this alphabet would know how to pronounce a word written in it, and upon hearing a word pronounced, would know how to write it using the alphabetic symbols. The inventors of this **International Phonetic Alphabet,** or **IPA,** knew that a phonetic alphabet should include enough symbols to represent the fundamental sounds of all languages. At the same time it should not, and cannot, include noncrucial variations of the fundamental sounds such as pitch, which may vary widely across speakers.

Table 6.1 is a list of the IPA symbols that we will use to represent English speech sounds. The symbols do not tell us everything about the sounds, which may vary from person to person and which may depend on their position in a word. They are not all the phonetic symbols needed for English sounds. When we discuss the sounds in more detail later in the chapter, we will add appropriate symbols.

TABLE 6.1 A Phonetic Alphabet for English Pronunciation

Consonants						Vowels			
p	pill	**t**	till	**k**	kill	**i**	beet	**ɪ**	bit
b	bill	**d**	dill	**g**	gill	**e**	bait	**ɛ**	bet
m	mill	**n**	nil	**ŋ**	ring	**u**	boot	**ʊ**	foot
f	feel	**s**	seal	**h**	heal	**o**	boat	**ɔ**	bore
v	veal	**z**	zeal	**l**	leaf	**æ**	bat	**a**	pot/bar
θ	thigh	**tʃ**	chill	**r**	reef	**ʌ**	butt	**ə**	sofa
ð	thy	**dʒ**	Jill	**j**	you	**aj**	bite	**aw**	bout
ʃ	shill	**ʍ**	which	**w**	witch	**ɔj**	boy		
ʒ	measure								

The symbol [ə] in *sofa* toward the bottom right of the chart is called a *schwa*. We use it only to represent vowels in syllables that are not emphasized in speaking and whose duration is very short. The schwa is pronounced with the mouth in a neutral position and is a brief, colorless vowel. The schwa is reserved for the vowel sound in all reduced syllables, even though its pronunciation may vary slightly according to its position in the word and who is speaking. All other vowel symbols in the chart occur in syllables that receive at least some emphasis.

Speakers from different parts of the country may pronounce some words differently. For example, some of you may pronounce the words *which* and *witch* identically. If you do, the initial sound of both words is symbolized by [w] in the chart. If you don't, the breathy *wh* of *which* is represented by [ʍ]. Some speakers of English pronounce *bought* and *pot* with the same vowel; others pronounce them with the vowel sounds in *bore* and *bar,* respectively. We have therefore listed both words in the chart of symbols. It is difficult to include all the phonetic symbols needed to represent all differences in English. There may be sounds in your speech that are not represented, and vice versa, but that's okay. English is a many-varied language when it comes to pronunciation.

The symbols in Table 6.1 are IPA symbols with one small exception. The IPA uses an upside-down "r" (ɹ) for the English sound *r.* We, and many writers, prefer the right-side up symbol r for clarity when writing for an English-reading audience. Apart from "r," some writers use different symbols for other sounds that once were traditional for transcribing American English. You may encounter these in other books. Here are some equivalents:

IPA	Alternative
ʃ	š
ʒ	ž
tʃ	č
dʒ	ǰ
ʊ	U

Using the IPA symbols, we can now unambiguously represent the pronunciation of words. For example, in the six words below, *ou* represents six distinct vowel sounds; the *gh* is silent in all but *rough,* where it is pronounced [f]; the *th* represents two sounds, and the *l* in *would* is also silent. However, the phonetic transcription gives us the actual pronunciation.

Spelling	Pronunciation
though	[ðo]
thought	[θɔt]
rough	[rʌf]
bough	[baw]
through	[θru]
would	[wʊd]

We always use square brackets around phonetic transcriptions to distinguish them from ordinary spelling.

Articulatory Phonetics

The voice is articulated by the lips and the tongue. . . . Man speaks by means of the air which he inhales into his entire body and particularly into the body cavities. When the air is expelled through the empty space it produces a sound, because of the resonances in the skull. The tongue articulates by its strokes; it gathers the air in the throat and pushes it against the palate and the teeth, thereby giving the sound a definite shape. If the tongue would not articulate each time, by means of its strokes, man would not speak clearly and would only be able to produce a few simple sounds.

HIPPOCRATES *(460–377 B.C.E.)*

The production of any sound involves the movement of air. Most speech sounds are produced by pushing lung air through the *vocal cords*—thin bands of membrane—up the throat, and into the mouth or nose, and finally out of the body. A brief anatomy lesson is in order. The *opening* between the vocal cords is the **glottis** and is located in the voice box or **larynx,** pronounced "lair rinks." The tubular part of the throat above the larynx is the **pharynx** (rhymes with *larynx*). What sensible people call "the mouth," we linguists call the **oral cavity** to distinguish it from the **nasal cavity,** which is the nose and the plumbing that connects it to the throat, plus your sinuses. All of it together is the **vocal tract.** Figure 6-1 should make these descriptions clearer. (The vocal cords and larynx are not specifically labeled in the figure.)

What distinguishes one sound from another? If you bang a large round drum you will get one sound; if you bang a small round drum you will get a different sound; if you bang a small oblong drum you will get still another sound. The size and shape of the vessel containing the air that is moving makes a difference. This is also true in the production of speech sounds. The vocal tract acts as the vessel of air. When it changes shape, different sounds are produced.

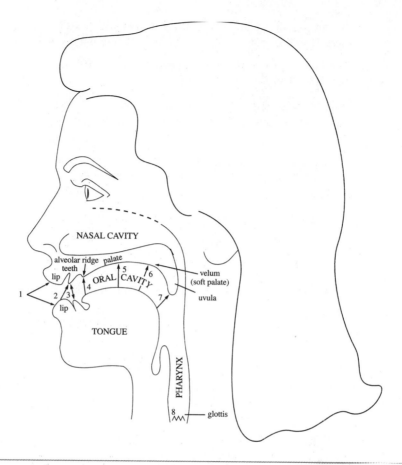

FIGURE 6.1 The vocal tract. Places of articulation: 1. bilabial; 2. labiodental; 3. interdental; 4. alveolar; 5. (alveo)palatal; 6. velar; 7. uvular; 8. glottal.

Consonants

The sounds of all languages fall into two classes: consonants and vowels. Consonants are produced with some restriction or closure in the vocal tract that impedes the flow of air from the lungs. In phonetics, the terms *consonant* and *vowel* refer to types of *sounds,* not to the letters that represent them. In speaking of the alphabet, we may call "a" a vowel and "b" a consonant, but that means only that we use the letter "a" to represent vowel sounds and the letter "b" to represent consonant sounds.

PLACES OF ARTICULATION

We classify consonants according to where in the vocal tract the airflow restriction occurs, called the **place of articulation.** Movement of the tongue and lips creates the constriction, reshaping the oral cavity in various ways to produce the various sounds. We are about to discuss the major places of articulation. As you read the description of each sound class, refer to Table 6.1, which provides key words containing the sounds.

As you pronounce these words, try to feel which articulators are moving. (Watching yourself in a mirror helps, too.) Look at Figure 6-1 for help with the terminology.

Bilabials [p] [b] [m] When we produce a [p], [b], or [m] we articulate by bringing both lips together.

Labiodentals [f] [v] We also use our lips to form [f] and [v]. We articulate these sounds by touching the bottom lip to the upper teeth.

Interdentals [θ] [ð] These sounds, both spelled *th,* are pronounced by inserting the tip of the tongue between the teeth. However, for some speakers the tongue merely touches behind the teeth, making a sound more correctly called **dental.** Watch yourself in a mirror and say *think* [θɪŋk] or *these* [ðiz] and see where *your* tongue tip goes.

Alveolars [t] [d] [n] [s] [z] [l] [r] All seven of these sounds are pronounced with the tongue raised in various ways to the **alveolar ridge.**

- For [t, d, n] the tongue tip is raised and touches the ridge, or slightly in front of it.
- For [s, z] the sides of the front of the tongue are raised, but the tip is lowered so that air escapes over it.
- For [l] the tongue tip is raised while the rest of the tongue remains down, permitting air to escape over its *sides.* Hence, [l] is called a **lateral** sound. You can feel this in the "la" of "tra la la."
- For [r] most English speakers either curl the tip of the tongue back behind the alveolar ridge—a **retroflex** sound—or they bunch up the top of the tongue behind the ridge.

Palatals [ʃ] [ʒ] [tʃ] [dʒ] [j] For these sounds, which occur in *mission* [mɪʃən], *measure* [mɛʒər], *cheap* [tʃip], *judge* [dʒʌdʒ], and *yoyo* [jojo], the constriction occurs by raising the front part of the tongue to the palate.

Velars [k] [g] [ŋ] Another class of sounds is produced by raising the back of the tongue to the soft palate or **velum.** The initial and final sounds of the words *kick* [kɪk] and *gig* [gɪg], and the final sounds of the words *back* [bæk], *bag* [bæg], and *bang* [bæŋ] are all velar sounds.

Uvulars [ʀ] [q] [ɢ] **Uvular** sounds are produced by raising the back of the tongue to the **uvula,** the fleshy protuberance that hangs down in the back of our throats. The *r* in French is often a uvular *trill* symbolized by [ʀ]. The uvular sounds [q] and [ɢ] occur in Arabic. These sounds do not ordinarily occur in English.

Glottals [h] [ʔ] The sound of [h] is from the flow of air through the open *glottis,* and past the tongue and lips as they prepare to pronounce a vowel sound, which always follows [h].

If the air is stopped completely at the glottis by tightly closed vocal cords, the sound upon release of the cords is a **glottal stop** [ʔ]. The interjection *uh–oh,* that you hope never to hear your dentist utter, has two glottal stops and is spelled phonetically [ʔʌʔo].

Table 6.2 summarizes the classification of the English consonants that we have discussed by their place of articulation.

TABLE 6.2 Place of Articulation of English Consonants

Bilabial	p	b	m				
Labiodental	f	v					
Interdental	θ	ð					
Alveolar	t	d	n	s	z	l	r
Palatal	ʃ	ʒ	tʃ	dʒ			
Velar	k	g	ŋ				
Glottal	h	ʔ					

MANNER OF ARTICULATION

We have described several classes of consonants according to their *place of articulation,* yet we are still unable to distinguish the sounds in each class from one another. What distinguishes [p] from [b] or [b] from [m]? All are bilabial sounds. What is the difference between [t], [d], and [n], which are all alveolar sounds?

Speech sounds also vary in the way the airstream is affected as it flows from the lungs up and out of the mouth and nose. It may be blocked or partially blocked; the vocal cords may vibrate or not vibrate. We refer to this as the **manner of articulation.**

Voiced and Voiceless Sounds If the vocal cords are apart when speaking, air flows freely through the glottis into the oral cavity. Sounds produced in this way are **voiceless:** [p] and [s] in *super* [supər] are two of the several voiceless sounds of English.

If the vocal cords are together, the airstream forces its way through and causes them to vibrate. Such sounds are **voiced.** [b] and [z] in *buzz* [bʌz] are two of the many voiced sounds of English. To get a sense of voicing, try putting a finger in each ear and say the voiced "z-z-z-z-z." You can feel the vibrations of the vocal cords. If you now say the voiceless "s-s-s-s-s," you will not sense these vibrations (although you might hear a hissing sound in your mouth). When you whisper, you are making all the speech sounds voiceless.

The voiced/voiceless distinction is very important in English. This phonetic property distinguishes the words in word pairs like the following:

rope/robe	fate/fade	rack/rag	wreath/wreathe
[rop]/[rob]	[fet]/[fed]	[ræk]/[ræg]	[riθ]/[rið]

The first word of each pair ends with a voiceless sound and the second word with a voiced sound. All other aspects of the sounds in each word pair are identical; the position of the lips and tongue is the same.

The voiced/voiceless distinction also occurs in the following pairs, where the first word begins with a voiceless sound and the second with a voiced sound:

fine/vine	seal/zeal	choke/joke
[fajn]/[vajn]	[sil/zil]	[tʃok]/[dʒok]
peat/beat	tote/dote	kale/gale
[pit]/[bit]	[tot]/[dot]	[kel]/[gel]

In our discussion of [p], we did not distinguish the initial sound in the word *pit* from the second sound in the word *spit.* There is, however, a phonetic difference in these two voiceless stops. During the production of voiceless sounds, the glottis is open and the air flows freely between the vocal cords. When a voiceless sound is followed by a voiced sound such as a vowel, the vocal cords must close so they can vibrate.

Voiceless sounds fall into two classes depending on the timing of the vocal cord closure. When we say *pit,* the vocal cords remain open for a very short time after the lips come apart to release the *p.* We call this *p* **aspirated** because a brief puff of air escapes before the glottis closes.

When we pronounce the *p* in *spit,* however, the vocal cords start vibrating as soon as the lips open. That *p* is **unaspirated.** Hold your palm about two inches in front of your lips and say *pit.* You will feel a puff of air, which you will not feel when you say *spit.* The *t* in *tick* and the *k* in *kin* are also aspirated voiceless stops, while the *t* in *stick* and the *k* in *skin* are unaspirated.

Finally, in the production of the voiced [b] (and [d] and [g] as well), the vocal cords are vibrating throughout the closure of the lips, and continue to vibrate during the vowel sound that follows after the lips part.

We indicate aspirated sounds by writing the phonetic symbol with a raised *h,* as in the following examples:

pool	[pʰul]	spool	[spul]
tale	[tʰel]	stale	[stel]
kale	[kʰel]	scale	[skel]

Figure 6.2 shows in diagrammatic form the timing of lip closure in relation to the state of the vocal cords.

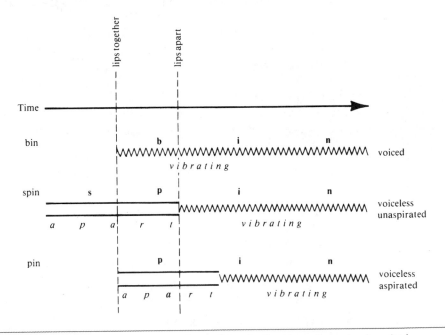

FIGURE 6.2 Timing of lip closure and vocal-cord vibrations for voiced, voiceless unaspirated, and voiceless aspirated bilabial stops. [b], [p], [pʰ].

Nasal and Oral Sounds The voiced/voiceless distinction differentiates the bilabials [b] and [p]. The sound [m] is also a bilabial, and it is voiced. What distinguishes it from [b]?

Figure 6.1 shows the roof of the mouth divided into the (hard) palate and the soft palate (or velum). The palate is a hard bony structure at the front of the mouth. You can feel it with your thumb. First, wash your hands. Now, slide your thumb along the hard palate back toward the throat; you will feel the velum, which is where the flesh becomes soft and pliable. The velum terminates in the uvula, which you can see in a mirror if you open your mouth wide and say "aaah." The velum is movable, and when it is raised all the way to touch the back of the throat, the passage through the nose is cut off and air can escape only through the mouth.

Sounds produced with the velum up, blocking the air from escaping through the nose, are **oral sounds,** because the air can escape only through the oral cavity. Most sounds in all languages are oral sounds. When the velum is not in its raised position, air escapes through both the nose and the mouth. Sounds produced this way are **nasal sounds.** The sound [m] is a nasal consonant. Thus [m] is distinguished from [b] because it is a nasal sound, whereas [b] is an oral sound.

The diagrams in Figure 6.3 show the position of the lips and the velum when [m], [b], and [p] are articulated. The sounds [p], [b], and [m] are produced by stopping the airflow at the lips; [m] and [b] differ from [p] by being voiced; [m] differs from [b] by being nasal.

The same oral/nasal difference occurs in *raid* [re**d**] and *rain* [re**n**], *rug* [rʌ**g**] and *rung* [rʌ**ŋ**]. The velum is raised in the production of [d] and [g], preventing the air from flowing through the nose, whereas for [n] and [ŋ] the velum is down, allowing the air out through both the nose and the mouth when the closure is released. The sounds [m], [n], and [ŋ] are therefore nasal sounds, and [b], [d], and [g] are oral sounds.

The presence or absence of these **phonetic features**—nasal and voiced—permit the division of all speech sounds into four classes: voiced, voiceless, nasal, and oral, as shown in Table 6.3.

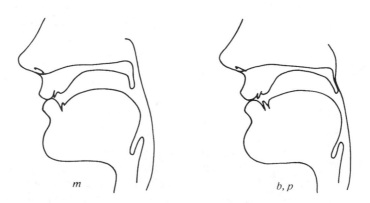

FIGURE **6.3** Position of lips and velum for *m* (lips together, velum down), and *b, p* (lips together, velum up).

TABLE 6.3 Four Classes of Speech Sounds

	Oral	Nasal
Voiced	b d g	m n ŋ
Voiceless	p t k	*

*Nasal consonants in English are usually voiced. Both voiced and voiceless nasal sounds occur in other languages.

We now have three ways of classifying consonants: by voicing, by place of articulation, and by nasalization. For example, [p] is a voiceless, bilabial, oral sound; [n] is a voiced, alveolar, nasal sound, and so on.

Stops [p] [b] [m] [t] [d] [n] [k] [g] [ŋ] [tʃ] [dʒ] [ʔ] We are seeing finer and finer distinctions of speech sounds. However, both [t] and [s] are voiceless, alveolar, oral sounds. What distinguishes them? After all, *tack* and *sack* are different words.

Stops are consonants in which the airstream is completely blocked in the *oral* cavity for a short period (tens of milliseconds). All other sounds are **continuants.** The sound [t] is a stop, but the sound [s] is not, and that is what makes them different speech sounds.

- [p], [b], and [m] are *bilabial stops,* with the airstream stopped at the mouth by the complete closure of the lips.
- [t], [d], and [n] are *alveolar stops;* the airstream is stopped by the tongue, making a complete closure at the alveolar ridge.
- [k], [g], and [ŋ] are *velar stops* with the complete closure at the velum.
- [tʃ] and [dʒ] are *palatal affricates* with complete stop closures. They will be further classified later.
- [ʔ] is a *glottal stop.* The air is completely stopped at the glottis.

We have been discussing the sounds that occur in English. Some sounds, including stops, occur in other languages but not in English. For example, in Quechua, spoken in Bolivia and Peru, uvular stops occur, where the back of the tongue is raised and moved rearward to form a complete closure with the uvula. The phonetic symbol [q] denotes the voiceless version of this stop, which is the initial sound in the name of the language "Quechua." The voiced uvular stop [ɢ] also occurs in Quechua.

Fricatives [f] [v] [θ] [ð] [s] [z] [ʃ] [ʒ] [x] [ɣ] [h] In the production of some continuants, the airflow is so severely obstructed that it causes friction, and the sounds are therefore called **fricatives.** The first of the following pairs of fricatives are voiceless; the second voiced.

- [f] and [v] are *labiodental fricatives;* the friction is created at the lips and teeth, where a narrow passage permits the air to escape.
- [θ] and [ð] are *interdental fricatives,* represented by *th* in *thin* and *then.* The friction occurs at the opening between the tongue and teeth.
- [s] and [z] are *alveolar fricatives,* with the friction created at the alveolar ridge.
- [ʃ] and [ʒ] are *palatal fricatives,* and contrast in such pairs as *mission* [mɪʃən] and *measure* [mɛʒər]. They are produced with friction created as the air

passes between the tongue and the part of the palate behind the alveolar ridge. In English, the voiced palatal fricative never begins words except for foreign words such as *genre*. The voiceless palatal fricative begins the words *shoe* [ʃu] and *sure* [ʃur] and ends the words *rush* [rʌʃ] and *push* [pʊʃ].

- [x] and [ɣ] denote *velar fricatives*. They are produced by raising the back of the tongue toward, but not quite touching, the velum. The friction is created as air passes through that narrow passage. These sounds do not commonly occur in English, except possibly in rapid speech, and in some forms of Scottish English, where the final sound of *loch* meaning "lake" is [x]. The final sound of the composer J. S. Bach's name is also pronounced [x], which is a far more common sound in German and is why German is said to sound guttural.
- [h] is a glottal fricative. It's relatively weak sound comes from air passing through the open glottis and pharynx.

All fricatives are continuants. Although the airstream is obstructed as it passes through the oral cavity, it is not completely stopped.

Affricates [tʃ], [dʒ] **Affricates** are produced by a stop closure followed immediately by a gradual release of the closure that produces an effect characteristic of a fricative. The palatal sounds that begin and end the words *church* and *judge* are voiceless and voiced affricates, respectively. Affricates are not continuants because of the initial stop closure.

Liquids [l] [r] In the production of the sounds [l] and [r], there is some obstruction of the airstream in the mouth, but not enough to cause any real constriction or friction. These sounds are **liquids.** They are articulated quite differently, as described in the earlier alveolar section, but are grouped as a class because they are acoustically similar. Because of that similarity, foreign speakers of English may confuse the two sounds and substitute one for the other. It also accounts for Dennis's confusion in the cartoon.

"WHO'S MAKING ALL THOSE MISTAKES? THEY'RE *ALWAYS* PASSING THE CORRECTION PLATE."

"Dennis the Menace"
© Hank Ketcham. Reprinted with permission of North America Syndicate.

Glides [j] [w] The sounds [j] and [w], the initial sounds of *you* [ju] and *we* [wi], are produced with little obstruction of the airstream. They are always followed directly by a vowel except when they are part of a diphthong (discussed later). After articulating [j] or [w], the tongue glides quickly into place for pronouncing the next vowel, hence the term **glide.** Glides are transitional sounds—halfway between consonants and vowels—and are sometimes called *semivowels.* However, we consider them to be consonants because like all consonants, they never form the nucleus of a syllable as do vowels.

The glide [j] is a palatal sound; the blade of the tongue (the front part minus the tip) is raised toward the hard palate in a position almost identical to that in producing the vowel sound [i] in the word *beat* [bit]. In pronouncing *you* [ju], the tongue moves rapidly from the [j] to the [u] vowel.

The glide [w] is produced by both raising the back of the tongue toward the velum and simultaneously rounding the lips. It is thus a **labio-velar** glide. Where speakers of English have different pronunciations for the words *which* and *witch,* the labio-velar glide in the first word is voiceless, symbolized as [ʍ] (an "upside-down" *w*). The position of the tongue and the lips for [w] is similar to that for producing the vowel sound [u] in *suit* [sut]. In pronouncing *we* [wi], the tongue moves rapidly from the [w] to the [i] vowel, as if you were saying *gooey* rapidly without the initial *g.*

Approximants In some books the sounds [w], [j], [r], and [l] are alternatively called approximants because the articulators approximate a frictional closeness, but no actual friction occurs. The first three are central approximants, whereas [l] is a lateral approximant.

Although in this chapter we focus on the sounds of English, the IPA has symbols and classifications for all the sounds of the world's languages. For example, many languages have sounds that are referred to as trills, and others have clicks. These are described in the following sections.

Trills and flaps The "*r*"-sound of many languages may be different than the English [r]. A trilled "*r*" is produced by rapid vibrations of an articulator. An alveolar **trill,** as in the Spanish word for dog, *perro,* is produced by vibrating the tongue tip against the alveolar ridge. Its IPA symbol is [r], strictly speaking, though we have co-opted [r] for the English liquid. Many French speakers articulate the initial sound of *rouge* as a uvular trill, produced by vibrating the uvula. Its IPA symbol is [ʀ].

Another "*r*"-sound is called a **flap** and is produced by a flick of the tongue against the alveolar ridge. It sounds like a "very fast *d.*" It occurs in Spanish in words like *pero* meaning "but." It may also occur in British English in words such as *very.* Its IPA symbol is [ɾ]. Most American speakers produce a flap instead of a [t] or [d] in words like *writer* and *rider,* which then sound identical and are spelled phonetically as [rajɾər].

Clicks These "exotic" sounds are made by moving air in the mouth between various articulators. The sound of disapproval often spelled *tsk* is an alveolar **click** that occurs in several languages of southern African such as Zulu. A lateral click, which is like the sound one makes to encourage a horse, occurs in Xhosa. In fact, the 'X' in Xhosa stands for that particular speech sound.

PHONETIC SYMBOLS FOR AMERICAN ENGLISH CONSONANTS

We are now capable of distinguishing all of the consonant sounds of English via the properties of voicing, nasality, and place and manner of articulation. For example, [f] is a voiceless, (oral), labiodental fricative; [n] is a (voiced), nasal, alveolar stop. The parenthesized features are usually not mentioned because they are redundant; all sounds are oral unless nasal is specifically mentioned, and all nasals are voiced in English.

Table 6.4 lists the consonants by their phonetic features. The rows stand for manner of articulation and the columns for place of articulation. The entries are sufficient to distinguish all words in English from one another. For example, the one symbol [p] for all voiceless bilabial stops (both aspirated and unaspirated), together with the symbol [b] for the voiced bilabial stop, are sufficient to differentiate the word *peat* [pit] from *beat*. If a narrower phonetic transcription of these words is desired, the symbol [pʰ] can be used as in [pʰit] as opposed to the [p] in [spid] *speed*.

TABLE 6.4 Some Phonetic Symbols for American English Consonants

	Bilabial	Labiodental	Interdental	Alveolar	Palatal	Velar	Glottal
Stop (oral)							
voiceless	p			t		k	ʔ
voiced	b			d		g	
Nasal (voiced)	m			n		ŋ	
Fricative							
voiceless		f	θ	s	ʃ		h
voiced		v	ð	z	ʒ		
Affricate							
voiceless					tʃ		
voiced					dʒ		
Glide							
voiceless	ʍ					ʍ	
voiced	w				j	w	
Liquid (voiced)							
lateral				l			
retroflex				r			

Examples of words in which these sounds occur are given in Table 6.5.

TABLE 6.5 Examples of Consonants in English Words

	Bilabial	Labiodental	Interdental	Alveolar	Palatal	Velar	Glottal
Stop (oral)							
voiceless	*p*ie			*t*ie		*k*ite	(ʔ)uh–(ʔ)oh
voiced	*b*uy			*d*ie		*g*uy	
Nasal (voiced)	*m*y			*n*ight		si*ng*	
Fricative							
voiceless		*f*ie	*th*igh	*s*ue	mi*ss*ion		*h*igh
voiced		*v*ie	*th*y	*z*oo	mea*s*ure		

TABLE 6.5 (Continued)

	Bilabial	Labiodental	Interdental	Alveolar	Palatal	Velar	Glottal
Affricate							
voiceless					*ch*ime		
voiced					*j*ive		
Glide							
voiceless	*wh*ich					*wh*ich	
voiced	*w*ipe				*y*ank	*w*ipe	
Liquid (voiced)							
lateral				*l*ye			
retroflex				*r*ye			

Vowels

"Frank and Ernest" © Thaves/Dist. by Newspaper Enterprise Association, Inc.

Vowels are pronounced with no significant blockage of the air as it is pushed out of the lungs. The quality of a vowel depends on the shape of the vocal tract as the air passes through. Different parts of the tongue may be high or low in the mouth; the lips may be spread or pursed; the velum may be raised or lowered.

Vowel sounds carry pitch and loudness; you can sing vowels or shout vowels. They may be longer or shorter in duration. Vowels can stand alone—they can be produced without consonants before or after them. You can say the vowels of *beat,* [bit], *bit* [bɪt], or *boot* [but], for example, without the initial [b] or the final [t], but you cannot say a [b] or a [t] alone without at least a "little bit" of vowel sound.

Linguists can describe vowels acoustically or electronically. We will discuss that topic in chapter 9. In this chapter we describe vowels by their articulatory features just as we described consonants. So just as we say a [d] is pronounced by raising the tongue tip to the alveolar ridge, we say an [i] is pronounced by raising the body of the tongue toward the palate. With a [b], the lips come together; for an [æ] (the vowel in *cat*) the tongue is low in the mouth with the tongue tip forward, behind the front teeth.

If you watch a side view of an X-ray (that's *-ray,* not *-rated!*) video of someone's tongue moving during speech, you will see various parts of the tongue rise up high and fall down low; at the same time you will see it move forward and backward in the mouth. These are the dimensions over which vowels are produced. We classify vowels according to three questions:

1. How high or low in the mouth is the tongue?
2. How forward or backward in the mouth is the tongue?
3. Are the lips rounded (pursed) or spread?

Tongue Position

Higgins: Tired of listening to sounds?

Pickering: Yes. It's a fearful strain. I rather fancied myself because I can pronounce twenty-four distinct vowel sounds, but your hundred and thirty beat me. I can't hear a bit of difference between most of them.

Higgins: Oh, that comes with practice. You hear no difference at first, but you keep on listening and presently you find they're all as different as A from B.

GEORGE BERNARD SHAW, Pygmalion

The upper two diagrams in Figure 6.4 show that the tongue is high in the mouth in the production of the vowels [i] and [u] in the words *he* [hi] and *who* [hu]. In *he* the front part (but not the tip) of the tongue is raised; in *who* it is the back of the tongue. (Prolong the vowels of these words and try to feel the raised part of your tongue.) These are both *high* vowels, and the [i] is a *high front* vowel while the [u] is a *high back* vowel.

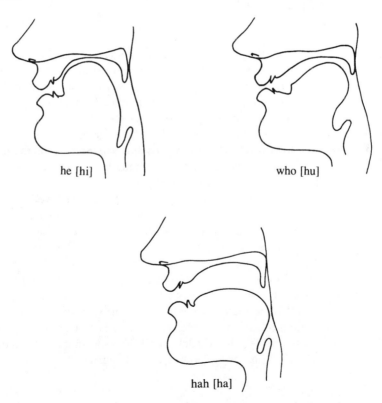

he [hi]

who [hu]

hah [ha]

FIGURE 6.4 Position of the tongue in producing the vowels in he, who, and hah.

To produce the vowel sound [a] of *hah* [ha], the back of the tongue is low in the mouth, as the lower diagram in Figure 6.4 shows. (The reason a doctor examining your throat may ask you to say "ah" is that the tongue is low and easy to see over.) This vowel is therefore a *low back* vowel.

The vowels [ɪ] and [ʊ] in the words *hit* [hɪt] and *put* [pʰʊt] are similar to those in *he* [hi] and *who* [hu] with slightly lowered tongue positions.

The vowel [æ] in *hack* [hæk] is produced with the front part of the tongue low in the mouth, similar to the low vowel [a], but with the front rather than the back part of the tongue lowered. Say "hack, hah, hack, hah, hack, hah, . . ." and you should feel your tongue moving forward and back in the low part of your mouth. Thus [æ] is a *low front* vowel.

The vowels [e] and [o] in *bait* [bet] and *boat* [bot] are *mid vowels,* produced by raising the tongue to a position midway between the high and low vowels just discussed. [ɛ] and [ɔ] in the words *bet* [bɛt] and *bore* [bɔr] are also mid vowels, produced with a slightly lower tongue position than [e] and [o]. Here, [e] and [ɛ] are *front;* [o] and [ɔ] are *back.*

To produce the vowel [ʌ] in the word *bu*tt [bʌt], the tongue is not strictly high nor low, front nor back. It is a lower midcentral vowel. The schwa vowel [ə], which occurs as the first sound in *about* [əbawt], or the final sound of *sofa* [sofə], is also articulated with the tongue in a more or less neutral position between the extremes of high/low, front/back. The schwa is used mostly to represent unstressed vowels. (We will discuss stress later.)

LIP ROUNDING

Vowels also differ as to whether the lips are rounded or spread. The vowels [u], [ʊ], [o], and [ɔ] in *boot, put, boat,* and *bore* are **rounded vowels.** They are produced with pursed or rounded lips. You can get a feel for the rounding by prolonging the word *who,* as if you were an owl: *whoooooooooo.* Now pose for the camera and say *cheese,* only say it with a prolonged vowel: *cheeeeeeeeeeese.* The high front [i] in *cheese* is unrounded, with the lips in the shape of a smile, and you can feel it or see it in a mirror. The low vowel [a] in the words *bar, bah,* and *aha* is the only (American) English back vowel that occurs without lip rounding. All other vowels in English (i.e., the nonback ones) are also unrounded.

This is not true of all languages. French and Swedish, for example, have front rounded vowels, which English lacks. English also lacks a high back *unrounded* vowel, but this sound occurs in Mandarin Chinese, Japanese, and the Cameroonian language FeʔFeʔ, among other languages. The IPA symbol for this vowel is [ɯ], and to show that roundedness is important, we note that in Mandarin Chinese the unrounded [sɯ] means "four," but the round [su] (like *sue*) means "speed."

Figure 6.5 shows the vowels based on tongue "geography." The position of the vowel relative to the horizontal axis is a measure of the vowel's front/back dimension. Its position relative to the vertical axis is a measure of tongue height. For example, we see that [i] is a high front vowel, [o] is a midback (rounded) vowel, and [ʌ] is a lower midcentral vowel, tending toward backness.

DIPHTHONGS

A **diphthong** is a sequence of two sounds, vowel plus glide. Diphthongs are present in the phonetic inventory of many languages, including English. The vowels we have

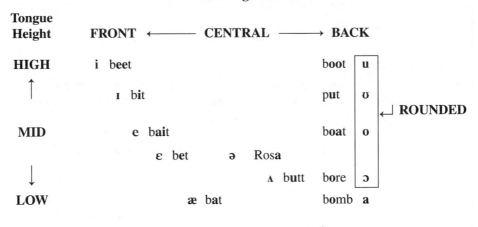

FIGURE 6.5 Classification of American English vowels.

studied so far are simple vowels, called **monophthongs.** The vowel sound in the word *bite* [bajt], however, is the [a] vowel sound of *father* followed by the [j] glide, resulting in the diphthong [aj]. Similarly, the vowel in *bout* [bawt] is [a] followed by the glide [w], resulting in [aw]. The third diphthong that occurs in English is the vowel sound in *boy* [bɔj], which is the vowel [ɔ] of *bore* followed by the palatal glide [j], resulting in [ɔj]. The pronunciation of any of these diphthongs may vary from our description because of the diversity of English speakers.

Nasalization of Vowels

Vowels, like consonants, can be produced with a raised velum that prevents the air from escaping through the nose, or with a lowered velum that permits air to pass through the nasal passage. When the nasal passage is blocked, *oral* vowels result; when the nasal passage is open, *nasal* (or *nasalized*) vowels result. In English, nasal vowels occur for the most part before nasal consonants in the same syllable, and oral vowels occur in all other places.

The words *bean, bone, bingo, boom, bam,* and *bang* are examples of words that contain nasalized vowels. To show the nasalization of a vowel in a phonetic transcription, an extra mark called a **diacritic**—the symbol ~ (tilde) in this case—is placed over the vowel, as in *bean* [bĩn] and *bone* [bõn].

In languages like French, Polish, and Portuguese, nasalized vowels occur without nasal consonants. The French word meaning "sound" is *son* [sõ]. The *n* in the spelling is not pronounced but indicates that the vowel is nasal.

Tense and Lax Vowels

Figure 6.5 shows that the vowel [i] has a slightly higher tongue position than [ɪ]. This is also true for [e] and [ɛ], [u] and [ʊ], and [o] and [ɔ]. The first vowel in each pair is generally produced with greater tension of the tongue muscles than its counterpart, and they are often a little longer in duration. These vowels can be distinguished from the shorter and less tense vowels by the features **tense** and **lax,** as shown in the following:

Tense		Lax	
i	beat	ɪ	bit
e	bait	ɛ	bet
u	boot	ʊ	put
o	boat	ɔ	bore

The tense vowels may be diphthongized somewhat by various speakers and within various communities of speakers of English. When they are, it's as if the tense front vowels are followed by a short [j] glide, so [ij] and [ej] are spoken in place of [i] and [e]. Similarly, the tense back vowels are followed by a short [w] glide, so [uw] and [ow] replace [u] and [o]. However, we will continue to denote these sounds as [i], [e], [u], and [o].

Additionally, [a] is a tense vowel but [æ], [ʌ], and of course [ə] are lax. Tense vowels may occur at the ends of words: [si], [se], [su], [so], and [pa] represent the English words *see, say, sue, sew,* and *pa.* Lax vowels mostly do not occur at the ends of words, so [sɪ], [sɛ], [sæ], [sʊ], and [sʌ] are not possible words in English. (The one exception to this generalization is lax [ɔ], which occurs in words such as [sɔ], *saw.*)

DIFFERENT (TONGUE) STROKES FOR DIFFERENT FOLKS

The vowels in Figure 6.5 do not represent all the vowels of all English speakers. They may not represent your particular vowel set. If you speak British English, there's a good chance that you have a low, back, rounded vowel in the word *hot* that the vowel chart lacks. Many British speakers highly diphthongize the tense vowels, much more so than most Americans, so for them *gate* is pronounced [gejt] and *go* is pronounced [gow]. On the other hand, Irish speakers of English tend to pronounce these vowels as pure monophthongs. Consonants, too, vary from region to region, if not from person to person. One person's "alveolar" stops may technically be dental stops, with the tongue hard behind the upper front teeth. In Britain, the substitution of the glottal stop where an American might use a [t] or [d] is common. It's very much the case throughout the English-speaking world that, as the old song goes, "I say "*tomayto*" [təmejto], you say "*tomahto*" [təmato]," and we lovers of language say "viva la différence."

Major Phonetic Classes

Biologists describe classes of life in broader or narrower terms. They may distinguish between animals and plants; or within animals, between vertebrates and invertebrates; and within vertebrates, between mammals and reptiles, and so on.

Linguists describe speech sounds similarly. All sounds are consonants or vowels. Within consonants, all are voiced or unvoiced, and so on. All the classes of sounds described so far in this chapter combine to form larger, more general classes that are important in the patterning of sounds in the world's languages.

NONCONTINUANTS AND CONTINUANTS

As we mentioned, stop sounds are **noncontinuants.** There is a total obstruction of the airstream in the *oral cavity.* They include the nasal stops (although air flows continuously out the nose) and the affricates. All other consonants, and all vowels, are continuants, in which the stream of air flows continuously out of the mouth.

OBSTRUENTS AND SONORANTS

The non-nasal stops, the fricatives, and the affricates form a major class of sounds called **obstruents.** The airstream may be fully obstructed, as in non-nasal stops and affricates, or partially obstructed, as in the production of fricatives. Fricatives are continuant obstruents. The air flows continuously out the mouth, though it is obstructed enough to cause the frictional sound that characterizes this class of consonants.

Non-nasal stops and affricates are noncontinuant obstruents; there is a complete blockage of the air during the production of these sounds. The closure of a stop is released abruptly as opposed to the closure of an affricate, which is released gradually, causing friction.

Sounds that are not obstruents are **sonorants.** Sonorants resonate. They are produced with relatively free airflow through either the mouth or nose. They have greater acoustic energy than obstruents, much of whose energy is absorbed in being forced through narrow passageways. Nasal stops are sonorants because, although the air is blocked in the mouth, it continues to resonate in the nasal cavity. Vowels, the liquids [l] and [r], and the glides [w] and [j] are also sonorants because the air resonates as it flows relatively undisturbed through the vocal tract.

CONSONANTAL

The sounds of all the languages of the world fall into two major classes—consonants and vowels. But not all consonants are created equal: some are more consonantal than others. Obstruents are the most consonantal and the least vowel-like. Nasals and liquids are less consonantal and more vowel-like because they resonate like vowels. Glides, however, are the least consonantal and the least vowel-like after the obstruents. In recognition of this sliding scale, linguists say that obstruents, liquids, and nasals all belong to a subclass of consonants called **consonantal.** Glides fail to make the cut and are not consonantal, and of course neither are vowels.

Here are some other terms used to form subclasses of consonantal sounds. These are not exhaustive, and a full course in phonetics would note further classes that we omit.

Labials [p] [b] [m] [f] [v] Labial sounds are those articulated with the involvement of the lips. They include the class of bilabial sounds—[p] [b] [m]—as well as the labiodentals, [f] and [v].

Coronals [θ] [ð] [t] [d] [n] [s] [z] [ʃ] [ʒ] [tʃ] [dʒ] [l] [r] Coronal sounds are articulated by raising the tongue blade. Coronals include the alveolars, [t] [d] [n] [s] [z]; the palatals, [ʃ] [ʒ]; the affricates, [tʃ] [dʒ]; and the liquids [l], [r].

Anteriors [p] [b] [m] [f] [v] [θ] [ð] [t] [d] [n] [s] [z] Anterior sounds are consonants produced in the front part of the mouth, that is, from the alveolar area forward. They include the labials, the interdentals, and the alveolars.

Sibilants [s] [z] [ʃ] [ʒ] [tʃ] [dʒ] Another class of consonantal sounds is characterized by an acoustic rather than an articulatory property of its members. The friction created by sibilants produces a hissing sound, which is a mixture of high-frequency sounds.

SYLLABIC SOUNDS

Sounds that may function as the core of a syllable possess the feature **syllabic.** Clearly, vowels are syllabic, but these are not the only sound classes around which syllables form.

Liquids and nasals can also be syllabic, as shown by the words *dazzle* [dæzl̩], *faker* [fekr̩], *rhythm* [rɪðm̩], and *button* [bʌtn̩]. (The diacritic mark under the [l̩], [r̩], [m̩], and [n̩] is the notation for syllabic.) Placing a schwa [ə] before the syllabic liquid or nasal also shows that these are separate syllables. The four words could be written as [dæzəl], [fekər], [rɪðəm], and [bʌtən]. We will use this transcription. Similarly, the vowel sound in words like *bird* and *verb* are sometimes written as a syllabic *r*, [br̩d] and [vr̩b]. For consistency we shall transcribe these words using the schwa—[bərd] and [vərb]—the only instances where a schwa represents a stressed vowel.

Obstruents and glides are never syllabic sounds because they are always accompanied by a vowel, and that vowel functions as the syllabic core.

Prosodic Features

Length, pitch, and the complex feature *stress* are **prosodic,** or **suprasegmental,** features. They are features *over and above* the segmental values of voicing or place of articulation, thus the "supra" in *suprasegmental*. The term *prosodic* comes from poetry, where it refers to the metrical structure of verse. One of the essential characteristics of poetry is the placement of stress on particular syllables, which defines the versification of the poem.

Speech sounds that are identical in their place or manner features may differ in length (duration). Tense vowels are generally longer than lax vowels, but only by a small amount, perhaps a few milliseconds. However, in some languages when a vowel is prolonged to around twice its normal length, it can make a difference between words. In Japanese the word *biru* [biru] with a regular *i* means "building," but with the *i* doubled as in *biiru,* spelled phonetically as [biːru], the meaning is "beer." (The colon-like : is the IPA symbol for segment length or doubling.)

Japanese, and many other languages such as Finnish and Italian, have long consonants that may contrast words. When a consonant is long, or doubled, either the closure or obstruction is prolonged. Pronounced with a short *k,* the word *saki* [saki] means "ahead" in Japanese; pronounced with a long *k*—prolonging the velar closure—the word *sakki* [sakːi] means "before."

English is not a language in which vowel or consonant length can change a word. You might say "stoooooooop!" to emphasize your desire to make someone stop, but the word is not changed. You may also say in English "Whatttttt a dump!" to express your dismay at a hotel room, prolonging the *t*-closure, but the word *what* is not changed.

When we speak, we also change the **pitch** of our voice. The pitch depends on how fast the vocal cords vibrate; the faster they vibrate, the higher the pitch. If the larynx is small, as in women and children, the shorter vocal cords vibrate faster and the pitch is higher, all other things being equal. That is why women and children have higher-pitched voices than men, in general. When we discuss tone languages later, we will see that pitch may affect the meaning of a word.

In many languages, certain syllables in a word are louder, slightly higher in pitch, and somewhat longer in duration than other syllables in the word. They are **stressed** syllables. For example, the first syllable of *digest,* the noun meaning "summation of articles," is stressed, whereas in *digest,* the verb meaning "to absorb food," the second syllable receives greater stress. Stress can be marked in several ways: for example, by putting an accent mark over the stressed vowel in the syllable, as in *dígest* versus *digést.*

English is a "stress" language. In general, at least one syllable is stressed in an English word. French is not a stress language. The syllables have approximately the same loudness, length, and pitch. When native English speakers attempt to speak French, they often stress syllables, so that native French speakers hear French with "an English accent." When French speakers speak English, they fail to put stress where a native English speaker would, and that contributes to what English speakers would call a "French accent."

Tone and Intonation

We have already seen how length and stress can make sounds with the same segmental properties different. In some languages, these differences make different words, such as the two *digests*. Pitch, too, can make a difference in certain languages.

Speakers of all languages vary the pitch of their voices when they talk. The effect of pitch on a syllable differs from language to language. In English, it doesn't matter whether you say *cat* with a high pitch or a low pitch. It will still mean "cat." But if you say [ba] with a high pitch in Nupe (a language spoken in Nigeria), it will mean "to be sour," whereas if you say [ba] with a low pitch, it will mean "to count." Languages that use the pitch of individual vowels or syllables to contrast meanings of words are called **tone languages.**

Most languages in the world are tone languages. There are more than one thousand tone languages spoken in Africa alone. Many languages of Asia, such as Mandarin Chinese, Burmese, and Thai, are tone languages. In Thai, for example, the same string of segmental sounds represented by [na:] will mean different things if one says the sounds with a low pitch, a midpitch, a high pitch, a falling pitch from high to low, or a rising pitch from low to high. Thai therefore has five linguistic tones, as illustrated as follows:

(Diacritics are used to represent distinctive tones in the phonetic transcriptions.)

[ˋ]	L	low tone	[nà:]	"a nickname"
[ˉ]	M	mid tone	[nā:]	"rice paddy"
[ˊ]	H	high tone	[ná:]	"young maternal uncle or aunt"
[ˆ]	HL	falling tone	[nâ:]	"face"
[ˇ]	LH	rising tone	[nǎ:]	"thick"

There are two kinds of tones. If the pitch is level across the syllable, we have a **register tone.** If the pitch changes across the syllable, whether from high to low or vice versa, we have a **contour tone.** Thai has three level and two contour tones. Commonly, tone languages will have two or three register tones, and possibly one or two contour tones.

In a tone language, it is not the absolute pitch of the syllables that is important but the relations among the pitches of different syllables. Thus men, women, and children, with differently pitched voices, can still communicate in a tone language.

Tones generally have a *lexical* function, that is, they make a difference between words. But in some languages tones may also have a *grammatical function,* as in Edo spoken in midwestern Nigeria. The tone on monosyllabic verbs followed by a direct object indicates the tense and transitivity of the verb. Low tone means present tense, transitive; high tone means past tense, transitive, as illustrated here:

òtà gbɛ̀   èbé
Ota write+PRES+TRANS   book
Ota writes a book.
òtà gbɛ́   èbé
Ota write+PAST+TRANS   book
Ota wrote a book.

In many tone languages we find a continual lowering of the absolute pitch on the tones throughout an utterance. The *relative* pitches remain the same, however. In the following sentence in Twi, spoken in Ghana, the relative pitch rather than the absolute pitch is important.

"Kofi searches for a little food for his friend's child."

Kòfí   hwèhwé   áduàŋ   kàkrá mà   ǹ' ádàmfò   bá
| | | | | | | | | | | | | |
L H   L   H   H   L   L   H L   L HL L L   H

The actual pitches of these syllables would be rather different from each other, as shown in the following musical staff–like figure (the higher the number, the higher the pitch):

7	fí								
6		hwé	á						
5	Kò				krá				
4		hwè					á		
3			duàŋ	kà					bá
2						mà ǹ'			
1							dàmfò		

The lowering of the pitch is called **downdrift.** In languages with downdrift, a high tone that occurs after a low tone, or a low tone after a high tone, is lower in pitch than the preceding similarly marked tone. Notice that the first high tone in the sentence is given the pitch value 7. The next high tone (which occurs after an intervening low tone) is 6; that is, it is lower in pitch than the first high tone.

This example shows that in analyzing tones, just as in analyzing segments, all the physical properties need not be considered. Only essential features are important in language—in this case, whether the tone is high or low *in relation to the other pitches.* The absolute pitch is inessential.

Languages that are not tone languages, such as English, are called **intonation** languages. The **pitch contour** of the utterance varies, but in an intonation language as opposed to a tone language, pitch is not used to distinguish words from each other. Intonation may affect the meaning of whole sentences, so that *John is here* spoken with falling pitch at the end is interpreted as a statement, but with rising pitch at the end, a question. We'll have more to say about intonation in the next chapter.

Phonetic Symbols and Spelling Correspondences

"Why do I have to keep writin' in these K's when they don't make any noise anyway?"

"Family Circus" © Bil Keane, Inc. Reprinted with permission of King Features Syndicate.

Table 6.6 shows the sound/spelling correspondences for American English consonants and vowels. (We have not given all possible spellings for every sound; however, these examples should help you relate English orthography to the English sound system.) We have included the symbols for the voiceless aspirated stops to illustrate that what speakers usually consider one sound—for example *p*—may occur phonetically as two sounds, [p], [pʰ].

Some of these pronunciations may differ from your own. For example, you may (or may not) pronounce the words *cot* and *caught* identically. In the form of English described here, *cot* and *caught* are pronounced differently, so *cot* is one of the examples of the vowel sound [a] as in *car*. *Caught* illustrates the vowel [ɔ] as in *core*.

There will be other differences, too, because English is a worldwide language and is spoken in many forms both within and without the United States. The English examples used in this book are a compromise among several varieties of American English, but this should not deter you. Our purpose is to teach phonetics in general, and to show you how phonetics might describe the speech sounds of any of the world's languages with the proper symbols and diacritics. We merely use American

English for illustration, and we provide the major phonetic symbols for American English to show you how such symbols may be used to describe the phonetics of any of the world's languages.

TABLE 6.6 Phonetic Symbol/English Spelling Correspondences

Consonants

Symbol	Examples
p	spit tip apple ample
pʰ	pit prick plaque appear
b	bit tab brat bubble
m	mitt tam smack Emmy camp comb
t	stick pit kissed write
tʰ	tick intend pterodactyl attack
d	Dick cad drip loved ride
n	nick kin snow mnemonic gnostic pneumatic know
k	skin stick scat critique elk
kʰ	curl kin charisma critic mechanic close
g	girl burg longer Pittsburgh
ŋ	sing think finger
f	fat philosophy flat phlogiston coffee reef cough
v	vat dove gravel
s	sip skip psychology pass pats democracy scissors fasten deceive descent
z	zip jazz razor pads kisses Xerox design lazy scissors maize
θ	thigh through wrath ether Matthew
ð	thy their weather lathe either
ʃ	shoe mush mission nation fish glacial sure
ʒ	measure vision azure casual decision rouge
tʃ	choke match feature rich righteous
dʒ	judge midget George magistrate residual
l	leaf feel call single
r	reef fear Paris singer
j	you yes feud use
w	witch swim queen
ʍ	which where whale (for speakers who pronounce *which* differently than *witch*)
h	hat who whole rehash
ʔ	bottle button glottal (for some speakers), (ʔ)uh–(ʔ)oh
ɾ	writer, rider, latter, ladder

TABLE 6.6 (Continued)

Vowels

Symbol	Examples
i	beet beat be receive key believe amoeba people Caesar Vaseline serene
ɪ	bit consist injury bin
e	gate bait ray great eight gauge reign they
ɛ	bet serenity says guest dead said
æ	pan act laugh comrade
u	boot lute who sewer through to too two move Lou
ʊ	put foot butcher could
ʌ	cut tough among oven does cover flood
o	coat go beau grow though toe own over
ɔ	caught stalk core saw ball awe
a	cot father palm sergeant honor hospital melodic
ə	sofa alone symphony suppose melody bird verb the
aj	bite sight by die dye Stein aisle choir liar island height sign
aw	about brown doubt coward
ɔj	boy doily

The "Phonetics" of Signed Languages

Earlier we noted that signed languages, like all other human languages, are governed by a grammatical system that includes syntactic and morphological rules. Signed languages are like spoken languages in another respect, which is that signs can be broken down into smaller units, which are in many ways analogous to the phonetic features we have discussed in this chapter. Just as spoken languages distinguish sounds according to place and manner of articulation, so signed languages distinguish signs according to the place and manner in which the signs are articulated by the hands. The signs of ASL, for example, are formed by four major features:

The configuration of the hand (handshape)

The movement of the hand and arms toward or away from the body

The location of the hands relative to the body

The orientation of the palm

For example, the sign meaning "arm" is a flat hand, moving to touch the upper arm. It has three features: *flat hand, motion upward, upper arm.*

As in spoken language, a change along one of these parameters can result in different words. So, for example, we saw that in English the voicing difference in the last sound of "rope" [rop] versus "robe" [rob] results in two different words. Similarly, in some languages supersegmental features such as tone distinguish words, for example, the difference in Thai between a word with a low tone, [nà:] meaning "a nickname," and the identical string with a midtone [nā:], meaning "rice paddy." In ASL a change in location, handshape, movement, or palm orientation can result in different signs with very different meanings. For example, the sign meaning "father" differs from the sign meaning "fine" only in their place of articulation. Both signs are formed with a spread five-finger handshape, but the thumb touches the signer's forehead in "father" and it touches his chest in "fine."

Figure 6.6 illustrates several sets of words that differ from each other along one or another of the phonetic parameters of ASL.

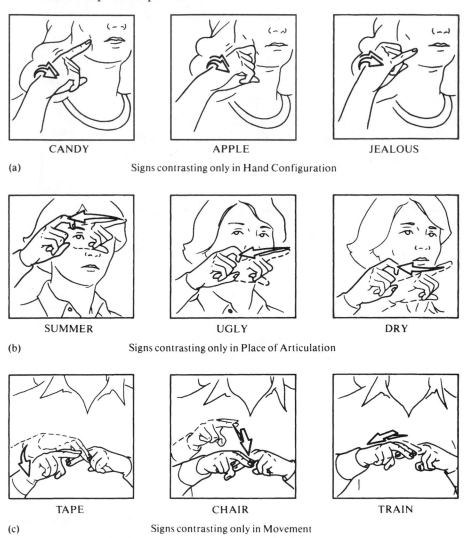

(a) Signs contrasting only in Hand Configuration

CANDY   APPLE   JEALOUS

(b) Signs contrasting only in Place of Articulation

SUMMER   UGLY   DRY

(c) Signs contrasting only in Movement

TAPE   CHAIR   TRAIN

FIGURE 6.6 Minimal contrasts illustrating major formational parameters.

Reprinted with permission of the publisher from *The Signs of Language* by Edward Klima and Ursula Bellugi, p. 42, Cambridge, Mass.: Harvard University Press, Copyright © 1979 by the President and Fellows of Harvard College.

Summary

The science of speech sounds is called **phonetics.** It aims to provide the set of properties necessary to describe and distinguish all the sounds in human languages throughout the world.

When we speak, the physical sounds we produce are continuous stretches of sound, which are the physical representations of strings of discrete linguistic **segments.** Knowledge of a language permits one to separate continuous speech into individual sounds and words.

The discrepancy between spelling and sounds in English and other languages motivated the development of phonetic alphabets in which one letter corresponds to one sound. The major **phonetic alphabet** in use is the **International Phonetic Alphabet (IPA),** which includes modified Roman letters and **diacritics,** by means of which the sounds of all human languages can be represented. To distinguish between **orthography** (spelling) and **phonetic transcriptions,** we write the latter between square brackets, as in [fənɛtɪk] for *phonetic*.

All English speech sounds come from the movement of lung air through the vocal tract. The air moves through the **glottis** (i.e., between the vocal cords), up the pharynx, through the oral (and possibly the nasal) cavity, and out the mouth or nose.

Human speech sounds fall into classes according to their phonetic properties. All speech sounds are either **consonants** or **vowels,** and all consonants are either **obstruents** or **sonorants.** Consonants have some obstruction of the airstream in the vocal tract, and the location of the obstruction defines their **place of articulation,** some of which are **bilabial, labiodental, alveolar, palatal, velar, uvular,** and **glottal.**

Consonants are further classified according to their **manner of articulation.** They may be **voiced** or **voiceless, oral** or **nasal,** long or short. They may be **stops, fricatives, affricates, liquids,** or **glides.** During the production of voiced sounds, the vocal cords are together and vibrating, whereas in voiceless sounds they are apart and not vibrating. Voiceless sounds may also be **aspirated** or **unaspirated.** In the production of aspirated sounds, the vocal cords remain apart for a brief time after the stop closure is released, resulting in a puff of air at the time of the release. Consonants may be grouped according to certain features to form larger classes such as **labials, coronals, anteriors,** and **sibilants.**

Vowels form the nucleus of syllables. They differ according to the position of the tongue and lips: high, mid, or low tongue; front, central, or back of the tongue; rounded or unrounded lips. The vowels in English may be **tense** or **lax.** Tense vowels are slightly longer in duration than lax vowels. Vowels may also be **stressed** (longer, higher in pitch, and louder) or **unstressed.** Vowels, like consonants, may be nasal or oral, although most vowels in all languages are oral.

Length, pitch, loudness, and stress are **prosodic,** or **suprasegmental,** features. They are imposed over and above the segmental values of the sounds in a syllable. In many languages, the pitch of the vowel in the syllable is linguistically significant. For example, two words with identical segments may contrast in meaning if one has a high pitch and another a low pitch. Such languages are tone languages. There are also **intonation** languages in which the rise and fall of pitch may contrast meanings of sentences. In English the statement *Mary is a teacher* will end with a fall in pitch, but as a question, *Mary is a teacher?* the pitch will rise.

English and other languages use stress to distinguish different words, such as *cóntent* and *contént*. In some languages, long vowels and long consonants contrast with their shorter counterparts. Thus *biru* and *biːru, saki* and *sakːi* are different words in Japanese.

Diacritics to specify such properties as nasalization, length, stress, and tone may be combined with the phonetic symbols for more detailed phonetic transcriptions. A phonetic transcription of *main* would use a tilde diacritic to indicate the nasalization of the vowel: [mẽn].

In sign languages, there are "phonetic" features analogous to those of spoken languages. In ASL these are handshape, movement, location, and palm orientation. As in spoken languages, changes along one of these parameters can result in a new word. In the following chapter, we discuss this meaning-changing property of features in much greater detail.

References for Further Reading

Abercrombie, D. 1967. *Elements of General Phonetics.* Chicago: Aldine.

Catford, J. C. 2001. *A Practical Introduction to Phonetics,* 2nd edition. New York: Oxford University Press.

Crystal, D. 2003. *A Dictionary of Linguistics and Phonetics,* 5th edition. Oxford, England: Blackwell Publishers.

Fromkin, V. A. (ed). 1978. *Tone: A Linguistic Survey.* New York: Academic Press.

International Phonetic Association. 1989. *Principles of the International Phonetics Association,* rev. ed. London: IPA.

Ladefoged, P. 2005. *Vowels and Consonants,* 2nd edition. Oxford, England: Blackwell Publishers.

Ladefoged, P. 2006. *A Course in Phonetics,* 5th edition. Boston, MA: Thomson Learning.

Ladefoged, P., and I. Maddieson. 1996. *The Sounds of the World's Languages.* Oxford, England: Blackwell Publishers.

MacKay, I. R. A. 1987. *Phonetics: The Science of Speech Production,* 2nd edition. Boston: Allyn and Bacon. (Appeared in 1991.)

Pullum, G. K., and W. A. Ladusaw. 1986. *Phonetic Symbol Guide.* Chicago: University of Chicago Press.

Exercises

1. Write the phonetic symbol for the first sound in each of the following words according to the way you pronounce it.

   Examples: ooze [u]   psycho   [s]

   a. judge   [ ]   **f.** thought   [ ]

   b. Thomas   [ ]   **g.** contact   [ ]

   c. though   [ ]   **h.** phone   [ ]

   d. easy   [ ]   **i.** civic   [ ]

   e. pneumonia [ ]   **j.** usual   [ ]

2. Write the phonetic symbol for the *last* sound in each of the following words.

   Example: boy [ɔj] (Dipththongs should be treated as one sound.)

a. fleece [ ]		**f.** cow	[ ]
b. neigh [ ]		**g.** rough	[ ]
c. long [ ]		**h.** cheese	[ ]
d. health [ ]		**i.** bleached	[ ]
e. watch [ ]		**j.** rags	[ ]

3. Write the following words in phonetic transcription, according to your pronunciation.

   Examples: *knot* [nat]; *delightful* [dilajtfəl] or [dəlajtfəl]. Some students may pronounce some words the same.

a. physics	**h.** Fromkin
b. merry	**i.** tease
c. marry	**j.** weather
d. Mary	**k.** coat
e. yellow	**l.** Rodman
f. sticky	**m.** heath
g. transcription	**n.** "your name"

4. Following is a phonetic transcription of a verse in the poem "The Walrus and the Carpenter" by Lewis Carroll. The speaker who transcribed it may not have exactly the same pronunciation as you; there are many correct versions. However, there is *one major error* in each line that is an impossible pronunciation for any American English speaker. The error may consist of an extra symbol, a missing symbol, or a wrong symbol in the word. Note that the phonetic transcription that is given is a **narrow** transcription; aspiration is marked, as is the nasalization of vowels. This is to illustrate a detailed transcription. However, none of the errors involve aspiration or nasalization of vowels.

   Write the word in which the error occurs in the correct phonetic transcription.

	Corrected Word
a. ðə tʰãjm hæz cʌ̃m	[kʰʌ̃m]
b. ðə wɔlrəs sed	
c. tʰu tʰɔlk əv mẽni θĩŋz	
d. əv ʃuz ãnd ʃɪps	
e. æ̃nd silĩŋ wæx	
f. əv kʰæbəgəz æ̃nd kʰĩŋz	
g. æ̃nd waj ðə si ɪs bɔjlĩŋ hat	
h. æ̃nd wɛθər pʰɪgz hæv wĩŋz	

5. The following are all English words written in a broad phonetic transcription (thus omitting details such as nasalization and aspiration). Write the words using normal English orthography.

   a. [hit]

   b. [strok]

   c. [fez]

    d. [ton]

    e. [boni]

    f. [skrim]

    g. [frut]

    h. [pritʃər]

    i. [krak]

6. Write the symbol that corresponds to each of the following phonetic descriptions, then give an English word that contains this sound.

    Example: voiced alveolar stop   [d] *dough*

    a. voiceless bilabial unaspirated stop   [ ]

    b. low front vowel   [ ]

    c. lateral liquid   [ ]

    d. velar nasal   [ ]

    e. voiced interdental fricative   [ ]

    f. voiceless affricate   [ ]

    g. palatal glide   [ ]

    h. mid lax front vowel   [ ]

    i. high back tense vowel   [ ]

    j. voiceless aspirated alveolar stop   [ ]

7. In each of the following pairs of words, the bold italicized sounds differ by one or more phonetic properties (features). Give the symbol for each italicized sound, state their differences and, in addition, state what properties they have in common.

    Example: ph*o*ne—ph*o*nic

        The *o* in *phone* is mid, tense, round.

        The *o* in *phonic* is low, unround.

        Both are back vowels.

    a. ba*th*—ba*th*e

    b. redu*c*e—redu*c*tion

    c. c*oo*l—c*o*ld

    d. wi*f*e—wi*v*es

    e. cat*s*—dog*s*

    f. i*m*polite—i*n*decent

8. Write a phonetic transcription of the italicized words in the following poem entitled "English" published long ago in a British newspaper.

I take it you already ***know***
Of ***tough*** and ***bough*** and ***cough*** and ***dough?***
Some may stumble, but not ***you,***
On ***hiccough, thorough, slough*** and ***through?***
So now you are ready, perhaps,
To learn of less familiar traps?
Beware of ***heard,*** a dreadful ***word***

That looks like *beard* and sounds like *bird.*
And *dead,* it's *said* like *bed,* not *bead;*
For goodness' sake, don't call it *deed!*
Watch out for *meat* and *great* and *threat.*
(They rhyme with *suite* and *straight* and *debt.*)
A *moth* is not a moth in *mother,*
Nor *both* in *bother, broth* in *brother.*

9. For each group of sounds listed, state the phonetic feature(s) they all share.

    Example: [p] [b] [m] Features: bilabial, stop, consonant

    a. [g] [p] [t] [d] [k] [b]

    b. [u] [ʊ] [o] [ɔ]

    c. [i] [ɪ] [e] [ɛ] [æ]

    d. [t] [s] [ʃ] [p] [k] [tʃ] [f] [h]

    e. [v] [z] [ʒ] [dʒ] [n] [g] [d] [b] [l] [r] [w] [j]

    f. [t] [d] [s] [ʃ] [n] [tʃ] [dʒ]

10. Write the following broad phonetic transcriptions in regular English spelling.

    a. nom tʃamski ɪz e lɪŋgwɪst hu titʃəz æt ɛm aj ti

    b. fənɛtɪks ɪz ðə stʌdi əv spitʃ sawndz

    c. ɔl spokən læŋgwɪdʒəz juz sawndz prədust baj ðə ʌpər rɛspərətɔri sɪstəm

    d. ɪn wʌn dajələkt əv ɪŋglɪʃ kat ðə nawn ænd kɔt ðə vərb ar prənawnst ðə sem

    e. sʌm pipəl θɪŋk fənɛtɪks ɪz vɛri ɪntərɛstɪŋ

    f. vɪktɔrijə framkən rabərt radmən ænd ninə hajəmz ar ðə ɔθərz əv ðɪs bʊk

11. What phonetic property or feature distinguishes the sets of sounds in column A from those in column B?

A	**B**
a. [i] [ɪ]	[u] [ʊ]
b. [p] [t] [k] [s] [f]	[b] [d] [g] [z] [v]
c. [p] [b] [m]	[t] [d] [n] [k] [g] [ŋ]
d. [i] [ɪ] [u] [ʊ]	[e] [ɛ] [o] [ɔ] [æ] [a]
e. [f] [v] [s] [z] [ʃ] [ʒ]	[tʃ] [dʒ]
f. [i] [ɪ] [e] [ə] [ɛ] [æ]	[u] [ʊ] [o] [ɔ] [a]

12. Which of the following sound pairs have the same manner of articulation, and what is that manner of articulation?

    a. [h] [ʔ]   **f.** [f] [ʃ]

    b. [r] [w]   **g.** [k] [θ]

    c. [m] [ŋ]   **h.** [s] [g]

    d. [ð] [v]   **i.** [j] [w]

    e. [r] [t]   **j.** [j] [dʒ]

13. **A.** Which of the following vowels are lax and which are tense.

    a. [i]   **b.** [ɪ]   **c.** [u]   **d.** [ʌ]   **e.** [ʊ]   **f.** [e]

    g. [ɛ]   **h.** [o]   **i.** [ɔ]   **j.** [æ]   **k.** [a]   **l.** [ə]

    m. [aj]   **n.** [aw]   **o.** [ɔj]

    (*Hint*: diphthongs are tense.)

    B. Think of ordinary, nonexclamatory English words with one syllable that end in [ʃ] preceded directly by each of these vowels. Are any such words impossible in English?

    Example: *fish* [fɪʃ] is such a word. Words ending in [-ajʃ] are not possible in English.

    C. In terms of tense/lax, which vowel type is found in most such words?

14. Write a made-up sentence in narrow phonetic transcription that contains at least six different monophthongal vowels and two different diphthongs.

15. The front vowels of English, [i, ɪ, e, ɛ, æ] are all unrounded. However, many languages have rounded front vowels, such as French. Here are three words in French with rounded front vowels. Transcribe them phonetically by finding out the correct IPA symbols for front rounded vowels: (*Hint:* Try one of the books given in the references, or Google around.)

    tu, "you," has a high front rounded vowel and is transcribed phonetically as [ ]?
    bleu, "blue," has a midfront rounded vowel and is transcribed phonetically as [ ]?
    heure, "hour," has a low midfront rounded vowel and is transcribed phonetically as [ ]?

    (*Hint*: the *h* is silent in *heure*.)

16. **a.** Take all of the vowels from Table 6.6 except the schwa and find a monosyllabic word containing that vowel followed directly by [t], giving both the spelling and the phonetic transcription.

    Example: *beat* [bit]   *foot* [fʊt]   etc.

    b. Now do the same thing for monosyllabic words ending in [r]. Indicate when such a word appears not to occur in your dialect of English.

    c. And do the same thing for monosyllabic words ending in [ŋ]. Indicate when such a word appears not to occur in your dialect of English.

    d. Is there a quantitative difference in the number of examples found as you go from **A** to **C**?

    e. Are most vowels that "work" in B tense or lax? How about in C?

    f. Write a brief summary of the difficulties you encountered in trying to do this exercise.

Phonology: The Sound Patterns of Language

7

Speech is human, silence is divine, yet also brutish and dead; therefore we must learn both arts.

THOMAS CARLYLE *(1795–1881)*

Phonology is the study of telephone etiquette.

A HIGH SCHOOL STUDENT

What do you think is greater: the number of languages in the world, or the number of speech sounds in all those languages? Well, there are thousands of languages, but only hundreds of speech sounds, some of which we examined in the previous chapter. Even more remarkable, only a few dozen features, such as *voicing* or *bilabial* or *stop*, are needed to describe every speech sound that occurs in every human language.

That being the case, why, you may ask, do languages sound so different? One reason is that the sounds form different patterns in different languages. English has nasalized vowels, but only in syllables with nasal consonants. French puts nasal vowels anywhere it pleases, with or without nasal consonants. The speech sound that ends the word *song*—the velar nasal [ŋ]—cannot begin a word in English, but it can in Vietnamese. The common Vietnamese name spelled *Nguyen* begins with this sound, and the reason few of us can pronounce this name correctly is that it doesn't follow the English pattern.

The fact that a sound such as [ŋ] is difficult for an English speaker to pronounce at the beginning of a word but easy for a Vietnamese speaker means that there is no general notion of "difficulty of articulation" that can explain all of the sound patterns of particular languages. Rather, the ease or difficulty of certain sounds and sound combinations depends on a speaker's unconscious knowledge of the sound patterns of her language.

The study of the way speech sounds form patterns is **phonology**. These patterns may be as simple as the fact that the velar nasal cannot begin a syllable in English, or as complex as why the *g* in *sign* is silent, but is pronounced in the related word *signature*. To see that this is a pattern and not a one-time exception, just consider the slippery *n* in *autumn* and *autumnal*, or the *b* in *bomb* and *bombard*.

The word *phonology* refers both to the linguistic knowledge that speakers have about the sound patterns of their language and to the description of that knowledge that linguists try to produce. Thus it is like the way we defined *grammar*: your mental knowledge of your language, or a linguist's description of that knowledge.

A speaker's phonological knowledge is nearly limitless: it includes the ability to recognize a foreign accent, to invent words, to make nouns plural, to put verbs in the past tense, to omit sounds without changing the word (you can say *general* with or without the middle vowel and it remains the same), to add sounds without changing the word (you can say *across* or *acrosst* and it's taken to be the same word). Phonology tells you what sounds are in your language and which ones are foreign; it tells you what combinations of sounds are legal, whether they make an actual word (*black*) or not (*blick*), and which ones aren't legal (**lbick*). It also explains why certain phonetic features are important to the meaning of a word, for example voicing in English as in *pat* versus *bat*, while other features, such as aspiration in English, are not crucial to meaning, as we noted in the previous chapter.

In this chapter we'll look at some of the phonological processes that you know, and have known since you were a child, and yet may initially appear to you to be unreasonably complex. Keep in mind that we are only making explicit what you already know, and its complexity is in a way a wondrous feature of your own mind.

The Pronunciation of Morphemes

> The *t* is silent as in Harlow.
>
> **MARGOT ASQUITH,** *referring to her name being mispronounced by Jean Harlow*

Knowledge of phonology determines how we pronounce words and the parts of words we call morphemes. Often, certain morphemes are pronounced differently depending on their context, and we will introduce a way of describing this variation with phonological rules. We begin with some examples from English, and then move on to examples from other languages.

The Pronunciation of Plurals

Nearly all English nouns have a plural form: *cat/cats, dog/dogs, fox/foxes*. But have you ever paid attention to how plural forms are *pronounced*. Listen to a native speaker of English (or yourself if you are one) pronounce the plurals of the following nouns.

A	B	C	D
cab	cap	bus	child
cad	cat	bush	ox
bag	back	buzz	mouse
love	cuff	garage	criterion

A	**B**	**C**	**D**
lathe	faith	match	sheep
cam		badge	
can			
bang			
call			
bar			
spa			
boy			

The final sound of the plural nouns from Column A is a [z]—a *voiced* alveolar fricative. For column B the plural ending is an [s]—a *voiceless* alveolar fricative. And for Column C it's [əz]. Here is our first example of a morpheme with different pronunciations: the regular plural morpheme is pronounced as [z], [s], or [əz]. Note also that there is a regularity in columns A, B, and C that does not exist in D. The plural forms in D—*children, oxen, mice, criteria, and sheep*—are a hodge-podge of special cases that are memorized individually when you learn English, whether natively or as a second language. This is because there is no way to predict the plural forms of these words.

How do we know how to pronounce this plural morpheme? The spelling, which adds *s* or *es*, is misleading—not a *z* in sight—yet if you know English, you pronounce it as we indicated. When faced with this type of question, it's useful to make a chart that records the phonological environments in which each variant of the morpheme is known to occur. (The more technical term for a variant is **allomorph**.) Writing the words from the first three columns in broad phonetic transcription, we have our first chart for the plural morpheme.

Allomorph	**Environment**
[z]	After [kæb], [kæd], [bæg], [lʌv], [leð], [kæm], [kæn], [bæŋ], [kɔl], [bar], [spa], [bɔj] e.g., [kæbz], [kædz] . . . [bɔjz]
[s]	After [kæp], [kæt], [bæk], [kʌf], [feθ], e.g., [kæps], [kæts] . . . [feθs]
[əz]	After [bʌs], [buʃ], [bʌz], [gəraʒ], [mætʃ], [bædʒ], e.g., [bʌsəz], [buʃəz] . . . [bædʒəz]

To discover the pattern behind the way plurals are pronounced, we look for a property of the environment associated with each group of allomorphs. For example, what is it about [kæb] or [lʌv] that determines that the plural morpheme will take the form [z] rather than [s] or [əz]?

To guide our search, we look for **minimal pairs** in our list of words. A minimal pair is two words with different meanings that are identical except for one sound segment that occurs in the same place in each word. For example, *cab* [kæb] and *cad* [kæd] are a minimal pair that differ only in their final segments, whereas *cat* [kæt] and *mat* [mæt] are a minimal pair that differ only in their initial segments. Other minimal pairs in our list include *cap/cab*, *bag/back*, and *bag/badge*.

Minimal pairs whose members take different allomorphs are particularly useful for our search. For example, consider *cab* [kæb] and *cap* [kæp], which take the allomorphs [z] and [s] to form the plural. Clearly, the final segment is responsible, because that is where the two words differ. Similarly for *bag* [bæg] and *badge* [bædʒ]. Their final segments determine the different plural allomorphs [z] and [əz].

Apparently, the distribution of allomorphs in English is conditioned by the final segment of the singular form. We can make our chart more concise by considering just the final segment. (We treat diphthongs such as [ɔj] as single segments.)

Allomorph	Environment
[z]	After [b], [d], [g], [v], [ð], [m], [n], [ŋ], [l], [r], [a], [ɔj]
[s]	After [p], [t], [k], [f], [θ]
[əz]	After [s], [ʃ], [z], [ʒ], [tʃ], [dʒ]

We now want to understand *why* the English plural follows this pattern. We *always* answer questions of this type by inspecting the *phonetic properties* of the conditioning segments. Such an inspection reveals that the segments that trigger the [əz] plural have in common the property of being *sibilants*. Of the nonsibilants, the *voiceless* segments take the [s] plural, and the *voiced* segments take the [z] plural. Now the rules can be stated in more general terms:

Allomorph	Environment
[z]	After voiced nonsibilant segments
[s]	After voiceless nonsibilant segments
[əz]	After sibilant segments

An even more concise way to express these rules is to assume that the basic or underlying form of the plural morpheme is /z/, with the meaning "plural." This is the "default" pronunciation. The rules tell us when the default does *not* apply:

1. Insert a [ə] before the plural morpheme /z/ when a regular noun ends in a sibilant, giving [əz].
2. Change the plural morpheme /z/ to a voiceless [s] when preceded by a voiceless sound.

These rules will derive the phonetic forms—that is, the pronunciations—of plurals for all regular nouns. Because the basic form of the plural is /z/, if no rule applies, then the plural morpheme will be realized as [z]. The following chart shows how the plurals of *bus, butt,* and *bug* are formed. At the top are the basic forms. The two rules apply or not as appropriate as one moves downward. The output of rule 1 becomes the input of rule 2. At the bottom are the phonetic realizations—the way the words are pronounced.

	bus + pl.	*butt* + pl.	*bug* + pl.
Basic representation	/bʌs + z/	/bʌt + z/	/bʌg + z/
Apply rule (1)	ə	NA*	NA
Apply rule (2)	NA	s	NA
Phonetic representation	[bʌsəz]	[bʌts]	[bʌgz]

*NA means "not applicable."

As we have formulated these rules, (1) must apply before (2). If we applied the rules in reverse order, we would derive an incorrect phonetic form for the plural of *bus*, as a diagram similar to the previous one illustrates:

Basic representation	/bʌs + z/
Apply rule (2)	s
Apply rule (1)	ə
Phonetic representation	*[bʌsəs]

The particular phonological rules that determine the phonetic form of the plural morpheme and other morphemes of the language are **morphophonemic rules**. Such rules concern the pronunciation of specific morphemes. Thus the plural morphophonemic rules apply to the plural morpheme specifically, not to all morphemes in English. If you find the terminology a bit daunting, you're not alone, as the following cartoon shows.

Additional Examples of Allomorphs

"Frank & Ernest" © Thaves/Dist. by Newspaper Enterprise Association, Inc.

The formation of the regular past tense of English verbs parallels the formation of regular plurals. Like plurals, some irregular past tenses conform to no particular rule and must be learned individually, such as *go/went, sing/sang,* and *hit/hit.* And also like plurals, there are three *phonetic* past-tense morphemes for regular verbs: [d], [t], and [əd]. Here are several examples in broad phonetic transcription. Study sets A, B, and C and try to see the regularity before reading further.

Set A: *grab* [græb], *grabbed* [græbd]; *hug* [hʌg], *hugged* [hʌgd]; *faze* [fez], *fazed* [fezd]; *roam* [rom], *roamed* [romd].

Set B: *reap* [rip], *reaped* [ript]; *poke* [pok], *poked* [pokt]; *kiss* [kɪs], *kissed* [kɪst]; *patch* [pætʃ], *patched* [pætʃt]

Set C: *gloat* [glɒt], *gloated* [glɒtəd], *raid* [red], *raided* [redəd]

Set A suggests that if the verb ends in a voiced segment, you add a voiced [d] to form the past tense. Set B suggests that if the verb ends in a voiceless segment, you add a voiceless [t] to form the past tense. Set C shows us that if the verb ends in the alveolar stops /t/ or /d/, a schwa plus [d] is added, reminding us of the insertion of a schwa to form the plural of nouns that end in sibilants.

Just as /z/ was the basic form of the plural morpheme, /d/ is the basic form of the past-tense morpheme, and the rules for past-tense formation of regular verbs is much like the rules for the plural formation of regular nouns. These are also *morphophonemic* rules as they apply specifically to the past-tense morpheme /d/. As with the plural rules, the output of Rule 1, if any, provides the input to Rule 2, and the rules must be applied in order.

1. Insert a [ə] before the past-tense morpheme when a regular verb ends in a non-nasal alveolar stop giving [əd].
2. Change the past-tense morpheme to a voiceless [t] when a voiceless sound precedes it.

Two further allomorphs in English are the possessive morphemes and the third-person singular morpheme, spelled *s* or *es*. These morphemes take on the same phonetic form as the plural morpheme *according to the same rules!* Add [s] to *ship* to get *ship's*; add [z] to *woman* to get *woman's*, and add [əz] to *judge* to get *judge's*. Similarly for the verbs *eat*, *need*, and *rush*, whose third-person singular forms are *eats* with a final [s], *needs* with a final [z], and *rushes* with a final [əz].

That the rules of phonology are based on properties of segments rather than on individual words is one of the factors that make it possible for young children to learn their native language in a relatively short period. The young child doesn't need to learn each plural, each past tense, each possessive form, and each verb ending, on a noun-by-noun or verb-by-verb basis. Once the rule is learned, thousands of word forms are automatically known. And as we will see when we discuss language development in chapter 8, children give clear evidence of learning morphophonemic rules such as the plural rules by applying the rule too broadly and producing forms such as *mouses, mans*, and so on, which are irregular in the adult language.

English is not the only language that has morphemes that are pronounced differently in different phonological environments. Most languages have morpheme variation that can be described by rules similar to the ones we have written for English. For example, the negative morpheme in the West African language Akan has three nasal allomorphs: [m] before *p*, [n] before *t*, and [ŋ] before *k*, as the following examples show ([mɪ] means "I"):

mɪ pɛ	"I like"	mɪ mpɛ	"I don't like"
mɪ tɪ	"I speak"	mɪ ntɪ	"I don't speak"
mɪ kɔ	"I go"	mɪ ŋkɔ	"I don't go"

The rule that describes the distribution of allomorphs is:

Change the place of articulation of the nasal negative morpheme to agree with the place of articulation of a following consonant.

The rule that changes the pronunciation of nasal consonants as just illustrated is called the **homorganic nasal rule**—*homorganic* means "same place"—because the place of articulation of the nasal is the same as for the following consonant. The homorganic nasal rule is a common rule in the world's languages.

Phonemes: The Phonological Units of Language

> In the physical world the naive speaker and hearer actualize and are sensitive to sounds, but what they feel themselves to be pronouncing and hearing are "phonemes."
>
> EDWARD SAPIR, *1933*

The phonological rules discussed in the preceding section apply only to particular morphemes. However, other phonological rules apply to the sounds in any morpheme in the language. These rules express our knowledge about the sound patterns of the entire language.

This section introduces the notions of **phoneme** and **allophone**. Phonemes are what we have been calling the basic form of a sound and are sensed in your mind rather than spoken or heard. Each phoneme has associated with it one or more sounds, called allophones, which represent the actual sound corresponding to the phoneme in various environments. For example, the phoneme /p/ is pronounced with the aspiration allophone [pʰ] in *pit* but without aspiration [p] in *spit*. Phonological rules operate on phonemes to make explicit which allophones are pronounced in which environments.

Vowel Nasalization in English as an Illustration of Allophones

English contains a general phonological rule that determines the contexts in which vowels are nasalized. In chapter 6 we noted that both oral and nasal vowels occur *phonetically* in English. The following examples show this:

bean	[bĩn]	bead	[bid]
roam	[rõm]	robe	[rob]

Taking oral vowels as basic—that is, as the phonemes—we have a phonological rule that states:

A vowel becomes nasalized before a nasal segment (within the same syllable).

This rule expresses your knowledge of English pronunciation: nasalized vowels occur only before nasal consonants and never elsewhere. The effect of this rule is exemplified in Table 7.1.

TABLE 7.1   Nasal and Oral Vowels: Words and Nonwords

Words						**Nonwords**		
be	[bi]	bead	[bid]	bean	[bĩn]	*[bĩ]	*[bĩd]	*[bin]
lay	[le]	lace	[les]	lame	[lẽm]	*[lẽ]	*[lẽs]	*[lem]
baa	[bæ]	bad	[bæd]	bang	[bæ̃ŋ]	*[bæ̃]	*[bæ̃d]	*[bæŋ]

As the examples in Table 7.1 illustrate, oral vowels in English occur in final position and before non-nasal consonants; nasalized vowels occur only before nasal consonants. The nonwords show us that nasalized vowels do not occur finally or before non-nasal consonants, nor do oral vowels occur before nasal consonants.

You may be unaware of this variation in your vowel production, but this is natural. Whether you speak or hear the vowel in *bean* with or without nasalization does not matter. Without nasalization, it might sound a bit strange, as if you had a foreign accent, but *bean* pronounced [bĩn] and *bean* pronounced [bin] would convey the same word. Likewise, if you pronounced *bead* as [bĩd], with a nasalized vowel, someone might suspect you had a cold, or that you spoke nasally, but the word would remain *bead*. Because nasalization is an inessential difference insofar as what the word actually is, we tend to be unaware of it.

Contrast this situation with a change in vowel height. If you intend to say *bead* but say *bad* instead, that makes a difference. The [i] in *bead* and the [æ] in *bad* are sounds from *different* phonemes. Substitute one for another and you get a different word (or no word). The [i] in *bead* and the [ĩ] in nasalized *bead* do not make a difference in meaning. These two sounds, then, belong to the same phoneme, an abstract high front vowel that we denote between slashes as /i/.

Phonemes are not physical sounds. They are abstract mental representations of the phonological units of a language, the units used to represent words in our mental lexicon. The phonological rules of the language apply to phonemes to determine the pronunciation of words.

The process of substituting one sound for another in a word to see if it makes a difference is a good way to identify the phonemes of a language. Here are twelve words differing only in their vowel:

beat	[bit]	[i]	boot	[but]	[u]
bit	[bɪt]	[ɪ]	but	[bʌt]	[ʌ]
bait	[bet]	[e]	boat	[bot]	[o]
bet	[bɛt]	[ɛ]	bought	[bɔt]	[ɔ]
bat	[bæt]	[æ]	bout	[bawt]	[aw]
bite	[bajt]	[aj]	bot	[bat]	[a]

Any two of these words form a *minimal pair*: two *different* words that differ in one sound. The two sounds that cause the word difference belong to different phonemes. The pair [bid] and [bĩd] are not different words; they are variants of the same word. Therefore, [i] and [ĩ] do *not* belong to different phonemes. They are two actualizations of the same phoneme.

From the minimal set of [b–t] words we can infer that English has a least twelve vowel phonemes. (We consider diphthongs to function as single vowel sounds.) To that total we can add a phoneme corresponding to [ʊ] resulting from minimal pairs such as *book* [bʊk] and *beak* [bik]; and we can add one for [ɔj] resulting from minimal pairs such as *boy* [bɔj] and *buy* [baj].

Our minimal pair analysis has revealed eleven monophthongal and three diphthongal vowel phonemes, namely /i ɪ e ɛ æ u ʊ o ɔ a ʌ/ and /aj aw ɔj/. (This set may differ slightly in other variants of English.) Importantly, each of these vowel phonemes has (at least) two allophones (i.e., two ways of being pronounced: orally as [i], [ɪ], [e], etc., and nasally as [ĩ], [ɪ̃], [ẽ], etc.), as determined by the phonological rule of nasalization.

A particular realization (pronunciation) of a phoneme is called a **phone**. The collection of phones that are the realizations of the same phoneme are called the *allophones* of that phoneme. In English, each vowel phoneme has both an oral and a nasalized allophone. The choice of the allophone is not random or haphazard; It is *rule-governed*.

To distinguish between a phoneme and its allophones, we use slashes / / to enclose phonemes and continue to use square brackets [ ] for allophones or phones. For example, [i] and [ī] are allophones of the phoneme /i/; [ɪ] and [ɪ̃] are allophones of the phoneme /ɪ/, and so on. Thus we will represent *bead* and *bean* phonemically as /bid/ and /bin/. We refer to these as *phonemic* transcriptions of the two words. The rule for the distribution of oral and nasal vowels in English shows that phonetically these words will be pronounced as [bid] and [bīn]. The pronunciations are indicated by phonetic transcriptions, and written between square brackets.

Allophones of /t/

KNOW YOUR OBJETS D'ART

BUST OF
PLATO

BUST OF
PLAY-DOH

5-13

Consonants, too, have allophones whose distribution is rule-governed. For /t/ the following examples illustrate the point.

  tick [tʰɪk]   stick [stɪk]   hits [hɪts]   bitter [bɪɾər]

In *tick* we normally find an aspirated [tʰ], whereas in *stick* and *hits* we find an unaspirated [t], and in *bitter* we find the flap [ɾ]. As with vowel nasalization, swapping these sounds around will not change word meaning. If we pronounce *bitter* with a [tʰ], it will not change the word; it will simply sound unnatural (to most Americans).

  We account for this knowledge of how *t* is pronounced by positing a phoneme /t/ with three allophones [tʰ], [t], and [ɾ]. We also posit phonological rules, which roughly state that the aspirated [tʰ] occurs before a stressed vowel, the unaspirated [t] occurs directly before or after /s/, and the flap [ɾ] occurs between a stressed vowel and an unstressed vowel. For many speakers, a glottal stop [ʔ] may be used in words such as *butler* [bʌʔlər]. Therefore, [ʔ] is yet another allophone of /t/.

Whether we pronounce *tick* as [tʰɪk], [tɪk], [ɾɪk], or [ʔɪk], we are speaking the same word, however strangely pronounced. The allophones of a phoneme do not *contrast*. If we change the voicing and say *Dick*, or the manner of articulation and say *sick*, or the nasalization and say *nick*, we get different words. Those sounds *do* contrast. *Tick, Dick, sick,* and *nick* thus form a minimal set that shows us that there are phonemes /t/, /d/, /s/, and /n/ in English. We may proceed in this manner to discover other phonemes by considering *pick, kick, Mick* (as in Jagger), *Vic, thick, chick, lick,* and *Rick* to infer the phonemes /p/, /k/, /m/, /v/, /θ/, /tʃ/, /l/, /r/. By finding other minimal pairs and sets, we would discover yet more consonant phonemes such as /ð/, which, together with /θ/, contrasts the words *thy* and *thigh,* or *either* and *ether*.

Each of these phonemes has its own set of allophones, even if that set consists of a single phone, which would mean there is only one pronunciation in all environments. Most phonemes have more than one allophone, and the phonological rules dictate when the different allophones occur. It should be clear at this point that pronunciation is not a random process. It is systematic and rule-governed, and while the systems and the rules may appear complex, they are no more than a compendium of the knowledge that every speaker has.

Minimal Pairs in ASL

There are minimal pairs in sign languages, just as there are in spoken languages. In chapter 6, p. 248, Figure 6-6 shows minimal contrasts involving hand configuration, place of articulation, and movement.

The signs meaning "candy," "apple," and "jealous" are articulated at the same location on the face and involve the same movement, but contrast minimally in hand configuration. "Summer," "ugly," and "dry" are a minimal set contrasting only in place of articulation, and "tape," "chair," and "train" contrast only in movement.

Complementary Distribution

Minimal pairs illustrate that some speech sounds are contrastive in a language, and these contrastive sounds represent the set of phonemes of that language. We also saw that some sounds are not distinct; they do not contrast meanings. The sounds [t] and [ʔ] were cited as examples that do not contrast. The substitution of one for the other does not create a minimal pair.

Oral and nasal vowels in English are also nondistinct sounds. What's more, the oral and nasal allophones of each vowel phoneme never occur in the same phonological context, as Table 7.2 illustrates.

TABLE 7.2 Distribution of Oral and Nasal Vowels in English Syllables

	In Final Position	Before Nasal Consonants	Before Oral Consonants
Oral vowels	Yes	No	Yes
Nasal vowels	No	Yes	No

Where oral vowels occur, nasal vowels do not occur, and vice versa. In this sense the phones are said to complement each other or to be in **complementary distribution**. By and large, the allophones of a phoneme are in complementary distribution—never occurring in identical environments. Complementary distribution is a fundamental concept of phonology, and interestingly enough, it shows up in everyday life. Here are a couple of examples that draw on the common experience of reading and writing English.

The first example focuses on *printed* letters such as those that appear on the pages of this book. Each printed letter of English has two main variants: lowercase and uppercase (or capital). If we restrict our attention to words that are not proper names or acronyms (such as Ron or UNICEF), we can formulate a simple rule that does a fair job of determining how letters will be printed:

> A letter is printed in uppercase if it is the first letter of a sentence; otherwise, it is printed in lowercase.

Even ignoring names and acronyms, this rule is only approximately right, but let's go with it anyway. It helps to explain why written sentences such as the following appear so strange:

> phonology is the study of the sound patterns of human languageS.
> pHONOLOGY iS tHE sTUDY oF tHE sOUND pATTERNS oF hUMAN lANGUAGES.

To the extent that the rule is correct, the lowercase and uppercase variants of an English letter *are in complementary distribution.* The uppercase variant occurs in one particular environment (namely, at the beginning of the sentence), and the lowercase variant occurs in every other environment (or elsewhere). Therefore, just as every English vowel phoneme has an oral and a nasalized allophone that occurs in different spoken environments, every letter of the English alphabet has two variants, or allographs, that occur in different written environments. In both cases, the two variants of a single mental representation (phoneme or letter) are in *complementary distribution* because they never appear in the same environment. And, substituting one for the other—a nasal vowel in place of an oral one, or an uppercase letter in place of a lowercase one—may sound or look unusual, but it will not change the meaning of what is spoken or written.

Our second example turns to *cursive* handwriting, which you are likely to have learned in elementary school. Writing in cursive is in one sense more similar to the act of speaking than printing is, because in cursive writing each letter of a word (usually) connects to the following letter—just as nearby sounds influence one another during speech. The following figure illustrates that the connections between the letters of a word in cursive writing create different variants of a letter in different environments:

Compare how the letter *l* appears after a *g* (as in *glue*) and after a *b* (as in *blue*). In the first case, the *l* begins near the bottom of the line, but in the second case, the *l* begins near the middle of the line (which is indicated by the dashes). In other words, the same letter *l* has two variants. It doesn't matter where the *l* begins, it's still an *l*. Likewise, it doesn't matter whether a vowel in English is nasalized or not, it's still that vowel. Which variant occurs in a particular word is determined by the immediately preceding letter. The variant that begins near the bottom of the line appears after letters like *g* that end near the bottom of the line. The variant that begins near the middle of the line appears after letters like *b* that end near the middle of the line. The two variants of *l* are therefore in complementary distribution.

This pattern of complementary distribution is not specific to *l* but occurs for other cursive letters in English. By examining the pairs *sat* and *vat*, *mill* and *will*, and *rack* and *rock*, you can see the complementary distribution of the variants of *a*, *i*, and *c*, respectively. In each case, the immediately preceding letter determines which variant occurs, with the consequence that the variants of a given letter are in complementary distribution.

We turn now to a general discussion of phonemes and allophones. When sounds are in complementary distribution, they do not contrast with each other. The replacement of one sound for the other will not change the meaning of the word, although it might not sound like typical English pronunciation. Given these facts about the patterning of sounds in a language, a phoneme can be defined as a set of phonetically similar sounds that are in complementary distribution. A set may consist of only one member. Some phonemes are represented by only one sound; they have one allophone. When there is more than one allophone in the set, the phones must be *phonetically similar*; that is, share most phonetic features. In English, the velar nasal [ŋ] and the glottal fricative [h] are in complementary distribution; [ŋ] does not occur word initially and [h] does not occur word finally. But they share very few phonetic features; [ŋ] is a voiced velar nasal stop; [h] is a voiceless glottal fricative. Therefore, they are not allophones of the same phoneme; [ŋ] and [h] are allophones of different phonemes.

Speakers of a language generally perceive the different allophones of a single phoneme as the same sound or phone. For example, most speakers of English are unaware that the vowels in *bead* and *bean* are different phones because mentally, speakers produce and hear phonemes, not phones.

Distinctive Features of Phonemes

We are generally not aware of the phonetic properties or features that distinguish the phonemes of our language. *Phonetics* provides the means to describe the phones (sounds) of language, showing how they are produced and how they vary. *Phonology* tells us how various sounds form patterns to create phonemes and their allophones.

For two phones to contrast meanings, there must be some phonetic difference between them. The minimal pairs *seal* [sil] and *zeal* [zil] show that [s] and [z] represent two contrasting phonemes in English. They cannot be allophones of one phoneme because one cannot replace the [s] with the [z] without changing the meaning of the word. Furthermore, they are not in complementary distribution; both occur word initially before the vowel [i]. They are therefore allophones of the two different phonemes /s/ and /z/. From the discussion of phonetics in chapter 6, we know that [s] and [z] differ in voicing: [s] is voiceless and [z] is voiced. The phonetic feature of voicing therefore distinguishes the two words. Voicing also distinguishes *feel* and *veal* [f]/[v] and *cap* and *cab* [p]/[b]. When a feature distinguishes one phoneme from another, hence one word from another, it is a **distinctive feature** or equivalently, a **phonemic feature**.

Feature Values

One can think of voicing and voicelessness as the presence or absence of a single feature, *voiced*. This single feature may have two values: plus (+), which signifies its presence, and minus (−), which signifies its absence. For example, [b] is [+ voiced] and [p] is [− voiced].

The presence or absence of nasality can similarly be designated as [+ nasal] or [− nasal], with [m] being [+ nasal] and [b] and [p] being [− nasal]. A [− nasal] sound is an oral sound.

We consider the phonetic and phonemic symbols to be *cover symbols* for sets of distinctive features. They are a shorthand method of specifying the phonetic properties of the segment. Phones and phonemes are not indissoluble units; they are composed of phonetic features, similar to the way that molecules are composed of atoms. A more explicit description of the phonemes /p/, /b/, and /m/ may thus be given in a **feature matrix** of the following sort.

	p	b	m
Stop	+	+	+
Labial	+	+	+
Voiced	−	+	+
Nasal	−	−	+

Aspiration is not listed as a phonemic feature in the specification of these units, because it is not necessary to include both [p] and [pʰ] as phonemes. In a phonetic transcription, however, the aspiration feature would be specified where it occurs.

A phonetic feature is distinctive when the + value of that feature in certain words contrasts with the − value of that feature in other words. At least one feature value difference must distinguish each phoneme from all the other phonemes in a language.

Because the phonemes /b/, /d/, and /g/ contrast by virtue of their place of articulation features—*labial*, *alveolar*, and *velar*—these place features are also distinctive in English. Because uvular sounds do not occur in English, the place feature *uvular* is not distinctive. The distinctive features of the voiced stops in English are shown in the following:

	b	m	d	n	g	ŋ
Stop	+	+	+	+	+	+
Voiced	+	+	+	+	+	+
Labial	+	+	−	−	−	−
Alveolar	−	−	+	+	−	−
Velar	−	−	−	−	+	+
Nasal	−	+	−	+	−	+

Each phoneme in this chart differs from all the other phonemes by at least one distinctive feature.

Vowels, too, have distinctive features. For example, the feature [± back] distinguishes the vowel in *rock* [rak] ([+ back]) from the vowel in *rack* [ræk] ([− back]), among others, and is therefore distinctive. Similarly [± tense] distinguishes [i] from [ɪ] (*beat* versus *bit*), among others, and is also a distinctive feature of the vowel system.

Nondistinctive Features

We have seen that nasality is a distinctive feature of English consonants, but it is a **nondistinctive feature** for English vowels. Given the arbitrary relationship between form and meaning, there is no way to predict that the word *meat* begins with a nasal bilabial stop [m] and that the word *beat* begins with an oral bilabial stop [b]. You learn this when you learn the words. On the other hand, the nasality feature value of the vowels in *bean, mean, comb,* and *sing* is predictable because they occur before nasal consonants. When a feature value is predictable by rule for a certain class of sounds, the feature is a nondistinctive or **redundant** or **predictable feature** *for that class*. (The three terms are equivalent.) Thus nasality is a redundant feature in English vowels, but a **nonredundant** (distinctive or phonemic) feature for English consonants.

This is not the case in all languages. In French, nasality is a distinctive feature for both vowels and consonants: *gars* pronounced [ga], "lad" contrasts with *gant* [gã], which means "glove"; and *bal* [bal] "dance" contrasts with *mal* [mal] "bad." Thus, French has both oral and nasal consonant phonemes and vowel phonemes; English has oral and nasal consonant phonemes, but only oral vowel phonemes.

Like French, the African language Akan (spoken in Ghana) has nasal vowel phonemes. Nasalization is a distinctive feature for vowels in Akan, as the following examples illustrate:

[ka]	"bite"	[kã]	"speak"
[fi]	"come from"	[fĩ]	"dirty"
[tu]	"pull"	[tũ]	"den"
[nsa]	"hand"	[nsã]	"liquor"
[tʃi]	"hate"	[tʃĩ]	"squeeze"
[pam]	"sew"	[pãm]	"confederate"

Nasalization is not predictable in Akan as it is in English. There is no nasalization rule in Akan, as shown by the minimal pair [pam] and [pãm]. If you substitute an oral vowel for a nasal vowel, or vice versa, you will change the word.

Two languages may have the same phonetic segments (phones) but have two different phonemic systems. Phonetically, both oral and nasalized vowels exist in English and Akan. However, English does not have nasalized vowel phonemes, but Akan does. The same phonetic segments function differently in the two languages. Nasalization of vowels in English is redundant and nondistinctive; nasalization of vowels in Akan is nonredundant and distinctive.

Another nondistinctive feature in English is aspiration. In the previous chapter we pointed out that in English both aspirated and unaspirated voiceless stops occur. The voiceless aspirated stops [pʰ], [tʰ], and [kʰ] and the voiceless unaspirated stops [p], [t], and [k] are in complementary distribution in English, as shown in the following:

Syllable Initial before a Stressed Vowel			After a Syllable Initial /s/			Nonword*		
[pʰ]	[tʰ]	[kʰ]	[p]	[t]	[k]			
pill	*till*	*kill*	*spill*	*still*	*skill*	[pɪl]*	[tɪl]*	[kɪl]*
[pʰɪl]	[tʰɪl]	[kʰɪl]	[spɪl]	[stɪl]	[skɪl]	[spʰɪl]*	[stʰɪl]*	[skʰɪl]*
par	*tar*	*car*	*spar*	*star*	*scar*	[par]*	[tar]*	[kar]*
[pʰar]	[tʰar]	[kʰar]	[spar]	[star]	[skar]	[spʰar]*	[stʰar]*	[skʰar]*

Where the unaspirated stops occur, the aspirated ones do not, and vice versa. You could say *spit* if you pleased with an aspirated [pʰ], as [spʰɪt], and it would be understood as *spit*, but listeners would probably think you were spitting out your words. Given this distribution, we see that aspiration is a redundant, nondistinctive feature in English; aspiration is predictable, occurring as a feature of voiceless stops when they occur initially in a stressed syllable.

This is the reason speakers of English usually perceive the [pʰ] in *pill* and the [p] in *spill* to be the same sound, just as they consider the [i] and [ī] that represent the phoneme /i/ in *bead* and *bean* to be the same. They do so because the difference between them is *predictable, redundant, nondistinctive*, and *nonphonemic* (all equivalent terms). This example illustrates why we refer to the phoneme as an abstract unit or as a mental unit. We do not utter phonemes; we produce phones, the allophones of the phonemes of the language. In English /p/ is a phoneme that is realized phonetically (pronounced) as both [p] and [pʰ], depending on context. The phones or sounds [p] and [pʰ] are allophones of the phoneme /p/.

Phonemic Patterns May Vary Across Languages

We have seen that the same phones may occur in two languages but pattern differently because the phonologies are different. English, French, and Akan have oral and nasal vowel phones; in English, oral and nasal vowels are allophones of one phoneme, whereas in French and Akan they represent distinct phonemes.

Aspiration of voiceless stops further illustrates the asymmetry of the phonological systems of different languages. Both aspirated and unaspirated voiceless stops occur in English and Thai, but they function differently in the two languages. Aspiration in English is not a distinctive feature because its presence or absence is predictable. In Thai it is not predictable, as the following examples show:

Voiceless Unaspirated		Voiceless Aspirated	
[paa]	*forest*	[pʰaa]	*to split*
[tam]	*to pound*	[tʰam]	*to do*
[kat]	*to bite*	[kʰat]	*to interrupt*

The voiceless unaspirated and the voiceless aspirated stops in Thai occur in minimal pairs; they contrast and are therefore phonemes. In both English and Thai, the phones [p], [t], [k], [pʰ], [tʰ], and [kʰ] occur. In English they represent the phonemes /p/, /t/, and /k/; in Thai they represent the phonemes /p/, /t/, /k/, /pʰ/, /tʰ/, and /kʰ/. Aspiration is a distinctive feature in Thai; it is a nondistinctive redundant feature in English.

The phonetic facts alone do not reveal what is distinctive or phonemic:

The *phonetic representation* of utterances shows what speakers know about the pronunciation of sounds.

The *phonemic representation* of utterances shows what speakers know about the patterning of sounds.

That *pot/pat* and *spot/spat* are phonemically transcribed with an identical /p/ reveals the fact that English speakers consider the [pʰ] in *pot* [pʰat] and the [p] in *spot* [spat] to be phonetic manifestations of the same phoneme /p/. This is also reflected in spelling, which is more attuned to phonemes than to individual phones.

In English, vowel length and consonant length are nonphonemic. Prolonging a sound in English will not produce a different word. In other languages, long and short vowels that are identical except for length are phonemic. In such languages, length is a nonpredictable distinctive feature. For example, vowel length is phonemic in Korean, as shown by the following minimal pairs: (Recall that the colon-like symbol ː indicates length.)

il	"day"	iːl	"work"
seda	"to count"	seːda	"strong"
kul	"oyster"	kuːl	"tunnel"

In Italian the word for "grandfather" is *nonno* /nonːo/, which contrasts with the word for "ninth," which is *nono* /nono/, so consonant length is phonemic in Rome. In Luganda, an African language, consonant length is also phonemic: /kula/ with a short /k/ means "grow up," whereas /kːula/ with a long /k/ means "treasure." Thus consonant length is unpredictable in Luganda, just as whether a word begins with a /b/ or a /p/ is unpredictable in English.

Natural Classes of Speech Sounds

It's as large as life, and twice as natural!

LEWIS CARROLL, *Through the Looking-Glass*

We show what speakers know about the predictable aspects of speech through phonological rules. In English, these rules determine the environments in which vowels are nasalized or voiceless stops aspirated. These rules apply to *all* the words in the language, and even apply to made-up words such as *sint, peeg,* or *sparg,* which would be /sɪnt/, /pig/, and /sparg/ phonemically and [sĩnt], [pʰig], and [sparg] phonetically.

The more linguists examine the phonologies of the world's languages, the more they find that similar phonological rules involve the same classes of sounds such as nasals or voiceless stops. For example, many languages besides English have a rule that nasalizes vowels before nasal consonants:

Nasalize a vowel when it precedes a nasal consonant in the same syllable.

The rule will apply to all vowel phonemes when they occur in a context preceding any segment marked [+ nasal] in the same syllable, and will add the feature [+ nasal] to the feature matrix of the vowel. Our description of vowel nasalization in English needs only this rule. It need not include a list of the individual vowels to which the rule applies or a list of the sounds that result from its application.

Many languages have rules that refer to [+ voiced] and [− voiced] sounds. For example, the aspiration rule in English applies to the class of [− voiced] noncontinuant sounds in word-initial position. As in the vowel nasality rule, we do not need to consider individual segments. The rule automatically applies to initial /p/, /t/, /k/, and /tʃ/.

Phonological rules often apply to **natural classes** of sounds. A natural class is a group of sounds described by a small number of distinctive features such as [− voiced], [− continuant], which describe /p/, /t/, /k/, and /tʃ/. Any individual member of a natural class would require more features in its description than the class itself, so /p/ is not only [− voiced], [− continuant], but also [+ labial].

The relationships among phonological rules and natural classes illustrate why segments are to be regarded as bundles of features. If segments were not specified as feature matrices, the similarities among /p/, /t/, /k/ or /m/, /n/, /ŋ/ would be lost. It would be just as likely for a language to have a rule such as

1. Nasalize vowels before *p, i,* or *z.*

as to have a rule such as

2. Nasalize vowels before *m, n,* or ŋ.

Rule 1 has no phonetic explanation, whereas Rule 2 does: the lowering of the velum in anticipation of a following nasal consonant causes the vowel to be nasalized. In Rule 1, the environment is a motley collection of unrelated sounds that cannot be described with a few features. Rule 2 applies to the natural class of nasal consonants, namely sounds that are [+ nasal], [+ consonantal].

The various classes of sounds discussed in chapter 6 also define natural classes to which the phonological rules of all languages may refer. They also can be specified by + and − feature values. Table 7.3 illustrates how these feature values combine to define some major classes of phonemes. The presence of +/− indicates that the sound may or may not possess a feature depending on its context. For example, word-initial nasals are [− syllabic] but some word-final nasals can be [+ syllabic], as in *button* [bʌtn̩].

TABLE 7.3 Feature Specification of Major Natural Classes of Sounds

Features	**Obstruents**	**Nasals**	**Liquids**	**Glides**	**Vowels**
Consonantal	+	+	+	−	−
Sonorant	−	+	+	+	+
Syllabic	−	+/−	+/−	−	+
Nasal	−	+	−	−	+/−

Feature Specifications for American English Consonants and Vowels

Here are feature matrices for vowels and consonants in English. By selecting all segments marked the same for one or more features, you can identify natural classes. For example, the natural class of high vowels /i, ɪ, u, ʊ/ is marked [+ high] in the vowel feature chart of Table 7.4; the natural class of voiced stops /b, m, d, n, g, ŋ, dʒ/ are the ones marked [+ voice] [− continuant] in the consonant chart of Table 7.5.

TABLE 7.5 Features of Some American English Consonants

Features	p	b	m	t	d	n	k	g	ŋ	f	v	θ	ð	s	z	ʃ	ʒ	tʃ	dʒ	l	r	j	w	h
Consonantal	+	+	+	+	+	+	+	+	+	+	+	+	+	+	+	+	+	+	+	+	+	−	−	−
Sonorant	−	−	+	−	−	+	−	−	+	−	−	−	−	−	−	−	−	−	−	+	+	+	+	+
Syllabic	−	−	−/+	−	−	−/+	−	−	−/+	−	−	−	−	−	−	−	−	−	−	−/+	−/+	−	−	−
Nasal	−	−	+	−	−	+	−	−	+	−	−	−	−	−	−	−	−	−	−	−	−	−	−	−
Voiced	−	+	+	−	+	+	−	+	+	−	+	−	+	−	+	−	+	−	+	+	+	+	+	−
Continuant	−	−	−	−	−	−	−	−	−	+	+	+	+	+	+	+	+	−	−	+	+	+	+	+
Labial	+	+	+	−	−	−	−	−	−	+	+	−	−	−	−	−	−	−	−	−	−	−	+	−
Alveolar	−	−	−	+	+	+	−	−	−	−	−	−	−	+	+	−	−	−	−	+	+	−	−	−
Palatal	−	−	−	−	−	−	−	−	−	−	−	−	−	−	−	+	+	+	+	−	−	+	−	−
Anterior	+	+	+	+	+	+	−	−	−	+	+	+	+	+	+	−	−	−	−	+	+	−	−	−
Velar	−	−	−	−	−	−	+	+	+	−	−	−	−	−	−	−	−	−	−	−	−	−	+	−
Coronal	−	−	−	+	+	+	−	−	−	−	−	+	+	+	+	+	+	+	+	+	+	+	−	−
Sibilant	−	−	−	−	−	−	−	−	−	−	−	−	−	+	+	+	+	+	+	−	−	−	−	−

Note: The phonemes /r/ and /l/ are distinguished by the feature [lateral], not shown here. /l/ is the only phoneme that would be [+ lateral].

TABLE 7.4   Features of Some American English Vowels

Features	i	ɪ	e	ɛ	æ	u	ʊ	o	ɔ	a	ʌ
High	+	+	−	−	−	+	+	−	−	−	−
Mid	−	−	+	+	−	−	−	+	+	−	+
Low	−	−	−	−	+	−	−	−	−	+	−
Back	−	−	−	−	−	+	+	+	+	+	−
Central	−	−	−	−	−	−	−	−	−	−	+
Round	−	−	−	−	−	+	+	+	+	−	−
Tense	+	−	+	−	−	+	−	+	−	+	−

The Rules of Phonology

But that to come

Shall all be done by the rule.

WILLIAM SHAKESPEARE, Antony and Cleopatra

Throughout this chapter we have emphasized that the relationship between the *phonemic* representations of words and the *phonetic* representations that reflect the pronunciation of these words is *rule-governed*. The phonological rules that relate the phonemic representations to the phonetic representations are part of a speaker's knowledge of the language.

The phonemic representations are *minimally specified* because some features or feature values are predictable. For example, in English all nasal consonants are voiced, so we don't need to specify voicing in the phonemic feature matrix for nasals. Similarly, we don't need to specify the feature *round* for non−low back vowels. If Table 7.5 was strictly phonemic, then instead of a + in the *voice*-row for *m, n,* and *ŋ,* the cells would be left blank, as would the cells in the *round*-row for *u, ʊ, o, ɔ.* Such underspecification reflects the redundancy in the phonology, which is also part of a speaker's knowledge of the sound system. The grammars we write aim at revealing this knowledge, so it is necessary to exclude predictable features. If we included them, we would fail in our goal of accurately representing what speakers know.

The phonemic representation, then, should include only the nonpredictable, distinctive features of the phonemes in a word. The phonetic representation, derived by applying the phonological rules, includes all of the linguistically relevant phonetic aspects of the sounds. It does not include all of the physical properties of the sounds of an utterance, however, because the physical signal may vary in many ways that have little to do with the phonological system. The absolute pitch of the sound, the rate of speech, or its loudness is not linguistically significant. The phonetic transcription is therefore also an abstraction from the physical signal; it includes the nonvariant phonetic aspects of the utterances, those features that remain relatively constant from speaker to speaker and from one time to another.

Although the specific rules of phonology differ from language to language, the kinds of rules, what they do, and the natural classes they refer to are the same throughout the world.

Assimilation Rules

We have seen that nasalization of vowels in English is nonphonemic because it is predictable by rule. The vowel nasalization rule is an **assimilation rule**, or a rule that makes neighboring segments more similar by duplicating a phonetic property. For the most part, assimilation rules stem from articulatory processes. There is a tendency when we speak to increase the **ease of articulation**, that is, to articulate efficiently. It is easier to lower the velum while a vowel is being pronounced before a nasal stop than to wait for the completion of the vowel and then force the velum to move suddenly.

We now wish to look more closely at the phonological rules we have been discussing. Previously, we stated the vowel nasalization rule as:

> Nasalize vowels when they occur before nasal consonants (within the same syllable).

This rule specifies the <u>class of sounds</u> affected by the rule:

> *Vowels*

It states what <u>phonetic change</u> will occur by applying the rule:

> *Change phonemic oral vowels to phonetic nasal vowels.*

And it specifies the context or <u>phonological environment</u>.

> *Before nasal consonants within the same syllable.*

A shorthand notation to write rules, similar to the way scientists and mathematicians use symbols, makes the rule statements more concise. Every physicist knows that $E = mc^2$ means "Energy equals mass times the square of the velocity of light." Children know that $2 + 6 = 8$ can be stated in words as "two plus six equals eight." We can use similar notations to state the nasalization rule as:

> V → [+ nasal] / __ [+ nasal] $

Let's look at the rule piece by piece.

V	→	[+ nasal]	/	__	[+ nasal]	$
Vowels	become	nasalized	in the environment	before	nasal segments	within a syllable

To the left of the arrow is the <u>class of sounds</u> affected. To the right of the arrow is the <u>phonetic change</u> that occurs. <u>The phonological environment</u> follows the slash. The underscore __ is the relative position of the sound to be changed within the environment, in this case *before* a nasal segment. The dollar sign indicates a syllable boundary and guarantees that the environment does not cross over to the next syllable.

This rule tells us that the vowels in such words as *den* /dɛn/ will become nasalized to [dɛ̃n], but *deck* /dɛk/ will not be affected and is pronounced [dɛk] because /k/ is not a nasal segment. As well, a word such as *den$tal* /dɛn$təl/ will be pronounced [dɛ̃n$təl], where we have showed the syllable boundary explicitly. However, the first vowel in *door$man*, /dɔr$mæn/, will not be nasalized, because the nasal segment does not precede the syllable boundary, so the "within a syllable" condition is not met.

Technically, our rule is not complete. It will not nasalize the vowel in *dent* or *dents*, because the rule doesn't allow for consonants to intervene between the nasal and the syllable boundary. One can indicate optional consonants within the syllable by using the cover symbol C for consonant and optionality by enclosing the C in parentheses. This rule has the following appearance and covers nearly all cases:

V → [+ nasal] / __ [+ nasal] (C) (C) $

We would read this rule as:

A vowel becomes nasalized before a nasal segment, possibly followed by one or two consonants within a syllable.

Any rule written in formal notation can be stated in words. The use of formal notation is a shorthand way of presenting the information. Notation also reveals the *function* of the rule more explicitly than words. It is easy to see in the formal statement of the rule that this is an assimilation rule because the change to [+ nasal] occurs before [+ nasal] segments. Assimilation rules in languages reflect **coarticulation**—the spreading of phonetic features either in the anticipation or in the perseveration (the "hanging on") of articulatory processes. The auditory effect is that words sound smoother.

The following example illustrates how the English vowel nasalization rule applies to the phonemic representation of words and shows the assimilatory nature of the rule; that is, the change from no nasal feature present for the vowel in the phonemic representation to a [+ nasal] in the phonetic representation:

	"bob"			"boom"		
Phonemic representation	/b	a	b/	/b	u	m/
Nasality: phonemic feature value	−	0	−	−	0	+
Apply nasal rule		NA*			↓	
Nasality: phonetic feature value	−	−	−	−	+	+
Phonetic representation	[b	a	b]	[b	ũ	m]

*NA means "not applicable." The 0 means not present on the phonemic level.

There are many assimilation rules in English and other languages. Recall that the voiced /z/ of the English regular plural suffix is changed to [s] after a voiceless sound, and that similarly the voiced /d/ of the English regular past-tense suffix is changed to [t] after a voiceless sound. These are instances of voicing assimilation. In these cases the value of the voicing feature goes from [+ voice] to [− voice] because of assimilation to the [− voice] feature of the final consonant of the stem, as in the derivation of *cats*:

/kæt + z/ → [kæts]

We saw a different kind of assimilation rule in Akan, where we observed that the nasal negative morpheme was expressed as [m] before /p/, [n] before /t/, and [ŋ] before /k/. (This is the homorganic nasal rule.) In this case the place of articulation—bilabial, alveolar, velar—of the nasal assimilates to the place of articulation of the following consonant. The same process occurs in English, where the negative morpheme prefix spelled *in-* or *im-* agrees in place of articulation with the word to which it is prefixed, so we have *impossible* [ĩmpʰasəbəl], *intolerant* [ĩntʰalərə̃nt], and *incongruous* [ĩŋkʰãngruəs]. In effect, the rule makes two consonants that appear next to each other more similar.

Dissimilation Rules

"Dennis the Menace" © Hank Ketcham. Reprinted with permission of North America Syndicate.

It is understandable that so many languages have assimilation rules; they permit greater ease of articulation. It might seem strange, then, to learn that languages also have **dissimilation rules**, in which a segment becomes less similar to another segment. Ironically, such rules have the same explanation: it is sometimes easier to articulate dissimilar sounds. The difficulty of tongue twisters like "the sixth sheik's sixth sheep is sick" is based on the repeated similarity of sounds. If one were to make some sounds less similar, as in "the fifth sheik's fourth sheep is sick," it would be easier to say. The cartoon makes the same point, with *toy boat* being more difficult to articulate repeatedly than *sail boat*, because the [ɔj] of *toy* is more similar to [o] than is the [e] of *sail*.

An example of easing pronunciation through dissimilation is found in some varieties of English, where there is a fricative dissimilation rule. This rule applies to sequences /fθ/ and /sθ/, changing them to [ft] and [st]. Here the fricative /θ/ becomes dissimilar to the preceding fricative by becoming a stop. For example, the words *fifth* and *sixth* come to be pronounced as if they were spelled *fift* and *sikst*.

A classic example of the same kind of dissimilation occurred in Latin, and the results of this process show up in the derivational morpheme /-ar/ in English. In Latin a derivational suffix *-alis* was added to nouns to form adjectives. When the suffix was added to a noun that contained the liquid /l/, the suffix was changed to *-aris*; that is, the liquid /l/ was changed to the liquid /r/. These words came into English as adjectives ending in *-al* or in its dissimilated form *-ar*, as shown in the following examples:

-al	**-ar**
anecdot-al	angul-ar
annu-al	annul-ar
ment-al	column-ar
pen-al	perpendicul-ar
spiritu-al	simil-ar
ven-al	vel-ar

All of the *-ar* adjectives contain an /l/, and as *columnar* illustrates, the /l/ need not be the consonant directly preceding the dissimilated segment.

Though dissimilation rules are rarer than assimilation rules, they are nevertheless found throughout the world's languages.

Feature-Changing Rules

The assimilation and dissimilation rules we have seen may all be thought of as *feature-changing rules*. In some cases a feature already present is changed. The /z/ plural morpheme has its voicing value changed from plus to minus when it follows a voiceless sound. Similarly, the /n/ in the phonemic negative prefix morpheme /ɪn/ undergoes a change in its place of articulation feature when preceding bilabials or velars. In the case of the Latin dissimilation rule, the feature [+ lateral] is changed to [− lateral], so that /l/ is pronounced [r].

The addition of a feature is the other way in which we have seen features change. The English vowel nasalization rule is a case in point. Phonemically, vowels are not marked for nasality; however, in the environment specified by the rule, the feature [+ nasal] is added.

Some feature-changing rules are neither assimilation nor dissimilation rules. The rule in English that aspirates voiceless stops at the beginning of a syllable simply adds a nondistinctive feature. Generally, aspiration occurs only if the following vowel is stressed. The /p/ in *pit* and *repeat* is an aspirated [pʰ], but the /p/ in *inspect* or *compass* is an unaspirated [p]. We also note that even with an intervening consonant, the aspiration takes place so that words such as *crib, clip*, and *quip* ([kʰrɪb], [kʰlɪp], and kʰwɪp]) all begin with an aspirated [kʰ]. And finally, the affricate /tʃ/ is subject to the rule, so *chip* is phonetically [tʃʰɪp]. We can now state the rule:

A voiceless, noncontinuant has [+aspirated] added to its feature matrix at the beginning of a syllable containing a stressed vowel with an optional, intervening consonant.

Aspiration is not specified in any phonemic feature matrices of English. The aspiration rule adds this feature for reasons having to do with the timing of the closure release rather than in an attempt to make segments more alike or not alike, as with assimilation and dissimilation rules.

Remember that /p/ and /b/ (and all such symbols) are simply cover symbols that do not reveal the phonemic distinctions. In phonemic and phonetic feature matrices, these differences are made explicit, as shown in the following phonemic matrices:

	p	**b**	
Consonantal	+	+	
Continuant	−	−	
Labial	+	+	
Voiced	−	+	← distinctive difference

The nondistinctive feature "aspiration" is not included in these phonemic representations because aspiration is predictable.

Segment Insertion and Deletion Rules

Phonological rules may add or delete entire segments. These are different from the feature-changing and feature-adding rules we have seen so far, which affect only parts of segments. The process of inserting a consonant or vowel is called **epenthesis**.

The rules for forming regular plurals, possessive forms, and third-person singular verb agreement in English all require an epenthesis rule. Here is the first part of that rule that we gave earlier for plural formation:

Insert a [ə] before the plural morpheme /z/ when a regular noun ends in a sibilant, giving [əz].

Letting the symbol ∅ stand for "null," we can write this *morphophonemic* epenthesis rule more formally as "null becomes schwa between two sibilants," or like this:

$$\varnothing \rightarrow \text{ə} \, / \, [+ \text{sibilant}] \, \underline{\quad} \, [+ \text{sibilant}]$$

Similarly, we recall the first part of the rule for regular past-tense formation in English:

Insert a [ə] before the past-tense morpheme when a regular verb ends in a nonnasal alveolar stop giving [əd].

This epenthesis rule may also be expressed in our more formal notation:

$\emptyset \rightarrow \vartheta$ / [− nasal, + alveolar, − continuant] _____ [− nasal, + alveolar, − continuant]

There is a plausible explanation for insertion of a [ə]. If we merely added a [z] to *squeeze* to form its plural, we would get [skwiːz], which would be hard for English speakers to distinguish from [skwiz]. Similarly, if we added just [d] to *load* to form its past tense, it would be [lodː], which would also be difficult to distinguish from [lod], because in English we do not contrast long and short consonants. These and other examples suggest that the morphological patterns in a language are closely related to other generalizations about the phonology of that language.

Segment deletion rules are commonly found in many languages and are far more prevalent than segment insertion rules. One such rule occurs in casual or rapid speech. We often delete the unstressed vowels that are shown in bold type in words like the following:

mys**te**ry general mem**o**ry funeral vig**o**rous Barb**a**ra

These words in casual speech sound as if they were written:

mystry genral memry funral vigrous Barbra

The silent *g* that torments spellers in such words as *sign* and *design* is actually an indication of a deeper phonological process, in this case, one of segment deletion. Consider the following examples:

A		**B**	
sign	[sãjn]	signature	[sɪgnətʃər]
design	[dəzãjn]	designation	[dɛzɪgneʃə̃n]
paradigm	[pʰærədãjm]	paradigmatic	[pʰærədɪgmærək]

In none of the words in column A is there a phonetic [g], but in each corresponding word in column B a [g] occurs. Our knowledge of English phonology accounts for these phonetic differences. The "[g]—no [g]" alternation is regular, and we apply it to words that we never have heard. Suppose someone says:

"He was a salignant [səlɪgnə̃nt] man."

Not knowing what the word means (which, of course, you couldn't since we made it up), you might ask:

"Why, did he salign [səlãjn] somebody?"

It is highly doubtful that a speaker of English would pronounce the verb form without the *-ant* as [səlɪgn], because the phonological rules of English would delete the /g/ when it occurred in this context. This rule might be stated as:

Delete a /g/ when it occurs before a final nasal consonant.

The rule is even more general, as evidenced by the pair *gnostic* [nastɪk] and *agnostic* [ægnastɪk], and by the silent *g*'s in the cartoon:

"Tumbleweeds" © Tom K. Ryan. Reprinted with permission of North America Syndicate.

This more general rule may be stated as:

Delete a /g/ when it occurs word initially before a nasal consonant or before a word-final nasal.

Given this rule, the phonemic representation of the stems in *sign/signature, design/designation, malign/malignant, phlegm/phlegmatic, paradigm/paradigmatic, gnosis/agnostic,* and so on will include a /g/ that will be deleted by the regular rule if a prefix or suffix is not added. By stating the class of sounds that follow the /g/ (nasal consonants) rather than any specific nasal consonant, the rule deletes the /g/ before both /m/ and /n/.

Students learning French often joke that for good pronunciation, leave off the second half of the word. This exaggeration is founded on the fact that final letters in French spelling are often silent. Thus in *petit* meaning "small," the *t* is not pronounced, nor is the *s* in *nos* meaning "our," and so on. It turns out that a single, simple segment deletion rule accounts for many of the unpronounced sounds in French:

Delete a word final consonant when the following word begins with an obstruent, a liquid, or a nasal consonant.

Table 7.6[1] illustrates the effect of this rule.

TABLE 7.6 Distribution of Word-Final Consonants in French

Environment	Phonemic	Phonetic	Translation
Before an obstruent:	/pətit tablo/	[pəti tablo]	"small picture"
	/noz tablo/	[no tablo]	"our pictures"
Before a liquid:	/pətit livr/	[pəti livr]	"small book"
	/noz livr/	[no livr]	"our books"
Before a nasal:	/pətit navet/	[pəti navɛ]	"small turnip"
	/noz navets/	[no navɛ]	"our turnips"
Before a vowel:	/pətit ami/	[pətit ami]	"small friend"
	/noz amis/	[noz ami]	"our friends"
Before a glide:	/pətit wazo/	[pətit wazo]	"small bird"
	/noz wazo/	[noz wazo]	"our birds"

[1] From *French Phonology and Morphology.* by Sanford Schane Copyright © 1968 MIT Press. Reprinted by permission of MIT Press.

From Table 7.3 we note that obstruents, liquids, and nasal consonants form the natural class of [+ consonantal] segments. We can now see why such natural classes are significant. Using the symbol ∅ to represent "null" again, and # to signify a word boundary, we can state the French rule simply as:

[+ consonantal] → ∅ / ___ # # [+ consonantal]

We can translate the formal statement of this rule as follows:

A [+ consonantal] segment (obstruent, liquid, or nasal) is deleted (→ ∅) in the environment (/) at the end of a word (___#), which is followed by a word beginning with an obstruent, liquid, or nasal (# [+ consonantal]).

Given this rule in the grammar of French, *petit* would be phonemically /pətit/. It need not be additionally represented as /pəti/, because the rule determines when the /t/ is not pronounced, and this would be true for all French words that end in /t/.

Movement (Metathesis) Rules

"The only reason I say 'aminal' is
I can't say 'animal'!"

"Family Circus" © Bil Keane, Inc. Reprinted with permission
of King Features Syndicate.

Phonological rules may also reorder sequences of phonemes, in which case they are called **metathesis** rules. For some speakers of English, the word *ask* is pronounced [æks], but the word *asking* is pronounced [æskɪŋ]. In this case a metathesis rule reorders the /s/ and /k/ in certain contexts. In Old English the verb was *aksian*, with the /k/ preceding the /s/. A historical metathesis rule switched these two consonants, producing *ask* in most dialects of English. Children's speech shows many cases of metathesis (which are corrected as the child approaches the adult grammar): *aminal* [æmə̃nəl] for *animal* and *pusketti* [pʰəskɛti] for *spaghetti* are common children's pronunciations. Dog lovers have metathesized the She*tl*and sheepdog into a she*lt*ie, and at least two presidents of the United States have been known to apply a metathesis rule to the word *nuclear*, which many Americans pronounce [nyu*k*liər], but is pronounced [nukyələr] by those leading statesmen.

We see, then, that phonological rules have several functions, among which are the following:

Function	**Example**
1. Change feature values	(nasal consonant assimilation rules in Akan and English).
2. Add new features	(aspiration in English).
3. Delete segments	(final consonant deletion in French).
4. Add segments	(schwa insertion in English plural and past tense).
5. Reorder segments	(metathesis rule relating [ask] and [aks]).

These rules, when applied to the phonemic representations of words and phrases, result in phonetic forms that differ from the phonemic forms. If such differences were unpredictable, it would be difficult to explain how we can understand what we hear or how we produce utterances that represent the meanings we wish to convey. The more we look at languages, however, the more we see that many aspects of the phonetic forms of utterances that appear at first to be irregular and unpredictable are actually rule-governed. We learn, or construct, these rules when we are acquiring the language as children (see chapter 8). The rules form an important part of the sound pattern that we acquire.

From One to Many and from Many to One

The relationship between the phonemes and phones of a language is complex and varied. Rarely is a single phoneme realized as one and only one phone. We often find one phoneme realized as several phones, as in the case with English voiceless stops that may be realized as aspirated or unaspirated, among other possibilities. And we find the same phone may be the realization of several different phonemes. Here is a dramatic example of that many-to-one relationship.

Consider the vowels in the following pairs of words:

	A			**B**	
/i/	compete	[i]		competition	[ə]
/ɪ/	medicinal	[ɪ]		medicine	[ə]
/e/	maintain	[e]		maintenance	[ə]
/ɛ/	telegraph	[ɛ]		telegraphy	[ə]
/æ/	analysis	[æ]		analytic	[ə]
/a/	solid	[a]		solidity	[ə]
/o/	phone	[o]		phonetic	[ə]
/ʊ/	Talmudic	[ʊ]		Talmud	[ə]

In column A all the boldfaced vowels are stressed vowels with a variety of vowel phones; in column B the boldfaced vowels are reduced and are pronounced as schwa [ə]. How can one explain the different pronunciations of the root morpheme that occurs in both words of each of these pairs? It wouldn't make sense for speakers of English to represent these root morphemes with distinct phonemic forms if some general rule relates the stressed vowels in column A to the reduced schwa vowel [ə] in column B. It would also miss the fact that the words in column A and the words in column B are related in a systematic way.

In these cases the stress rules of English, taking into account the different suffixes in the words, change the stress pattern of the word. The vowel that is stressed in one form becomes reduced in a different form and is therefore pronounced as [ə]. The phonemic representations of all of the root morphemes contain an unreduced vowel such as /i/ or /e/ that is phonetically [ə] when it is reduced. We can conclude, then, that [ə] is an allophone of all English vowel phonemes. The rule to derive the schwa is simple to state:

Change a vowel to a [ə] when the stress rules mark it as reduced.

In the phonological description of a language, it is not always straightforward to determine phonemic representations from phonetic transcriptions. How would we deduce the /o/ in *phonetic* from its pronunciation as [fənɛtɪk] without a complete phonological analysis? However, given the phonemic representation and the phonological rules, we can always derive the correct phonetic representation. In our internal mental grammars this derivation is no problem, because the words occur in their phonemic forms in our mental lexicons and we know the rules of the language.

Another example will illustrate this aspect of phonology. In English, /t/ and /d/ are both phonemes, as is illustrated by the minimal pairs *tie/die* and *bat/bad*. When /t/ or /d/ occurs between a stressed and an unstressed vowel, they both become a flap [ɾ]. For many speakers of English, *writer* and *rider* are pronounced identically as [rajɾər]. Yet these speakers know that *writer* has a phonemic /t/ because of *write* /rajt/, whereas *rider* has a phonemic /d/ because of *ride* /rajd/. The flap rule may be stated as:

An alveolar stop becomes a voiced flap when preceded by a stressed vowel and followed by an unstressed vowel.

The application of this rule is illustrated as follows:

Phonemic representation	write /rajt/	writer /rajt + ər/ ↓	ride /rajd/	rider /rajd + ər/ ↓
Apply rule	NA	ɾ	NA	ɾ
Phonetic representation	[rajt]	[rajɾər]	[rajd]	[rajɾər]

This is another example, this time with consonants, that illustrates the fact that two distinct phonemes may be realized phonetically by the same phone.

Such cases show that we cannot arrive at a phonological analysis by simply inspecting the phonetic representation of utterances. If we just looked for minimal pairs as the only evidence for phonology, we would have to conclude that [ɾ] is a phoneme in English because it contrasts phonetically with other phonetic units: *rider/writer* [rajɾər], *riper* [rajpər], *rhymer* [rãjmər], *riser* [rajzər], and so forth. The fact that *write* and *ride* change their phonetic forms when suffixes are added shows that there is an intricate mapping between phonemic representations of words and phonetic pronunciations.

The allophone derived from the different phonemes /t/ and /d/ by the flap rule is different in features from all other phonemes in the language. That is, there is no /ɾ/ phoneme, but there is a [ɾ] phone. This was also true of aspirated voiceless stops and nasalized vowels. The set of phones is larger than the set of phonemes and contains elements whose feature matrices are different from any feature matrix of any phoneme.

The English flap rule also illustrates an important phonological process called **neutralization**; the voicing contrast between /t/ and /d/ is neutralized in the specified environment. That is, /t/ never contrasts with /d/ in the environment between a stressed and an unstressed vowel.

Similar rules exist in other languages that show that there is no one-to-one relationship between phonemes and phones. For example, in German both voiced and voiceless obstruents occur as phonemes, as is shown by the following minimal pair:

Tier [tiːr] "animal" *dir* [diːr] "to you"

However, when voiced obstruents occur at the end of a word or syllable, they become voiceless. So, at the end of a German word, only [t] occurs. The words meaning "bundle" *Bund* /bʊnd/ and "colorful" *bunt* /bʊnt/ are phonetically identical and pronounced [bʊnt] with a final [t]. Obstruent voicing is neutralized in syllable-final position.

The German devoicing rule changes the specifications of features. In German, the phonemic representation of the final stop in *Bund* is /d/, specified as [+ voiced]; it is changed by rule to [− voiced] to derive the phonetic [t] in word-final position. Again, this shows there is no simple relationship between phonemes and their allophones. German presents us with this picture:

German Phonemes   /d/   /t/

German Phones   [d]   [t]

The devoicing rule in German provides a further illustration that we cannot discern the phonemic representation of a word given only the phonetic form; [bʊnt] can be derived from either /bʊnd/ or /bʊnt/. The phonemic representations and the phonological rules together determine the phonetic forms.

The Function of Phonological Rules

The function of the phonological rules in a grammar is to provide the phonetic information necessary for the pronunciation of utterances. We may illustrate this point in the following way:

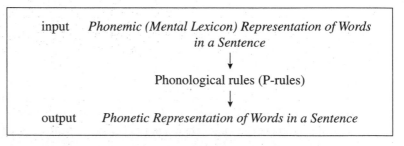

input   *Phonemic (Mental Lexicon) Representation of Words in a Sentence*

Phonological rules (P-rules)

output   *Phonetic Representation of Words in a Sentence*

The input to the P-rules is the phonemic representation. The P-rules apply to the phonemic strings and produce as output the phonetic representation.

The application of rules in this way is called a **derivation**. We have given examples of derivations that show how plurals are derived, how phonemically oral vowels become nasalized, and how /t/ and /d/ become flaps in certain environments. A derivation is thus an explicit way of showing both the effects and the function of phonological rules in a grammar.

All the examples of derivations we have so far considered show the application of just one phonological rule, except the plural and past-tense rules, which are actually one rule with two parts. In any event, it is common for more than one rule to apply to a word. For example, the word *tempest* is phonemically /tempɛst/ (as shown by the pronunciation of *tempestuous* [tʰɛ̃mpʰɛstʃuəs]) but phonetically [tʰɛ̃mpəst]. Three rules apply to it: the aspiration rule, the vowel nasalization rule, and the schwa rule. We can derive the phonetic form from the phonemic representation as follows:

Underlying phonemic representation	/ t	ɛ	m	p	ɛ	s t /
Aspiration rule	tʰ					
Nasalization rule		ɛ̃				
Schwa rule					ə	
Surface phonetic representation	[tʰ	ɛ̃	m	p	ə	s t]

We are using phonetic symbols instead of matrices in which the feature values are changed. These notations are equivalent, however, as long as we understand that a phonetic symbol is a cover term representing a matrix with all distinctive features marked either + or − (unless, of course, the feature is nondistinctive, such as the nasality value for phonemic vowels in English).

Slips of the Tongue: Evidence for Phonological Rules

Slips of the tongue, or **speech errors**, in which we deviate in some way from the intended utterance, show phonological rules in action. We all make speech errors, and they tell us interesting things about language and its use. Consider the following speech errors:

Intended Utterance	Actual Utterance
1. gone to seed	god to seen
[gãn tə sid]	[gad tə sĩn]
2. stick in the mud	smuck in the tid
[stɪk ĩn ðə mʌd]	[smʌk ĩn ðə tʰɪd]
3. speech production	preach seduction
[spitʃ pʰrədʌkʃən]	[pʰritʃ sədʌkʃən]

In the first example, the final consonants of the first and third words were reversed. Notice that the reversal of the consonants also changed the nasality of the vowels. The vowel [ã] in the intended utterance is replaced by [a]. In the actual utterance, the nasalization was lost because it no longer occurred before a nasal consonant. The vowel in the third word, which was the non-nasal [i] in the intended utterance, became [ĩ] in the error, because it was followed by /n/. The nasalization rule applied.

In the other two errors, we see the application of the aspiration rule. In the intended *stick*, the /t/ would have been realized as an unaspirated [t] because it follows the syllable initial /s/. When it was switched with the /m/ in *mud*, it was pronounced as the aspirated [tʰ], because it occurred initially. The third example also illustrates the aspiration rule in action. More than being simply amusing, speech errors are linguistically interesting because they provide further evidence for phonological rules and for the decomposition of speech sounds into features.

We will learn more about speech errors in chapter 9 on language processing.

Prosodic Phonology

Syllable Structure

"Hi & Lois" © King Features Syndicate. Reprinted with permission of King Features Syndicate.

Words are composed of one or more syllables. A **syllable** is a phonological unit composed of one or more phonemes. Every syllable has a **nucleus**, which is usually a vowel (but which may be a syllabic liquid or nasal). The nucleus may be preceded by one or more phonemes called the syllable **onset** and followed by one or more segments called the **coda**. From a very early age, children learn that certain words rhyme. In rhyming words, the nucleus and the coda of the final syllable of both words are identical, as in the following jingle:

> Jack and **Jill**
> Went up the h**ill**
> To fetch a pail of water.
> Jack fell d**own**
> And broke his cr**own**
> And Jill came tumbling after.

For this reason, the nucleus + coda constitute the subsyllabic unit called a **rime** (note the spelling).

A syllable thus has a hierarchical structure. Using the Greek letter *sigma*, σ, as the symbol for the phonological unit syllable, the hierarchical structure of the mono-syllabic word *splints* can be shown:

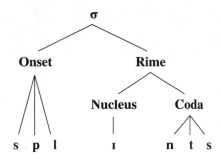

Word Stress

In many languages, including English, one or more of the syllables in every content word (i.e., every word except for function words like *to, the, a, of*) are stressed. A stressed syllable, which can be marked by an acute accent (´), is perceived as more prominent than unstressed syllables in the following examples:

pérvert	(noun)	as in	"My neighbor is a pervert."
pervért	(verb)	as in	"Don't pervert the idea."
súbject	(noun)	as in	"Let's change the subject."
subjéct	(verb)	as in	"He'll subject us to criticism."

These pairs show that stress can be contrastive in English. In these cases it distinguishes between nouns and verbs.

Some words may contain more than one stressed vowel, but exactly one of the stressed vowels is more prominent than the others. The vowel that receives primary stress is marked by an acute accent. The other stressed vowels are indicated by a grave accent (`) over the vowels (these vowels receive secondary stress).

rèsignátion	lìnguístics	sỳstemátic
fùndaméntal	ìntrodúctory	rèvolútion

Generally, speakers of a language know which syllable receives primary stress, which ones receive secondary stress, and which ones are reduced (are unstressed). It is part of their knowledge of the language. It's usually easy to distinguish between stressed and reduced syllables, because the vowel in reduced syllables is pronounced as a schwa [ə], except at the ends of certain words such as *confetti* or *laboratory*. It may be harder to distinguish between primary and secondary stress. If you are unsure of where the primary stress is in a word (and you are a good speaker of English), try shouting the word as if talking to a person across a busy street. Often, the difference in stress becomes more apparent.

The stress pattern of a word may differ among English-speaking people. For example, in most varieties of American English the word *láboratòry* [lǽbərətòri] has two stressed syllables, but in most varieties of British English it receives only one stress [ləbɔ́rətri]. Because vowel qualities in English are closely related to stress—vowels generally reduce to schwa or delete when they are not stressed—the British and American vowels differ in this word. In fact, in the British version the fourth vowel is deleted because it is not stressed.

There are several ways to represent stress. We have used acúte accent marks for primary stress and gràve accent marks for secondary stress. We can also specify which syllable in the word is stressed by marking the syllable *s* if strongly stressed, *w* if weakly stressed, and unmarked if unstressed (reduced).

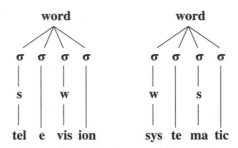

Stress is also sometimes shown by placing a 1 over the primary stressed syllable, a 2 over the syllable with secondary stress, and leaving unstressed vowels unmarked.

2	1		2	1			1	2
fundamental			introductory			secondary		

Stress is a property of the syllable rather than a segment; it is a prosodic or suprasegmental feature. To produce a stressed syllable, one may change the pitch (usually by raising it), make the syllable louder, or make it longer. We often use all three of these phonetic means to stress a syllable.

Sentence and Phrase Stress

"Bimbo's Circus" © Howie Schneider/Dist. by Newspaper Enterprise Association, Inc.

When words are combined into phrases and sentences, one syllable receives greater stress than all others. That is, just as there is only one primary stress in a word spoken in isolation, only one of the vowels in a phrase (or sentence) receives primary stress or **accent**. All of the other stressed vowels are reduced to secondary stress. This is illustrated by these examples:

$$
\begin{array}{cccc}
1 & 1 & 1 & 2 \\
\end{array}
$$
tight + rope → tightrope   ("a rope for acrobatics")
$$
\begin{array}{cccc}
1 & 1 & 2 & 1 \\
\end{array}
$$
tight + rope → tight rope   ("a rope drawn taut")

$$
\begin{array}{cccc}
1 & 1 & 1 & 2 \\
\end{array}
$$
hot + dog → hotdog   ("frankfurter")
$$
\begin{array}{cccc}
1 & 1 & 2 & 1 \\
\end{array}
$$
hot + dog → hot dog   ("an overheated dog")

$$
\begin{array}{cccc}
1 & 1 & 1 & 2 \\
\end{array}
$$
red + coat → Redcoat   ("a British soldier")
$$
\begin{array}{cccc}
1 & 1 & 2 & 1 \\
\end{array}
$$
red + coat → red coat   ("a coat that is red")

$$
\begin{array}{cccc}
1 & 1 & 1 & 2 \\
\end{array}
$$
white + house → White House   ("the President's house")
$$
\begin{array}{cccc}
1 & 1 & 2 & 1 \\
\end{array}
$$
white + house → white house   ("a house painted white")

Speaking naturally, say these examples aloud, and at the same time listen or feel the stress pattern. This may not work if English is not your native language, for which we apologize, but we suggest you listen to a native speaker say them.

In English we place primary stress on the adjectival part of a compound noun (which may be written as one word, two words separated by a hyphen, or two separate words), but we place the stress on the noun when the words are a noun phrase consisting of an adjective followed by a noun. The differences between the following pairs are therefore predictable:

Compound Noun	Adjective + Noun
tíghtrope	tight rópe
Rédcoat	red cóat
hótdog	hot dóg
White House	white hóuse

These pairs show that stress may be predictable from the morphology and syntax. The phonology interacts with the other components of the grammar. The stress differences between the noun and verb pairs discussed in the previous section (*subject* as noun or verb) are also predictable from the syntactic word category.

Intonation

In chapter 6, we discussed pitch as a phonetic feature in reference to tone languages and intonation languages. In this chapter we have discussed the use of phonetic features to distinguish meaning. We can now see that pitch is a *phonemic* feature in tone languages such as Chinese, Thai, and Akan. We refer to these relative pitches as **contrasting tones**. In intonation languages such as English, pitch still plays an important role, but in the form of the **pitch contour** or **intonation** of the phrase or sentence.

In English, intonation may reflect syntactic or semantic differences. If we say *John is going* with a falling pitch at the end, it is a statement, but if the pitch rises at the end, it may be interpreted as a question. Similarly, *What's in the tea, honey?* may, depending on intonation, be a query to someone called "honey" regarding the contents of the tea (falling intonation on *honey*), or may be a query regarding whether the tea contains honey (rising intonation on *honey*).

A sentence that is ambiguous in writing may be unambiguous when spoken because of differences in the pitch contour, as we saw in the previous paragraph. Here is a somewhat more subtle example. Written, sentence 1 is unclear as to whether Tristram intended for Isolde to read and follow directions, or merely to follow him:

1. Tristram left directions for Isolde to follow.

Spoken, if Tristram wanted Isolde to follow him, the sentence would be pronounced with a rise in pitch on the first syllable of *follow*, followed by a fall in pitch, as indicated (oversimplistically) in sentence 2.

Tristram left directions for Isolde to follow.

In this pronunciation of the sentence, the primary stress is on the word *follow*.

If the meaning is to read and follow a set of directions, the highest pitch comes on the second syllable of *directions*, as illustrated, again oversimplistically, in sentence 3.

Tristram left directions for Isolde to follow.

The primary stress in this pronunciation is on the word *directions*.

The way we have indicated pitch ignores much detail. Before the big rise in pitch, the voice does not remain on the same monotone low pitch. These pitch diagrams merely indicate when there is a special change in pitch.

Pitch plays an important role in both tone languages and intonation languages, but in different ways, depending on the phonological system of the respective languages.

Sequential Constraints of Phonemes

The one-l lama,
He's a priest.
The two-l llama,
He's a beast.
And I will bet
A silk pajama
There isn't any
Three-l lllama.

OGDEN NASH, *"The Lama"*[2]

---

[2] From "Candy Is Dandy: The Best of Ogden Nash" by Ogden Nash; published by André Deutsch. Copyright © 1931 by Ogden Nash, renewed. Reprinted by permission of Curtis Brown, Ltd.

Suppose you were given the following four phonemes of English and asked to arrange them to form all *possible* words:

/b/   /ɪ/   /k/   /l/

You would most likely produce the following:

/b   l   ɪ   k /
/k   l   ɪ   b /
/b   ɪ   l   k /
/k   ɪ   l   b /

These are the only permissible arrangements of these phonemes in English. */lbkɪ/, */ɪlbk/, */bkɪl/, and */ɪlkb/ are not possible English words. Although /blɪk/ and /klɪb/ are not now existing words, if you heard someone say:

"I just bought a beautiful new blick."

you might ask: "What's a blick?"

If, on the other hand, you heard someone say:

"I just bought a beautiful new bkli."

you might reply, "You just bought a new *what?*"

Your knowledge of English phonology includes information about what sequences of phonemes are permissible, and what sequences are not. After a consonant like /b/, /g/, /k/, or /p/, another stop consonant in the same syllable is not permitted by the phonology. If a word begins with an /l/ or an /r/, the next segment must be a vowel. That is why */lbɪk/ does not sound like an English word. It violates the restrictions on the sequencing of phonemes. People who like to work crossword puzzles are often more aware of these constraints than the ordinary speaker, whose knowledge, as we have emphasized, may not be conscious.

Other such constraints exist in English. If the initial sounds of *chill* or *Jill* begin a word, the next sound must be a vowel. The words / tʃʌt/ or / tʃon/ or / tʃæk/ are possible in English, as are /dʒæl/ or /dʒil/ or /dʒalɪk/, but */tʃlɔt/ and */dʒpurz/ are not. No more than three sequential consonants can occur at the beginning of a word, and these three are restricted to /s/ + /p, t, k/ + /l, r, w, y/. There are even restrictions if this condition is met. For example, /stl/ is not a permitted sequence, so *stlick* is not a possible word in English, but *strick* is, along with *spew* /spju/, *sclaff* /sklæf/ (to strike the ground with a golf club), and *squat* /skwat/.

Other languages have different sequential restrictions. In Polish *zl* and *kt* are permissible syllable−initial combinations, as in /zlev/, "a sink," and /kto/, "who." Croatian permits words like the name *Mladen*. Japanese has severe constraints on what may begin a syllable; most combinations of consonants (e.g., /br/, /sp/) are impermissible.

The limitations on sequences of segments are called **phonotactic constraints**. Phonotactic constraints have as their basis the syllable, rather than the word. That is, only the clusters that can begin a syllable can begin a word, and only a cluster that can end a syllable can end a word.

In multisyllabic words, clusters that seem illegal may occur, for example the /kspl/ in *explicit* /ɛksplɪsɪt/. However, there is a syllable boundary between the /ks/

and /pl/, which we can make explicit using $: /ɛk $ splɪs $ ɪt/. Thus we have a permitted syllable coda /k/ that ends a syllable adjoined to a permitted onset /spl/ that begins a syllable. On the other hand, English speakers know that "condstluct" is not a possible word because the second syllable would have to start with an impermissible onset, either /stl/ or /tl/.

In Twi, a word may end only in a vowel or a nasal consonant. The sequence /pik/ is not a possible Twi word because it breaks the phonotactic rules of the language, whereas /mba/ is not a possible word in English, although it is a word in Twi.

All languages have constraints on the permitted sequences of phonemes, although different languages have different constraints. Just as spoken language has sequences of sounds that are not permitted in the language, so sign languages have forbidden combinations of features. They differ from one sign language to another, just as the constraints on sounds and sound sequences differ from one spoken language to another. A permissible sign in a Chinese sign language may not be a permissible sign in ASL, and vice versa. Children learn these constraints when they acquire the spoken or signed language, just as they learn what the phonemes are and how they are related to phonetic segments.

Lexical Gaps

The words *bot* [bat] and *crake* [krek] are not known to all speakers of English, but they are words. On the other hand [bʊt] (to rhyme with *put*), *creck* [krɛk], *cruke* [kruk], *cruk* [krʌk], and *crike* [krajk] are not now words in English, although they are possible words.

Advertising professionals often use possible but nonoccurring words for the names of new products. Although we would hardly expect a new product or company to come on the market with the name *Zhleet* [ʒlit]—an impossible word in English—we do not bat an eye at *Bic, Xerox* /zɪraks/, Kodak, Glaxo, or Spam (a meat product, not junk mail), because those once nonoccurring words obey the phonotactic constraints of English.

A *possible word* contains phonemes in sequences that obey the phonotactic constraints of the language. An actual, occurring word is the union of a possible word with a meaning. Possible words without meaning are sometimes called **nonsense words** and are also referred to as **accidental gaps** in the lexicon, or **lexical gaps**. Thus "words" such as *creck* and *cruck* are nonsense words and represent accidental gaps in the lexicon of English.

Why Do Phonological Rules Exist?

A very important question that we have not addressed thus far is: why do grammars have phonological rules at all? In other words, why don't underlying or phonemic forms surface intact rather than undergoing various changes?

In the previous section we discussed *phonotactic constraints,* which are part of our knowledge of phonology. As we saw, phonotactic constraints specify which sound sequences are permissible in a particular language, so that in English *blick* is a possible word but *lbick* isn't. Many phonologists believe that phonological rules exist to ensure that the surface or phonetic forms of words do not violate phonotactic constraints. If underlying forms remained unmodified, they would often violate the phonotactics of the language.

Consider, for example, the English past-tense rule and recall that it has two sub-rules. The first inserts a schwa when a regular verb ends in an alveolar stop (/t/ or /d/), as in *mated* [metəd]. The second devoices the past-tense morpheme /d/ when it occurs after a voiceless sound, as in *reaped* [ript] or *peaked* [pikt]. Notice that the part of the rule that devoices /d/ reflects the constraint that English words may not end in a sequence consisting of a voiceless stop + d. Words such as [lɪpd] and [mɪkd] do not exist, nor could they exist. They are impossible words of English, just as [bkɪl] is.

More generally, there are no words that end in a sequence of obstruents whose voicing features do not match. Thus words such as [kasb], where the final two obstruents are [− voice] [+ voice] are not possible, nor are words such as [kabs] whose final two obstruents are [+ voice] [− voice]. On the other hand, [kasp] and [kɛbz] are judged to be possible words because the final two segments agree in voicing. Thus, there appears to be a general constraint in English, stated as follows:

> (A) Obstruent sequences may not differ with respect to their voice feature at the end of a word.

We can see then that the devoicing part of the past-tense rule changes the underlying form of the past-tense morpheme to create a surface form that conforms to this general constraint.

Similarly, the schwa insertion part of the past-tense rule creates possible sound sequences from impossible ones. English does not generally permit sequences of sounds within a single syllable that are very similar to each other, such as [kk], [kg], [gk], [gg], [pp], [sz], [zs], and so on. (Words spelled *egg* or *puppy* are phonetically [ɛg] and [pʌpi].) Thus the schwa insertion rule separates sequences of sounds that are otherwise not permitted in the language because they are too similar to each other, for example, the sequence of /d/ and /d/ in /mɛnd+d/, which becomes [mɛndəd] *mended*, or /t/ and /d/ in /part+d/, which becomes [partəd] *parted*. The relevant constraint is stated as follows;

> (B) Sequences of obstruents that differ at most with respect to voicing are not permitted within English words.

Constraints such as (A) and (B) are far more general than particular rules like the past-tense rule. For example, constraint B might also explain why an adjective such as *smooth* turns into the abstract noun *smoothness*, rather than taking the affix −*th* ([θ]), as in *wide-width, broad-breadth,* and *deep-depth.* Suffixing *smooth* with −*th* would result in a sequence of too similar obstruents, smoo[ðθ], which differ only in their voicing feature. This suggests that languages may satisfy constraints in various grammatical situations.

Thus, phonological rules exist because languages have general principles that constrain possible sequences of sounds. The rules specify minimal modifications of the underlying forms that bring them in line with the surface constraints. Therefore, we find different variants of a particular underlying form depending on the phonological context.

It has also been proposed that a universal set of phonological constraints exists, and that this set is ordered, with some constraints being more highly ranked than others.

The higher the constraint is ranked, the more influence it exerts on the language. This proposal, known as **Optimality Theory**, also holds that the particular constraint rankings can differ from language to language, and that the different rankings generate the different sound patterns shown across languages. For example, constraint B is highly ranked in English; and so we have the English past-tense rule, as well as many other rules, including the plural rule (with some modification), that modify sequences of sounds that are too similar. Constraint B is also highly ranked in other languages, for example, Modern Hebrew, in which suffixes that begin with /t/ are always separated from stems ending in /t/ or /d/ by inserting [e], as in /kiʃat + ti/ → [kiʃateti] meaning "I decorated." In Berber, similar consonants such as tt, dd, ss, and so on can surface at the end of words. In this language, constraint B is not highly ranked; other constraints outrank it and therefore exert a stronger effect on the language, notably constraints that want the surface forms not to deviate from corresponding underlying forms. These constraints, known as *faithfulness constraints*, compete in the rankings with constraints that modify the underlying forms. Faithfulness constraints reflect the drive among languages to want a morpheme to have a single identifiable form, a drive that is in competition with constraints such as A and B. In the case of the English past-tense morpheme, the drive toward a single morpheme shows up in the spelling, which is always *-ed*.

In our discussion of syntactic rules in chapter 4, we noted that there are principles of Universal Grammar (UG) operating in the syntax. Two examples of this are the principle that transformational rules are structure dependent and the constraint that movement rules may not move phrases out of coordinate structures. If Optimality Theory is correct, and universal phonological constraints exist that differ among languages only in their rankings, then phonological rules, like syntactic rules, are constrained by universal principles. The differences in constraint rankings across languages are in some ways parallel to the different parameter settings that exist in the syntax of different languages, also discussed in chapter 4. We noted that in acquiring the syntax of her language, the young child must set the parameters of UG at the values that are correct for the language of the environment. Similarly, in acquiring the phonology of her language, the child must determine the correct constraint rankings as evidenced in the input language. We will have more to say about language acquisition in the following chapter.

Phonological Analysis: Discovering Phonemes

Out of clutter, find simplicity.
From discord, find harmony.

ALBERT EINSTEIN

Children recognize phonemes at an early age without being taught, as we shall see in chapter 8. Before reading this book, or learning anything about phonology, you knew a *p* sound was a phoneme in English because it contrasts words like *pat* and *cat, pat* and *sat, pat* and *mat.* But you probably did not know that the *p* in *pat* and the *p* in *spit* are different sounds. There is only one /p/ phoneme in English, but that phoneme has more than one allophone, including an aspirated one and an unaspirated one.

If a non-English-speaking linguist analyzed English, how could this fact about the sound *p* be discovered? More generally, how do linguists discover the phonological system of a language?

To do a phonemic analysis, the words to be analyzed must be transcribed in great phonetic detail, because we do not know in advance which phonetic features are distinctive and which are not.

Consider the following Finnish words:

1.	[kudot]	"failures"		**5.**	[madon]	"of a worm"
2.	[kate]	"cover"		**6.**	[maton]	"of a rug"
3.	[katot]	"roofs"		**7.**	[ratas]	"wheel"
4.	[kade]	"envious"		**8.**	[radon]	"of a track"

Given these words, do the voiceless/voiced alveolar stops [t] and [d] represent different phonemes, or are they allophones of the same phone?

Here are a few hints as to how a phonologist might proceed:

1. Check to see if there are any minimal pairs.
2. Items (2) and (4) are minimal pairs: [kate] "cover" and [kade] "envious."
   Items (5) and (6) are minimal pairs: [madon] "of a worm" and [maton] "of a rug."
3. [t] and [d] in Finnish thus represent the distinct phonemes /t/ and /d/.

That was an easy problem.

Now consider these data from Greek, focusing on the following sounds:

[x] voiceless velar fricative
[k] voiceless velar stop
[c] voiceless palatal stop
[ç] voiceless palatal fricative

1.	[kano]	"do"		**9.**	[çeri]	"hand"
2.	[xano]	"lose"		**10.**	[kori]	"daughter"
3.	[çino]	"pour"		**11.**	[xori]	"dances"
4.	[cino]	"move"		**12.**	[xrima]	"money"
5.	[kali]	"charms"		**13.**	[krima]	"shame"
6.	[xali]	"plight"		**14.**	[xufta]	"handful"
7.	[çeli]	"eel"		**15.**	[kufeta]	"bonbons"
8.	[ceri]	"candle"		**16.**	[oçi]	"no"

To determine the status of [x], [k], [c], and [ç], you should answer the following questions.

1. Are there are any minimal pairs in which these sounds contrast?
2. Are any noncontrastive sounds in complementary distribution?
3. If noncontrasting phones are found, what are the phonemes and their allophones?
4. What are the phonological rules by which the allophones can be derived?

1. By analyzing the data, we find that [k] and [x] contrast in a number of minimal pairs, for example, in [kano] and [xano]. [k] and [x] are therefore distinctive. [c] and [ç] also contrast in [çino] and [cino] and are therefore distinctive. But what about the velar fricative [x] and the palatal fricative [ç]? And the velar stop [k] and the palatal stop [c]? We can find no minimal pairs that would conclusively show that these represent separate phonemes.

2. We now proceed to answer the second question: Are these noncontrasting phones, namely [x]/[ç] and [k]/[c], in complementary distribution? One way to see if sounds are in complementary distribution is to list each phone with the environment in which it is found, as follows:

Phone	Environment
[k]	before [a], [o], [u], [r]
[x]	before [a], [o], [u], [r]
[c]	before [i], [e]
[ç]	before [i], [e]

We see that [k] and [x] are not in complementary distribution; they both occur before back vowels. Nor are [c] and [ç] in complementary distribution. They both occur before front vowels. But the stops [k] and [c] are in complementary distribution; [k] occurs before back vowels and [r], and never occurs before front vowels. Similarly, [c] occurs only before front vowels and never before back vowels or [r]. Finally, [x] and [ç] are in complementary distribution for the same reason. We therefore conclude that [k] and [c] are allophones of one phoneme, and the fricatives [x] and [ç] are also allophones of one phoneme. The pairs of allophones also fulfill the criterion of phonetic similarity. The first two are [− anterior] stops; the second are [− anterior] fricatives. (This similarity discourages us from pairing [k] with [ç], and [c] with [x], which are less similar to each other.)

3. Which of the phone pairs are more basic, and hence the ones whose features would define the phoneme? When two allophones can be derived from one phoneme, one selects as the underlying segment the allophone that makes the rules and the phonemic feature matrix as simple as possible, as we illustrated with the English unaspirated and aspirated voiceless stops.

In the case of the velar and palatal stops and fricatives in Greek, the rules appear to be equally simple. However, in addition to the simplicity criterion, we wish to state rules that have natural phonetic explanations. Often these turn out to be the simplest solution. In many languages, velar sounds become palatal before front vowels. This is an assimilation rule; palatal sounds are produced toward the front of the mouth, as are front vowels. Thus we select /k/ as a phoneme with the allophones [k] and [c], and /x/ as a phoneme with the allophones [x] and [ç].

4. We can now state the rule by which the palatals can be derived from the velars.

Palatalize velar consonants before front vowels.

Using feature notation we can state the rule as:

$$[+ \text{ velar}] \rightarrow [+ \text{ palatal}] / \underline{\quad\quad} [- \text{ back}]$$

Because only consonants are marked for the feature [velar], and only vowels for the feature [back], it is not necessary to include the features [consonantal] or [syllabic] in the rule. We also do not need to include any other features that are redundant in defining the segments to which the rule applies or the environment in which the rule applies. Thus [+ palatal] in the change part of the rule is sufficient, and the feature [− back] also suffices to specify the front vowels. The simplicity criterion constrains us to state the rule as simply as we can.

Summary

Part of one's knowledge of a language is knowledge of the **phonology** or sound system of that language. It includes the inventory of **phones**—which are the phonetic sounds that occur in the language—and the ways in which they pattern. This patterning determines the inventory of **phonemes**—the abstract basic units that differentiate words.

Phonetic segments are enclosed in square brackets, [ ], and phonemes between slashes, / /. When similar phones occur in **complementary distribution**, they are **allophones**—predictable phonetic variants—of phonemes. For example, in English, aspirated voiceless stops such as the initial sound in *pill* are in complementary distribution with the unaspirated voiceless stops in words such as *spill*. Thus the aspirated [pʰ] and the unaspirated [p] are allophones of the phoneme /p/. This generalizes also to the voiceless stops /t/ and /k/. On the other hand, phones in the same environment that differentiate words, like the [b] and [m] in *boat* [bot] and *moat* [mot], represent two distinct phonemes, /b/ and /m/.

Some phones may be allophones of more than one phoneme. There is no one-to-one correspondence between the phonemes of a language and their allophones. In English, for example, stressed vowels become unstressed according to regular rules, and ultimately reduce to schwa [ə], which is an allophone of each English vowel.

Phonological segments—phonemes and phones—are composed of **phonetic features** such as voiced, nasal, labial, and continuant, whose presence or absence is indicated by + or − signs. They distinguish one segment from another. When a phonetic feature causes a word contrast, as nasal does in *boat* and *moat*, it is a distinctive feature. Thus, in English, the binary valued feature [± nasal] is a distinctive feature, whereas [± aspiration] is not.

When two distinct words are distinguished by a single phone occurring in the same position, they constitute a **minimal pair**. Some pairs, such as *boat* and *moat*, contrast by means of a single distinctive feature, in this case [± nasal], where /b/ is [− nasal] and /m/ is [+ nasal]. Other minimal pairs may show sounds contrasting in more than one feature, for example, *dip* versus *sip*, where /d/, a voiced alveolar stop, is [+ voiced, − continuant] and /s/, a voiceless alveolar fricative, is [− voiced, + continuant]. Minimal pairs and sets also occur in sign languages. Signs may contrast by hand configuration, place of articulation, movement, and palm position.

Phonetic features that are **predictable** are nondistinctive and **redundant**. The nasality of vowels in English is a redundant feature because all vowels are nasalized before nasal consonants. One can thus predict the + or − value of this feature in vowels. A feature may therefore be distinctive in one class of sounds and **nondistinctive** in another. Nasality is distinctive for English consonants and nondistinctive predictable for English vowels. Phonetic features that are nondistinctive in one language may be distinctive in another. Aspiration is distinctive in Thai and nondistinctive in English; both aspirated and unaspirated voiceless stops are phonemes in Thai.

Words in some languages may also be phonemically distinguished by prosodic or suprasegmental features, such as pitch, stress, and segment duration or length. Languages in which syllables or words are contrasted by pitch are called **tone languages**. **Intonation** languages may use pitch variations to distinguish meanings of phrases and sentences.

In English, words and phrases may be differentiated by stress, as in the contrast between the noun *pérvert*, in which the first syllable is stressed, and the verb *pervért*, in which the final syllable is stressed. In the compound noun *hótdog* versus the adjective + noun phrase *hot dóg*, the former is stressed on *hot*, the latter on *dog*.

Vowel length and consonant length may be phonemic features. Both are contrastive in Japanese, Finnish, Italian, and many other languages.

The relationship between the phonemic representation of words and sentences and the phonetic representation (the pronunciation of these words and sentences) is determined by phonological rules. Phonological rules in a grammar apply to phonemic strings and alter them in various ways to derive their phonetic pronunciation:

1. They may be **assimilation rules**, which change feature values of segments, thus spreading phonetic properties. The rule that nasalizes vowels in English before nasal consonants is such a rule.
2. They may be **dissimilation rules**, which change feature values to make two phonemes in a string more dissimilar, like the Latin liquid rule.
3. They may *add* **nondistinctive features**, which are predictable from the context. The rule that aspirates voiceless stops at the beginning of words and syllables in English is such a rule.
4. They may *insert* segments that are not present in the phonemic string. Insertion is also called **epenthesis**. The schwa insertion part of the rule of English plural formation is an example of epenthesis (e.g., *kisses* [kʰɪsəz]).
5. They may *delete* phonemic segments in certain contexts. French has a rule deleting final consonants in certain environments, so that the final /t/ in *petit livre* is not pronounced.
6. They may *transpose* or move segments in a string. These **metathesis** rules occur in many languages. The rule in certain varieties of American English that changes an *sk* to [ks] in final position illustrates a metathesis rule.

Phonological rules generally refer to entire classes of sound. These are **natural classes**, characterized by the phonetic features that pertain to all the members of the class, such as voiced sounds, which are represented in feature notation as [+ voiced]. A natural class can be defined by fewer features than required to distinguish a member of that class.

In the writing of rules, one can use formal notations, which often reveal linguistic generalizations of phonological processes. The formal statement of the vowel nasalization rule (V → [+ nasal] / __ [+ nasal] $) reveals that it's an assimilation rule because the feature [+ nasal] occurs both as a change and in the rule's environment.

A morpheme may have different phonetic representations; these are determined by **morphophonemic rules**, a type of phonological rule that applies to specific morphemes, but not in general. Thus the regular plural morpheme is phonetically [z], [s], or [əz], depending on the final phoneme of the noun to which it is attached.

The phonology of a language also includes constraints on the sequences of phonemes in the language (**phonotactics**), as illustrated by the fact that in English two stop consonants may not occur together at the beginning of a word. Similarly, the final sound of the word *sing*, the velar nasal, never occurs word initially. These sequential constraints determine what are *possible* but nonoccurring words in a language, and what phonetic strings are impermissible. For example, *blick* [blɪk] is not now an English word, but it could become one, whereas *kbli* [kbli] or *ngos* [ŋɔs] could not. Possible but nonoccurring words constitute **accidental gaps** and are **nonsense words**.

Phonological rules exist in part to enforce phonotactic constraints. The English plural rule includes the insertion of a schwa ([ə]) to prevent the phonotactically illegal sequence [sz]. **Optimality Theory** hypothesizes a universal set of ranked constraints with higher ranked constraints taking precedence over lower ranked ones, with the entire system motivating and governing the nature and order of the phonological rules.

To discover the phonemes of a language, linguists (or students of linguistics) can use a methodology such as looking for minimal pairs of words, or for sounds that are in complementary distribution. The feature matrix of the allophone of a phoneme that results in the simplest statement of the phonological rules is selected as the underlying phoneme from which all the phonetic allophones are derived.

The phonological rules in a language show that the phonemic shape of words or phrases is not identical with their phonetic form. The phonemes are not the actual phonetic sounds, but are abstract mental constructs that are realized as sounds by the operation of rules such as those described in this chapter. No one is taught these rules, yet everyone knows them subconsciously.

References for Further Reading

Anderson, S. R. 1985. *Phonology in the Twentieth Century: Theories of Rules and Theories of Representations*. Chicago: University of Chicago Press.

Bybee, J. 2002. *Phonology and Language Use*. Cambridge, UK: Cambridge University Press.

Chomsky, N., and M. Halle. 1968. *The Sound Pattern of English*. New York: Harper & Row.

Clark, J., and C. Yallop. 1990. *An Introduction to Phonetics and Phonology*. Oxford, England: Basil Blackwell.

Clements, G. N., and S. J. Keyser. 1983. *CV Phonology: A Generative Theory of the Syllable*. Cambridge, MA: MIT Press.

Dell, F. 1980. *Generative Phonology*. London, England: Cambridge University Press.

Goldsmith, J. A. (ed.). 1995. *The Handbook of Phonological Theory*. Cambridge, MA: Blackwell.

Hogg, R., and C. B. McCully. 1987. *Metrical Phonology: A Coursebook*. Cambridge, England: Cambridge University Press.

Hyman, L. M. 1975. *Phonology: Theory and Analysis*. New York: Holt, Rinehart & Winston.

Kaye, Jonathan. 1989. *Phonology: A Cognitive View*. Hillsdale, NJ: Erlbaum.

Kenstowicz, M. J. 1994. *Phonology in Generative Grammar*. Oxford: Blackwell Publications.

Exercises

All the data in languages other than English are given in phonetic transcription without square brackets unless otherwise stated. The phonetic transcriptions of English words are given within square brackets.

1. The following sets of minimal pairs show that English /p/ and /b/ contrast in initial, medial, and final positions.

Initial	Medial	Final
pit/bit	rapid/rabid	cap/cab

Find similar sets of minimal pairs for each pair of consonants given:

a. /k/−/g/ **d.** /b/−/v/ **g.** /s/−/ʃ/

b. /m/−/n/ **e.** /b/−/m/ **h.** /tʃ/−/dʒ/

c. /l/−/r/ **f.** /p/−/f/ **i.** /s/−/z/

2. A young patient at the Radcliffe Infirmary in Oxford, England, following a head injury, appears to have lost the spelling-to-pronunciation and pronunciation-to-spelling rules that most of us can use to read and write new words or nonsense strings. He also is unable to get to the phonemic representation of words in his lexicon. Consider the following examples of his reading pronunciation and his writing from dictation:

Stimulus	Reading Pronunciation	Writing from Dictation
fame	/fæmi/	FAM
café	/sæfi/	KAFA
time	/tajmi/	TIM
note	/noti/ or /nɔti/	NOT
praise	/pra-aj-si/	PRAZ
treat	/tri-æt/	TRET
goes	/go-ɛs/	GOZ
float	/flɔ-æt/	FLOT

What rules or patterns relate his reading pronunciation to the written stimulus? What rules or patterns relate his spelling to the dictated stimulus? For example, in reading, *a* corresponds to /a/ or /æ/; in writing from dictation /e/ and /æ/ correspond to written A.

3. Consider the distribution of [r] and [l] in Korean in the following words: (Some simplifying changes have been made in these transcriptions, and those in exercise 4, that have no bearing on the problems.)

rubi	"ruby"	mul	"water"
kir-i	"road (nom.)"	pal	"arm"
saram	"person"	səul	"Seoul"
irum-i	"name (nom.)"	ilgop	"seven"
ratio	"radio"	ibalsa	"barber"

Are [r] and [l] allophones of one or two phonemes?

a. Do they occur in any minimal pairs?

b. Are they in complementary distribution?

c. In what environments does each occur?

d. If you conclude that they are allophones of one phoneme, state the rule that can derive the phonetic allophonic forms.

4. Here are some additional data from Korean:

son	"hand"	ʃihap	"game"
som	"cotton"	ʃilsu	"mistake"

sosəl	"novel"	ʃipsam	"thirteen"
sɛk	"color"	ʃinho	"signal"
isa	"moving"	maʃita	"is delicious"
sal	"flesh"	oʃip	"fifty

a. Are [s] and [ʃ] allophones of the same phoneme, or is each an allophone of a separate phoneme? Give your reasons.

b. If you conclude that they are allophones of one phoneme, state the rule that can derive the phonetic allophones.

5. In Southern Kongo, a Bantu language spoken in Angola, the nonpalatal segments [t, s, z] are in complementary distribution with their palatal counterparts [tʃ, ʃ, ʒ], as shown in the following words:

tobola	"to bore a hole"	tʃina	"to cut"
tanu	"five"	tʃiba	"banana"
kesoka	"to be cut"	ŋkoʃi	"lion"
kasu	"emaciation"	nselele	"termite"
kunezulu	"heaven"	aʒimola	"alms"
nzwetu	"our"	lolonʒi	"to wash house"
zevo	"then"	zeŋga	"to cut"
ʒima	"to stretch"		

a. State the distribution of each pair of segments. (Assume that the nonoccurrence of [t] before [e] is an accidental gap.)

Example: [t]—[tʃ]: [t] occurs before [o], [a], and [u]; [tʃ] occurs before [i].

         [s]—[ʃ]:

         [z]—[ʒ]:

b. Using considerations of simplicity, which phone should be used as the underlying phoneme for each pair of nonpalatal and palatal segments in Southern Kongo?

c. State in your own words the *one* phonological rule that will derive all the phonetic segments from the phonemes. Do not state a separate rule for each phoneme; a general rule can be stated that will apply to all three phonemes you listed in b. Try to give a formal statement of your rule.

6. In some dialects of English, the following words have different vowels, as is shown by the phonetic transcriptions:

A		**B**		**C**	
bite	[bʌjt]	bide	[bajd]	die	[daj]
rice	[rʌjs]	rise	[rajz]	by	[baj]
ripe	[rʌjp]	bribe	[brajb]	sigh	[saj]
wife	[wʌjf]	wives	[wajvz]	rye	[raj]
dike	[dʌjk]	dime	[dãjm]	guy	[gaj]
		nine	[nãjn]		
		rile	[rajl]		
		dire	[dajr]		
		writhe	[rajð]		

a. How may the classes of sounds that end the words in columns A and B be characterized? That is, what feature specifies all the final segments in A and all the final segments in B?

b. How do the words in column C differ from those in columns A and B?

c. Are [ʌj] and [aj] in complementary distribution? Give your reasons.

d. If [ʌj] and [aj] are allophones of one phoneme, should they be derived from /ʌj/ or /aj/? Why?

e. Give the phonetic representations of the following words as they would be spoken in the dialect described here:

life _____ lives _____ lie _____

file _____ bike _____ lice _____

f. Formulate a rule that will relate the phonemic representations to the phonetic representations of the words given above.

7. Pairs like *top* and *chop, dunk* and *junk, so* and *show*, and *Caesar* and *seizure* reveal that /t/ and /tʃ/, /d/ and /dʒ/, /s/ and /ʃ/, and /z/ and /ʒ/ are distinct phonemes in English. Consider these same pairs of nonpalatalized and palatalized consonants in the following data. (The palatal forms are optional forms that often occur in casual speech.)

Nonpalatalized

[hɪt mi]	"hit me"
[lid hĩm]	"lead him"
[pʰæs ʌs]	"pass us"
[luz ðɛm]	"lose them"

Palatalized

[hɪtʃ ju]	"hit you"
[lidʒ ju]	"lead you"
[pʰæʃ ju]	"pass you"
[luʒ ju]	"lose you"

Formulate the rule that specifies when /t/, /d/, /s/, and /z/ become palatalized as [tʃ], [dʒ], [ʃ], and [ʒ]. Restate the rule using feature notations. Does the formal statement reveal the generalizations?

8. Here are some Japanese words in a broad phonetic transcription. Note that [ts] is an alveolar affricate and should be taken as a *single* symbol just like the palatal fricative [tʃ]. It is pronounced as the initial sound in *ts*unami. Japanese words (except certain loan words) never contain the phonetic sequences *[ti] or *[tu].

tatami	"mat"	tomodatʃi	"friend"	utʃi	"house"
tegami	"letter"	totemo	"very"	otoko	"male"
tʃitʃi	"father"	tsukue	"desk"	tetsudau	"help"
ʃita	"under"	ato	"later"	matsu	"wait"
natsu	"summer"	tsutsumu	"wrap"	tʃizu	"map"
kata	"person"	tatemono	"building"	te	"hand"

a. Based on these data, are [t], [tʃ], and [ts] in complementary distribution?

b. State the distribution—first in words, then using features—of these phones.

c. Give a phonemic analysis of these data insofar as [t], [tʃ], and [ts] are concerned. That is, identify the phonemes and the allophones.

d. Give the phonemic representation of the phonetically transcribed Japanese words shown as follows. Assume phonemic and phonetic representations are the same except for [t], [tʃ], and [ts].

tatami _____	tsukue _____	tsutsumu _____
tomodatʃi _____	tetsudau _____	tʃizu _____
utʃi _____	ʃita _____	kata _____
tegami _____	ato _____	koto _____
totemo _____	matsu _____	tatemono _____
otoko _____	degutʃi _____	te _____
tʃitʃi _____	natsu _____	tsuri _____

9. The following words are Paku, a language spoken by the Pakuni in the NBC television series *Land of the Lost* (a language created by V. Fromkin). The acute accent indicates a stressed vowel.

   a. ótu   "evil" (N)   **h.** mpósa   "hairless"

   b. túsa   "evil" (Adj)   **i.** ámpo   "hairless one"

   c. etógo   "cactus" (sg)   **j.** ãmpṍni   "hairless ones"

   d. etogṍni   "cactus" (pl)   **k.** ámi   "mother"

   e. Pákũ   "Paku" (sg)   **l.** ãmíni   "mothers"

   f. Pakṹni   "Paku" (pl)   **m.** áda   "father"

   g. épo   "hair"   **n.** adáni   "fathers"

   (1) Is stress predictable? If so, what is the rule?

   (2) Is nasalization a distinctive feature for vowels? Give the reasons for your answer.

10. Consider the following English verbs. Those in column A have stress on the next-to-last syllable (called the *penultimate*), whereas the verbs in column B and C have their last syllable stressed.

A	B	C
astónish	collápse	amáze
éxit	exíst	impróve
imágine	resént	surpríse
cáncel	revólt	combíne
elícit	adópt	belíeve
práctice	insíst	atóne

   a. Transcribe the words under columns A, B, and C phonemically. (Use a schwa for the unstressed vowels even if they can be derived from different phonemic vowels. This should make it easier for you.)

   e.g., *astonish* /əstanɪʃ/, *collapse* /kəlæps/, *amaze* /əmez/

   b. Consider the phonemic structure of the stressed syllables in these verbs. What is the difference between the final syllables of the verbs in columns A and B? Formulate a rule that predicts where stress occurs in the verbs in columns A and B.

   c. In the verbs in column C, stress also occurs on the final syllable. What must you add to the rule to account for this fact? (*Hint*: For the forms in columns A and B, the final consonants had to be considered; for the forms in column C, consider the vowels.)

11. Following are listed the phonetic transcriptions of ten "words." Some are English words, some are not words now but are possible words or nonsense words, and others are not possible because they violate English sequential constraints.

Write the English words in regular spelling. Mark the other words as *possible* or *not possible*. For each word you mark as "not possible," state your reason.

	Word	Possible	Not Possible	Reason
Example:				
[θrot]	throat			
[slig]		X		
[lsig]			X	No English word can begin with a liquid followed by an obstruent.

	Word	Possible	Not Possible	Reason
a. [pʰril]				
b. [skritʃ]				
c. [kʰno]				
d. [maj]				
e. [gnostɪk]				
f. [jũnəkʰɔrn]				
g. [fruit]				
h. [blaft]				
i. [ŋar]				
j. [æpəpʰlɛksi]				

12. Consider these phonetic forms of Hebrew words:

[v]–[b]		**[f]–[p]**	
bika	"lamented"	litef	"stroked"
mugbal	"limited"	sefer	"book"
ʃavar	"broke" (masc.)	sataf	"washed"
ʃavra	"broke" (fem.)	para	"cow"
ʔikev	"delayed"	mitpaxat	"handkerchief"
bara	"created"	haʔalpim	"the Alps"

Assume that these words and their phonetic sequences are representative of what may occur in Hebrew. In your answers, consider classes of sounds rather than individual sounds.

a. Are [b] and [v] allophones of one phoneme? Are they in complementary distribution? In what phonetic environments do they occur? Can you formulate a phonological rule stating their distribution?

b. Does the same rule, or lack of a rule, that describes the distribution of [b] and [v] apply to [p] and [f]? If not, why not?

c. Here is a word with one phone missing. A blank appears in place of the missing sound: hid___ik.

Check the one correct statement.

(1) [b] but not [v] could occur in the empty slot.

(2) [v] but not [b] could occur in the empty slot.

(3) Either [b] or [v] could occur in the empty slot.

(4) Neither [b] nor [v] could occur in the empty slot.

d. Which of the following statements is correct about the incomplete word ___ana?

(1) [f] but not [p] could occur in the empty slot.

(2) [p] but not [f] could occur in the empty slot.

(3) Either [p] or [f] could fill the blank.

(4) Neither [p] nor [f] could fill the blank.

e. Now consider the following possible words (in phonetic transcription):

laval   surva   labal   palar   falu   razif

If these words actually occurred in Hebrew, would they:

(1) Force you to revise the conclusions about the distribution of labial stops and fricatives you reached on the basis of the first group of words given above?

(2) Support your original conclusions?

(3) Neither support nor disprove your original conclusions?

13. In the African language Maninka, the suffix *-li* has more than one pronunciation (like the *-ed* past-tense ending on English verbs, as in *reaped* [t], *robbed* [d], and *raided* [əd]). This suffix is similar to the derivational suffix *-ing*, which, when added to the verb *cook*, makes it a noun as in "Her cooking was great," or the suffix *-ion*, which also derives a noun from a verb as in *create* + *ion*.

Consider these data from Maninka:

bugo	"hit"	bugoli	"hitting"
dila	"repair"	dilali	"repairing"
don	"come in"	donni	"coming in"
dumu	"eat"	dumuni	"eating"
gwen	"chase"	gwenni	"chasing"

a. What are the two forms of the "ing" morpheme?

(1) _____ (2) _____

b. Can you predict which phonetic form will occur? If so, state the rule.

c. What are the "-ing" forms for the following verbs?

da   "lie down" _____   famu   "understand" _____

men   "hear"_____   sunogo "sleep" _____

14. Consider the following phonetic data from the Bantu language Luganda. (The data have been somewhat altered to make the problem easier.) In each line except the last, the same root occurs in both columns A and B, but it has one prefix in column A, meaning "a" or "an," and another prefix in column B, meaning "little."

A		**B**	
ẽnato	"a canoe"	aka:to	"little canoe"

A		B	
ẽnapo	"a house"	aka:po	"little house"
ẽnobi	"an animal"	akaobi	"little animal"
ẽmpipi	"a kidney"	akapipi	"little kidney"
ẽŋko:sa	"a feather"	akako:sa	"little feather"
ẽm:ã:m:o	"a peg"	akabã:m:o	"little peg"
ẽŋ:õ:m:e	"a horn"	akagõ:m:e	"little horn"
en:īmiro	"a garden"	akadīmiro	"little garden"
ẽnugẽni	"a stranger"	akatabi	"little branch"

Base your answers to the following questions on only these forms. Assume that all the words in the language follow the regularities shown here. (*Hint:* You may write long segments such as /m:/ as /mm/ to help you visualize more clearly the phonological processes taking place.)

a. Are nasal vowels in Luganda phonemic?

Are they predictable?

b. Is the phonemic representation of the morpheme meaning "garden" /dimiro/?

c. What is the phonemic representation of the morpheme meaning "canoe"?

d. Are [p] and [b] allophones of one phoneme?

e. If /am/ represents a bound prefix morpheme in Luganda, can you conclude that [ãmdãno] is a possible phonetic form for a word in this language starting with this prefix?

f. Is there a homorganic nasal rule in Luganda?

g. If the phonetic representation of the word meaning "little boy" is [akapo:be], give the phonemic and phonetic representations for "a boy."

Phonemic_____ Phonetic _____

h. Which of the following forms is the phonemic representation for the prefix meaning "a" or "an"?

(1) /en/   (2) /ẽn/   (3) /ẽm/   (4) /em/   (5) /eŋ/

i. What is the *phonetic* representation of the word meaning "a branch"?

j. What is the *phonemic* representation of the word meaning "little stranger"?

k. State the three phonological rules revealed by the Luganda data.

15. Here are some Japanese verb forms given in a broad phonetic transcription. They represent two styles (informal and formal) of present-tense verbs. Morphemes are separated by +. (*Cf.* exercise 8.)

Gloss	Informal	Formal
call	yob + u	yob + imasu
write	kak + u	kak + imasu
eat	tabe + ru	tabe + masu
see	mi + ru	mi + masu
leave	de + ru	de + masu
go out	dekake + ru	dekake + masu
die	ʃin + u	ʃin + imasu
close	ʃime + ru	ʃime + masu
swindle	kata + ru	kata + masu

wear	ki + ru	ki + masu
read	yom + u	yom + imasu
lend	kas + u	kaʃ + imasu
wait	mats + u	matʃ + imasu
press	os + u	oʃ + imasu
apply	ate + ru	ate + masu
drop	otos + u	otoʃ + imasu
have	mots + u	motʃ + imasu
win	kats + u	katʃ + imasu
steal a lover	neto + ru	neto + masu

   a. List each of the Japanese verb roots in their phonemic representations.

   b. Formulate the rule that accounts for the different phonetic forms of these verb roots.

   c. There is more than one allomorph for the suffix designating formality and more than one for the suffix designating informality. List the allomorphs of each. Formulate the rule or rules for their distribution.

16. Consider these data from the Native American language Ojibwa.[3] (The data have been somewhat altered for the sake of simplicity; /c/ is a palatal stop.)

anokːiː	"she works"	nitanokːiː	"I work"
aːkːosi	"she is sick"	nitaːkːosi	"I am sick"
ayeːkːosi	"she is tired"	kiʃayeːkːosi	"you are tired"
ineːntam	"she thinks"	kiʃineːntam	"you think"
maːcaː	"she leaves"	nimaːcaː	"I leave"
takoʃːin	"she arrives"	nitakoʃːin	"I arrive"
pakiso	"she swims"	kipakiso	"you swim"
wiːsini	"she eats"	kiwiːsini	"you eat"

   a. What forms do the morphemes meaning "I" and "you" take; that is, what are the allomorphs?

   b. Are the allomorphs for "I" in complementary distribution? How about for "you"?

   c. Assuming that we want one phonemic form to underlie each allomorph, what should it be?

   d. State a rule that derives the phonetic forms of the allomorphs. Make it as general as possible; that is, refer to a broad natural class in the environment of the rule. You may state the rule formally, in words, or partially in words with some formal abbreviations.

   e. Is the rule a morphophonemic rule; that is, does it (most likely) apply to specific morphemes but not in general? What evidence do you see in the data to suggest your answer?

17. Consider these data from the Burmese language, spoken in Myanmar (formally called Burma). The small ring under the nasal consonants indicates a voiceless nasal. Tones have been omitted as they play no role in this problem.

ma	"health"	n̥ej	"unhurried"
na	"pain"	m̥i	"flame"

---

[3] From *The Logical Problem of Language Acquisition* by C. L. Baker & John McCarthy. Copyright © 1981 MIT Press. Reprinted by permission of MIT Press.

mjiʔ	"river"	m̥on	"flour"
nwe	"to flex"	m̥a	"order"
nwa	"cow"	ŋ̥wej	"heat (verb)"
mi	"flame"	n̥a	"nostril"

Are [m] and [m̥] and [n] and [n̥] allophones or phonemic? Present evidence to support your conclusion.

18. Here are some short sentences in a made-up language called wakanti. (Long consonants are written as doubled letters to make the analysis easier.)

[aba]	"I eat"	[amma]	"I don't eat"
[idej]	"You sleep"	[innej]	"You don't sleep"
[aguw]	"I go"	[aŋŋuw]	"I don't go"
[upi]	"We come"	[umpi]	"We don't come"
[atu]	"I walk"	[antu]	"I don't walk"
[ika]	"You see"	[iŋka]	"You don't see"
[ijama]	"You found out"	[injama]	"You didn't find out"
[aweli]	"I climbed up"	[amweli]	"I didn't climb up"
[ioa]	"You fell"	[inoa]	"You didn't fall"
[aie]	"I hunt"	[anie]	"I don't hunt"
[ulamaba]	"We put on top"	[unlamaba]	"We don't put on top"

a. What is the phonemic form of the negative morpheme based on these data?

b. What are its allomorphs?

c. State a rule that derives the phonetic form of the allomorphs from the underlying, phonemic form.

d. Another phonological rule applies to these data. State explicitly what the rule does and to what natural class of consonants it applies.

e. Give the phonemic forms for all the negative sentences.

19. Consider these pairs of semantically related phonetic forms and glosses in a commonly known language: (The + indicates a morpheme boundary.)

phonetic	gloss	phonetic	gloss
[bãm]	explosive device	[bãmb+ard]	to attack with explosive devices
[kʰrʌ̃m]	a morsel or bit	[kʰrʌ̃mb+əl]	to break into bits
[ajæ̃m]	a metrical foot	[ajæ̃mb+ɪc]	consisting of metrical feet
[θʌ̃m]	an opposable digit	[θʌ̃mb+əlĩnə]	a tiny woman of fairy tales

a. What are the two allomorphs of the root morpheme in each line of data?

b. What is the phonemic form of the underlying root morpheme? (*Hint:* Consider pairs such as *atom/atomic* and *form/formal* before you decide.)

c. State a rule that derives the allomorphs.

d. If you know English, spell these words using the English alphabet.

20. Consider these data from Hebrew: (*ts* is an alveolar sibilant fricative and should be considered one sound, just as *sh* stands for the palatal fricative [ʃ]. The word *lehit* is a reflexive pronoun.)

Nonsibilant–Initial Verbs		**Sibilant–Initial Verbs**	
kabel	"to accept"	*tsadek*	"to justify"
lehit-kabel	"to be accepted"	*lehits-tadek*	"to apologize"
		(not *lehit-tsadek*)	
pater	"to fire"	*shamesh*	"to use for"
lehit-pater	"to resign"	*lehish-tamesh*	"to use"
		(not *lehit-shamesh*)	
bayesh	"to shame"	*sader*	"to arrange"
lehit-bayesh	"to be ashamed"	*lehis-tader*	"to arrange oneself"
		(not *lehit-sader*)	

a. Describe the phonological change taking place in the second column of Hebrew data.

b. Describe in words as specifically as possible a phonological rule that accounts for the change. Make sure your rule doesn't affect the data in the first column of Hebrew.

21. Here are some Japanese data, many of them from exercise 8, in a fine enough phonetic transcription to show voiceless vowels (the ones with the little ring under them).

Word	**Gloss**	**Word**	**Gloss**	**Word**	**Gloss**
tatami	mat	tomodatʃi	friend	utʃi	house
tegami	letter	totemo	very	otoko	male
sṷkiyaki	sukiyaki	kịsetsu	season	busata	silence
tʃịtʃi	father	tsṵkue	desk	tetsudau	help
ʃịta	under	kịta	north	matsu	wait
degutʃi	exit	tsuri	fishing	kịsetsu	mistress
natsu	summer	tsṵtsumu	wrap	tʃizu	map
kata	person	fṵton	futon	fugi	discuss
matsṵshịta	a name	etsṵko	girl's name	fṵkuan	a plan

a. Which vowels may occur voiceless?

b. Are they in complementary distribution with their voiced counterparts? If so, state the distribution.

c. Are the voiced/voiceless pairs allophones of the same phoneme?

d. State in words, or write in formal notation if you can, the rule for determining the allophones of the vowels that have voiceless allophones.

22. With regard to the plural and past-tense rules, we observed that the two parts of the rules must be carried out in the proper order. If we reverse the order, we would get *[bʌsəs] instead of [bʌsəz] for the plural of *bus* (as illustrated in the text), and *[stetət] instead of [stetəd] for the past tense of *state*. Although constraints A and B (given below) are the motivation for the plural and past-tense rules, both the correct and incorrect plural and past-tense forms are consistent with those constraints. What additional constraint is needed to prevent [bʌsəs] and [stetət] from being generated?

(A) Obstruent sequences may not differ with respect to their voice feature at the end of a word.

(B) Sequences of obstruents that differ at most with respect to voicing are not permitted within English words.

23. We described a rule of word-final obstruent devoicing in German. (Recall that German /bund/ is pronounced [bunt]). This rule is actually a manifestation of the constraint:

Voiced obstruents are not permitted at the end of a word.

Given that this constraint is universal, how would you explain that English *band* is nevertheless pronounced [bænd], not [bænt] in terms of Optimality Theory (OT).

24. For many English speakers, word-final /z/ is devoiced when the /z/ represents a separate morpheme. These speakers pronounce plurals such as *dogs*, *days*, and *dishes* as [dɔgs], [des], and [dɪʃəs] instead of [dɔgz], [dez], and [dɪʃəz]. Furthermore, they pronounce possessives such as *Dan's, Jay's,* and *Liz's* as [dæns], [dʒes], and [lɪzes] instead of [dænz], [dʒez], and [lɪzez]. Finally, they pronounce third-person singular verb forms such as *reads, goes,* and *fusses* as [rids], [gos], and [fʌsəs] instead of [ridz], [goz], and [fʌsəz].

(However, words such as *daze* and *Franz* are still pronounced [dez] and [frænz], because the /z/ is not a separate morpheme. Interestingly, in this dialect Franz and Fran's are not homophones.) How might OT explain this phenomenon?

25. In German the third-person singular suffix is *-t*. Following are three German verb stems (underlying forms) and the third-person forms of these verbs:

Stem	Third person	
/loːb/	[loːpt]	he praises
/zag/	[zakt]	he says
/rajz/	[rajst]	he travels

The final consonant of the verb *stem* undergoes devoicing in the third-person form, even though it is not at the end of the word. What constraint is operating to devoice the final stem consonant? How is this similar or different from the constraint that operates in the English plural and past tense?

PART
3

The Psychology
of Language

The field of psycholinguistics, or the psychology of language, is concerned with discovering the psychological processes that make it possible for humans to acquire and use language.

JEAN BERKO GLEASON AND NAN BERNSTEIN RATNER, Psycholinguistics *(1993)*

8

Language Acquisition

The acquisition of language "is doubtless the greatest intellectual feat any one of us is ever required to perform."

LEONARD BLOOMFIELD, Language *(1933)*

The capacity to learn language is deeply ingrained in us as a species, just as the capacity to walk, to grasp objects, to recognize faces. We don't find any serious differences in children growing up in congested urban slums, in isolated mountain villages, or in privileged suburban villas.

DAN SLOBIN, The Human Language Series 2 *(1994)*

Language is extremely complex. Yet very young children—before the age of five—already know most of the intricate system that comprises the grammar of a language. Before they can add 2 + 2, children are conjoining sentences, asking questions, using appropriate pronouns, negating sentences, forming relative clauses, and inflecting verbs and nouns, and in general have acquired the syntactic, phonological, morphological, and semantic rules of the grammar.

It is obvious that children do not learn a language simply by memorizing the sentences of the language and storing them in some giant mental dictionary. The list of words is finite, but no dictionary can hold all the sentences of a language, which are infinite in number. Rather, children acquire a system of rules that enables them to construct and understand sentences, most of which they have never produced or heard before. Children, like adults, are creative in their use of language.

No one teaches children the rules of the grammar. Their parents are no more aware of the phonological, morphological, syntactic, and semantic rules than are the children. Even if you remember your early years, do you remember anyone telling you to form a sentence by adding a verb phrase to a noun phrase, or to add [s] or [z] to form plurals? Children seem to act like efficient linguists equipped with a perfect theory of language, and they use this theory to construct the grammar of the language they are exposed to.

In the preceding chapters you saw something of the richness and complexity of human language (but only a bit). How do children acquire such an intricate system so quickly and effortlessly? This task is rendered even more difficult by the fact that the child must figure out the rules of language from very "noisy" data. She hears sentence fragments, false starts, speech errors, and interruptions. No one tells her "this is a grammatical utterance and that is not." Yet, somehow she is able to recreate the grammar of the language of her speech community based on the language she hears around her. How the child accomplishes this phenomenal task is the subject of this chapter.

Mechanisms of Language Acquisition

There have been various proposals concerning the psychological mechanisms involved in acquiring a language. Early theories of language acquisition were heavily influenced by behaviorism, a school of psychology prevalent in the 1950s. As the name implies, behaviorism focused on people's behaviors, which are directly observable, rather than on the mental systems underlying these behaviors. Language was viewed as a kind of verbal behavior, and it was proposed that children learn language through imitation, reinforcement, analogy, and similar processes. B. F. Skinner, one of the founders of behaviorist psychology, proposed a model of language acquisition in his book *Verbal Behavior* (1957). Two years later, in a devastating reply to Skinner, *Review of Verbal Behavior* (1959), Noam Chomsky showed that language is a complex cognitive system that could not be acquired by behaviorist principles.

Do Children Learn through Imitation?

Child: My teacher holded the baby rabbits and we patted them.
Adult: Did you say your teacher held the baby rabbits?

Child: Yes.
Adult: What did you say she did?
Child: She holded the baby rabbits and we patted them.
Adult: Did you say she held them tightly?
Child: No, she holded them loosely.

At first glance the question of how children acquire language doesn't seem to be such a difficult one to answer. Don't children just listen to what is said around them and imitate the speech they hear? **Imitation** is involved to some extent, but the early words and sentences that children produce show that they are not simply imitating adult speech. Children do not hear words like *holded* or *tooths* or sentences such as *Cat stand up table* or many of the other utterances they produce between the ages of two and three, such as the following:[1]

a my pencil

two foot

what the boy hit?

other one pants

Mommy get it my ladder

cowboy did fighting me

Even when children are trying to imitate what they hear, they are unable to produce sentences that they would not spontaneously produce. The following are the child's attempt to imitate what the adult has said:

Adult: He's going out.   *Child*: He go out
Adult: That's an old-time train.   *Child*: Old-time train.
Adult: Adam, say what I say.
             Where can I put them?   *Child*: Where I can put them?

Imitation cannot account for another important phenomenon: children who are unable to speak for neurological or physiological reasons learn the language spoken to them and understand it. When they overcome their speech impairment, they immediately use the language for speaking.

Do Children Learn through Reinforcement?

Child: Nobody don't like me.
Mother: No, say "Nobody likes me."
Child: Nobody don't like me.
        (dialogue repeated eight times)
Mother: Now, listen carefully, say *"Nobody likes me."*
Child: Oh, nobody don't likes me.

---

[1]Many of the examples of child language in this chapter are taken from CHILDES (Child Language Data Exchange System), a computerized database of the spontaneous speech of children acquiring English and many other languages. B. MacWhinney and C. Snow. 1985. "The Child Language Data Exchange System," *Journal of Child Language* 12:271–96.

Another proposal, in the behaviorist tradition, is that children learn to produce correct (grammatical) sentences because they are positively reinforced when they say something right and negatively reinforced when they say something wrong. One kind of reinforcement is correction of "bad grammar" and reward for "good grammar." Roger Brown and his colleagues at Harvard University studied parent–child interactions. They report that reinforcement seldom occurs, and when it does, it is usually mispronunciations or incorrect reporting of facts that is corrected. They note, for example, that the ungrammatical sentence "Her curl my hair" was not corrected because the child's mother was in fact curling her hair. However, when the child uttered the grammatical sentence "Walt Disney comes on Tuesday," she was corrected because the television program was shown on Wednesday. Brown concludes that it is "truth value rather than syntactic well-formedness that chiefly governs explicit verbal reinforcement by parents—which renders mildly paradoxical the fact that the usual product of such a training schedule is an adult whose speech is highly grammatical but not notably truthful."

Even if adults did correct children's syntax more often than they do, it would still not explain how or what children learn from such adult responses, or how children discover and construct the correct rules. In fact, attempts to correct a child's language are doomed to failure. Children do not know what they are doing wrong and are unable to make corrections even when they are pointed out, as shown by the preceding example and the following one:

Child: Want other one spoon, Daddy.
Father: You mean, you want *the other spoon*.
Child: Yes, I want other one spoon, please, Daddy.
Father: Can you say "the other spoon"?
Child: Other . . . one . . . spoon.
Father: Say . . . "other."
Child: Other.
Father: Spoon.
Child: Spoon.
Father: Other . . . spoon.
Child: Other . . . spoon. Now give me other one spoon?

Such conversations between parents and children do not occur often; this conversation was between a linguist studying child language and his child. Mothers and fathers are usually delighted that their young children are talking and consider every utterance a gem. The "mistakes" children make are cute and repeated endlessly to anyone who will listen.

Do Children Learn Language through Analogy?

It has also been suggested that children put words together to form phrases and sentences by **analogy**, by hearing a sentence and using it as a sample to form other sentences. But this doesn't work, as Lila Gleitman points out:

> . . . suppose the child has heard the sentence "I painted a red barn." So now, by analogy, the child can say "I painted a blue barn." That's exactly the kind of theory that we want. You hear a sample and you extend it to all of the new

cases by similarity. . . . In addition to "I painted a red barn" you might also hear the sentence "I painted a barn red." So it looks as if you take those last two words and switch their order. . . . So now you want to extend this to the case of seeing, because you want to look at barns instead of paint them. So you have heard, "I saw a red barn." Now you try (by analogy) a . . . new sentence—"I saw a barn red." Something's gone wrong. This is an analogy, but the analogy didn't work. It's not a sentence of English.

This problem arises constantly. Consider another example. The child hears the following pair of sentences:

The boy was sleeping.   Was the boy sleeping?

Based on pairs of sentences like this, he formulates a rule for forming questions, "move the auxiliary to the position preceding the subject." He then acquires the more complex relative clause construction:

The boy who is sleeping is dreaming about a new car.

He now wants to form a question. What does he do? If he forms a question on analogy to the simple yes-no question, he will move the first auxiliary *is* as follows:

*Is the boy who sleeping is dreaming about a new car?

Studies of spontaneous speech, as well as experiments, show that children never make mistakes of this sort. As discussed in chapter 4, sentences have structure, and the rules of grammar, such as the rule that moves the auxiliary, are sensitive to structure and not to linear order. Children seem to know about the structure dependency of rules at a very early age.

Recently, a computer model of language representation and acquisition called **connectionism** has been proposed that relies in part on behaviorist learning principles such as analogy and reinforcement. In the connectionist model, no grammatical rules are stored anywhere. Linguistic knowledge, such as knowledge of the past tense, is represented by a set of neuron-like connections between different phonological forms (e.g., between *play* and *played*, *dance* and *danced, drink* and *drank*). Repeated exposure to particular verb pairs in the input reinforces the connection between them, mimicking rule-like behavior. Based on similarities between words, the model can produce a past-tense form that it was not previously exposed to. On analogy to *dance-danced*, it will convert *prance* to *pranced*; on analogy to *drink-drank* it will convert *sink* to *sank*.

As a model of language acquisition, connectionism faces some serious challenges. The model assumes that the language of the child's environment has very specific properties. However, investigation of the input that children actually receive shows that it is not consistent with those assumptions. Another problem is that rules such as formation of past tense cannot be based on phonological form alone but must also be sensitive to information in the lexicon. For example, the past tense of a verb derived from a noun is always regular even if an irregular form exists. When a fly ball is caught in a baseball game, we say the batter *flied out,* not *flew out.* Similarly, when an irregular plural is part of a larger noun, it may be regularized. When we see several images of Walt Disney's famous rodent, we describe them as Mickey Mouses, not Mickey Mice.

Do Children Learn through Structured Input?

Yet another suggestion is that children are able to learn language because adults speak to them in a special "simplified" language sometimes called **motherese**, or **child-directed speech** (CDS) (or more informally, **baby talk**.) This hypothesis places a lot of emphasis on the role of the environment in facilitating language acquisition.

In our culture adults do typically talk to young children in a special way. We tend to speak more slowly and more clearly, we exaggerate our intonation, and sentences are generally grammatical. However, motherese is not syntactically simpler. It contains a range of sentence types, including syntactically complex sentences such as questions: *Do you want your juice now?* Embedded sentences: *Mommy thinks you should sleep now.* Imperatives: *Pat the dog gently!* Negatives with tag questions: *We don't want to hurt him, do we?* And adults do not simplify their language by dropping inflections from verbs and nouns or omitting function words such as determiners and auxiliaries. It is fortunate that motherese is not syntactically restricted. If it were, children might not have sufficient information to extract the rules of their language.

Although infants prefer to listen to motherese than to normal adult speech, controlled studies show that motherese does not significantly affect the child's language development. In many cultures, adults do not use a special register with children, and there are even communities in which adults hardly talk to babies at all. Nevertheless, children around the world acquire language in much the same way, irrespective of these varying circumstances. Adults seem to be the followers rather than the leaders in this enterprise. The child does not develop linguistically because he is exposed to ever more adultlike language. Rather, the adult adjusts his language to the child's increasing linguistic sophistication. The exaggerated intonation and other properties of motherese may be useful for getting a child's attention and holding it, but it is not a driving force behind language development.

Analogy, imitation, and reinforcement cannot account for language development because they are based on the (implicit or explicit) assumption that what the child acquires is a set of sentences or forms rather than a set of grammatical rules. Theories that assume that acquisition depends on a specially structured input also place too much emphasis on the environment rather than on the grammar-making abilities of the child. These proposals do not explain the creativity that children show in acquiring language, why they go through stages, or why they make some kinds of "errors" but not others, for example, "Give me other one spoon" but not "Is the boy who sleeping is dreaming about a new car?"

Children Construct Grammars

> We are designed to walk. . . . That we are taught to walk is impossible. And pretty much the same is true of language. Nobody is taught language. In fact you can't prevent the child from learning it.
>
> **NOAM CHOMSKY,** The Human Language Series 2 *(1994)*

Language acquisition is a creative process. Children are not given explicit information about the rules, by either instruction or correction. They must somehow extract the rules of the grammar from the language they hear around them, and their linguistic environment does not need to be special in any way for them to do this. Observations of children acquiring different languages under different cultural and social circumstances reveal that the developmental stages are similar, possibly universal. Even deaf children of deaf signing parents go through stages in their signing development that parallel those of children acquiring spoken languages. These factors lead many linguists to believe that children are equipped with an innate template or blueprint for language—which we have referred to as Universal Grammar (UG)—and this blueprint aids the child in the task of constructing a grammar for her language. This is referred to as the **innateness hypothesis**.

The Innateness Hypothesis

"WHAT'S THE BIG SURPRISE? ALL THE LATEST THEORIES OF LINGUISTICS SAY WE'RE BORN WITH THE INNATE CAPACITY FOR GENERATING SENTENCES."

© ScienceCartoonsPlus.com

The innateness hypothesis receives its strongest support from the observation that the grammar a person ends up with is vastly underdetermined by linguistic experience. In other words, we end up knowing far more about language than is exemplified in the language we hear around us. This argument for the innateness of UG is called the **poverty of the stimulus**.

Although children hear many utterances, the language they hear is incomplete, noisy, and unstructured. We said earlier that child-directed speech is largely well formed, but children are also exposed to adult–adult interactions. These utterances include slips of the tongue, false starts, ungrammatical and incomplete sentences, and no information as to which utterances are well formed and which are not. But most important is the fact that children come to know aspects of the grammar about which they receive *no* information. In this sense, the data they are exposed to is **impoverished**. It is less than what is necessary to account for the richness and complexity of the grammar they attain.

For example, we noted that the rules children construct are **structure dependent**. Children do not produce questions by moving the first auxiliary as in (1). Instead, they correctly invert the auxiliary of the main clause, as in (2). (We use ____ to mark the position from which a constituent moves.)

1. *Is the boy who ____ sleeping is dreaming of a new car.
2. Is the boy who is sleeping ____ dreaming of a new car.

To come up with a rule that moves the auxiliary of the main clause rather than the first auxiliary, the child must know something about the structure of the sentence. Children are not told about structure dependency. They are not told about constituent structure. The input they get is a sequence of sounds, not a set of phrase structure trees. No amount of imitation, reinforcement, analogy, or structured input will lead the child to formulate a phrase structure tree much less a principle of structure dependency. Yet, children do create phrase structures, and the rules they acquire are sensitive to this structure.

The knowledge that children and adults have of abstract principles (principles not identified in the input) can be shown in countless ways. The rules for the formation of *wh* questions provide another illustration. To ask a question, the child learns to replace the noun phrase (NP) *Jack, Jill, ice cream,* or *school,* or the coordinate NPs *Jack and Jill* or *bagels and lox* with the appropriate *wh* question word, *who* or *what* or *where,* as in the following examples:

Statement	**Question**
<u>Jack</u> went up the hill.	<u>Who</u> went up the hill?
<u>Jack and Jill</u> went up the hill.	<u>Who</u> went up the hill?
Jack and <u>Jill</u> went home.	Jack and <u>who</u> went home?
Jill ate <u>bagels and lox</u>.	Jill ate <u>what</u>?
Jill ate cookies and <u>ice cream</u>.	Jill ate cookies and <u>what</u>?

The *wh* phrase can replace any subject or object NP, but in coordinate structures, the *wh* phrase must stay in the original NP position. It can't be moved, as the following sentences show:

*Who did Jack and ____ go up the hill?
*What did Jill eat bagels and ____?

The coordinate structure constraint discussed in chapter 4 prohibits the movement of a *wh* phrase out of a coordinate structure. It is part of the grammar of all languages that linguists have investigated. Children do make errors in their early *wh* questions, but they never produce sentences such as the starred sentences just shown. No one has told them that these sentences are impossible. No one corrects them, because children never utter them to begin with. How do children know that *wh* phrases are frozen inside a coordinate structure? According to the innateness hypothesis, children come "prewired" with knowledge of Universal Grammar, including structure dependency and the coordinate structure constraint, among many other principles.

The child must also learn many aspects of grammar from her specific linguistic environment. English-speaking children learn that the subject comes first and that the verb precedes the object inside the VP, that is, that English is an SVO language. Japanese children acquire an SOV language. They learn that the object precedes the verb. Japanese children also learn that to form a yes-no question, the morpheme *-ka* is suffixed to a verb stem. In Japanese, sentence constituents are not rearranged.

English-speaking children must learn that yes-no questions are formed by moving the auxiliary to the beginning of the sentence, as follows:

You will come home. → Will you ____ come home?

Because this rule is learned, errors can occur. Children may initially form questions with uninverted auxiliaries as follows:

Where Mommy is going?

What you can do?

But they never make the mistake of moving the wrong auxiliary in a complex sentence. English-speaking children learn that in *wh* questions, the *wh* phrase moves as follows (with the additional complexity of inserting *do*):

You like who. → Who do you like ____?

Children acquiring Mandarin Chinese and many other Asian languages learn to form questions by leaving the question word in its original position, which is correct in these languages, as shown in the following Mandarin example:

Ni xihuan shei
"You like who"

According to the innateness hypothesis, the child extracts from the linguistic environment those rules of grammar that are language specific, such as word order and movement rules. But he does not need to learn universal principles like structure dependency and the coordinate structure constraint, or general rules of sentence formation such as the fact that heads of categories can take complements. They are part of the innate blueprint for language that children use to construct the grammar of their language.

The innateness hypothesis provides an answer to *the logical problem of language acquisition* posed by Chomsky: What accounts for the ease, rapidity, and uniformity of language acquisition in the face of impoverished data? The answer is that children acquire a complex grammar quickly and easily without any particular help beyond exposure to the language because they do not start from scratch. UG helps them to extract the rules of their language and to avoid many grammatical errors. Because the child constructs his grammar according to an innate blueprint, all children proceed through similar developmental stages, as we will discuss in the next section.

The innateness hypothesis also predicts that all languages will conform to the principles of UG. We are still far from understanding the full nature of the principles of UG. Research on more languages provides a way to test principles like the coordinate structure constraint, which linguists propose are part of our genetic makeup for language. If we investigate a language in which posited UG principles are absent, we will have to correct our theory and substitute other principles, as scientists must do in any field. But there is little doubt that human languages conform to abstract universal principles and that the human brain is specially equipped for acquisition of human language grammars.

Stages in Language Acquisition

> . . . for I was no longer a speechless infant; but a speaking boy. This I remember; and have since observed how I learned to speak. It was not that my elders taught me words . . . in any set method; but I . . . did myself . . . practice the sounds in my memory. . . . And thus by constantly hearing words, as they occurred in various sentences . . . I thereby gave utterance to my will.
>
> St. Augustine, Confessions

Children do not wake up one fine morning with a fully formed grammar in their heads. Relative to the complexity of the adult grammar that they eventually attain, the process of language acquisition is fast, but it is not instantaneous. From first words to virtual adult competence takes three to four years, during which time children pass through linguistic stages. They begin by babbling, they then acquire their first words, and in just a few months they begin to put words together into sentences.

Observations of children acquiring different languages reveal that the stages are similar, possibly universal. The earliest studies of child language acquisition come from diaries kept by parents. More recent studies include the use of tape recordings, videotapes, and controlled experiments. Linguists record the spontaneous utterances of children and purposefully elicit other utterances to study the child's production and comprehension. Researchers have also invented ingenious techniques for investigating the linguistic abilities of infants, who are not yet speaking.

Children's early utterances may not look exactly like adult sentences, but child language is not just a degenerate form of adult language. The words and sentences that the child produces at each stage of development conform to the set of grammatical rules he has developed to that point. Although child grammars and adult grammars differ in certain respects, they also share many formal properties. Like adults, children have grammatical categories such as NP and VP, rules for building phrase structures and for moving constituents, as well as phonological, morphological, and semantic rules, and they adhere to universal principles such as structure dependency.

Sentences such as *Nobody don't like me* and *want 'nother one spoon, daddy* may contain errors from the perspective of the adult grammar, but they are not errors from the child's point of view. They reflect his current grammar. The so-called errors that children make provide us with a window into their grammar.

The Perception and Production of Speech Sounds

> An infant crying in the night:
> An infant crying for the light:
> And with no language but a cry.
>
> ALFRED LORD TENNYSON, *"In Memoriam H.H.S."*

The old idea that the neonate is born with a mind that is like a blank slate is belied by a wealth of evidence that infants are highly sensitive to some subtle distinctions in their environment and not to others. That is, the mind appears to be attuned at birth to receive certain kinds of information.

Experiments have shown that infants will increase their sucking rate when stimuli (visual or auditory) presented to them are varied, but will decrease the sucking rate when the same stimuli are presented repeatedly. Infants will respond to visual depth and distance distinctions, to differences between rigid and flexible physical properties of objects, and to human faces rather than to other visual stimuli.

Similarly, a newborn will respond to phonetic contrasts found in human languages even when these differences are not phonemic in the language spoken in the baby's home. A baby hearing a human voice over a loudspeaker saying [pa] [pa] [pa] will slowly decrease her rate of sucking. If the sound changes to [ba] or even [pʰa], the sucking rate increases dramatically. Controlled experiments show that adults find it difficult to differentiate between the allophones of one phoneme, but for infants it comes naturally. Japanese infants can distinguish between [r] and [l] whereas their parents cannot; babies can hear the difference between aspirated and unaspirated stops even if students in an introductory linguistics course cannot. Babies can discriminate between sounds that are phonemic in other languages and nonexistent in the language of their parents. For example, in Hindi, there is a phonemic contrast between a retroflex [t] and the alveolar [t]. To English-speaking adults, these sound the same; to their infants, they do not.

Infants can perceive voicing contrasts such as [pa] versus [ba], contrasts in place of articulation such as [da] versus [ga], and contrasts in manner of articulation such as [ra] versus [la], or [ra] versus [wa], among many others. Babies will not react, however, to distinctions that never correspond to phonemic contrasts in any human language, such as sounds spoken more or less loudly or sounds that lie between two phonemes. Furthermore, a vowel that we perceive as [i], for example, is a different physical sound when produced by a male, female, or child, but babies ignore the non-linguistic aspects of the speech signal just as adults do. Yet, computational linguists still have difficulty programming computers to recognize these different-sounding [i]s as the same.

Infants appear to be born with the ability to perceive just those sounds that are phonemic in some language. It is therefore possible for children to learn any human language they are exposed to. During the first years of life, the infant's job is to uncover the sounds of this language. From around six months, he begins to lose the ability to discriminate between sounds that are not phonemic in his own language. His linguistic environment molds the infant's initial perceptions. Japanese infants can no longer hear the difference between [r] and [l], which do not contrast in Japanese, whereas babies in English-speaking homes retain this perception. They have begun to learn the sounds of the language of their parents. Before that, they appear to know the sounds of human language in general.

The shaping by the linguistic environment that we see in perception also occurs in the speech the infant is producing. At around six months, the infant begins to babble. The sounds produced in this period include many sounds that do not occur in the language of the household. However, **babbling** is not linguistic chaos. The twelve most frequent consonants in the world's languages make up 95 percent of the consonants infants use in their babbling. There are linguistic constraints even during this very early stage. The early babbles consist mainly of repeated consonant-vowel sequences, like *mama, gaga,* and *dada.* Later babbles are more varied.

Gradually, the child's babbles come to include only those sounds and sound combinations that occur in the target language. Babbles begin to sound like words, although they may not have any specific meaning attached to them. At this point adults can distinguish the babbles of an English-babbling infant from those of an infant babbling in Cantonese or Arabic. During the first year of life, the infant's perceptions and productions are being fine-tuned to the language(s) of the surroundings.

Deaf infants produce babbling sounds that are different from those of hearing children. Babbling is related to auditory input and is linguistic in nature. Studies of vocal babbling of hearing children and manual babbling of deaf children support the view that babbling is a linguistic ability related to the kind of language input the child receives. These studies show that four- to seven-month-old hearing infants exposed to spoken language produce a restricted set of phonetic forms. At the same age, deaf children exposed to sign language produce a restricted set of signs. In each case the forms are drawn from the set of possible sounds or possible gestures found in spoken and signed languages.

Babbling illustrates the readiness of the human mind to respond to linguistic input from a very early stage. During the babbling stage, the intonation contours produced by hearing infants begin to resemble the intonation contours of sentences spoken by adults. The different intonation contours are among the first linguistic contrasts that children perceive and produce. During this same period, the vocalizations produced by deaf babies are random and nonrepetitive. Similarly, the manual gestures produced by hearing babies differ greatly from those produced by deaf infants exposed to sign language. The hearing babies move their fingers and clench their fists randomly with little or no repetition of gestures. The deaf infants, however, use more than a dozen different hand motions repetitively, all of which are elements of American Sign Language or the other sign languages used in deaf communities of other countries.

The generally accepted view is that humans are born with a predisposition to discover the units that serve to express linguistic meanings, and that at a genetically specified stage in neural development, the infant will begin to produce these units— sounds or gestures—depending on the language input the baby receives. This suggests that babbling is the earliest stage in language acquisition, in opposition to an earlier view that babbling was prelinguistic and merely neuromuscular in origin. The "babbling as language acquisition" hypothesis is supported by recent neurological studies that link babbling to the language centers of the left hemisphere, also providing further evidence that the brain specializes for language functions at a very early age, as discussed in chapter 2.

First Words

> From this golden egg a man, Prajapati, was born. . . . A year having passed, he
> wanted to speak. He said bhur and the earth was created. He said bhuvar and
> the space of the air was created. He said suvar and the sky was created. That is
> why a child wants to speak after a year. . . . When Prajapati spoke for the first
> time, he uttered one or two syllables. That is why a child utters one or two syl-
> lables when he speaks for the first time.
>
> HINDU MYTH

"The Middletons" by Ralph Dunagin/Dana Summers. Copyright 1994 Tribune Media Services, Inc. Reprinted with permission.

Some time after the age of one, children begin to use repeatedly the same string of
sounds to mean the same thing. At this stage children realize that sounds are related
to meanings. They have produced their first true words. This is an amazing feat. How
do they discover where one word begins and another leaves off? Speech is a continuous stream broken only by breath pauses. Children are in the same fix that you might
be in if you tuned in a foreign-language radio station. You wouldn't have the foggiest
idea of what was being said or what the words were. Remarkably, infants solve the
problem in a relatively short time. The age of the child when this occurs varies and
has nothing to do with the child's intelligence. (It is reported that Einstein did not
start to speak until he was three or four years old.)

The child's first utterances differ from adult language. The following words of
one child, J. P., at the age of 16 months, illustrate the point:

[ʔaw]	"not," "no," "don't"	[sː]	"aerosol spray"
[bʌʔ]/[mʌʔ]	"up"	[sʲuː]	"shoe"
[da]	"dog"	[haj]	"hi"
[iʔo]/[siʔo]	"Cheerios"	[sr]	"shirt" "sweater"
[sa]	"sock"	[sæː]/[əsæː]	"what's that?" "hey, look!"
[aj]/[ʌj]	"light"	[ma]	"mommy"
[baw]/[daw]	"down"	[dæ]	"daddy"

Most children go through a stage in which their utterances consist of only one
word. This is called the **holophrastic** stage (from *holo*, "complete" or "undivided,"
and *phrase*, "phrase" or "sentence") because these one-word utterances seem to convey a more complex message. For example, when J. P. says "down" he may be making a request to be put down, or he may be commenting on a toy that has fallen down

from the shelf. When he says "cheerios" he may simply be naming the box of cereal in front of him, or he may be asking for some Cheerios. This suggests that children have a more complex mental representation than their language at this point allows them to express. Comprehension experiments confirm the hypothesis that children's grammatical competence is ahead of their productive abilities.

There is some evidence that deaf babies develop their first signs earlier than hearing children speak their first words. This has led to the development of Baby Sign, a technique in which hearing parents learn and model for their babies various signs, such as a sign for "milk," "hurt," and "mother." The idea is that this will enable the baby to communicate his needs and desires even before he is able to articulate spoken words. Promoters of Baby Sign (and many parents) say that this leads to less frustration and less crying. To the extent that Baby Sign is successful it provides further support for the hypothesis that the ability to speak lags behind linguistic competence (in this case, knowledge of words).

The Development of Grammar

Children are biologically equipped to acquire all aspects of grammar. In this section we will look at development in each of the components of language, and we will illustrate the role that Universal Grammar plays in this development.

THE ACQUISITION OF PHONOLOGY

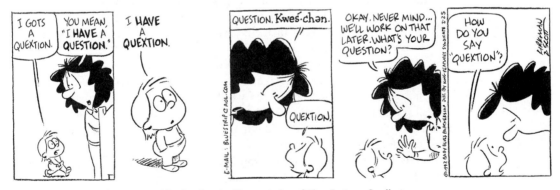

"Baby Blues" © Baby Blues Partnership. Reprinted with permission of King Features Syndicate.

In terms of his phonology, J. P. is like most children at this stage. His first words are generally monosyllabic with a CV (consonant-vowel) form. The vowel part may be a diphthong, depending on the language being acquired. His phonemic or phonetic inventory—at this stage they are equivalent—is much smaller than is found in the adult language. The linguist Roman Jakobson suggested that children first acquire the small set of sounds common to all languages of the world, no matter what language they hear, and in later stages a child acquires the less common sounds of his own language. For example, most languages have the sounds [p] and [s], but [θ] is a rare sound. J. P.'s sound system was as Jakobson's theory predicted. His phonological inventory at an early stage included the consonants [b, m, d, k], which are frequently occurring sounds in the world's languages.

In general, the order of acquisition of classes of sounds goes by manner of articulation: nasals are acquired first, then glides, stops, liquids, fricatives, and affricates.

Natural classes characterized by place of articulation features also appear in children's utterances according to an ordered series: labials, velars, alveolars, and palatals. It is not surprising that *mama* is an early word for many children.

If the first year is devoted to figuring out the phonetic inventory of the target language, the second year involves learning how these sounds are used in the phonology of the language, especially which contrasts are phonemic. When they first begin to contrast one set (i.e., when they learn that /p/ and /b/ are distinct phonemes), they also begin to distinguish between /t/ and /d/, /s/ and /z/, and all the other voiceless–voiced phonemic pairs. As we would expect, the generalizations refer to natural classes of speech sounds.

Controlled experiments show that children at this stage can perceive or comprehend many more phonological contrasts than they can produce. The same child who says [wæbɪt] instead of "rabbit," and who does not seem to distinguish [w] and [r], will not make mistakes on a picture identification task in which she must point to either a ring or a wing. In addition, children sometimes produce a sound in a way that makes it indiscernible to adult observers. Acoustic analyses of children's utterances show that the child's pronunciation of *wing* and *ring* are physically different sounds, although they may seem the same to the adult ear. As a further example, a spectrographic analysis of *ephant,* "elephant," produced by a three-year-old child, clearly showed an [l] in the representation of the word even though the adult experimenter could not hear it.

Many anecdotal reports also show the disparity between the child's production and perception at this stage. An example is the exchange between the linguist Neil Smith and his two-year-old son Amahl. (At this age Amahl's pronunciation of "mouth" is [maws].)

NS: What does [maws] mean?
 A: Like a cat.
NS: Yes, what else?
 A: Nothing else.
NS: It's part of your head.
 A: [fascinated]
NS: [touching A's mouth] What's this?
 A: [maws]

According to Smith, it took Amahl a few seconds to realize his word for "mouse" and for "mouth" were the same. It is not that Amahl and other children do not hear the correct adult pronunciation. They do, but they are unable in these early years to produce it themselves. Another linguist's child (yes, linguists love to experiment on their own children) pronounced the word *light* as *yight* [jajt] but would become very angry if someone said to him, "Oh, you want me to turn on the yight." "No no," he would reply, "not yight—yight!"

Therefore, even at this stage, it is not possible to determine the extent of the grammar of the child—in this case, the phonology—simply by observing speech production. It is sometimes necessary to use various experimental and instrumental techniques to tap the child's competence.

A child's first words show many substitutions of one feature for another or one phoneme for another. In the preceding examples, *mouth* [mawθ] is pronounced *mouse* [maws], with the alveolar fricative [s] replacing the less common interdental fricative [θ]; *light* [lajt] is pronounced *yight* [jajt], with the glide [j] replacing the liquid [l]; and *rabbit* is pronounced *wabbit*, with the glide [w] replacing the liquid [r]. Glides are acquired earlier than liquids, and hence substitute for them. These substitutions are simplifications of the adult pronunciation. They make articulation easier until the child achieves greater articulatory control.

Children's early pronunciations are not haphazard, however. The phonological substitutions are rule governed. The following is an abridged lexicon for another child, Michael, between the ages of 18 and 21 months:

[pun]	"spoon"	[majtl]	"Michael"
[peyn]	"plane"	[dajtər]	"diaper"
[tɪs]	"kiss"	[pati]	"Papi"
[taw]	"cow"	[mani]	"Mommy"
[tin]	"clean"	[bərt]	"Bert"
[polər]	"stroller"	[bərt]	"(big) Bird"

Michael systematically substituted the alveolar stop [t] for the velar stop [k] as in his words for "cow," "clean," "kiss," and his own name. He also replaced labial [p] with [t] when it occurred in the middle of a word, as in his words for "Papi" and "diaper." He reduced consonant clusters in "spoon," "plane," and "stroller," and he devoiced final stops as in "Big Bird." In devoicing the final [d] in "bird," he created an ambiguous form [bərt] referring both to Bert and Big Bird. No wonder only parents understand their children's first words!

Michael's substitutions are typical of the phonological rules that operate in the very early stages of acquisition. Other common rules are reduplication—"bottle" becomes [baba], "water" becomes [wawa]; and the dropping of a final consonants—"bed" becomes [be], "cake" becomes [ke]. These two rules show that the child prefers a simple CV syllable.

Of the many phonological rules that children create, no one child will necessarily use all rules. Early phonological rules generally reflect natural phonological processes that also occur in adult languages. For example, various adult languages have a rule of syllable-final consonant devoicing (German does, English does not). Children do not create bizarre or whimsical rules. Their rules conform to the possibilities made available by UG.

THE ACQUISITION OF WORD MEANING

> Suddenly I felt a misty consciousness as of something forgotten—a thrill of returning thought; and somehow the mystery of language was revealed to me. . . . Everything had a name, and each name gave birth to a new thought.
>
> HELEN KELLER

In addition to phonological regularities, the child's early vocabulary provides insight into how children use words and construct word meaning. For J. P. the word *up* was originally used only to mean "Get me up!" when he was either on the floor or in his high chair, but later he used it to mean "Get up!" to his mother as well. J. P. used his word for *sock* not only for socks but also for other undergarments that are put on over the feet, such as undershorts. This illustrates how a child may extend the meaning of a word from a particular referent to encompass a larger class.

When J. P. began to use words, the object had to be physically present, but that requirement did not last very long. He first used "dog" only when pointing to a real dog, but later he used the word for pictures of dogs in various books. A new word that entered J. P.'s vocabulary at seventeen months was "uh-oh," which he would say after he had an accident like spilling juice, or when he deliberately poured his yogurt over the side of his high chair. His use of this word shows his developing use of language for social purposes. At this time he added two new words meaning "no," [doː] and [no], which he used when anyone attempted to take something from him that he wanted, or tried to make him do something he did not want to do. He used them either with the imperative meaning of "Don't do that!" or with the assertive meaning of "I don't want to do that." Even at this early stage, J. P. was using words to convey a variety of ideas and feelings, as well as his social awareness.

But how do children learn the meanings of words? Most people do not see this aspect of acquisition as posing a great problem. The intuitive view is that children look at an object, the mother says a word, and the child connects the sounds with the object. However, this is not as easy as it seems, as the following quote demonstrates:

> A child who observes a cat sitting on a mat also observes . . . a mat supporting a cat, a mat under a cat, a floor supporting a mat and a cat, and so on. If the adult now says "The cat is on the mat" even while pointing to the cat on the mat, how is the child to choose among these interpretations of the situation?[2]

Even if the mother simply says "cat," and the child by accident associates the word with the animal on the mat, the child may interpret cat as "Cat," the name of a particular animal, or of an entire species. In other words, to learn a word for a class of objects such as "cat" or "dog," children have to figure out exactly what the word refers to. Upon hearing the word *dog* in the presence of a dog, how does the child know that "dog" can refer to any four-legged, hairy, barking creature? Should it include poodles, tiny Yorkshire terriers, bulldogs, and great Danes, all of which look rather different from one another? What about cows, lambs, and other four-legged mammals? Why are they not "dogs"? The important and very difficult question is: What relevant features define the class of objects we call *dog*, and how does a child acquire knowledge of them? Even if a child succeeds in associating a word with an object, nobody provides explicit information about how to extend the use of that word to other objects to which that word refers.

It is not surprising, therefore, that children often overextend a word's meaning, as J. P. did with the word *sock*. A child may learn a word such as *papa* or *daddy,* which she first uses only for her own father, and then extend its meaning to apply to all men, just as she may use the word *dog* to mean any four-legged creature. After the child has acquired her first seventy-five to one hundred words, the overextended meanings start to narrow until they correspond to those of the other speakers of the language. How this occurs is still not entirely understood.

The mystery surrounding the acquisition of word meanings has intrigued philosophers and psychologists as well as linguists. We know that all children view the world in a similar fashion and apply the same general principles to help them determine a

[2]L. R. Gleitman and E. Wanner. 1982. *Language Acquisition: The State of the Art.* Cambridge, England: Cambridge University Press, p. 10.

word's meaning. For example, overextensions are usually based on physical attributes such as size, shape, and texture. *Ball* may refer to all round things, *bunny* to all furry things, and so on. However, children will not make overextensions based on color. In experiments, children will group objects by shape and give them a name, but they will not assign a name to a group of red objects.

If an experimenter points to an object and uses a nonsense word like *blick* to a child, saying *that's a blick*, the child will interpret the word to refer to the whole object, not one of its parts or attributes. Given the poverty of stimulus for word learning, principles like the "form over color principle" and the "whole object principle" help the child organize experience in ways that facilitate word learning. Without such principles, it is doubtful that children could learn words as quickly as they do. Children learn approximately 14 words a day for the first six years of their lives. That averages to about 5,000 words per year. How many students know 10,000 words of a foreign language after two years of study?

THE ACQUISITION OF MORPHOLOGY

"Baby Blues" © Baby Blues Partnership. Reprinted with permission of King Features Syndicate.

The child's acquisition of morphology provides the clearest evidence of rule learning. Children's errors in morphology reveal that the child acquires the regular rules of the grammar and overgeneralizes them. This **overgeneralization** occurs when children treat irregular verbs and nouns as if they were regular. We have probably all heard children say *bringed, goed, drawed,* and *runned,* or *foots, mouses, sheeps,* and *childs*.

These mistakes tell us much about how children learn language because such forms could not arise through imitation; children use them in families in which the parents never speak "bad English." In fact, children generally go through three phases in the acquisition of an irregular form:

Phase 1	Phase 2	Phase 3
broke	breaked	broke
brought	bringed	brought

In phase 1 the child uses the correct term such as *brought* or *broke*. At this point the child's grammar does not relate the form *brought* to *bring*, or *broke* to *break*. The words are treated as separate lexical entries. Phase 2 is crucial. This is when the child constructs a rule for forming the past tense and attaches the regular past-tense morpheme to all verbs—*play, hug, help*, as well as *break* and *bring*. Children look for general patterns, for systematic occurrences. What they do not know at phase 2 is that there are exceptions to the rule. Now their language is more regular than the adult language. During phase 3 the child learns that there are exceptions to the rule, and then once again uses *brought* and *broke*, with the difference being that these irregular forms will be related to the root forms.

The child's morphological rules emerge quite early. In a classic study, preschool children and children in the first, second, and third grades were shown a drawing of a nonsense animal like the funny creature shown in the following picture. Each "animal" was given a nonsense name. The experimenter would then say to the child, pointing to the picture, "This is a wug."

Then the experimenter would show the child a picture of two of the animals and say, "Now here is another one. There are two of them. There are two _____?"

The child's task was to give the plural form, "wugs" [wʌgz]. Another little make-believe animal was called a "bik," and when the child was shown two biks, he or she again was to say the plural form [bɪks]. The children applied the regular plural formation rule to words they had never heard. Their ability to add [z] when the animal's name ended with a voiced sound, and [s] when there was a final voiceless consonant, showed that the children were using rules based on an understanding of natural classes of phonological segments, and not simply imitating words they had previously heard.

More recently, studies of children acquiring languages with richer inflectional morphologies than English reveal that they learn agreement and case distinctions at a very early age. For example, Italian verbs must be inflected for number and person to agree with the subject. This is similar to the English agreement rule "add *s* to the verb" for third-person, singular subjects—*He giggles a lot* but *We giggle a lot*—except that in Italian more verb forms must be acquired. Italian-speaking children between the ages of 1;10 (one year, ten months) and 2;4 correctly inflect the verb, as the following utterances of Italian children show:

Tu legg**i** il libro.	"You (second-person singular) read the book."
Io vad**o** fuori.	"I go (first-person singular) outside."
Dorm**e** miao dorme.	"Sleeps (third-person singular) cat sleeps."
Legg**iamo** il libro.	"(We) read (first-person plural) the book."

Children acquiring other richly inflected languages such as Spanish, German, Catalan, and Swahili quickly acquire agreement morphology. It is rare for them to make agreement errors, just as it is rare for an English-speaking child to say "I goes."

In these languages there is also gender and number agreement between the head noun and the article and adjectives inside the noun phrase. Children as young as two years old respect these agreement requirements, as shown by the following Italian examples:

E mia gonn**a**.	"(It) is my (feminine singular) skirt."
Questo mi**o** bimbo.	"This my (masculine singular) baby."
Guarda **la** mela piccolin**a**.	"Look at the little (feminine singular) apple."
Guarda **il** topo piccolin**o**.	"Look at the little (masculine singular) mouse."

Many languages have case morphology, where nouns have different forms depending on their grammatical function: subject, object, possessor, and so on. Studies show that children acquiring Russian and German, two languages with extensive case systems, acquire case morphology at a very early age.

Children also show knowledge of the derivational rules of their language and use these rules to create novel words. In English, for example, we can derive verbs from nouns. From the noun *microwave* we now have a verb *to microwave;* from the noun *e(lectronic) mail* we derived the verb *to e-mail.* Children acquire this derivational rule early and use it often because there are lots of gaps in their verb vocabulary.

Child Utterance	Adult Translation
You have to scale it.	"You have to weigh it."
I broomed it up.	"I swept it up."
He's keying the door.	"He's opening the door (with a key)."

These novel forms provide further evidence that language acquisition is a creative process and that children's utterances reflect their internal grammars, which include both derivational and inflectional rules.

THE ACQUISITION OF SYNTAX

"Doonesbury" © 1984 G. B. Trudeau. Reprinted with permission of Universal Press Syndicate. All rights reserved.

When children are still in the holophrastic stage, adults listening to the one-word utterances often feel that the child is trying to convey a more complex message. New experimental techniques show that at that stage (and even earlier), children have knowledge of some syntactic rules. In these experiments the infant sits on his mother's lap and hears a sentence over a speaker while seeing two video displays depicting different actions, one of which corresponds to the sentence. Infants tend to look longer at the video that matches the sentence they hear. This methodology allows researchers to tap the linguistic knowledge of children who are only using single words or who are not talking at all. Results show that children as young as seventeen months can understand the difference between sentences such as "Ernie is tickling Bert" and "Bert is tickling Ernie." Because these sentences have all the same words, the child cannot be relying on the words alone to understand the meanings. He must also understand the word-order rules and how they determine the grammatical relations of subject and object. Results such as these strongly suggest that children's syntactic competence is ahead of their productive abilities, which is also how their phonology develops.

Around the time of their second birthday, children begin to put words together. At first these utterances appear to be strings of two of the child's earlier holophrastic utterances, each word with its own single-pitch contour. Soon, they begin to form actual two-word sentences with clear syntactic and semantic relations. The intonation contour of the two words extends over the whole utterance rather than being separated by a pause between the two words. The following utterances illustrate the kinds of patterns that are found in children's utterances at this stage:

allgone sock	hi Mommy
byebye boat	allgone sticky
more wet	it ball
Katherine sock	dirty sock

These early utterances can express a variety of semantic and syntactic relations. For example, noun + noun sentences such as *Mommy sock* can express a subject + object relation in the situation when the mother is putting the sock on the child, or a possessive relation when the child is pointing to Mommy's sock. Two nouns can also be used to show a subject-locative relation, as in *sweater chair* to mean "The sweater is on the chair," or to show attribution as in *dirty sock*. Children often have a variety of modifiers such as *allgone, more*, and *bye bye*.

Because children mature at different rates and the age at which children start to produce words and put words together varies, chronological age is not a good measure of a child's language development. Instead, researchers use the child's **mean length of utterances** (MLU) to compare children's progress. MLU is the average length of the utterances the child is producing at a particular point. MLU is usually measured in terms of morphemes rather than words, so the words *boys, danced*, and *crying* are each two morphemes long. Children with the same MLU are likely to have similar grammars even though they are different ages.

In their earliest multiword utterances, children are inconsistent in their use of function words (grammatical morphemes) such as *to* and *the*, auxiliary verbs such as *can* and *is,* and verbal inflection. Many (though not all) utterances consist only of open-class or content words, while some or all of the function words, auxiliaries, and verbal inflection may be missing. During this stage children often sound as if they are sending an e-message or reading an old-fashioned telegram (containing only the required words for basic understanding), which is why such utterances are sometimes called **telegraphic speech**:

Cat stand up table.

What that?

He play little tune.

Andrew want that.

Cathy build house.

No sit there.

J. P.'s early sentences were similar. (The words in parentheses are missing from J. P.'s sentences):

Age in Months

25	[danʔ ɪʔ tˢɪʔ]	"Don't eat (the) chip."
	[bʷaʔ tat]	"Block (is on) top."
26	[mamis tu hæs]	"Mommy's two hands."
	[mo bʌs go]	"Where bus go?"
	[dædi go]	"(Where) Daddy go?"
27	[ʔaj gat tu dʲus]	"I got two (glasses of) juice."
	[do bajʔ mi]	"Don't bite (kiss) me."
	[kʌdər sʌni ber]	"Sonny color(ed a) bear."
28	[ʔaj gat pwe dɪs]	"I('m) play(ing with) this."
	[mamis tak mɛns]	"Mommy talk(ed to the) men."

It can take many months before children use all the grammatical morphemes and auxiliary verbs consistently. However, the child does not deliberately leave out function words as would an adult sending an instant message. The sentences reflect the child's grammar at that particular stage of language development. Although these sentences may lack certain morphemes, they nevertheless appear to have hierarchical constituent structures and syntactic rules similar to those in the adult grammar. For example, children almost never violate the word-order rules of their language. In languages with relatively fixed word order such as English, children use SVO order from the earliest stage.

Telegraphic speech is also very good evidence against the hypothesis that children learn sentences by imitation. Adults—even those speaking motherese—do not drop function words when they speak to children.

In languages with freer word order, like Turkish and Russian, grammatical relations such as subject and object are generally marked by inflectional morphology, such as case markers. Children acquiring these languages quickly learn the morphological case markers. For example, two-year-old Russian-speaking children mark subjects with nominative case and objects with accusative case with very few errors. Most errors arise with words that have an idiosyncratic or irregular case ending. This is reminiscent of the overgeneralization errors that children make with irregular verb morphology in English. Children take longer to acquire aspects of grammar that are not predictable by rule.

The correct use of word order, case marking, and agreement rules shows that even though children may often omit function morphemes, they are aware of constituent structure and syntactic rules. Their utterances are not simply words randomly strung together. From a very early stage onward, children have a grasp of the principles of phrase and sentence formation and of the kinds of structure dependencies mentioned in chapter 4, as revealed by these constituent structure trees:

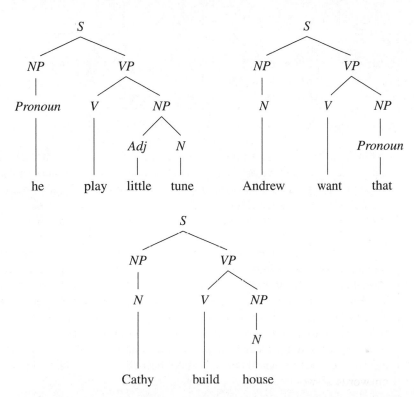

Sometime between the ages of 2;6 and 3;6, a virtual language explosion occurs. At this point it is difficult to identify distinct stages because the child is undergoing so much development so rapidly. By the age of 3;0, most children are consistent in their use of function morphemes. Moreover, they have begun to produce and understand complex structures, including coordinated sentences and embedded sentences of various kinds, such as the following:

He was stuck and I got him out.

I want this doll because she's big.

I know what to do.

I like to play with something else.

I think she's sick.

Look at the train Ursula bought.

I gon' make it like a rocket to blast off with.

It's too early for us to eat.

THE ACQUISITION OF PRAGMATICS

"Baby Blues" © Baby Blues Partnership. Reprinted with permission of King Features Syndicate.

In addition to acquiring the rules of grammar, children must learn the appropriate use of language in context, or pragmatics. The cartoon is funny because of the inappropriateness of the interaction, showing that Zoe hasn't completely acquired the pragmatic "maxims of conversation" discussed in chapter 5.

Context is needed to determine the reference of pronouns. A sentence such as, "Amazingly, he loves her" is uninterpretable unless both speaker and hearer understand who the pronouns *he* and *her* refer to. If the sentence were preceded by "I saw John and Mary kissing in the park," then the referents of the pronouns would be clear. Children are not always sensitive to the needs of their interlocutors, and they may fail to establish the referents for pronouns. It is not unusual for a three- or four-year-old (or even older children) to use pronouns out of the blue, like the child who cries to his mother "He hit me" when mom has no idea who did the deed.

The speaker and listener form part of the context of an utterance. The meaning of *I* and *you* depends on who is talking and who is listening, which changes from situation to situation. Younger children (around age two) have difficulty with the "shifting reference" of these pronouns. A typical error that children make at this age is to refer to themselves as "you," for example, saying "You want to take a walk" when he means "I want to take a walk."

Children also show a lack of pragmatic awareness by the way they sometimes use articles. Like pronouns, the interpretation of articles depends on context. The definite article (*the*), as in "the boy," can be used felicitously only when it is clear to speaker and hearer what boy is being discussed. In a discourse the indefinite article (*a/an*) must be used for the first mention of a new referent, but the definite article (or pronoun) may be used in subsequent mentions, as illustrated following:

A boy walked into the class.

He was in the wrong room.

The teacher directed the boy to the right classroom.

Children do not always respect the pragmatic rules for articles. In experimental studies, three-year-olds are just as likely to use the definite article as the indefinite article for introducing a new referent. In other words, the child tends to assume that his listener knows who he is talking about without having established this in a linguistically appropriate way.

It may take a child several months or years to master those aspects of pragmatics that involve establishing the reference for function morphemes such as determiners and pronouns. Other aspects of pragmatics are acquired very early. Children in the holophrastic stage use their one-word utterances with different illocutionary force. The utterance "up" spoken by J. P. at sixteen months might be a simple statement such as "The teddy is up on the shelf," or a request "Pick me up."

THE DEVELOPMENT OF AUXILIARIES: A CASE STUDY

We have seen in this chapter that language acquisition involves development in various components—the lexicon, phonology, morphology, and syntax, as well as pragmatics. These different modules interact in complex ways to chart an overall course of language development.

As an example, let us take the case of the English auxiliaries. As noted earlier, children in the telegraphic stage do not typically use auxiliaries such as *can*, *will*, or *do*, and they often omit *be* and *have* from their utterances. Several syntactic constructions in English depend on the presence of an auxiliary, the most central of which are questions and negative sentences. To negate a main verb requires the auxiliary *do* or a modal, as in the following examples:

I don't like this movie.

I won't see this movie.

An adult does not say "I not read this book."

Similarly, as discussed in chapter 4, English yes-no and *wh* questions are formed by moving an auxiliary to precede the subject, as in the following examples:

Can I leave now?

Where should John put the book?

Although the two-year-old does not have productive control of auxiliaries, she is able to form negative sentences and questions. During the telegraphic stage, the child produces questions of the following sort:

Yes-No Questions

I ride train?

Mommy eggnog?

Have some?

These utterances have a rising intonation pattern typical of yes-no questions in English, but because there are no auxiliaries, there can be no auxiliary movement. In *wh* questions there is also no auxiliary, but there is generally a *wh* phrase that has moved to the beginning of the sentence. English-speaking children do not produce sentences such as "Cowboy doing what?" in which the *wh* phrase remains in its deep structure position.

The two-year-old has an insufficient lexicon. The lack of auxiliaries means that she cannot use a particular syntactic device associated with question formation in English—auxiliary movement. However, she has the pragmatic knowledge of how to make a request or ask for information, and she has the appropriate prosody, which depends on knowledge of phonology and the syntactic structure of the question. She also knows the grammatical rule that requires *wh* phrases to be in a fronted position. Many components of language must be in place to form an adultlike question.

In languages that do not require auxiliaries to form a question, children appear more adultlike. For example, in Dutch and Italian, the main verb moves. Because many main verbs are acquired before auxiliaries, Dutch and Italian children in the telegraphic stage produce questions that follow the adult rule:

Dutch

En wat doen ze daar?	and what do they there	"And what are they doing there?"
Wordt mama boos?	becomes mama angry	"Is mommy angry?"
Weet je n kerk?	know you a church	"Do you know a church?"

Italian

Cosa fanno questi bambini?	what do these children	"What are these babies doing?"
Chando vene a mama?	when comes the mommy	"When is Mommy coming?"
Vola cici?	flies birdie	"Is the birdie flying?"

The Dutch and Italian children show us there is nothing intrinsically difficult about syntactic movement rules. The delay that English-speaking children show in producing adultlike questions may simply be because auxiliaries are acquired later than main verbs, and English is idiosyncratic in forming questions by moving only auxiliaries.

The lack of auxiliaries during the telegraphic stage also affects the formation of negative sentences. An English-speaking child's negative sentences look like the following:

He no bite you.

Wayne not eating it.

Kathryn not go over there.

You no bring choo-choo train.

That no fish school.

Because of the absence of auxiliaries, these utterances do not look very adultlike. However, children at this stage understand the pragmatic force of negation. The child who says "no!" when asked to take a nap knows exactly what he means.

As children acquire the auxiliaries, they generally use them correctly; that is, the auxiliary usually appears before the subject, but not always.

Yes-No Questions

Does the kitty stand up?

Can I have a piece of paper?

Will you help me?

We can go now?

Wh Questions

Which way they should go?

What can we ride in?

What will we eat?

The introduction of auxiliaries into the child's grammar also affects negative sentences. We now find correctly negated auxiliaries, though *be* is still missing in many cases.

Paul can't have one.

Donna won't let go.

I don't want cover on it.

I am not a doctor.

It's not cold.

Paul not tired.

I not crying.

The child always places the negation in the correct position in relation to the auxiliary or *be*. Main verbs follow negation and *be* precedes negation. Children virtually never produce errors such as "Mommy dances not" or "I not am going."

In languages such as French and German, which are like Italian and Dutch in having a rule that moves inflected verbs, the verb shows up before the negative marker. French and German children respect this rule, as follows. (In the German examples *nich* is the baby form of *nicht*.)

French

Veux pas lolo.	want not water	"I don't want water."
Marche pas.	walks not	"She doesn't walk."
Ça tourne pas.	that turns not	"That doesn't turn."

German

Macht nich aua.	makes not ouch	"It doesn't hurt."
Brauche nich lala.	need not pacifier	"I don't need a pacifier."
Schmeckt auch nich.	tastes also not	"It doesn't taste good either."

Whether they are acquiring Dutch, German, Italian, French, or any other language, all children pass through a "telegraphic" stage, which is but one of many stages that a child goes through on the way to adult linguistic competence. Each of these stages corresponds to a system of rules that the child has internalized—a grammar—and includes a lexicon and pragmatic rules. Although the child's language may not look exactly like the adult language, it is rule-governed and not simply a haphazard approximation to the adult language.

Though the stages of language development are universal, they are shaped by the grammar of the particular adult language the child is acquiring. German, French, Italian, and English-speaking children all go through a telegraphic stage in which they do not use auxiliaries, but they form negative sentences and questions in different ways because the rules of question and negative formation are different in the respective adult languages. This tells us something essential about language acquisition: Children are sensitive to the rules of the adult language at the earliest stages of development. Just as their phonology is quickly fine-tuned to the adult language, so is their syntactic system.

The ability of children to form complex rules and construct grammars of the languages used around them in a relatively short time is phenomenal. The similarity of the language acquisition stages across diverse peoples and languages shows that children are equipped with special abilities to know what generalizations to look for and what to ignore, and how to discover the regularities of language.

Children develop language the way they develop the ability to sit up, stand, crawl, or walk. They are not taught to do these things, but all normal children begin to do them at around the same age. Learning to walk or learning language is different from learning to read or to ride a bicycle. Many people never learn to read because they are not taught to do so, and large groups of people in many parts of the world have no *written* language. However, they all have language.

Setting Parameters

Children acquire some aspects of syntax very quickly, even while they are still in the telegraphic stage. Most of these early developments correspond to what we earlier referred to as the **parameters** of UG. One such parameter that we discussed in chapter 4, the Head Parameter, determines whether the head of a phrase comes before or after its complements; for example, whether the order of the VP is verb-object (VO) as in English or OV as in Japanese. Children produce the correct word order of their language in their earliest multiword utterances, and they understand word order even when they are in the one-word stage of production. According to the parameter model of UG, the child does not actually have to formulate a word-order rule. Rather, he must choose between two already specified values: head first or head last? He determines the correct value based on the language he hears around him. The English-speaking child can quickly figure out that the head comes before its complements; a Japanese-speaking child can equally well determine that his language is head final.

Other parameters of UG involve the verb movement rules. In some languages the verb can move out of the VP to higher positions in the phrase structure tree. We saw this in the Dutch and Italian questions discussed in the last section. In other languages, such as English, verbs do not move (only auxiliaries do). The verb movement parameters provide the child with an option: my language does/does not allow verb movement. As we saw, Dutch- and Italian-speaking children quickly set the verb movement parameters to the "does allow" value, and so they form questions by moving the verb. English-speaking children never make the mistake of moving the verb, even when they don't yet have auxiliaries. In both cases, the children have set the parameter at the correct value for their language. Even after English-speaking children acquire the auxiliaries and the Aux movement rule, they never overgeneralize this movement to include verbs. This supports the hypothesis that the parameter is set early in development and cannot be undone. In this case as well, the child does not have to formulate a rule of verb movement; he does not have to learn when the verb moves and where it moves to. This is all given by UG. He simply has to decide whether verb movement is possible in his language.

The parameters of UG limit the grammatical options to a small well-defined set—is my language head first or head last, does my language have verb movement, and so on. Parameters greatly reduce the acquisition burden on the child and contribute to explaining the ease and rapidity of language acquisition.

The Acquisition of Signed Languages

Deaf children who are born to deaf signing parents are naturally exposed to sign language just as hearing children are naturally exposed to spoken language. Given the universal aspects of sign and spoken languages, it is not surprising that language development in these deaf children parallels the stages of spoken language acquisition. Deaf children babble, they then progress to single signs similar to the single words in the holophrastic stage, and finally they begin to combine signs. There is also a telegraphic stage in which the function signs may be omitted. Use of function signs becomes consistent at around the same age for deaf children as function words in spoken languages. The ages at which signing children go through each of these stages are comparable to the ages of children acquiring a spoken language.

Like the acquisition of spoken languages, the acquisition of signed languages involves the interaction of universal and language-particular components. In our discussion of the acquisition of questions in English, we saw that children easily acquire *wh* movement, which is governed by universal principles, but they show some delay in their use of Aux movement, because they first must learn the auxiliaries, which are specific to English.

In *wh* questions in ASL, the *wh* word can move or it can be left in its original position. Both of the following sentences are grammatical:

_____whq

WHO BILL SEE YESTERDAY?

_____whq

BILL SAW WHO YESTERDAY?

(*Note*: We follow the convention of writing the glosses for signs in uppercase letters.)

There is no Aux movement in ASL, but a question is accompanied by a facial expression with furrowed brows and the head tilted back. This is represented by the "whq" above the ASL glosses. This *non-manual marker* is part of the grammar of ASL. It is like the rising intonation we use when we ask questions in English and other spoken languages.

In one study of the acquisition of *wh* questions in ASL, researchers found that children easily learned the rules associated with the *wh* phrase. The children would sometimes move the *wh* phrase and sometimes leave it in place, as adult signers do. But the children often omitted the non-manual marker, which is not possible in the adult language.

Sometimes the parallels between the acquisition of signed and spoken languages are surprising. Some of the grammatical morphemes in ASL are semantically transparent or **iconic**, that is, they look like what they mean. For example, the sign for the pronoun "I" involves the speaker pointing to his chest. The sign for the pronoun "you" is a point to the chest of the addressee. As we discussed earlier, at around age two, children acquiring spoken languages often reverse the pronouns "I" and "you." Interestingly, at this same age signing children make this same error. They will point to themselves when they mean "you" and point to the addressee when they mean "I." Children acquiring ASL make this error despite the transparency or iconicity of these particular signs, because signing children (like signing adults) treat these pronouns as linguistic symbols and not simply as pointing gestures. As part of the language, the shifting reference of these pronouns presents the same problem for signing children that it does for speaking children.

Hearing children of deaf parents acquire both sign language and spoken language when exposed to both. Studies show that Canadian bilingual children who acquire Langues des Signes Quebecoise (LSQ), or Quebec Sign Language, develop the two languages exactly as bilingual children acquiring two spoken languages. The LSQ–French bilinguals reached linguistic milestones in each of their languages in parallel with Canadian children acquiring French and English. They produced their first words, as well as their first word combinations, at the same time in each language. In reaching these milestones, neither group showed any delay as compared to monolingual children.

Deaf children of hearing parents who are not exposed to sign language from birth suffer a great handicap in acquiring language. It may be many years before these children are able to use a spoken language or before they encounter a conventional sign language. Yet the instinct to acquire language is so strong in humans that these deaf children begin to develop their own manual gestures to express their thoughts and desires. A study of six such children revealed that they not only developed individual signs but joined pairs and formed sentences with definite syntactic order and systematic constraints. Although these "home signs," as they are called, are not fully developed languages like ASL or LSQ, they have a linguistic complexity and systematicity that could not have come from the input, because there was no input. Cases such as these demonstrate not only the strong drive that humans have to communicate through language, but also the innate basis of language structure.

Knowing More Than One Language

> He that understands grammar in one language, understands it in another as far as the essential properties of Grammar are concerned. The fact that he can't speak, nor comprehend, another language is due to the diversity of words and their various forms, but these are the accidental properties of grammar.
>
> ROGER BACON *(1214–1294)*

People can acquire a second language under many different circumstances. You may have learned a second language when you began middle school, or high school, or college. Moving to a new country often means acquiring a new language. Other people live in communities or homes in which more than one language is spoken and may acquire two (or more) languages simultaneously. The term **second language acquisition**, or **2 acquisition**, generally refers to the acquisition of a second language by someone (adult or child) who has already acquired a first language. **Bilingual language acquisition** refers to the (more or less) simultaneous acquisition of two languages beginning in infancy (or before the age of three years).

Childhood Bilingualism

> *Bilingual Hebrew-English-speaking child*: "I speak Hebrew and English."
> *Monolingual English-speaking child*: "What's English?"

Approximately half of the people in the world are native speakers of more than one language. This means that as children they had regular and continued exposure to those languages. In many parts of the world, especially in Africa and Asia, bilingualism (even multilingualism) is the norm. In contrast, many Western countries (though by no means all of them) view themselves as monolingual, even though they may be home to speakers of many languages. In the United States and many European countries, bilingualism is often viewed as a transitory phenomenon associated with immigration.

Bilingualism is an intriguing topic. People wonder how it's possible for a child to acquire two (or more) languages at the same time. There are many questions, such as: Doesn't the child confuse the two languages? Does bilingual language development take longer than monolingual development? Are bilingual children brighter or does acquiring two languages negatively affect the child's cognitive development in some way? How much exposure to each language is necessary for a child to become bilingual?

Much of the early research into bilingualism focused on the fact that bilingual children sometimes mix the two languages in the same sentences, as the following examples from French-English bilingual children illustrate. In the first example, a French word appears in an otherwise English sentence. In the other two examples, all of the words are English but the syntax is French.

His nose is perdu.	"His nose is lost."
A house pink	"A pink house"
That's to me.	"That's mine."

In early studies of bilingualism, this kind of language mixing was viewed negatively. It was taken as an indication that the child was confused or having difficulty with the two languages. In fact, many parents, sometimes on the advice of educators or psychologists, would stop raising their children bilingually when faced with this issue. However, it now seems clear that some amount of language mixing is a normal part of the early bilingual acquisition process and not necessarily an indication of any language problem.

THEORIES OF BILINGUAL DEVELOPMENT

These mixed utterances raise an interesting question about the grammars of bilingual children. Does the bilingual child start out with only one grammar that is eventually differentiated, or does she construct a separate grammar for each language right from the start? The **unitary system hypothesis** says that the child initially constructs only one lexicon and one grammar. The presence of mixed utterances such as the ones just given is often taken as support for this hypothesis. In addition, at the early stages, bilingual children often have words for particular objects in only one language. For example, a Spanish-English bilingual child may know the Spanish word for milk, *leche*, but not the English word, or she may have the word *water* but not *agua*. This kind of complementarity has also been taken as support for the idea that the child has only one lexicon.

However, careful examination of the vocabularies of bilingual children reveals that although they may not have exactly the same words in both languages, there is enough overlap to make the single lexicon idea implausible. The reason children may not have the same set of words in both languages is that they use their two languages in different circumstances and acquire the vocabulary appropriate to each situation. For example, the bilingual English-Spanish child may hear only Spanish during meal-time, and so he will first learn the Spanish words for foods. Also, bilingual children initially have smaller vocabularies in each of their languages than the monolingual child has in her one language. This makes sense because a child can only learn so many words a day, and the bilingual child has two lexicons to build. For these reasons the bilingual child may have more lexical gaps than the monolingual child at a comparable stage of development, and those gaps may be different for each language.

The **separate systems hypothesis** says that the bilingual child builds a distinct lexicon and grammar for each language. To test the separate systems hypothesis, it is necessary to look at how the child acquires those pieces of grammar that are different in his two languages. For example, if both languages have SVO word order, this would not be a good place to test this hypothesis. Several studies have shown that where the two languages diverge, children acquire the different rules of each language. Spanish-English and French-German bilingual children have been shown to use the word orders appropriate to each language, as well as the correct agreement morphemes for each language. Other studies have shown that children set up two distinct sets of phonemes and phonological rules for their languages.

The separate systems hypothesis also receives support from the study of the LSQ-French bilinguals discussed earlier. These children have semantically equivalent words in the two languages, just as spoken-spoken bilinguals do. In addition, these children, like all bilingual children, were able to adjust their language choice to the language of their addressees, showing that they differentiated the two languages. Like most bilingual children, the LSQ-French bilinguals produced mixed utterances that had words from both languages. What is especially interesting is that these children showed simultaneous language mixing. They would produce an LSQ sign and a French word at the same time, something that is only possible if one language is spoken and the other signed. However, this finding has implications for bilingual language acquisition in general. It shows that the language mixing of bilingual children is not caused by confusion, but is rather the result of two grammars operating simultaneously.

If bilingual children have two grammars and two lexicons, what explains the mixed utterances? Various explanations have been offered. One suggestion is that children mix because they have lexical gaps; if the French-English bilingual child does not know the English word *lost*, she will use the word she does know, *perdu*— the "any port in a storm strategy." Another possibility is that the mixing in child language is like the special language usage of many adult bilinguals referred to as **code-switching** (discussed in chapter 10). In specific social situations, bilingual adults may switch back and forth between their two languages in the same sentence, for example, "I put the forks en las mesas" (I put the forks on the tables). Code-switching reflects the grammars of both languages working simultaneously; it is not "bad grammar" or "broken English." Adult bilinguals code-switch only when speaking to other bilingual speakers. It has been suggested that the mixed utterances of bilingual children are a form of code-switching. In support of this proposal, various studies have shown that bilingual children as young as two make contextually appropriate language choices: In speaking to monolinguals the children use one language, and in speaking to bilinguals they mix the two languages.

TWO MONOLINGUALS IN ONE HEAD

Although we must study many bilingual children to reach any firm conclusions, the evidence accumulated so far seems to support the idea that children construct multiple grammars at the outset. Moreover, it seems that bilingual children develop their grammars along the same lines as monolingual children. They go through a babbling stage, a holophrastic stage, a telegraphic stage, and so on. During the telegraphic stage they show the same characteristics in each of their languages as the monolingual children. For example, monolingual English-speaking children omit verb endings in sentences such as "Eve play there," "Andrew want that," and German-speaking children use infinitives as in "S[ch]okolade holen" (chocolate get-infinitive). Spanish- and Italian-speaking monolinguals never omit verbal inflection or use infinitives in this way. Remarkably, two-year-old German-Italian bilinguals use infinitives when speaking German but not when they speak Italian. Young Spanish-English bilingual children drop the English verb endings but not the Spanish ones, and German-English bilinguals omit verbal inflection in English and use the infinitive in German. Results such as these have led some researchers to suggest that the bilingual child is like "two monolinguals in one head."

THE ROLE OF INPUT

One issue that concerns researchers studying bilingualism, as well as parents of bilingual children, is the relationship between language input and proficiency. What role does input play in helping the child to separate the two languages? One input condition that is thought to promote bilingual development is *une personne–une langue* (one person, one language). In this condition, each person, say Mom and Dad, speaks only one language to the child. The idea is that keeping the two languages separate in the input will make it easier for the child to keep them separate. Whether this affects bilingual development in some important way has not been established. In practice this "ideal" input situation may be difficult to attain. It may also be unnecessary. We saw earlier that babies are attuned to various phonological properties of the input language such as prosody and phonotactics. This may provide a sufficient basis for the bilingual child to keep the two languages separate.

Another question is, how much input does a child need in each language to become "native" in both? The answer is not straightforward. It seems intuitively clear that if a child hears 12 hours of English a day and only 2 hours of Spanish, he will probably develop English much more quickly and completely than Spanish. In fact, under these conditions he may never achieve the kind of grammatical competence in Spanish that we associate with the normal monolingual Spanish speaker. In reality, bilingual children are raised in varying circumstances. Some may have more or less equal exposure to the two languages; some may hear one language more than the other but still have sufficient input in the two languages to become "native" in both; some may ultimately have one language that is dominant to a lesser or greater degree. Researchers simply do not know how much language exposure is necessary in the two languages to produce a balanced bilingual. For practical purposes, the rule of thumb is that the child should receive roughly equal amounts of input in the two languages to achieve native proficiency in both.

COGNITIVE EFFECTS OF BILINGUALISM

Another issue is the effect of bilingualism on intellectual or cognitive development. Does being bilingual make you more or less intelligent, more or less creative, and so on? Historically, research into this question has been fraught with methodological problems and has often been heavily influenced by the prevailing political and social climate. Many early studies (before the 1960s) showed that bilingual children did worse than monolingual children on IQ and other cognitive and educational tests. The results of more recent research indicate that bilingual children outperform monolinguals in certain kinds of problem solving. Also, bilingual children seem to have better **metalinguistic awareness**, which refers to a speaker's conscious awareness *about* language and the use of language. This is in contrast to linguistic knowledge, which, as we have seen, is knowledge *of* language and is unconscious. Bilingual children have an earlier understanding of the arbitrary relationship between an object and its name, for instance. And they have sufficient metalinguistic awareness to speak the contextually appropriate language, as we mentioned.

Whether children enjoy some cognitive or educational benefit from being bilingual seems to depend a great deal on extralinguistic factors such as the social and economic position of the child's group or community, the educational situation, and the relative "prestige" of the two languages. Studies that show the most positive effects (e.g., better school performance) generally involve children reared in societies where both languages are valued and whose parents were interested and supportive of their bilingual development.

Second Language Acquisition

> With each newly learned language you acquire a new soul.
>
> **SLOVAKIAN PROVERB**

In contrast to the bilinguals just discussed, many people are introduced to a second language (L2) after they have achieved native competence in a first language (L1). If you have had the experience of trying to master a second language as an adult, no doubt you found it to be a challenge quite unlike your first language experience.

IS L2 ACQUISITION THE SAME AS L1 ACQUISITION?

With some exceptions, adults do not simply pick up a second language. It usually requires conscious attention, if not intense study and memorization, to become proficient in a second language. Again, with the exception of some remarkable individuals, adult second-language learners (L2ers) do not often achieve nativelike grammatical competence in the L2, especially with respect to pronunciation. They generally have an accent, and they may make syntactic or morphological errors that are unlike the errors of children acquiring their first language (L1ers). For example, L2ers often make word order errors, especially early in their development, as well as morphological errors in grammatical gender and case. L2 errors may **fossilize** so that no amount of teaching or correction can undo them.

Unlike L1 acquisition, which is uniformly successful across children and languages, adults vary considerably in their ability to acquire an L2 completely. Some people are very talented language learners. Others are hopeless. Most people fall somewhere in the middle. Success may depend on a range of factors, including age, talent, motivation, and whether you are in the country where the language is spoken or sitting in a classroom five mornings a week with no further contact with native speakers. For all these reasons, many people, including many linguists who study L2 acquisition, believe that second language acquisition is something different from first language acquisition. This hypothesis is referred to as the **fundamental difference hypothesis** of L2 acquisition.

In certain important respects, however, L2 acquisition is like L1 acquisition. Like L1ers, L2ers do not acquire their second language overnight; they go through stages. Like L1ers, L2ers construct grammars. These grammars reflect their competence in the L2 at each stage, and so their language at any particular point, though not native-like, is rule-governed and not haphazard. The intermediate grammars that L2ers create on their way to the target have been called **interlanguage grammars**.

Consider word order in the interlanguage grammars of Romance (e.g., Italian, Spanish, and Portuguese) speakers acquiring German as a second language. The word order of the Romance languages is Subject-(Auxiliary)-Verb-Object (like English). German has two basic word orders depending on the presence of an auxiliary. Sentences with auxiliaries have Subject-Auxiliary-Object-Verb, as in (1). Sentences without auxiliaries have Subject-Verb-Object, as in (2). (Note that as with the child data above, these L2 sentences may contain various "errors" in addition to the word order facts we are considering.)

1. Hans hat ein Buch gekauft.   "Hans has a book bought."
2. Hans kauft ein Buch.   "Hans is buying a book."

Studies show that Romance speakers acquire German word order in pieces. During the first stage they use German words but the S-Aux-V-O word order of their native language, as follows:

Stage 1:   Mein Vater hat gekauft ein Buch.
        "My father has bought a book."

At the second stage, they acquired the VP word order Object-Verb.

Stage 2:   Vor Personalrat auch meine helfen.
        in the personnel office [a colleague] me helped
        "A colleague in the personnel office helped me."

At the third stage they acquired the rule that places the verb or (auxiliary) in second position.

Stage 3:   Jetzt kann sie mir eine Frage machen.
        now can she me a question ask
        "Now she can ask me a question."

        I kenne nich die Welt.
        I know not the world.
        "I don't know the world."

These stages differ from those of children acquiring German as a first language. For example, German children know early on that the language has SOV word order.

Like L1ers, L2ers also attempt to uncover the grammar of the target language, but with varying success, and they often do not reach the target. Proponents of the *fundamental difference hypothesis* believe that L2ers construct grammars according to different principles than those used in L1 acquisition, principles that are not specifically designed for language acquisition, but for the problem-solving skills used for tasks like playing chess or learning math. According to this view, L2ers lack access to the specifically linguistic principles of UG that L1ers have to help them.

Opposing this view, others have argued that adults are superior to children in solving all sorts of nonlinguistic problems. If they were using these problem-solving skills to learn their L2, shouldn't they be uniformly more successful than they are? Also, linguistic savants such as Christopher, discussed in chapter 2, argue against the view that L2 acquisition involves only nonlinguistic cognitive abilities. Christopher's IQ and problem-solving skills are minimal at best, yet he has become proficient in several languages.

Many L2 acquisition researchers do not believe that L2 acquisition is fundamentally different from L1 acquisition. They point to various studies that show that interlanguage grammars do not generally violate principles of UG, which makes the process seem more similar to L1 acquisition. In the German L2 examples above, the interlanguage rules may be wrong for German, or wrong for Romance, but they are not impossible rules. These researchers also note that although L2ers may fall short of L1ers in terms of their final grammar, they appear to acquire rules in the same way as L1ers.

Native Language Influence in L2 Acquisition

One respect in which L1 acquisition and L2 acquisition are clearly different is that adult L2ers already have a fully developed grammar of their first language. As discussed in chapter 1, linguistic competence is unconscious knowledge. We cannot suppress our ability to use the rules of our language. We cannot decide not to understand English. Similarly, L2ers—especially at the beginning stages of acquiring their L2—seem to rely on their L1 grammar to some extent. This is shown by the kinds of errors L2ers make, which often involve the **transfer of grammatical rules** from their L1. This is most obvious in phonology. L2ers generally speak with an accent because they may transfer the phonemes, phonological rules, or syllable structures of their first language to their second language. We see this in the Japanese speaker, who does not distinguish between *write* [rajt] and *light* [lajt] because the r/l distinction is not phonemic in Japanese; in the French speaker, who says "ze cat in ze hat" because French does not have [ð]; in the German speaker, who devoices final consonants, saying [hæf] for *have;* and in the Spanish speaker, who inserts a schwa before initial consonant clusters, as in [əskul] for *school* and [əsnab] for *snob.*

Similarly, English speakers may have difficulty with unfamiliar sounds in other languages. For example, in Italian long (or double) consonants are phonemic. Italian has minimal pairs such as the following:

ano	"anus"	anno	"year"
pala	"shovel"	palla	"ball"
dita	"fingers"	ditta	"company"

English-speaking L2 learners of Italian have difficulty in hearing and producing the contrast between long and short consonants. This can lead to very embarrassing situations, for example on New Year's Eve, when instead of wishing people *buon anno* (good year), you wish them *buon ano.*

Native language influence is also found in the syntax and morphology. Sometimes this influence shows up as a wholesale transfer of a particular piece of grammar. For example, a Spanish speaker acquiring English might drop subjects in nonimperative sentences because this is possible in Spanish, as illustrated by the following examples:

Hey, is not funny.

In here have the mouth.

Live in Columbia.

Or speakers may begin with the word order of their native language, as we saw in the Romance-German interlanguage examples.

Native language influence may show up in more subtle ways. For example, people whose L1 is German acquire English yes-no questions faster than Japanese speakers do. This is because German has a verb movement rule for forming yes-no questions that is very close to the English Aux movement rule, while in Japanese there is no syntactic movement in question formation.

THE CREATIVE COMPONENT OF L2 ACQUISITION

It would be an oversimplification to think that L2 acquisition involves only the transfer of L1 properties to the L2 interlanguage. There is a strong creative component to L2 acquisition. Many language-particular parts of the L1 grammar do not transfer. Items that a speaker considers irregular, infrequent, or semantically difficult are not likely to transfer to the L2. For example, speakers will not typically transfer L1 idioms such as *He hit the roof* meaning "He got angry." They are more likely to transfer structures in which the semantic relations are transparent. For example, a structure such as (1) will transfer more readily than (2).

1. It is awkward to carry this suitcase.
2. This suitcase is awkward to carry.

In (1) the NP "this suitcase" is in its logical direct object position, while in (2) it has been moved to the subject position away from the verb that selects it.

Many of the "errors" that L2ers do make are not derived from their L1. For example, in one study Turkish speakers at a particular stage in their development of German used S-V-Adv (Subject-Verb-Adverb) word order in embedded clauses (the *wenn* clause in the following example) in their German interlanguage, even though both their native language and the target language have S-Adv-V order:

Wenn	ich	geh	zuruck	ich	arbeit elektriker	in der Türkei.
if	I	go	back,	I	work (as an) electrician	in Turkey

The embedded S-V-Adv order is most likely an overgeneralization of the verb second requirement in main clauses that we discussed previously. As we noted earlier, overgeneralization is a clear indication that a rule has been acquired.

Why certain L1 rules transfer to the interlanguage grammar and others don't is not well understood. It is clear, however, that although construction of the L2 grammar is influenced by the L1 grammar, developmental principles—possibly universal—also operate in L2 acquisition. This is best illustrated by the fact that speakers with different L1s go through similar L2 stages. For example, Turkish, Serbo-Croatian, Italian, Greek, and Spanish speakers acquiring German as an L2 all drop articles to some extent. Because some of these L1s have articles, this cannot be caused by transfer but must involve some more general property of language acquisition.

IS THERE A CRITICAL PERIOD FOR L2 ACQUISITION?

> I don't know how you manage, Sir, amongst all the foreigners; you never know what they are saying. When the poor things first come here they gabble away like geese, although the children can soon speak well enough.
>
> MARGARET ATWOOD, Alias Grace

Age is a significant factor in L2 acquisition. The younger a person is when exposed to a second language, the more likely she is to achieve nativelike competence.

In an important study of the effects of age on ultimate attainment in L2 acquisition, Jacqueline Johnson and Elissa Newport tested several groups of Chinese and Korean speakers who had acquired English as a second language. The subjects, all of whom had been in the United States for at least five years, were tested on their knowledge of specific aspects of English morphology and syntax. They were asked to judge the grammaticality of sentences such as:

The little boy is speak to a policeman.

The farmer bought two pig.

A bat flewed into our attic last night.

Johnson and Newport found that the test results depended heavily on the age at which the person had arrived in the United States. The people who arrived as children (between the age of three and eight) did as well on the test as American native speakers. Those who arrived between the ages of eight and fifteen did not perform like native speakers. Moreover, every year seemed to make a difference for this group. The person who arrived at age nine did better than the one who arrived at age ten; those who arrived at age eleven did better than those who arrived at age twelve, and so on. The group that arrived between the ages of seventeen and thirty-one had the lowest scores.

Does this mean that there is a critical period for L2 acquisition, an age beyond which it is *impossible* to acquire the grammar of a new language? Most researchers would hesitate to make such a strong claim. Although age is an important factor in achieving nativelike L2 competence, it is certainly possible to acquire a second language as an adult. Many teenage and adult L2 learners become proficient, and a few highly talented ones even manage to pass for native speakers.

It is more appropriate to say that L2 acquisition abilities gradually decline with age and that there are "sensitive periods" for the nativelike mastery of certain aspects of the L2. The sensitive period for phonology is the shortest. To achieve nativelike pronunciation of an L2 generally requires exposure during childhood. Other aspects of language, such as syntax, may have a larger window.

Recent research with learners of their "heritage language" (the ancestral language not learned as a child such as Gaelic in Ireland) provides additional support for the notion of sensitive periods in L2 acquisition. UCLA psychologist Terry Au and her colleagues investigated the acquisition of Spanish by college students who had overheard the language as children (and sometimes knew a few words), but who did not otherwise speak or understand Spanish. The overhearers were compared to people who had no exposure to Spanish before the age of fourteen. All of the students were native speakers of English studying their heritage language as a second language. Au's results showed that the overhearers acquired a more nativelike accent whereas the other students did not. However, the overhearers did not show any advantage in acquiring the grammatical morphemes of Spanish. Early exposure may leave an imprint that facilitates the late acquisition of certain aspects of language.

Recent research on the neurological effects of acquiring a second language shows that left hemisphere cortical density is increased in bilinguals relative to monolinguals and that this increase is more pronounced in early versus late second-language learners. The study also shows a positive relationship between brain density and second-language proficiency. The researchers concluded that the structure of the human brain is altered by the experience of acquiring a second language.

Second-Language Teaching Methods

Many approaches to second or foreign language teaching have been developed over the years. Though these methods can differ significantly from one another, many experts believe that there is no single best method for teaching a second language. All methods have something to offer, and virtually any method can succeed with a gifted, native or near-native speaker teacher, motivated students, and appropriate teaching materials. All methods are most effective when they fit a given educational setting and when they are understood and embraced by the teacher.

Second-language teaching methods fall into two broad categories: the *synthetic approach* and the *analytic approach*. As the name implies, the synthetic approach stresses the teaching of the grammatical, lexical, phonological, and functional units of the language step by step. This is a bottom-up method. The task of the learner is to put together—or synthesize—the discrete elements that make up the language. The more traditional language teaching methods, which stress grammar instruction, fall into this category.

An extreme example of the synthetic approach is the **grammar translation** method favored up until the mid-1960s, in which students learned lists of vocabulary, verb paradigms, and grammatical rules. Learners translated passages from the target language into their native language. The teacher typically conducted class in the students' native language, focusing on the grammatical parsing of texts, and there was little or no contextualization of the language being taught. Reading passages were carefully constructed to contain only vocabulary and structures to which learners had already been exposed, and errors in translation were corrected on the spot. Learners were tested on their mastery of rules, verb paradigms, and vocabulary. The students did not use the target language very much except in reading translated passages aloud.

Analytic approaches are more top-down. The goal is not to explicitly teach the component parts or rules of the target language. Rather, the instructor selects topics, texts, or tasks that are relevant to the needs and interests of the learner, whose job it is to then discover the constituent parts of the language. This approach assumes that adults can extract the rules of the language from unstructured input, more or less like a child does when acquiring his first language.

Currently, one of the most widely practiced analytic approaches is *content-based instruction,* in which the focus is on making the language meaningful and on getting the student to communicate in the target language. Learners are encouraged to discuss issues and express opinions on various topics of interest to them in the target language. Topics for discussion might include "Online Romance" or "Taking Responsibility for Our Environment." Grammar rules are taught on an as-needed basis, and fluency takes precedence over grammatical accuracy. Classroom texts (both written and aural) are generally taken from sources that were not created specifically for language learners, based on the view that these will be more interesting and relevant to the student. Assessment is based on the learner's comprehension of the target language.

Not all second-language teaching methods fall clearly into one or the other category. The synthetic and analytic approaches should be viewed as the opposite ends of a continuum along which various second-language methods may fall. Also, teachers practicing a given method may not strictly follow all the principles of the method. Actual classroom practices tend to be more eclectic, with teachers using techniques that work well for them and to which they are accustomed—even if these techniques are not in complete accordance with the method they are practicing.

Can Chimps Learn Human Language?

> It is a great baboon, but so much like man in most things . . . I do believe it already understands much English; and I am of the mind it might be taught to speak or make signs.
>
> ENTRY IN SAMUEL PEPYS'S Diary, *August 1661*

In this chapter, the discussion has centered on human language acquisition. Recently, much effort has been expended to determine whether nonhuman primates (e.g., chimpanzees, monkeys, gorillas) can learn human language.

In their natural habitat, primates communicate with each other in systems that include visual, auditory, olfactory, and tactile signals. Many of these signals seem to have meaning associated with the animals' immediate environment or emotional state. They can signal danger and can communicate aggressiveness and subordination. Females of some species emit a specific call to indicate that they are anestrus (sexually quiescent), which inhibits attempts by males to copulate. However, the natural sounds and gestures produced by all nonhuman primates show their signals to be highly stereotyped and limited in the type and number of messages they convey. Their basic vocabularies occur primarily as emotional responses to particular situations. They have no way of expressing the anger they felt yesterday or the anticipation of tomorrow.

Despite their limited natural systems of communication, these animals have provoked an interest in whether they have the capacity to acquire complex linguistic systems that are similar to human language.

In the 1930s, Winthrop and Luella Kellogg raised their infant son with an infant chimpanzee named Gua to determine whether a chimpanzee raised in a human environment and given language instruction could learn a human language. Gua understood about one hundred words at sixteen months, more words than their son at that age, but she never went beyond that. Moreover, comprehension of language involves more than understanding the meanings of isolated words. When their son could understand the difference between *I say what I mean* and *I mean what I say*, Gua could not understand either sentence.

A chimpanzee named Viki was raised by Keith and Cathy Hayes, and she too learned many individual words, even learning to articulate, with great difficulty, the words *mama, papa, cup,* and *up.* That was the extent of her language production.

Psychologists Allen and Beatrice Gardner recognized that one disadvantage suffered by the primates was their physical inability to pronounce many different sounds. Without a sufficient number of phonemic contrasts, spoken human language is impossible. Many species of primates are manually dexterous, and this fact inspired the Gardners to attempt to teach American Sign Language to a chimpanzee that they named Washoe, after the Nevada county in which they lived. Washoe was brought up in much the same way as a human child in a deaf community, constantly in the presence of people who used ASL. She was deliberately taught to sign, whereas children raised by deaf signers acquire sign language without explicit teaching, as hearing children learn spoken language.

By the time Washoe was four years old (June 1969), she had acquired eighty-five signs with such meanings as "more," "eat," "listen," "gimme," "key," "dog," "you," "me," "Washoe," and "hurry." According to the Gardners, Washoe was also able to produce sign combinations such as "baby mine," "you drink," "hug hurry," "gimme flower," and "more fruit."

At about the same time that Washoe was growing up, psychologist David Premack and his wife Ann Premack raised a chimp named Sarah in their home and attempted to teach her an artificial language designed to resemble human languages in some aspects. The "words" of Sarah's "language" were plastic chips of different shapes and colors that had metal backs. Sarah and her trainers "talked" to each other by arranging these symbols on a magnetic board. Sarah was taught to associate particular symbols with particular meanings. The form-meaning relationship of these "morphemes" or "words" was arbitrary; a small red square meant "banana," and a small blue rectangle meant "apricot," while the color red was represented by a gray chip and the color yellow by a black chip. Sarah learned a number of "nouns," "adjectives," and "verbs," symbols for abstract concepts like "same as" and "different from," "negation," and "question."

There were drawbacks to the Sarah experiment. She was not allowed to "talk" spontaneously, but only in response to her trainers. And there was the possibility that her trainers unwittingly provided cues that Sarah responded to.

To avoid these and other problems, Duane and Sue Rumbaugh and their associates at the Yerkes Regional Primate Research Center began in 1973 to teach a different kind of artificial language, called Yerkish, to three chimpanzees: Lana, Sherman, and Austin. The words of Yerkish, called *lexigrams,* are geometric symbols displayed on a computer keyboard. Certain fixed orders of these lexigrams constitute grammatical sentences in Yerkish. The computer records every button pressed so that a complete 24/7 record of the chimps' "speech" was obtained. The researchers are particularly interested in the ability of primates to communicate using abstract, functional symbols.

Another experiment aimed at teaching sign language to primates involved a gorilla named Koko, who was taught by her trainer, Francine "Penny" Patterson. Patterson claims that Koko has learned several hundred signs, is able to put signs together to make sentences, and is capable of making linguistic jokes and puns, composing rhymes such as BEAR HAIR (which is a rhyme in spoken language but not ASL), and inventing metaphors such as FINGER BRACELET for ring.

The psychologist H. S. Terrace and his associates studied a chimpanzee named Nim Chimpsky in a project specifically designed to test the linguistic claims that had emerged from prior primate experiments. An experienced teacher of ASL taught Nim to sign. Under carefully controlled experimental conditions that included thorough record-keeping and many hours of videotaping, Nim's teachers hoped to show beyond a reasonable doubt that chimpanzees had a humanlike linguistic capacity, in contradiction to the view put forth by Noam Chomsky (after whom Nim was ironically named) that human language is species-specific.

In the nearly four years of study, Nim learned about 125 signs, and during the last two years Nim's teachers recorded more than 20,000 utterances that included two or more signs. Nim produced his first ASL sign (DRINK) after just four months, which greatly encouraged the research team at the start of the study. Their enthusiasm soon diminished when he never seemed to go much beyond the two-word stage. Terrace concluded that "his three-sign combinations do not . . . provide new information. . . . Nim's most frequent two- and three-sign combinations [were] PLAY ME and PLAY ME NIM. Adding NIM to PLAY ME is simply redundant," writes Terrace. This kind of redundancy is illustrated by a sixteen-sign utterance of Nim's: GIVE ORANGE ME GIVE EAT ORANGE ME EAT ORANGE GIVE ME EAT ORANGE GIVE ME YOU. Other typical sentences do not sound much like the early sentences of children we cited earlier.

Nim eat Nim eat.

Drink eat me Nim.

Me Eat Me eat.

You me banana me banana you.

Nim rarely signed spontaneously as children do when they begin to use language (spoken or sign). Only 12 percent of his utterances were spontaneous. Most of Nim's signing occurred only in response to prompting by his trainers and was related to eating, drinking, and playing; that is, it was stimulus-controlled. As much as 40 percent of his output was simply repetitions of signs made by the trainer. Children initiate conversations more frequently as they grow older, and their utterances repeat less of the adult's prior utterance. Some children rarely imitate anything they've heard in conversation. Children become increasingly more creative in their language use, but Nim showed almost no tendency toward such creativity. Furthermore, children's utterances increase in length and complexity as time progresses, finally mirroring the adult grammar, whereas Nim's language did not.

The lack of spontaneity and the excessive noncreative imitative nature of Nim's signing led to the conclusion that Nim's acquisition and use of language is qualitatively different from a child's. After examining the films of Washoe, Koko, and others, Terrace drew similar conclusions regarding the signing of the other primates.

Signing chimpanzees are also unlike humans in that when several of them are together they do not sign to each other as freely as humans would under similar circumstances. There is also no evidence to date that a signing chimp (or one communicating with plastic chips or computer symbols) will teach another chimp language, or that offspring will acquire language from their parent.

Like Terrace, the Premacks and the Rumbaughs suggest that the sign-language studies lacked sufficient control and that the reported results were too anecdotal to support the view that primates are capable of acquiring a human language. They also question whether all attempts to teach sign language to primates suffer from what has come to be called the Clever Hans phenomenon.

Clever Hans was a performing horse that became famous at the end of the nineteenth century because of his apparent ability to do arithmetic, read, spell, and even solve problems of musical harmony. He answered the questions posed by his interrogators by stamping out numbers with his hoof. It turned out, not surprisingly, that Hans did not know that $2 + 2 = 4$, but he was clever enough to pick up subtle cues conveyed unconsciously by his trainer as to when he should stop tapping his foot.

Sarah, like Clever Hans, took prompts from her trainers and her environment to produce the plastic-chip sentences. In responding to the string of chips standing for

SARAH INSERT APPLE PAIL BANANA DISH

all Sarah had to figure out was to place certain fruits in certain containers, and she could decide which by merely seeing that the apple symbol was next to the pail symbol, and the banana symbol was next to the dish symbol. There is no evidence that Sarah actually grouped strings of words into constituents. There is also no indication that Sarah would understand a new compound sentence of this type. The creative ability that is so much a part of human language is not demonstrated by this act.

Problems also exist in Lana's acquisition of Yerkish. Thompson and Church studied the Lana project and were able to simulate Lana's behavior with a computer model. They concluded that the chimp's "linguistic" behavior can all be accounted for by her learning to associate lexigrams with objects, persons, or events, and to produce one of several "stock sentences" depending on situational cues (like Clever Hans).

How Sarah and Lana learned to manipulate symbols differs in several significant respects from how children learn language. In the case of the chimpanzees, each new rule or sentence form was introduced in a deliberate, highly constrained way. When parents speak to children, however, they do not confine themselves to a few words in a particular order for months, rewarding the child with a chocolate bar or a banana each time the child correctly responds to a command. Nor do they wait until the child has mastered one rule of grammar before going on to a different structure. Unless they were linguists, parents wouldn't know how to do such a thing. Young children require no special language training.

Research on the linguistic ability of nonhuman primates continues. Two investigators, Patricia Greenfield and Sue Savage-Rumbaugh, studied a different species of chimp, a male bonobo (or pygmy chimpanzee) named Kanzi. They used the same plastic lexigrams and computer keyboard as used with Lana. They concluded that Kanzi not only learned but also invented grammatical rules that may well be as complex as those used by two-year-old children. The grammatical rule referred to was the combination of a lexigram (such as that meaning "dog") followed by a gesture meaning "go." After combining these gestures, Kanzi would then go to an area where dogs were located to play with them. Greenfield and Savage-Rumbaugh claim that this "ordering" rule was not an imitation of Kanzi's caretakers' utterances, who they say use an opposite ordering, in which "go" was followed by "dogs."

The investigators report that Kanzi's acquisition of "grammatical skills" was slower than that of children, taking about three years (starting when he was five and a half years old). Most of Kanzi's so-called sentences are fixed formulas with little if any internal structure. Kanzi has not yet exhibited the linguistic knowledge of a human three-year-old, whose complexity level includes knowledge of structure dependencies and hierarchical structure. Moreover, unlike Kanzi, who used a different word order from her caretakers, children rapidly set the word order parameters of UG to correspond to the input.

As often happens in science, the search for the answers to one kind of question leads to answers to other questions. The linguistic experiments with primates have led to many advances in our understanding of primate cognitive ability. Premack has gone on to investigate other capacities of the chimp mind, such as causality; the Rumbaughs and Greenfield are continuing to study the ability of chimpanzees to use symbols. These studies also point out how remarkable it is that children, by the age of three and four, without explicit teaching, and without overt reinforcement, create new and complex sentences never spoken and never heard before.

Summary

When children acquire a language, they acquire the grammar of that language—the phonological, morphological, syntactic, and semantic rules. They also acquire the pragmatic rules of the language as well as a lexicon. Children are not taught language. Rather, they extract the rules (and much of the lexicon) from the language around them.

Several learning mechanisms have been suggested to explain the acquisition process. Imitations of adult speech, reinforcement, and analogy have all been proposed. None of these possible learning mechanisms account for the fact that children creatively form new sentences according to the rules of their language, or for the fact that children make certain kinds of errors but not others. Empirical studies of the **motherese** hypothesis show that grammar development does not depend on structured input. **Connectionist models** of acquisition also depend on the child having specially structured input.

The ease and rapidity of children's language acquisition and the uniformity of the stages of development for all children and all languages, despite the **poverty of the stimulus** they receive, suggest that the language faculty is innate and that the infant comes to the complex task already endowed with a Universal Grammar. UG is not a grammar like the grammar of English or Arabic, but represents the principles to which all human languages conform. Language acquisition is a creative process. Children create grammars based on the linguistic input and are guided by UG.

Language development proceeds in stages, which are universal. During the first year of life, children develop the sounds of their language. They begin by producing and perceiving many sounds that do not exist in their language input, the **babbling** stage. Gradually, their productions and perceptions are fine-tuned to the environment. Children's late babbling has all the phonological characteristics of the input language. Deaf children who are exposed at birth to sign languages also produce manual babbling, showing that babbling is a universal first stage in language acquisition that is dependent on the linguistic input received.

At the end of the first year, children utter their first words. During the second year, they learn many more words and they develop much of the phonological system of the language. Children's first utterances are one-word "sentences" (the **holophrastic** stage). After a few months, the child puts two or more words together. These early sentences are not random combinations of words: The words have definite patterns and express both syntactic and semantic relationships.

During the **telegraphic stage**, the child produces longer sentences that often lack function or grammatical morphemes. The child's early grammar still lacks many of the rules of the adult grammar, but is not qualitatively different from it. Children at this stage have correct word order and rules for agreement and case, which show their knowledge of structure.

Children make specific kinds of errors while acquiring their language. For example, they will **overgeneralize** morphology by saying *bringed* or *mans*. This shows that they are acquiring rules of their particular language. Children never make errors that would involve violating principles of Universal Grammar.

Deaf children exposed to **sign language** show the same stages of language acquisition as do hearing children exposed to spoken languages.

Children may acquire more than one language at a time. **Bilingual** children seem to go through the same stages as monolingual children except that they develop two grammars and two lexicons simultaneously. This is true for children acquiring two spoken languages as well as for children acquiring a spoken language and a signed language. Whether the child will be equally proficient in the two languages depends on the input she receives and the social conditions under which the languages are acquired.

Like first-language learners, **L2 learners** construct grammars of the target language and they also go through stages—called **interlanguage grammars**. In **second language acquisition**, influence from the speaker's first language makes L2 acquisition appear different from L1 acquisition. Adults often do not achieve nativelike competence in their L2, especially in pronunciation. The difficulties encountered in attempting to learn languages after puberty may be because there are sensitive periods for L2 acquisition. Some theories of second language acquisition suggest that the same principles operate that account for first language acquisition. A second view suggests that the acquisition of a second language in adulthood involves general learning mechanisms rather than the specifically linguistic principles used by the child.

Several second-language teaching methods have been proposed. Some of them focus more on the grammatical aspects of the target language, and others focus more on getting students to communicate in the target language, with less regard for grammatical accuracy.

Questions as to whether language is unique to the human species have led researchers to attempt to teach nonhuman primates systems of communication that purportedly resemble human language. Chimpanzees like Sarah and Lana have been taught to manipulate symbols to gain rewards, and other chimpanzees, like Washoe and Nim Chimpsky, have been taught some ASL signs. A careful examination of the utterances in ASL by these chimps shows that unlike children, their language exhibits little spontaneity, is highly imitative (echoic), and reveals little syntactic structure. It has been suggested that the pygmy chimp Kanzi shows grammatical ability greater than the other chimps studied, but he still does not have the ability of even a three-year-old child.

The universality of the language acquisition process, of the stages of development, of the relatively short period in which the child constructs a complex grammatical system without overt teaching, and the limited results of the chimpanzee experiments suggest that the human species is innately endowed with special language acquisition abilities and that language is biologically and genetically part of the human neurological system.

All normal children everywhere learn language. This ability is not dependent on race, social class, geography, or even intelligence (within a normal range). This ability is uniquely human.

References for Further Reading

Brown, R. 1973. *A First Language: The Early Stages*. Cambridge, MA: Harvard University Press.

Cairns, H. 1996. *The Acquisition of Language*. Austin, TX: PRO-ED.

Crain, S., and D. Lillo-Martin. 1999. *An Introduction to Linguistic Theory and Language Acquisition*. Oxford: Blackwell Publishers.

Gass, S., and L. Selinker. 1994. *Second Language Acquisition*. Hillsdale, NJ: Lawrence Erlbaum Associates.

Golinkoff, R., and K. Hirsh-Pasek. 1996. *The Origins of Grammar*. Cambridge, MA: MIT Press.

Guasti, M. T. 2002. *Language Acquisition: The Growth of Grammar*. Cambridge, MA: MIT Press.

Hakuta, K. 1986. *Mirror of Language: The Debate on Bilingualism*. New York: Basic Books.

Hyltenstam, K., and L. Obler. 1989. *Bilingualism Across the Lifespan: Aspects of Acquisition, Maturity and Loss*. Cambridge, England: Cambridge University Press.

Ingram, D. 1989. *First Language Acquisition: Method, Description and Explanation*. New York: Cambridge University Press.

Jakobson, R. 1971. *Studies on Child Language and Aphasia*. The Hague: Mouton.

Jusczyk, P. W. 1997. *The Discovery of Spoken Language*. Cambridge, MA: MIT Press.

Klima, E. S., and U. Bellugi. 1979. *The Signs of Language*. Cambridge, MA: Harvard University Press.

Landau, B., and L. R. Gleitman. 1985. *Language and Experience: Evidence from the Blind Child*. Cambridge, MA: Harvard University Press.

Premack, A. J., and D. Premack. 1972. "Teaching Language to an Ape." *Scientific American* (October): 92–99.

Sebeok, T. A., and J. Umiker-Sebeok. 1980. *Speaking of Apes: A Critical Anthology of Two-Way Communication with Man*. New York: Plenum Press.

Terrace, H. S. 1979. *Nim: A Chimpanzee Who Learned Sign Language*. New York: Knopf.

White, L. 2003. *Second Language Acquisition and Universal Grammar*. Cambridge: Cambridge University Press.

Exercises

1. *Baby talk* is a term used to label the word forms that many adults use when speaking to children. Examples in English are *choo-choo* for "train" and *bow-wow* for "dog." Baby talk seems to exist in every language and culture. At least two things seem to be universal about baby talk: The words that have baby-talk forms fall into certain semantic categories (e.g., food and animals), and the words are phonetically simpler than the adult forms (e.g., "tummy" /tʌmi/ for "stomach" /stʌmɪk/). List all the baby-talk words you can think of in your native language; then (1) separate them into semantic categories, and (2) try to state general rules for the kinds of phonological reductions or simplifications that occur.

2. In this chapter we discussed the way children acquire rules of question formation. The following examples of children's early questions are from a stage that is later than those discussed in the chapter. Formulate a generalization to describe this stage.

Can I go?   Can I can't go?
Why do you have one tooth?   Why you don't have a tongue?
What do frogs eat?   What do you don't like?
Do you like chips?   Do you don't like bananas?

3. Find a child between two and four years old and play with the child for about thirty minutes. Keep a list of all words and/or "sentences" that are used inappropriately. Describe what the child's meanings for these words probably are. Describe the syntactic or morphological errors (including omissions). If the child is producing multiword sentences, write a grammar that could account for the data you have collected.

4. Noam Chomsky has been quoted as saying:

> It's about as likely that an ape will prove to have a language ability as that there is an island somewhere with a species of flightless birds waiting for human beings to teach them to fly.

In the light of evidence presented in this chapter, comment on Chomsky's remark. Do you agree or disagree, or do you think the evidence is inconclusive?

5. Roger Brown and his coworkers at Harvard University studied the language development of three children, referred to in the literature as Adam, Eve, and Sarah. The following are samples of their utterances during the "two-word stage."

see boy   push it
see sock   move it
pretty boat   mommy sleep
pretty fan   bye-bye melon
more taxi   bye-bye hot
more melon

A. Assume that these utterances are grammatical sentences in the children's grammars.

    (1) Write a minigrammar that would account for these sentences.

        Example: One rule might be: VP → V N

    (2) Draw phrase structure trees for each utterance. *Example*:

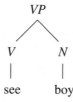

B. One observation made by Brown was that many of the sentences and phrases produced by the children were ungrammatical from the point of view of the adult grammar. The research group concluded, based on utterances such as those below, that a rule in the children's grammar for a noun phrase was:

NP → M N (where M = any modifier)

A coat	My stool	Poor man
A celery	That knee	Little top
A Becky	More coffee	Dirty knee
A hands	More nut	That Adam
My mummy	Two tinker-toy	Big boot

(3) Mark with an asterisk any of the above NPs that are ungrammatical in the adult grammar of English.

(4) State the "violation" for each starred item.

For example, if one of the utterances were *Lotsa book,* you might say: "The modifier *lotsa* must be followed by a plural noun."

6. In the holophrastic (one-word) stage of child language acquisition, the child's phonological system differs in systematic ways from that in the adult grammar. The inventory of sounds and the phonemic contrasts are smaller, and there are greater constraints on phonotactic rules. (See chapter 7 for a discussion of these aspects of phonology.)

A. For each of the following words produced by a child, state what the substitution is, and any other differences that result.

Example:
spook [pʰuk] Substitution: initial cluster [sp] reduced to single consonant; /p/ becomes aspirated, showing that child has acquired aspiration rule.

(1) don't	[dot]
(2) skip	[kʰɪp]
(3) shoe	[su]
(4) that	[dæt]
(5) play	[pʰe]
(6) thump	[dʌp]
(7) bath	[bæt]
(8) chop	[tʰap]
(9) kitty	[kɪdi]
(10) light	[wajt]
(11) dolly	[dawi]
(12) grow	[go]

B. State general rules that account for the children's deviations from the adult pronunciations.

7. Children learn demonstrative words such as *this, that, these, those*; temporal terms such as *now, then, tomorrow*; and spatial terms such as *here, there, right, behind* relatively late. What do all these words have in common? Why might that factor delay their acquisition?

8. We saw in this chapter how children overgeneralize rules such as the plural rule, producing forms such as *mans* or *mouses*. What might a child learning English use instead of the adult words given?

    a. children

    b. went

    c. better

    d. best

    e. brought

    f. sang

    g. geese

    h. worst

    i. knives

    j. worse

9. The following words are from the lexicons of two children ages one year six months (1;6) and two (2;0) years old. Compare the pronunciation of the words to adult pronunciation.

Child 1 (1;6)

soap	[doʊp]	bib	[bɛ]
feet	[bit]	slide	[daj]
sock	[kak]	dog	[da]
goose	[gos]	cheese	[tʃis]
dish	[dɪtʃ]	shoes	[dus]

Child 2 (2.0)

light	[wajt]	bead	[biː]
sock	[sʌk]	pig	[pɛk]
geese	[gis]	cheese	[tis]
fish	[fɪs]	biz	[bɪs]
sheep	[ʃip]	bib	[bɪp]

    a. What happens to final consonants in the language of these two children? Formulate the rule(s) in words. Do all final consonants behave the same way? If not, which consonants undergo the rule(s)? Is this a natural class?

    b. On the basis of these data, do any pairs of words allow you to identify any of the phonemes in the grammars of these children? What are they? Explain how you were able to determine your answer.

10. Make up a "wug test" to test a child's knowledge of the following morphemes:

comparative	-er	(as in *bigger*)
superlative	-est	(as in *biggest*)
progressive	-ing	(as in *I am dancing*)
agentive	-er	(as in *writer*)

11. Children frequently produce sentences such as the following:

Don't giggle me.
I danced the clown.
Yawny Baby – you can push her mouth open to drink her.
Who deaded my kitty cat?
Are you gonna nice yourself?

    a. How would you characterize the difference between the grammar or lexicon of children who produce such sentences and adult English?

    b. Can you think of similar, but well-formed, examples in adult English?

12. Many Arabic speakers tend to insert a vowel in their pronunciation of English words. The first column has examples from L2ers whose L1 is Egyptian Arabic

and the second column from L2ers who speak Iraqi Arabic (consider [tʃ] to be a single consonant):

L1 = Egyptian Arabic

[bilastik]	plastic
[θiriː]	three
[tiransilet]	translate
[silayd]	slide
[firɛd]	Fred
[tʃildiren]	children

L1 = Iraqi Arabic

[ifloːr]	floor
[ibleːn]	plane
[tʃilidren]	children
[iθriː]	three
[istadi]	study
[ifrɛd]	Fred

a. What vowel do the Egyptian Arabic speakers insert and where?

b. What vowel do the Iraqi Arabic speakers insert and where?

c. Based on the position of the epenthetic vowel in the third example, can you guess which list, A or B, belongs to Egyptian Arabic and which belongs to Iraqi Arabic?

Arabic A

kitabta	"I wrote him"
kitabla	"He wrote to him"
kitabɪtla	"I wrote to him"

Arabic B

katabtu	"I wrote him"
katablu	"He wrote to him"
katabtɪlu	"I wrote to him"

13. The following sentences were uttered by children in the telegraphic stage (The second column contains a word-by-word gloss, and the last column is a translation of the sentence that includes elements that the child omitted.):

	Child's utterance	Gloss	Translation
Swedish	Se, blomster har	look flowers have	"Look, (I) have flowers"
English	Tickles me		"It tickles me"
French	Mange du pain	eat some bread	"S/he eats some bread"
German	S[ch]okolade holen	chocolate get	"I/we get chocolate"
Dutch	Earst kleine boekje lezen	first little book read	"First, I/we read a little book"

In each of the children's sentences, the subject is missing, although this is not grammatical in the respective adult languages (in contrast to languages such as Spanish and Italian in which it is grammatical to omit the subject):

A. Develop two hypotheses as to why the child might omit sentence subjects during this stage. For example, one hypothesis might be "children are limited in the length of sentence they can produce, so they drop subjects."

B. Evaluate the different hypotheses. For example, an objection to the hypothesis given in A might be "If length is the relevant factor, why do children consistently drop subjects but not objects?"

9

Language Processing: Humans and Computers

No doubt a reasonable model of language use will incorporate, as a basic component, the generative grammar that expresses the speaker-hearer's knowledge of the language; but this generative grammar does not, in itself, prescribe the character or functioning of a perceptual model or a model of speech production.

NOAM CHOMSKY, Aspects of a Theory of Syntax

The Human Mind at Work: Human Language Processing

Psycholinguistics is the area of linguistics that is concerned with linguistic performance—how we use our linguistic competence—in speech (or sign) production and comprehension. The human brain is able not only to acquire and store the mental lexicon and grammar, but also to access that linguistic storehouse to speak and understand language in real time.

How we process knowledge depends largely on the nature of that knowledge. If, for example, language were not open-ended, and were merely a finite store of fixed phrases and sentences in the memory, then speaking might simply consist of finding a sentence that expresses a thought we wished to convey. Comprehension could be the reverse—matching the sounds to a stored string that has been memorized with its meaning. Of course this is ridiculous! It is not possible because of the creativity of language. In chapter 8, we saw that children do not learn language by imitating and storing sentences, but by constructing a grammar. When we speak, we access our lexicon to find the words, and we use the rules of grammar to construct novel sentences and to produce the sounds that express the message we wish to convey. When we listen to speech and understand what is being said, we also access the lexicon and grammar to assign a structure and meaning to the sounds we hear.

Speaking and comprehending speech can be viewed as a speech chain, a kind of "brain-to-brain" linking, as shown in Figure 9.1.

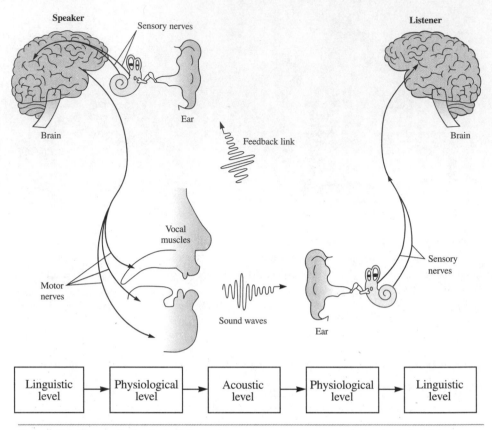

| Linguistic level | → | Physiological level | → | Acoustic level | → | Physiological level | → | Linguistic level |

FIGURE 9.1 The speech chain.[1] A spoken utterance starts as a message in the speaker's brain/mind. It is put into linguistic form and interpreted as articulation commands, emerging as an acoustic signal. The signal is processed by the listener's ear and sent to the brain/mind, where it is interpreted.

The grammar relates sounds and meanings, and contains the units and rules of the language that make speech production and comprehension possible. However, other psychological processes are used to produce and understand utterances. Certain mechanisms enable us to break the continuous stream of speech sounds into linguistic units such as phonemes, syllables, and words in order to comprehend, and to compose sounds into words in order to produce meaningful speech. Other mechanisms determine how we pull words from the mental lexicon, and still others explain how we construct a phrase structure representation of the words we retrieve.

We usually have no difficulty understanding or producing sentences in our language. We do it without effort or conscious awareness of the processes involved. However, we have all had the experience of making a speech error, of having a word on the "tip of our tongue," or of failing to understand a perfectly grammatical sentence, such as sentence (1):

[1] The figure is taken from P. B. Denes and E. N. Pinson, eds. 1963. *The Speech Chain.* Philadelphia, PA: Williams & Wilkins, p. 4. Reprinted with permission of Lucent Technologies, Inc./Bell Labs.

1. The horse raced past the barn fell.

Many individuals, on hearing this sentence, will judge it to be ungrammatical, yet will judge as grammatical a sentence with the same syntactic structure, such as:

2. The bus driven past the school stopped.

Similarly, people will have no problem with sentence (3), which has the same meaning as (1).

3. The horse that was raced past the barn fell.

Conversely, some ungrammatical sentences are easily understandable, such as sentence (4). This mismatch between grammaticality and interpretability tells us that language processing involves more than grammar.

4. *The baby seems sleeping.

A theory of linguistic performance tries to detail the psychological mechanisms that work with the grammar to facilitate language production and comprehension.

Comprehension

"I quite agree with you," said the Duchess; "and the moral of that is—'Be what you would seem to be'—or, if you'd like it put more simply—'Never imagine yourself not to be otherwise than what it might appear to others . . . to be otherwise.'"

"I think I should understand that better," Alice said very politely, "if I had it written down: but I can't quite follow it as you say it."

LEWIS CARROLL, *Alice's Adventures in Wonderland*

The sentence uttered by the Duchess provides another example of a grammatical sentence that is difficult to understand. The sentence is very long and contains several words that require extra resources to process, for example, multiple uses of negation and words like *otherwise*. Alice notes that if she had a pen and paper she could "unpack" this sentence more easily. One of the aims of psycholinguistics is to describe the processes people normally use in speaking and understanding language. The various breakdowns in performance, such as tip of the tongue phenomena, speech errors, and failure to comprehend tricky sentences, can tell us a great deal about how the language processor works, just as children's acquisition errors tell us a lot about the mechanisms involved in language development.

THE SPEECH SIGNAL

Understanding a sentence involves analysis at many levels. To begin with, we must comprehend the individual speech sounds we hear. We are not conscious of the complicated processes we use to understand speech any more than we are conscious of the complicated processes of digesting food and utilizing nutrients. We must study these processes deliberately and scientifically. One of the first questions of linguistic performance concerns segmentation of the acoustic signal. To understand this process, some knowledge of the signal can be helpful.

In chapter 6 we described speech sounds according to the ways in which they are produced. These involve the position of the tongue, the lips, and the velum; the state of the vocal cords; whether the articulators obstruct the free flow of air; and so on. All of these articulatory characteristics are reflected in the physical characteristics of the sounds produced.

Speech sounds can also be described in physical, or **acoustic**, terms. Physically, a sound is produced whenever there is a disturbance in the position of air molecules. The ancient philosophers asked whether a sound is produced if a tree falls in the middle of the forest with no one to hear it. This question has been answered by the science of acoustics. Objectively, a sound is produced; subjectively, there is no sound. In fact, there are sounds we cannot hear because our ears are not sensitive to the full range of frequencies. *Acoustic phonetics* is concerned only with speech sounds, all of which can be heard by the normal human ear.

When we push air out of the lungs through the glottis, it causes the vocal cords to vibrate; this vibration in turn produces pulses of air that escape through the mouth (and sometimes also the nose). These pulses are actually small variations in the air pressure caused by the wavelike motion of the air molecules.

The sounds we produce can be described in terms of how fast the variations of the air pressure occur. This determines the **fundamental frequency** of the sounds and is perceived by the hearer as *pitch*. We can also describe the magnitude, or **intensity**, of the variations, which determines the loudness of the sound. The quality of the speech sound—whether it's an [i] or an [a] or whatever—is determined by the shape of the vocal tract when air is flowing through it. This shape modulates the fundamental frequency into a spectrum of frequencies of greater or lesser intensity, and the particular combination of "greater or lesser" is heard as a particular sound.

An important tool in acoustic research is a computer program that decomposes the speech signal into its frequency components. When speech is fed into a computer (from a microphone or a recording), an image of the speech signal is displayed. The patterns produced are called **spectrograms** or, more vividly, **voiceprints**. A spectrogram of the words *heed, head, had,* and *who'd* is shown in Figure 9.2.

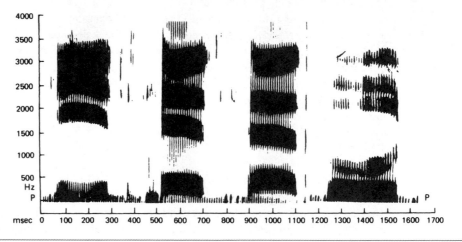

FIGURE 9.2 A spectrogram of the words *heed, head, had,* and *who'd*, spoken with a British accent (speaker: Peter Ladefoged, February 16, 1973).
Courtesy of Peter Ladefoged.

Time in milliseconds moves horizontally from left to right on the x axis; on the y axis the graph represents pitch (or, more technically, frequency). The intensity of each frequency component is indicated by the degree of darkness: the more intense, the darker. Each vowel is characterized by dark bands that differ in their placement according to their frequency. They represent the strongest harmonics produced by the shape of the vocal tract and are called the **formants** of the vowels. (A harmonic is a special frequency that is a multiple (2, 3, etc.) of the fundamental frequency.) Because the tongue is in a different position for each vowel, the formant frequencies differ for each vowel. The frequencies of these formants account for the different vowel qualities you hear. The spectrogram also shows, although not very conspicuously, the pitch of the entire utterance (intonation contour) on the voicing bar marked P. The striations are the thin vertical lines that indicate a single opening and closing of the vocal cords. When the striations are far apart, the vocal cords are vibrating slowly and the pitch is low; when the striations are close together, the vocal cords are vibrating rapidly and the pitch is high.

By studying spectrograms of all speech sounds and many different utterances, acoustic phoneticians have learned a great deal about the basic acoustic components that reflect the articulatory features of speech sounds.

SPEECH PERCEPTION AND COMPREHENSION

Speech is a continuous signal. In natural speech, sounds overlap and influence each other, and yet listeners have the impression that they are hearing discrete units such as words, morphemes, syllables, and phonemes. A central problem of speech perception is to explain how listeners carve up the continuous speech signal into meaningful units. This is referred to as the "segmentation problem."

Another question is, how does the listener manage to recognize particular speech sounds when they occur in different contexts and when they are spoken by different people? For example, how can a speaker tell that a [d] spoken by a man with a very deep voice is the same unit of sound as the [d] spoken in the high-pitched voice of a little child? Acoustically, they are distinct. In addition, a [d] that occurs before the vowel [i] is somewhat different acoustically from a [d] that occurs before the vowel [u]. How does a listener know that two physically distinct instances of a sound are the same? This is referred to as the "lack of invariance problem."

In addressing the latter problem, experimental results show that listeners can calibrate their perceptions to control for differences in the size and shape of the vocal tract of the speaker. Similarly, listeners adjust how they interpret timing information in the speech signal as a function of how quickly the speaker is talking. These *normalization* procedures enable the listener to understand a [d] as a [d] regardless of the speaker or the speech rate. More complicated adjustments are required to factor out the effects of a preceding or following sound.

As we might expect, the units we can perceive depend on the language we know. Speakers of English can perceive the difference between [l] and [r] because these phones represent distinct phonemes in the language. Speakers of Japanese have great difficulty in differentiating the two because they are allophones of one phoneme in their language. Recall from our discussion of language development in chapter 8 that these perceptual biases develop during the first year of life.

Returning to the segmentation problem, spoken words are seldom surrounded by boundaries such as pauses. Nevertheless, words are obviously units of perception. The spaces between them in writing support this view. How do we find the words in the speech stream?

Suppose you heard someone say:

A sniggle blick is procking a slar.

and you were able to perceive the sounds as

[ə s n ɪ g ə l b l ɪ k ɪ z p r a k ĩ ŋ ə s l a r]

You would still be unable to assign a meaning to the sounds, because the meaning of a sentence relies mainly on the meaning of its words, and the only English lexical items in this string are the morphemes *a, is*, and *-ing*. The sentence lacks any English content words. (However, you would accept it as grammatically well-formed because it conforms to the rules of English syntax.)

You can decide that the sentence has no meaning only if you attempt (unconsciously or consciously) to search your mental lexicon for the phonological strings you decide are possible words. This process is called **lexical access**, or word recognition, discussed in detail later. Finding that there are no entries for *sniggle, blick, prock,* and *slar*, you can conclude that the sentence contains nonsense strings. The segmentation and search of these "words" relies on knowing the grammatical morphemes and the syntax. It may not always be possible to find a unique segmentation when unfamiliar words are involved, however, as Sally's difficulties in the cartoon illustrate.

"Peanuts" © United Feature Syndicate, Inc.

If instead you heard someone say *The cat chased the rat*, a similar lexical look-up process would lead you to conclude that an event concerning a cat, a rat, and the activity of chasing had occurred. You could only know this by segmenting the words in the continuous speech signal, analyzing them into their phonological word units, and matching these units to similar strings stored in your lexicon, which also includes the meanings attached to these phonological representations. (This still would not enable you to tell who chased whom, because that requires syntactic analysis.)

Stress and intonation provide some clues to syntactic structure. We know, for example, that the different meanings of the sentences *He lives in the white house* and *He lives in the White House* can be signaled by differences in their stress patterns. Such prosodic aspects of speech also help to segment the speech signal into words and phrases. For example, syllables at the end of a phrase are longer in duration than at the beginning, and intonation contours mark boundaries of clauses.

BOTTOM-UP AND TOP-DOWN MODELS

> I have experimented and experimented until now I know that [water] never does run uphill, except in the dark. I know it does in the dark, because the pool never goes dry; which it would, of course, if the water didn't come back in the night. It is best to prove things by experiment; then you know; whereas if you depend on guessing and supposing and conjecturing, you will never get educated.
>
> MARK TWAIN, Eve's Diary

> In this laboratory the only one who is always right is the cat.
>
> MOTTO IN LABORATORY OF ARTURO ROSENBLUETH

Language comprehension is very fast and automatic. We understand an utterance as fast as we hear it or read it. But we know this understanding must involve (at least) the following suboperations: segmenting the continuous speech signal into phonemes, morphemes, words, and phrases; looking up the words and morphemes in the mental lexicon; finding the appropriate meanings of ambiguous words; parsing them into tree structures; choosing among different possible structures when syntactic ambiguities arise; interpreting the sentence; taking a mental model of the discourse and updating it to reflect the meaning of the new sentence; and other things we do not have space to go into here. This seems like a great deal of work to be done in a very short time: we can understand spoken language at a rate of twenty phonemes per second. One might conclude that there must be some sort of a trick that makes it all possible. In a certain sense there is. Because of the sequential nature of language, a certain amount of guesswork is involved in online comprehension. Many psycholinguists suggest that language perception and comprehension involve **top-down processing** in addition to **bottom-up processing**.

Top-down processes proceed from semantic and syntactic information to the lexical information gained from the sensory input. Through use of such higher-level information, we can try to predict what is to follow in the signal. For example, upon hearing the determiner *the*, the speaker begins constructing an NP and expects that the next word could be a noun, as in *the boy*. In this instance the knowledge of phrase structure would be the source of information.

Bottom-up processing moves step-by-step from the incoming acoustic (or visual) signal to semantic interpretation, building each part of the structure based on the sensory data and accompanying lexical information alone. According to this model the speaker waits until hearing *the* and *boy* before constructing an NP, and then waits for the next word, and so on.

Evidence for top-down processing is found in experiments that require subjects to identify spoken words in the presence of noise. Listeners make more errors when the words occur in isolation than when they occur in sentences. Moreover, they make more errors if the words occur in anomalous, or nonsense, sentences; and they make the most errors if the words occur in ungrammatical sentences. Apparently, subjects are using their knowledge of syntactic and semantic relations to help them narrow down the set of candidate words.

Top-down processing is also supported by a different kind of experiment. Subjects hear recorded sentences in which some part of the signal is removed and a cough or buzz is substituted, such as the underlined "s" in the sentence *The state governors met with their respective legislatures convening in the capital city*. Their experience is that they "hear" the sentence as complete, without any phonemes missing, and, in fact, have difficulty saying exactly where in the word the noise occurred. This effect is called *phoneme restoration*. It would not be surprising simply to find that subjects can guess that the word containing the cough was *legislatures*. What is remarkable is that they really believe they are hearing the [s], even if they are told it is not there. In this case, top-down information apparently overrides bottom-up information.

There is also a role for context (top-down information) in segmentation. In some instances even an utterance containing all familiar words can be divided in more than one way. For example, the sequence [grede] in a discussion of meat or eggs is likely to be heard as *Grade A*, but in a discussion of the weather as *grey day*. In other cases, although the sequence of phonemes might be compatible with two segmentations (e.g., [najtret]), the phonetic details of pronunciation can signal where the word boundary is. In *night rate*, the first [t] is part of the coda of the first syllable and thus unaspirated, whereas in *nitrate* it begins the onset of the second syllable and is therefore aspirated, a fact apparently lost on the writer's of Wiley's Dictionary:

"B.C." © 2001 Creators Syndicate Inc. By permission of John L. Hart FLP, and Creators Syndicate, Inc.

LEXICAL ACCESS AND WORD RECOGNITION

Oh are you from Wales?
Do you know a fella named Jonah?
He used to live in whales for a while.

GROUCHO MARX

Psycholinguists have conducted a great deal of research on *lexical access* or *word recognition*, the process by which we obtain information about the meaning and syntactic properties of a word from our mental lexicon. Several experimental techniques have been used in studies of lexical access.

One technique involves asking subjects to decide whether a string of letters (or sounds if auditory stimuli are used) is or is not a word. They must respond by pressing one button if the stimulus is an actual word and a different button if it is not, so they are making a **lexical decision**. During these and similar experiments, measurements of *response time*, or *reaction time* (often referred to as RTs), are taken. The assumption is that the longer it takes to respond to a particular task, the more processing is involved. RT measurements show that lexical access depends to some extent on word *frequency*; more commonly used words (both spoken and written) such as *car* are responded to more quickly than words that we rarely encounter such as *fig*.

Many properties of lexical access can be examined using lexical decision experiments. In the following example, the relationship between the current word and the immediately preceding word is manipulated. For example, making a lexical decision on the word *doctor* will be faster if you just made a lexical decision on *nurse* than if you just made one on a semantically unrelated word such as *flower*. This effect is known as **semantic priming**: we say that the word *nurse* primes the word *doctor*. This effect might arise because semantically related words are located in the same part of the mental lexicon, so when we hear a priming word and look it up in the lexicon, semantically related, nearby words are "awakened" and more readily accessible for a few moments.

Recent neurolinguistic research is showing the limits of the lexical decision technique. It is now possible to measure electrical brain activity in subjects while they perform a lexical decision experiment, and compare the patterns in brain responses to patterns in RTs. (The technique is similar to the event-related brain potentials mentioned in chapter 2.) Such experiments have provided results that directly conflict with the RT data. For example, measures of brain activity show priming to pairs of verb forms such as *teach/taught* during the early stages of lexical access, whereas such pairs do not show priming in lexical decision RTs. This is because lexical decision involves several stages of processing, and patterns in early stages may be obscured by different patterns in later stages. Brain measures, by contrast, are taken continuously and therefore allow researchers to separately measure early and later processes.

One of the most interesting facts about lexical access is that listeners retrieve all meanings of a word even when the sentence containing the word is biased toward one of the meanings. This is shown in experiments in which the ambiguous word primes words related to both of its meanings. For example, suppose a subject hears the sentence:

The gypsy read the young man's palm for only a dollar.

Palm primes the word *hand*, so in a lexical decision about *hand*, a shorter RT occurs than in a comparable sentence not containing the word *palm*. However, a shorter RT also occurs for the word *tree*. The other meaning of *palm* (as in *palm tree*) is apparently activated even though that meaning is not a part of the meaning of the priming sentence.

In listening or reading, then, all of the meanings represented by a string of letters and sounds will be triggered. This argues for a limit on the effects of top-down processing because the individual word *palm* is heard and processed somewhat independently of its context, and so is capable of priming words related to all its lexical meanings. However, the disambiguating information in the sentence is used very quickly (within 250 milliseconds) to discard the meanings that are not appropriate to the sentence. If we check for priming after the word *only* instead of right after the word *palm* in the previous example, we find it for *hand* but no longer for *tree*.

Another experimental technique, called the **naming task**, asks the subject to read aloud a printed word. (A variant of the naming task is also used in studies of people with aphasia, who are asked to name the object shown in a picture.) Subjects read irregularly spelled words like *dough* and *steak* just slightly more slowly than regularly spelled words like *doe* and *stake*, but still faster than invented strings like *cluff*. This suggests that people can do two different things in the naming task. They can look for the string in their mental lexicon, and if they find it (i.e., if it is a real word), they can pronounce the stored phonological representation for it. They can also "sound it out," using their knowledge of how certain letters or letter sequences (e.g., "gh," "oe") are most commonly pronounced. The latter is obviously the only way to come up with a pronunciation for a nonexisting word.

The fact that irregularly spelled words are slower than regularly spelled real words suggests that the mind "notices" the irregularity. This may be because the brain is trying to do two tasks—lexical look-up and sounding out the word—in parallel in order to perform naming as fast as possible. When the two approaches yield inconsistent results, a conflict arises that takes some time to resolve.

Syntactic Processing

Teacher Strikes Idle Kids
Enraged Cow Injures Farmer with Ax
Killer Sentenced to Die for Second Time in 10 Years
Stolen Painting Found by Tree

AMBIGUOUS HEADLINES

Psycholinguistic research has also focused on syntactic processing. In addition to recognizing words, the listener must figure out the syntactic and semantic relations among the words and phrases in a sentence, what we earlier referred to as "parsing." The parsing of a sentence is largely determined by the rules of the grammar, but it is also strongly influenced by the sequential nature of language.

Listeners actively build a phrase structure representation of a sentence as they hear it. They must therefore decide for each "incoming" word what its grammatical category is and how it attaches to the tree that is being constructed. Many sentences present temporary ambiguities, such as a word or words that belong to more than one syntactic category. For example, the string *The warehouse fires* . . . could continue in one of two ways:

1. . . . were set by an arsonist.
2. . . . employees over sixty.

Fires is part of a compound noun in sentence (1) and is a verb in sentence (2). As noted earlier, experimental studies of such sentences show that both meanings and categories are activated when a subject encounters the ambiguous word. The ambiguity is quickly resolved (hence the term *temporary ambiguity*) based on syntactic and semantic context, and on the frequency of the two uses of the word. The disambiguations are so quick and seamless that unintentionally ambiguous newspaper headlines such as those at the head of this section are scarcely noticeable except to linguists who collect them.

Another important type of temporary ambiguity concerns sentences in which the phrase structure rules allow two possible attachments of a constituent, as illustrated by the following example:

After the child visited the doctor prescribed a course of injections.

Experiments that track eye movements of people when they read such sentences show that there may be attachment preferences that operate independently of the context or meaning of the sentence. When the mental syntactic processor, or parser, receives the word *doctor*, it attaches it as a direct object of the verb *visit* in the subordinate clause. For this reason, subjects experience a strange perceptual effect when they encounter the verb *prescribed*. They must "change their minds" and attach *the doctor* as subject of the main clause instead. Sentences that induce this effect are called **garden path sentences**. The sentence presented at the beginning of this chapter, *The horse raced past the barn fell*, is also a garden path sentence. People naturally interpret *raced* as the main verb, when in fact the main verb is *fell*.

The initial attachment choices that lead people astray may reflect general principles used by the parser to deal with syntactic ambiguity. Two such principles that have been suggested are known as **Minimal Attachment** and **Late Closure**. Minimal Attachment says "Build the simplest structure consistent with the grammar of the language." In the string *The horse raced . . .*, the simpler structure is the one in which *the horse* is the subject and *raced* the main verb; the more complex structure is similar to *The horse that was raced . . .* We can think of simple versus complex here in terms of the amount of structure in the syntactic tree for the sentence so far.

The second principle, Late Closure, says "Attach incoming material to the phrase that is currently being processed." Late Closure is exemplified in the following sentence:

The doctor said the patient will die yesterday.

Readers often experience a garden path effect at the end of this sentence because their initial inclination is to construe *yesterday* as modifying *will die*, which is semantically incongruous. Late Closure explains this: The hearer encounters *yesterday* as he is processing the embedded clause, of which *die* is the main verb. On the other hand, the verb *said*, which *yesterday* is supposed to modify, is part of the root clause, which hasn't been worked on for the past several words. The hearer must therefore backtrack to attach *yesterday* to the clause containing *said*.

The comprehension of sentences depends on syntactic processing that uses the grammar in combination with special parsing principles to construct trees. Garden path sentences like those we have been discussing suggest that the mental parser sometimes makes a strong commitment to one of the possible parses. Whether it always does so, and whether this means it completely ignores all other parses, are open questions that are still being investigated by linguists.

Another striking example of processing difficulty is a rewording of a Mother Goose poem. In its original form we have:

This is the dog that worried the cat that killed the rat that ate the malt that lay in the house that Jack built.

No problem understanding that? Now try this equivalent description:

> *Jack built the house that the malt that the rat that the cat that the dog worried killed ate lay in.*

No way, right?

Although the confusing sentence follows the rules of relative clause formation— you have little difficulty with *the cat that the dog worried*—it seems that once is enough, and when you apply the same process twice, getting *the rat that the cat that the dog worried killed*, it becomes quite difficult to process. If we apply the process three times, as in *the malt that the rat that the cat that the dog worried killed ate*, all hope is lost.

The difficulty in parsing this kind of sentence is related to memory constraints. In processing the sentence, you have to keep *the malt* in mind all the way until *ate*, but while doing that you have to keep *the rat* in mind all the way until *killed*, and while doing that . . . It's a form of structure juggling that is difficult to perform; we evidently don't have enough memory capacity to keep track of all the necessary items. Though we have the competence to create such sentences—in fact we have the competence to make a sentence with 10,000 words in it—performance limitations prevent creation of such monstrosities.

Various experimental techniques are used to study sentence comprehension. In addition to the priming and reading tasks, in a **shadowing task** subjects are asked to repeat what they hear as rapidly as possible. Exceptionally good shadowers can follow what is being said only about a syllable behind (300 milliseconds). Most of us, however, shadow with a delay of 500 to 800 milliseconds, which is still quite fast. More interestingly, fast shadowers often correct speech errors or mispronunciations unconsciously and add inflectional endings if they are absent. Even when they are told that the speech they are to shadow includes errors and they should repeat the errors, they are rarely able to do so. Corrections are more likely to occur when the target word is predictable from what has been said previously.

These shadowing experiments make at least two points: (1) they support extremely rapid use of top-down information: differences in predictability have an effect within about one-quarter of a second; and (2) they show how fast the mental parser does grammatical analysis, because some of the errors that are corrected, such as missing agreement inflections, depend on successfully parsing the immediately preceding words.

The ability to comprehend what is said to us is a complex psychological process involving the internal grammar, parsing principles such as Minimal Attachment and Late Closure, frequency factors, memory, and both linguistic and nonlinguistic context.

Speech Production

> Speech was given to the ordinary sort of men whereby to communicate their mind; but to wise men, whereby to conceal it.
>
> **ROBERT SOUTH,** Sermon *(1676)*

As we saw, the speech chain starts with a speaker who, through some complicated set of neuromuscular processes, produces an acoustic signal that represents a thought, idea, or message to be conveyed to a listener, who must then decode the signal to arrive at a similar message. It is more difficult to devise experiments that provide information about how the speaker proceeds than to do so from the listener's side of the process. Much of the best information has come from observing and analyzing spontaneous speech.

PLANNING UNITS

We might suppose that speakers' thoughts are simply translated into words one after the other via a semantic mapping process. Grammatical morphemes would be added as demanded by the syntactic rules of the language. The phonetic representation of each word in turn would then be mapped onto the neuromuscular commands to the articulators to produce the acoustic signal representing it.

We know, however, that this is not a true picture of speech production. Although sounds within words and words within sentences are linearly ordered, speech errors, or slips of the tongue (also discussed in chapter 7), show that the prearticulation stages involve units larger than the single phonemic segment or even the word, as illustrated by the "U.S. Acres" cartoon. That error is an example of a **spoonerism**, named after William Archibald Spooner, a distinguished head of an Oxford College in the early 1900s who is reported to have referred to Queen Victoria as "That queer old dean" instead of "That dear old queen," and berated his class of students by saying, "You have hissed my mystery lecture. You have tasted the whole worm" instead of the intended, "You have missed my history lecture. You have wasted the whole term."

In fact, phrases and even whole sentences can be constructed before the production of a single sound. Errors show that features, segments, words, and phrases can be anticipated, that is, produced earlier than intended, or reversed (as in typical spoonerisms), so the later words or phrases in which those elements are intended to occur must already be conceptualized. This point is illustrated in the following examples of speech errors (the intended utterance is to the left of the arrow; the actual utterance, including the error, is to the right of the arrow):

1. The *h*iring of minority faculty. $\rightarrow$ The *f*iring of minority faculty.
   (The intended *h* is replaced by the *f* of *faculty*, which occurs later in the intended utterance.)
2. *a*d h*o*c $\rightarrow$ *o*dd h*a*ck
   (The vowels /æ/ of the first word and /ɑ/ of the second are exchanged or reversed.)

3. *b*ig and *f*at → *p*ig and *v*at
(The values of a single feature are switched: in *big* [+ voiced] becomes [−voiced] and in *fat* [− voiced] becomes [+ voiced].)

4. There are many ministers in our church. → There are many churches in our minister.
(The stem morphemes *minister* and *church* are exchanged; the grammatical plural morpheme remains in its intended place in the phrase structure.)

5. Seymour sliced the salami with a knife. → Seymour sliced a knife with the salami.
(The entire noun phrases—article + noun—were exchanged.)

In these errors, the intonation contour (primary stressed syllables and variations in pitch) remained the same as in the intended utterances, even when the words were rearranged. In the intended utterance of (5), the highest pitch would be on *knife*. In the misordered sentence, the highest pitch occurred on the second syllable of *salami*. The pitch rise and increased loudness are thus determined by the syntactic structure of the sentence and are independent of the individual words. Thus syntactic structures exist independent of the words that occupy them, and intonation contours can be mapped onto those structures without being associated with particular words.

Errors like those just cited are constrained in interesting ways. Phonological errors involving segments or features, as in (1), (2), and (3), primarily occur in content words, and not in grammatical morphemes, showing the distinction between these lexical classes. In addition, while words and lexical morphemes may be interchanged, grammatical morphemes may not be. We do not find errors like *The boying are sings* for *The boys are singing*. Typically, as example (4) illustrates, the inflectional endings are left behind when lexical morphemes switch and subsequently attach, in their proper phonological form, to the moved lexical morpheme.

Errors like those in (1)–(5) show that speech production operates in real time with features, segments, morphemes, words, phrases—the very units that exist in the grammar. They also show that when we speak, words are chosen and sequenced quite a while ahead of when they are articulated. Thus, we do not select one word from our mental dictionary and say it, then select another word and say it.

LEXICAL SELECTION

> Humpty Dumpty's theory, of two meanings packed into one word like a portmanteau, seems to me the right explanation for all. For instance, take the two words "fuming" and "furious." Make up your mind that you will say both words but leave it unsettled which you will say first. Now open your mouth and speak. If . . . you have that rarest of gifts, a perfectly balanced mind, you will say "frumious."
>
> **LEWIS CARROLL,** *Preface to* The Hunting of the Snark

In chapter 5, word substitution errors were used to illustrate the semantic properties of words. Such substitutions are seldom random; they show that in our attempt to express our thoughts by speaking words in the lexicon, we may make an incorrect lexical selection based on partial similarity or relatedness of meanings.

Blends, in which we produce part of one word and part of another, further illustrate the lexical selection process in speech production; we may select two or more words to express our thoughts and instead of deciding between them, we produce them as "portmanteaus," as Humpty Dumpty calls them. Such blends are illustrated in the following errors:

1. splinters/blisters   →   splisters
2. edited/annotated   →   editated
3. a swinging/hip chick   →   a swip chick
4. frown/scowl   →   frowl

These blend errors are typical in that the segments stay in the same position within the syllable as they were in the target words. This is not true in the previous example made up by Lewis Carroll: a much more likely blend of *fuming* and *furious* would be *fumious* or *furing*.

APPLICATION AND MISAPPLICATION OF RULES

> I thought . . . four rules would be enough, provided that I made a firm and constant resolution not to fail even once in the observance of them.
>
> **RENÉ DESCARTES** *(1596–1650)*

Spontaneous errors show that the rules of morphology and syntax, discussed in earlier chapters as part of competence, may also be applied (or misapplied) when we speak. It is difficult to see this process in normal error-free speech, but when someone says *groupment* instead of *grouping*, *ambigual* instead of *ambiguous*, or *bloodent* instead of *bloody*, it shows that regular rules are applied to combine morphemes and form possible but nonexistent words.

Inflectional rules also surface. The UCLA professor who said *We swimmed in the pool* knows that the past tense of *swim* is *swam*, but he mistakenly applied the regular rule to an irregular form.

Morphophonemic rules also appear to be performance rules as well as rules of competence. Consider the *a/an* alternation rule in English. Errors such as *an istem* for the intended *a system* or *a burly bird* for the intended *an early bird* show that when segmental misordering changes a noun beginning with a consonant to a noun beginning with a vowel, or vice versa, the indefinite article is also changed so that it conforms to the grammatical rule.

Speakers hardly ever produce errors like *an burly bird* or *a istem*, which tells us something about the stages in the production of an utterance. The rule that determines whether *a* or *an* should be produced (*an* precedes a vowel; *a* precedes a consonant) must apply after the stage at which *early* has slipped to *burly*; that is, the stage at which /b/ has been anticipated. If *a/an* were selected first, the article would be *an* (or else the rule must reapply after the initial error has occurred). Similarly, an error such as *bin beg* for the intended *Big Ben* shows that phonemes are misordered before allophonic rules apply. That is, the intended *Big Ben* phonetically is [bɪg bɛ̃n] with an oral [ɪ] before the [g], and a nasal [ɛ̃] before the [n]. In the utterance that was produced, however, the [ɪ] is nasalized because it now occurs before the misordered [n], whereas the [ɛ̃] is oral before the misordered [g]. If the misordering occurred after the phonemes had undergone allophonic rules such as nasalization, the result would have been the phonetic utterance [bɪ̃n bɛg].

Nonlinguistic Influences

The discussion on speech comprehension suggested that nonlinguistic factors can be involved in—and sometimes interfere with—linguistic processing. They also affect speech production. The individual who said *He made hairlines* instead of *He made headlines* was referring to a barber. The fact that the two compound nouns both start with the same sound, are composed of two syllables, have the same stress pattern, and contain the identical second morphemes undoubtedly played a role in producing the error, but the relationship between hairlines and barbers may also have been a contributing factor. Similar comments apply to the congressional representative who said, "It can deliver a large *payroll*" instead of "It can deliver a large *payload*," in reference to a bill to fund the building of bomber aircraft.

Other errors show that thoughts unrelated in form to the intended utterance may have an influence on what is said. One speaker said, "I've never heard of classes *on April 9*" instead of the intended *on Good Friday*. Good Friday fell on April 9 that year. The two phrases are not similar phonologically or morphologically, yet the nonlinguistic association seems to have influenced what was said.

Both normal conversational data and experimentally elicited data provide the psycholinguist with evidence for the construction of models both of speech production and of comprehension, the beginning and ending points of the speech chain of communication.

Computer Processing of Human Language

> Man is still the most extraordinary computer of all.
>
> JOHN F. KENNEDY

Until a few decades ago, language was strictly "humans only—others need not apply." Today, it is common for computers to process language. **Computational linguistics** is a subfield of linguistics and computer science that is concerned with the interactions of human language and computers.

Computational linguistics includes the analysis of written texts and spoken discourse, the translation of text and speech from one language into another, the use of *human* (not computer) languages for communication between computers and people, and the modeling and testing of linguistic theories.

Frequency Analysis, Concordances, and Collocations

> [The professor had written] all the words of their language in their several moods, tenses and declensions [on tiny blocks of wood, and had] emptied the whole vocabulary into his frame, and made the strictest computation of the general proportion there is in books between the numbers of particles, nouns, and verbs, and other parts of speech.
>
> JONATHAN SWIFT, Gulliver's Travels

Jonathan Swift prophesied one application of computers to language: statistical analysis. The relative frequencies (i.e., the "general proportions") of letters and sounds, morphemes, words, word categories, types of phrases, and so on may be swiftly and accurately computed for any textual or spoken input, or **corpus**.

A frequency analysis of one million words of written American English reveals the ten most frequently occurring words: *the, of, and, to, a, in, that, is, was*, and *he*. These "little" words accounted for about 25 percent of the words in the corpus, with *the* leading the pack at 7 percent. A similar analysis of *spoken* American English produced somewhat different results. The "winners" were *I, and, the, to, that, you, it, of, a*, and *know*, accounting for nearly 30 percent. This is but one of the differences between spoken and written language demonstrated by corpus analysis. All English prepositions except *to* occur more frequently in written than in spoken English, and not surprisingly, profane and taboo words (see chapter 10) were far more numerous in spoken than written language.

A **concordance** takes frequency analysis one step further by specifying the location within the text of each word and its surrounding context. A concordance of the previous paragraph would not only show that the word *words* occurred five times, but would indicate in which line of the paragraph it appeared, and provide its context. If one chose a "window" of three words on either side for context, the concordance would look like this for *words*:

of one million	**words**	of written American
most frequently occurring	**words**:	*the, of, and,*
These "little"	**words**	accounted for about
percent of the	**words**,	in the corpus
profane and taboo	**words**	(see chapter 10)

A concordance, as you can see, might be of limited usefulness because of its "raw" nature. A way to refine a concordance is through **collocation analysis**. A collocation is the occurrence of two or more words within a short space of each other in a corpus. The point is to find evidence that the presence of one word in the text affects the occurrence of other words. Such an analysis must be statistical and involve large samples to show significant results. In the previous concordance of *words*, there is not enough data to be significant. If we performed a concordance on this entire book, patterns would emerge that would show that *words* and *written, words* and *taboo*, and *words* and *of*, are more likely to occur close together than, say, *words* and *million*.

Such analyses can be conducted on existing texts (such as the works of Shakespeare or the Bible) or on any corpus of utterances gathered from spoken or written sources. Authorship attribution is one motivation for these studies. By analyzing the various books of the Bible, for instance, it is possible to get a sense of who wrote what passages. In a notable study of The Federalist Papers, the authorship of a disputed paper was attributed to James Madison rather than to Alexander Hamilton. This was accomplished by comparing the statistical analyses of the paper in question with those of known works by the two writers.

A concordance of sounds by computer may reveal patterns in poetry that would be nearly impossible for a human to detect. An analysis of the *Iliad* showed that many of the lines with an unusual number of etas (/i/) related to youth and lovemaking; the line with the most alphas (/a/) was interpreted as being an imitation of stamping feet, the marching of armies. The use of computers permits literary scholars to study poetic and prosaic features such as assonance, alliteration, meter, and rhythm. Today, computers can do the tedious mechanical work that once had to be done painstakingly with paper and pencil.

Information Retrieval and Summarization

Hired
Tired
Fired

A CAREER SUMMARY, *source obscure*

Many people use the search features of the Internet to find information. Typically, one enters a keyword, or perhaps several, and magically the computer returns the location of Web sites that contain information relating to that keyword. This process is an example of **information retrieval**. It may be as trivial as finding Web sites that contain the keyword exactly as it is entered, but usually some linguistic analysis is applied. Web sites are returned, and even ranked, according to the frequency of occurrence of the keyword, different morphological forms of the keyword, synonyms of the keyword, and concepts semantically related to the keyword. For example, the keyword *bird* might retrieve information based on *bird, birds, to bird* (verb infinitive), *bird feeders, water birds, avian, sparrow, feathers, flight, migration,* and so on.

In general, information retrieval is the use of computers to locate and display data gleaned from possibly very large databases. The input to an information retrieval system consists of words, statements, or questions, which the computer analyzes linguistically and then uses the results to sift through the database for pertinent information. Nowadays, complex information retrieval systems identify useful patterns or relationships in corpuses or other computer repositories using advanced linguistic and statistical analyses. The term **data mining** is used currently for the highly evolved information retrieval systems.

A keyword as general as *bird* may return far more information than could be read in ten lifetimes if a thorough search of the Web occurs. (A search on the day of this writing produced 122,000,000 hits.) Much of the data would repeat, and some information would outweigh other information. Through **summarization** programs, computers can eliminate redundancy and identify the most salient features of a body of information. World leaders, corporate executives, and even university professors—all of whom may wish to digest large volumes of textual material such as reports, newspapers, and scholarly articles—can benefit through summarization processes providing the material is available in computer-readable form, which is increasingly the case in the first few years of the twenty-first century.

A typical scenario would be to use information retrieval to access, say, a hundred articles about birds. The articles may average 5,000 words each. Summarization programs, which can be set to reduce an article by a certain amount, say 1/10 or 1/100, are applied. The human reads the final output. Thus 500,000 words can be reduced to 5,000 or 10,000 words containing the most pertinent information, which may then be read in 10 or 20 minutes. Former President Bill Clinton—a fast reader—could absorb the contents of relevant articles from more than 100 news sources from around the world with the help of aides using computer summarizations.

Summarization programs range from the simplistic "print the first sentence of every paragraph" to complex programs that analyze the document semantically to identify the important points, often using "concept vectors." A *concept vector* is a list of meaningful keywords whose presence in a paragraph is a measure of the paragraph's significance, and therefore an indication of whether the content of that paragraph should be included in a summarization. The summary document contains concepts from as many of the key paragraphs as possible, subject to length constraints.

Spell Checkers

Take care that you never spell a word wrong . . . It produces great praise to a lady to spell well.

THOMAS JEFFERSON

Spell checkers, and perhaps in the future, pronunciation checkers, are an application of computational linguistics that vary in sophistication from mindless, brute-force lookups in a dictionary, to enough intelligence to flag *your* when it should be *you're*, or *bear* when *bare* is intended. One often finds spell checkers as front ends to information retrieval systems, checking the keywords to prevent misspellings from misleading the search. However, as the following poem reveals, spell checkers cannot replace careful editing:

I have a spelling checker.
It came with my PC.
It plane lee marks four my revue
Miss steaks aye can knot sea.
A checker is a bless sing,
It freeze yew lodes of thyme.
It helps me right awl stiles to reed,
And aides me when aye rime.
To rite with care is quite a feet
Of witch won should bee proud,
And wee mussed dew the best wee can,
Sew flaws are knot aloud.

"Candidate for a Pullet Surprise," **THE JOURNAL OF IRREPRODUCIBLE RESULTS** *(www.jir.com)*

Machine Translation

Egad, I think the interpreter is the hardest to be understood of the two!

R. B. SHERIDAN, The Critic

There exist extremely simple sentences in English—and . . . for any other natural language—which would be uniquely . . . and unambiguously translated into any other language by anyone with a sufficient knowledge of the two languages involved, though I know of no program that would enable a machine to come up with this unique rendering.

YEHOSHUA BAR-HILLEL

President Clinton required information from sources written in many languages, and translators worked hard to fulfill the president's demand. Scholars and business personnel have a similar need, and that need has existed since the dawn of human writing (see chapter 12).

The first use of computers for natural language processing began in the 1940s with the attempt to develop **automatic machine translation**. During World War II, Allied scientists, without the assistance of computers, deciphered coded enemy communications and proved their skill in coping with difficult language problems. The idea of using deciphering techniques to translate from one language into another was expressed in a letter written to cyberneticist Norbert Wiener by Warren Weaver, a pioneer in the field of computational linguistics: "When I look at any article in Russian, I say: 'This is really written in English, but it has been coded in some strange symbols. I will now proceed to decode it.'"[2]

The aim in automatic translation is to input a written passage in the **source language** and to receive a grammatical passage of equivalent meaning in the **target language** (the output). In the early days of machine translation, it was believed that this task could be accomplished by entering into the memory of a computer a dictionary of a source language and a dictionary with the corresponding morphemes and words of a target language. The translating program attempted to match the morphemes of the input sentence with those of the target language. Unfortunately, what often happened was a process that early experimenters with machine translation called "language in, garbage out."

Translation is more than word-for-word replacement. Often there is no equivalent word in the target language, and the order of words may differ, as in translating from an SVO language like English to an SOV language like Japanese. There is also difficulty in translating idioms, metaphors, jargon, and so on. Human translators cope with these problems because they know the grammars of the two languages and draw on general knowledge of the subject matter and the world to arrive at the intended meaning. Machine translation is often impeded by lexical and syntactic ambiguities, structural disparities between the two languages, morphological complexities, and other cross-linguistic differences. It is often difficult to get good translations even when humans do the translating, as is illustrated by some of the "garbage" printed on signs in non-English-speaking countries as "aids" to tourists:

> The lift is being fixed for the next day. During that time we regret that you will be unbearable. (Bucharest hotel lobby)
>
> The nuns harbor all diseases and have no respect for religion. (Swiss nunnery hospital)
>
> All the water has been passed by the manager. (German hotel)
>
> Because of the impropriety of entertaining guest of the opposite sex in the bedroom, it is suggested that the lobby be used for this purpose. (Hotel in Zurich)
>
> The government bans the smoking of children. (Turkey)

Similar problems are evident in this brief excerpt of the translation of an interview of the entertainer Madonna in the Hungarian newspaper *Blikk*:

> *Blikk*: Madonna, let's cut toward the hunt: Are you a bold hussy-woman that feasts on men who are tops?

---

[2] W. N. Locke and A. D. Boothe, eds. 1955. *Machine Translation of Languages*. New York: Wiley.

> *Madonna*: Yes, yes, this is certainly something that brings to the surface my longings. In America it is not considered to be mentally ill when a woman advances on her prey in a discotheque setting with hardy cocktails present.

Such "translations" represent the difficulties of finding the right words, but word choice is not the only problem in automatic translation. There are challenges in morphology when translating between languages. A word like *ungentlemanliness* is certainly translatable into any language, but few languages are likely to have an exact word with that meaning, so a phrase of several words is needed. Similarly, *mbuki-mvuki* is a Swahili word that means "to shuck off one's clothes in order to dance." English does not have a word for that practice, but not for lack of need.

Syntactic problems are equally challenging. English is a language that allows possessive forms of varying syntactic complexity, such as *that man's son's dog's food dish*, or *the guy that my roommate is dating's cousin*. Translating these sentences without a loss of meaning into languages that prohibit such structures requires a great deal of sentence restructuring.

We have been implicitly discussing translation of written texts. What about the translation of speech from one language to another? On the one side, speech recognition is needed—or "speech-to-text." On the other side, "text-to-speech" is required. The most general machine translation scenario—that of speech-to-speech—encapsulates the areas of computational linguistics concerned with computers utilizing human grammars to communicate with humans, or to assist humans in communicating with each other. Diagrammatically, we have a progression like the flowchart in Figure 9.3.

FIGURE 9.3 Logic flow of machine translation of speech.

Computers That Talk and Listen

> The first generations of computers had received their inputs through glorified typewriter keyboards, and had replied through high-speed printers and visual displays. Hal could do this when necessary, but most of his communication with his shipmates was by means of the spoken words. Poole and Bowman could talk to Hal as if he were a human being, and he would reply in the perfect idiomatic English he had learned during the fleeting weeks of his electronic childhood.
>
> **ARTHUR C. CLARKE,** 2001, A Space Odyssey

The ideal computer is multilingual; it should "speak" computer languages such as FORTRAN and Java, and human languages such as French and Japanese. For many purposes it would be helpful if we could communicate with computers as we communicate with other humans, through our native language, but the computers portrayed in films and on television as capable of speaking and understanding human language do not yet exist.

The translation processes of Figure 9.3 summarize the areas of computational linguistics concerned with human-machine communication. Speech-to-text on the one end, and text-to-speech on the other end, are the chief concern of **computational phonetics and phonology**. The tasks of machine understanding and of language generation, whether for purposes of translation into a target language or as part of the human-machine communication process, encompasses **computational morphology**, **computational syntax**, **computational semantics**, and **computational pragmatics**, all of which are discussed in the following sections.

COMPUTATIONAL PHONETICS AND PHONOLOGY

Computational phonetics and phonology has two concerns. The first is with programming computers to analyze the speech signal into its component phones and phonemes. The second is to send the proper signals to an electronic speaker so that it enunciates the phones of the language and combines them into morphemes and words. The first of these is **speech recognition**; the second is **speech synthesis**.

Speech Recognition

> When Frederic was a little lad he proved so brave and daring,
> His father thought he'd 'prentice him to some career seafaring.
> I was, alas! his nurs'rymaid, and so it fell to my lot
> To take and bind the promising boy apprentice to a pilot—
> A life not bad for a hardy lad, though surely not a high lot,
> Though I'm a nurse, you might do worse than make your boy a pilot.
> I was a stupid nurs'rymaid, on breakers always steering,
> And I did not catch the word aright, through being hard of hearing;
> Mistaking my instructions, which within my brain did gyrate
> I took and bound this promising boy apprentice to a pirate.
>
> THE PIRATES OF PENZANCE, Gilbert and Sullivan, *1877*

When you listen to someone speak a foreign language, you notice that it is continuous except for breath pauses, and that it is difficult to segment the speech into sounds and words. It's all run together. The computer faces this situation when it tries to do speech recognition.

Early speech recognizers did not even attempt to "hear" individual sounds. Programmers stored the acoustic patterns of words in the memory of the computer and programmed it to look for those patterns in the speech signal. The computer had a fixed, small vocabulary. Moreover, it best recognized the speech of the same person who provided the original word patterns. It would have trouble "understanding" a different speaker, and if a word outside the vocabulary was uttered, the computer was clueless. If the words were run together, recognition accuracy also fell, and if the words were not fully pronounced, say *missipi* for Mississippi, failure generally ensued. Coarticulation effects also muddied the waters. The computer might have [hɪz] as its representation of the word *his*, but in the sequence *his soap*, pronounced [hɪssop], the *his* is pronounced [hɪs] with a voiceless [s]. In addition, the vocabulary best consisted of words that were not too similar phonetically, avoiding confusion between words like *pilot* and *pirate*, which might, as with the young lad in the song, have grave consequences.

Today, many interactive phone systems have a speech recognition component. They will invite you to "press 1 or say 'yes'; press 2 or say 'no,'" or something similar. These systems have very small vocabularies and so can search the speech signal for anything resembling prestored acoustic patterns of a keyword and generally get it right.

The more sophisticated speech recognizers that can be purchased for use on a personal computer have much larger vocabularies, upwards of 25,000 words. To be highly accurate they must be trained to the voice of a specific person, and they must be able to detect individual phones in the speech signal. The training consists in the user making multiple utterances known in advance to the computer, which extracts the acoustic patterns of each phone typical of that user. Later the computer uses those patterns to aid in the recognition process.

Because no two utterances are ever identical, and because there is generally noise (nonspeech sounds) in the signal, the matching process that underlies speech recognition is statistical. On the phonetic level, the computations may classify some stretch of sound in its input as [l] with 65 percent confidence and [r] with 35 percent confidence. Other factors may be used to help the decision. For example, if the computer is confident that the preceding sound is [d] and begins the word, then [r] is the likely candidate, because no words begin with /dl/ in English. The system takes advantage of its (i.e., the programmer's) knowledge of sequential constraints (see chapter 7). If, on the other hand, the sound occurs at the beginning of the word, further information is needed to determine whether it is the phoneme /l/ or /r/. If the following sounds are [up] then /l/ is the one, because *loop* is a word but **roop* is not. If the computer is unable to decide, it may offer a list of choices such as *lack, rack,* and ask the person using the system to decide.

Even these modern systems are brittle. They break when circumstances become unfavorable. If the user speaks rapidly with lots of coarticulation (*whatcha* for *what are you*), and there is a lot of background noise, recognition accuracy plummets. People do better. If someone mumbles, you can generally make out what they are saying because you have context to help you. In a noisy setting such as a party, you are able to converse with your dance partner despite the background noise because your brain has the ability to filter out irrelevant sounds and zero in on the voice of a single speaker. This effect is so striking it is given a name: the **cocktail party effect**. Computers are not nearly as capable of coping with noise as people, although research directed at the problem is beginning to show positive results.

Speech Synthesis

> Machines which, with more or less success, imitate human speech, are the most difficult to construct, so many are the agencies engaged in uttering even a single word—so many are the inflections and variations of tone and articulation, that the mechanician finds his ingenuity taxed to the utmost to imitate them.
>
> *SCIENTIFIC AMERICAN (January 14, 1871)*

> Speak clearly, if you speak at all; carve every word before you let it fall.
>
> OLIVER WENDELL HOLMES, SR.

Early efforts toward building "talking machines" were concerned with machines that could produce sounds that imitated human speech. In 1779, Christian Gottlieb Kratzenstein won a prize for building such a machine. It was "an instrument constructed like the vox humana pipes of an organ which . . . accurately express the sounds of the vowels." In building this machine he also answered a question posed by the Imperial Academy of St. Petersburg: "What is the nature and character of the sounds of the vowels *a, e, i, o, u* [that make them] different from one another?" Kratzenstein constructed a set of "acoustic resonators" similar to the shapes of the mouth when these vowels are articulated and set them resonating by a vibrating reed that produced pulses of air similar to those coming from the lungs through the vibrating vocal cords.

Twelve years later, Wolfgang von Kempelen of Vienna constructed a more elaborate machine with bellows to produce a stream of air to simulate the lungs, and with other mechanical devices to simulate the different parts of the vocal tract. Von Kempelen's machine so impressed the young Alexander Graham Bell, who saw a replica of the machine in Edinburgh in 1850, that he, with his brother Melville, attempted to construct a "talking head," making a cast from a human skull. They used various materials to form the velum, palate, teeth, lips, tongue, cheeks, and so on, and installed a metal larynx with vocal cords made by stretching a slotted piece of rubber. They used a keyboard control system to manipulate all the parts with an intricate set of levers. This ingenious machine produced vowel sounds, some nasal sounds, and even a few short combinations of sounds.

With the advances in the acoustic theory of speech production, and the technological developments in electronics, machine production of speech sounds has made great progress. We no longer have to build physical models of the speech-producing mechanism; we can now imitate the process by producing the physical signals electronically.

Research on speech has shown that all speech sounds can be reduced to a small number of acoustic components. One way to produce synthetic speech is to mix these important parts together in the proper proportions, depending on the speech sounds to be imitated. It is rather like following a recipe for making soup, which might read: "Take two quarts of water, add one onion, three carrots, a potato, a teaspoon of salt, a pinch of pepper, and stir it all together."

This method of producing synthetic speech would include a recipe that might read:

1. Start with a tone at the same frequency as vibrating vocal cords (higher if a woman's or child's voice is being synthesized, lower for a man's).
2. Emphasize the harmonics corresponding to the formants required for a particular vowel, liquid, or nasal quality.
3. Add hissing or buzzing for fricatives.
4. Add nasal resonances for nasal sounds.
5. Temporarily cut off sound to produce stops and affricates.
6. and so on. . . .

All of these ingredients are blended electronically, using computers to produce highly intelligible, more or less natural-sounding speech. Because item 2 is central to the process, this method of speech synthesis is called **formant synthesis**.

Most synthetic speech still has a machinelike quality or accent, caused by small inaccuracies in simulation, and because suprasegmental factors such as changing intonation and stress patterns are not yet fully understood. If not correct, such factors may be more confusing than mispronounced phonemes. Currently, the chief area of research in speech synthesis is concerned precisely with discovering and programming the rules of rhythm and timing that native speakers apply. Still, speech synthesizers today are no harder to understand than a person speaking a dialect slightly different from one's own, and when the context is sufficiently narrow, as in a synthetic voice reading a weather report (a common application), there are no problems.

An alternative approach to formant synthesis is **concatenative synthesis**. The basic units of concatenative synthesis are recorded units such as phones, syllables, morphemes, words, phrases, and sentences. The recordings are made by human speakers. The synthesis aspect is in the assembling of the individual units to form the desired computer-spoken utterance.

The challenge in concatenative synthesis is designing the concatenation process to be smooth and natural so that its output possesses the fluidity of human speech. At this time, with the exception of simple phrases such as telephone numbers (this is the technique used by the phone company's information services), concatenative speech still has a stilted sound to it as the units do not always fit together seamlessly.

To provide input to the speech synthesizer, a computer program called **text-to-speech** converts written text into the basic units of the synthesizer. For formant synthesizers, the text-to-speech process translates the input text into a phonetic representation. This task is like the several exercises at the end of chapter 6, in which we asked you for a phonetic transcription of written words. Naturally, the text-to-speech process *precedes* the electronic conversion to sound.

For concatenative synthesizers, the text-to-speech process translates the input text into a representation based on whatever units are to be concatenated. For a syllable-based synthesizer, the text-to-speech program would take *The number is 5557766* as input and produce [θə] [nʌ̃m] [bər] [ɪz] [fajv] [fajv] [fajv] [sɛv] [ə̃n] [sɛv] [ə̃n] [sɪks] [sɪks] as output. The synthesizer would look up the various syllables in its memory and concatenate them, with further electronic processing supplied to smooth over the syllable boundaries.

The difficulties of text-to-speech are legion. We will mention two. The first is the problem of words spelled alike but pronounced differently. *Read* may be pronounced like *red* in *She has read the book*, but like *reed* in *She will read the book*. How does the text-to-speech system know which is which? Make no mistake about the answer; the machine must have structural knowledge of the sentence to make the correct choice, just as humans do. Unstructured, linear knowledge will not suffice. For example, we might program the text-to-speech system to pronounce *read* as *red* when the previous word is a form of *have*, but this approach fails in several ways. First, the *have* governs the pronunciation at a distance, both from the left and the right, as in *Has the girl with the flaxen hair read the book?* and *Oh, read a lot of books, has he!* The underlying structure needs to be known, namely that *has* is an auxiliary verb for the main verb *to read*. If we try the ploy of pronouncing *read* as *red* whenever *have* is "in the vicinity," we run into sentences like *The teacher said to have the girl read the book by tomorrow*, where this version of *read* gets the *reed* pronunciation. Even worse for the linear analysis are sentences like *Which girl did the teacher have read from the book?* where the words *have read* occur next to each other. Of course you know that this occurrence of *read* is of the *reed* type, because you know English and therefore know English syntactic structures. Only through structural knowledge can the "spelled-the-same-pronounced-differently" problem be approached effectively. We'll learn more about this in the section on computational syntax later in the chapter.

The second difficulty is inconsistent spelling, which is well illustrated by the first two lines of a longer poem:

I take it you already know
Of *tough* and *bough* and *cough* and *dough*

Each of the *ough* words is phonetically different, but it is difficult to find rules that dictate when *gh* should be [f] and when it is silent, or how to pronounce the *ou*. Modern computers have sufficient storage capacity to store the recorded pronunciation of every word in the language, its alternative pronunciations, and its likely pronunciations, which may be determined by an extensive statistical analysis. This list may include acronyms, abbreviations, foreign words, proper names, numbers including fractions, and special symbols such as #, &, *, %, and so on. Such a list is helpful—it is like memorizing rather than figuring out the pronunciations—and encompasses a large percentage of items, including the *ough* words. This is the basis of word-level concatenative synthesis. However, the list can never be complete. New words, new word forms, proper names, abbreviations, and acronyms are constantly being added to the language and cannot be anticipated. The text-to-speech system requires conversion rules for items not in its dictionary, and these must be output by a formant synthesizer or a concatenative synthesizer based on units smaller than the word if they are to be spoken. The challenges here are similar to those faced when learning to read aloud, which are considerable and, when it comes to the pronunciation of proper names or foreign words, utterly daunting.

Speech synthesis has important applications. It benefits visually impaired persons in the form of "reading machines," now commercially available. Mute patients with laryngectomies or other medical conditions that prevent normal speech can use synthesizers to express themselves. For example, researchers at North Carolina State University developed a communication system for an individual with so severe a form of multiple sclerosis that he could utter no sound and was totally paralyzed except for nodding his head. Using a head movement for "yes" and its absence as "no," this individual could select words displayed on a computer screen and assemble sentences to express his thoughts, which were then spoken by a synthesizer.

COMPUTATIONAL MORPHOLOGY

If we wish our computers to speak and understand grammatical English, we must teach them morphology (see chapter 3). We can't have machines going around saying, "*The cat is sit on the mat," or "*My five horse be in the barn." Similarly, if computers are to understand English, they need to know that *sitting* contains two morphemes, *sit+ing*, whereas *spring* is one morpheme, and *reinvent* is two but they are *re+invent*, not *rein+vent*.

The processing of word structures by computers is computational morphology. The computer needs to understand the structure of words both to understand the words and to use the words in a grammatically correct way. To process words, the computer is programmed to look for roots and affixes. In some cases this process is straightforward. *Books* is easily broken into *book+s*, *walking* into *walk+ing*, *fondness* into *fond+ness*, and *unhappy* into *un+happy*. These cases, and many like them, are the easy ones, because the spelling is well behaved, and the morphological processes are general. Other words are more difficult, such as *profundity = profound+ity*, *galactic = galaxy+ic*, and *democracy = democrat+y*.

One approach is to place all the morphological forms of all the words in the language in the computer's dictionary. Although today's computers can handle such a high computational load—many millions of forms—there would still be problems because of the generality of the processes. As soon as a new word enters the language, as *fax* did some years ago, a whole family of words is possible: *faxes, fax's, faxing, faxed, refax*, and *faxable*; and many others are not possible: **faxify, *exfax, *disfax*, and so on. The dictionary would be continually out of date.

Moreover, not all forms are predictable. Although *uglify* is not a dictionary word, if you hear it you know, and the computer should know, that it means "to make ugly." Likewise, compounding is a general process, and it would be impossible to predict all possible compounds of English. When *podcast* was coined from *pod+cast*, no computer could have had it in its dictionary.

The computer needs to have the ability to break words correctly into their component morphemes, and to understand each morpheme and its effect on the word's meaning, and where the word can be placed in a sentence. Computational morphology, then, is a host of interwoven rules, exceptions, and word/morpheme forms, all with the purpose of comprehending the internal structure of words.

Difficult problems always remain. If the computer sees *resent*, how does it know if it's the monomorphemic *resent* (with a /z/), or *re+sent?* A broader context is needed, and that is the topic of the next section.

COMPUTATIONAL SYNTAX

Good order is the foundation of all things.

EDMUND BURKE

In the beginning, there was ELIZA.

Patient: Men are all alike.

Eliza: In what way?

Patient: They're always bugging me about something or other.

Eliza: Can you think of a specific example?

Patient: Well, my boyfriend made me come here.

Eliza: Your boyfriend made you come here?

Patient: He says I'm depressed much of the time.

Eliza: I am sorry to hear you are depressed.

ELIZA is a computer program designed to simulate a nondirective psychiatrist talking to a patient. ELIZA has a collection of prepared phrases stored in memory such as "In what way?" or "Tell me more" that help keep the conversation going when it doesn't "understand" the patient. When ELIZA recognizes certain syntactic patterns, however, it turns them around to make a sensible response, as when it echoes "Your boyfriend made you come here?" ELIZA was programmed with a small bit of syntactic knowledge, which allowed it to make grammatical utterances based on the patient's statements, but no semantic knowledge at all. If a patient says "My sniggle is untherible," ELIZA would respond with "How long has your sniggle been untherible?" ELIZA was designed by the MIT scientist Joseph Weizenbaum in the 1960s. Though its syntactic sophistication is low by today's standards, ELIZA is one of the earliest attempts at human-machine communication that took the syntax of English into account.

Twenty-five years after ELIZA, computer scientists at Duke University and North Carolina State University programmed the "Circuit Fix-It Shop," a system designed to help a technician repair a faulty circuit. Unlike ELIZA, which accepted only typed input and produced printed output, the Circuit Fix-It Shop accepted speech input and spoke its responses. It had its own syntax and was capable both of understanding and speaking syntactically complex utterances, as the following excerpt from a repair session shows:

Computer: This is the circuit fix-it shop. How may I help you?

Technician: I need to fix the RS111 circuit.

Computer: I am familiar with that circuit. The LED is supposed to be displaying alternately blinking one and seven.

Technician: Where is the LED?

Computer: In the middle right of the blue region is the LED.

Technician: No light.

Computer: What is the switch at when the LED is off?

Technician: The switch is down.

Computer: You put up the switch.

Once the computer has understood the technician's utterance, it uses rules of semantics and syntax, together with a lexicon of words and morphemes, to formulate a grammatical, sensible response, which it then speaks through its synthesizer. The rules in many cases are similar to the phrase structure rules seen in chapter 4, such as "Form a noun phrase from an article followed by a noun." It also has semantic rules that tell it to use *the* with the word *switch* since its "world knowledge" tells it that there is only one switch in that particular circuit.

To understand a sentence, you must know its syntactic structure. If you didn't know the structure of *dogs that chase cats chase birds*, you wouldn't know whether dogs or cats chase birds. Similarly, machines that understand language must also determine syntactic structure. A **parser** is a computer program that attempts to replicate what we have been calling the "mental parser." Like the mental parser, the parser in a computer uses a grammar to assign a phrase structure to a string of words. Parsers may use a phrase structure grammar and lexicon similar to those discussed in chapter 4.

For example, a parser may contain the following rules: S → NP VP, NP → Det N, and so forth. Suppose the machine is asked to parse *The child found the kittens*. A *top-down* parser proceeds by first consulting the grammar rules and then examining the input string to see if the first word could begin an S. If the input string begins with a Det, as in the example, the search is successful, and the parser continues by looking for an N, and then a VP. If the input string happened to be *child found the kittens*, the parser would be unable to assign it a structure because it doesn't begin with a determiner, which is required by this grammar to begin an S. It would report that the sentence is ungrammatical.

A *bottom-up* parser takes the opposite tack. It looks first at the input string and finds a Det (*the*) followed by an N (*child*). The rules tell it that this phrase is an NP. It would continue to process *found*, *the*, and *kittens* to construct a VP, and would finally combine the NP and VP to make an S.

Parsers may run into difficulties with words that belong to several syntactic categories. In a sentence like *The little orange rabbit hopped*, the parser might mistakenly assume *orange* is a noun. Later, when the error is apparent, the parser backtracks to the decision point, and retries with *orange* as an adjective. Such a strategy works on confusing but grammatical sentences like *The old man the boats* and *The Russian women loved died*, which cause a garden path effect for human (mental) parsers.

Another way to handle such ambiguous situations is for the computer to try every parse that the grammar allows *in parallel*. Only parses that finish are accepted as valid. In such a strategy, two parses of *The Russian women loved died* would be explored simultaneously: *Russian* would be an adjective in one and a noun in the other. The adjective parse would get as far as *The Russian women loved* but then fail since *died* cannot occur in that position of a verb phrase. (The parser must not allow ungrammatical sentences such as *The young women loved died.*) This parse does not finish because it leaves the word *died* without an analysis. The other parse, when it sees the two nouns *Russian women* together, deduces the presence of a relative clause, which would have been obvious if the word *that* had preceded *women* (but English allows it to be left out). The parser is then able to assign the category of noun phrase to *The Russian women loved.* The sentence is completed with the verb *died*, which can form a verb phrase, and the parse finishes successfully.

Interestingly, it is not established whether the human parser uses backtracking or parallelism to deal with ambiguity, or perhaps a combination, or some alternative strategy. This remains a challenge for psycholinguists. Figuring this out is difficult because people usually handle ambiguity and arrive at the intended meaning easily, and we do not see much evidence that they are doing lots of extra work to deal with additional possible meanings. Fiendish linguists must toil long and hard to come up with examples like the garden path sentences discussed earlier that confuse the human parser.

Computers may outperform humans in certain cases, however. For example, try to figure out all the possible meanings of the sentence *Time flies like an arrow.* (*Hint*: Several of the words can belong to more than one syntactic category.) It turns out there are five (at least). The usual sense is "The way that time flies is the way that an arrow flies" (i.e., quickly). But it can also mean that a particular species of flies, namely "time flies," are fond of an arrow. Or, it can be a command: "(Please) time (a bunch of) flies in the same way that you would time an arrow!" (e.g., with a stopwatch). Another reading is again a command to time something, but in this case the things to be timed are "flies (that are) like an arrow." There is one more (even less plausible) reading: can you find it?[3]

Most people cannot find these alternative sentence structures and their corresponding meanings. A computer parser with a few simple rules and a lexicon in which *time, flies,* and *like* each have two entries of different categories will find the four other meanings just as easily as it finds the (only) one that humans readily discover. One reason for this is that the computer is not burdened with the task of semantic analysis, whereas the human parser is, and the unlikelihood of most of the interpretations appears to be a deterrent to the parsing process. For the human parser, syntax and semantics are inextricably bound together.

We not only want computers to understand language, we also want them to be able to produce new sentences—ones that are not pre-stored—and this also requires

---

3

"(Please) time (a bunch of) flies in the same way that an (animate) arrow with a stopwatch would time them."

knowledge of the syntactic rules of the grammar. In some cases the programming may be done simplistically. For example, a computer program to generate insults in the style of Shakespeare takes three columns of words, where the first column is a list of simple adjectives, the second a list of hyphenated adjectives, and the third a list of nouns:

Simple Adjectives	Hyphenated Adjectives	Nouns
bawdy	beetle-headed	baggage
churlish	clay-brained	bladder
goatish	fly-bitten	codpiece
lumpish	milk-livered	hedge-pig
mewling	pox-marked	lout
rank	rump-fed	miscreant
villainous	toad-spotted	varlet

The program chooses a word from each column at random to produce a noun phrase insult. Instantaneous insults guaranteed, you goatish, pox-marked bladder, you lumpish, milk-livered hedge-pig.

In less simplistic language generation, the computer works from the meaning of what is to be said, which may be the output of a translation system or simply the information that the computer is to supply in its next turn in a dialogue, as in the Circuit Fix-It Shop.

The generation system first assigns lexical items to the ideas and concepts to be expressed. These, then, must be fit into phrases and sentences that comply with the syntax of the output language. As in parsing, there are two approaches: top-down and bottom-up. In the top-down approach, the system begins with the highest-level categories such as S(entence). Lower levels are filled in progressively, beginning with noun phrases and verb phrases, and descending to determiners, nouns, verbs, and other sentence parts, always conforming to the syntactic rules. The bottom-up approach begins with the lexical items needed to express the desired meaning, and proceeds to combine them to form the higher-level categories. (Here, too, it is not yet known to what extent human language production employs one or other of these approaches.)

A **transition network** is a convenient way to visualize and program the use of a grammar to ensure proper syntactic output. A transition network is a complex of **nodes** (circles) and **arcs** (arrows). A network equivalent to the phrase structure rule S → NP VP is illustrated in Figure 9.4.

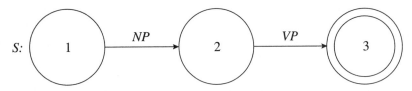

FIGURE 9.4 Transition network for S → NP VP.

The nodes are numbered to distinguish them; the double circle is the "final" node. The object of the generation is to traverse the arcs from the first to the final node.

The generator would start at node 1 and realize that a noun phrase is necessary to begin the output. The appropriate concept is assigned to that noun phrase. Other transition networks, in particular, one for NP, determine the structure of the noun phrase.

For example, one part of a transition network for a noun phrase would state that an NP may be a pronoun, corresponding to the phrase structure rule NP → Pronoun. It would look like Figure 9.5.

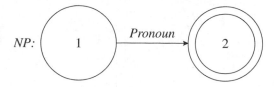

FIGURE 9.5 Transition network for NP → Pronoun.

To satisfy the NP *arc* in the S network, the *entire NP network* is traversed. In this case, the NP is to be a Pronoun, as determined by the concept needed. The NP arc is then traversed in the S network, and the system is at node 2. To finish, an appropriate verb phrase must be constructed according to the concept to be communicated. That concept is made to comply with the structure of the VP, which is also expressed as a transition network. To get past the VP arc in the S network, the entire VP network is traversed. Figure 9.6 shows one part of the VP complex of transition networks, corresponding to VP → V NP:

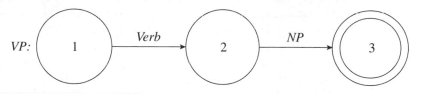

FIGURE 9.6 Transition network for VP → V NP.

Once the VP network is completed, the VP arc in the S network is traversed to the final node, and the system sends the sentence out to be spoken or printed.

The final sentence of the Circuit Fix-It Shop dialogue is, *You put up the switch.* The concept is a command to the user (*you*) to move the switch to the up position. It chooses the verb *put up* to represent this concept, and the noun phrase *the switch* to represent the switch that the computer knows the user is already familiar with. The syntax begins in the S network, then moves to the NP network, which is finished by producing the subject of the sentence, the pronoun *you*. The NP arc is traversed to node 2 in the S network. Now the syntax requires a VP. The scene of action moves to the VP network. The first arc is traversed and gives the verb *put up*. An NP network is again required so that the VP can finish up. This network (not shown) indicates that an NP may be a determiner followed by a noun, in this case, *the* and *switch*. When that network is finished, the NP arc in the VP network is traversed, the VP network is finished, the VP arc in the S network is traversed, the S network is finished, and the final output is the sentence, *You put up the switch.*

Because a reference to any network may occur in any other network, or even in the same network (thus capturing the recursive property of the syntax), a relatively small number of networks can generate the large number of sentences that may be needed by a natural language system. The networks must be designed so that they generate only grammatical, never ungrammatical, utterances.

COMPUTATIONAL SEMANTICS

"ZITS" copyright © 2001 ZITS Partnership. Reprinted with permission of King Features Syndicate, Inc.

The question of how to represent meaning is one that has been debated for thousands of years, and it continues to engender much research in linguistics, philosophy, psychology, cognitive science, and computer science. In chapter 5 we discussed many of the semantic concepts that a natural language system would incorporate into its operation. For simplicity's sake, we consider computational semantics to be the representation of the meaning of words and morphemes in the computer, as well as the meanings derived from their combinations.

Computational semantics has two chief concerns. One is to produce a semantic representation in the computer of language input; the other is to take a semantic representation and produce natural language output that conveys the meaning. These two concerns dovetail in a machine translation system. Ideally—and systems today are *not* ideal—the computer takes input from the source language, creates a semantic representation of its meaning, and from that semantic representation produces output in the target language. Meaning (ideally) remains constant across the entire process. In a dialogue system such as the Circuit Fix-It Shop, the computer must create a semantic representation of the user's input, act on it, and thus produce another semantic representation, which it then outputs to the user in ordinary language.

To generate sentences, the computer tries to find words that fit the concepts incorporated into its semantic representation. In the Circuit Fix-It Shop system, the computer had to decide what it wanted to talk about next: the switch, the user, the light, wire 134, or whatever. It needed to choose words corresponding to whether it wanted to declare the state of an object, ask about the state of an object, make a request of the user, tell the user what to do next, and so forth. If the query involved the user, the pronoun *you* would be chosen; if the state of the switch were the chief concern, the words *the switch,* or *a switch above the blue light*, would be chosen. When the components of meaning are assembled, the syntactic rules that we have seen already are called upon to produce grammatical output.

To achieve **speech understanding** the computer tries to find concepts in its semantic representation capabilities that fit the words and structures of the input. When the technician says *I need to fix the RS111 circuit*, the system recognizes that *I* means the user, that *need* represents something that the user lacks and the computer must provide. It further knows that if fixing is what is needed, it has to provide information about the workings of something. It recognizes *the RS111 circuit* as a circuit with certain properties that are contained in certain of its files. It infers that the workings of that particular circuit will be central to the ensuing dialogue.

A computer can represent concepts in numerous ways, none of them perfect or preferable to others. All methods share one commonality: a lexicon of words and morphemes that it is prepared to speak or understand. Such a lexicon would contain morphological, syntactic, and semantic information, as discussed in chapters 3, 4, and 5. Exactly how that information is structured depends on the particular applications it is to be suited for.

On a higher level, the relationships between words are conveniently represented in networks similar (but different in objective) to the transition networks we saw previously. The nodes represent words, and the arcs represent thematic roles (see chapter 5) between the words. *You put up the switch*, then, might have the representation in Figure 9.7.

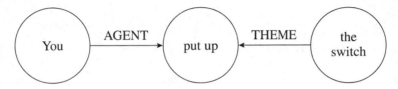

FIGURE 9.7 Semantic network for *You put up the switch.*

This means that the user (*you*) is the agent, or doer, and *put up* is what is to be done, and it is to be done to the theme, which is *the switch*.

Some systems draw on formal logic for semantic representations. *You put up the switch* would be represented in a function/argument form, which is its logical form:

PUT UP(YOU, THE SWITCH)

where PUT UP is a "two-place predicate" in the jargon of logicians, and the arguments are YOU and THE SWITCH. The lexicon indicates the appropriate relationships between the arguments of the predicate PUT UP.

A two-place predicate is the logical form of a transitive verb, with the first argument being the subject, and the second argument being the direct object. In chapter 5 on semantics we noted that one way to represent the meaning of a transitive verb such as *put up* was the set of pairs of elements (x,y) for which it is true that "x puts up y." This is consistent with the current notation in that the argument of the predicate is in the form of a pair of entities. Thus given the sentence "you put up the switch," and representing it as PUT UP(YOU, THE SWITCH), its meaning—whether it is true or false—is easily computed by seeing if the pair comprising the meaning of YOU and the meaning of THE SWITCH is in the set of ordered pairs that represent the meaning of PUT UP.

Two well-known natural language processing systems from the 1970s used the predicate-argument approach to semantic representation. One, named SHRDLU by its developer Terry Winograd, demonstrated several abilities, such as being able to interpret questions, draw inferences, learn new words, and even explain its actions. It operated in the context of a "blocks world," consisting of a table, blocks of various shapes, sizes, and colors, and a robot arm for moving the blocks. Using simple sentences, one could ask questions about the blocks and give commands to have blocks moved from one location to another.

The second system, LUNAR developed by William Woods, was capable of answering questions phrased in simple English about the lunar rock samples brought back from the Moon by the astronauts. LUNAR translated English questions into a logical representation, which it then used to query a database of information about the lunar samples.

COMPUTATIONAL PRAGMATICS

"Baby Blues" copyright © 1996 Baby Blues Partnership. Reprinted with permission of King Features Syndicate, Inc.

Pragmatics, as discussed in chapter 5, is the interaction of the "real world" with the language system. In the Circuit Fix-It Shop the computer knows that there is only one switch, that there is no other switch in the (its) universe, and hence that the determiner *the* is correct for this item. If the human mentioned *a wire*, however, the computer would ask *which wire* because it knows that there are several wires in the circuit. This is simple, computational pragmatics in action.

When a sentence is structurally ambiguous, such as *He sells synthetic buffalo hides* (are they buffalo hides that are synthetic, or hides from synthetic buffalo?), the parser will compute each structure. Semantic processing may eliminate some of the structures if they are anomalous (in this case, a hide can be synthetic but an animal, unless we count cloning, cannot be, so the second parse can be ruled out), but often some ambiguity remains. For example, the structurally ambiguous sentence *John found a book on the Oregon Trail* is semantically acceptable in both its meanings. To decide which meaning is intended, situational knowledge is needed. If John is in the library researching history, the "book *about* the Oregon Trail" meaning is most likely; if John is on a two-week hike to Oregon, the "book *upon* the Oregon Trail" meaning is more plausible.

Many natural language processing systems have a knowledge base of contextual and world knowledge. The semantic processing routines can refer to the knowledge base in cases of ambiguity. For example, the syntactic component of the Circuit Fix-It Shop will have two structures for *The LED is in the middle of the blue region at the top*. The sentence is ambiguous. Both meanings are semantically well formed and conceivable. However, the Circuit Fix-It Shop's knowledge base "knows" that the LED is in the middle of the blue region, and the blue region is at the top of the work area, rather than that the LED is in the middle, top of the blue region. It uses pragmatic knowledge, knowledge of the world, to disambiguate the sentence.

To conclude this section, we return to the subject of machine translation. All of the computational subsystems (e.g., phonology, morphology, syntax) bear on the ability of computers to translate from a source language to a target language. The greater recognition of the role of syntax, and the application of the linguistic principles of semantics and pragmatics that have evolved over the past fifty years, have made it possible to use computers to translate simple texts—ones in a constrained context such as a mathematical proof—grammatically and accurately between well-studied languages such as English and Russian. More complex texts require human intervention if the translation is to be grammatical and semantically faithful. The use of computers to aid the human translator can improve efficiency by a factor of ten or more, but the day when travelers can whip out a "pocket translator," hold it up to the mouth of a native speaker, and receive a translation in their own language is as yet beyond the horizon.[4]

Computer Models of Grammar

I am never content until I have constructed a . . . model of the subject I am studying. If I succeed in making one, I understand; otherwise I do not.
WILLIAM THOMSON (LORD KELVIN), Molecular Dynamics and the Wave Theory of Light

A theory has only the alternative of being right or wrong. A model has a third possibility: it may be right, but irrelevant.
MANFRED EIGEN, The Physicist's Conception of Nature

The grammars used by computers for parsing may not be the same as the grammars linguists construct for human languages, which are models of linguistic competence; nor are they similar, for the most part, to models of linguistic performance. Computers and people are different, and they achieve similar ends differently. Just as an efficient flying machine is not a replica of any bird, efficient grammars for computers do not resemble human language grammars in every detail.

Computers are often used to model physical or biological systems, which allows researchers to study those systems safely and sometimes even cheaply. For example, the performance of a new aircraft can be simulated and the test pilot informed about safe limits in advance of actual flight.

Computers can also be programmed to model the grammar of a language. An accurate grammar—one that is a true model of a speaker's mental grammar—should be able to generate all and only the sentences of the language. Failure to generate a grammatical sentence indicates an error in the grammar, because the human mental grammar has the capacity to generate all possible grammatical sentences—an infinite set. In addition, if the grammar produces a string that speakers consider ungrammatical, that too indicates a defect in the grammar; although in actual speech performance we often produce ungrammatical strings—sentence fragments, slips of the tongue, and so on—we will judge them to be ill-formed if we notice them. Our grammars do not generate these strings.

One computer model of a grammar was developed in the 1960s to test a generative grammar of English written by syntacticians at UCLA. More recently, computational linguists are developing computer programs to generate the sentences of a language and to simulate human parsing of these sentences using the rules included in various current linguistic theories. The computational models show that it is possible to use a written-down grammar in language production and comprehension, but it is still controversial whether such grammars are true models of human language processing.

Because linguistic competence and performance are so complex, computers are being used as a tool in the attempt to understand human language and its use. We have emphasized some of the differences in the ways human beings and computers process

---

[4] At this writing, one of the authors of your book is on a project to put a speech recognizer on a PDA. That would be a first step toward a pocket translator.

language. For example, humans appear to do speech recognition, parsing, semantic interpretation, and contextual disambiguation more or less simultaneously and smoothly while hearing and comprehending speech. Computers, on the other hand, usually have different components, loosely connected, and perform these functions individually.

One reason for this is that, typically, computers have only a single, powerful processor, capable of performing a single task at a time. Currently, computers are being designed with multiple processors, albeit less powerful ones, which are interconnected. The power of these computers lies both in the individual processors and in the connections. Such computers are capable of **parallel processing**, or carrying out several tasks simultaneously.

With a parallel architecture, computational linguists may be better able to program machine understanding in ways that blend all the stages of processing, from speech recognition through contextual interpretation, and hence approach more closely the way humans process language.

Summary

Psycholinguistics is concerned with **linguistic performance** or processing, the use of linguistic knowledge (competence) in speech production and comprehension.

Comprehension, the process of understanding an utterance, requires the ability to access the mental lexicon to match the words in the utterance to their meanings. Comprehension starts with the perception of the **acoustic speech signal**. The speech signal can be described in terms of the **fundamental frequency**, perceived as pitch; the intensity, perceived as loudness; and the quality, perceived as differences in speech sounds, such as between an [i] and an [a]. The speech wave can be displayed visually as a **spectrogram**, sometimes called a **voiceprint**. In a spectrogram, vowels exhibit dark bands where frequency intensity is greatest. These are called **formants** and result from the emphasis of certain *harmonics* of the fundamental frequency, as determined by the shape of the vocal tract. Each vowel has a unique formant pattern.

The speech signal is a continuous stream of sounds. Listeners have the ability to segment the stream into linguistic units and to recognize acoustically distinct sounds as the same linguistic unit.

The perception of the speech signal is necessary but not sufficient for the comprehension of speech. To get the full meaning of an utterance, we must **parse** the string into syntactic structures, because meaning depends on word order and constituent structure in addition to the meaning of words. Some psycholinguists believe we use both **top-down processing** and **bottom-up processing** during comprehension. Top-down processing uses semantic and syntactic information in addition to the lexical information drawn from the sensory input; bottom-up processing uses only information contained in the sensory input.

Psycholinguistic experimental studies are aimed at uncovering the units, stages, and processes involved in linguistic performance. Several experimental techniques have proven to be very helpful. In a **lexical decision** task, subjects are asked to respond to spoken or written stimuli by pressing a button if they consider the stimulus to be a word. In **naming** tasks, subjects read from printed stimuli. The measurement of response times, RTs, in naming and other tasks shows that it takes longer to process less frequent words compared to more frequent words, longer to produce irregularly spelled versus regularly spelled words, and longer to pronounce nonsense forms as opposed to real words. In addition to using behavioral data such as RT, researchers can now use various measures of electrical brain activity to learn about language processing.

A word may **prime** another word if the words are related in some way such as semantically, phonetically, or even through similar spelling. The semantic priming effect is shown by experiments in which a word such as *nurse* is spoken in a sentence, and it is found that words related to *nurse* such as *doctor* have lower RTs in lexical decision tasks. If an ambiguous word like *mouse* is used in an unambiguous context such as *My spouse has been chasing a mouse*, words related to both meanings of mouse are primed (e.g., *rat* and *computer*).

Eye tracking techniques can determine the points of a sentence at which readers have difficulty and have to backtrack to an earlier point of the sentence. These experiments provide strong evidence that the parser has preferences in how it constructs trees, which may give rise to **garden path** effects.

Another technique is **shadowing**, in which subjects repeat as fast as possible what is being said to them. Subjects often correct errors in the stimulus sentence, suggesting that they use linguistic knowledge rather than simply echoing sounds they hear. Other experiments reveal the processes involved in accessing the mental grammar and the influence of nonlinguistic factors in comprehension.

The units and stages in speech production have been studied by analyzing spontaneously produced speech errors. Anticipation errors, in which a sound is produced earlier than in the intended utterance, and **spoonerisms**, in which sounds or words are exchanged or reversed, show that we do not produce one sound or one word or even one phrase at a time. Rather, we construct and store larger units with their syntactic structures specified.

Word substitutions and blends show that words are connected to other words phonologically and semantically. The production of ungrammatical utterances also shows that morphological, inflectional, and syntactic rules may be wrongly applied or fail to apply when we speak, but at the same time shows that such rules are actually involved in speech production.

Computational linguistics is the study of how computers can process language. Computers aid scholars in analyzing literature and language, translate between languages, and communicate in natural language with human users.

To analyze a **corpus**, or body of data, a computer can do a frequency analysis of words, compute a **concordance**, which locates words in the corpus and gives their immediate context, and compute a **collocation**, which measures how the occurrence of one word affects the probability of the occurrence of other words. Computers are also useful for **information retrieval** based on keywords, automatic **summarization**, and **spell checking**.

Soon after their invention, computers were used to try to translate from one language to another. This is a difficult, complex task, and the results are often humorous as the computer struggles to translate text (or speech) in the **source language** into the **target language**, without loss of meaning or grammaticality.

Whether translating from one language to another, or communicating with a human being, computers must be capable of **speech recognition**, processing the speech signal into phonemes, morphemes, and words. They also must be able to speak its output. **Speech synthesis** is a two-step process in which a **text-to-speech** program first converts text to phones or other basic units such as words or syllables. **Formant synthesis** simulates the sounds of phones electronically; **concatenative synthesis** is based on assembling prerecorded units such as words to produce complete utterances.

To recognize speech is not to understand speech, and to speak a text does not necessarily mean that the computer knows what it is saying. To either understand or generate speech, the computer must process phonemes, morphemes, words, phrases, and sentences, and it must be aware of the meanings of these units (except for phonemes). The computational linguistics of speech understanding and speech generation has the subfields of **computational phonetics and phonology**, **computational morphology**, **computational syntax**, **computational semantics**, and **computational pragmatics**.

Computational phonetics and phonology relates phonemes to the acoustic signal of speech. It is fundamental to speech recognition and synthesis. Computational morphology deals with the structure of words, so it determines that the meaning of *bird* applies as well to *birds*, which has in addition the meaning of plural. Computational syntax is concerned with the syntactic categories of words and with the larger syntactic units of phrases and sentences. It is further concerned with analyzing a sentence into these components for speech understanding, or assembling these components into larger units for speech generation. A formal device called a **transition network** may be used to model the actions of syntactic processing.

Computational semantics is concerned with representing meaning inside the computer, or **semantic representation**. To communicate with a person, the computer creates a semantic representation of what the person says to it, and another semantic representation of what it wants to say back. In a machine translation environment, the computer produces a semantic representation of the source language input, and outputs that meaning in the target language.

Semantic representations may be based on logical expressions involving predicates and arguments, on **semantic networks**, or on other formal devices to represent meaning.

Computational pragmatics may influence the understanding or the response of the computer by taking into account knowledge that the computer system has about the real world, for example, that there is a unique element in the environment, so the determiner *the* can be used appropriately to refer to it.

Computers may be programmed to model a grammar of a human language and thus rapidly and thoroughly test that grammar. Modern computer architectures include **parallel processing** machines that can be programmed to process language more as humans do insofar as carrying out many linguistic tasks simultaneously.

References for Further Reading

Allen, J. 1987. *Natural Language Understanding*. Menlo Park, CA: Benjamin/Cummings.

Barnbrook, G. 1996. *Language and Computers: A Practical Introduction to the Computer Analysis of Language*. Edinburgh, Scotland: Edinburgh University Press.

Barr, A., and E. A. Feigenbaum, eds. 1981. *The Handbook of Artificial Intelligence*. Los Altos, CA: William Kaufmann.

Berwick, R. C., and A. S. Weinberg. 1984. *The Grammatical Basis of Linguistic Performance: Language Use and Acquisition*. Cambridge, MA: MIT Press.

Caron, J. 1992. *An Introduction to Psycholinguistics*. Tim Pownall, trans. Toronto, Canada: University of Toronto Press.

Carroll, D. W. 2004. *Psychology of Language*, 4th edition. Belmont, CA: Wadsworth.

Clark, H., and E. Clark. 1977. *Psychology and Language: An Introduction to Psycholinguistics*. New York: Harcourt Brace Jovanovich.

Fodor, J. A., T. G. Bever, and M. Garrett. 1974. *The Psychology of Language*. New York: McGraw-Hill.

Fromkin, V. A., ed. 1980. *Errors in Linguistic Performance*. New York: Academic Press.

Garrett, M. F. 1988. "Processes in Sentence Production." In F. Newmeyer, ed., *The Cambridge Linguistic Survey, Volume 3*. Cambridge, England: Cambridge University Press.

Gazdar, G., and C. Mellish. 1989. *Natural Language Processing in PROLOG: An Introduction to Computational Linguistics*. Reading, MA: Addison-Wesley.

Harley, T. A. 2001. *The Psychology of Language: From Data to Theory*, 2nd edition. Hove, UK: Psychology Press.

Hockey, S. 1980. *A Guide to Computer Applications in the Humanities*. London, England: Duckworth.

Johnson, M. 1989. "Parsing as Deduction: The Use of Knowledge in Language," *Journal of Psycholinguistic Research* 18(1):105–28.

Jurafsky, D., and J. H. Martin. 2000. *Speech and Language Processing*. Upper Saddle River, NJ: Prentice-Hall (Pearson Higher Education).

Ladefoged, P. 1996. *Elements of Acoustic Phonetics*, 2nd edition. Chicago, IL: University of Chicago Press.

Lea, W. A. 1980. *Trends in Speech Recognition*. Englewood Cliffs, NJ: Prentice-Hall.

Levelt, W. J. M. 1993. *Speaking: From Intention to Articulation*. Cambridge, MA: MIT Press.

Marcus, M. P. 1980. *A Theory of Syntactic Recognition for Natural Language*. Cambridge, MA: MIT Press.

Miller, G., and P. Johnson-Laird. 1976. *Language and Perception*. Cambridge, MA: Harvard University Press.

Miller, J. L., and P. D. Eimas, eds. 1995. *Speech, Language, and Communication*. San Diego, CA: Academic Press.

Osherson, D., and H. Lasnik, eds. 1990. *Language: An Invitation to Cognitive Science, Volume 1*. Cambridge, MA: MIT Press.

Slocum, J. 1985. "A Survey of Machine Translation: Its History, Current Status, and Future Prospects." *Computational Linguistics* 11(1).

Smith, R., and R. Hipp. 1994. *Spoken Natural Language Dialog Systems*. New York: Oxford University Press.

Sowa, J., ed. 1991. *Principles of Semantic Networks*. San Mateo, CA: Morgan Kaufmann.

Stabler, E. P., Jr. 1992. *The Logical Approach to Syntax: Foundations, Specifications and Implementations of Theories of Government and Binding*. Cambridge, MA: MIT Press.

Tartter, V. C. 1998. *Language and its Normal Processing*. Thousand Oaks, CA: Sage Publications.

Weizenbaum, J. 1976. *Computer Power and Human Reason*. San Francisco: W. H. Freeman.

Whitney, P. 1998. *The Psychology of Language*. Boston: Houghton Mifflin.

Winograd, T. 1972. *Understanding Natural Language*. New York: Academic Press.

———. 1983. *Language as a Cognitive Process*. Reading, MA: Addison-Wesley.

Witten, I. H. 1986. *Making Computers Talk*. Englewood Cliffs, NJ: Prentice-Hall.

Exercises

....

1. Speech errors (i.e., "slips of the tongue" or "bloopers") illustrate a difference between linguistic competence and performance, because our recognition of them as errors shows that we have knowledge of well-formed sentences. Furthermore, errors provide information about the grammar. The following utterances are part of the UCLA corpus of more than 5,000 English speech errors. Most of them were actually observed. One is attributed to Dr. Spooner.

   a. For each speech error, state what kind of linguistic unit or rule is involved (i.e., phonological, morphological, syntactic, lexical, or semantic).

   b. State, to the best of your ability, the nature of the error, or the mechanisms that produced it.

   (*Note*: The intended utterance is to the left of the arrow; the actual utterance to the right.)

   Example: ad hoc → odd hack

      a. phonological vowel segment   **b.** reversal or exchange of segments

   Example: she gave it away → she gived it away

      a. inflectional morphology   **b.** incorrect application of regular past-tense rule to exceptional verb

   Example: When will you leave? → When you will leave?

      a. syntactic rule   **b.** failure to move the auxiliary to form a question

    (1) brake fluid → blake fruid

    (2) drink is the curse of the working classes → work is the curse of the drinking classes (Spooner)

    (3) I have to smoke a cigarette with my coffee → . . . smoke my coffee with a cigarette

    (4) untactful → distactful

    (5) an eating marathon → a meeting arathon

    (6) executive committee → executor committee

    (7) lady with the dachshund → lady with the Volkswagen

    (8) are we taking the bus back → are we taking the buck bass

    (9) he broke the crystal on my watch → he broke the whistle on my crotch

  (10) a phonological rule → a phonological fool

  (11) pitch and stress → piss and stretch

  (12) Lebanon → Lemadon

  (13) speech production → preach seduction

  (14) he's a New Yorker → he's a New Yorkan

  (15) I'd forgotten about that → I'd forgot abouten that

2. The use of spectrograms for speaker identification is based on the fact that no two speakers have exactly the same speech characteristics. List some differences you have noticed in the speech of several individuals. Can you think of any reasons for such differences?

3. Using a bilingual dictionary of any language, attempt to translate the following English sentences by looking up each word:

The children will eat the fish.
Send the professor a letter from your new school.
The fish will be eaten by the children.
Who is the person that is hugging that dog?
The spirit is willing, but the flesh is weak.

A. Have a person who knows the target language give a correct translation of each sentence. What difficulties are brought to light by comparing the two translations? Mention five of them.

B. Have a different person who knows the target language translate the grammatical translation back into English. What problems do you observe? Are they related to any of the difficulties you mentioned in part A?

4. Suppose you were given a manuscript of a play and were told that it is either by Christopher Marlowe or William Shakespeare (both born in 1564). Suppose further that this work, and all works by Marlowe and Shakespeare, were in a computer. Describe how you would use the computer to help determine the true authorship of the mysterious play.

5. Speech synthesis is useful because it allows computers to convey information without requiring the user to be sighted. Think of five other uses for speech synthesis in our society.

6. Some advantages of speech recognition are similar to those of speech synthesis. A computer that understands speech does not require a person to use hands or eyes to convey information to the computer. Think of five other possible uses for speech recognition in our society.

7. Consider the following ambiguous sentences. Explain the ambiguity, give the most likely interpretation, and state what a computer would have to have in its knowledge base to achieve that interpretation.

   Example: A cheesecake was on the table. It was delicious and was soon eaten.

   a. Ambiguity: "It" can refer to the cheesecake or the table.

   b. Likely: "It" refers to the cheesecake.

   c. Knowledge: Tables are not usually eaten.

   (1) For those of you who have children and don't know it, we have a nursery downstairs. (Sign in a church)

   (2) The police were asked to stop drinking in public places.

   (3) Our bikinis are exciting; they are simply the tops. (Bathing suit ad in newspaper)

   (4) It's time we made smoking history. (Antismoking campaign slogan)

   (5) Do you know the time? (*Hint*: This is a pragmatic ambiguity.)

   (6) Concerned with spreading violence, the president called a press conference.

   (7) The ladies of the church have cast off clothing of every kind and they may be seen in the church basement Friday. (Announcement in a church bulletin)

   The following three items are newspaper headlines:

   (8) Red Tape Holds Up New Bridge

   (9) Kids Make Nutritious Snacks

   (10) Sex Education Delayed, Teachers Request Training

8. Google ELIZA. The first hit or so will give you a Web site where you can try ELIZA out by asking questions like "Why am I unhappy?" or asking ELIZA to respond to statements like "My friends all hate me."

A. List five "intelligent" responses to questions or statements that you formulate, and why they are intelligent. For example, if you tell ELIZA, "My friends all hate me," ELIZA will respond "Why do you say your friends all hate you?" This is intelligent because it makes sense, it's syntactically correct, the tense is appropriate, and it correctly changed the first-person *me* to the second-person *you*.

B. What are some of the "stock" responses that ELIZA makes? For example, when ELIZA doesn't "understand" you, she says "Please go on."

C. Try to identify some ways in which ELIZA uses your input to formulate its response. For example, if you mention "brother" or "mother," ELIZA will respond with a phrase containing "family member."

9. A. Here are some sentences along with a possible representation in predicate logic notation. Based on the examples in the text, and those in part B of this exercise, give a *semantic network* representation for each example.

(1) Birds fly. FLY (BIRDS)

(2) The student understands the question. UNDERSTAND (THE STUDENT, THE QUESTION)

(3) Penguins do not fly. NOT (FLY [PENGUINS])

(4) The wind is in the willows. IN (THE WIND, THE WILLOWS)

(5) Kathy loves her cat. LOVE (KATHY, [POSSESSIVE (KATHY, CAT)])

B. Here are five more sentences and a semantic network representation for each. Give a representation of each of them using the *predicate logic* notation.

(6) Seals swim swiftly.

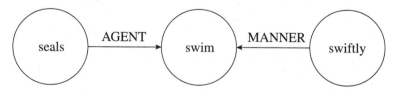

(7) The student doesn't understand the question.

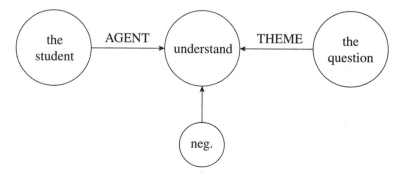

(8) The pen is on the table.

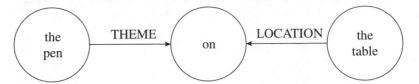

(9) My dog eats bones.

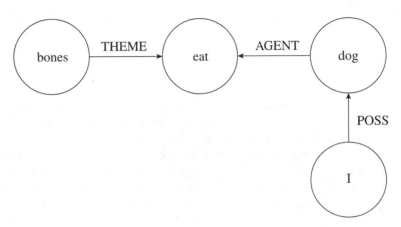

(10) Emily gives money to charity. (*Hint: Give* is a three-place predicate.)

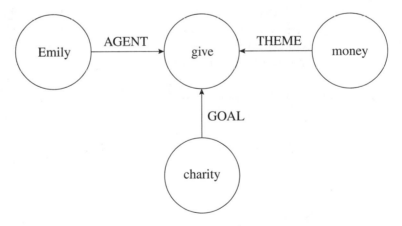

10. Let's play "torment the computer." Imagine a fairly good morphological parser. Give it *kindness*, it returns *kind + ness;* give it *upchuck*, it returns *up + chuck*, but if you give it *catsup* and it returns *cat + s + up*, you will scold it. Think of ten more words that are likely to lead to false analyses.

11. A major problem with text-to-speech is pronouncing proper names. Oh, how the telephone companies would like to solve this one! But it is difficult. Open a telephone directory at random, point at random, and try to pronounce surnames one after another, as they occur alphabetically. How far do you get before you are

unsure—not clueless, which you may be if you ran across Duke University's basketball coach *Mike Krzyzewski*—but merely unsure. As we write this exercise, we are doing it. Here is what we got:

Honeycutt
Honeywell
Hong
Hongtong
Honig
Honkanen
Honnigford
Honorato
Honore
Honour
Honrine
Hontz

We think we could do the first four correctly, but there is some doubt regarding the first vowel in *Honig*: is it [o], [ɔ], [a], or even the [ʌ] of *honey?* We also are unsure where to place the primary stress in *Honkanen*, and is the last letter in *Honore* pronounced as in Balzac's first name, and is *Honrine* pronounced to rhyme with *benzine* or *hemline?* Oh, and are all those *h*'s pronounced, or are some silent, as in *honor?* Do this exercise ten times to see the average number of surnames you can pronounce with confidence before becoming unsure. This gives some measure of the vast difficulty facing computers that have to read names.

12. What similarities and differences might there between looking up a word in a dictionary and the processes called *lexical access* and *lexical selection* in speech comprehension and production? Consider the functions that these different processes have to perform.

PART 4

Language and Society

Language is not an abstract construction of the learned, or of dictionary-makers, but is something arising out of the work, needs, ties, joys, affections, tastes, of long generations of humanity, and has its bases broad and low, close to the ground.

WALT WHITMAN

10

Language in Society

Language is a city to the building of which every human being brought a stone.
RALPH WALDO EMERSON, Letters and Social Aims

Dialects

A language is a dialect that has an army and a navy.

MAX WEINREICH

All speakers of English can talk to each other and pretty much understand each other. Yet, no two speak exactly alike. Some differences are the result of age, sex, social situation, and where and when the language was learned. These differences are reflected in word choices, the pronunciation of words, and grammatical rules. The unique characteristics of the language of an individual speaker are referred to as the speaker's **idiolect**. English may then be said to consist of more than 450 million idiolects, or the number equal to the number of speakers of English (which seems to be growing every day).

Like individuals, different groups of people who speak the same language speak it differently. Bostonians, New Yorkers, Blacks in Chicago, Whites in Denver, and Hispanics in Albuquerque all exhibit systematic variation in the way they speak English. When there are systematic differences in the way different groups speak a language, we say that each group speaks a **dialect** of that language. Dialects are *mutually intelligible* forms of a language that *differ in systematic ways. Every* speaker, whether rich or poor, regardless of region or racial origin, speaks at least one dialect, just as each individual speaks an idiolect. A dialect is *not* an inferior or degraded form of a language, and logically could not be so because a language is a collection of dialects.

It is not always easy to decide whether the systematic differences between two speech communities reflect two dialects or two languages. A rule-of-thumb definition can be used: When dialects become mutually *un*intelligible—when the speakers of one dialect group can no longer understand the speakers of another dialect group—these dialects become different languages. However, to define mutually intelligible is a difficult task. Danes speaking Danish and Norwegians speaking Norwegian and Swedes speaking Swedish can converse with each other. Nevertheless, Danish and Norwegian and Swedish are considered separate languages because they are spoken in separate countries and because there are regular differences in their grammars. Similarly, Hindi and Urdu are mutually intelligible languages spoken in Pakistan and India, although the differences between them are not much greater than those between the English spoken in America and Australia. On the other hand, the various languages spoken in China, such as Mandarin and Cantonese, although mutually unintelligible when spoken, have nevertheless been referred to as dialects of Chinese because they are spoken within a single country and have a common writing system.

It is also not easy to draw a distinction between dialects and languages on strictly linguistic grounds. Dialects and languages reflect the underlying rule systems—grammars—of their speakers. It would be completely arbitrary to say, for example, that grammars that differ from one another by, say, 20 rules represent different languages whereas grammars that differ by less than 20 rules are dialects. Why not 10 rules or 30 rules? In truth dialects and language exist on a continuum. Because neither mutual intelligibility, degree of grammatical difference, nor the existence of political or social boundaries is decisive, it is not surprising that a clear-cut distinction between language and dialect has evaded linguistic scholars. We shall, however, use the rule-of-thumb definition and refer to dialects of one language as mutually intelligible versions of the same basic grammar, with systematic differences among them.

Regional Dialects

Phonetics . . . the science of speech. That's my profession. . . . (I) can spot an Irishman or a Yorkshireman by his brogue. I can place any man within six miles. I can place him within two miles in London. Sometimes within two streets.

GEORGE BERNARD SHAW, Pygmalion

Dialect diversity develops when people are separated geographically and socially. The changes that occur in the language spoken in one area or group do not necessarily spread to another. Within a single group of speakers who are in regular contact with one another, the changes spread and are acquired by children. However, when some communication barrier separates groups of speakers—be it a physical barrier such as an ocean or a mountain range, or social barriers of a political, racial, class, or religious kind—linguistic changes do not spread so readily, and the differences between groups are reinforced and grow in number.

Dialect differences tend to increase proportionately to the degree of communicative isolation of the groups. *Communicative isolation* refers to a situation such as existed between America, Australia, and England in the eighteenth century. There was some contact through commerce and emigration, but an Australian was much less likely to talk to an Englishman than to another Australian. Today the isolation is less pronounced because of mass media and air travel, but even within a single country, a certain degree of isolation persists between regions, and we find many regional dialects.

Dialect leveling is movement toward greater uniformity and less variation among dialects. Though one might expect dialect leveling to occur as a result of the ease of travel and mass media, little evidence supports this theory. Dialect variation in the United Kingdom is maintained although only a few major dialects are spoken on national radio and television. There may actually be an increase in dialects in urban areas, where different groups attempt to maintain their distinctness. On the other hand, dialects die out, and do so for several reasons. This topic is discussed in chapter 11 in the section on extinct and endangered languages.

Changes in the grammar do not take place all at once in a speech community. They occur gradually, often originating in one region and spreading slowly to others, and often over the life spans of several generations of speakers. A change that occurs in one region and fails to spread to other regions of the language community creates dialect differences. When enough such differences accumulate in a particular region (e.g., the city of Boston or the southern area of the United States), the language spoken has its own character, and that version of the language is referred to as a **regional dialect**.

ACCENTS

> The educated Southerner has no use for an r except at the beginning of a word.
>
> **MARK TWAIN,** Life on the Mississippi

Regional phonological or phonetic distinctions are often referred to as different **accents**. A person is said to have a Boston or Brooklyn or Midwestern accent, a Southern drawl, an Irish brogue, and so on. Thus, *accent* refers to the characteristics of speech that convey information about the speaker's dialect, which may reveal in what country or in what part of the country the speaker grew up, or to which sociolinguistic group the speaker belongs. People in the United States often refer to someone as having a British accent or an Australian accent; in Britain they refer to an American accent.

The term *accent* is also used to refer to the speech of non-native speakers, that is, someone who has learned the language as a second language. For example, a native French speaker's English is described as having a French accent. In this sense, *accent* refers to phonological differences with, or interference from, one's native language. Unlike regional dialect accents, such foreign accents do not reflect differences in the speech of the community where the language was learned.

DIALECTS OF ENGLISH

"Hagar the Horrible" copyright © 1996 King Features Syndicate. Reprinted with permission of King Features Syndicate.

A radio comedian once remarked that "the Mason-Dixon line is the dividing line between *you-all* and *youse-guys*," pointing to the varieties of English in the United States. Regional dialects tell us a great deal about how languages change, which is discussed in the next chapter. The origins of many regional dialects of American English can be traced to the people who settled in North America in the seventeenth and eighteenth centuries. The early settlers came from different parts of England, already speaking different dialects of English. Regional dialect differences existed in the original thirteen American colonies.

By the time of the American Revolution, there were three major dialect areas in the British colonies: the Northern dialect spoken in New England and around the Hudson River; the Midland dialect spoken in Pennsylvania; and the Southern dialect. These dialects differed from one another and from the English spoken in England, in systematic ways. Some of the changes that occurred in British English spread to the colonies; others did not.

How regional dialects develop is illustrated by changes in the pronunciation of words with an *r*. The British in southern England were already dropping their *r*'s before consonants and at the ends of words as early as the eighteenth century. Words such as *farm, farther*, and *father* were pronounced as [faːm], [faːðə], and [faːðə], respectively. By the end of the eighteenth century, this practice was a general rule among the early settlers in New England and the southern Atlantic seaboard. Close commercial ties were maintained between the New England colonies and London, and Southerners sent their children to England to be educated, which reinforced the *r*-dropping rule. The *r*-less dialect still spoken today in Boston, New York, and Savannah maintained this characteristic. Later settlers, however, came from northern England, where the *r* had been retained; as the frontier moved westward, so did the *r*. Pioneers from all three dialect areas spread westward. The mingling of their dialects leveled many of their dialect differences, which is why the English used in large sections of the Midwest and the West is similar.

Other waves of immigration brought speakers of other dialects and other languages to different regions. Each group left its imprint on the language of the communities in which they settled. For example, the settlers in various regions developed different dialects—the Germans in the southeastern section, the Welsh west of Philadelphia, the Germans and Scotch-Irish in the Midlands area of Pennsylvania.

The last half of the twentieth century brought hundreds of thousands of Spanish-speaking immigrants from Cuba, Puerto Rico, Central America, and Mexico to both the east and west coasts of the United States. In addition, English is being enriched by the languages spoken by the large numbers of new residents coming from the Pacific Rim countries of Japan, China, Korea, Samoa, Malaysia, Vietnam, Thailand, the Philippines, and Indonesia. Large new groups of Russian and Armenian speakers also contribute to the richness of the vocabulary and culture of American cities. The language of the regions where the new immigrants settle may thus be differentially affected by the native languages of the settlers, further adding to the varieties of American English.

English is the most widely spoken language in the world if one counts all those who use it as a native language or as a second or third language. It is the national language of several countries, such as the United States, large parts of Canada, the British Isles, Australia, and New Zealand. For many years it was the official language in countries that were once colonies of Britain, including India, Nigeria, Ghana, Kenya, and the other "anglophone" countries of Africa. Dialects of English are spoken in these countries for the reasons just discussed. It is likely that more than one billion human beings can speak English with useful fluency.

Phonological Differences

I have noticed in traveling about the country a good many differences in the pronunciation of common words. . . . Now what I want to know is whether there is any right or wrong about this matter. . . . If one way is right, why don't we all pronounce that way and compel the other fellow to do the same? If there isn't any right or wrong, why do some persons make so much fuss about it?

Letter quoted in "The Standard American," in J. V. Williamson and V. M. Burke, eds., A Various Language

A comparison of the *r*-less and other dialects illustrates the many phonological differences among dialects of American English. These variations created difficulties for us in writing chapter 6 (phonetics), where we wished to illustrate the different sounds of English by reference to words in which the sounds occur. As mentioned, some students pronounce *caught* [kɔt] with the vowel [ɔ] and *cot* [kat] with [a], whereas other students pronounce them both [kat]. Some readers pronounce *Mary, merry,* and *marry* the same; others pronounce the three words differently as [meri], [mɛri], and [mæri]; and still others pronounce two of them the same. In the southern area of the country, *creek* is pronounced with a tense [i] as [krik], and in the north Midlands, it is pronounced with a lax [ɪ] as [krɪk]. Many speakers of American English pronounce *pin* and *pen* identically, whereas others pronounce the first [pĭn] and the second [pɛ̆n]. If variety is the spice of life, then American English dialects add zest to our existence.

The pronunciation of British English (or many dialects of it) differs in systematic ways from pronunciations in many dialects of American English. In a survey of hundreds of American and British speakers conducted via the Internet, 48 percent of the Americans pronounced the mid consonants in *luxury* as voiceless [lʌkʃəri], whereas 96 percent of the British pronounced them as voiced [lʌgʒəri]. Sixty-four percent of the Americans pronounced the first vowel in *data* as [e] and 35 percent as [æ], as opposed to 92 percent of the British pronouncing it with an [e] and only 2 percent with [æ]. The most consistent difference occurred in the placement of primary stress, with most Americans putting stress on the first syllable and most British on the second or third in polysyllabic words like *cigarette, applicable, formidable, kilometer,* and *laboratory.*

The United Kingdom also has many regional dialects. The British vowels described in the phonetics chapter are used by speakers of the dialect called RP for "received pronunciation" because it is "received" (accepted) in the court of the monarch. In this dialect, *h* is pronounced at the beginning of both *head* and *herb,* whereas in most American English dialects *h* is not pronounced in *herb.* In some English dialects the *h* is regularly dropped from most words in which it is pronounced in American, such as *house,* pronounced [aws], and *hero,* pronounced [iro].

There are many other phonological differences in the various dialects of English used around the world.

Lexical Differences Regional dialects may differ in the words people use for the same object, as well as in phonology. Hans Kurath, an eminent dialectologist, in his paper "What Do You Call It?" asked:

Do you call it a *pail* or a *bucket*? Do you draw water from a *faucet* or from a *spigot*? Do you pull down the *blinds*, the *shades*, or the *curtains* when it gets dark? Do you *wheel* the baby, or do you *ride* it or *roll* it? In a *baby carriage*, a *buggy*, a *coach*, or a *cab*?

"Liberty Meadows" copyright © 1998. By permission of Frank Cho and Creators Syndicate, Inc.

People take a *lift* to the *first floor* (our *second floor*) in England, but an *elevator* in the United States; they get five gallons of *petrol* (not *gas*) in London; in Britain a *public school* is "private" (you have to pay), and if a student showed up there wearing *pants* ("underpants") instead of *trousers* ("pants"), he would be sent home to get dressed.

If you ask for a *tonic* in Boston, you will get a drink called *soda* or *soda-pop* in Los Angeles; and a *freeway* in Los Angeles is a *thruway* in New York, a *parkway* in New Jersey, a *motorway* in England, and an *expressway* or *turnpike* in other dialect areas.

Dialect Atlases Kurath published **dialect maps** and **dialect atlases** of a region (see Figure 10.1), on which dialect differences are geographically plotted. The dialectologists who created the map noted the places where speakers use one word or another word for the same item. For example, the area where the term *Dutch cheese* is used is not contiguous; there is a small pocket mostly in West Virginia where speakers use that term for what other speakers call *smearcase* (from the Dutch word *smeerkaas* a compound made from the verb *smeren* "to spread" and *kaas* "cheese").

In similar maps, areas were differentiated based on the variation in pronunciation of the same word, such as [krik] and [krɪk] for *creek*. The concentrations defined by different word usages and varying pronunciations, among other linguistic differences, form **dialect areas**.

A line drawn on the map to separate the areas is called an **isogloss**. When you cross an isogloss, you are passing from one dialect area to another. Sometimes several isoglosses coincide, often at a political boundary or at a natural barrier such as a river or mountain range. Linguists call these groupings a *bundle* of isoglosses. Such a bundle can define a regional dialect.

DARE is the acronym for the *Dictionary of American Regional English,* whose chief editor was the distinguished American dialectologist Frederick G. Cassidy (1907–2000).

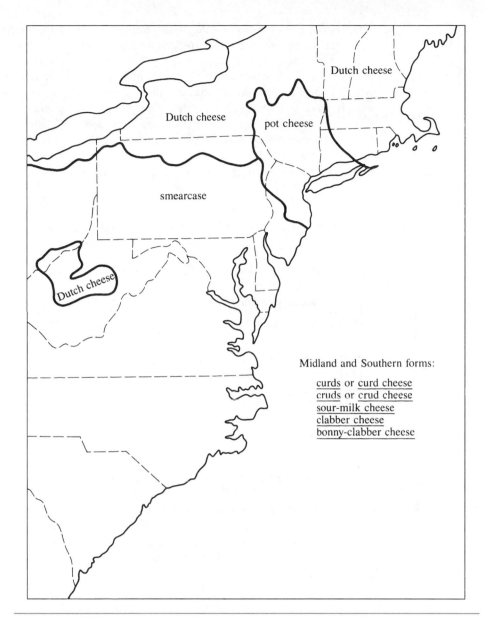

FIGURE 10.1 A dialect map showing the isoglosses separating the use of different words that refer to the same cheese.

Kurath, Hans. *A Word Geography of the Eastern United States*. Ann Arbor, MI: University of Michigan Press, copyright © 1949. Reprinted with permission of University of Michigan Press.

This work represents decades of research and scholarship by Cassidy and other American dialectologists and is a major resource for those interested in American English dialects. Its first four volumes, covering *A* through *Sk,* are published; volume 5, covering *Sk* through *Z*, is due out in 2009. Its purpose is described on its Web site as follows:

The *Dictionary of American Regional English (DARE)* is a reference tool unlike any other. Its aim is not to prescribe how Americans should speak, or even to describe the language we use generally, the "standard" language. Instead, it seeks to document the varieties of English that are **not** found everywhere in the United States—those words, pronunciations, and phrases that vary from one region to another, that we learn at home rather than at school, or that are part of our oral rather than our written culture. Although American English is remarkably homogeneous considering the tremendous size of the country, there are still many thousands of differences that characterize the various dialect regions of the United States. It is these differences that *DARE* records.

Syntactic Differences Systematic syntactic differences also distinguish dialects. In most American dialects, sentences may be conjoined as follows:

1. John will eat and Mary will eat. → John and Mary will eat.

In the Ozark dialect of southern Missouri, the following conjoining is also possible:

2. John will eat and Mary will eat. → John will eat and Mary.

Both shortened conjoined sentences are the result of deletion transformations similar to the ones discussed in Exercise 19 of chapter 4. It was shown there that the ambiguous sentence *George wants the presidency more than Martha* may be derived from two possible d-structures:

3. George wants the presidency more than he wants Martha.
4. George wants the presidency more than Martha wants the presidency.

In this case a deletion transformation either deletes *he wants* from the structure of (3) or *wants the presidency* from the structure of (4). A similar transformation derives *John and Mary will eat* by deleting the first occurrence of the verb phrase (VP) *will eat*, as illustrated in (1). Most dialects of English, however, do not have a rule that deletes the second VP in conjoined sentences, as illustrated in (2), and in those dialects *John will eat and Mary* is ungrammatical. The Ozark dialect differs in allowing the second VP deletion rule.

Speakers of some American dialects say *Have them come early!* where others would say *Have them **to** come early!* Many speakers of the latter dialect also exhibit "double modals," and expressions like *He **might could** do it*, or *You **might should** go home* are grammatical. While Aux recursion (see chapter 4) is permitted in all English dialects, most dialects constrain verb phrases to contain no more than one modal verb.

Some of the dialects that permit double modals (e.g., Appalachian English) also exhibit double objects (e.g., *I caught me a fish)*; and *a*-prefixing with progressives, *He came a-runnin'*. The several distinguishing syntactic characteristics, then, would contribute to a *bundle* of syntactic isoglosses that separate these regional dialects.

In several American English dialects, the pronoun *I* occurs when *me* would be used in other dialects. This difference is a syntactically conditioned morphological difference.

Dialect 1

between you and I
Won't he let you and I swim?
*Won't he let I swim?

Dialect 2

between you and me
Won't he let you and me swim?

The use of *I* in these structures is only permitted in a conjoined NP, as the starred (ungrammatical) sentence shows. *Won't he let me swim?* however is grammatical in both dialects. Dialect 1 is growing, and these forms are becoming Standard English, spoken by TV announcers, political leaders, and university professors, although language purists still frown on this usage.

In British English the pronoun *it* in the sentence *I could have done it* can be deleted. British speakers say *I could have done*, which is not in accordance with the syntactic rules in American English grammars. American English, however, permits the deletion of *done it*, and Americans say *I could have*, which does not accord with the British syntactic rules.

Despite such differences, we are still able to understand speakers of other English dialects. Although regional dialects differ in pronunciation, vocabulary, and syntactic rules, the differences are minor when compared with the totality of the grammar. Dialects typically share most rules and vocabulary, which explains why the dialects of a language are mutually intelligible.

Social Dialects

> The limits of my language mean the limits of my world.
>
> **LUDWIG WITTGENSTEIN**

In many respects, social boundaries and class differences are as confining as the physical barriers that often define regional dialects. It is therefore not surprising that different dialects of a language evolve within social groups. Communication within a particular group is free and unconstrained, as it is in a particular region. Communication among social groups, however, may be as severely limited as if a physical boundary such as an ocean existed between them.

"For Better or for Worse" copyright © 2005 Lynn Johnston Productions. Dist. by Universal Press Syndicate. Reprinted with permission. All rights reserved.

The social boundaries that give rise to dialect variation are numerous. They may be based on socioeconomic status, ethnic or racial differences, country of origin, and even gender. Middle-class American and British speakers are often distinguishable from working-class speakers; in America, many speakers of African descent speak a different dialect than those of European, Asian, or Hispanic descent; and, as we shall see, women and men each have their own distinguishing speech characteristics.

Dialect differences that seem to come about because of social factors are called **social dialects**, as opposed to *regional dialects*, which are spawned by geographical factors. However, there are regional aspects to social dialects and, clearly, social aspects to regional dialects, so the distinction is not entirely cut and dried.

THE "STANDARD"

> We don't talk fancy grammar and eat anchovy toast. But to live under the kitchen doesn't say we aren't educated.
>
> **MARY NORTON,** The Borrowers

> Standard English is the customary use of a community when it is recognized and accepted as the customary use of the community. Beyond this is the larger field of good English, any English that justifies itself by accomplishing its end, by hitting the mark.
>
> **GEORGE PHILIP KRAPP,** Modern English: Its Growth and Present Use

Even though every language is a composite of dialects, many people talk and think about a language as if it were a well-defined fixed system with various dialects diverging from this norm. This is false, although it is a falsehood that is widespread. One writer of books on language accused the editors of *Webster's Third New International Dictionary*, published in 1961, of confusing "to the point of obliteration the older distinction between standard, substandard, colloquial, vulgar, and slang," attributing to them the view that "good and bad, right and wrong, correct and incorrect no longer exist." In the next section we argue that such criticisms are ill founded.

Language Purists

> A woman who utters such depressing and disgusting sounds has no right to be anywhere—no right to live. Remember that you are a human being with a soul and the divine gift of articulate speech: that your native language is the language of Shakespeare and Milton and The Bible; and don't sit there crooning like a bilious pigeon.
>
> **GEORGE BERNARD SHAW,** Pygmalion

Prescriptive grammarians, or language purists, usually consider the dialect used by political leaders and national newscasters as the correct form of the language. (See chapter 1 for a discussion of prescriptive grammars.) This is the dialect taught in "English" or "grammar" classes in school, and it is closer to the written form of the language than many other dialects, which also lends it an air of superiority.

Otto Jespersen, the great Danish linguist, ridiculed the view that a particular dialect is better than any other when he wrote: "We set up as the best language that which is found in the best writers, and count as the best writers those that best write the language. We are therefore no further advanced than before."

"Rose Is Rose" copyright © 2001 United Feature Syndicate, Inc. Reprinted by permission.

The dominant, or **prestige**, dialect is often called the standard dialect. **Standard American English (SAE)** is a dialect of English that many Americans *nearly* speak; divergences from this "norm" are labeled "Philadelphia dialect," "Chicago dialect," "African American English," and so on.

SAE is an idealization. Nobody speaks this dialect; and if somebody did, we would not know it, because SAE is not defined precisely (like most dialects, none of which are easy to clearly define). Teachers and linguists held a conference in the 1990s that attempted to come up with a precise definition of SAE. This meeting did not succeed in satisfying everyone as to what SAE should be. The language used by national news broadcasters used to represent SAE, but today many of these people speak a regional dialect or violate the English preferred by the purists. Similarly, the British Broadcasting Corporation (BBC) once used mostly speakers of RP English, but today speakers of Irish, Welsh, Scottish, and other regional dialects of English are commonly heard on BBC programs. The BBC describes its English as "the speech of educated professionals."

According to some language pundits, deviations from the indefinable Standard constitute a language "crisis." One prescriptivist goes so far as to ask, "Will Americans be the death of English?" and answers, "My mature, considered opinion is that they will." Languages do die, as discussed in chapter 11, but certainly the cause of death is not corruption. All this fuss is reminiscent of Mark Twain's cable to the Associated Press, after reading his obituary: "The reports of my death are greatly exaggerated."

The idea that language change equals corruption goes back at least as far as the Greek grammarians at Alexandria (200–100 B.C.E.). They were concerned that the Greek spoken in their time was different from the Greek of Homer, and they believed that the earlier forms were purer. They tried to correct the imperfections but failed as miserably as do any modern counterparts. Similarly, the Muslim Arabic grammarians working at Basra in the eighth and ninth centuries attempted to purify Arabic to restore it to the perfection of the Arabic in the Koran.

For many years after the American Revolution, British writers and journalists railed against American English. Thomas Jefferson was an early target in a commentary on his *Notes on the State of Virginia*, which appeared in the *London Review*:

For shame, Mr. Jefferson! Why, after trampling upon the honour of our country, and representing it as little better than a land of barbarism—why, we say, perpetually trample also upon the very grammar of our language . . . Freely, good sir, we will forgive all your attacks, impotent as they are illiberal, upon our *national character*; but for the future spare—O spare, we beseech you, our mother-tongue!

The fears of the British journalists in 1787 proved unfounded, and so will the fears of modern-day purists. From a linguistic point of view, one dialect is neither better nor worse than another, nor purer nor more corrupt, nor more or less logical, nor more or less expressive. It is simply different. More precisely, it is a simply a different set of rules or lexical items represented in the minds of its speakers.

No academy and no guardians of language purity can stem the tide of language change, nor should anyone attempt to do so, because such change does not mean corruption. The fact that for most American English speakers *criteria* and *data* are now mass nouns like *information* is no cause for concern. Information can include one fact or many facts, but one would still say "The information is." For some speakers it is equally correct to say "The criteria is" or "The criteria are." Those who say "The data are" would or could say "The datum (singular) is."

A standard dialect (or prestige dialect) of a particular language may have social functions. Its use in a group may bind people together or provide a common written form for multidialectal speakers. If it is the dialect of the wealthy, influential, and powerful members of society, this may have important implications for the entire society. All speakers who aspire to become successful may be required to speak that dialect even if it isn't their own.

In 1954 the British scholar Alan Ross published *Linguistic Class-Indicators in Present-Day English*, in which he compared the speech habits of the English upper class, whom he labeled "U," with the speech habits of "non-U" speakers. Ross concluded that although the upper class had words and pronunciations peculiar to it, the main characteristic of U speech is the avoidance of non-U speech; and the main characteristic of non-U speech is, ironically, the effort to sound U. "They've a lovely home," for example, is pure non-U, because it is an attempt to be refined. Non-U speakers say "wealthy" and "ever so"; U speakers say "rich" and "very." Non-U speakers "recall"; U-speakers simply "remember."

Non-U speech habits often include **hypercorrections**, deviations from the norm *thought* to be "proper English," such as pronouncing *often* with a [t], or saying *between you and I*. U speakers, being generally less insecure about their dialect, persist in saying [ɔfən] for *often* and *between you and me*. Ironically, in some cases non-U speech is so pervasive it eventually becomes part of the prestige dialect, as we are seeing today with *often* and *between you and I/me*.

No dialect, however, is more expressive, more logical, more complex, or more regular than any other dialect or language. Any judgments, therefore, as to the superiority or inferiority of a particular dialect or language are social judgments, which have no linguistic or scientific basis.

Banned Languages Language purists wish to prevent language or dialect differentiation because of their false belief that some languages are better than others, or that change leads to corruption. Languages and dialects have also been banned as a means of political control. Russian was the only legal language permitted by the Russian tsars, who banned the use of Ukrainian, Lithuanian, Georgian, Armenian, Azeri, and all the other languages spoken by national groups under the rule of Russia.

Cajun English and French were banned in southern Louisiana by practice if not by law until about twenty years ago. Individuals over the age of fifty years report that they were often punished in school if they spoke French, even though many of them had never heard English before attending school.

For many years, American Indian languages were banned in federal and state schools on reservations. Speaking Faroese was formerly forbidden in the Faroe Islands. A proscription against speaking Korean was imposed by the Japanese during their occupation of Korea between 1910 and 1945. Throughout history many languages and dialects have been banned to various degrees.

As recently as 2001, the *New York Times* reported that "Singapore's leaders want English, not Singlish." Although Standard English is the common language of Singapore's multiethnic population, many who do not learn English as their native language speak *Singlish,* a form of English with elements of Malay, Tamil, Mandarin Chinese, and other Chinese dialects (languages). They are the target of Singapore's "Speak Good English Movement."

In France, a notion of the "standard" as the only correct form of the language is propagated by an official academy of "scholars" who determine what usage constitutes the "official French language." Some years ago, this academy enacted a law forbidding the use of "Franglais," which are words of English origin like *le parking, le weekend,* and *le hotdog.* The French, of course, continue to use them, and because such words are notorious, they are widely used in advertising, where being noticed is more important than being correct. Only in government documents can these proscriptions be enforced.

The academy also disapproves of the use of the hundreds of local village dialects, or *patois* [patwa], although some of them are actually separate languages, derived from Latin (as are French, Spanish, and Italian). This diverse, rich collection of dialects and languages of France have one thing in common: they are not officially approved French. There are political as well as misguided linguistic motivations behind the efforts to maintain only one official language.

In the past (and to some extent in the present), a French citizen from the provinces who wished to succeed in French society nearly always had to learn the Parisian French dialect—the prestige dialect of France. Then, several decades ago, members of regional autonomy movements demanded the right to use their own languages in their schools and for official business. In the section of France known as l'Occitanie, the popular singers sing in Langue d'oc, a Romance language of the region, both as a protest against the official language policy and as part of the cultural revival movement. Here is the final chorus of a popular song in Langue d'oc (shown with its French and English translations):

Langue d'oc	French	English
Mas perqué, perqué	Mais pourquoi, pourquoi	But why, why
M'an pas dit à l'escóla	Ne m'a-t-on pas dit à l'école	Did they not speak to me at school
La lega de mon pais?	La langue de mon pays?	The language of my country?

In the French province of Brittany, there has also been a strong movement favoring the use of Breton in the schools. Breton is not a Romance language like French; it is a Celtic language in the same family as Irish, Gaelic, and Welsh. (We will discuss such family groupings in chapter 11.) It is not, however, the structure of the language or the genetic family grouping that has led to the Breton movement. It is rather the pride of a people who speak a language not considered as good as the "standard," and who wish to preserve it by opposing the political view of language use.

These efforts have proved successful. In 1982, the newly elected French government decreed that the languages and cultures of Brittany (Breton), the southern Languedoc region, and other areas would be promoted through schooling, exhibitions, and festivals. No longer would schoolchildren who spoke Breton be punished by having to wear a wooden shoe tied around their necks, as had been the custom.

In many places in the world (including the United States), the use of sign languages of the deaf was banned. Children in schools for the deaf, where the aim was to teach them to read lips and to communicate through sound, were often punished if they used any gestures at all. This view prevented early exposure to language. It was mistakenly thought that children, if exposed to sign, would not learn to read lips or produce sounds. Individuals who become deaf after learning a spoken language are often able to use their knowledge to learn to read lips and continue to speak. This is, however, very difficult if one has never heard speech sounds. Furthermore, even the best lip readers can comprehend only about one-third of the sounds of spoken language. Imagine trying to decide whether *lid* or *led* was said by reading the speaker's lips. Mute the sound on a TV set and see what percentage of a news broadcast you can understand, even if recorded and played back in slow motion, and even if you know the subject matter.

There is no reference to a national language in the U.S. Constitution. John Adams proposed that a national academy be established—similar to the French Academy—to standardize American English, but this view was roundly rejected as not in keeping with the goals of "liberty and justice for all."

In recent years in the United States, a movement has arisen in an attempt to establish English as an official language by amending the Constitution. An "Official English" initiative was passed by the electorate in California in 1986; in Colorado, Florida, and Arizona in 1988; and in Alabama in 1990. Such measures have also been adopted by seventeen state legislatures. This kind of linguistic chauvinism is opposed by civil-rights minority-group advocates, who point out that such a measure could be used to prevent large numbers of non-English-speaking citizens from participating in civil activities such as voting, and from receiving the benefits of a public education, for which they pay through taxes. Fortunately, as of this writing, the movement appears to have lost momentum.

The Revival of Languages

> None of your living languages for Miss Blimber. They must be dead—stone dead—and then Miss Blimber dug them up like a Ghoul.
>
> CHARLES DICKENS, Dombey and Son

The attempts to ban certain languages and dialects are countered by the efforts of certain peoples to preserve their languages and cultures. This attempt to slow down or reverse the dying out of a language is illustrated by the French in Quebec. In 1961, the Quebec Office of the French Language was formed to standardize the dialect of French spoken in Quebec, but ironically refuses to do so for fear of reducing the interintelligibility with other French-speaking communities. It is believed that standardization would linguistically isolate Quebecers and lead to the extinction of French in Canada. Instead, the office uses its powers to promote the use of French, irrespective of dialect, in the daily lives of Quebecers.

Across the Atlantic, Gaelic, or Irish, is being taught again in hundreds of schools in Ireland and Northern Ireland, and there are numerous first-language learners of this once-moribund language. But such "antilinguicide" movements should not include the enforced banning of any language.

A dramatic example of the revival of a dormant language occurred in Israel. The Academy of the Hebrew Language in Israel undertook a task that had never been done in the history of humanity—to awaken an ancient written language to serve the daily colloquial needs of the people. Twenty-three lexicologists worked with the Bible and the Talmud to add new words to the language. While there is some attempt to keep the language "pure," the academy has given way to popular pressure. Thus, a bank check is called a *check* [tʃɛk] in the singular and pluralized by adding the Hebrew plural suffix *-im* to form *check-im*, although the Hebrew word *hamcha'ah* was proposed. Similarly, *lipstick* has triumphed over *s'faton* and *pajama* over *chalifat-sheinah* (lit. sleeping suit).

AFRICAN AMERICAN ENGLISH

> The language, only the language. . . . It is the thing that black people love so much—the saying of words, holding them on the tongue, experimenting with them, playing with them. It's a love, a passion. Its function is like a preacher's: to make you stand up out of your seat, make you lose yourself and hear yourself. The worst of all possible things that could happen would be to lose that language.
>
> TONI MORRISON, *interview in* The New Republic, *March 21, 1981*

Most regional dialects of the United States are largely free from stigma. Some regional dialects, like the *r*-less Brooklynese, are the victims of so-called humor, and speakers of one dialect may deride the "drawl" of southerners or the "nasal twang" of Texans (even though not all speakers of southern dialects drawl, nor do all Texans twang).

There is, however, a *social* dialect of North American English that has been a victim of prejudicial ignorance. This dialect, **African American English (AAE)**, is spoken by a large population of Americans of African descent.[1] The distinguishing features of this English dialect persist for social, educational, and economic reasons. The historical discrimination against African Americans has created the social boundaries that permit this dialect to thrive. In addition, particularly in recent years, many blacks have embraced their dialect as a means of positive identification.

Since the onset of the civil rights movement in the 1960s, AAE has been the focus of national attention. Some critics attempt to equate its use with inferior genetic intelligence and cultural deprivation, justifying these incorrect notions by stating that AAE is a "deficient, illogical, and incomplete" language. Such epithets cannot be applied to any language, and they are as unscientific in reference to AAE as to Russian, Chinese, or Standard American English. The cultural-deprivation myth is as false as the idea that some dialects or languages are inferior. A person may be "deprived" of one cultural background, but be rich in another.

---

[1]AAE is actually a group of closely related dialects also called African American Vernacular English (AAVE), Black English (BE), Inner City English (ICE), and Ebonics.

Some people, white and black, think they can identify the race of a person by speech alone, believing that different races inherently speak differently. This belief is patently false. A black child raised in Britain will speak the British dialect of the household. A white child raised in an environment where AAE is spoken will speak AAE. Children construct grammars based on the language they hear.

AAE is discussed here more extensively than other American dialects because it provides an informative illustration of the regularities of a dialect of a major language, and the systematic differences from the so-called standard dialects of that language. A vast body of research shows that there are the same kinds of linguistic differences between AAE and SAE as occur between many of the world's major dialects.

Phonology of African American English Some of the differences between AAE and SAE phonology are discussed in this section. Because AAE is not a single, monolithic dialect, but rather refers to a collection of tightly related dialects, not everything discussed in this section applies to all speakers of AAE.

R-Deletion

Like several dialects of both British and American English, AAE includes a rule of *r-deletion* that deletes /r/ everywhere except before a vowel. Pairs of words like *guard* and *god, nor* and *gnaw, sore* and *saw, poor* and *Poe, fort* and *fought*, and *court* and *caught* are pronounced identically in AAE because of this phonological rule.

L-Deletion

There is also an *l-deletion* rule for some speakers of AAE, creating identically pronounced pairs like *toll* and *toe, all* and *awe, help* and *hep.*

Consonant Cluster Reduction

A *consonant cluster reduction* rule in AAE simplifies consonant clusters, particularly at the ends of words and when one of the two consonants is an alveolar (/t/, /d/, /s/, /z/). The application of this rule may delete the past-tense morpheme so that *meant* and *mend* are both pronounced as *men,* and *past* and *passed* (*pass + ed*) may both be pronounced like *pass.* When speakers of this dialect say *I pass the test yesterday*, they are not showing an ignorance of past and present-tense forms of the verb, but are pronouncing the past tense according to this rule in their grammar.

The deletion rule is optional; it does not always apply, and studies have shown that it is more likely to apply when the final [t] or [d] does not represent the past-tense morpheme, as in nouns like *paste* [pes] as opposed to verbs like *chased* [tʃest], where the final past tense [t] will not always be deleted. This has also been observed with final [s] or [z], which will be retained more often by speakers of AAE in words like *seats* /sit + s/, where the /s/ represents plural, than in words like *Keats* /kits/, where it is more likely to be deleted to yield the surface form [kit].

Consonant cluster reduction is not unique to AAE. It exists optionally for many speakers of other dialects including SAE. For example, the medial [d] in *didn't* is often deleted, producing [dĩnt]. Furthermore, nasals are commonly deleted before final voiceless stops, to result in [hĩt] versus [hĩnt].

Neutralization of [ɪ] and [ɛ] before Nasals

AAE shares with many regional dialects a lack of distinction between /ɪ/ and /ɛ/ before nasal consonants, producing identical pronunciations of *pin* and *pen, bin* and *Ben, tin* and *ten*, and so on. The vowel sound in these words is roughly between the [ɪ] of *pit* and the [ɛ] of *pet*.

DIPHTHONG REDUCTION

AAE has a rule

$$/ɔj/ \rightarrow /ɔ/$$

that reduces the diphthong /ɔj/ (particularly before /l/) to the simple vowel [ɔ] without the glide, so that *boil* and *boy* are pronounced [bɔ]. This rule is common throughout the regional dialects of the south, spoken both by whites and blacks.

LOSS OF INTERDENTAL FRICATIVES

A regular feature is the change of a /θ/ to /f/ and /ð/ to /v/ so that *Ruth* is pronounced [ruf] and *brother* is pronounced [brʌver]. This [θ]-[f] correspondence also is true of some dialects of British English, where /θ/ is not even a phoneme in the language. *Think* is regularly [fɪnk] in Cockney English.

Initial /ð/ in such words as *this, that, these*, and *those* are pronounced as [d]. This is again not unique to AAE, but a common characteristic of certain regional, nonethnic dialects of English, many found in the state of New Jersey as well as in New York City and Boston.

GLOTTAL STOP SUBSTITUTION

Another regular feature found in many varieties of AAE (and non-AAE) is the substitution of a glottal stop for an alveolar stop at the end of non-word-final syllables, thus the name *Rodman* is pronounced [raʔmə̃n], but the word *rod* is pronounced [rad]. In fact, we observed in chapter 6 on phonetics that the glottal stop [ʔ] is a common allophone of /t/ in many dialects of English.

All of these differences are systematic and rule-governed and similar to the kinds of phonological variations that are found in languages all over the world, including Standard English.

Syntactic Differences between AAE and SAE

> And of his port as meeke as is a mayde
>
> He nevere yet no vileynye ne sayde
>
> **GEOFFREY CHAUCER,** The Canterbury Tales, Prologue, *69–70*

Syntactic differences also exist between dialects. They have often been used to illustrate the illogic of AAE, and yet these differences are evidence that AAE is as syntactically complex and as logical as SAE.

MULTIPLE NEGATIVES

Constructions with multiple negatives akin to AAE *He don't know nothing* are commonly found in languages of the world, including such prestigious languages as French, Italian, and the English of Chaucer, as illustrated in the epigraph from the *Canterbury Tales*. The multiple negatives of AAE are governed by rules of syntax and are not illogical, nor are speakers of AAE somehow illogical thinkers for not knowing that two negatives make a positive, which may be true in algebra, but depends on the rules of semantics in linguistics.

DELETION OF THE VERB "BE"

In most cases, if in Standard English the verb can be contracted, in African American English sentences it is deleted; where it can't be contracted in SAE, it can't be deleted in AAE, as shown in the following sentences:

SAE	AAE
He is nice/He's nice.	He nice.
They are mine/They're mine.	They mine.
I am going to do it/I'm gonna do it.	I gonna do it.
He is/he's as nice as he says he is.	He as nice as he say he is.
*He's as nice as he says he's	*He as nice as he say he
How beautiful you are.	How beautiful you are.
*How beautiful you're	*How beautiful you
Here I am.	Here I am.
*Here I'm	*Here I

These examples show that syntactic reduction rules operate in both dialects although they show small systematic differences.

HABITUAL "BE"

In SAE, the sentence *John is happy* can be interpreted to mean *John is happy* now or *John is generally happy*. One can make the distinction clear in SAE only by lexical means, that is, the addition of words. One would have to say *John is generally happy* or *John is a happy person* to disambiguate the meaning from *John is presently happy*.

In AAE, this distinction is made syntactically; an uninflected form of *be* is used if the speaker is referring to *habitual* state.

John be happy.	"John is always happy."
John happy.	"John is happy now."
*John be happy at the moment.	
He be late.	"He is habitually late."
He late.	"He is late this time."
*He be late this time.	
Do you be tired?	"Are you generally tired?"
You tired?	"Are you tired now?"
*Do you be tired today?	

The ungrammatical sentences are caused by a conflict of the habitual meaning with the momentary meaning conveyed by *at the moment, this time,* and *today*. The syntactic distinction between habitual and nonhabitual aspect also occurs in SAE, but with verbs other than *be*. In SAE eventive verbs such as *eat* and *dance*, when marked with the present-tense *-s* morpheme, have only a habitual meaning and cannot refer to an ongoing situation, in contrast to stative verbs such as *think* or *love*, as exemplified by the following sentences:

John dances every Saturday night.

*John dances now.

John loves Mary now and forever.

History of African American English It is simple to date the beginning of AAE—the first black people were brought in chains to Virginia in 1619. There are, however, different theories about the factors that led to the systematic differences between AAE and other American English dialects.

One view suggests that African American English originated when the African slaves learned English from their colonial masters as a second language. Although the basic grammar was learned, many surface differences persisted, which were reflected in the grammars constructed by the children of the slaves, who heard English primarily from their parents. If the children had been exposed to the English spoken by the whites, their grammars would have been more similar if not identical to the general Southern dialect. The dialect differences persisted and grew because social and racial barriers isolated blacks in America. The proponents of this theory point to the fact that the grammars of AAE and Standard American English are identical except for a few syntactic and phonological rules that produce surface differences.

Another view that is receiving increasing support is that many of the unique features of AAE are traceable to influences of the African languages spoken by the slaves. During the seventeenth and eighteenth centuries, Africans who spoke different languages were purposefully grouped together to discourage communication and to prevent slave revolts. In order to communicate, the slaves were forced to use the one common language all had access to, namely English. They invented a simplified form—called a pidgin (discussed in a following section)—that incorporated many features from West African languages. According to this view, the differences between AAE and other dialects result more from deep syntactic differences than from surface distinctions.

It is apparent that AAE is closer to Southern dialects of American English than to other dialects. This supports the idea that the Negro slaves learned the English of white Southerners as a second language. It might also be explained by the fact that for many decades a large number of Southern white children were raised by black women and played with black children. It is possible that many of the distinguishing features of Southern dialects were acquired from African American English in this way. A publication of the American Dialect Society in 1908–1909 by noted folklorist L. W. Payne makes this point clearly:

> For my part, after a somewhat careful study of east Alabama dialect, I am convinced that the speech of the white people, the dialect I have spoken all my life and the one I tried to record here, is more largely colored by the language of the negroes [*sic*] than by any other single influence.

The two-way interchange still goes on. Standard American English is constantly enriched by words, phrases, and usage originating in AAE; and AAE, whatever its origins, is influenced by the changes that go on in the many other dialects of English.

LATINO (HISPANIC) ENGLISH

A major group of American English dialects is spoken by native Spanish speakers or their descendants. The Southwest was once part of Mexico, and for more than a century large numbers of immigrants from Spanish-speaking countries of South and Central America have been enriching the country with their language and culture. Among these groups are native speakers of Spanish who have learned or are learning English as a second language. There are also those born in Spanish-speaking homes whose native language is English, some of whom are monolingual, and others who speak Spanish as a second language.

One cannot speak of a homogeneous Latino dialect. In addition to the differences between bilingual and monolingual speakers, the dialects spoken by Puerto Rican, Cuban, Guatemalan, and El Salvadoran immigrants or their children are somewhat different from one another and also from those spoken by many Mexican Americans in the Southwest and California, called Chicano English (ChE).

A description of the Latino dialects of English is complicated by historical and social factors. While many Latinos are bilingual, as many as 20 percent of Chicanos may be monolingual English speakers. Recent studies also show that the shift to monolingual English is growing rapidly. Furthermore, the bilingual speakers are not a homogeneous group; a native Spanish speaker's knowledge of English may range from passive (ability to understand but not speak) to full competence. The Spanish influence on both immigrant and native English speakers is reinforced by border contact between the United States and Mexico and the social cohesion of a large segment of this population.

When speaking English, bilingual Latinos may insert a Spanish word or phrase into a single sentence or move back and forth between Spanish and English, a process called **code-switching**. This is a universal language-contact phenomenon that reflects the grammars of both languages working simultaneously. Quebecois in Canada switch from French to English and vice versa; the Swiss switch between French and German. Code-switching occurs wherever groups of bilinguals speak the same two languages. Furthermore, code-switching occurs in specific social situations, enriching the repertoire of the speakers.

Because most people do not know about code-switching, a common misconception is that bilingual Latinos speak a sort of "broken" English, sometimes called Spanglish or Tex-Mex. This is not the case. In fact, the phrases inserted into a sentence are always in keeping with the syntactic rules of that language. For example, in a Spanish noun phrase, the adjective usually follows the noun, as opposed to the English NP in which it precedes, as shown by the following:

> English: My mom fixes **green tamales**. Adj N
> Spanish: Mi mamá hace **tamales verdes**. N Adj

A bilingual Spanish-English speaker might, in a code-switching situation, say:

> My mom fixes **tamales verdes**.
> or Mi mamá hace **green tamales**.

but would not produce the sentences

> *My mom fixes **verdes tamales**.
> or *Mi mamá hace **tamales green**.

because the Spanish word order was reversed in the inserted Spanish NP and the English word order was reversed in the English NP.

What needs to be emphasized is that these individuals know not one, but two languages, and that code-switching, like linguistic knowledge in general, is governed by grammatical principles.

Chicano English (ChE) We have seen that there is no one form of Latino English, just as there is no single dialect of SAE or American English. Nor is the Chicano English dialect homogeneous. Nevertheless, we can still recognize it as a distinct dialect of American English, one that is acquired as a first language by many children and that is the native language of hundreds of thousands, if not millions, of Americans. It is not English with a Spanish accent nor an incorrect version of SAE but, like African American English, it is a mutually intelligible dialect that differs systematically from SAE. Many of the differences, however, depend on the social context of the speaker. (This is also true of AAE and most "minority" dialects.) Linguistic differences of this sort that vary with the social situation of the speaker are termed **sociolinguistic variables**. For example, the use of nonstandard forms like double negation is often associated with pride of ethnicity, which is part of the social context. Many Chicano speakers (and speakers of AAE) are bidialectal; they can use either ChE (or AAE) or SAE, depending on the social situation.

PHONOLOGICAL VARIABLES OF ChE

Like other dialects, ChE is the result of many factors. One major factor is the influence of Spanish. Phonological differences between ChE and SAE reveal this influence.

Here are some systematic differences:

1. Chapters 6 and 7 discussed the fact that English has eleven stressed vowel phonemes (not counting the three diphthongs): / i, ɪ, e, ɛ, æ, u, ʊ, o, ɔ, a, ʌ/. Spanish, however, has only five: /i, e, u, o, a/. Chicano speakers whose native language is Spanish may substitute the Spanish vowel system for the English. When this is done, several homonyms result that have distinct pronunciations in SAE. Thus *ship* and *sheep* are both pronounced like *sheep*; *rid* is pronounced like *read*, and so on. Chicano speakers whose native language is English may *choose to speak the ChE dialect* despite having knowledge of the full set of American English vowels.
2. Alternation of *ch* and *sh*; *shook* is pronounced as if spelled with a *ch* and *check* as if spelled with an *sh*.
3. Devoicing of some consonants, such as /z/ in *easy* [isi] and *guys* [gajs].
4. The substitution of /t/ for /θ/ and /d/ for /ð/ word initially, as in [tin] for *thin* and [de] for *they*.
5. Word-final consonant cluster reduction. *War* and *ward* are both pronounced like *war*; *star* and *start* like *star*. This process may also delete past-tense suffixes (*poked* is pronounced like *poke*) and third-person singular agreement suffixes (*He loves her* becomes *he love her*). Word-final alveolar-cluster reduction (e.g., pronouncing *fast* as if it were spelled *fas*) has become widespread among all dialects of English including SAE. Although this process is often singled out for speakers of ChE and AAE, it is actually no longer dialect specific.
6. Prosodic aspects of speech in ChE such as vowel length and intonation patterns may also differ from SAE and give ChE a distinctive flavor.
7. The Spanish sequential constraint, which does not permit a word to begin with an /s/ cluster, is sometimes carried over to ChE. Thus *scare* may be pronounced as if it were spelled *escare*, and *school* as if it were spelled *eschool*.

Syntactic Variables in ChE

There are also regular syntactic differences between ChE and SAE. In Spanish, a negative sentence includes a negative morpheme before the verb even if another negative appears; thus negative concord (the multiple negatives mentioned earlier) is a regular rule of ChE syntax:

SAE	ChE
I don't have any money.	I don have no money.
I don't want anything.	I no want nothin.

Another regular difference between ChE and SAE is in the use of the comparative *more* to mean *more often* and the preposition *out from* to mean *away from*, as in the following:

SAE	ChE
I use English more often.	I use English more.
They use Spanish more often.	They use more Spanish.
They hope to get away from their problems.	They hope to get out from their problems.

Lexical differences also occur, such as the use of *borrow* in ChE for *lend* in SAE (*Borrow me a pencil*), as well as many other often subtle differences. This is entirely expected and occurs between any two dialects—for example, American Southern use of the verb *mash* to mean *push,* as in *Mash the third-floor button,* spoken in an elevator.

Genderlects

Dialects are defined in terms of groups of speakers, and speakers are most readily grouped by geography. There's little confusion in seeing that people live in England or America and speak British or American dialects. Regional dialects are the most apparent and generally are what people mean when they use the word *dialect*. Social groups are more amorphous than regional groups, and social dialects correspondingly less well delineated and, until recently, less well studied. Surprisingly, the most obvious division of humankind into groups—women and men—has not engendered (if you'll pardon the expression) much dialectal attention until relatively recently.

In 1973, the linguist Robin Lakoff wrote the first article specifically concerned with women and language to be published in a major linguistics journal.[2] Lakoff's study suggested that women spoke more "proper" English (e.g., saying *Whom do you like?* rather than *who do you like?*) than men because of an insecurity caused by sexism in society. Since Lakoff's study an increasing number of scholars have been conducting research on language, gender, and sexism, investigating the differences between male and female speech and their underlying causes.

Recent research by the linguist and writer Deborah Tannen has revealed other dialectal differences between the sexes. For example, women "hedge" their speech more often than men with expressions like *I suppose, I would imagine, This is probably wrong, but . . . ,* and so on. Women frequently use tag questions to weaken or qualify their statements (e.g., *He's not a very good actor, is he?*), and women use words of politeness (e.g., *please, thank you*) more often than men. Tannen calls the different

---

[2]Lakoff, R. 1973. "Language and Woman's Place," *Language in Society* 2:45–80.

variants of English used by men and women "genderlects" (a blend of *gender* and *dialect*). She attributes the differences, roughly speaking, to a greater desire on the part of women than men to be cooperative and nonconfrontational.

Variations in the language of men and women occur in many, if not all languages. In Japanese, women may choose to speak a distinct female dialect, although they know the standard dialect used by both men and women. The Japanese language has many *honorific* words—words intended to convey politeness and lesser social status in addition to their regular meaning. Studies have shown that statistically, women use polite forms more often than men. Japanese has formal and informal verbal inflections (see exercise 15, chapter 7), and again, women use the formal speech more frequently. There are also words in Japanese reserved for women's use, although they can be used by both sexes. The overall impression is that Japanese women speak a dialect of Japanese that is distinct from that spoken by men.

One effect of the different genderlects of Japanese shows in the training of guide and helper dogs. The animals learn their commands in English because the sex of the owner is not known in advance, and it is easier for an impaired person to use English commands than it is to train the dog in both language styles.

The differences discussed by Tannen, as well as those in Japanese genderlects, have more to do with language use than with grammatical rules. There are, however, cases in which the language spoken by men and women differ in their grammars. In the Muskogean language Koasati, spoken in Louisiana, words that end in an /s/ when spoken by men, end in /l/ or /n/ when used by women; for example, the word meaning "lift it" is *lakawhol* for women and *lakawhos* for men. Early explorers reported that the men and women of the Carib Indians used different dialects. In Chiquitano, a Bolivian language, the grammar of male language includes a noun-class gender distinction, with names for males and supernatural beings morphologically marked in one way, and nouns referring to females marked in another. In Thai, utterances may end with "politeness particles," k^hrap for men and k^ha for women (tones omitted); and Thai also has differing pronouns and fixed expressions like *please* and *thank you* that give each genderlect a distinctive character.

One obvious characteristic of female speech is its relatively higher pitch, caused mainly by shorter vocal tracts. Nevertheless, studies have shown that the difference in pitch between male and female voices is generally greater than could be accounted for by physiology alone, suggesting that some social factors may be at work, possibly beginning as early as girls' language acquisition.

SOCIOLINGUISTIC ANALYSIS

Speakers from different socioeconomic classes often display systematic speech differences, even when region and ethnicity are not factors. These social-class dialects differ from other dialects in that their sociolinguistic variables, while still systematic, are often statistical in nature. With regional and social dialects, a differing factor is either present or absent (for the most part), so regional groups who say *faucet* say it pretty much all the time, as do the regional groups who say *spigot*. Speakers of AAE dialects will say *she pretty* meaning "she is pretty" with great regularity, other factors being equal. But social-class dialects differentiate themselves in a more quantitative way; for example, one class of speakers may apply a certain rule 80 percent of the time to distinguish it from another that applies the same rule 40 percent of the time.

The linguist William Labov carried out a sociolinguistic analysis in New York City that focused on the rule of *r*-dropping that we discussed earlier, and its use by upper-, middle-, and lower-class speakers.[3] In this classic study, which teaches us much about how to conduct a sociolinguistic analysis, Labov first identified three department stores that catered primarily to the three classes: Sak's Fifth Avenue, Macy's, and S. Klein—upper, middle, and lower, respectively. To elicit data, he would go to the three stores and ask questions that he knew would evoke the words *fourth* and *floor*. People who applied the *r*-dropping rule would pronounce these words [fɔθ] and [flɔ], whereas ones who did not apply the rule would say [fɔrθ] and [flɔr].

The methodology behind much of Labov's research is important to note. Labov interacted with all manner of people in their own environment where they were comfortable, although he took care when analyzing the data to take into account ethnic and gender differences. In gathering data he was careful to elicit naturally spoken language through his casual, unassuming manner. Finally, he would evoke the same answer twice by pretending not to hear or understand, and in that way was able to collect both informal, casual utterances, and utterances spoken (the second time) with more care.

In Sak's 62 percent of respondents pronounced the *r* at least some of the time; in Macy's it was 52 percent, and in Klein's a mere 21 percent. The *r*-dropping rule, then, is socially "stratified," to use Labov's terminology, with the lower socio-class dialects applying the rule most often. What makes Labov's work so distinctive (and distinguished!) is his methodology and his discovery that the systematic differences among dialects can be usefully defined on a quantitative basis of rule applications rather than the strict presence or absence of a rule. He also showed that social context and the sociolinguistic variables that it governs play an important role in language change (discussed in chapter 11).

Languages in Contact

"Bizarro" copyright © 1994 by Dan Piraro. Reprinted with permission of King Features Syndicate. All rights reserved.

---

[3]Labov, W. 1966. *The Social Stratification of English in New York City*. Washington, DC: Center for Applied Linguistics.

Even a dog we do know is better company than a man whose language we know not.

ST. AUGUSTINE

Human beings are great travelers and traders and colonizers. The mythical tales of nearly all cultures tell of the trials and tribulations of travel and exploration, such as those of Odysseus (Ulysses) in Homer's *Odyssey*. Surely one of the tribulations of ranging outward from your home is that sooner or later you will encounter people who do not speak your language, nor you theirs. In some parts of the world, you may not have to travel farther than next door to find the language disconnect, and in other parts you may have to cross an ocean. Because this situation is so common in human history and society, several solutions for bridging this communication gap have arisen.

Lingua Francas

Language is a steed that carries one into a far country.

ARAB PROVERB

Many areas of the world are populated by people who speak diverse languages. In such areas, where groups desire social or commercial communication, one language is often used by common agreement. Such a language is called a **lingua franca**.

In medieval times, a trade language based largely on the languages that became modern Italian and Provençal came into use in the Mediterranean ports. That language was called Lingua Franca, "Frankish language." The term *lingua franca* was generalized to other languages similarly used. Thus, any language can be a lingua franca.

English has been called "the lingua franca of the whole world." French, at one time, was "the lingua franca of diplomacy." Latin was a lingua franca of the Roman Empire and of western Christendom for a millennium, just as Greek served eastern Christendom as its lingua franca. Among Jews, Yiddish has long served as a lingua franca, permitting Jews of all nationalities to communicate among themselves.

More frequently, lingua francas serve as trade languages. East Africa is populated by hundreds of villages, each speaking its own language, but most Africans of this area learn at least some Swahili as a second language, and this lingua franca is used and understood in nearly every marketplace. A similar situation exists in Nigeria, where Hausa is the lingua franca.

Hindi and Urdu are the lingua francas of India and Pakistan. The linguistic situation of this area of the world is so complex that there are often regional lingua francas—usually a local language surrounding a commercial center. Thus the Dravidian language Kannada is a lingua franca for the area surrounding the southwestern Indian city of Mysore. A similar situation existed in Imperial China.

In modern China, 94 percent of the people speak Han languages, which can be divided into eight major dialects (or language groups) that for the most part are mutually unintelligible. (Roughly speaking, the Han languages are comparable to the Germanic languages such as Dutch, English, German, and Norwegian, which have a common origin but are not mutually intelligible. This situation is fully discussed in chapter 11.) Within each group there are hundreds of dialects. In addition to the Han languages, there are more than fifty "national minority" languages, including the five principal ones: Mongolian, Uighur, Tibetan, Zhuang, and Korean. The situation is complex, and therefore an extensive language reform policy was inaugurated to spread a standard language as a lingua franca, called *Putonghua*, which embodies the pronunciation of the Beijing dialect, the grammar of northern Chinese dialects, and the vocabulary of modern colloquial Chinese. The native languages and dialects are not considered inferior. Rather, the approach is to spread the "common speech" (the literal meaning of Putonghua), so that all may communicate with one another in this lingua franca.

Certain lingua francas arise naturally; others are instituted by government policy and intervention. In many parts of the world, however, people still cannot speak with their neighbors only a few miles away.

Pidgins

> I include 'pidgin-English' . . . even though I am referred to in that splendid language as 'Fella belong Mrs. Queen.'
>
> **PRINCE PHILIP,** *Husband of Queen Elizabeth II*

A lingua franca is typically a language with a broad base of native speakers, likely to be used and learned by persons whose native language is in the same language family. Often in history, however, traders and missionaries from one part of the world have visited and attempted to communicate with peoples residing in another distant part. In such cases, the contact is too specialized, and the cultures too widely separated, for one language to function effectively as a lingua franca. Instead, the two (or possibly more) groups use their native languages as a basis for a rudimentary lingua franca with few lexical items and less complex grammatical rules. Generally, most of the lexical items are chosen from a dominant language, called the **lexifier language**. The other language or languages contribute marginally to the lexicon and grammar. A language cobbled together in such a way is known as a **pidgin**.

During the seventeenth, eighteenth, and nineteenth centuries, many pidgins sprang up along the coasts of China, Africa, and the New World to accommodate the Europeans. Chinook Jargon was a pidgin widely used in the Pacific Northwest of the United States. It had features both from indigenous languages of the area such as Chinook and Nootka, as well as French and English. Various tribes used it as a lingua franca among themselves for commercial purposes, as well as with the European traders.

Some linguists have suggested that Proto-Germanic (the earliest form of the Germanic languages) was originally a pidgin, arguing that ordinary linguistic change cannot explain certain striking differences between the Germanic tongues and other Indo-European languages. They theorized that in the first millennium B.C.E. the primitive Germanic tribes that resided along the Baltic Sea traded with the more sophisticated, seagoing cultures. The two peoples communicated by means of a pidgin, which either grossly affected Proto-Germanic or actually became Proto-Germanic. If this is true, English, German, Dutch, and Yiddish had humble beginnings as a pidgin.

Although pidgins are in some sense rudimentary, they are not devoid of rules. The phonological system is rule-governed, as in any human language. The inventory of phonemes is generally small, and each phoneme may have many allophonic pronunciations. In one English-based pidgin, for example, [s], [ʃ], and [tʃ] are all possible pronunciations of the phoneme /s/; [masin], [maʃin], and [matʃin] all mean "machine."

There are also some grammatical rules. For example, in several English-based pidgins, verbs that take a direct object must have the suffix *-m* or *-im*, even if the direct object is absent. Here are some examples of the application of this rule:

Mi driman long kil*im* wanpela snek.
*Mi driman long kil wanpela snek.
I dream of killing a snake.

Bandarap i bin kuk*im*.
*Bandarap i bin kuk.
Bandarap cooked (it).

Nevertheless, one of the characteristics of pidgins is that speakers from different linguistic backgrounds may have different sets of rules, giving the language a more haphazard feel than one gets from a fully developed language. Japanese is an SOV (verb last) language, and a Japanese speaker of an English-based pidgin may put the verb last, as in *The poor people all potato eat*. On the other hand, a Filipino speaker of Tagalog, a VSO language, may put the verb first as in *Work hard these people*.

The set of pronouns is often simpler in pidgins. In an English-based pidgin spoken in Cameroon (CP), the pronoun system does not show gender or all the case differences that exist in Standard English (SE).

CP			SE		
a	mi	ma	I	me	my
yu	yu	yu	you	you	your
i	i/am	i	he	him	his
i	i/am	i	she	her	her
wi	wi	wi	we	us	our
wuna	wuna	wuna	you	you	your
dɛm	dɛm/am	dɛm	they	them	their

Pidgins also may have fewer prepositions than the languages on which they are based. In CP, for example, *fɔ* means "to," "at," "in," "for," and "from," as shown in the following examples:

Gif di buk fɔ mi.	"Give the book to me."
I dei fɔ fam.	"She is at the farm."
Dɛm dei fɔ chɔs.	"They are in the church."
Du dis wan fɔ mi, a bɛg.	"Do this for me, please."
Di mɔni dei fɔ tebul.	"The money is on the table."
You fit muf tɛn frank fɔ ma kwa.	"You can take ten francs from my bag."

With their small vocabularies, however, pidgins are not good at expressing fine distinctions of meaning. Many lexical items bear a heavy semantic burden, with context relied on to remove ambiguity. The word *muckamuck* in Chinook Jargon could mean "eat," "drink," or other activities performed with the mouth. Much circumlocution and metaphorical extension is necessary. All of these factors combine to give pidgins a unique flavor. What could be a friendlier definition of "friend" than *him brother belong me*, or more poetic than this description of the sun: *lamp belong Jesus*? A policeman is *gubmint catchum-fella*, whiskers are *grass belong face*, and when a man is thirsty *him belly allatime burn*.

Pidgin has come to have negative connotations, perhaps because many pidgins were associated with European colonial empires. The *Encyclopedia Britannica* once described pidgins as "an unruly bastard jargon, filled with nursery imbecilities, vulgarisms and corruptions." It no longer uses such a definition. In recent times there is greater recognition that pidgins reflect human creative linguistic ability, as is beautifully revealed by the Chinese servant asking whether his master's prize sow had given birth to a litter: *Him cow pig have kittens?* as well as the description of Prince Philip, the husband of Queen Elizabeth II of England, quoted in the epigraph to this section.

Some people would like to eradicate pidgins. Through massive education, English replaced a pidgin spoken on New Zealand by the Maoris. The government of China at the time forbade the use of Chinese Pidgin English. It died out by the end of the nineteenth century because the Chinese gained access to English, which proved to be more useful in communicating with non-Chinese speakers.

Pidgins have been unjustly maligned; they may serve a useful function. For example, a person can learn an English-based pidgin well enough in six months to begin many kinds of semiprofessional training. To learn English for the same purpose might require ten times as long. In areas with many mutually unintelligible languages, a pidgin can play a vital role in unifying similar cultures.

In general, pidgins are short-lived, perhaps spanning several human generations, though a few have lasted much longer. Pidgins may die out because the speakers all come to share a common language. This was the fate of Chinook Jargon, a pidgin once widely spoken in the American Northwest, whose speakers all learned English. Also, because pidgins are often disdained, there is social pressure for speakers to learn a "standard" language, usually the one on which the pidgin is based. Finally, and ironically, the death of a pidgin language may come about because of its success in uniting diverse communities; the pidgin proves so useful and becomes so widespread, that successive generations in the communities in which it is spoken adopt it as their native tongue. But as it is acquired by children as a first language, it ceases to be a pidgin and becomes a creole.

Creoles

Padi dɛm; kɔntri; una ɔl we de na Rom.
Mɛk una ɔl kak una yes. A kam bɛr Siza,
a nɔ kam prez am.

WILLIAM SHAKESPEARE, Julius Caesar, *3.2, translated to Krio by Thomas Decker*

When children are exposed to a pidgin as their linguistic input, they develop a language that is no longer a pidgin but that shares many of the fundamental characteristics of a nonpidgin human language, one that is far richer and more complex than the pidgin that the children heard when growing up. Such a language is called a **creole**. The question arises as to how children are able to construct a creole based on the rudimentary input of the pidgin. The answer is that the pidgin is reanalyzed by the children, whose innate grammatical abilities immensely enrich it, and so it becomes a full-fledged language.

Creoles often arose on slave plantations in certain areas where Africans of many different tribes could communicate only via the plantation pidgin. Haitian Creole, based on French, developed in this way, as did the "English" spoken in parts of

Jamaica. Gullah is an English-based creole spoken by the descendants of African slaves on islands off the coast of Georgia and South Carolina. Louisiana Creole, related to Haitian Creole, is spoken by large numbers of blacks and whites in Louisiana. Krio, the language spoken by as many as a million Sierra Leoneans, and illustrated in the epigraph to this section, developed at least in part from an English-based pidgin.

Tok Pisin is a creole that evolved from Melanesian Pidgin English, once a widely spoken lingua franca of Papua New Guinea. It had its roots in English-based pidgins developed in the nineteenth century for use between English-speaking traders and the native population. Because New Guinea is so linguistically diverse—more than 800 different languages were once spoken throughout the island—the pidgin came to be used as a lingua franca among the indigenous population as well.

Tok Pisin was gradually creolized throughout the twentieth century. (Creolization is not an instantaneous process and may take several generations to fully develop and spread throughout the area where the pidgin is spoken.) While Creoles retain some of the simplicity of the underlying pidgin—for example, the pronominal system may have fewer distinctions as discussed earlier for Cameroonian Pidgin—they nevertheless are equal to noncreole languages in their creativity and flexibility.

Tok Pisin has its own writing system, its own literature, and its own newspapers and radio programs; it has even been used to address a United Nations meeting. Papers in (not *on*!) Tok Pisin have been presented at linguistics conferences in Papua New Guinea, and it is commonly used for debates in the parliament of the country. Today, Tok Pisin is one of the three recognized national languages of The Independent State of Papua New Guinea, alongside English and Kiri Motu, another creole.

Sign languages may also be pidgins. In Nicaragua in the 1980s, adult deaf people came together and constructed a crude system more like pantomiming than sign language in order to communicate. It had the characteristics of a pidgin in that different people used it differently and the grammatical rules were few and varied. However, when young deaf children joined the community, an amazing event took place. The crude sign language of the adults was tremendously enhanced by the children learning it, so much so that it emerged as a fully viable sign language called Idioma de Signos Nicaragüense, or Nicaraguan Sign Language. This is another example of how a fully developed human language sprang from a crudely developed pidgin—a process of creolization that, because of the absence of a model language, can only be explained by appeal to the human child's innate knowledge of certain fundamental aspects of grammar.

The study of pidgins and creoles has contributed a great deal to our understanding of the nature of human language and the genetically determined constraints on grammars.

Language in Use

One of the themes of this book is that you have a lot of linguistic knowledge that you may not be aware of, but that can be made explicit through the rules of phonology, morphology, syntax, and semantics. You also have a deep social knowledge of your language. You know the appropriate way to talk to your parents, your friends, your clergy, and your teachers. You know when it's okay to say *ain't*, and when it ain't okay; you know when to use cool language and when to speak formally; you know when to refer to the male sex organ as a dick, and when to call it, well, a male sex

"Jump Start" copyright © 2001 United Feature Syndicate, Inc. Reprinted by permission.

organ. You even know, especially if you have been born in the past thirty years, about "politically correct" (PC) language, to say "mail *carrier*," "fire*fighter*," and "police *officer*," and not to say "nigger," "wop," and "bitch." In short, you know how to use your language appropriately, even if you sometimes choose not to.

Just as your regional dialect groups you geographically, and your social dialect(s) groups you socially, the way you use language may also indicate an inclination on your part to belong to a group. Gang members adopt a certain (tough) style of talk that helps them identify with the gang. Members of a profession identify themselves through the use of special terminology like *morphophonemics*, or by ascribing a special meaning to words like *grammar* and *linguist*. Gay men and women may choose to use language to express themselves in a style that identifies them with the gay community. This section discusses some of the many ways in which the use of language varies in society.

Styles

Most speakers of a language speak one way with friends, another on a job interview or presenting a report in class, another talking to small children, another with their parents, and so on. These "situation dialects" are called **styles**, or **registers**.

Nearly everybody has at least an informal and a formal style. In an informal style, the rules of contraction are used more often, the syntactic rules of negation and agreement may be altered, and many words are used that do not occur in the formal style.

Informal styles, although permitting certain abbreviations and deletions not permitted in formal speech, are also rule-governed. For example, questions are often shortened with the subject *you* and the auxiliary verb deleted. One can ask *Running the marathon?* or *You running the marathon?* instead of the more formal *Are you running the marathon?* but you cannot shorten the question *to *Are running the marathon?* Similarly, *Are you going to take the Linguistics 1 course?* can be abbreviated to *You gonna take the Ling 1 course?* or simply *Gonna take Ling 1?* but not to **Are gonna take Ling 1?* Informal talk is not anarchy and even informal registers are rule-governed, but the rules of deletion, contraction, and word choice are different from those of the formal language.

It is common for speakers to have competence in several styles, ranging between the two extremes of formal and informal. Speakers of minority dialects sometimes display virtuosic ability to slide back and forth along a continuum of styles that range from the informal patterns of street talk to formal standard classroom talk. When

William Labov was studying African American English used by Harlem youths, he encountered difficulties because the youths (subconsciously) adopted a different style in the presence of strangers. It took time and effort to gain their confidence to the point where they would forget that their conversations were being recorded and so use their less formal style. Labov, famously, also noted the use of styles as a means of identification with a particular group (e.g., a family, gang, or church), and/or nonidentification with groups believed to be hostile or undesirable.

Many cultures have rules of social behavior that govern style. Some Indo-European languages distinguish between "you (familiar)" and "you (polite)." German *du* and French *tu* are to be used only with "intimates"; *Sie* and *vous* are more formal and used with nonintimates. French even has a verb *tutoyer*, which means "to use the *tu* form," and German uses the verb *duzen* to refer to the informal or less honorific style of speaking.

Other languages have a much more elaborate code of style usage. For example, speakers of Thai have various words for "eat." They use *kin* when conversing with intimates, *thaan* when conversing with nonintimates, *rabprathaan* on formal occasions or when conversing with dignitaries or esteemed persons (such as professors), and *chan* exclusively when referring to Buddhist monks. The situation is even more complex than that. Because *kin* is the most informal word, used around the family dinner table, it is also used when referring to animals for which a more formal term would be inappropriate. Further, *kin* may be used with nonintimates who are disliked in order to show disrespect or contempt, the idea being that such individuals are unworthy of the more formal word. Japanese and Javanese are also languages with elaborate styles that must be adhered to in certain social situations.

Slang

> Slang is language which takes off its coat, spits on its hands—and goes to work.
>
> CARL SANDBURG

> Don't bogart that joint my friend.
>
> ELLIOT INGBER

One mark of an informal style is the frequent occurrence of **slang**. Slang is something that nearly everyone uses and recognizes, but nobody can define. The use of slang has introduced many new words into the language by recombining old words into new meanings. *Spaced out, right on, hang-up*, and *rip-off* have all gained a degree of acceptance. Slang also introduces entirely new words such as *barf, flub*, and *dis*. Finally, slang often consists of ascribing entirely new meanings to old words. *Rave* has broadened its meaning to "an all-night dance party," where *ecstasy* (slang for a kind of drug) is taken to provoke wakefulness; *crib* refers to one's home and *posse* to one's cohorts. *Grass* and *pot* widened their meaning to "marijuana"; *pig* and *fuzz* are derogatory terms for "police officer"; *rap, cool, dig, stoned, bread, split*, and *suck* have all extended their semantic domains.

The words we have cited may sound slangy because they have not gained total acceptability. Words such as *dwindle, freshman, glib*, and *mob* are former slang words that in time overcame their "unsavory" origin. It is not always easy to know where to draw the line between slang words and regular words. This confusion seems to have always been around. In 1890, John S. Farmer, coeditor with W. E. Henley of *Slang and*

Its Analogues, remarked: "The borderland between slang and the 'Queen's English' is an ill-defined territory, the limits of which have never been clearly mapped out."

In 1792, Friedrich Christian Laukhard wrote: "It is common knowledge that students have a language that is quite peculiar to them and that is not understood very well outside student society." The situation has not changed. Many college campuses publish a slang dictionary that gives college students the hip words they need to be cizool ("cool"), many of them for drinking and sex.

One generation's slang is another generation's standard vocabulary. *Fan* (as in "Dodger fan") was once a slang term, short for *fanatic. Phone*, too, was once a slangy, clipped version of *telephone*, as *TV* was of *television*. In Shakespeare's time, *fretful* and *dwindle* were slang, and more recently *blimp* and *hot dog* were both "hard-core" slang.

The use of slang varies from region to region, so slang in New York and slang in Los Angeles differ. The word *slang* itself is slang in British English for "scold."

Slang words and phrases are often "invented" in keeping with new ideas and customs. They may represent "in" attitudes better than the more conservative items of the vocabulary. Their importance is shown by the fact that it was thought necessary to give the returning Vietnam prisoners of war a glossary of eighty-six new slang words and phrases, from *acid* to *zonked*. The words on this list—prepared by the Air Force—had come into use in merely five years. Furthermore, by the time the words were published, many of them had already passed out of the language, and many new ones had been added.

Many slang words have entered English from the underworld, such as *crack* for a special form of cocaine, *payola, C-note, G-man, to hang paper* ("to write 'bum' checks"), *sawbuck*, and so forth. Prison slang has given us *con* ("a convicted prisoner"), *brek* ("young offender," from *breakfast*), *burn* (tobacco or cigarettes), *peter* ("cell"), and *screw* (prison officer).

Slang even emanates from the White House of the U.S. Capitol. Writers are called *pencils*, newspaper photographers are *stills,* TV camera operators are *sticks* (a reference to their tripods), and the *football* refers to the black box of national security secrets that the president's *mil aide* carries everywhere.

The now ordinary French word meaning "head," *tête*, was once a slang word derived from the Latin *testa*, which meant "earthen pot." Some slang words persist in the language, never changing their status from slang to "respectable." Shakespeare used the expression *beat it* to mean "scram" (or more politely, "leave!"), and most English speakers would still consider *beat it* a slang expression. Similarly, the use of the word *pig* for "policeman" goes back at least as far as 1785, when a writer of the time called a Bow Street police officer a "China Street pig."

Jargon and Argot

Police are notorious for creating new words by shortening existing ones, such as *perp* for perpetrator, *ped* for pedestrian and *wit* for witness. More baffling to court reporters is the gang member who . . . might testify that he was in his *hoopty* around *dimday* when some *mud duck* with a *tray-eight* tried to take him *out of the box*. Translation: The man was in his car about dusk when a woman armed with a .38 caliber gun tried to kill him.

Los Angeles Times, *August 11, 1986*

Practically every conceivable science, profession, trade, and occupation has its own set of words, some of which are considered slang and others technical, depending on the status of the people using these "in" words. Such words are sometimes called **jargon**, or **argot**. Linguistic jargon, some of which is used in this book, consists of terms such as *phoneme, morpheme, case, lexicon, phrase structure rule*, and so on. Part of the reason for specialized terminology is for clarity of communication, but part is also for speakers to identify themselves with the group, the set of colleagues with whom they share professional interests.

An intriguing female *written* argot arose in the Jiangyong Prefecture of Hunan Province, China, with roots as early as the third century C.E. It is called *Nushu*, literally "woman's writing." Women were not taught to read and write in sexually oppressive Imperial China, and so to express themselves among themselves, and to exclude men from the expression of their deepest thoughts and feelings, they invented an ideographic system similar to, but distinct from, ordinary Chinese ideographic writing. Nushu was passed down from generation to generation of Chinese women, who carefully preserved its secrecy well into the twentieth century. Through Nushu, women shared their every thought, from diaries and poetry to recipes and medical treatments. Today only a handful of women, and now a few men, can read and write Nushu, which is dying out because women, freer and less oppressed in modern China, have less need for this secret writing. Nushu is a stunning example of how the sharing of a language characteristic can provide a bonding mechanism for a particular group.

A French argot called *verlan* is widely used by youths, drug users, and criminals as a sign of bonding among group members and to confound authority figures. In verlan, a word is pronounced by reversing the pronunciation of its syllables and putting them back together with modifications so that the phonotactic rules of the language are obeyed. The word *verlan* comes from French *l'envers* ("reverse") by first syllabifying it to *l'en vers*, reversing to *vers l'en*, and removing the *s* to get *verl'en*, which is spelled *verlan* in accordance with French orthography. Other examples are *meuf* for *femme* ("woman") and *céfran* for *français* ("French"). What is interesting is that criminal or not, you cannot break the rules of language, so that phonotactic and orthographic constraints are adhered to.

Because the jargon used by different professional and social groups is so extensive (and so obscure in meaning), court reporters in the Los Angeles Criminal Courts Building have a library that includes books on medical terms, guns, trade names, and computer jargon, as well as street slang.

The computer age not only ushered in a technological revolution, it also introduced a huge jargon of "computerese" used by computer "hackers" and others. So vast is this specialized vocabulary that *Webster's New World Computer Dictionary* has 400 pages and contains thousands of computer terms as entries. A few such words that are familiar to most people are *modem* (from **mod**ulator-**dem**odulator), *bit* (from **b**inary dig**it**), and *byte* (eight *bits*). Acronyms and alphabetic abbreviations abound in computer jargon. *ROM* (read-only memory), *RAM* (random-access memory), *CPU* (central processing unit), and DVD (digital video disk) are a small fraction of what's out there.

Many jargon terms pass into the standard language. Jargon, like slang, spreads from a narrow group that originally embraced it until it is used and understood by a large segment of the population.

Taboo or Not Taboo?

Sex is a four-letter word.

BUMPER STICKER SLOGAN

"There are some words I will not tolerate in this house—and 'awesome' is one of them."

An item in a newspaper once included the following paragraph:

> "This is not a Sunday school, but it is a school of law," the judge said in warning the defendants he would not tolerate the "use of expletives during jury selection." "I'm not going to have my fellow citizens and prospective jurors subjected to filthy language," the judge added.

How can language be filthy? In fact, how can it be clean? The filth or beauty of language must be in the ear of the listener, or in the collective ear of society. The writer Paul Theroux points this out:

> A foreign swear-word is practically inoffensive except to the person who has learned it early in life and knows its social limits.

Nothing about a particular string of sounds makes it intrinsically clean or dirty, ugly or beautiful. If you say that you pricked your finger when sewing, no one would raise an eyebrow, but if you refer to your professor as a prick, the judge quoted previously would undoubtedly censure this "dirty" word.

You know the obscene words of your language, and you know the social situations in which they are desirable, acceptable, forbidden, and downright dangerous to utter. Most people remember acquiring these words as a child, often repeating them innocently in the presence of an adult and—surprise, surprise—little Suzy or Johnny has just learned something new about the force of words.

Certain words are considered **taboo** in all societies—they are not to be used, or at least not in "polite company." The word *taboo* was borrowed from Tongan, a Polynesian language, in which it refers to acts that are forbidden or to be avoided. When an act is taboo, reference to this act may also become taboo. That is, first you are forbidden to do something, then you are forbidden to talk about it.

Forbidden acts or words reflect the particular customs and views of the society. Some words may be used in certain circumstances and not in others. Among the Zuni Indians, it is improper to use the word *takka*, meaning "frogs," during a religious ceremony; a complex compound word must be used instead, which literally translated would be "several-are-sitting-in-a-shallow-basin-where-they-are-in-liquid."

In the world of Harry Potter, the evil Voldemort is not to be named, but is referred to as "You-Know-Who." In certain societies, words that have religious connotations are considered profane if used outside of formal or religious ceremonies. In many religions believers are forbidden to "take the Lord's name in vain," and this prohibition often extends to the use of curses, which are believed to have magical powers. Thus *hell* and *damn* are changed to *heck* and *darn*, perhaps with the belief or hope that this change will fool the "powers that be." Imagine the last two lines of Act II, Scene 1, of *Macbeth* if they were "cleaned up:"

> Hear it not, Duncan; for it is a knell
> That summons thee to heaven, or to heck

Loses a little something, wouldn't you say?

Words that are taboo in one locale may be acceptable in another, and vice versa, and the acceptance changes over time. In the 1830s, a British visitor to America, Fanny Trollope, remarked:

> Hardly a day passed in which I did not discover something or other which I had been taught to consider as natural as eating, was held in abhorrence by those around me; many words to which I had never heard an objectionable meaning attached, were totally interdicted, and the strangest paraphrastic phrases substituted.

Some of the words that were taboo at that time in America but not in England were *corset, shirt, leg*, and *woman*. Fanny Trollope remarked:

> The ladies here have an extreme aversion to being called women . . . Their idea is, that that term designates only the lower or less-refined classes of female human-kind. This is a mistake which I wonder they should fall into, for in all countries in the world, queens, duchesses, and countesses, are called women.

In England the word *bloody* is, or perhaps was, a taboo word. In Shaw's *Pygmalion* the following lines "startled London and indeed, flustered the whole Empire," according to the British scholar Eric Partridge, when the play was first produced in London in 1910.

> "Are you walking across the Park, Miss Doolittle?"
> "Walk! Not bloody likely. I am going in a taxi."

Partridge adds, "Much of the interest in the play was due to the heroine's utterance of this banned word. It was waited for with trembling, heard shudderingly."

The *Oxford English Dictionary* states that *bloody* has been in general colloquial use from the Restoration and is "now constantly in the mouths of the lowest classes, but by respectable people considered 'a horrid word' on a par with obscene or profane language, and usually printed in the newspapers 'b____y.'" The origin of the term is not quite certain. One view is that the word is derived from an oath involving the "blood of Christ"; another that it relates to menstruation. The scholars do not agree, and the public has no idea. This uncertainty gives us a clue about vulgarities: People who use them often do not know why they are taboo, only that they are, and to some extent they remain in the language to give vent to strong emotion.

Words relating to sex, sex organs, and natural bodily functions make up a large part of the set of taboo words of many cultures. Some languages have no native words to mean "sexual intercourse" but have to borrow such words from neighboring people. Other languages have many words for this common and universal act, most of which are taboo.

Two or more words or expressions can have the same linguistic meaning, with one acceptable and the others the cause of embarrassment or horror. In English, words borrowed from Latin sound "scientific" and therefore appear to be technical and "clean," whereas native Anglo-Saxon counterparts are taboo. This fact reflects the opinion that the vocabulary used by the upper classes was superior to that used by the lower classes, a distinction going back at least to the Norman Conquest in 1066, when "a duchess perspired and expectorated and menstruated—while a kitchen maid sweated and spat and bled." Such pairs of words are illustrated as follows:

Anglo-Saxon Taboo Words	Latinate Acceptable Words
cunt	vagina
cock	penis
prick	penis
tits	mammary gland
shit	feces

There is no grammatical reason why the word *vagina* [vədʒājnə] is "clean" whereas *cunt* [kʌ̃nt] is "dirty," or why *prick* or *cock* is taboo but *penis* is acknowledged as referring to part of the male anatomy, or why everyone *defecates* but only vulgar people *shit*. Many people even avoid words like *breasts, intercourse,* and *testicles* as much as words like *tits, fuck,* and *balls*. Although there is no grammatical basis for such preferences, there certainly are sociolinguistic reasons to embrace or eschew such usages, just as there are sociolinguistic reasons for speaking formally, respectfully, disrespectfully, informally, jargon riddled, and so on.

Euphemisms

Banish the use of the four-letter words
Whose meaning is never obscure.
The Anglos, the Saxons, those bawdy old birds
Were vulgar, obscene, and impure.

But cherish the use of the weaseling phrase
That never quite says what it means;
You'd better be known for your hypocrite ways
Than vulgar, impure, and obscene.

Folk song attributed to Wartime Royal Air Force of Great Britain

The existence of taboo words and ideas motivates the creation of **euphemisms**. A euphemism is a word or phrase that replaces a taboo word or serves to avoid frightening or unpleasant subjects. In many societies, because death is feared, there are many euphemisms related to this subject. People are less apt to *die* and more apt to *pass on* or *pass away*. Those who take care of your loved ones who have passed away are more likely to be *funeral directors* than *morticians* or *undertakers*. And then there's *feminine protection* . . .

The use of euphemisms is not new. It is reported that the Greek historian Plutarch in the first century C.E. wrote that "the ancient Athenians . . . used to cover up the ugliness of things with auspicious and kindly terms, giving them polite and endearing names. Thus they called harlots *companions*, taxes *contributions*, and prison a *chamber*."

The aforementioned poem exhorts against such euphemisms, as another verse demonstrates:

When in calling, plain speaking is out;
When the ladies (God bless 'em) are milling about,
You may wet, make water, or empty the glass;
You can powder your nose, or the "johnny" will pass.
It's a drain for the lily, or man about dog
When everyone's drunk, it's condensing the fog;
But sure as the devil, that word with a hiss,
It's only in Shakespeare that characters ____.

Some scholars are bemused with the attitudes revealed by the use of euphemisms. A journal, *Maledicta*, subtitled *The International Journal of Verbal Aggression* and edited by Reinhold Aman, "specializes in uncensored glossaries and studies of all offensive and negatively valued words and expressions, in all languages and from all cultures, past and present." A review of this journal by Bill Katz in the *Library Journal* (November 1977) points out, "The history of the dirty word or phrase is the focus of this substantial . . . journal [whose articles] are written in a scholarly yet entertaining fashion by professors . . . as well as by a few outsiders."

A scholarly study of Australian English euphemisms shows the considerable creativity involved:

urinate: drain the dragon
siphon the python
water the horse
squeeze the lemon
drain the spuds
wring the rattlesnake
shake hands with the wife's best friend
point Percy at the porcelain
train Terence on the terracotta

have intercourse: shag
root
crack a fat
dip the wick
play hospital
hide the ferret
play cars and garages
hide the egg roll (sausage, salami)
boil bangers
slip a length
go off like a belt fed motor
go like a rat up a rhododendron
go like a rat up a drain pipe
have a northwest cocktail

These euphemisms, as well as the difference between the accepted Latinate "genteel" terms and the "dirty" Anglo-Saxon terms, show that a word or phrase has not only a linguistic **denotative meaning** but also a **connotative meaning** that reflects attitudes, emotions, value judgments, and so on. In learning a language, children learn which words are taboo, and these taboo words differ from one child to another, depending on the value system accepted in the family or group in which the child grows up.

Racial and National Epithets

The use of epithets for people of different religions, nationalities, or races tells us something about the users of these words. The word *boy* is not a taboo word when used generally, but when a twenty-year-old white man calls a forty-year-old African American man "boy," the word takes on an additional meaning; it reflects the racist attitude of the speaker. So also, words like *kike* (for Jew), *wop* (for Italian), *nigger* or *coon* (for African American), *slant* (for Asian), *towelhead* (for Middle Eastern Arab), and so forth reflect racist and chauvinist views of society.

Such epithets are found under surprising circumstances. The chairman of the Raleigh Convention and Visitors Bureau in North Carolina was quoted in the newspaper[4] as saying: "If we had a shabby-looking place, we wouldn't have a Chinaman's chance of attracting the people we need to do business with." One is tempted to observe that the chances of attracting any of the 1.2 billion potential Chinese tourists might be diminished by such statements. Even words that sound like epithets are perhaps to be avoided (see exercise 13). An administrator in Washington, D.C. described a fund he administers as "niggardly," meaning stingy. He resigned his position under fire for using a word "so close to a degrading word."

The use of the verbs to *jew* or to *gyp/jip* also reflect the stereotypical views of Jews and Gypsies. Most people do not realize that *gyp*, which is used to mean "cheat," comes from the view that Gypsies are duplicitous. In time these words would either disappear or lose their racist connotations if bigotry and oppression ceased to exist, but because they show no signs of doing so, the use of such words reflects racism, perpetuates stereotypes, and separates one people from another.

---

[4]*Raleigh News and Observer*, February 22, 1999.

Language, however, is creative, malleable, and ever changing. The epithets used by a majority to demean a minority may be reclaimed as terms of bonding and friendship among members of the minority. Thus, for some—we emphasize *some*—African Americans, the word *nigger* is used to show affection. Similarly, the ordinarily degrading word *queer* is used among *some* gay persons as a term of endearment, as is *cripple* or *crip* among *some* individuals who share a disability.

Language and Sexism

doctor, n. . . . a man of great learning.

THE AMERICAN COLLEGE DICTIONARY, 1947

A businessman is aggressive; a businesswoman is pushy. A businessman is good on details; she's picky. . . . He follows through; she doesn't know when to quit. He stands firm; she's hard. . . . His judgments are her prejudices. He is a man of the world; she's been around. He isn't afraid to say what is on his mind; she's mouthy. He exercises authority diligently; she's power mad. He's closemouthed; she's secretive. He climbed the ladder of success; she slept her way to the top.

FROM "HOW TO TELL A BUSINESSMAN FROM A BUSINESSWOMAN,"
Graduate School of Management, UCLA, The Balloon XXII, (6).

The discussion of obscenities, blasphemies, taboo words, and euphemisms showed that words of a language are not intrinsically good or bad, but reflect individual or societal values. In addition, one speaker may use a word with positive connotations while another may select a different word with negative connotations to refer to the same person. For example, a person may be called a *terrorist* or a *freedom fighter* depending on who is doing the calling. A woman may be a *castrating female* (or *ballsy women's libber*) or may be a *courageous feminist advocate,* again depending on who is talking. The words we use to refer to certain individuals or groups reflect our individual nonlinguistic attitudes and may reflect the culture and views of society.

Dictionaries often give clues to social attitudes. In the 1969 edition of the *American Heritage Dictionary*, examples used to illustrate the meaning of words include "manly courage" and "masculine charm." Women do not fare as well, as exemplified by "womanish tears" and "feminine wiles." In *Webster's New World Dictionary of the American Language* (1961), *honorarium* is defined as "a payment to a professional man for services on which no fee is set or legally obtainable." Attempts to deflect the inherent sexism in such definitions by claiming that *man* actually means "human" was deftly parried in 1973:

If a woman is swept off a ship into the water, the cry is *Man overboard*. If she is killed by a hit-and-run driver, the charge is *manslaughter*. If she is injured on the job, the coverage is *workmen's compensation*. But if she arrives at the threshold marked *Men Only*, she knows the admonition is not intended to bar animals or plants or inanimate objects. It is meant for her.[5]

---

[5]A. Graham. December 1973. "How to Make Troubles: The Making of a Nonsexist Dictionary," *Ms.*

Until 1972, at Columbia University, the women's faculty toilet doors were labeled "Women," whereas the men's doors were labeled "Officers of Instruction." Yet, linguistically, the word *officer* is not marked semantically for gender. There were apparently few women professors at Columbia at that time, which was reflected in these designations. This shows that nonlinguistic aspects of society may influence our interpretation of the meaning of words. Thus, until recently, most people hearing *My cousin is a professor* (or a *doctor*, or *the Chancellor of the University*, or a *steel worker*) would assume that the cousin is a man.

On the other hand, if you heard someone say *My cousin is a nurse* (or *elementary school teacher*, or *clerk-typist*, or *house worker*), you would probably conclude that the speaker's cousin is a woman. It is less evident why the sentence *My neighbor is a blond* (or a *redhead* or a *brunette*) is understood as referring to a woman. Apparently, in our society at least, hair color is a primary category of classification for women, but whether that fact is part of the *meaning* of such words is debatable.

Studies analyzing the language used by men in reference to women, which often has derogatory or sexual connotations, indicate that such terms go far back into history, and sometimes enter the language with no pejorative implications but gradually gain them. Thus, from Old English *huswif*, "housewife," the word *hussy* was derived. In their original employment, a laundress made beds, a needlewoman came to sew, a spinster tended the spinning wheel, and a nurse cared for the sick. But all apparently acquired secondary duties in some households, because all became euphemisms for a mistress or a prostitute at some time during their existence.

Words for women—all with abusive or sexual overtones—abound: *dish, tomato, piece, piece of ass, piece of tail, bunny, chick, pussy, pussycat, bitch, doll, slut, cow, eye candy*—to name just a few. Far fewer such sexual terms exist for men, and those that do, such as *boy toy, stud muffin, hunk,* or *jock,* are not pejorative in the same way.

It's clear that language can be used to promote sexism. It can be used to promote any cause, good or evil, just or unjust. Languages are infinitely flexible and expressive. It is another question to ask whether there is something about language, or a particular language, that abets sexism. Before we attempt to answer that question, let's look more deeply into the subject, using English as the illustrative language.

MARKED AND UNMARKED FORMS

Long afterward, Oedipus, old and blinded, walked the roads. He smelled a familiar smell. It was the Sphinx. Oedipus said, "I want to ask one question. Why didn't I recognize my mother?" "You gave the wrong answer," said the Sphinx. "But that was what made everything possible," said Oedipus. "No," she said. "When I asked, 'What walks on four legs in the morning, two at noon, and three in the evening,' you answered, 'Man.' You didn't say anything about woman." "When you say Man," said Oedipus, "you include women too. Everyone knows that." She said, "That's what you think."

MURIEL RUKEYSER, Myth[6]

---

[6] Reprinted by permission of International Creative Management, Inc. Copyright © 1973 Muriel Rukeyser. From *The Collected Poems of Muriel Rukeyser*, University of Pittsburgh Press 2005.

One striking fact about the asymmetry between male and female terms in many languages is that when there are male/female pairs, the male form for the most part is unmarked and the female term is created by adding a bound morpheme or by compounding. We have many such examples in English:

Male	Female
prince	princess
author	authoress
count	countess
actor	actress
host	hostess
poet	poetess
heir	heiress
hero	heroine
Paul	Pauline

Since the advent of the feminist movement, many of the marked female forms have been replaced by the male forms, which are used to refer to either sex. Thus women, as well as men, are authors, actors, poets, heroes, and heirs. Women, however, remain countesses, duchesses, and princesses, if they are among this small group of female aristocrats.

Other male/female gender pairs have interesting meaning differences. Although a governor governs a state, a governess takes care of children; a mistress, in its most widely used meaning, is not a female master, nor is a majorette a woman major. We talk of "unwed mothers" but not "unwed fathers," of "career women" but not "career men," because there has been historically no stigma for a bachelor to father a child, and men are supposed to have careers. It is only recently that the term *househusband* has come into being, again reflecting changes in social customs.

Possibly as a protest against the reference to new and important ideas as *seminal* (from *semen*), Clare Booth Luce updated Ibsen's drama *A Doll's House* by having Nora tell her husband that she is pregnant "in the way only men are supposed to get pregnant." When he asks, "Men pregnant?" she replies, "With ideas. Pregnancies there (she taps her head) are masculine. And a very superior form of labor. Pregnancies here (she taps her stomach) are feminine—a very inferior form of labor."

Other linguistic asymmetries exist, such as the fact that most women continue to adopt their husbands' names in marriage. This name change can be traced back to early legal practices, some of which are perpetuated currently. Thus we often refer to a woman as Mrs. Jack Fromkin, but seldom refer to a man as Mr. Vicki Fromkin, except in an insulting sense. This convention, however, is not true in other cultures. We talk of Professor and Mrs. John Smith but seldom, if ever, of Mr. and Dr. Philippa Kerr. At a UCLA alumni association dinner, place cards designated where "Dr. Fromkin" and "Mrs. Fromkin" were to sit, although both individuals have doctoral degrees.

It is insulting to a woman to be called a *spinster* or an *old maid*, but it is not insulting to a man to be called a *bachelor*. There is nothing inherently pejorative about the word *spinster*. The connotations reflect the different views society has about an unmarried woman as opposed to an unmarried man.

THE GENERIC "HE"

> If the English language had been properly organized . . . then there would be a word which meant both "he" and "she," and I could write, "If John or Mary comes, heesh will want to play tennis," which would save a lot of trouble.
>
> **A. A. MILNE,** The Christopher Robin Birthday Book

The unmarked, or male, nouns (e.g., *actor, host, lion*) also serve as general terms, as do the male pronouns (e.g., *he, him, his*). The *brotherhood of man* includes women, but *sisterhood* does not include men. *My neighbor likes his new car* allows for the neighbor to be female, but *My neighbor likes her new car* does not allow for a male neighbor.

When Thomas Jefferson wrote in the Declaration of Independence that "all *men* are created equal" and "governments are instituted among *men* deriving their just powers from the consent of the governed," he was not using *men* as a general term to include women. His use of the word *men* was precise at the time that women could not vote. In the sixteenth and seventeenth centuries, masculine pronouns were not used as the generic terms; the various forms of *he* were used when referring to males, and of *she* when referring to females. The pronoun *they* was used to refer to people of either sex even if the referent was a singular noun, as shown by Lord Chesterfield's statement in 1759: "If a person is born of a gloomy temper . . . they cannot help it."

By the eighteenth century, grammarians (males to be sure) created the rule designating the male pronouns as the general term, but the rule wasn't applied widely until the nineteenth century, after an act of Britain's Parliament in 1850 sanctioned its use. But this generic use of *he* was ignored. In 1879, women doctors were barred from membership in the all-male Massachusetts Medical Society on the basis that the bylaws of the organization referred to members by the pronoun *he*.

Changes in English are taking place that indicate a growing awareness on the part of both men and women that language may reflect attitudes of society and reinforce stereotypes and bias. More and more, the word *people* is replacing *mankind, personnel* is used instead of *manpower, nurturing* instead of *mothering*, and to *operate* instead of *to man. Chair* or *moderator* is used instead of *chairman* (particularly by those who do not like the awkwardness of *chairperson*), and terms like *postal worker, firefighter*, and *public safety officer* or *police officer* are replacing *mailman, fireman*, and *policeman*.

Many suggestions for a single, genderless third person pronoun for English have been proposed (e.g., *e, hesh, po, tey, co, jhe, ve, xe, he'er, thon, na*), but there seems to be no inclination on the part of speakers to adopt any of them, and it appears likely that *he* and *she* are going to be with us for a while.

The Sapir-Whorf hypothesis, discussed in chapter 1, proposes that the way a language encodes—puts into words—different categories like male and female subtly affects the way speakers of the language think about those categories. Thus, it may be argued that because English speakers are often urged to choose *he* as the unmarked pronoun (*One should love **his** neighbor*), and to choose *she* only when the referent is overtly female, they tend to think of the male sex as predominant. Likewise, the fact that nouns require special affixes to make them feminine forces people to think in terms of male and female, with the female somehow more derivative because of affixing. The different titles, Mr., Mrs., Miss, and Ms., also emphasize the male/female distinction. (Compare Japanese, which although it has distinctive genderlects, has the gender-neutral morpheme *-san* for polite address.) Finally, the preponderance of words denigrating females in English and many other languages may create a climate that is more tolerant of sexist behavior.

Nevertheless, although people can undoubtedly be sexist and even cultures can be sexist, can language be sexist? That is, can we be molded by our language to be something we may not want to be? Or does language merely facilitate any natural inclinations we may have? Is it simply a reflection of societal values? These questions are disputed today by linguists, anthropologists, psychologists, and philosophers, and no definitive answer has yet emerged.

Secret Languages and Language Games

Throughout the world and throughout history, people have invented secret languages and language games. They have used these special languages as a means of identifying with their group and/or to prevent outsiders from knowing what is being said, as in the case of *Verlan*, discussed previously as an argot, or *Nushu*, the woman's writing of Chinese. Often, though, it's merely for fun, as with the Elvish language from "Lord of the Rings."

When the aim is secrecy, several methods are used; immigrant parents sometimes use their native language when they do not want their children to understand what they are saying, or parents may spell out words. American slaves developed an elaborate code that could not be understood by the slave owners. References to "the promised land" or the "flight of the Israelites from Egypt" sung in spirituals were codes for the north and the Underground Railroad.

One special language is Cockney rhyming slang. No one is completely sure how it first arose. One view is that it began as a secret language among the criminals of the underworld in London in the midnineteenth century to confuse the "peelers" (i.e., the police). Another view is that during the building of the London docks at the beginning of the century, the Irish immigrant workers invented rhyming slang to confuse the non-Irish workers. Still another view is that it was spread by street chanters who went from market to market in England telling tales, reporting the news, and reciting ballads.

This language game is played by creating a rhyme as a substitute for a specific word. Thus, for *table* the rhymed slang may be *Cain and Abel*; *missus* is called *cows and kisses*; *stairs* are *apples and pears*; *head* is *loaf of bread*, often shortened to *loaf* as in "use yer loaf." Several cockney rhyming slang terms have crossed the ocean to America. *Bread* meaning *money* in American slang comes from cockney *bread and honey;* and *brass tacks*—those things that Americans love to get down to—is derived from the cockney rhyming slang for *facts*.

Other language games, such as Pig Latin,[7] are used for amusement by and of children and adults. They exist in all the world's languages and take a wide variety of forms. In some, a suffix is added to each word; in others a syllable is inserted after each vowel; there are rhyming games and games in which phonemes are reversed. A game in Brazil substitutes an /i/ for all the vowels; Indian children learn a Bengali language game in which the syllables are reversed (reminiscent of verlan), as in pronouncing *bisri,* "ugly," as *sribi*.

---

[7]Dog is pronounced *og-day, parrot* as *arrot-pay,* and *elephant* as *elephant-may,* etc., but see exercise 6.

A language game based on writing disguises a forbidden word by adding strokes to alter letters. Thus FUCK becomes ENOR by altering its four letters; CUNT becomes OOMF, and now the innocent-sounding nonsense words are codes for the vulgarities.

The Walbiri, natives of central Australia, play a language game in which the meanings of words are distorted. In this play language, all nouns, verbs, pronouns, and adjectives are replaced by a semantically contrastive word. Thus, the sentence *Those men are small* means *This woman is big*.

These language games provide evidence for the phonemes, words, morphemes, semantic features, and so on that are posited by linguists for descriptive grammars. They also illustrate the boundless creativity of human language and human speakers.

Summary

Every person has a unique way of speaking, called an **idiolect**. The language used by a group of speakers is a **dialect**. The dialects of a language are the mutually intelligible forms of that language that differ in systematic ways from each other. Dialects develop because languages change, and the changes that occur in one group or area may differ from those that occur in another. **Regional dialects** and **social dialects** develop for this reason. Some differences in U.S. regional dialects may be traced to the dialects spoken by colonial settlers from England. Those from southern England spoke one dialect and those from the north spoke another. In addition, the colonists who maintained close contact with England reflected the changes occurring in British English, while earlier forms were preserved among Americans who spread westward and broke communication with the Atlantic coast. The study of regional dialects has produced **dialect atlases**, with **dialect maps** showing the areas where specific dialect characteristics occur in the speech of the region. A boundary line called an **isogloss** delineates each area.

Social dialects arise when groups are isolated socially, such as Americans of African descent in the United States, many of whom speak dialects collectively called African American (Vernacular) English, which are distinct from the dialects spoken by non-Africans.

Dialect differences include phonological or pronunciation differences (often called **accents**), vocabulary distinctions, and syntactic rule differences. The grammar differences among dialects are not as great as the similarities, thus permitting speakers of different dialects to communicate.

In many countries, one dialect or dialect group is viewed as the **standard**, such as **Standard American English (SAE)**. Although this particular dialect is not linguistically superior, some language purists consider it the only correct form of the language. Such a view has led to the idea that some nonstandard dialects are deficient, as is erroneously suggested regarding **African American English** (sometimes referred to as **Ebonics**), a collection of dialects used by some African Americans. A study of African American English shows it to be as logical, complete, rule-governed, and expressive as any other dialect. This is also true of the dialects spoken by Latino Americans whose native language or those of their parents is Spanish. There are bilingual and monolingual Latino speakers of English. One Latino dialect spoken in the Southwest, referred to as **Chicano English (ChE)**, shows systematic phonological and syntactic differences from SAE that stem from the influence of Spanish. Other differences are shared with many nonstandard ethnic and nonethnic dialects. **Code-**

switching is when bilingual persons switch from one language to another, also within a single sentence. It reflects both grammars working simultaneously and does not represent a form of "broken" English or Spanish or whatever.

Attempts to legislate the use of a particular dialect or language have been made throughout history and exist today, even extending to banning the use of languages other than the preferred one.

In areas where many languages are spoken, one language may become a **lingua franca** to ease communication among people. In other cases, where traders, missionaries, or travelers need to communicate with people who speak a language unknown to them, a **pidgin** based on one language—the **lexifier language**—may develop, which is simplified lexically, phonologically, and syntactically. When a pidgin is widely used, and constitutes the primary linguistic input to children, it is *creolized*. The grammars of **creole** languages are similar to those of other languages, and languages of creole origin now exist in many parts of the world and include sign languages of the deaf.

Besides regional and social dialects, speakers may use different **styles**, or **registers**, depending on the context. **Slang** is not often used in formal situations or writing but is widely used in speech; **argot** and **jargon** refer to the unique vocabulary used by particular groups of people to facilitate communication, provide a means of bonding, and exclude outsiders.

In all societies, certain acts or behaviors are frowned on, forbidden, or considered **taboo**. The words or expressions referring to these taboo acts are then also avoided or considered "dirty." Language cannot be obscene or clean; attitudes toward specific words or linguistic expressions reflect the views of a culture or society toward the behaviors and actions of the language users. At times, slang words may be taboo where scientific or standard terms with the same meaning are acceptable in "polite society." Taboo words and acts give rise to **euphemisms**, which are words or phrases that replace the expressions to be avoided. Thus, *powder room* is a euphemism for *toilet*, which started as a euphemism for *lavatory*, which is now more acceptable than its replacement.

Just as the use of some words may indicate society's views toward sex, natural bodily functions, or religious beliefs, some words may also indicate racist, chauvinist, or sexist attitudes. Language is not intrinsically racist or sexist but reflects the views of various sectors of a society. However, the availability of offensive terms, and particular grammatical peculiarities such as the lack of a genderless third-person singular pronoun, may perpetuate and reinforce biased views and be demeaning and insulting to those addressed. Thus culture influences language, and, arguably, language may have an influence on the culture in which it is spoken.

The invention or construction of secret languages and language games like verlan and Pig Latin attest to human creativity with language and the unconscious knowledge that speakers have of the phonological, morphological, and semantic rules of their language.

References for Further Reading

Bickerton, D. 1981. *Roots of Language*. Ann Arbor, MI: Karoma.

Cameron, D. 1992. *Feminism and Linguistic Theory*, 2nd edition. London: Macmillan.

Carver, C. M. 1987. *American Regional Dialects: A Word Geography*. Ann Arbor, MI: University of Michigan Press.

Cassidy, F. G. (chief ed.). 1985, 1991, 1996, 2002. *Dictionary of American Regional English,* Volumes 1, 2, 3, 4. Cambridge, MA: Harvard University Press.

Chambers, J., and P. Trudgill. 1998. *Dialectology,* 2nd edition. Cambridge, UK: Cambridge University Press.

Coates, J. 1993. *Women, Men and Language: A Sociolinguistic Account of Sex Differences in Language.* Upper Saddle River, NJ: Pearson Education.

Fasold, R. 1990. *Sociolinguistics of Language.* London: Blackwell Publishers.

Ferguson, C., and S. B. Heath, eds. 1981. *Language in the USA.* Cambridge, UK: Cambridge University Press.

Holm, J. 2000. *An Introduction to Pidgins and Creoles.* Cambridge, UK: Cambridge University Press.

Labov, W. 1966. *The Social Stratification of English in New York City.* Washington, DC: Center for Applied Linguistics.

_____. 1969. *The Logic of Nonstandard English.* Georgetown University 20th Annual Round Table, Monograph Series on Languages and Linguistics, No. 22.

_____. 1972. *Sociolinguistic Patterns.* Philadelphia: University of Pennsylvania Press.

Lakoff, R. 1990. *Talking Power: The Politics of Language.* New York: Basic Books.

Simpson, J. 2005. *The Oxford Dictionary of Modern Slang.* Oxford, UK: Oxford University Press.

Tannen, D. 1990. *You Just Don't Understand: Women and Men in Conversation.* New York: Ballantine.

_____. 1994. *Gender and Discourse.* New York: Oxford University Press.

Thorne, B., C. Kramarae, and N. Henley, eds. 1983. *Language, Gender, and Society.* Rowley, MA: Newbury House.

Trudgill, P. 2001. *Sociolinguistics, An Introduction to Language and Society,* 4th edition. London: Penguin Books.

Williamson, J. V., and V. M. Burke. 1971. *A Various Language: Perspectives on American Dialects.* New York: Holt, Rinehart, and Winston.

Wolfram, W., and N. Schilling-Estes. 1998. *American English Dialects and Variation.* London: Blackwell Publishers.

Exercises

1. Each pair of words is pronounced as shown phonetically in at least one American English dialect. Write in phonetic transcription your pronunciation of each word that you pronounce differently.

a. horse	[hɔrs]		hoarse	[hors]		
b. morning	[mɔrnĩŋ]		mourning	[mornĩŋ]		
c. for	[fɔr]		four	[for]		
d. ice	[ʌjs]		eyes	[ajz]		
e. knife	[nʌjf]		knives	[najvz]		
f. mute	[mjut]		nude	[njud]		
g. din	[dĩn]		den	[dẽn]		
h. hog	[hɔg]		hot	[hat]		
i. marry	[mæri]		Mary	[meri]		
j. merry	[mɛri]		marry	[mæri]		
k. rot	[rat]		wrought	[rɔt]		
l. lease	[lis]		grease (v.)	[griz]		

m. what	[ʌʌat]	watt	[wat]
n. ant	[ænt]	aunt	[ãnt]
o. creek	[kʰrɪk]	creak	[kʰrik]

2. Below is a passage from *The Gospel According to St. Mark* in Cameroon English Pidgin. See how much you can understand before consulting the English translation given below. State some of the similarities and differences between CEP and SAE.

   a. Di fos tok fo di gud nuus fo Jesus Christ God yi Pikin.

   b. I bi sem as i di tok fo di buk fo Isaiah, God yi nchinda (Prophet), "Lukam, mi a di sen man nchinda fo bifo yoa fes weh yi go fix yoa rud fan."

   c. Di vos fo som man di krai fo bush: "Fix di ples weh Papa God di go, mek yi rud tret."

   Translation:

   a. The beginning of the gospel of Jesus Christ, the Son of God.

   b. As it is written in the book of Isaiah the prophet, "Behold, I send my messenger before thy face, which shall prepare thy way before thee."

   c. The voice of one crying in the wilderness, "Prepare ye the way of the Lord, make his paths straight."

3. In the period from 1890 to 1904, *Slang and Its Analogues*, by J. S. Farmer and W. E. Henley, was published in seven volumes. The following entries are included in this dictionary. For each item (1) state whether the word or phrase still exists; (2) if not, state what the modern slang term would be; and (3) if the word remains but its meaning has changed, provide the modern meaning.

   all out: completely, as in "All out the best." (The expression goes back to as early as 1300.)
   to have apartments to let: be an idiot; one who is empty-headed.
   been there: in "Oh, yes, I've been there." Applied to a man who is shrewd and who has had many experiences.
   belly-button: the navel.
   berkeleys: a woman's breasts.
   bitch: most offensive appellation that can be given to a woman, even more provoking than that of *whore*.
   once in a blue moon: seldom.
   boss: master; one who directs.
   bread: employment. (1785 — "out of bread" = "out of work.")
   claim: to steal.
   cut dirt: to escape.
   dog cheap: of little worth. (Used in 1616 by Dekker: "Three things there are dog-cheap, learning, poorman's sweat, and oathes.")
   funeral: as in "It's not my funeral." "It's no business of mine."
   to get over: to seduce, to fascinate.
   groovy: settled in habit; limited in mind.
   grub: food.
   head: toilet (nautical use only).
   hook: to marry.

hump: to spoil.

hush money: money paid for silence; blackmail.

itch: to be sexually excited.

jam: a sweetheart or a mistress.

leg bags: stockings.

to lie low: to keep quiet; to bide one's time.

to lift a leg on: to have sexual intercourse.

looby: a fool.

malady of France: syphilis (used by Shakespeare in 1599).

nix: nothing.

noddle: the head.

old: money. (1900 — "Perhaps it's somebody you owe a bit of the old to, Jack.")

to pill: talk platitudes.

pipe layer: a political intriguer; a schemer.

poky: cramped, stuffy, stupid.

pot: a quart; a large sum; a prize; a urinal; to excel.

puny: a freshman.

puss-gentleman: an effeminate.

4. Suppose someone asked you to help compile items for a new dictionary of slang. List ten slang words, and provide a short definition for each.

5. Below are some words used in British English for which different words are usually used in American English. See if you can match the British and American equivalents.

British

a. clothes peg	**k.** biscuits
b. braces	**l.** queue
c. lift	**m.** torch
d. pram	**n.** underground
e. waistcoat	**o.** high street
f. shop assistant	**p.** crisps
g. sweets	**q.** lorry
h. boot (of car)	**r.** holiday
i. bobby	**s.** tin
j. spanner	**t.** knock up

American

A. candy	**K.** baby buggy
B. truck	**L.** elevator
C. line	**M.** can
D. main street	**N.** cop
E. crackers	**O.** wake up
F. suspenders	**P.** trunk
G. wrench	**Q.** vest
H. flashlight	**R.** subway
I. potato chips	**S.** clothes pin
J. vacation	**T.** clerk

6. Pig Latin is a common language game of English; but even Pig Latin has dialects, forms of the "language game" with different rules.

   A. Consider the following data from three dialects of Pig Latin, each with its own rule applied to words beginning with vowels:

	Dialect 1	Dialect 2	Dialect 3
"eat"	[itme]	[ithe]	[ite]
"arc"	[arkme]	[arkhe]	[arke]
"expose"	[ɛkspozme]	[ɛkspozhe]	[ɛkspoze]

(1) State the rule that accounts for the Pig Latin forms in each dialect.

(2) How would you say *honest*, *admire*, and *illegal* in each dialect? Give the phonetic transcription of the Pig Latin forms.

B. In one dialect of Pig Latin, the word "strike" is pronounced [ajkstre], and in another dialect it is pronounced [trajkse]. In the first dialect "slot" is pronounced [atsle] and in the second dialect, it is pronounced [latse].

(1) State the rules for each of these dialects that account for these different Pig Latin forms of the same words.

(2) Give the phonetic transcriptions for *spot*, *crisis*, and *scratch* in both dialects.

7. Below are some sentences representing different English language games. Write each sentence in its undistorted form; state the language-game "rule."

a. /aj-o tʊk-o maj-o dag-o awt-o sajd-o/

b. /hirli ɪzli əli mɔrli kamliplɪlikelitədli gemli/

c. Mary-shmary can-shman talk-shmalk in-shmin rhyme-shmyme.

d. Bepeterper latepate thanpan nepeverper.

e. thop-e fop-oot bop-all stop-a dop-i op-um blop-ew dop-own /ðapə fapʊt bapɔl stape dapi apəm blapu dapawn/

f. /kʌbæn jʌbu spʌbik ðʌbɪs kʌbajnd ʌbəv ʌbɪŋglʌbɪʃ/ (This sentence is in "Ubby Dubby" from a children's television program popular in the 1970s.)

8. Below are sentences that might be spoken between two friends chatting informally. For each, state what the nonabbreviated full sentence in SAE would be. In addition, state in your own words (or formally if you wish) the rule or rules that derived the informal sentences from the formal ones.

a. Where've ya been today?

b. Watcha gonna do for fun?

c. Him go to church?

d. There's four books there.

e. Who ya wanna go with?

9. Compile a list of argot (or jargon) terms from some profession or trade (e.g., lawyer, musician, doctor, longshoreman). Give a definition for each term in non-jargon terms.

10. "Translate" the first paragraph of any well-known document or speech—such as the Declaration of Independence, the Gettysburg Address, or the Preamble to the U.S. Constitution—into informal, colloquial language.

11. In Column A are Cockney rhyming slang expressions. Match these to the items in Column B to which they refer.

A	B
a. drip dry	(1) balls (testicles)
b. In the mood	(2) bread

    c. Insects and ants   (3) ale

    d. orchestra stalls   (4) cry

    e. Oxford scholar   (5) food

    f. strike me dead   (6) dollar

    g. ship in full sail   (7) pants

Now construct your own version of Cockney rhyming slang for the following words:

    h. chair

    i. house

    j. coat

    k. eggs

    l. pencil

12. Column A lists euphemisms for words in Column B. Match each item in A with its appropriate B word.

A	B
a. Montezuma's revenge	(1) condom
b. joy stick	(2) genocide
c. friggin'	(3) fire
d. ethnic cleansing	(4) diarrhea
e. French letter (old)	(5) masturbate
f. diddle oneself	(6) kill
g. holy of holies	(7) urinate
h. spend a penny (British)	(8) penis
i. ladies' cloak room	(9) die
j. knock off (from 1919)	(10) waging war
k. vertically challenged	(11) vagina
l. hand in one's dinner pail	(12) women's toilet
m. sanitation engineer	(13) short
n. downsize	(14) fuckin'
o. peace keeping	(15) garbage collector

13. Defend or criticize the following statement in a short essay:

A person who uses the word *niggardly* in a public hearing should be censured for being insensitive and using a word that resembles a degrading, racist word.

14. The words *waitron* and *waitperson* are currently fighting it out to see which, if either, will replace *waitress* as a gender-neutral term. Using dictionaries, the Internet, and whatever other resources you can think of, predict the winner, or the failure of both candidates. Give reasons for your answers.

15. If you have access to the Internet, search for Tok Pisin. You will quickly find Web sites where it is possible to hear Tok Pisin spoken. Listen to a passage several times. How much of it can you understand without looking at the text or the translation? Then follow along with the text (generally provided) until you can hear the individual words. Now try a new passage. Does your comprehension improve? How much practice do you think you would need before you could understand roughly half of what is being said the first time you heard it?

16. A language game that is so popular it has appeared in the *Washington Post* is to take a word or (well-known) expression and alter it by adding, subtracting, or changing one letter, and supplying a new (clever) definition. Read the following examples, try to figure out the expression from which they are derived, and then try to produce ten on your own. (*Hint*: lots of Latin)

Cogito eggo sum	I think, therefore I am a waffle.
Foreploy	A misrepresentation about yourself for the purpose of getting laid
Veni, vipi, vici	I came, I am important, I conquered.
Giraffiti	Dirty words sprayed very, very high
Ignoranus	A person who is both stupid and an asshole
Rigor Morris	The cat is dead.
Felix navidad	Our cat has a boat.
Veni, vidi, vice	I came, I saw, I smoked.
Glibido	All talk, no action
Haste cuisine	Fast French food
L'état, c'est moo	I'm bossy around here.
Intaxication	The euphoria that accompanies a tax refund
Ex post fucto	"Lost in the mail"

17. In his original, highly influential novel *1984*, George Orwell introduces Newspeak, a government-enforced language designed to keep the masses subjugated. He writes:

> Its vocabulary was so constructed as to give exact and often very subtle expression to every meaning that a Party member could properly wish to express, while excluding all other meanings and also the possibility of arriving at them by indirect methods. This was done partly by the invention of new words, but chiefly by eliminating undesirable words and by stripping such words as remained of unorthodox meanings, and so far as possible of all secondary meanings whatever. To give a single example. The word *free* still existed in Newspeak, but it could only be used in such statements as "This dog is free from lice" or "This field is free from weeds." It could not be used in its old sense of "politically free" or "intellectually free," since political and intellectual freedom no longer existed even as concepts, and were therefore of necessity nameless.

Critique Newspeak. Will it achieve its goal? Why or why not? (*Hint*: You may want to review concepts such as language creativity and arbitrariness as discussed in the first few pages of chapter 1.)

18. In *1984* Orwell proposed that if a concept does not exist, it is nameless. In the passage quoted below, he suggests that if a crime were nameless, it would be unimaginable, hence impossible to commit:

    > A person growing up with Newspeak as his sole language would no more know that . . . *free* had once meant "intellectually free," than, for instance, a person who had never heard of chess would be aware of the secondary meanings attaching to *queen* and *rook*. There would be many crimes and errors which it would be beyond his power to commit, simply because they were nameless and therefore unimaginable.

    Critique this notion.

19. One aspect of different English genderlects is lexical choice. For example, women say *darling* and *lovely* more frequently than men; men use sports word metaphors such as *home run* and *slam dunk* more than women. Think of other lexical usages that appear to be asymmetric between the sexes.

20. Research question: Throughout history many regimes have banned languages. Write a report in which you mention several such regimes, the languages they banned, and possible reasons for banning them (e.g., you might have discovered that the Basque language was banned in Spain under the regime of Francisco Franco (1936–1975) owing in part to the separatist desires of the Basque people and because the Basques opposed his dictatorship).

21. Abbreviated English (AE) is a register of written English used in newspaper headlines and elsewhere. Some examples follow:

    CLINTON IN BULGARIA THIS WEEK
    OLD MAN FINDS RARE COIN
    BUSH HIRES WIFE AS SECRETARY
    POPE DIES IN VATICAN

    AE does not involve an arbitrary omission of parts of the sentence, but is regulated by grammatical rules.

    A. Translate each of these headlines into Standard American English (SAE).

    B. What features or rules distinguish AE from SAE?

    C. Are there other contexts (besides headlines) in which we find AE? If so, provide examples.

    Challenge questions:

    A. What is the time reference of the above headlines (e.g., present, recent past, remote past, future)?

    B. Is there a difference in possible tense interpretations when the predicate is eventive (e.g., *dies*) than when it is stative (e.g., *in Bulgaria*)?

11

Language Change:
The Syllables of Time

> No language as depending on arbitrary use and custom can ever be permanently the same, but will always be in a mutable and fluctuating state; and what is deem'd polite and elegant in one age, may be accounted uncouth and barbarous in another.
>
> **BENJAMIN MARTIN,** *Lexicographer*

All living languages change with time. It is fortunate that they do so rather slowly compared to the human life span. It would be inconvenient to have to relearn our native language every twenty years. Stargazers find a similar situation. Because of the movement of individual stars, the constellations are continuously changing their shape. Fifty thousand years from now we would hardly recognize Orion or the Big Dipper, but from season to season the changes are imperceptible. Linguistic change is also slow, in human—if not astronomical—terms. As years pass we hardly notice any change. Yet if we were to turn on a radio and miraculously receive a broadcast in our "native language" from the year 3000, we would probably think we had tuned in a foreign language station. Many language changes are revealed in written records. We know a great deal of the history of English because it has been a written language for about 1,000 years. Old English, spoken in England around the end of the first millennium, is scarcely recognizable as English. (Of course, our linguistic ancestors did not call their language Old English!) A speaker of Modern English would find the language unintelligible. There are college courses in which Old English is studied as a foreign language.

A line from *Beowulf* illustrates why Old English must be translated:[1]

Wolde guman findan þone þe him on sweofote sare geteode.
He wanted to find the man who harmed him while he slept.

Approximately five hundred years after *Beowulf*, Chaucer wrote *The Canterbury Tales* in what is now called Middle English, spoken from around 1100 to 1500. It is more easily understood by present-day readers, as seen by looking at the opening of the *Tales*:

Whan that Aprille with his shoures soote
The droght of March hath perced to the roote . . .
When April with its sweet showers
The drought of March has pierced to the root . . .

Two hundred years after Chaucer, in a language that can be considered an earlier form of Modern English, Shakespeare's Hamlet says:

A man may fish with the worm that hath eat of a king, and eat of the fish that hath fed of that worm.

The stages of English are Old English (449–1100 C.E.), Middle English (1100–1500), and Modern English (1500–present). This division is somewhat arbitrary, being marked by dates of events in English history, such as the Norman Conquest of 1066, the results of which profoundly influenced the English language. Thus the history of English and the changes in the language reflect nonlinguistic history to some extent, as suggested by the following dates:

449–1066 Old English	449	Saxons invade Britain
	6th century	Religious literature
	8th century	*Beowulf*
	1066	Norman Conquest
1066–1500 Middle English	1387	*Canterbury Tales*
	1476	Caxton's printing press
	1500	Great Vowel Shift
1500–Modern English	1564	Birth of Shakespeare

Changes in a language are changes in the grammars of people who speak the language and are perpetrated as new generations of children acquire the altered language and make further changes to the grammar. This is true of sign languages as well as spoken languages. Like all living languages, American Sign Language continues to change. Not only have new signs entered the language over the past 200 years, but also the forms of the signs have changed in ways similar to the historical changes in spoken languages.

An examination of the past 1,500 years of English shows changes in the lexicon as well as to the phonological, morphological, syntactic, and semantic components of the grammar. No part of the grammar remains the same over the course of history. Although most of the examples in this chapter are from English, the histories of all languages show similar changes.

---

[1]The letter þ is called *thorn* and is pronounced [θ] in this example.

The Regularity of Sound Change

> That's not a regular rule: you invented it just now.
>
> **LEWIS CARROLL,** Alice's Adventures in Wonderland

The southern United States represents a major dialect area of American English. For example, words pronounced with the diphthong [aj] in non-Southern English will usually be pronounced with the monophthong [aː] in the South. Local radio and TV announcers at the 1996 Olympics in Atlanta called athletes to the [haː] "high" jump, and local natives invited visitors to try Georgia's famous pecan [paː] "pie." The [aj]-[aː] correspondence of these two dialects is an example of a **regular sound correspondence**. When [aj] occurs in a word in non-Southern dialects, [aː] occurs in the Southern dialect, and *this is true for all such words*.

The different pronunciations of *I*, *my*, *high*, *pie*, and such did not always exist in English. This chapter will discuss how such dialect differences arose and why the sound differences are usually regular and not confined to just a few words.

Sound Correspondences

In Middle English a *mouse* [maws] was called a *mūs* [muːs], and this *mūs* may have lived in someone's *hūs* [huːs], the way *house* [haws] was pronounced at that time. In general, Middle English speakers pronounced [uː] where we now pronounce [aw]. This is a regular correspondence like the one between [aj] and [aː]. Thus *out* [awt] was pronounced [uːt], *south* [sawθ] was pronounced [suːθ], and so on. Many such regular correspondences show the relation of older and newer forms of English.

The regular sound correspondences we observe between older and modern forms of a language are the result of phonological changes that affect certain sounds, or classes of sounds, rather than individual words. Centuries ago English underwent a phonological change called a **sound shift** in which [uː] became [aw].

Phonological changes can also account for dialect differences. At an earlier stage of American English a sound shift of [aj] to [aː] took place among certain speakers in the southern region of the United States. The change did not spread beyond the South because the region was somewhat isolated. Many dialect differences in pronunciation result from sound shifts whose spread is limited.

Regional dialect differences may also arise when innovative changes occur everywhere but in a particular region. The regional dialect may be conservative relative to other dialects. The pronunciation of *it* as *hit*, found in the Appalachian region of the United States, was standard in older forms of English. The dropping of the [h] was the innovation.

Ancestral Protolanguages

Many modern languages were first regional dialects that became widely spoken and highly differentiated, finally becoming separate languages. The Romance languages—French, Spanish, and so on—were once dialects of Latin spoken in the Roman Empire. There is nothing degenerate about regional pronunciations. They result from natural sound changes that occur wherever human language is spoken.

In a sense, the Romance languages are the offspring of Latin, their metaphorical parent. Because of their common ancestry, the Romance languages are **genetically**

related. Early forms of English and German, too, were once dialects of a common ancestor called **Proto-Germanic**. A **protolanguage** is the ancestral language from which related languages have developed. Both Latin and Proto-Germanic were descendants of an older language called **Indo-European** or **Proto-Indo-European**. Thus, Germanic languages such as English and German are genetically related to the Romance languages such as French and Spanish. All these important national languages were once regional dialects.

How do we know that the Germanic and Romance languages have a common ancestor? One clue is the large number of sound correspondences. If you have studied a Romance language such as French or Spanish, you may have noticed that where an English word begins with *f*, the corresponding word in a Romance language often begins with *p*, as shown in the following examples:

English /f/	French /p/	Spanish /p/
father	père	padre
fish	poisson	pescado

This /f/-/p/ correspondence is another example of a regular sound correspondence. There are many such correspondences between the Germanic and Romance languages, and their prevalence cannot be explained by chance. What then accounts for them? A reasonable guess is that a common ancestor language used a *p* in words for *fish*, *father*, and so on. We posit a /p/ rather than an /f/ because more languages show a /p/ in these words. At some point speakers of this language separated into two groups that lost contact with each other. In one of the groups a sound change of *p* → *f* took place. The language spoken by this group eventually became the ancestor of the Germanic languages. This ancient sound change left its trace in the *f-p* sound correspondence that we observe today, as illustrated in the diagram.

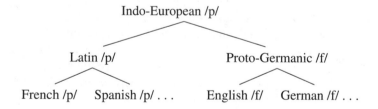

Indo-European /p/

Latin /p/   Proto-Germanic /f/

French /p/   Spanish /p/ . . .   English /f/   German /f/ . . .

Phonological Change

Etymologists . . . for whom vowels did not matter and who cared not a jot for consonants.

Voltaire

Regular sound correspondences illustrate changes in the phonological system. In earlier chapters we discussed speakers' knowledge of their phonological system, including knowledge of the phonemes and phonological rules of the language. Any of these aspects of the phonology is subject to change.

The velar fricative /x/ is no longer part of the phonemic inventory of most Modern English dialects. *Night* used to be pronounced [nɪxt] and *drought* was pronounced [druxt]. This phonological change—the loss of /x/—took place between the times of Chaucer and Shakespeare. All words once pronounced with an /x/ no longer include this sound. In some cases it disappeared altogether, as in *night* and *light*. In other cases the /x/ became a /k/, as in *elk* (Old English *eolh* [ɛɔlx]). In yet other cases it disappeared to be replaced by a vowel, as in *hollow* (Old English *holh* [hɔlx]). Dialects of Modern English spoken in Scotland have retained the /x/ sound in some words, such as *loch* [lax] meaning "lake."

These examples show that changes in the inventory of sounds in a language can occur through the loss of phonemes. The inventory can also change through the addition of phonemes. Old English did not have the phoneme /ʒ/ of *leisure* [liʒər]. Through a process of palatalization—a change in place of articulation to the palatal region—certain occurrences of /z/ were pronounced [ʒ]. Eventually the [ʒ] sound became a phoneme in its own right, reinforced by the fact that it occurs in French words familiar to many English speakers such as *azure* [æʒər].

An allophone of a phoneme may, through sound change, become a phoneme in its own right. Old English lacked a /v/ phoneme. The phoneme /f/, however, had the allophone [v] when it occurred between vowels. Thus *ofer* /ofer/ meaning "over" was pronounced [ɔvər] in Old English.

Old English also had a long consonant phoneme /fː/ that contrasted with /f/ between vowels. The name *Offa* /ofːa/ was pronounced [ɔfːa]. A sound change occurred in which the pronunciation of /fː/ was simplified to [f]. Now /fː/ was pronounced [f] between vowels so it contrasted with [v]. This made it possible for English to have minimal pairs involving [f] and [v]. Speakers therefore perceived the two sounds as separate phonemes, in effect, creating a new phoneme /v/.

Similar changes occur in the history of all languages. Neither /tʃ/ nor /ʃ/ were phonemes of Latin, but /tʃ/ is a phoneme of modern Italian and /ʃ/ a phoneme of modern French, both of which evolved from Latin. In American Sign Language many signs that were originally formed at the waist or chest level are now produced at a higher level near the neck or upper chest, a reflection of changes in the "phonology."

Thus in language change phonemes may be lost (/x/), or added (/ʒ/), or result from a change in the status of allophones (the [v] allophone of /f/ becoming /v/).

Phonological Rules

An interaction of phonological rules may result in changes in the lexicon. The nouns *house* and *bath* were once differentiated from the verbs *house* and *bathe* by the fact that the verbs ended with a short vowel sound. Furthermore, the same rule that realized /f/ as [v] between vowels, also realized /s/ and /θ/ as the allophones [z] and [ð] between vowels. This general rule added voicing to intervocalic fricatives. Thus the /s/ in the verb *house* was pronounced [z], and the /θ/ in the verb *bathe* was pronounced [ð].

Later a rule was added to the grammar of English deleting unstressed short vowels at the end of words (even though the final vowel still appears in the written words). A contrast between the voiced and voiceless fricatives resulted, and the new phonemes /z/ and /ð/ were added to the phonemic inventory. The verbs *house* and *bathe* were now represented in the mental lexicon with final voiced consonants.

Eventually, both the unstressed vowel deletion rule and the intervocalic-voicing rule were lost from the grammar of English. The set of phonological rules can change both by addition and loss of rules.

Changes in phonological rules can, and often do, result in dialect differences. In the previous chapter we discussed the addition of an *r*-dropping rule in English (/r/ is not pronounced unless followed by a vowel) that did not spread throughout the language. Today, we see the effect of that rule in the *r*-less pronunciation of British English and of American English dialects spoken in the northeastern and the southern United States.

From the standpoint of the language as a whole, phonological changes occur gradually over the course of many generations of speakers, although a given speaker's grammar may or may not reflect the change. The changes are not planned any more than we are presently planning what changes will take place in English by the year 2300. In a single generation changes are evident only through dialect differences.

The Great Vowel Shift

A major change in English that resulted in new phonemic representations of words and morphemes took place approximately between 1400 and 1600. It is known as the **Great Vowel Shift**. The seven long, or tense, vowels of Middle English underwent the following change:

Shift			Example			
Middle English		**Modern English**	**Middle English**		**Modern English**	
[iː]	→	[aj]	[miːs]	→	[majs]	mice
[uː]	→	[aw]	[muːs]	→	[maws]	mouse
[eː]	→	[iː]	[geːs]	→	[giːs]	geese
[oː]	→	[uː]	[goːs]	→	[guːs]	goose
[ɛː]	→	[eː]	[brɛːken]	→	[breːk]	break
[ɔː]	→	[oː]	[brɔːken]	→	[broːk]	broke
[aː]	→	[eː]	[naːmə]	→	[neːm]	name

By diagramming the Great Vowel Shift on a vowel chart (Figure 11.1), we can see that the high vowels [iː] and [uː] became the diphthongs [aj] and [aw], while the long vowels underwent an increase in tongue height, as if to fill in the space vacated by the high vowels. In addition, [aː] was fronted to become [eː].

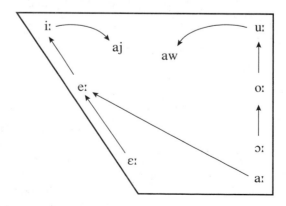

FIGURE 11.1 The Great Vowel Shift.

These changes are among the most dramatic examples of regular sound shift. The phonemic representation of many thousands of words changed. Today, some reflection of this vowel shift is seen in the alternating forms of morphemes in English: *please—pleasant*; *serene—serenity*; *sane—sanity*; *crime—criminal*; *sign—signal*; and so on. Before the Great Vowel Shift, the vowels in each pair were the same. Then the vowels in the second word of each pair were shortened by the **Early Middle English Vowel Shortening** rule. As a result, the Great Vowel Shift, which occurred later, affected only the first word in each pair. The second word, with its short vowel, was unaffected. This is why the vowels in the morphologically related words are pronounced differently today, as shown in Table 11.1.

TABLE 11.1 Effect of Vowel Shift on Modern English

Middle English Vowel	Shifted Vowel	Short Vowel	Word with Shifted Vowel	Word with Short Vowel
ī	aj	ɪ	divine	divinity
ū	aw	ʊ	profound	profundity
ē	i	ɛ	serene	serenity
ō	u	a	fool	folly
ā	e	æ	sane	sanity

The Great Vowel Shift is a primary source of many spelling inconsistencies of English because our spelling system still reflects the way words were pronounced before the Great Vowel Shift.

Morphological Change

And is he well content his son should find
No nourishment to feed his growing mind,
But conjugated verbs and nouns declin'd?

WILLIAM COWPER, Tirocinium

Like phonological rules, rules of morphology may be lost, added, or changed. We can observe some of these changes by comparing older and newer forms of the language or by looking at different dialects.

Extensive changes in morphological rules have occurred in the history of the Indo-European languages. Latin had **case endings**, suffixes on the noun based on its grammatical relationship to the verb. These are no longer found in the Romance languages. (See chapter 5 for a more extensive discussion of grammatical case.) The following is a **declension**, or list of cases, for the Latin noun *lupus*, "wolf":

Noun	Noun Stem	Case Ending	Case	Example
lupus	lup	+ us	nominative	The *wolf* runs.
lupī	lup	+ ī	genitive	A sheep in *wolf's* clothing.
lupō	lup	+ ō	dative	Give food to *the wolf*.
lupum	lup	+ um	accusative	I love *the wolf*.
lupe	lup	+ e	vocative	*Wolf*, come here!

In *Alice's Adventures in Wonderland,* Lewis Carroll has Alice give us a brief lesson in grammatical case. Alice has become very small and is swimming around in a pool of her own tears with a mouse that she wishes to befriend:

"Would it be of any use, now," thought Alice, "to speak to this mouse? Everything is so out-of-the-way down here, that I should think very likely it can talk: at any rate, there's no harm in trying." So she began: "O Mouse, do you know the way out of this pool? I am very tired of swimming about here, O Mouse!" (Alice thought this must be the right way of speaking to a mouse: she had never done such a thing before, but she remembered having seen in her brother's Latin Grammar, "A mouse-of a mouse-to a mouse-a mouse-O mouse!")

Alice gives the English corresponding to the nominative, genitive, dative, accusative, and vocative cases.

Ancient Greek and Sanskrit also had extensive case systems expressed morphologically through noun suffixing, as did Old English, as illustrated by the following noun forms:

Case	OE Singular		OE Plural	
nominative	stān	"stone"	stānas	"stones"
genitive	stānes	"stone's"	stāna	"stones'"
dative	stāne	"stone"	stānum	"stones"
accusative	stān	"stone"	stānas	"stones"

Lithuanian and Russian retain much of the early Indo-European case system, but changes have all but obliterated it in most modern Indo-European languages. In English, phonological changes over the centuries resulted in the loss of many case endings.

English retains the genitive case, which is written with an apostrophe *s*, as in *Robert's dog,* but that's all that remains as far as nouns are concerned. Pronouns retain a few more traces: *he/she* are nominative, *him/her* accusative and dative, and *his/hers* genitive.

English has replaced its depleted case system with an equally expressive system of prepositions. For example the dative case is often indicated by the preposition *to* and the genitive case by the preposition *of.* A noun occurring after a verb with no intervening preposition is often in the accusative case.

English and most of the Indo-European languages, then, have undergone extensive morphological changes over the past 1,000 years, many of them induced by changes that took place in the phonological rules of the language.

Syntactic Change

Understanding changes in grammar is a key component in understanding changes in language.

DAVID LIGHTFOOT, The Development of Language

When we see a word-for-word translation of older forms of English, we are most highly struck by the differences in word order. Consider again the opening lines of the *Canterbury Tales,* this time translated word-for-word:

Whan that Aprille with his shoures soote
When that April with its showers sweet
The droght of March hath perced to the roote . . .
The drought of March has pierced to the root . . .

In modern English, adjectives generally precede the nouns they modify, thus we would say *sweet showers* in place of *showers sweet*. Moreover, direct objects generally follow their verb so that *has pierced* **the drought of March** *to the root* would be a modern rendering of the second line.

There are other changes such as the occurrence of the complementizer *that*, which, in modern English, is not possible following a *wh*-word such as *when*. Nevertheless, it is safe to say that syntactic change in English and other languages is most evident in the changes of permitted word orders.

Syntactic change in English is a good illustration of the interrelationship of the various modules of the grammar. Changes in syntax were influenced by changes in morphology, and these in turn by changes in the phonology of the language.

When the rich system of case-endings of Old English became simplified in part because of phonological changes, speakers of English were forced to rely more heavily on word order to convey the function of noun phrases. A sentence such as

sē		*man*	*þone*		*kyning*	*sloh*
the (nominative)		man	the (accusative)		king	slew

was understood to mean "the man slew the king" because of the case markings (given in parentheses). There would have been no confusion on the listeners' part as to who did what to whom. Also, in earlier stages of English the verb had a richer system of subject-verb agreement. For example, the verb *to sing* had the following forms: *singe* (I sing), *singest* (you sing), *singeth* (he sings), and *singen* (we, plural you, they sing). It was therefore also possible in many cases to identify the subject on the basis of verb inflection. In modern English the only marker of agreement is the third-person singular *-s* in *He sings*.

Thus, in Modern English *the man the king slew* is only grammatical as a relative clause meaning "the man that the king slew," with the subject and object of *slew* reversed. To convey the meaning "the man slew the king," Modern English speakers must rely on word order—subject-verb-object—or other syntactical devices like ones found in sentences such as *It was the king that the man slew*.

The change in English word order reflects a change in the rules of grammar. The Old English VP was head final, as indicated by the following PS rule:

VP → NP V

The Old English phrase structure was like the phrase structure of Dutch and German, closely related languages. The English VP (but not German and Dutch) underwent a change in parameter setting and became head initial as follows:

VP → V NP

Thus Modern English has SVO word order whereas Old English (and modern Dutch and German) have a basic SOV word order. However, Modern English still has remnants of the original SOV word order in "old-fashioned" kinds of expressions such as *I thee wed*.

This was only one of many ramifications of the morphological simplification that took place in English. In short, as morphological distinctions vanished over the centuries, word order became stricter. For example, older grammars of English were more apt than current grammars to permit Noun-Adjective constructs, even though the Adjective-Noun word order has been the most common since Old English times.

As discussed in chapter 4, in today's English we form questions by moving an auxiliary verb, if there is one, before the NP subject:

Can the girl kiss the boy?

Will the girl kiss the boy?

Has the girl kissed the boy yet?

Was the girl kissing the boy when you arrived?

However, if an auxiliary verb is absent, modern English requires the word *do* to support the tense of the sentence:

Does the girl kiss the boy often?

*Kisses the girl the boy often?

Older forms of English had a more general rule that moved the first verbal element in the verb phrase to precede the NP subject, *even if it was a main verb*. The question

Kisses the girl the boy often?

was grammatical in English through the time of Shakespeare. This more general verb movement rule still exists in languages like Dutch and German. In English the rule of question formation changed, so that it now moves only auxiliary verbs. If no auxiliary verb is present, a "place-holding" auxiliary verb *do* fills its role. This rule change was motivated in part by the fact that in Old English, *the girl* and *the boy* would have been marked for case, so there was no possibility of misunderstanding who was kissing whom. In effect, the sentence would be:

Kisses the (nominative) girl the (accusative) boy often?

In modern English, which has only a rudimentary case system, if the main verb were moved to the front in forming questions, the usual configuration in which the NP following the main verb is the direct object would be violated. The introduction of *do* allows the main verb to remain in its base position, and thus the sentence retains the SVO word order that most plainly indicates the subject and object of the sentence.

The big picture here is that the loss of information that came with morphological simplification is compensated for by more rigid rules of word order. Such syntactic changes may take centuries to be completed, and there are often intermediate stages.

The syntactic rules relating to the English negative construction also underwent several changes from Old English to the present. In Modern English, negation is expressed by adding *not* or *do not*. We may also express negation with words like *never* or *no*.

I am going → I am not going

I went → I did not go

I go to school → I never go to school

I want food → I don't want any food; I want no food

In Old English the main negation element was *ne*. It usually occurred before a verbal element:[2]

þæt	he	*na*	siþþan	geboren	*ne*	wurde
that	he	never	after	born	not	would-be

that he should never be born after that

ac	hie	*ne*	dorston	þær	on	cuman
but	they	not	dared	there	on	come

but they dared not land there

In the first example, the word order is different from that of Modern English, and there are two negatives: *na* (a contraction of *ne* + *a*, "not" + "ever" = "never") and *ne*. As shown, a double negative was grammatical in Old English. Although double negatives are ungrammatical in Modern Standard American English, they are grammatical in some English dialects (e.g., the Rolling Stones' *I can't get no satisfaction*).

In addition to the contraction of *ne* + *a* → *na*, other negative contractions occurred in Old English: *ne* could be attached to *habb-* "have," *wes-* "be," *wit-* "know," and *will-* "will" to form *nabb-, nes-, nyt-*, and *nyll-*, respectively.

Modern English also has contraction rules that change *do* + *not* into *don't*, *will* + *not* into *won't*, and so on. In these contractions the phonetic form of the negation element always comes at the *end* of the word because Modern English word order puts the *not* after the auxiliary verb. In Old English, the negative element occurred at the beginning of the contraction because it preceded the auxiliary verb. The rules determining the position of the negative morpheme relative to the auxiliary have changed.

Another syntactic change in English affected the rules of comparative and superlative constructions. Today we form the comparative by adding *-er* to the adjective or by inserting *more* before it; the superlative is formed by adding *-est* or by inserting *most*. In Malory's *Tales of King Arthur*, written in 1470, double comparatives and double superlatives occur, which today are ungrammatical: *more gladder, more lower, moost royallest, moost shamefullest*.

Both Old English and Middle English permitted *split genitives*, that is, possessive constructs in which the words that describe the possessor occur on both sides of the head noun:

Inwæres	broþur	ond	Healfdenes (Old English)
Inwær's	brother	and	Healfden's

"Inwær's and Healfden's brother"

The Wife's tale of Bath (Middle English)

"The Wife of Bath's tale"

Modern English does not permit such constructs, but it does permit rather complex genitive expressions when the words describing the possessor occur entirely to the left of the head noun:

The man with the two small children's hat

The girl whose sister I'm dating's roommate

---

[2]From E. C. Traugott. 1972. *The History of English Syntax*. New York: Holt, Rinehart, and Winston.

It is important to note that when we study a language solely from written records, which is necessarily the case with languages such as Old or Middle English, we see only sentences that are grammatical unless ungrammatical sentences are used deliberately. Without native speakers to query, we can only infer what was ungrammatical. Such inference leads us to believe that expressions like *the Queen of England's crown* were ungrammatical in earlier periods of English. The title *The Wife's Tale of Bath* (rather than *The Wife of Bath's Tale*) in *The Canterbury Tales* supports this inference.

Once again it was the loss of case endings that resulted in this syntactic change. As the case system weakened, there was insufficient noun morphology to carry the semantic burden of expressing possession. Over the centuries the use of *'s* replaced the defunct genitive case, and in so doing generalized to syntactic units larger than merely the noun. And, as has been the theme of this entire section on syntactic change, the word order allowed in possessive constructs became more fixed and split genitives are now ungrammatical.

Lexical Change

"Get Fuzzy" © Darby Conley/Dist. by United Feature Syndicate, Inc.

Changes in the lexicon also occur. Among them are changes in the lexical categories in which a word may function.

The words *food* and *verb* are ordinarily used as nouns, but Bucky the cat refuses to be so restricted and "wordifies" them into verbs. If we speakers of English adopt Bucky's usage, then *food* and *verb* will take on the additional lexical category of verb in our mental lexicons. Recently, a radio announcer said that Congress was "to-ing and fro-ing" on a certain issue, to mean "wavering." This strange compound verb is derived from the adverb *to and fro*. In British English, *hoover* is a verb meaning "to vacuum up," derived from the proper noun *Hoover*, the name of a vacuum cleaner manufacturer. American police *Mirandize* arrested persons, meaning to read them their rights according to the Miranda rule. Since the judicial ruling was made in 1966, we have a complete history of how a proper name became a verb. Even the French, not known for their tolerance of linguistic innovation, have fallen prey to "wordification." A widespread advertisement says *Voulez-vous Cointreau avec moi*, literally, "Would you like to Cointreau with me?" Here the proper noun Cointreau, a brand of orange-flavored liqueur, is "verbed."

The word *telephone* was coined exclusively as a noun in 1844 and meant "acoustic apparatus." Alexander Graham Bell appropriated the word for his invention in 1876, and in 1877 the word was first used as a verb, meaning "to speak by telephone." In languages where verbs have a specific morphological form, such as the *-er* ending in French (*parler*, to speak) or the *-en* ending in German (*sprechen,* to speak), such changes are less common than in English. Thus the French noun *téléphone* cannot be a verb, but becomes the different word *téléphoner* as a verb.

Other categorical changes may occur historically. The word *remote* was once only an adjective, but with the invention of control-at-a-distance devices, the compound *remote control* came into usage, which ultimately was shortened to *remote*, which now functions as a noun; witness the half dozen remotes every modern household loses track of.

A recent announcement at North Carolina State University invited "all faculty to sandwich in the Watauga Seminar." We were not invited to squeeze together, but rather to bring our lunches. Although the verb *to sandwich* exists, the new verbal usage is derived from the noun *sandwich* rather than the verb.

Addition of New Words

And to bring in a new word by the head and shoulders, they leave out the old one.
MONTAIGNE

In chapter 3 we discussed ways in which new words can enter the language. These included deriving words from names (*sandwich*), blends (*smog*), back-formations (*edit*), acronyms (*NATO*), and abbreviations or clippings (*ad*). We also saw that new words may be formed by derivational processes, as in *uglification, finalize*, and *finalization.*

Compounding is a particularly productive means of creating words. Thousands of common English words have entered the language by this process, including *afternoon, bigmouth, cyberspace, day-tripper, egghead, force feed, global warming, icecap, jet set, kilowatt-hour, laptop, moreover, newsgroup, 9-11, offshore, pothole, railroad, skybox, takeover, username, water cooler, x-ray*, and *zookeeper*. (Recall that compounds are written in three different ways: as one word, as two words, and hyphenated.)

Other methods for enlarging the vocabulary that were discussed include word coinage. Societies often require new words to describe changes in technology, sports, entertainment, and so on. Languages are accommodating and inventive in meeting these needs. The words may be entirely new, as *steganography*, the concealment of information in an electronic document, or *micropolitan*, a city of less than 10,000 people. Or they may be words originally coined for one purpose, but put to work to serve a related purpose, such as *google*, meaning "to use the Google search engine on the Internet."

Even new bound morphemes may enter the language. The prefix *e-*, as in *e-commerce, e-mail, e-trade*, meaning "electronic," is barely two decades old, and most interestingly has given rise to the prefix *s-* as in *s-mail* to contrast with *e-mail*. The suffix *-gate,* meaning "scandal," derived from the Watergate scandal of the 1970s, may now be suffixed to a word to convey that meaning. Thus *Irangate* meant a scandal involving Iran, and *Dianagate*, a British usage, referred to a scandal involving wiretapped conversations of the late Princess of Wales, Diana. A change currently under way is the use of -*peat* to mean "win a championship so many years in succession," as in *threepeat* and *fourpeat,* which we have observed in the newspaper. What with Lance Armstrong having just won his seventh Tour de France bicycle race at this writing, we are waiting with bated breath for—you guessed it—*sevenpeat.*

A word so new that its spelling is still in doubt is *dot com,* also seen in magazines as .*com* and *dot.com.* It means "a company whose primary business centers on the Internet." The expression written 24/7, and pronounced *twenty-four seven,* meaning "all the time," also appears to be a new entry not yet found in dictionaries, but seen in newspapers and heard during news broadcasts. Also so new that it hasn't made the dictionaries are words that take -*zilla* as a bound suffix with the meaning "huge or extreme," as in *shopzilla, bridezilla,* and the British band *Dogzilla,* with its source being the world-famous Japanese movie monster "Godzilla."

Borrowings or Loan Words

> Neither a borrower, nor a lender be.
>
> **WILLIAM SHAKESPEARE,** Hamlet, *I. iii*

Languages ignore the "precept" of Polonius quoted above. Many of them are avid borrowers. **Borrowing** words from other languages is an important source of new words. Borrowing occurs when one language adds a word or morpheme from another language to its own lexicon. The pronunciation of the borrowed item is often altered to fit the phonological rules of the borrowing language. The borrowed word remains in the source language, so there is no need for its return. Most languages are borrowers, so their lexicons can be divided into native and non-native words, called **loan words**. A native word is one whose history or **etymology** can be traced back to the earliest known stages of the language.

A language may borrow a word directly or indirectly. A direct borrowing means that the borrowed item is a native word in the language from which it is borrowed. *Feast* was borrowed directly from French and can be traced back to Latin *festum.* On the other hand, the word *algebra* was borrowed from Spanish, which in turn had borrowed it from Arabic. Thus *algebra* was indirectly borrowed from Arabic, with Spanish as an intermediary. Some languages are heavy borrowers. Albanian has borrowed so heavily that few native words are retained. On the other hand, most Native American languages borrowed little from their neighbors.

English has borrowed extensively. Of the 20,000 or so words in common use, about three-fifths are borrowed. On the other hand, of the 500 most frequently used words only two-sevenths are borrowed, and because these words are used repeatedly in sentences—they're mostly function words—the actual frequency of appearance of native words is about 80 percent. The frequently used words *and, be, have, it, of, the, to, will, you, on, that,* and *is* are all native to English.

HISTORY THROUGH LOAN WORDS

> A morsel of genuine history is a thing so rare as to be always valuable.
>
> **THOMAS JEFFERSON**

We may trace the history of the English-speaking peoples by studying the kinds of loan words in their language, their source, and when they were borrowed. Until the Norman Conquest in 1066, the Angles, the Saxons, and the Jutes inhabited England.

They were of Germanic origin when they came to Britain in the fifth century to eventually become the English. Originally, they spoke Germanic dialects, from which Old English developed directly. These dialects contained some Latin borrowings but few foreign elements beyond that. These Germanic tribes had displaced the earlier Celtic inhabitants, whose influence on Old English was confined to a few Celtic place-names. (The modern languages Welsh, Irish, and Scots Gaelic are descended from the Celtic dialects.)

The Normans spoke French, and for three centuries after the Conquest, French was used for all affairs of state and for most commercial, social, and cultural matters. The West Saxon literary language was abandoned, but regional varieties of English continued to be used in homes, churches, and the marketplace. During these three centuries, vast numbers of French words entered English, of which the following are representative:

government	crown	prince	estate	parliament
nation	jury	judge	crime	sue
attorney	saint	miracle	charity	court
lechery	virgin	value	pray	mercy
religion	chapel	royal	money	society

Until the Normans came, when an Englishman slaughtered an ox for food, he ate *ox*. If it was a pig, he ate *pig*. If it was a sheep, he ate *sheep*. However, "ox" served at the Norman tables was *beef* (*boeuf*), "pig" was *pork* (*porc*), and "sheep" was *mutton* (*mouton*). These words were borrowed from French into English, as were the food-preparation words *boil*, *fry*, *stew*, and *roast*. Over the years French foods have given English a flood of borrowed words for menu preparers:

aspic	bisque	bouillon	brie	brioche
canapé	caviar	consommé	coq au vin	coupe
crêpe	croissant	croquette	crouton	escargot
fondue	mousse	pâté	quiche	ragout

English borrowed many "learned" words from foreign sources during the Renaissance. In 1475 William Caxton introduced the printing press in England. By 1640, 55,000 books had been printed in English. The authors of these books used many Greek and Latin words, and as a result, many words of ancient Greek and Latin entered the language. From Greek came *drama*, *comedy*, *tragedy*, *scene*, *botany*, *physics*, *zoology*, and *atomic*. Latin loan words in English are numerous. They include:

bonus	scientific	exit	alumnus	quorum	describe

During the ninth and tenth centuries, Scandinavian raiders, who eventually settled in the British Isles, left their traces in the English language. The pronouns *they*, *their*, and *them* are loan words from Old Norse, the predecessor of modern Danish, Norwegian, and Swedish. This period is the only time that English ever borrowed pronouns.

Bin, *flannel*, *clan*, *slogan*, and *whisky* are all words of Celtic origin, borrowed at various times from Welsh, Scots Gaelic, or Irish. Dutch was a source of borrowed words, too, many of which are related to shipping: *buoy*, *freight*, *leak*, *pump*, *yacht*. From German came *quartz*, *cobalt*, and—as we might guess—*sauerkraut*. From Italian, many musical terms, including words describing opera houses, have been borrowed: *opera*, *piano*, *virtuoso*, *balcony*, and *mezzanine*. Italian also gave us *influenza*, which was derived from the Italian word for "influence" because the Italians were convinced that the disease was *influenced* by the stars.

Many scientific words were borrowed indirectly from Arabic, because early Arab scholarship in these fields was quite advanced. *Alcohol*, *algebra*, *cipher*, and *zero* are a small sample. Spanish has loaned us (directly) *barbecue*, *cockroach*, and *ranch*, as well as *California*, literally "hot furnace." In America, the English-speaking colonists borrowed from Native American languages. They provided us with *hickory*, *chipmunk*, *opossum*, and *squash*, to mention only a few. Nearly half the names of U.S. states are borrowed from one American Indian language or another.

English has borrowed from Yiddish. Many non-Jews as well as non-Yiddish-speaking Jews use Yiddish words. There was once even a bumper sticker proclaiming: "Marcel Proust is a yenta." *Yenta* is a Yiddish word meaning "gossipy woman" or "shrew." *Lox*, "smoked salmon," and *bagel*, "a doughnut dipped in cement," now belong to English, as well as Yiddish expressions like *chutzpah*, *schmaltz*, *schlemiel*, *schmuck*, *schmo*, and *kibitz*.

English is also a lender of copious numbers of words to other languages, especially in the areas of technology, sports, and entertainment. Words and expressions such as *jazz*, *whisky*, *blue jeans*, *rock music*, *supermarket*, *baseball*, *picnic*, and *computer* have been borrowed into languages as diverse as Twi, Hungarian, Russian, and Japanese.

Loan translations are compound words or expressions whose parts are translated literally into the borrowing language. *Marriage of convenience* is a loan translation from French *mariage de convenance*. Spanish speakers eat *perros calientes*, a loan translation of *hot dogs* with an adjustment reversing the order of the adjective and noun, as required by the rules of Spanish syntax.

Loss of Words

Pease porridge hot
Pease porridge cold
Pease porridge in the pot nine days old

NURSERY RHYME

Languages can also lose words, although the departure of an old word is never as striking as the arrival of a new one. When a new word comes into vogue, its unusual presence draws attention, but a word is lost through inattention—nobody thinks of it, nobody uses it, and it fades away.

A reading of Shakespeare's works shows that English has lost many words, such as these taken from *Romeo and Juliet*: *beseem*, "to be suitable," *mammet*, "a doll or puppet," *wot*, "to know," *gyve*, "a fetter," *fain*, "gladly," and *wherefore*, "why," as in Juliet's plaintive cry: "O Romeo, Romeo! wherefore art thou Romeo," in which she is questioning why he is so named, not his current location.

More recently, it appears that the expression *two bits*, meaning "twenty-five cents," is no longer used by the younger generation and is in the process of being lost along with *lickety-split*, meaning "very fast," and far more likely to be understood by your grandparents than by you. The word *stile*, meaning "steps crossing a fence or gate," is no longer widely understood. Other similar words for describing rural objects are fading out of the language as a result of urbanization. *Pease*, from which *pea* is a back-formation, is gone, and *porridge*, meaning "boiled cereal grain," is falling out of usage, although it is sustained by a discussion of its ideal serving temperature in the children's story *Goldilocks and the Three Bears* and its appearance on Harry Potter's breakfast table.

Technological change may also be the cause for the loss of words. *Acutiator* once meant "sharpener of weapons," and *tormentum* once meant "siege engine." Advances in warfare have put these terms out of business. Although one still finds the words *buckboard, buggy, dogcart, hansom, surrey,* and *tumbrel* in the dictionary—all of them referring to subtly different kinds of horse-drawn carriages—progress in transportation is likely to render these terms obsolete and eventually they will be lost.

Semantic Change

> The language of this country being always upon the flux, the Struldbruggs of one age do not understand those of another, neither are they able after two hundred years to hold any conversation (farther than by a few general words) with their neighbors the mortals, and thus they lie under the disadvantage of living like foreigners in their own country.
>
> **JONATHAN SWIFT,** Gulliver's Travels

We have seen that a language may gain or lose lexical items. Additionally, the meaning or semantic representation of words may change, by becoming broader or narrower, or by shifting.

BROADENING

When the meaning of a word becomes broader, that word means everything it used to mean and more. The Middle English word *dogge* meant a specific breed of dog, but it was eventually **broadened** to encompass all members of the species *canis familiaris*. The word *holiday* originally meant a day of religious significance, from "holy day." Today the word signifies any day on which we do not have to work. *Picture* used to mean "painted representation," but today you can take a picture with a camera, not to mention a cell phone. *Quarantine* once had the restricted meaning of "forty days' isolation."

More recent broadenings, spurred by the computer age, are *computer, mouse, cookie, cache, virus,* and *bundle. Footage* use to refer to a certain length of film or videotape, but nowadays it means any excerpt from the electronic video media such as DVDs, irrespective of whether its length can be measured in feet. And here is where we go out on a limb: we predict that *google*, which currently means "use the Google search engine on the Internet," will be broadened in meaning to "use a search engine on the Internet."

NARROWING

In the King James Version of the Bible (1611 C.E.), God says of the herbs and trees, "to you they shall be for meat" (Genesis 1:29). To a speaker of seventeenth-century English, *meat* meant "food," and *flesh* meant "meat." Since that time, semantic change has **narrowed** the meaning of *meat* to what it is in Modern English. The word *deer* once meant "beast" or "animal," as its German cognate *Tier* still does. The meaning of *deer* has been narrowed to a particular kind of animal. Similarly, the word *hound* used to be the general term for "dog," like the German *Hund*. Today *hound* means a special kind of dog, one used for hunting. The word *davenport* once meant "sofa" or "small writing desk." Today, in American English, its meaning has narrowed to "sofa" alone.

MEANING SHIFTS

The third kind of semantic change that a lexical item may undergo is a shift in meaning. The word *knight* once meant "youth" but shifted to "mounted man-at-arms." *Lust* used to mean simply "pleasure," with no negative or sexual overtones. *Lewd* was merely "ignorant," and *immoral* meant "not customary." *Silly* used to mean "happy" in Old English. By the Middle English period it had come to mean "naive," and only in Modern English does it mean "foolish." The overworked Modern English word *nice* meant "ignorant" a thousand years ago. When Juliet tells Romeo, "I am too *fond*," she is not claiming she likes Romeo too much. She means "I am too *foolish*."

Reconstructing "Dead" Languages

> The living languages, as they were called by the Harvard fellows, were little more than cheap imitations, low distortions. Italian, like Spanish and German, particularly represented the loose political passions, bodily appetites, and absent morals of decadent Europe.
>
> **MATTHEW PEARL,** The Dante Club

"Shoe" by Gary Brookins/Chris Cassatt. Copyright 1989 Tribune Media Services. Reprinted with permission.

The branch of linguistics that deals with how languages change, what kinds of changes occur, and why they occurred is called **historical and comparative linguistics**. It is "historical" because it deals with the history of particular languages; it is "comparative" because it deals with relations among languages.

The Nineteenth-Century Comparativists

> When agreement is found in words in two languages, and so frequently that rules may be drawn up for the shift in letters from one to the other, then there is a fundamental relationship between the two languages.
>
> **RASMUS RASK**

The nineteenth-century historical and comparative linguists based their theories on observations of regular sound correspondences among certain languages. They proposed that languages displaying systematic similarities and differences must have descended from a common source language—that is, were genetically related.

The chief goal of these linguists was to develop and elucidate the genetic relationships that exist among the world's languages. They aimed to establish the major language families of the world and to define principles for the classification of languages. Their work grew out of earlier research.

As a child, Sir William Jones had an astounding propensity for learning languages, including so-called dead ones such as Ancient Greek and Latin. As an adult he found it best to reside in India because of his sympathy for the rebellious American colonists. There he distinguished himself both as a jurist, holding a position on the Bengal Supreme Court, and as an "Orientalist," as certain linguists were then called.

In Calcutta he took up the study of Sanskrit and in 1786 delivered a paper in which he observed that Sanskrit bore to Greek and Latin "a stronger affinity . . . than could possibly have been produced by accident." Jones suggested that these three languages had "sprung from a common source" and that probably Germanic and Celtic had the same origin.

About thirty years after Jones delivered his important paper, the German linguist Franz Bopp pointed out the relationships among Sanskrit, Latin, Greek, Persian, and Germanic. At the same time, a young Danish scholar named Rasmus Rask corroborated these results, and brought Lithuanian and Armenian into the relationship as well. Rask was the first scholar to describe formally the regularity of certain phonological differences of related languages.

Rask's investigation of these regularities inspired the German linguist Jakob Grimm (of fairy-tale fame), who published a four-volume treatise (1819–1822) that specified the regular sound correspondences among Sanskrit, Greek, Latin, and the Germanic languages. Not only did the similarities intrigue Grimm and the other linguists, but also the systematic nature of the differences. Where Latin has a [p], English often has an [f]; where Latin has a [t], English often has a [θ]; where Latin has a [k], English often has an [h].

Grimm pointed out that certain phonological changes that did not take place in Sanskrit, Greek, or Latin must have occurred early in the history of the Germanic languages. Because the changes were so strikingly regular, they became known as **Grimm's law**, which is illustrated in Figure 11.2.

Grimm's Law can be expressed in terms of natural classes of speech sounds: Voiced aspirates become unaspirated; voiced stops become voiceless; voiceless stops become fricatives.

Earlier stage:[a]	bh	dh	gh	b	d	g	p	t	k
	↓	↓	↓	↓	↓	↓	↓	↓	↓
Later stage:	b	d	g	p	t	k	f	θ	x (or h)

---

[a] This "earlier stage" is Indo-European. The symbols bh, dh, and gh are breathy voiced stop consonants. These phonemes are often called "voiced aspirates."

FIGURE 11.2 Grimm's Law, an early Germanic sound shift.

COGNATES

Cognates are words in related languages that developed from the same ancestral root, such as English *horn* and Latin *cornū*. Cognates often, but not always, have the same meaning in the different languages. From cognates we can observe sound correspondences and from them deduce sound changes. In Figure 11.3 the regular correspondence *p-p-f* of cognates from Sanskrit, Latin, and Germanic (represented by English) indicates that the languages are genetically related. Indo-European **p* is posited as the origin of the *p-p-f* correspondence.[3]

"Shouldn't a unicorn be
called a uniHORN?"

"Family Circus" © Bil Keane, Inc. Reprinted
with permission of King Features Syndicate.

Indo-European	Sanskrit	Latin	English
*p	**p**	**p**	**f**
	pitar-	pater	father
	pad-	ped-	foot
	No cognate	piscis	fish
	paśu[a]	pecu	fee

[a] ś is a sibilant pronounced differently than *s* was pronounced.

FIGURE 11.3 Cognates of Indo-European *p.

[3]The asterisk before a letter indicates a reconstructed sound, not an unacceptable form. This use of asterisk occurs only in this chapter.

Figure 11.4 is a more detailed chart of correspondences, where a single representative example of each regular correspondence is presented. In most cases cognate sets exhibit the same correspondence, which leads to the reconstruction of the Indo-European sound shown in the first column.

Indo-European	Sanskrit		Latin		English	
*p	p	pitar-	p	pater	f	father
*t	t	trayas	t	trēs	θ	three
*k	ś	śun	k	canis	h	hound
*b	b	No cognate	b	labium	p	lip
*d	d	dva-	d	duo	t	two
*g	j	ajras	g	ager	k	acre
*bh	bh	bhrātar-	f	frāter	b	brother
*dh	dh	dhā	f	fē-ci	d	do
*gh	h	vah-	h	veh-ō	g	wagon

Figure 11.4 Some Indo-European sound correspondences.

Sanskrit underwent the fewest consonant changes, Latin somewhat more, and Germanic (under Grimm's Law) underwent almost a complete restructuring. Still, the fact that the phonemes and phonological rules change and not individual words has resulted in the remarkably regular correspondences that allow us to reconstruct much of the Indo-European sound system.

Exceptions can be found to these regular correspondences, as Grimm was aware. He stated: "The sound shift is a general tendency; it is not followed in every case." Karl Verner explained some of the exceptions to Grimm's Law in 1875. He formulated **Verner's Law** to show why Indo-European p, t, and k failed to correspond to f, θ, and x in certain cases:

> *Verner's Law*: When the preceding vowel was unstressed, f, θ, and x underwent a further change to b, d, and g.

A group of young linguists known as the **Neo-Grammarians** went beyond the idea that such sound shifts represented only a tendency, and claimed that sound laws have no exception. They viewed linguistics as a natural science and therefore believed that laws of sound change were unexceptionable natural laws. The "laws" they put forth often had exceptions, however, which could not always be explained as dramatically as Verner's Law explained the exceptions to Grimm's Law. Still, the work of these linguists provides important data and insights into language change and why such changes occur.

The linguistic work of the early nineteenth century had some influence on Charles Darwin, and in turn, Darwin's theory of evolution had a profound influence on linguistics and on all science. Some linguists thought that languages had a "life cycle" and developed according to evolutionary laws. In addition, it was believed that every language could be traced to a common ancestor. This theory of biological naturalism has an element of truth to it, but it is an oversimplification of how languages change and evolve into other languages.

Comparative Reconstruction

> . . . Philologists who chase
> A panting syllable through time and space
> Start it at home, and hunt it in the dark,
> To Gaul, to Greece, and into Noah's Ark.
>
> **WILLIAM COWPER**, *"Retirement"*

When languages resemble one another in ways not attributable to chance or borrowing, we may conclude they are related. That is, they evolved via linguistic change from an ancestral protolanguage.

The similarity of the basic vocabulary of languages such as English, German, Danish, Dutch, Norwegian, and Swedish is too pervasive for chance or borrowing. We therefore conclude that these languages have a common parent, Proto-Germanic. There are no written records of Proto-Germanic, and certainly no native speakers alive today. Proto-Germanic is a hypothetical language whose properties have been deduced based on its descendants. In addition to related vocabulary, the Germanic languages share grammatical properties such as similar sets of irregular verbs, particularly the verb *to be*, further supporting their relatedness.

Once we know or suspect that several languages are related, their protolanguage may be partially determined by **comparative reconstruction**. One proceeds by applying the **comparative method**, which we illustrate with the following brief example.

Restricting ourselves to English, German, and Swedish, we find the word for "man" is *man* [mæn], *Mann* [man], and *man* [man], respectively. This is one of many word sets in which we can observe the regular sound correspondence [m]-[m]-[m] and [n]-[n]-[n] in the three languages. Based on this evidence, the comparative method has us reconstruct **mVn* as the word for "man" in Proto-Germanic. The *V* indicates a vowel whose quality we are unsure of because, despite the similar spelling, the vowel is phonetically different in the various Germanic languages, and it is unclear how to reconstruct it without further evidence.

Although we are confident that we can reconstruct much of Proto-Germanic with relative accuracy, we can never be sure, and many details remain obscure. To build confidence in the comparative method, we can apply it to Romance languages such as French, Italian, Spanish, and Portuguese. Their protolanguage is the well-known Latin, so we can verify the method. Consider the following data, focusing on the initial consonant of each word. In these data, *ch* in French is [ʃ], and *c* in the other languages is [k].

French	Italian	Spanish	Portuguese	English
cher	**c**aro	**c**aro	**c**aro	"dear"
champ	**c**ampo	**c**ampo	**c**ampo	"field"
chandelle	**c**andela	**c**andela	**c**andeia	"candle"

The French [ʃ] corresponds to [k] in the three other languages. This regular sound correspondence, [ʃ]-[k]-[k]-[k], supports the view that French, Italian, Spanish, and Portuguese descended from a common language. The comparative method leads to the reconstruction of [k] in "dear," "field," and "candle" of the parent language, and shows that [k] underwent a change to [ʃ] in French, but not in Italian, Spanish, or Portuguese, which retained the original [k] of the parent language, Latin.

To use the comparative method, analysts identify regular sound correspondences in the cognates of potentially related languages. For each correspondence, they deduce the most likely sound in the parent language. In this way, much of the sound system of the parent may be reconstructed. The various phonological changes in the development of each daughter language as it descended and changed from the parent are then identified. Sometimes the sound that analysts choose in their reconstruction of the parent language is the one that appears most frequently in the correspondence. This is the "majority rules" principle, which we illustrated with the four Romance languages.

Other considerations may outweigh the majority rules principle. The likelihood of certain phonological changes may persuade the analyst to reconstruct a less frequently occurring sound, or even a sound that does not occur in the correspondence. Consider the data in these four hypothetical languages:

Language A	Language B	Language C	Language D
hono	hono	fono	vono
hari	hari	fari	veli
rahima	rahima	rafima	levima
hor	hor	for	vol

Wherever Languages A and B have an *h*, Language C has an *f* and Language D has a *v*. Therefore, we have the sound correspondence *h-h-f-v*. Using the comparative method's majority rules principle, we might first consider reconstructing the sound *h* in the parent language, but from other data on historical change, and from phonetic research, we know that *h* seldom becomes *v*. The reverse, /f/ and /v/ becoming [h], occurs both historically and as a phonological rule and has an acoustic explanation. Therefore, linguists reconstruct an **f* in the parent, and posit the sound change "*f* becomes *h*" in Languages A and B, and "*f* becomes *v*" in Language D. One obviously needs experience and knowledge to conclude this.

The other correspondences are not problematic as far as these data are concerned. They are:

o-o-o-o   n-n-n-n   a-a-a-e   r-r-r-l   m-m-m-m

They lead to the reconstructed forms **o, **n, **a, **r*, and **m* for the parent language, and the sound changes "*a* becomes *e*" and "*r* becomes *l*" in Language D. These are natural sound changes found in many of the world's languages.

It is now possible to reconstruct the words of the protolanguage. They are **fono, **fari, **rafima,* and **for*. Language D, in this example, is the most innovative of the three languages, because it has undergone three sound changes. Language C is the most conservative in that it is identical to the protolanguage insofar as these data are concerned.

The sound changes seen in the previous illustrations are examples of **unconditioned sound change**. The changes occurred irrespective of phonetic context. Following is an example of **conditioned sound change**, taken from three dialects of Italian:

Standard	Northern	Lombard	
fisːo	fiso	fis	"fixed"
kasːa	kasa	kasə	"cabinet"

The correspondence sets are:

f-f-f   i-i-i   sː-s-s   o-o-<>[4]   k-k-k   a-a-a   a-a-ə

---

[4]The empty angled brackets indicate a loss of the sound.

It is straightforward to reconstruct *f, *i, and *k. Knowing that a long consonant like *s:* commonly becomes *s* (recall Old English *f:* became *f*), we reconstruct *s: for the s:-s-s correspondence. A shortening change took place in the Northern and Lombard dialects.

There is evidence in these (very limited) data for a weakening of word-final vowels, again a change we discussed earlier for English. We reconstruct *o for o-o-<> and *a for a-a-ə. In Lombard, conditioned sound changes took place. The sound *o* was deleted in *word-final position*, but remained *o* elsewhere. The sound *a* became ə in word-final position and remained *a* elsewhere. As far as we can tell from the data presented, the conditioning factor is word-final position. Vowels in other position do not undergo change. We reconstruct the protodialect as having had the words *fis:o* meaning "fixed" and *kas:a* meaning "cabinet."

It is by means of the comparative method that nineteenth-century linguists were able to initiate the reconstruction of the long-lost ancestral language so aptly conceived by Jones, Bopp, Rask, and Grimm, a language that flourished about 6,000 years ago, the language that we have been calling Indo-European.

Historical Evidence

You know my method. It is founded upon the observance of trifles.
SIR ARTHUR CONAN DOYLE, *"The Boscombe Valley Mystery,"*
The Memoirs of Sherlock Holmes

The comparative method is not the only way to explore a language or language family's past. Moreover, the comparative method may prove unable to answer certain questions because data are lacking, or reconstructions are untenable. For example, how do we know positively how Shakespeare or Chaucer or the author of *Beowulf* pronounced their versions of English? The comparative method leaves many details in doubt, and we have no recordings that give us direct knowledge.

For many languages, written records go back more than a thousand years. Linguists study these records to find out how languages were once pronounced. The spelling in early manuscripts tells us a great deal about the sound systems of older forms of modern languages. Two words spelled differently were probably pronounced differently. Once several orthographic contrasts are identified, good guesses can be made as to actual pronunciation. For example, because we spell *Mary, merry*, and *marry* with three different vowels, we may conclude that at one time most speakers pronounced them differently, probably [meri], [mɛri], and [mæri]. For at least one modern American dialect, only /ɛ/ can occur before /r/, so the three words are all pronounced [mɛri]. That dialect is the result of a sound shift in which both /e/ and /æ/ shifted to /ɛ/ when followed immediately by /r/. This is another instance of a conditioned sound shift.

Another clue to earlier pronunciation is provided by non-English words that appear in English manuscripts. Suppose a French word known to contain the vowel [o] is borrowed into English. The way the borrowed word is spelled reveals a particular letter-sound correspondence.

Other documents can be examined for evidence. Private letters are an excellent source of data. Linguists prefer letters written by naive spellers, who will misspell words according to the way they pronounce them. For instance, at one point in English history, all words spelled with *er* in their stems were pronounced as if they were spelled with *ar*, just as in modern British English *clerk* and *derby* are pronounced "clark" and "darby." Some poor speller kept writing *parfet* for *perfect*, which helped linguists discover the older pronunciation.

Clues are also provided by the writings of the prescriptive grammarians of the period. Between 1550 and 1750, a group of prescriptivists in England known as orthoepists attempted to preserve the "purity" of English. In prescribing how people should speak, they told us how people actually spoke. An orthoepist alive in the United States today might write in a manual: "It is incorrect to pronounce *Cuba* with a final *r*." Future scholars would know that some speakers of English pronounced it that way.

Some of the best clues to earlier pronunciation are provided by puns and rhymes in literature. Two words rhyme if the vowels and final consonants are the same. When a poet rhymes the verb *found* with the noun *wound*, it strongly suggests that the vowels of these two words were identical:

> *Benvolio*: . . . 'tis in vain to seek him here that means not to be found.
> *Romeo*:   He jests at scars that never felt a wound.

Shakespeare's rhymes are helpful in reconstructing the sound system of Elizabethan English. The rhyming of *convert* with *depart* in Sonnet XI strengthens the conclusion that *er* was pronounced as *ar*.

Most powerfully, the above techniques may be combined with the comparative methods. Dialect differences discovered through written records may permit comparison of the pronunciation of various words in several dialects. On that basis we can draw conclusions about earlier forms and see what changes took place in the inventory of sounds and in the phonological rules.

The historical comparativists working on languages with written records have a challenging job, but not nearly as challenging as that of scholars who are attempting to discover genetic relationships among languages with no written history. Linguists must first transcribe large amounts of language data from all the languages, analyze them phonologically, morphologically, and syntactically, and establish a basis for relatedness such as similarities in basic vocabulary and regular sound correspondences not resulting from chance or borrowing. Only then can the comparative method be applied to reconstruct the extinct protolanguage.

Linguists proceeding in this manner have discovered many relationships among Native American languages and have successfully reconstructed Amerindian protolanguages. Similar achievements have been made with the numerous languages spoken in Africa. Linguists have been able to group the large number of languages of Africa into four overarching families: Afroasiatic, Nilo-Saharan, Niger-Congo, and Khoisan. For example, Somali is in the Afroasiatic family; Zulu is in the Niger-Congo family; and Hottentot, spoken in South Africa, is in the Khoisan family. These familial divisions are subject to revision if new discoveries or analyses deem it necessary.

Extinct and Endangered Languages

> Any language is the supreme achievement of a uniquely human collective genius, as divine and unfathomable a mystery as a living organism.
>
> MICHAEL KRAUSS

> I am always sorry when any language is lost, because languages are
> the pedigree of nations.
>
> SAMUEL JOHNSON

A language dies and becomes extinct when no children learn it. Linguists have identified four primary types of language death:

1. **Sudden language death** occurs when all of the speakers of the language die or are killed. Such was the case with Tasmanian languages, once spoken on the island of Tasmania, and Nicoleño, a Native American Indian language once spoken in California.

2. **Radical language death** is similar to sudden language death in its abruptness. Rather than the speakers dying, however, they all stop speaking the language. Often, the reason for this abrupt change is survival under the threat of political repression or even genocide. Indigenous languages embedded in other cultures suffer death this way. In order to avoid being identified as "natives," speakers simply stop speaking their native language. Children are unable to learn a language that is not spoken in their environment, and when the last speaker dies, the language dies.

3. **Gradual language death** is the most common way for a language to become extinct. It happens to minority languages that are in contact with a dominant language, much as American Indian languages are in contact with English. In each generation, fewer and fewer children learn the language until there are no new learners. The language is said to be dead when the last generation of speakers dies out. Cornish suffered this fate in Britain in the eighteenth century, as have many Native American languages in both North and South America.

4. **Bottom-to-top language death** describes a language that survives only in specific contexts, such as a liturgical language. Latin and, at one time, Hebrew are such languages. It contrasts with gradual language death, which in its dying throes is spoken casually and informally in homes and villages. People stopped speaking Latin in daily situations centuries ago, and its usage is confined to scholarly and religious contexts.

Language death has befallen, and is befalling, many Native American languages. According to the linguist Michael Krauss, only 20 percent of the remaining native languages in the United States are being acquired by children. Hundreds have already been lost. Once widely spoken American Indian languages such as Comanche, Apache, and Cherokee have fewer native speakers every generation.

Doomed languages have existed throughout time. The Indo-European languages Hittite and Tocharian no longer exist. Hittite passed away 3,500 years ago, and both dialects of Tocharian gave up the ghost around 1000 C.E.

Linguists have placed many languages on an endangered list. They attempt to preserve these languages by studying and documenting their grammars—the phonetics, phonology, and so on—and by recording for posterity the speech of the last few speakers. Through its grammar, each language provides new evidence on the nature of human cognition. In its literature, poetry, ritual speech, and word structure, each language stores the collective intellectual achievements of a culture, offering unique perspectives on the human condition. The disappearance of a language is tragic; not only are these insights lost, but the major medium through which a culture maintains and renews itself is gone as well.

Dialects, too, may become extinct. Many dialects spoken in the United States are considered endangered by linguists. For example, the sociolinguist Walt Wolfram is studying the dialect spoken on Ocracoke Island off the coast of North Carolina. One reason for the study is to preserve the dialect, which is in danger of extinction because so many young Ocracokers leave the island and raise their children else-where, a case of gradual *dialect* death. Vacationers and retirees are diluting the dialect-speaking population, because they are attracted to the island by its unique character, including, ironically, the quaint speech of the islanders.

Linguists are not alone in their preservation efforts. Under the sponsorship of language clubs, and occasionally even governments, adults and children learn an endangered language as a symbol of the culture. Gael Linn is a private organization in Ireland that runs language classes in Irish (Gaelic) for adults. Hundreds of public schools in Ireland and Northern Ireland are conducted entirely in Gaelic. In the U.S. state of Hawaii, a movement is under way to preserve and teach Hawaiian, the native language of the island.

The United Nations, too, is concerned about endangered languages. In 1991, the United Nations Educational, Scientific, and Cultural Organization (UNESCO) passed a resolution that states:

> As the disappearance of any one language constitutes an irretrievable loss to mankind, it is for UNESCO a task of great urgency to respond to this situation by promoting . . . the description—in the form of grammars, dictionaries, and texts—of endangered and dying languages.

Occasionally, a language is resurrected from written records. For centuries, classical Hebrew was used only in religious ceremonies, but today, with some modernization, and through a great desire among Jews to speak the language of their forefathers, it has become the national language of Israel.

The documentation of dying languages is not only important for social and cultural reasons. There is also a scientific reason for studying these languages. Through examining a wide array of different types of languages, linguists can develop a comprehensive theory of language that accounts for both its universal and language-specific traits.

The Genetic Classification of Languages

> The Sanskrit language, whatever be its antiquity, is of a wonderful structure, more perfect than the Greek, more copious than the Latin, and more exquisitely refined than either, yet bearing to both of them a stronger affinity, both in the roots of verbs and in the forms of grammar, than could possibly have been produced by accident; so strong, indeed, that no philologer could examine all three, without believing that they have sprung from some common source, which, perhaps, no longer exists. . . .
>
> SIR WILLIAM JONES *(1786)*

We have discussed how different languages evolve from one language and how historical and comparative linguists classify languages into families such as Germanic or Romance and reconstruct earlier forms of the ancestral language. When we examine the languages of the world, we perceive similarities and differences among them that provide evidence for degrees of relatedness or for nonrelatedness.

Counting to five in English, German, and Vietnamese shows similarities between English and German not shared by Vietnamese (shown with tones omitted):

English	German	Vietnamese
one	eins	mot
two	zwei	hai
three	drei	ba
four	vier	bon
five	fünf	nam

The similarity between English and German is pervasive. Sometimes it is extremely obvious (*man/Mann*), but at other times a little less obvious (*child/Kind*). No regular similarities or differences apart from those resulting from chance are found between them and Vietnamese.

Pursuing the metaphor of human genealogy, we say that English, German, Norwegian, Danish, Swedish, Icelandic, and so on are sisters in that they descended from one parent and are more closely related to one another than any of them are to non-Germanic languages such as French or Russian.

The Romance languages are also sister languages whose parent is Latin. If we carry the family metaphor to an extreme, we might describe the Germanic languages and the Romance languages as cousins, because their respective parents, Proto-Germanic and early forms of Latin, were siblings.

As anyone from a large family knows, there are cousins, and then there are distant cousins, encompassing nearly anyone with a claim to family bloodlines. This is true of the Indo-European family of languages. If the Germanic and Romance languages are truly cousins, then languages such as Greek, Armenian, Albanian, and even the extinct Hittite and Tocharian are distant cousins. So are Irish, Scots Gaelic, Welsh, and Breton, whose protolanguage, Celtic, was once spoken widely throughout Europe and the British Isles. Breton is spoken in Brittany in the northwest coastal regions of France. It was brought there by Celts fleeing from Britain in the seventh century.

Russian is also a distant cousin, as are its sisters, Bulgarian, Serbo-Croatian, Polish, Czech, and Slovak. The Baltic language Lithuanian is related to English, as is its sister language, Latvian. A neighboring language, Estonian, however, is not a relative. Sanskrit, as pointed out by Sir William Jones, although far removed geographically, is nonetheless a relative. Its offspring, Hindi and Bengali, spoken primarily in South Asia, are distantly related to English. Persian (or Farsi), spoken in modern Iran, is a distant cousin of English, as is Kurdish, spoken in Iran, Iraq, and Turkey, and Pashto spoken in Afghanistan and Pakistan. All these languages, except for Estonian, are related, more or less distantly, to one another because they all descended from Indo-European.

Figure 11.5 is an abbreviated family tree of the Indo-European languages that gives a genealogical and historical classification of the languages shown. This diagram is somewhat simplified. For example, it appears that all the Slavic languages are sisters. This suggests the comical scenario of speakers of Proto-Slavic dividing themselves

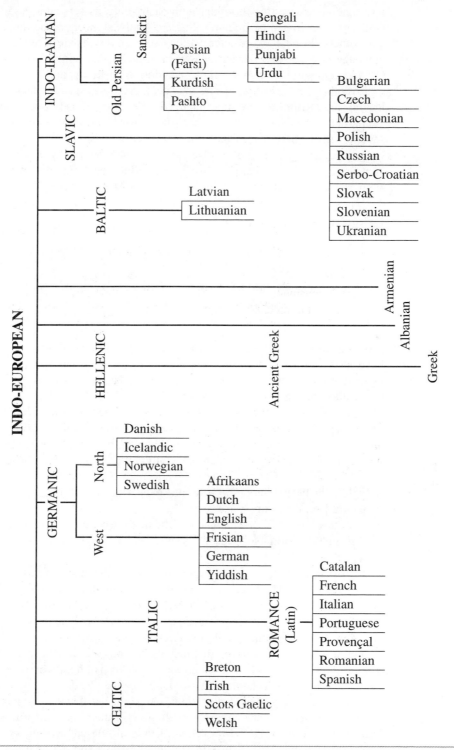

FIGURE 11.5 The Indo-European family of languages.

into nine clans one fine morning, with each going its separate way. In fact the nine languages shown can be organized hierarchically, showing some more closely related than others. In other words, the various separations that resulted in the nine Slavic languages we see today occurred several times over a long stretch of time. Similar remarks apply to the other families, including Indo-European.

Another simplification is that the "dead ends"—languages that evolved and died leaving no offspring—are not included. We have already mentioned Hittite and Tocharian as two such Indo-European languages. The family tree also fails to show several intermediate stages that must have existed in the evolution of modern languages. Languages do not evolve abruptly, which is why comparisons with the genealogical trees of biology have limited usefulness. Finally, the diagram fails to show some Indo-European languages because of lack of space.

Languages of the World

And the whole earth was of one language, and of one speech.

GENESIS 11:1

Let us go down, and there confound their language, that they may not understand one another's speech.

GENESIS 11:7

Most of the world's languages do not belong to the Indo-European family. Linguists have also attempted to classify the non-Indo-European languages according to their genetic relationships. The task is to identify the languages that constitute a family and the relationships that exist among them.

The two most common questions asked of linguists are: "How many languages do you speak?" and "How many languages are there in the world?" Both questions are difficult to answer precisely. Most linguists have varying degrees of familiarity with several languages, and many are **polyglots**, persons who speak and understand several languages. Charles V, the Holy Roman Emperor from 1519 to 1558, was a polyglot, for he proclaimed: "I speak Spanish to God, Italian to women, French to men, and German to my horse."

As to the second question, it's difficult to ascertain the precise number of languages in the world because of disagreement as to what comprises a language as opposed to a dialect.

A difficulty with both these questions is that the answers rely on a sliding scale. Familiarity with a language is not an all-or-nothing affair, so how much of a language do you have to know before you can be said to "speak and understand" that language? And how different must two dialects be before they become separate languages? One criterion is that of mutual intelligibility. As long as two dialects remain mutually intelligible, it is generally believed that they cannot be considered separate languages. But mutual intelligibility is a relative notion, as all of us know who have conversed with persons speaking dialects of our native language that we do not understand completely.

The Indo-Iranian languages Hindi and Urdu are listed as separate languages in Figure 11.5, yet they are mutually intelligible in their spoken form and are arguably dialects of one language. However, each uses a different writing system and each is spoken in communities of differing religious beliefs and nationalities. (Hindi, for the most part, is spoken in India by Hindus; Urdu is spoken in Pakistan by Muslims.) So what constitutes a separate language is not always determined by linguistic factors alone. On the other hand, mutually unintelligible languages spoken in China are often thought of as dialects because they have a common writing system and culture, and are spoken within a single political boundary.

Recent estimates place the number of languages in the world today (2006) at somewhat less than 7,000, including sign languages. (See URL http://www.ethnologue .com/web.asp for more detail.) In the city of Los Angeles alone, more than 80 languages are spoken. Students at Hollywood High School go home to hear their parents speak Amharic, Armenian, Arabic, Marshallese, Urdu, Sinhalese, Ibo, Gujarati, Hmong, Afrikaans, Khmer, Ukrainian, Cambodian, Spanish, Tagalog, and Russian, among others.

It is often surprising to discover which languages are genetically related and which ones are not. Nepali, the language of remote Nepal, is an Indo-European language, whereas Hungarian, surrounded on all sides by Indo-European languages, is not.

It is not possible in an introductory text to give an exhaustive table of families, subfamilies, and individual languages. Besides, some genetic relationships have not yet been firmly established. For example, linguists are divided as to whether Japanese and Turkish are related. We simply mention several language families in the following paragraphs with a few of their members. These language families do not appear to be related to one another or to Indo-European. This, however, may be an artifact of being unable to delve into the past far enough to see common features that time has erased. We cannot eliminate the possibility that the entire world's languages spring ultimately from a single source, an "ur-language" that some have termed **Nostratic,** which is buried, if not concealed, in the depths of the past. Readers interested in this fascinating topic may wish to read the writings of Professor Johanna Nichols of the University of California at Berkeley. And as always, more can be found by googling *nostratic*.

Uralic is the other major family of languages, besides Indo-European, spoken on the European continent. Hungarian, Finnish, and Estonian are the major representatives of this group.

Afro-Asiatic languages comprise a large family spoken in northern Africa and the Middle East. They include the modern *Semitic* languages of Hebrew and Arabic, as well as languages spoken in biblical times such as Aramaic, Babylonian, Canaanite, and Moabite.

The *Sino-Tibetan* family includes Mandarin, the most populous language in the world, spoken by around one billion Chinese. This family also includes all of the Chinese dialects, as well as Burmese and Tibetan.

Most of the languages of Africa belong to the *Niger-Congo* family. These include more than nine hundred languages grouped into subfamilies such as Kordofanian and Atlantic-Congo. The latter includes individual languages such as Swahili and Zulu.

Equally numerous, the *Austronesian* family contains about nine hundred languages, spoken over a wide expanse of the globe, from Madagascar, off the coast of Africa, to Hawaii. Hawaiian is an Austronesian language, as are Maori, spoken in New Zealand; Tagalog, spoken in the Philippine Islands; and Malay, spoken in Malaysia and Singapore, to mention just a few.

Dozens of families and hundreds of languages are, or were, spoken in North and South America. Knowledge of the genetic relationships among these families of languages is often tenuous, and because so many of the languages are approaching extinction, there may be little hope for as thorough an understanding of the Amerindian language families as linguists have achieved for Indo-European.

Types of Languages

All the Oriental nations jam tongue and words together in the throat, like the Hebrews and Syrians. All the Mediterranean peoples push their enunciation forward to the palate, like the Greeks and the Asians. All the Occidentals break their words on the teeth, like the Italians and Spaniards. . . .

ISIDORE OF SEVILLE, *seventh century c.e.*

There are many ways to classify languages. One way already discussed in this chapter is according to the language family—the genetic classification. This method would be like classifying people according to whether they were related by blood. Another way of classifying languages is by certain linguistic traits, regardless of family. With people, this method would be like classifying them according to height and weight, political preference, religion, degree of wealth, and so on.

So far in this book we have hinted at the widely varied ways that languages might be classified. From a phonological point of view, we have tone languages versus intonation languages—Thai versus English. We have languages with varying numbers of vowel phonemes, from as few as three to as high as a dozen or more. Languages may be classified according to what combinations of consonants and vowels may comprise syllables. Japanese and Hawaiian allow few syllable types (CV and V, mostly), whereas English and most Indo-European languages allow a much wider variety. Languages may use length to contrast phonemes, or not. They may have nasal vowel phonemes, or not. They may have affricates, or not. They may use stress phonemically (English), or not (French).

From a morphological standpoint, languages may be classified according to the richness of verb and noun morphology. For example, Vietnamese has little if any word morphology, so its words are monomorphemic; there are no plural affixes on nouns or agreement affixes on verbs. Languages like English have a middling amount of morphology, much less than Old English or Latin once had, or than Russian has today. Some languages—termed *polysynthetic* by linguists—have extraordinarily rich morphologies in which a single word may have ten or more affixes and carry the semantic load of an entire English sentence.

From a lexical standpoint, languages are classifiable as to whether they have articles like *the* and *a* in English; as to their system of pronouns and what distinctions are made regarding person, number, and gender; as to their vocabulary for describing family members; as to whether they have noun classes such as the masculine, feminine, and neuter nouns of German, or the multiple noun classes present in Swahili that we observed in chapter 3, and so on.

Every language has sentences that include a subject (S), an object (O), and a verb (V), although individual sentences may not contain all three elements. From the point of view of syntax, languages have been classified according to the basic or most common order in which these elements occur in sentences. There are six possible orders—SVO (subject, verb, object), SOV, VSO, VOS, OVS, OSV—permitting six possible language types. Of these, SVO and SOV languages comprise nearly 90 percent of investigated languages in roughly equal proportions. English, Spanish, and Thai are SVO; German, Dutch, and Japanese illustrate SOV languages.

In SVO languages, auxiliary verbs precede main verbs, adverbs follow main verbs, and prepositions precede their head noun. Here are English examples:

They are eating. (Aux-V)
They sing beautifully. (V-Adv) (*Cf.*, *They beautifully sing.)
They are from Tokyo. (Prep-V)

In SOV languages, the opposite tendencies are true. Auxiliary verbs follow the main verb, adverbs precede main verbs, and "prepositions," now called *postpositions,* follow their head noun. Here are Japanese examples:

Akiko	wa	sakana	o	tabete	iru (V-Aux)
Akiko	*topic marker*	fish	*object marker*	eating	is

"Akiko is eating fish."

Akiko	wa	hayaku	tabemasu	(Adv-V)
Akiko	*topic marker*	quickly	eats	

"Akiko eats quickly."

Akiko	wa	Tokyo	kara	desu	(V-PostP)
Akiko	*topic marker*	Tokyo	from	is	

"Akiko is from Tokyo."

These differences, and many more like them, stem from a single underlying parameter choice: the placement of the head of phrase. SVO languages are head-final; SOV languages are head-initial.

The question of why SVO and SOV languages are dominant is not completely understood, but linguists have observed that two principles or constraints are favored:

Subjects precede objects.
There is a VP constituent—either VO or OV.

SVO and SOV are the only two types that obey both principles. The next most common type is VSO, here illustrated by Tagalog, which is widely spoken in the Philippine Islands:

Sumagot	siya	sa	propesor
answered	he	the	professor

"He answered the professor."

VSO languages comprise nearly 10 percent of languages investigated—the lion's share of what's left over after SVO and SOV languages. With VSO, the principle that the subject precedes the object still holds, but there is no VP constituent (VS cannot be a constituent). Thus it appears that the subject-precedes-object principle is the most pervasive.

Of the remaining types, VOS and OVS both have VP constituents but do not obey the subject-precedes-object constraint. These types are rare, comprising just a small percent of languages observed. Finally, OSV languages, in which neither principle is obeyed, may or may not exist. Some linguists claim that in the two or three languages put forth as OSV, the OSV word order is derived from a different more basic order.

That a language is SVO does not mean that SVO is the only possible word order. The correlations between language type and the word order of syntactic categories in sentences are *preferred* word orders, and for the most part are violable tendencies. Different languages follow them to a greater or lesser degree. Thus, when a famous comedian said "Believe you me" on network TV, he was understood and imitated despite the VSO word order. Yoda, the Jedi Master of *Star Wars* fame, speaks a strange but perfectly understandable style of English that achieves its eccentricity by being OSV. (Objects may be complements other than Noun Phrases.) Some of Yoda's utterances are:

Sick I've become.
Around the survivors a perimeter create.
Strong with the Force you are.
Impossible to see the future is.
When nine hundred years you reach, look as good you will not.

For linguists, the many languages and language families provide essential data for the study of universal grammar. Although these languages are diverse in many ways, they are also remarkably similar in many ways. We find that languages from northern Greenland to southern New Zealand, from the oriental nations to the occidental nations, all have similar sounds, similar phonological and syntactic rules, and similar semantic systems.

Why Do Languages Change?

Some method should be thought on for ascertaining and fixing our language forever. . . . I see no absolute necessity why any language should be perpetually changing.

JONATHAN SWIFT *(1712)*

Stability in language is synonymous with rigor mortis.

ERNEST WEEKLEY

No one knows exactly how or why languages change. As we have shown, linguistic changes do not happen suddenly. Speakers of English did not wake up one morning and decide to use the word *beef* for "ox meat," nor do all the children of one particular generation grow up to adopt a new word. Changes are more gradual, particularly changes in the phonological and syntactic system.

Certain changes may occur instantaneously for any one speaker. When someone acquires a new word, it is not acquired gradually, although full appreciation for all of its possible uses may come slowly. When a new rule enters a speaker's grammar, it is either in or not in the grammar. It may at first be an optional rule, so that sometimes it is used and sometimes it is not, possibly determined by social context or other external factors, but the rule is either there and available for use or not. What is gradual about language change is the spread of certain changes through an entire speech community.

A basic cause of change is the way children acquire the language. No one teaches a child the rules of the grammar. Each child constructs a personal grammar alone, generalizing rules from the linguistic input she receives. As discussed in chapter 8, the child's language develops in stages until it approximates the adult grammar. The child's grammar is never exactly like that of the adult community, because children receive diverse linguistic input. Certain rules may be simplified or overgeneralized, and vocabularies may show small differences that accumulate over several generations.

The older generation may be using certain rules optionally. For example, at certain times they may say "It's I" and at other times "It's me." The less formal style is usually used with children, who, as the next generation, may use only the "me" form of the pronoun in this construction. In such cases the grammar will have changed.

The reasons for some changes are relatively easy to understand. Before television there was no such word as *television*. It soon became a common lexical item. Borrowed words, too, generally serve a useful purpose, and their entry into the language is not mysterious. Other changes are more difficult to explain, such as the Great Vowel Shift in English.

One plausible source of change is *assimilation*, a kind of *ease of articulation* process in which one sound influences the pronunciation of an adjacent or nearby sound. Because of assimilation, vowels are frequently nasalized before nasal consonants because it is easiest to lower the velum to produce nasality in advance of the actual consonant articulation. This results in the preceding vowel being nasalized. Once the vowel is nasalized, the contrast that the nasal consonant provided can be equally well provided by the nasalized vowel alone, and the redundant consonant may be deleted. The contrast between oral and nasal vowels that exists in many languages of the world today resulted from just such a historical sound change.

In reconstructing older versions of French, it has been hypothesized that *bol,* "basin," *botte*, "high boot," *bog*, "a card game," *bock*, "Bock beer," and *bon*, "good," were pronounced [bɔl], [bɔt], [bɔg], [bɔk], and [bɔ̃n], respectively. The nasalized vowel in *bon* resulted from the final nasal consonant. Because of a conditioned sound change that deleted nasal consonants in word-final position, *bon* is pronounced [bɔ̃] in modern French. The nasal vowel alone maintains the contrast with the other words.

Another example from English illustrates how such assimilative processes can change a language. In Old English, word initial [kʲ] (like the initial sound of *cute*), when followed by /i/, was further palatalized to become our modern palatal affricate /tʃ/, as illustrated by the following words:

Old English (c = [kʲ])	Modern English (ch = [tʃ])
ciese	cheese
cinn	chin
cild	child

The process of palatalization is found in the history of many languages. In Twi, the word meaning "to hate" was once pronounced [ki]. The [k] became first [kʲ] and then finally [tʃ], so that today "to hate" is [tʃi].

Ease of articulation processes, which make sounds more alike, are countered by the need to maintain contrast. Thus sound change also occurs when two sounds are acoustically similar, with risk of confusion. We saw a sound change of /f/ to /h/ in an earlier example that can be explained by the acoustic similarity of [f] to other sounds.

Analogic change is a generalization of rules that results in a reduction of the number of exceptional or irregular morphemes that must be individually learned and remembered. It was by analogy to *plow/plows* and *vow/vows* that speakers started saying *cows* as the plural of *cow* instead of the earlier plural *kine*. In effect, the plural rule became more general.

The plural rule continues to undergo analogic change as exemplified by the regularization of exceptional plural forms. We have borrowed words like *datum/data, agendum/agenda, curriculum/curricula, memorandum/memoranda, medium/media, criterion/criteria,* and *virtuoso/virtuosi,* to name just a few. The irregular plurals of these nouns are being replaced by regular plurals among many speakers: *agendas, curriculums, memorandums, criterias,* and *virtuosos.* In some cases the borrowed original plural forms were considered to be the singular (as in *agenda* and *criteria*), and the new plural (e.g., *agendas*) is therefore a "plural-plural." In addition, many speakers now regard *data* and *media* as nouns that do not have plural forms, like *information.* All these changes are "economy of memory" changes and lessen the number of irregular forms that must be remembered.

The past-tense rule is also undergoing generalization. By analogy to *bake/baked* and *ignite/ignited,* many children and adults now say *I waked last night* (instead of *woke*) and *She lighted the bonfire* (instead of *lit*). These regular past-tense forms are found in today's dictionaries next to the irregular forms, with which they currently coexist.

Assimilation and analogic change account for some linguistic changes, but they cannot account for others. Simplification and regularization of grammars occur, but so does elaboration or complication. Old English rules of syntax became more complex, imposing a stricter word order on the language, at the same time that case endings were being simplified. A tendency toward simplification is counteracted by the need to limit potential ambiguity. Much of language change is a balance between the two.

Many factors contribute to linguistic change: simplification of grammars, elaboration to maintain intelligibility, borrowing, and so on. Changes are actualized by children learning the language, who incorporate them into their grammar. The exact reasons for linguistic change are still elusive, although it is clear that the imperfect learning of the adult dialects by children is a contributing factor. Perhaps language changes for the same reason all things change: it is the nature of things to change. As Heraclitus pointed out centuries ago, "All is flux, nothing stays still. Nothing endures but change."

Summary

Languages change. Linguistic change such as **sound shift** is found in the history of all languages, as evidenced by the **regular sound correspondences** that exist between different stages of the same language, different dialects of the same language, and different languages. Languages that evolve from a common source are **genetically related**. Genetically related languages were once dialects of the same language. For example, English, German, and Swedish were dialects of an earlier form of Germanic called **Proto-Germanic**, whereas earlier forms of Romance languages, such as Spanish, French, and Italian, were dialects of Latin. Going back even further in time, earlier forms of Proto-Germanic, Latin, and other languages were dialects of **Indo-European**.

All components of the grammar may change. Phonological, morphological, syntactic, lexical, and semantic changes occur. Words, morphemes, phonemes, and rules of all types may be added, lost, or altered. The meaning of words and morphemes may **broaden**, **narrow**, or shift. The lexicon may expand by **borrowing**, which results in **loan words** in the vocabulary. It also grows through word coinage, blends, compounding, acronyms, and other processes of word formation. On the other hand, the lexicon may shrink as certain words like *typewriter* are no longer used and become obsolete.

The study of linguistic change is called **historical and comparative linguistics**. Linguists use the **comparative method** to identify regular sound correspondences among the **cognates** of related languages and systematically reconstruct an earlier **protolanguage**. This **comparative reconstruction** allows linguists to peer backward in time and determine the linguistic history of a language family, which may then be represented in a tree diagram similar to Figure 11.5.

Recent estimates place the number of languages in the world today (2006) at somewhat less than 7,000, including sign languages. These languages are grouped into families, subfamilies, and so on, based on their genetic relationships. A vast number of these languages are dying out because in each generation fewer children learn them. However, attempts are being made to preserve dying languages and dialects for the knowledge they bring to the study of Universal Grammar and the culture in which they are spoken.

No one knows all the causes of linguistic change. Some sound changes result from assimilation, a fundamentally physiological process of ease of articulation. Others, like the **Great Vowel Shift**, are more difficult to explain. Some grammatical changes are **analogic changes**, generalizations that lead to more regularity, such as *cows* instead of *kine* and *waked* instead of *woke*.

Change comes about through the restructuring of the grammar by children learning the language. Grammars may appear to change in the direction of simplicity and regularity, as in the loss of the Indo-European case morphology, but such simplifications may be compensated for by other complexities, such as stricter word order. A balance is always present between simplicity—languages must be learnable—and complexity—languages must be expressive and relatively unambiguous.

References for Further Reading

Aitchison, J. 2001. *Language Change: Progress or Decay?* 3rd edition. Cambridge, New York, Melbourne: Cambridge University Press.

Anttila, R. 1989. *Historical and Comparative Linguistics.* New York: John Benjamins.

Baugh, A. C., and T. Cable. 2002. *A History of the English Language*, 5th edition. Upper Saddle River, NJ: Pearson Education.

Campbell, L. 2004. *Historical Linguistics: An Introduction,* 2nd edition. Cambridge, MA: MIT Press.

Comrie, B., ed. 1990. *The World's Major Languages.* New York: Oxford University Press.

Hock, H. H., and B. D. Joseph. 1996. *Language History, Language Change, and Language Relationship:An Introduction to Historical and Comparative Linguistics.* New York: Mouton de Gruyter.

Lehmann, W. P. 1992. *Historical Linguistics: An Introduction*, 3rd edition. London, New York: Routledge.

Lightfoot, D. 1999. *The Development of Language: Acquisition, Change and Evolution.* Oxford, England: Blackwell.

Pyles, T., and J. Algeo. 2005. *The Origins and Development of the English Language,* 5th edition. New York: Thomson/Wadsworth.

Trask, R. L. 1996. *Historical Linguistics.* London: Hodder Arnold.

Traugott, E. C. 1972. *A History of English Syntax.* New York: Holt, Rinehart and Winston.

Wolfram, W. 2001. "Language Death and Dying," In Chambers, J. K., Trudgill, P., and Schilling-Estes, N. (eds.). *The Handbook on Language Variation and Change.* Oxford, UK: Basil Blackwell.

Exercises

1. Many changes in the phonological system have occurred in English since 449 C.E. Below are some Old English words (given in their spelling and phonetic forms) and the same words as we pronounce them today. They are typical of regular sound changes that took place in English. What sound changes have occurred in each case?

   Example: OE hlud [xluːd] → Mod. Eng. loud

   Changes: (1) The [x] was lost.

   (2) The long vowel [uː] became [aw].

   OE   **Mod E**

   a. crabba [kraba] → crab

   Changes:

   b. fisc [fɪsk] → fish

   Changes:

   c. fūl [fuːl] → foul

   Changes:

   d. gāt [gaːt] → goat

   Changes:

   e. lǣfan [læːvãn] → leave

   Changes:

   f. tēþ [teːθ] → teeth

   Changes:

2. The Great Vowel Shift left its traces in Modern English in such meaning-related pairs as:

   (1) serene/serenity [i]/[ɛ]

   (2) divine/divinity [aj]/[ɪ]

   (3) sane/sanity [e]/[æ]

   List five such meaning-related pairs that relate [i] and [ɛ] as in example 1, five that relate [aj] and [ɪ] as in example 2, and five that relate [e] and [æ] as in example 3.

	[i]/[ɛ]	**[aj]/[ɪ]**	**[e]/[æ]**
(1)			
(2)			
(3)			
(4)			
(5)			

3. Below are given some sentences taken from Old English, Middle English, and early Modern English texts, illustrating some changes that have occurred in the syntactic rules of English grammar. (*Note*: In the sentences, the earlier spelling forms and words have been changed to conform to Modern English. That is, the OE sentence *His suna twegen mon brohte to þæm cynige* would be written as *His sons two one brought to that king*, which in Modern English would be *His two sons were brought to the king*.) Underline the parts of each sentence that differ from Modern English. Rewrite the sentence in Modern English. State what changes must have occurred.

   Example: It *not* belongs to you. (Shakespeare, *Henry IV*)

   Mod. Eng.: It does not belong to you.

   Change: At one time a negative sentence simply had a *not* before the verb. Today, the word *do*, in its proper morphological form, must appear before the *not*.

   a. It nothing pleased his master.

   b. He hath said that we would lift them whom that him please.

   c. I have a brother is condemned to die.

   d. I bade them take away you.

   e. I wish you was still more a Tartar.

   f. Christ slept and his apostles.

   g. Me was told.

4. Yearbooks and almanacs (including ones online) often publish a new word list. In the 1990s several new words, such as *Teflon* and *e-business*, entered the English language. Before that, new words such as *byte* and *modem* arrived together with the computer age. Other words have been expanded in meaning, such as *memory* to refer to the storage part of a computer and *crack* meaning a form of cocaine. Sports-related new words include *threepeat* and *skybox*, as well as other compounds such as *air ball*, *contact hitter*, and *nose guard*. Some very recent arrivals came with the new millennium and include *Viagra*, *Botox*, *Sudoku*, and *Sambuca* (an aniseed liqueur served with a flaming coffee bean).

   a. Find five other words or compound words that have entered the language in the last ten years. Describe briefly the source of the word.

   b. Think of three words that might be on the way out. (*Hint*: Consider *flapper*, *groovy*, and *slay/slew*. Dictionary entries that say "archaic" are a good source.)

   c. Think of three words whose dictionary entries do not say they are verbs, but which you've heard or seen used as verbs. *Example*: "He went to piano over at the club," meaning (we guess) "He went to play the piano at the club."

   d. Think of three words that have become, or are becoming, obsolete as a result of changes in technology. *Example*: *Mimeograph*, a method of reproduction, is on the way out because of advances in xerographic duplication technology.

5. Here is a table showing, in phonemic form, the Latin ancestors of ten words in modern French (given in phonetic form):

Latin	French	Gloss
kor	kœr[5]	heart
kantāre	ʃãte	to sing
klārus	kler	clear
kervus	sɛr	deer
karbō	ʃarbɔ̃	coal
kwandō	kã	when
kentum	sã	hundred
kawsa	ʃoz	thing
kinis	sãdrə	ashes
kawda/koda[6]	kø[5]	ṭail

Are the following statements true or false? Justify your answer.

	True	**False**
a. The modern French word for "thing" shows that a /k/, which occurred before the vowel /o/ in Latin, became [ʃ] in French.	_____	_____
b. The French word for "tail" probably derived from the Latin word /koda/ rather than from /kawda/.	_____	_____
c. One historical change illustrated by these data is that [s] became an allophone of the phoneme /k/ in French.	_____	_____
d. If there were a Latin word *kertus*, the modern French word would probably be [sɛr]. (Consider only the initial consonant.)	_____	_____

6. Here is how to count to five in a dozen languages, using standard Roman alphabet transcriptions. Six of these languages are Indo-European and six are not. Which are Indo-European? (Just for fun, how many of the languages can you identify? If you get all twelve correct, we'll mention your school in the next edition. You may email your answer and institutional affiliation to either author Rodman or Hyams.)

	L1	**L2**	**L3**	**L4**	**L5**	**L6**
1.	en	jedyn	i	eka	ichi	echad
2.	twene	dwaj	liang	dvau	ni	shnayim
3.	thria	tři	san	trayas	san	shlosha
4.	fiuwar	štyri	ssu	catur	shi	arbaʔa
5.	fif	pjeć	wu	pañca	go	chamishsha

	L7	**L8**	**L9**	**L10**	**L11**	**L12**
1.	mot	ün	hana	yaw	uno	nigen
2.	hai	duos	tul	daw	dos	khoyar
3.	ba	trais	set	dree	tres	ghorban
4.	bon	quatter	net	tsaloor	cuatro	durben
5.	nam	tschinch	tasŏt	pindze	cinco	tabon

---

[5]œ and ø are front, rounded vowels.
[6]/kawda/ and /koda/ are the word for "tail" in two Latin dialects.

7. Recommend three ways in which society can act to preserve linguistic diversity. Be realistic and concrete. For example, "encourage children of endangered languages to learn the language" is *not* a good answer, being neither sufficiently realistic (why should they want to?), nor sufficiently concrete (what is meant by "encourage"?).

8. The vocabulary of English consists of native words as well as thousands of loan words. Look up the following words in a dictionary that provides their etymologies. Speculate how each word came to be borrowed from the particular language.

   Example: *Skunk* was a Native American term for an animal unfamiliar to the European colonists, so they borrowed that word into their vocabulary so they could refer to the creature.

a. size	**h.** robot	**o.** skunk	**v.** pagoda
b. royal	**i.** check	**p.** catfish	**w.** khaki
c. aquatic	**j.** banana	**q.** hoodlum	**x.** shampoo
d. heavenly	**k.** keel	**r.** filibuster	**y.** kangaroo
e. skill	**l.** fact	**s.** astronaut	**z.** bulldoze
f. ranch	**m.** potato	**t.** emerald	
g. blouse	**n.** muskrat	**u.** sugar	

9. Analogic change refers to a tendency to generalize the rules of language, a major cause of language change. We mentioned two instances, the generalization of the plural rule (*cow/kine* becoming *cow/cows*) and the generalization of the past-tense formation rule (*light/lit* becoming *light/lighted*). Think of at least three other instances of nonstandard usage that are analogic; they are indicators of possible future changes in the language. (*Hint*: Consider fairly general rules and see if you know of dialects or styles that overgeneralize them, for example, comparative formation by adding -*er*.)

10. Study the following passage from Shakespeare's *Hamlet*, Act IV, Scene iii, and identify every difference in expression between Elizabethan and current Modern English that is evident (e.g., in line 3, *thou* is now *you*.).

    Hamlet: A man may fish with the worm that hath eat of a king, and eat of the fish that hath fed of that worm.

    King: What dost thou mean by this?

    Hamlet: Nothing but to show you how a king may go a progress through the guts of a beggar.

    King: Where is Polonius?

    Hamlet: In heaven. Send thither to see. If your messenger find him not there, seek him i' the other place yourself. But indeed, if you find him not within this month, you shall nose him as you go up the stairs into the lobby.

11. Here are some data from four Polynesian languages.

Maori	Hawaiian	Samoan	Fijian	Gloss	Proto-Polynesian (to be completed)
pou	pou	pou	bou	"post"	*
tapu	kapu	tapu	tabu	"forbidden"	*

Maori	Hawaiian	Samoan	Fijian	Gloss	Proto-Polynesian (to be completed)
taŋi	kani	taŋi	taŋi	"cry"	*
takere	kaʔele	taʔele	takele	"keel"	*
hono	hono	fono	vono	"stay, sit"	*
marama	malama	malama	malama	"light, moon"	*
kaho	ʔaho	ʔaso	kaso	"thatch"	*

a. Find the correspondence sets. (*Hint*: There are 14. For example: o–o–o–o, p–p–p–b.)

b. For each correspondence set, reconstruct a proto-sound. Mention any sound changes that you observe. For example:

o–o–o–o   *o

p–p–p–b   *p   p → b in Fijian.

c. Complete the table by filling in the reconstructed words in Proto-Polynesian.

12. Consider these data from two American Indian languages:

Yerington Paviotso = YP	Northfork Monachi = NM	Gloss
mupi	mupi	"nose"
tama	tawa	"tooth"
piwɨ	piwɨ	"heart"
sawaʔpono	sawaʔpono	"a feminine name"
nɨmɨ	nɨwɨ	"liver"
tamano	tawano	"springtime"
pahwa	pahwa	"aunt"
kuma	kuwa	"husband"
wowaʔa	wowaʔa	"Indians living to the west"
mɨhɨ	mɨhɨ	"porcupine"
noto	noto	"throat"
tapa	tape	"sun"
ʔatapɨ	ʔatapɨ	"jaw"
papiʔi	papiʔi	"older brother"
patɨ	petɨ	"daughter"
nana	nana	"man"
ʔatɨ	ʔetɨ	"bow," "gun"

a. Identify each sound correspondence. (*Hint*: There are ten correspondence sets of consonants and six correspondence sets of vowels: for example, *p–p, m–w, a–a,* and *a–e.*)

b. (1) For each correspondence you identified in A not containing an *m* or *w,* reconstruct a proto-sound (e.g., for *h–h, *h; o–o, *o.*).

(2) If the proto-sound underwent a change, indicate what the change is and in which language it took place.

c. (1) Whenever a *w* appears in YP, what appears in the corresponding position in NM?

(2) Whenever an *m* occurs in YP, what two sounds may correspond to it in NM?

(3) On the basis of the position of *m* in YP words, can you predict which sound it will correspond to in NM words? How?

d. (1) For the three correspondences you discovered in (a) involving *m* and *w*, should you reconstruct two or three proto-sounds?

(2) If you chose three proto-sounds, what are they and what did they become in the two daughter languages, YP and NM?

(3) If you chose two proto-sounds, what are they and what did they become in the daughter languages? What further statement do you need to make about the sound changes? (*Hint*: One proto-sound will become two different pairs, depending on its phonetic environment. It is an example of a conditioned sound change.)

e. Based on the above, reconstruct all the words given in the common ancestor from which both YP and NM descended (e.g., "porcupine" is reconstructed as *mihi.).

13. The people of the Isle of Eggland once lived in harmony on a diet of soft-boiled eggs. They spoke proto-Egglish. Contention arose over which end of the egg should be opened first for eating, the big end or the little end. Each side retreated to its end of the island, and spoke no more to the other. Today, Big-End Egglish and Little-End Egglish are spoken in Eggland. Below are data from these languages.

A. Find the correspondence sets for each pair of cognates, and reconstruct the proto-Egglish word from which the cognates descended.

B. Identify the sound changes that have affected each language. Use *classes* of sounds to express the change when possible. (*Hint*: There are three conditioned sounds changes.)

Big-End Egglish	Little-End Egglish	Gloss	Proto-Egglish (to be completed)
ʃur	kul	omelet	*
ve	vet	yoke	*
rɔ	rɔk	egg	*
ver	vel	egg shell	*
ʒu	gup	soufflé	*
vel	vel	egg white	*
pe	pe	hard-boiled (obscene)	*

Writing: The ABCs of Language

The Moving Finger writes; and, having writ,
Moves on: nor all thy Piety nor Wit
Shall lure it back to cancel half a Line,
Nor all thy Tears wash out a Word of it.

OMAR KHAYYÁM, Rubáiyát

The palest ink is better than the sharpest memory.

CHINESE PROVERB

Throughout this book we have emphasized the spoken form of language. The grammar, which represents one's linguistic knowledge, is viewed as a system for relating sound (sign) and meaning. The ability to acquire and use language represents a vital evolutionary development. No individual or peoples discovered or created language. The human language faculty appears to be biologically and genetically determined.

This is not true of the written form of human languages. Children learn to speak naturally through exposure to language, without formal teaching. To become literate—to learn to read and write—one must make a conscious effort and receive instruction.

Before the invention of writing, useful knowledge had to be memorized. Messengers carried information in their heads. Crucial lore passed from the older to the newer generation through speaking. Even in today's world, many spoken languages lack a writing system, and oral literature still abounds. However, human memory is short-lived, and the brain's storage capacity is limited.

Writing overcomes such problems and allows communication across space and through time. Writing permits a society to permanently record its literature, its history and science, and its technology. The creation and development of writing systems is therefore one of the greatest of human achievements.

By *writing* we mean any of the many visual (nongestural) systems for representing language, including handwriting, printing, and electronic displays of these written forms. It might be argued that today we have electronic means of recording sound and cameras to produce films and television, so writing is becoming obsolete. If writing became extinct, however, there would be no knowledge of electronics for engineers to study; there would be, in fact, little technology in years to come. There would be no film or TV scripts, no literature, no books, no mail, no newspapers. There would be some advantages—no junk mail, poison-pen letters, or "fine print"—but the losses would far outweigh the gains.

The History of Writing

An Egyptian legend relates that when the god Thoth revealed his discovery of the art of writing to King Thamos, the good King denounced it as an enemy of civilization. "Children and young people," protested the monarch, "who had hitherto been forced to apply themselves diligently to learn and retain whatever was taught them, would cease to apply themselves, and would neglect to exercise their memories."

WILL DURANT, The Story of Civilization 1

There are many legends and stories about the invention of writing. Greek legend has it that Cadmus, Prince of Phoenicia and founder of the city of Thebes, invented the alphabet and brought it with him to Greece. In one Chinese fable, the four-eyed dragon-god Cang Jie invented writing, but in another, writing first appeared as markings on the back of the chi-lin, a white unicorn of Chinese legend. In other myths, the Babylonian god Nebo and the Egyptian god Thoth gave humans writing as well as speech. The Talmudic scholar Rabbi Akiba believed that the alphabet existed before humans were created; and according to Islamic teaching, the alphabet was created by Allah himself, who presented it to humans but not to the angels.

Although these are delightful stories, it is evident that before a single word was written, uncountable billions were spoken. The invention of writing comes relatively late in human history, and its development was gradual. It is highly unlikely that a particularly gifted ancestor awoke one morning and decided, "Today I'll invent a writing system."

Pictograms and Ideograms

One picture is worth a thousand words.

CHINESE PROVERB

The seeds from which writing developed were probably the early drawings made by ancient humans. Cave drawings, called **petroglyphs**, such as those found in the Altamira cave in northern Spain, drawn by humans living over twenty thousand years ago, can be "read" today. They are literal portrayals of life at that time. We don't know why they were produced; they may be aesthetic expressions rather than pictorial communications. Later drawings, however, are clearly "picture writings," or **pictograms**.

Unlike modern writing systems, each picture or pictogram is a direct image of the object it represents. There is a nonarbitrary relationship between the form and meaning of the symbol. Comic strips minus captions are pictographic—literal representations of the ideas to be communicated. This early form of writing represented objects in the world directly rather than through the linguistic names given to these objects. Thus they did not represent the words and sounds of spoken language.

Pictographic writing has been found throughout the world, ancient and modern: among Africans, Native Americans including the Inuits of Alaska and Canada, the Incas of Peru, the Yukagirians of Siberia, and the people of Oceania. Pictograms are used today in international road signs, where the native language of the region might not be understood by all travelers. Such symbols can be understood by anyone because they do not depend on the words of any language. To understand the signs used by the National Park Service, for example, a visitor does not need to know English. (See Figure 12.1.)

FIGURE 12.1 Six of seventy-seven symbols developed by the National Park Service for use as signs indicating activities and facilities in parks and recreation areas. These symbols denote, from left to right: environmental study area, grocery store, men's restroom, women's restroom, fishing, and amphitheater. Certain symbols are available with a prohibiting slash—a diagonal red bar across the symbol that means that the activity is forbidden.

National Park Service, U.S. Department of the Interior

Once a pictogram was accepted as the representation of an object, its meaning was extended to attributes of that object, or concepts associated with it. A picture of the sun could represent warmth, heat, light, daytime, and so on. Pictograms thus began to represent ideas rather than objects. Such generalized pictograms are called **ideograms** ("idea pictures" or "idea writing").

The difference between pictograms and ideograms is not always clear. Ideograms tend to be less direct representations, and one may have to learn what a particular ideogram means. Pictograms tend to be more literal. For example, the no parking symbol consisting of a black circle with a slanting red line through it is an ideogram. It represents the idea of no parking abstractly. A no parking symbol showing an automobile being towed away is more literal, more like a pictogram.

Inevitably, pictograms and ideograms became stylized and formulaic so that the masses of people could read them. The simplifying conventions that developed so distorted the literal representations that it was no longer easy to interpret symbols without learning the system. The ideograms became linguistic symbols as they came also to stand for the sounds that represented the ideas—that is, for the words of the language. This stage represented a revolutionary step in the development of writing systems.

Cuneiform Writing

> Bridegroom, let me caress you,
> My precious caress is more savory than honey,
> In the bed chamber, honey-filled,
> Let me enjoy your goodly beauty,
> Lion let me caress you
>
> TRANSLATION OF A SUMERIAN POEM WRITTEN IN CUNEIFORM

Much of what we know about writing stems from the records left by the Sumerians, an ancient people of unknown origin, who built a civilization in southern Mesopotamia (modern Iraq) more than 6,000 years ago. They left innumerable clay tablets containing business documents, epics, prayers, poems, proverbs, and so on. So copious are these written records that scholars studying the Sumerians are publishing a seventeen-volume dictionary of their written language. The first of these volumes appeared in 1984.

The writing system of the Sumerians is the oldest one known. They were a commercially oriented people, and as their business deals became increasingly complex, the need for permanent records arose. An elaborate pictography was developed, along with a system of tallies. Some examples are shown here:

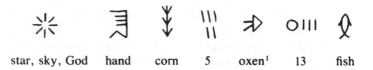

| star, sky, God | hand | corn | 5 | oxen[1] | 13 | fish |

Over the centuries the Sumerians simplified and conventionalized their pictography. They began to produce the symbols of their written language by using a wedge-shaped stylus that was pressed into soft clay tablets. The tablets hardened in the desert sun to produce permanent records that were far hardier than modern paper or electronic documents. Had the original American Declaration of Independence been written this way, it would not be in need of restoration and preservation. This form of writing is called **cuneiform**—literally, "wedge-shaped" (from Latin *cuneus*, "wedge"). Here is an illustration of the evolution of Sumerian pictograms to cuneiform:

✳	became	✳	became	⊱╂	star
⫘	became			⊟	hand
◊	became			╎╎◁	fish

---

[1]The pictograph for "ox" evolved, much later, into the letter *A*.

The cuneiform symbols in the right-most column do little to remind us (or the Sumerians) of the meaning represented. As cuneiform evolved, its users began to think of the symbols more in terms of the name of the thing represented than of the thing itself. Eventually cuneiform script came to represent words of the language. Such a system is called **logographic**, or **word writing**. In this oldest type of writing system, the symbol stands for both the word and the concept, which it may still resemble, however abstractly. Thus **logograms**, the symbols of a word-writing system, are ideograms that represent in addition to the concept, the word or morpheme in the language for that concept.

The cuneiform writing system spread throughout the Middle East and Asia Minor. The Babylonians, Assyrians, and Persians borrowed it. In adopting cuneiform characters, the borrowers often used them to represent the sounds of the syllables in their own languages. In this way cuneiform evolved into a **syllabic writing** system.

In a syllabic writing system, each syllable in the language is represented by its own symbol, and words are written syllable by syllable. Cuneiform writing was never purely syllabic. A large residue of symbols remained that stood for whole words. The Assyrians retained many word symbols, even though every word in their language could be written out syllabically if it were desired. Thus they could write ⟨symbol⟩ *mātu* "country" as:

⟨ma⟩		⟨a⟩		⟨tu⟩
ma	+	a	+	tu

The Persians (ca. 600–400 B.C.E.) devised a greatly simplified syllabic alphabet for their language, which made little use of word symbols. By the reign of Darius I (521–486 B.C.E.), this writing system was in wide use. The following characters illustrate it:

⟨symbol⟩	da
⟨symbol⟩	di
⟨symbol⟩	fa
⟨symbol⟩	ma
⟨symbol⟩	tu

Emoticons are strings of text characters that, when viewed sideways, form a face expressing a particular emotion. They are used mostly in e-mail and text messaging to express a feeling. They are a modern, pictographic system similar to cuneiform in that the same symbols are combined in different manners to convey different concepts. Most everyone who uses e-mail recognizes the smiley face **:-)** to mean "not serious" or "just joking." Several less common emoticons, and their generally accepted meanings, are shown here:

:'–("crying"

:–S   "bizarre"

:^D   "love it!"

:–)~   "drooling"

The invention, use, and acceptance of emoticons reflect on a small scale how a writing system such as cuneiform might have spread throughout a country.

The Rebus Principle

"B.C." © 1985 Creators Syndicate, Inc. Reprinted by permission of John L. Hart FLP and Creators Syndicate, Inc.

When a graphic sign no longer has a visual relationship to the word it represents, it becomes a **phonographic symbol**, standing for the sounds that represent the word. A single sign can then be used to represent all words with the same sounds—the homophones of the language. If, for example, the symbol ⊙ stood for *sun* in English, it could then be used in a sentence like *My ⊙ is a doctor*. This sentence is an example of the **rebus principle**.

A rebus is a representation of words by pictures of objects whose names sound like the word. Thus 👁 might represent *eye* or the pronoun *I*. The sounds of the two words are identical, even though the meanings are not. Similarly, 🐝🍃 could represent *belief* (*be + lief = bee + leaf =* /bi/ + /lif/), and 🐝🍃🍃 could be *believes*.

Proper names can also be written in such a way. If the symbol | is used to represent *rod* and the symbol ♟ represents *man*, then | ♟ could represent *Rodman*, although nowadays the name is unrelated to either rods or men. Such combinations often become stylized or shortened so as to be more easily written. *Rodman*, for example, might be written in such a system as |✶ or even ⋏.

Jokes, riddles, and advertising use the rebus principle. A well-known ice-cream company advertises "31derful flavors."

This is not an efficient system because in many languages words cannot be divided into sequences of sounds that have meaning by themselves. It would be difficult, for example, to represent the word *English* (/ɪŋ/ + /glɪʃ/) in English according to the rebus principle. *Eng* by itself does not mean anything, nor does *glish*.

From Hieroglyphics to the Alphabet

"You'd better phrase that more politely.
We no longer use the 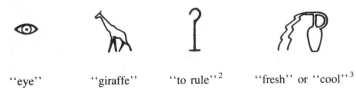 word."

At the time that Sumerian pictography was flourishing (around 4000 B.C.E.), a similar system was being used by the Egyptians, which the Greeks later called hieroglyphics (*hiero*, "sacred," + *glyphikos*, "carvings"). These sacred carvings originated as pictography as shown by the following:

"eye"	"giraffe"	"to rule"[2]	"fresh" or "cool"[3]

---

[2]The symbol portrays the Pharaoh's staff.
[3]Water trickling out of a vase.

Eventually, these pictograms came to represent both the concept and the word for the concept. Once this happened, hieroglyphics became a bona fide logographic writing system. Through the rebus principle, hieroglyphics also became a syllabic writing system.

The Phoenicians, a Semitic people who lived in what is today Lebanon, were aware of hieroglyphics as well as the offshoots of Sumerian writing. By 1500 B.C.E., they had developed a writing system of twenty-two characters, the West Semitic Syllabary. Mostly, the characters stood for consonants alone. The reader provided the vowels, and hence the rest of the syllable, through knowledge of the language. (Cn y rd ths?) Thus the West Semitic Syllabary was both a **syllabary** and a **consonantal alphabet**.

The ancient Greeks tried to borrow the Phoenician writing system, but it was unsatisfactory as a syllabary because Greek has too complex a syllable structure. In Greek, unlike Phoenician, vowels cannot be determined by grammatical context, so a writing system for Greek required that vowels have their own independent representations. Fortuitously, Phoenician had more consonants than Greek, so when the Greeks borrowed the system, they used the leftover consonant symbols to represent vowel sounds. The result was **alphabetic writing**, a system in which both consonants and vowels are symbolized. (The word *alphabet* is derived from *alpha* and *beta*, the first two letters of the Greek alphabet.)

Most alphabetic systems in use today derive from the Greek system. The Etruscans knew this alphabet and through them it became known to the Romans, who used it for Latin. The alphabet spread with Western civilization, and eventually most nations of the world were exposed to, and had the option of using, alphabetic writing.

According to one view, the alphabet was not invented, it was discovered. If language did not include discrete individual sounds, no one could have invented alphabetic letters to represent such sounds. When humans started to use one symbol for one phoneme, they merely brought their intuitive knowledge of the language sound system to consciousness: They discovered what they already "knew." Furthermore, children (and adults) can learn an alphabetic system only if each separate sound has some psychological reality.

Modern Writing Systems

. . . but their manner of writing is very peculiar, being neither from the left to the right, like the Europeans; nor from the right to the left, like the Arabians; nor from up to down, like the Chinese; nor from down to up, like the Cascagians, but aslant from one corner of the paper to the other, like ladies in England.

JONATHAN SWIFT, *Gulliver's Travels*

We have already mentioned the various types of writing systems used in the world: word or logographic writing, syllabic writing, consonantal alphabet writing, and alphabetic writing. Most of the world's written languages use alphabetic writing. Even Chinese and Japanese, whose native writing systems are not alphabetic, have adopted alphabetic transcription systems for special purposes such as communicating with foreigners, computers, and over the Internet.

Word Writing

"Peanuts" copyright © United Feature Syndicate, Inc. Reprinted by permission.

In a word-writing or logographic writing system, a written character represents both the meaning and pronunciation of each word or morpheme. Such systems are cumbersome, containing thousands of different characters. On the other hand, the editors of *Webster's Third New International Dictionary* claim more than 450,000 entries. All of these words may be written using only twenty-six alphabetic symbols, a dot, a hyphen, an apostrophe, and a space. It is understandable why, historically, word writing gave way to alphabetic systems in most places in the world.

The major exceptions are the writing systems used in China and Japan. The Chinese writing system has an uninterrupted history that goes back more than 3,500 years. For the most part it is a word-writing system, each character representing an individual word or morpheme. Longer words may be formed by combining two words or morphemes, as shown by the word meaning "business," māimai, which is formed by combining the words meaning "buy" and "sell." This is similar to compounding in English.

A word-writing system would be awkward for English and other Indo-European languages because of the pervasiveness of inflectional morphemes such as the *in-*, *im-*, and *iŋ-* of *intolerant*, *impossible*, and *incontinent*, inflected verb forms such as *take*, *takes*, *taken*, *took*, and *taking*, and inflected noun forms such as *cat*, *cats*, and *cat's*. These are difficult to represent without a huge proliferation of characters. Chinese, on the other hand, has little inflection.

Even without the need to represent inflectional forms, Chinese dictionaries contain tens of thousands of characters. A person need know "only" about 5,000, however, to read a newspaper. To promote literacy, the Chinese governments undertake character simplification programs from time to time. This process was first tried in 213 B.C.E., when the scholar Li Si published an official list of over 3,000 characters whose written forms he had simplified by omitting unneeded strokes. This would be analogous to dictionary writers simplifying *amoeba* to *ameba*, eliminating the superfluous *o*. Since that time, successive generations of Chinese scholars have added new characters and modified old ones, creating redundancy, ambiguity, and complexity. Recent character-simplification efforts continue the ages-old tradition of trying to make the system learnable and usable, while retaining its basic form.

The Chinese government has adopted a spelling system using the Roman alphabet called **Pinyin**, which is now used for certain purposes along with the regular system of characters. Many city street signs are printed in both systems, which is helpful to foreign visitors. It is not the government's intent to replace the traditional writing, which is viewed as an integral part of Chinese culture. To the Chinese, writing is an art—**calligraphy**—and thousands of years of poetry, literature, and history are preserved in the old system.

An additional reason for keeping the traditional system is that it permits all literate Chinese to communicate even though their spoken languages are not mutually intelligible. Thus writing has served as a unifying factor throughout Chinese history, in an area where hundreds of languages and dialects coexist. A Chinese proverb states "people separated by a blade of grass cannot understand each other." The unified writing system is a scythe that cuts across linguistic differences and allows the people to communicate.

This use of written Chinese characters is similar to the use of Arabic numerals, which mean the same in many countries. The character 5, for example, stands for a different sequence of sounds in English, French, and Finnish. In English it is *five* /fajv/, in French it is *cinq* /sɛ̃k/, and in Finnish *viisi* /viːsi/, but in all these languages, 5, whatever its phonological form, means "five." Similarly, the spoken word for "rice" is different in the various Chinese languages, but the written character is the same. If the writing system in China were to become alphabetic, each language would be as different in writing as in speaking, and written communication would no longer be possible among the various language communities.

Syllabic Writing

Syllabic writing systems are more efficient than word-writing systems, and they are certainly less taxing on the memory. However, languages with a rich structure of syllables containing many consonant clusters (such as *tr* or *spl*) cannot be efficiently written with a syllabary. To see this difficulty, consider the syllable structures of English:

I	/aj/	V	ant	/ænt/	VCC
key	/ki/	CV	pant	/pænt/	CVCC
ski	/ski/	CCV	stump	/stʌmp/	CCVCC
spree	/spri/	CCCV	striped	/strajpt/	CCCVCC
an	/æn/	VC	ants	/ænts/	VCCC
seek	/sik/	CVC	pants	/pænts/	CVCCC
speak	/spik/	CCVC	sports	/spɔrts/	CCVCCC
scram	/skræm/	CCCVC	splints	/splɪnts/	CCCVCCC

Even this table is not exhaustive; there are syllables whose codas may contain four consonants such as *strengths* /strɛnkθs/ and *triumphs* /trajəmpfs/. With more than thirty consonants and over twelve vowels, the number of different possible syllables is astronomical, which is why English, and Indo-European languages in general, are unsuitable for syllabic writing systems.

The Japanese language, on the other hand, is more suited for syllabic writing, because all words in Japanese can be phonologically represented by about one hundred syllables, mostly of the consonant-vowel (CV) type, and there are no underlying consonant clusters. To write these syllables, the Japanese have two syllabaries, each containing forty-six characters, called **kana**. The entire Japanese language can be written using kana. One syllabary, **katakana**, is used for loan words and for special effects similar to italics in European writing. The other syllabary, **hiragana**, is used for native words. Hiragana characters may occur in the same word as ideographic characters, which are called **kanji**, and are borrowed Chinese characters. Thus Japanese writing is part word writing, part syllable writing.

During the first millennium, the Japanese tried to use Chinese characters to write their language. However, spoken Japanese is unlike spoken Chinese. (They are genetically unrelated languages.) A word-writing system alone was not suitable for Japanese, which is a highly inflected language in which verbs may occur in thirty or more different forms. Scholars devised syllabic characters, based on modified Chinese characters, to represent the inflectional endings and other grammatical morphemes. Thus, in Japanese writing, kanji is commonly used for the verb roots, and hiragana symbols for the inflectional markings.

For example, 行 is the character meaning "go," pronounced [i]. The word for "went" in formal speech is *ikimashita*, written 行きました, where the hiragana symbols きました represent the syllables *ki*, *ma*, *shi*, *ta*. Nouns, on the other hand, are not inflected in Japanese, and they can generally be written using Chinese characters alone.

In theory, all of Japanese could be written in hiragana. However, in Japanese, there are many homographs (like *lead* in "lead pipe" or "lead astray"), and the use of kanji disambiguates a word that might be ambiguous if written syllabically, similar to the ambiguity of *can* in "He saw that gasoline can explode." In addition, kanji writing is an integral part of Japanese culture, and it is unlikely to be abandoned.

In America in 1821, the Cherokee Sequoyah invented a syllabic writing system for his native language. Sequoyah's script, which survives today essentially unchanged, proved useful to the Cherokee people and is justifiably a point of great pride for them. The syllabary contains eighty-five symbols, many of them derived from Latin characters, which efficiently transcribe spoken Cherokee. A few symbols are shown here:

Ꭷ	gu
Ꮁ	hu
Ꮺ	we
Ꮤ	ta
Ꮀ	mi

In some languages, an alphabetic character can be used in certain words to write a syllable. In a word such as bar-b-q, the single letters represent syllables (*b* for [bi] or [bə], *q* for [kju]).

Consonantal Alphabet Writing

Semitic languages, such as Hebrew and Arabic, are written with alphabets that consist only of consonants. Such an alphabet works for these languages because consonants form the root of most words. For example, the consonants *ktb* in Arabic form the root of words associated with "write." Thus *katab* means "to write," *aktib* means "I write," *kitab* means "a book," and so on. Inflectional and derivational processes can be expressed by different vowels inserted into the triconsonantal roots.

Because of this structure, vowels can sometimes be figured out by a person who knows the spoken language, jst lk y cn rd ths phrs, prvdng y knw nglsh. English, however, is unrelated to the Semitic languages, and its structure is such that vowels are usually crucial for reading and writing. The English phrase *I like to eat out* would be incomprehensible without vowels, viz. *lk t t t.*

Semitic alphabets provide a way to use diacritic marks to express vowels. This is partly out of the desire to preserve the true pronunciations of religious writings, and partly out of deference to children and foreigners learning to read and write. In Hebrew, dots or other small figures are placed under, above, or even in the center of the consonantal letter to indicate the accompanying vowel. For example, ל represents an l-sound in Hebrew writing. Unadorned, the vowel that follows would be determined by context. However לֶ (with a tiny triangle of dots below it) indicates that the vowel that follows is [ε], so in effect לֶ represents the syllable [lε].

These systems are called consonantal alphabets because only the consonants are fully developed symbols. Sometimes they are considered syllabaries because once the reader or writer perceives the vowel, the consonantal letter *seems* to stand for a syllable. With a true syllabary, however, a person need know only the phonetic value of each symbol to pronounce it correctly and unambiguously. Once you learn a Japanese syllabary, you can read Japanese in a (more or less) phonetically correct way without any idea of what you are saying. (The syllabic text doesn't always show word boundaries, and there is no indication of prosodic features such as intonation.) Anyway, this would be impossible for Arabic or Hebrew.

Alphabetic Writing

Alphabetic writing systems are easy to learn, convenient to use, and maximally efficient for transcribing any human language.

The term **sound writing** is sometimes used in place of *alphabetic writing*, but it does not truly represent the principle involved in the use of alphabets. One-sound ↔ one-letter is inefficient and unintuitive, because we do not need to represent the [pʰ] in *pit* and the [p] in *spit* by two different letters. It is confusing to represent non-phonemic differences in writing because the sounds are seldom perceptible to speakers. Except for the phonetic alphabets, whose function is to record the sounds of all languages for descriptive purposes, most, if not all, alphabets have been devised on the **phonemic principle**.

In the twelfth century, an Icelandic scholar developed an orthography derived from the Latin alphabet for the writing of the Icelandic language of his day. Other scholars in this period were also interested in orthographic reform, but the Icelander, who came to be known as "the First Grammarian" (because his anonymous paper was the first entry in a collection of grammatical essays), was the only one of the time who left a record of his principles. The orthography he developed was clearly based on the phonemic principle. He used minimal pairs to show the distinctive contrasts. He did not suggest different symbols for voiced and unvoiced [θ] and [ð], nor for [f] or [v], nor for velar [k] and palatal [tʃ], because these pairs, according to him, represented allophones of the phonemes /θ/, /f/, and /k/, respectively. He did not use these modern technical terms, but the letters of this alphabet represent the distinctive phonemes of Icelandic of that century.

King Seijong of Korea (1397–1450) realized that the same principles held true for Korean when, with the assistance of scholars, he designed a phonemic alphabet. The king was an avid reader and realized that the more than 30,000 Chinese characters used to write Korean discouraged literacy. The fruit of the king's labor was the Korean alphabet called **Hangul**, which had seventeen consonants and eleven vowels.

The Hangul alphabet was designed on the phonemic principle. Although Korean has the sounds [l] and [r], Seijong represented them by a single letter because they are allophonic variants of the same phoneme. (See exercise 3, chapter 7.) The same is true for the sounds [s] and [ʃ], and [ts] and [tʃ].

Seijong showed further ingenuity in the design of the characters themselves. The consonants are drawn so as to depict the place and manner of articulation. Thus the letter for /g/ is ㄱ to suggest the raising of the back of the tongue to the velum. The letter for /m/ is the closed figure □ to suggest the closing of the lips. Vowels are drawn as long vertical or horizontal lines, sometimes with smaller marks attached to them. Thus ㅣ represents /i/, ㅜ represents /u/, and ㅏ represents /a/. They are easily distinguishable from the blockier consonants.

In Korean writing, the Hangul characters are grouped into squarish blocks, each corresponding to a syllable. The syllabic blocks, though they consist of alphabetic characters, make Korean look as if it were written in a syllabary. If English were written that way, "Now is the winter of our discontent" would have this appearance:

No	i	th	wi te	o	ou	di co te
w	s	e	n r	f	r	s n nt

The space between letters is less than the space between syllables, which is less than the space between words. An example of Korean writing can be found in exercise 9, item 10 at the end of the chapter, or on the Internet.

These characteristics make Korean writing unique in the world, unlike that of the Europeans, the Arabians, the Chinese, the Cascagians, or even "ladies in England."

Many languages have their own alphabet, and each has developed certain conventions for converting strings of alphabetic characters into sequences of sound (reading), and converting sequences of sounds into strings of alphabetic characters (writing). As we have illustrated with English, Icelandic, and Korean, the rules governing the sound system of the language play an important role in the relation between sound and character.

Most European alphabets use Latin (Roman) letters, adding diacritic marks to accommodate individual characteristics of a particular language. For example, Spanish uses /ñ/ to represent the palatalized nasal phoneme of *señor*, and German has added an umlaut for certain of its vowel sounds that did not exist in Latin (e.g., in über). Diacritic marks supplement the forty-six kana of the Japanese syllabaries to enable them to represent the more than 100 syllables of the language. Diacritic marks are also used in writing systems of tone languages such as Thai to indicate the tone of a syllable.

Some languages use two letters together—called a **digraph**—to represent a single sound. English has many digraphs, such as *sh* /ʃ/ as in *she*, *ch* /tʃ/ as in *chop*, *ng* as in *sing* (/sɪŋ/), and *oa* as in *loaf* /lof/.

Besides the European languages, languages such as Turkish, Indonesian, Swahili, and Vietnamese have adopted the Latin alphabet. Other languages that have more recently developed a writing system use some of the IPA phonetic symbols in their alphabet. Twi, for example, uses ɔ, ɛ, and ŋ.

Many Slavic languages, including Russian, use the Cyrillic alphabet, named for St. Cyril. It is derived directly from the Greek alphabet without Latin mediation.

Many contemporary alphabets, such as those used for Arabic, Farsi (spoken in Iran), Urdu (spoken in Pakistan), and many languages of the Indian subcontinent, including Hindi, are ultimately derived from the ancient Semitic syllabaries.

Figure 12.2 shows a coarse time line of the development of the Roman alphabet.

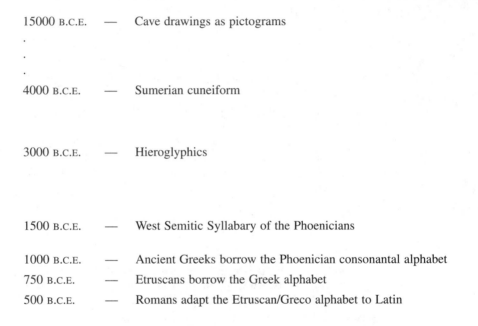

15000 B.C.E.	—	Cave drawings as pictograms
4000 B.C.E.	—	Sumerian cuneiform
3000 B.C.E.	—	Hieroglyphics
1500 B.C.E.	—	West Semitic Syllabary of the Phoenicians
1000 B.C.E.	—	Ancient Greeks borrow the Phoenician consonantal alphabet
750 B.C.E.	—	Etruscans borrow the Greek alphabet
500 B.C.E.	—	Romans adapt the Etruscan/Greco alphabet to Latin

FIGURE 12.2 Timeline of the development of the Roman alphabet.

Reading, Writing, and Speech

> . . . Ther is so great diversite
> In English, and in wryting of oure tonge,
> So prey I god that non myswrite thee . . .
>
> **GEOFFREY CHAUCER,** Troilus and Cressida

The development of writing freed us from the limitations of time and geography, but spoken language still has primacy and is the principle concern of most linguists. Nevertheless, writing systems are of interest for their own sake.

The written language reflects, to a certain extent, the elements and rules that together constitute the grammar of the language. The letters of the alphabet represent the system of phonemes, although not necessarily in a direct way. The independence of words is revealed by the spaces between them in most writing systems. However, written Japanese and Thai do not require spaces between words, although speakers and writers are aware of the individual words. On the other hand, no writing system shows the individual morphemes within a word in this way, even though speakers know what they are. (The hyphen occasionally serves this purpose in English, as in *two-fold* or *bone-dry*.)

Languages vary in regard to how much punctuation is used in writing. Some have little or none, such as Chinese. German uses capitalization, a form of punctuation, for all nouns. English uses punctuation to set apart sentences and phrases, and to indicate questions, intonation, stress, and contrast.

Consider the difference in meaning between (1) and (2):

1. Jack, thinks Jill, is smart.
2. Jack thinks Jill is smart.

With commas as in (1), it's Jack who's thought to be smart. Without commas as in (2), it's Jill who's thought to be smart. The commas fill in for the pauses of speech that would have made the meaning clear.

Similarly, by using an exclamation point or a question mark, the intention of the writer can be made clearer.

3. The children are going to bed at eight o'clock. (a simple statement)
4. The children are going to bed at eight o'clock! (an order)
5. The children are going to bed at eight o'clock? (a question)

In sentences 6 and 7, the use of the comma and quotation marks affects the syntax. In 6 *he* may refer either to John or to someone else, but in sentence 7 the pronoun must refer to someone other than John:

6. John said he's going.
7. John said, "He's going."

The apostrophe used in contractions and possessives also provides syntactic information not always available in the spoken utterance.

8. My cousin's friends (one cousin)
9. My cousins' friends (two or more cousins)

Writing, then, somewhat reflects the spoken language, and punctuation may even distinguish between two meanings not revealed in the spoken forms, as shown in sentences 8 and 9. However, often the spoken language conveys meaning that the written language does not.

In the normal written version of sentence 10,

10. John whispered the message to Bill and then he whispered it to Mary *he* can refer to either John or Bill. In the spoken sentence, if *he* receives extra stress (called **contrastive stress**), it must refer to Bill; if *he* receives normal stress, it refers to John.

A speaker can usually emphasize any word in a sentence by using contrastive stress. Writers sometimes attempt to show emphasis by using all capital letters, italics, or underlining the emphasized word. This is nicely illustrated by the Garfield cartoon.

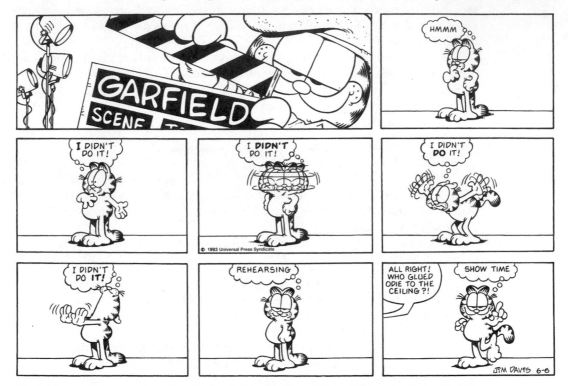

In the first panel we understand Garfield as meaning, "I didn't do it, someone else did." In the second panel the meaning is "I didn't do it, even though you think I did." In the third, the contrastive stress conveys the meaning "I didn't do it, it just happened somehow." In the fourth panel Garfield means, "I didn't do it, though I may be guilty of other things." In each case the boldfaced word is contrasted with something else.

Although such visual devices can help in English, it is not clear that they can be used in a language such as Chinese. In Japanese, however, this kind of emphasis can be achieved by writing a word in katakana.

The use of italics has many functions in written language. One use is to indicate reference to the italicized word, as in "*sheep* is a noun." A children's riddle, which is sung aloud, plays on this distinction:

Railroad crossing, watch out for cars

How do you spell it without any *r*'s?

The answer is "i-t." The joke is that the second line, were it written, would be:

How do you spell *it* without any *r*'s?

Written language is more conservative than spoken language. That is why the English spelling system is replete with vestiges left over from the Great Vowel Shift discussed in chapter 11. When we write we are more apt to obey the prescriptive rules taught in school than when we speak. We may write "it is I" but we say "it's me." Such informalities abound in spoken language, but may be "corrected" by copy editors, diligent English teachers, and careful writers. A linguist wishing to describe the language that people regularly use therefore cannot depend on written records alone, except when nothing else is available, as in the study of dead languages (see chapter 11).

Reading

"Baby Blues" © Baby Blues Partnership. Reprinted with permission of King Features Syndicate.

In chapter 8 we discussed how young children acquire their native language. We noted that language development (whether of a spoken or sign language) is a biologically driven process with a substantial innate component. Parents do not teach their children the grammatical rules of their language. Indeed, they are not even aware of the rules themselves. Rather, the young child is naturally predisposed to uncover these rules from the language he hears around him. In Western cultures most children also learn to read and write. The way we learn to be literate, however, is quite different from the way we acquire the spoken/signed language.

First, and most obviously, children learn to talk (or sign) at a very young age, while reading typically begins when the child is school-age (around 5 or 6 years old in most cases, although some children are not reading-ready until even later). A second important difference is that across cultures and languages, all children acquire a spoken/signed language while many children never learn to read or write. This may be because they are born into cultures that are not literate; that is, there is no written form of their language. For example, many American Indian languages, such as Chickasaw or Zapotec, have only recently developed writing systems, often through the efforts of linguists who are trying to help save these endangered languages from extinction. It is also unfortunately the case that even some children born into literate societies do not learn to read, either because they suffer from a specific reading disability—**dyslexia**—or because they have not been properly taught to read. It is important to recognize, however, that even illiterate children and adults have a mental grammar of their language and are able to speak/sign and understand perfectly well.

The most important respect in which spoken/signed language development differs from learning to read is that reading requires specific instruction and conscious effort, whereas language acquisition does not. Which kind of instruction works best for teaching reading has been a topic of considerable debate for many decades Three main approaches have been tried. The first—the *whole-word approach*—teaches children to recognize a vocabulary of some 50 to 100 words by rote learning, often by seeing the words used repeatedly in a story, for example, *Run, Spot, Run* from the Dick and Jane series well-known to people who learned to read in the 1950s. Other words are acquired gradually. This approach does not teach children to "sound out" words according to the individual sounds that make up the words. Rather, it treats the written language as though it were a logographic system, such as Chinese, in which a single written character corresponds to a whole word or word root. In other words, the whole-word approach fails to take advantage of the fact that English (and the writing sytems of most literate societies) is based on an alphabet, in which the symbols correspond to the individual sounds (roughly phonemes) of the language. This is ironic because alphabetic writing systems are the easiest to learn and are maximally efficient for transcribing any human language. For the past half-century, children in China have been taught to read Chinese words using the Roman alphabet. In Japan, reading instruction begins with the *hiragana*, the syllabary that directly and unambiguously represents the sounds of Japanese words. And the writing systems developed for indigenous languages are typically phonemically based.

A system of reading instruction that emphasizes the correspondence between letters and the sounds associated with them is called the *phonics approach*, which is familiar to the baby boomer generation. Phonics instruction begins by teaching children the letters of the alphabet and then encourages them to sound out words based on their knowledge of the sound-letter correspondences. So, if you have learned to read the word *gave* (understanding that the *e* is silent), then it is easy to read *save* and *pave*.

However, as we discussed in chapter 6, English and many other languages do not show a perfect correspondence between sounds and letters. So, for example, the rule for *gave, save*, and *pave* does not extend to *have*. The existence of many such exceptions has encouraged some schools to adopt another approach to reading, the *whole-language approach* (also called "literature-based" or "guided reading"), which was most popular in the 1990s. A key principle of this approach is that phonics should not be taught directly. Rather, the child is supposed to make the connections between sounds and letters herself based on exposure to text. For example, she would be encouraged to figure out an unfamiliar word based on the context of the sentence or by looking for clues in the story line or the pictures rather than by sounding it out, as she would in the phonics approach. The philosophy behind the whole-language approach is that learning to read, like learning to speak, is a natural act that children can basically do on their own—an assumption that, as we noted earlier, is questionable at best. With the whole-language approach, the main job of the teacher is to make the reading experience an enjoyable one. To this end, children are presented with engaging books and are encouraged to write stories of their own as a way of instilling a love of reading and words.

Despite the intuitive appeal of the whole-language approach—after all, who would deny the educational value of good literature and creative expression in learning—research has clearly shown that understanding the relationship between letters and sounds is critically important in reading. One of the assumptions of the whole-language approach is that skilled adult readers do not sound out words when reading, so proponents question the value of focusing on sounding out in reading instruction. However, research shows that the opposite is true: skilled adult readers *do* sound out words mentally, and they do so very rapidly. Another study compared groups of college students who were taught to read unfamiliar symbols such as Arabic letters, one group by a phonics approach and the other with a whole-word approach. Those trained with phonics could read many more new words. Similar results have been obtained through computer modeling of how children learn to read. Classroom studies have also compared phonics with whole-word or whole-language approaches and have shown that systematic phonics instruction produces better results for beginning readers.

The advantage of phonics is not contradicted by studies showing that deaf children who have fully acquired a sign language have difficulty learning to read. This is understandable because the alphabetic principle requires an understanding of sound-symbol regularities, which deaf children do not have. It seems reasonable, then, that hearing children should not be deprived of the advantage they would have if their unconscious knowledge of phonemes is made conscious.

At this point, the consensus among psychologists and linguists who do research on reading—and a view shared by many teachers—is that reading instruction must be grounded in a firm understanding of the connections between letters and sounds, and that whole-language activities that make reading fun and meaningful for children should be used to supplement phonics instruction. Based on such research, the federal govenment now promotes the inclusion of phonics in reading programs across the United States.

Spelling

"Do you spell it with a 'v' or a 'w'?" inquired the judge.
"That depends upon the taste and fancy of the speller, my Lord," replied Sam.

CHARLES DICKENS, The Pickwick Papers

If writing represented the spoken language perfectly, spelling reforms would never have arisen. In chapter 6 we discussed some of the problems in the English orthographic system. These problems prompted George Bernard Shaw to write:

> . . . It was as a reading and writing animal that Man achieved his human eminence above those who are called beasts. Well, it is I and my like who have to do the writing. I have done it professionally for the last sixty years as well as it can be done with a hopelessly inadequate alphabet devised centuries before the English language existed to record another and very different language. Even this alphabet is reduced to absurdity by a foolish orthography based on the notion that the business of spelling is to represent the origin and history of a word instead of its sound and meaning. Thus an intelligent child who is bidden to spell *debt*, and very properly spells it *d-e-t*, is caned for not spelling it with a *b* because Julius Caesar spelt the Latin word for it with a *b*.[4]

The irregularities between graphemes (letters) and phonemes have been cited as one reason "why Johnny can't read." Homographs such as *lead* /lid/ and *lead* /lɛd/ have fueled the flames of spelling reform movements. Different spellings for the same sound, silent letters, and missing letters also are cited as reasons that English needs a

---

[4]G. B. Shaw. 1948. Preface to R. A. Wilson, *The Miraculous Birth of Language.* New York: Philosophical Library.

new orthographic system. The following examples illustrate the discrepancies between spelling and sounds in English:

Same Sound, Different Spelling	Different Sound, Same Spelling		Silent Letters	Missing Letters	
/aj/	thought	/θ/	listen	use	/juz/
	though	/ð/	debt	fuse	/fjuz/
aye	Thomas	/t/	gnome		
buy			know		
by	ate	/e/	psychology		
die	at	/æ/	right		
hi	father	/a/	mnemonic		
Thai	many	/ɛ/	science		
height			talk		
guide			honest		
			sword		
			bomb		
			clue		
			Wednesday		

The spelling of most English words today is based on English as spoken in the fourteenth, fifteenth, and sixteenth centuries. Spellers in those times saw no need to spell the same word consistently. Shakespeare spelled his own name in several ways. In his plays, he spelled the first person singular pronoun variously as *I, ay,* and *aye.*

When the printing press was introduced in the fifteenth century, archaic and idiosyncratic spellings became widespread and more permanent. Words in print were frequently misspelled outright because many of the early printers were not native speakers of English.

Spelling reformers saw the need for consistent spelling that correctly reflected the pronunciation of words. To that extent, spelling reform was necessary, but many scholars became overzealous. Because of their reverence for Classical Greek and Latin, these scholars changed the spelling of English words to conform to their etymologies. Where Latin had a *b*, they added a *b* even if it was not pronounced. Where the original spelling had a *c* or *p* or *h*, these letters were added, as shown by these few examples:

Middle English Spelling		Reformed Spelling
indite	→	indict
dette	→	debt
receit	→	receipt
oure	→	hour

Such spelling habits inspired Robert N. Feinstein to compose the following poem, entitled *Gnormal Pspelling:*[5]

Gnus and gnomes and gnats and such
Gnouns with just one G too much.
Pseudonym and psychedelic

[5]Robert N. Feinstein, "Gnormal Pspelling," *National Forum: The Phi Kappa Phi Journal,* Summer 1986. Reprinted with permission.

P becomes a psurplus relic.
Knit and knack and knife and knocked
Kneedless Ks are overstocked.
Rhubarb, rhetoric and rhyme
Should lose an H from thyme to time.

Even today spelling reform is an issue. Advertisers often spell *though* as *tho*, *through* as *thru*, and *night* as *nite*. The *Chicago Tribune* once used such spellings, but it gave up the practice in 1975. Spelling habits are hard to change, and many people regard revised spelling as substandard.

The current English spelling system is based primarily on the earlier pronunciations of words. The many changes that have occurred in the sound system of English since then are not reflected in the current spelling, which was frozen due to widespread printed material and scholastic conservatism.

For these reasons, modern English orthography does not always represent what we know about the phonology of the language. The disadvantage is partially offset by the fact that the writing system allows us to read and understand what people wrote hundreds of years ago without the need for translations. If there were a one-to-one correspondence between our spelling and the sounds of our language, we would have difficulty reading the *U.S. Constitution* or the *Declaration of Independence*, let alone the works of Shakespeare and Dickens.

Languages change. It is not possible to maintain a perfect correspondence between pronunciation and spelling, nor is it 100 percent desirable. For instance, in the case of homophones, it is helpful at times to have different spellings for the same sounds, as in the following pair:

The book was red. The book was read.

Lewis Carroll makes the point with humor:

"And how many hours a day did you do lessons?" said Alice.

"Ten hours the first day," said the Mock Turtle, "nine the next, and so on."

"What a curious plan!" exclaimed Alice.

"That's the reason they're called lessons," the Gryphon remarked, "because they lessen from day to day."

There are also reasons for using the same spelling for different pronunciations. A morpheme may be pronounced differently when it occurs in different contexts. The identical spelling reflects the fact that the different pronunciations represent the same morpheme. This is the case with the plural morpheme. It is always spelled with an *s* despite being pronounced [s] in *cats* and [z] in *dogs*. The sound of the morpheme is determined by rules, in this case and elsewhere.

Similarly, the phonetic realizations of the vowels in the following forms follow a regular pattern:

aj/ɪ	**i/ɛ**	**e/æ**
divine/divinity	serene/serenity	sane/sanity
child/children	obscene/obscenity	profane/profanity
sign/signature	clean/cleanse	humane/humanity

These considerations have led some scholars to suggest that in addition to being phonemic, English has a **morphophonemic orthography**. To read English correctly, morphophonemic knowledge is required. This contrasts with a language such as Spanish, whose orthography is almost purely phonemic.

Other examples provide further motivation for spelling irregularities. The *b* in "*debt*" may remind us of the related word *debit*, in which the *b* is pronounced. The same principle is true of pairs such as *sign/signal*, *bomb/bombardier*, and *gnosis/ prognosis/agnostic*.

There are also different spellings that represent the different pronunciations of a morpheme when confusion would arise from using the same spelling. For example, there is a rule in English phonology that changes a /t/ to an /s/ in certain cases:

democrat → democracy

The different spellings have resulted partly because this rule does not apply to all morphemes, so that *art* + *y* is *arty*, not **arcy*. Regular phoneme-to-grapheme rules determine in many cases when a morpheme is to be spelled identically and when it is to be changed.

Other subregularities are apparent. A *c* always represents the /s/ sound when it is followed by a *y*, *i*, or *e*, as in *cynic*, *citizen*, and *censure*. Because it is always pronounced [k] when it is the final letter in a word or when it is followed by any other vowel (*coat*, *cat*, *cut*, and so on), no confusion results. The *th* spelling is usually pronounced voiced [ð] between vowels (the result of an historical intervocalic voicing rule), and in function words such as *the*, *they*, *this*, and *there*. Elsewhere it is the voiceless [θ].

There is another important reason why spelling should not always be tied to the phonetic pronunciation of words. Different dialects of English have divergent pronunciations. Cockneys drop their "(h)aitches," and Bostonians and Southerners drop their *r*'s; *neither* is pronounced [niðər], [najðər], and [niðə] by Americans, [najðə] by the British, and [neðər] by the Irish; some Scots pronounce *night* [nɪxt]; people say "Chicago" and "Chicawgo," "hog" and "hawg," "bird" and "boyd"; *four* is pronounced [fɔː] by the British, [fɔr] in the Midwest, and [foə] in the South; *orange* is pronounced in at least two ways in the United States: [arəndʒ] and [ɔrəndʒ].

Although dialectal pronunciations differ, the common spellings indicate the intended word. It is necessary for the written language to transcend local dialects. With a uniform spelling system, a native of Atlanta and a native of Glasgow can communicate through writing. If each dialect were spelled according to its pronunciation, written communication among the English-speaking peoples of the world would suffer.

Spelling Pronunciations

For pronunciation, the best general rule is to consider those as the most elegant speakers who deviate least from written words.

SAMUEL JOHNSON *(1755)*

Write with the learned, pronounce with the vulgar.

BENJAMIN FRANKLIN, Poor Richard's Almanac

Despite the primacy of the spoken word over the written language, the written word is often regarded with excessive reverence. The stability, permanency, and graphic nature of writing cause some people to favor it over ephemeral and elusive speech.

Humpty Dumpty expressed a rather typical attitude when he said: "I'd rather see that done on paper."

Writing has affected speech only marginally, however, most notably in the phenomenon of **spelling pronunciation**. Since the sixteenth century, we find that spelling has to some extent influenced standard pronunciation. The most important of such changes stem from the eighteenth century under the influence and decrees of the dictionary makers and the schoolteachers. The struggle between those who demanded that words be pronounced according to the spelling and those who demanded that words be spelled according to their pronunciation generated great heat in that century. The preferred pronunciations were given in the many dictionaries printed in the eighteenth century, and the "supreme authority" of the dictionaries influenced pronunciation in this way.

Spelling also has influenced pronunciation of words that are infrequently used in normal daily speech. In many words that were spelled with an initial *h*, the *h* was silent as recently as the eighteenth century. Then, no [h] was pronounced in *honest*, *hour*, *habit*, *heretic*, *hotel*, *hospital*, and *herb*. Common words like *honest* and *hour* continued *h*-less, despite the spelling. The other less frequently used words were given a "spelling pronunciation," and the *h* is sounded today. *Herb* is currently undergoing this change. In British English the *h* is pronounced, whereas in American English it generally is not.

Similarly, the *th* in the spelling of many words was once pronounced like the /t/ in *Thomas*. Later most of these words underwent a change in pronunciation from /t/ to /θ/, as in *anthem*, *author*, and *theater*. Nicknames may reflect the earlier pronunciations: "Ka*t*e" for "Ca*t*herine," "Be*tty*" for "Eliza*beth*," "Ar*t*" for "Ar*th*ur." *Often* is often pronounced with the *t* sounded, though historically it is silent, and up-to-date dictionaries now indicate this pronunciation as an alternative.

The clear influence of spelling on pronunciation is observable in the way place-names are pronounced. *Berkeley* is pronounced [bʊrkli] in California, although it stems from the British [baːkli]; *Worcester* [wʊstər] or [wʊstə] in Massachusetts is often pronounced [wʊrtʃɛstər] in other parts of the country. *Salmon* is pronounced [sæmə̃n] in most parts of the United States, but many southern speakers pronounce the [l] and say [sælmə̃n].

Although the written language has some influence on the spoken, it does not change the basic system—the grammar—of the language. The writing system, conversely, reflects, in a more or less direct way, the grammar that every speaker knows.

Summary

Writing is a basic tool of civilization. Without it, the world as we know it could not exist. The precursor of writing was "picture writing," which used **pictograms** to represent objects directly and literally. Pictograms are called **ideograms** when the drawing becomes less literal, and the meaning extends to concepts associated with the object originally pictured. When ideograms become associated with the words for the concepts they signify, they are called **logograms**. Logographic systems are true writing systems in the sense that the symbols stand for words of a language.

The Sumerians first developed a pictographic writing system to keep track of commercial transactions. It was later expanded for other uses and eventually evolved into the highly stylized (and stylus-ized) **cuneiform** writing. Cuneiform was generalized to other writing systems by application of the **rebus principle**, which uses the symbol of one word or syllable to represent another word or syllable pronounced the same.

The Egyptians also developed a pictographic system known as **hieroglyphics**. This system influenced many peoples, including the Phoenicians, who developed the West Semitic Syllabary. The Greeks borrowed the Phoenician system, and in adapting it to their own language they used the symbols to represent both consonant and vowel sound segments, thus inventing the first alphabet.

There are four types of writing systems: (1) **logographic** (word writing), where every symbol or character represents a word or morpheme (as in Chinese); (2) **syllabic**, where each symbol represents a syllable (as in Japanese); (3) **consonantal alphabetic**, where each symbol represents a consonant and vowels may be represented by diacritical marks (as in Hebrew); and (4) **alphabetic**, where each symbol represents (for the most part) a vowel or consonant (as in English).

Reading and writing, unlike speaking and understanding, must be deliberately taught. Three methods of teaching reading have been used in the United States: *whole-word*, *whole-language*, and *phonics*. In the whole-word and whole-language approaches, children are taught to recognize entire words without regard to individual letters and sounds. The phonics approach emphasizes the spelling-sound corresondences of the language, and thus draws on the child's innate phonological knowledge.

The writing system may have some small effect on the spoken language. Languages change in time, but writing systems tend to be more conservative. Thus spelling no longer accurately reflects pronunciation. Also, when the spoken and written forms of the language diverge, some words may be pronounced as they are spelled, sometimes as a result of the efforts of pronunciation reformers.

There are advantages to a conservative spelling system. A common spelling permits speakers whose dialects have diverged to communicate through writing, as is best exemplified in China, where the dialects are mutually unintelligible. We are also able to read and understand the language as it was written centuries ago. In addition, despite a certain lack of correspondences between sound and spelling, the spelling often reflects speakers' morphological and phonological knowledge.

References for Further Reading

Adams, M. J. 1996. *Beginning to Read*. Cambridge, MA: MIT Press.

Biber, D. 1988. *Variation across Speech and Writing*. Cambridge, England: Cambridge University Press.

Coulmas, F. 1989. *The Writing Systems of the World*. Cambridge, MA: Blackwell Publishers.

Cummings, D. W. 1988. *American English Spelling*. Baltimore, MD: The Johns Hopkins University Press.

Daniels, P. T., and W. Bright, eds. 1996. *The World's Writing Systems*. New York: Oxford University Press.

DeFrancis, J. 1989. *Visible Speech: The Diverse Oneness of Writing Systems*. Honolulu: University of Hawaii Press.

Gaur, A. 1984. *A History of Writing*. London, England: The British Library.

Sampson, G. 1985. *Writing Systems: A Linguistic Introduction*. Stanford, CA: Stanford University Press.

Senner, W. M., ed. 1989. *The Origins of Writing*. Lincoln: University of Nebraska Press.

Exercises

1. **A.** "Write" the following words and phrases, using pictograms that you invent:

    a. eye

    b. a boy

    c. two boys

    d. library

    e. tree

    f. forest

    g. war

    h. honesty

    i. ugly

    j. run

    k. Scotch tape

    l. smoke

   B. Which words are most difficult to symbolize in this way? Why?

   C. How does the following sentence reveal the problems in pictographic writing? "A grammar represents the unconscious, internalized linguistic competence of a native speaker."

2. A *rebus* is a written representation of words or syllables that uses pictures of objects whose names resemble the sounds of the intended words or syllables. For example, ◁◉▷ might be the symbol for "eye" or "I" or the first syllable in "idea."

   A. Using the rebus principle, "write" the following words:

    a. tearing

    b. icicle

    c. bareback

    d. cookies

   B. Why would such a system be a difficult system in which to represent all words in English? Illustrate with an example.

3. **A.** Construct non-Roman alphabetic letters to replace the letters used to represent the following sounds in English:

    t r s k w tʃ i æ f n

   B. Use these symbols plus the regular alphabet symbols for the other sounds to write the following words in your "new" orthography.

    a. character

    b. guest

    c. cough

    d. photo

    e. cheat

    f. rang

    g. psychotic

    h. tree

4. Suppose the English writing system were a *syllabic* system instead of an *alphabetic* system. Use capital letters to symbolize the necessary syllabic units for the following words, and list your "syllabary." *Example*: Given the words *mate*, *inmate*, *intake*, and *elfin*, you might use: A = mate, B = in, C = take, and D = elf. In addition, write the words using your syllabary. *Example*: inmate—BA; elfin—DB; intake—BC; mate—A. (Do not use more syllable symbols than you absolutely need.)

    a. childishness

    b. childlike

    c. Jesuit

    d. lifelessness

    e. likely

    f. zoo

    g. witness

    h. lethal

    i. jealous

    j. witless

    k. lesson

5. In the following pairs of English words, the bold-faced portions are pronounced the same but spelled differently. Can you think of any reason why the spelling should remain distinct? (*Hint*: *Reel* and *real* are pronounced the same, but *reality* shows the presence of a phonemic /æ/ in *real*.)

A	B	Reason
a. I **am**	i**amb**	
b. g**oose**	pr**oduce**	
c. **fashion**	com**plication**	
d. New**ton**	or**gan**	
e. **no**	**know**	
f. hy**mn**	**him**	

6. In the following pairs of words, the bold-faced portions are spelled the same but pronounced differently. Try to state some reasons why the spelling of the words in column B should not be changed.

A	B	Reason
a. mi**ng**le	lo**ng**	The *g* is pronounced in *longer*.
b. li**ne**	childre**n**	

	A	B	Reason
c.	sonar	resound	
d.	cent	mystic	
e.	crumble	bomb	
f.	cats	dogs	
g.	stagnant	design	
h.	serene	obscenity	

7. Each of the following sentences is ambiguous in the written form. How can these sentences be made unambiguous when they are spoken?

   Example: John hugged Bill and then he kissed him.

   For the meaning "John hugged and kissed Bill," use normal stress (*kissed* receives stress). For the meaning "Bill kissed John," contrastive stress is needed on both *he* and *him*.

   a. What are we having for dinner, Mother?

   b. She's a German language teacher.

   c. They formed a student grievance committee.

   d. Charles kissed his wife and George kissed his wife too.

8. In the written form, the following sentences are not ambiguous, but they would be if spoken. State the devices used in writing that make the meanings explicit.

   a. They're my brothers' keepers.

   b. He said, "He will take the garbage out."

   c. The red book was read.

   d. The flower was on the table.

9. Match the ten samples of writing and the ten languages. There are enough hints in this chapter to get most of them. (The source of these examples, and many others, is *Languages of the World* by Kenneth Katzner, 1975, New York: Funk & Wagnalls.)

   a. _____ Cherokee

   b. _____ Chinese

   c. _____ German (Gothic style)

   d. _____ Greek

   e. _____ Hebrew

   f. _____ Icelandic

   g. _____ Japanese

   h. _____ Korean

   i. _____ Russian

   j. _____ Twi

   1. 仮に勝手に変えるようなことをすれば、

   2. Κι ό νοῦς του ἀγκάλιασε πονετικά τὴν Κρήτη.

   3. «Что это? я падаю? у меня ноги подкашиваются»,

   4. וְהָיָה ׀ בְּאַחֲרִית הַיָּמִים נָכוֹן יִהְיֶה הַר

   5. Saá sáre yi bɛ̀ŋ atɛkyé bí â mpɔ̀torɔ áhyɛ́

   6. 既然必须和新的群众的时代相结合。

   7. *ᏗᏎ Ꭵ ᎠᏓ ᎫᏕᏋ ᏔᏫᎩ ᏋᎣᏘᏲ.*

   8. Þótt þú langförull legðir sérhvert land undir fót,

   9. Pharao's Unblick war wunderbar.

   10. 스위스는 독특한 체제

10. The following appeared on the safety card of a Spanish airline. Identify each language.

1. **Para su seguridad**
2. **For your safety**
3. **Pour votre sécurité**
4. **Für ihre Sicherheit**
5. **Per la Vostra sicurezza**
6. **Para sua segurança**
7. **あなたの安全のために**
8. **Для Вашей безопасности**
9. **Dla bezpieczeństwa pasażerów**
10. **Za vašu sigurnost**
11. **Γιά τήν ἀσφάλειά σας**
12. **Kendi emniyetiniz için**
13. **من أجل سلامتك**

11. Diderot and D'Alembert, the French "Encyclopedists," wrote:

> The Chinese have no alphabet; their very language is incompatible with one, since it is made up of an extremely limited number of sounds. It would be impossible to convey the sound of Chinese through our alphabet or any other alphabet.

Comment on this.

12. Here are several emoticons. See if you can assign a meaning to each one. There is no one correct answer because they haven't been in the language long enough to become conventionalized. One possible set of answers is printed upside down in the footnote.[6]

a. >:−(

b. :−#

c. 8:—(

d. :D

e. :-(o)

f. :−(O)

g. |−)

h. :/)

13. Just as words may be synonyms (*sad*, *unhappy*), so may emoticons. Thus **:–>** and **:–)** are both used to mean "just kidding."

---

a. Annoyance. **b.** My lips are sealed. **c.** Condescension **d.** Ha, ha. **e.** Surprise. **f.** I'm yelling. **g.** See no evil. **h.** Not that funny.

    A. If you are a user of electronic communication, try to think of three instances in which different emoticons have approximately the same meaning.

    B. Emoticons may also be ambiguous, that is, subject to different interpretations. You may have discovered that in the previous exercise. Cite three instances in which a single emoticon may be given two different interpretations.

14. Make up five or ten emoticons along with their meaning. Don't just look them up somewhere. Be creative! For example, **3:>8** to mean "bull!"

15. Punctuate the following with periods, commas, semicolons, and capital letters so that it makes sense:

> *that that is is that that is not is not that that is not is not that that is that that is is not that that is not*

16. Think of three (or more) "majority rules" sound-spelling correspondences, and then the several exceptions to each one that make learning to read English difficult. In the text we noted words like *brave, cave, Dave, gave, slave,* etc. in which *a* followed by "silent *e*" is pronounced [e], but *have* is exceptional in that the *a* is pronounced [æ]. Another example might be the *ea* spelling in *beak, leak, peak, weak, teak,* where it is pronounced [i], with exceptions such as *steak* or the president's name *Reagan,* where the *ea* is pronounced [e], or the past tense of *read* where it is pronounced [ɛ].

17. Investigate *nushu* using the time-honored template of answering: *what, who, where, when,* and *why.* Using the Internet, a good library, or any other source, answer the questions:

    a. What is nushu?

    b. Who was involved with nushu?

    c. Where did nushu exist?

    d. When did nushu exist?

    e. Why did nushu exist?

    f. **Speculative**: Can you think of a situation in your own country that might give rise to a "nushu-like situation"?

Glossary

AAE Abbreviates **African American English**.[1] See **Ebonics, AAVE**.

AAVE Abbreviates **African American Vernacular English**. See **Ebonics, AAE**.

abbreviation Shortened form of a word, e.g., *prof* from *professor*. See **clipping**.

accent (1) Prominence. See **stressed syllable**; (2) the phonology or pronunciation of a specific regional dialect, e.g., southern accent; (3) the pronunciation of a language by a non-native speaker, e.g., French accent.

accidental gap Phonological or morphological form that constitutes possible but nonoccurring lexical items, e.g., *blick, unsad*.

acoustic Pertaining to physical aspects of sound.

acoustic phonetics The study of the physical characteristics of speech sounds.

acoustic signal The sound waves produced by any sound source, including speech.

acquired dyslexia Loss of ability to read correctly following brain damage of persons who were previously literate.

acronym Word composed of the initials of several words and pronounced as such, e.g., *PET* scan from *positron-emission tomography* scan. See **alphabetic abbreviations**.

active sentence A sentence in which the noun phrase subject in D-structure is also the noun phrase subject in S-structure, e.g., *The dog chased the car.* See **passive sentence**.

adjective (Adj) The syntactic category, also lexical category, of words that function as the head of an **adjective phrase**, and that have the semantic effect of qualifying or describing the referents of nouns, e.g., *tall, bright, intelligent*. See **adjective phrase**.

adjective phrase (AP) A syntactic category, also phrasal category, whose head is an adjective possibly accompanied by premodifiers, that occurs inside noun phrases and as complements of the verb *to be*, e.g., *worthy of praise, several miles high, green, more difficult*.

adjunction A movement operation that copies an existing node and creates a new level to which the moved category is appended.

adverb (Adv) The syntactic category, also lexical category, of words that qualify the verb such as manner adverbs like *quickly* and time adverbs like *soon*. The position of the adverb in the sentence depends on its semantic type, e.g., *John will soon eat lunch, John eats lunch quickly*.

affix A bound morpheme attached to a stem or root. See **prefix, suffix, infix, circumfix, stem, root**.

---

[1]Bold words in definitions have a separate entry in this glossary, regardless of whether the bold word or term is preceded by the expression *See*.

affricate A sound produced by a stop closure followed immediately by a slow release characteristic of a fricative; phonetically a sequence of stop + fricative, e.g., the *ch* in *chip*, which is [tʃ] and like [t] + [ʃ].

African American (Vernacular) English (AA(V)E) Dialects of English spoken by some Americans of African descent, or by any person raised from infancy in a place where AAE is spoken. See **Ebonics**.

agent The thematic role of the noun phrase whose referent does the action described by the verb, e.g., *George* in *George hugged Martha*.

agrammatic aphasics Persons suffering from **agrammatism**.

agrammatism Language disorder usually resulting from damage to Broca's region in which the patient has difficulty with certain aspects of syntax, especially functional categories. See **Broca's area**.

agreement The process by which one word in a sentence is altered depending on a property of another word in that sentence, such as gender or number, e.g., the addition of *s* to a regular verb when the subject is third-person singular (in English).

allomorph Alternative phonetic form of a morpheme; e.g., the /-s/, /-z/, and /-əz/ forms of the plural morpheme in *cats*, *dogs*, and *kisses*.

allophone A predictable phonetic realization of a phoneme, e.g., [p] and [pʰ] are allophones of the phoneme /p/ in English.

alphabetic abbreviation A word composed of the initials of several words and pronounced letter-by-letter, e.g., *MRI* from *magnetic resonance imaging*. See **acronyms**.

alphabetic writing A writing system in which each symbol typically represents one sound segment.

alveolar A sound produced by raising the tongue to the alveolar ridge, e.g., [s], [t], [n].

alveolar ridge The part of the hard palate directly behind the upper front teeth.

ambiguous, ambiguity The terms used to describe a word, phrase, or sentence with multiple meanings.

American Sign Language (ASL) The sign language used by the deaf community in the United States. See **sign languages**.

analogic change A language change in which a rule spreads to previously unaffected forms, e.g., the plural of *cow* changed from the earlier *kine* to *cows* by the generalization of the plural formation rule or by analogy to regular plural forms. Also called **internal borrowing**.

analogy The use of one form as an exemplar by which other forms can be similarly constructed, e.g., based on *bow/bows*, *sow/sows*, English speakers began to say *cows* instead of the older *kine*. Analogy also leads speakers to say **brang* as a past tense of *bring* based on *sing/sang/sung*, *ring/rang/rung*, and so on.

analytic Describes a sentence that is true by virtue of its meaning alone, irrespective of context, e.g., *Kings are male*. See **contradiction**.

anomalous Semantically ill-formed, e.g., *Colorless green ideas sleep furiously*.

anomaly A violation of semantic rules resulting in expressions that seem nonsensical, e.g., *The verb crumpled the milk*.

anomia A form of **aphasia** in which patients have word-finding difficulties.

antecedent A noun phrase with which a pronoun is coreferential, e.g., *the man who is eating* is the antecedent of the pronoun *himself* in the sentence *The man who is eating bit himself*.

anterior A phonetic feature of consonants whose place of articulation is in front of the palato-alveolar area, including **labials**, **interdentals**, and **alveolars**.

antonymic pair Two words that are pronounced the same (i.e., are homonyms) but spelled differently and whose meanings are opposite, e.g., *raise* and *raze*. See **autoantonym**.

antonyms Words that are opposite with respect to one of their semantic properties, e.g., *tall/short* are both alike in that they describe height, but opposite in regard to the extent of the height. See **gradable pair**, **complementary pair**, **relational opposites**.

aphasia Language loss or disorders following brain damage.

arbitrary Describes the property of language, including sign language, whereby there is no natural or intrinsic relationship between the way a word is pronounced (or signed) and its meaning.

arc Part of the graphical depiction of a transition network represented as an arrow, often labeled, connecting two nodes. See **node**, **transition network**.

argot The specialized words used by a particular group, such as pilots or linguists, e.g., *morphophonemics* in linguistics.

arguments The various NPs that occur with a verb, e.g., *Jack* and *Jill* are arguments of *loves* in *Jack loves Jill*.

argument structure The various NPs that occur with particular verbs, called its arguments, e.g., **intransitive** verbs take a subject NP only; **transitive** verbs take both a subject and direct object NP.

article (Art) One of several subclasses of determiners, e.g., *the*, *a*.

articulatory phonetics The study of how the vocal tract produces speech sounds; the physiological characteristics of speech sounds.

aspirated Describes a voiceless stop produced with a puff of air that results when the vocal cords remain open for a brief period after the release of the stop, e.g., the [p^h] in *pit*. See **unaspirated**.

assimilation rules/assimilation A phonological process that changes feature values of segments to make them more similar, e.g., a vowel becomes [+ nasal] when followed by [+ nasal] consonant. Also called **feature spreading rules**.

asterisk The symbol [*] used to indicate ungrammatical or anomalous examples, e.g., **cried the baby*, **sincerity dances*. Also used in historical and comparative linguistics to represent a reconstructed form.

auditory phonetics The study of the perception of speech sounds.

autoantonym A word that has two opposite meanings, e.g., *cleave*, "to split apart" or "to cling together." See **antonymic pair**.

automatic machine translation The use of computers to translate from one language to another. See **source language**, **target language**.

aux A syntactic category containing auxiliary verbs and abstract tense morphemes. It is also called **INFL** and functions as the **head** of a **sentence**.

auxiliary verb Verbal elements, traditionally called "helping verbs," that co-occur with, and qualify, the main verb in a verb phrase with regard to such properties as tense, e.g., *have*, *be*, *will*.

babbling Sounds produced in the first few months after birth that gradually come to include only sounds that occur in the language of the household. Deaf children babble with hand gestures.

baby talk A certain **style** of speech that many adults use when speaking to children that includes among other things exaggerated intonation. See **motherese**, **child-directed speech** (**CDS**).

back-formation Creation of a new word by removing an affix from an old word, e.g., *donate* from *donation*; or by removing what is mistakenly considered an affix, e.g., *edit* from *editor*.

backtracking The process of undoing an analysis—usually a top-down analysis—when sensory data indicates it has gone awry, and beginning again at a point where the analysis is consistent with the data, e.g., in the syntactic analysis of *The little orange car sped*, analyzing *orange* as a noun, and later reanalyzing it as an adjective. See **top-down processing**.

base Any root or stem to which an affix is attached.

bilabial A sound articulated by bringing both lips together.

bilingual language acquisition The (more or less) simultaneous acquisition of two or more languages before the age of three years such that each language is acquired with native competency.

birdcall One or more short notes that convey messages associated with the immediate environment, such as danger, feeding, nesting, and flocking.

bird song A complex pattern of notes used to mark territory and to attract mates.

blend A word composed of the parts of more than one word, e.g., *smog* from *smoke + fog*.

blocked A derivation that is prevented by a prior application of morphological rules, e.g., when *Commun + ist* entered the language, words such as *Commun + ite* (as in *Trotsky + ite*) or *Commun + ian* (as in *grammar + ian*) were not needed and were not formed.

borrowing The incorporating of a loan word from one language into another, e.g., English borrowed *buoy* from Dutch. See **loan word**.

bottom-to-top language death The cessation of use of a language except in special circumstances, e.g., a liturgical language like Latin. See **sudden language death**, **radical language death**, **gradual language death**.

bottom-up processing Data-driven analysis of linguistic input that begins with the small units like phones and proceeds stepwise to increasingly larger units like words and phrases until the entire input is processed, often ending in a complete sentence and semantic interpretation. See **top-down processing**.

bound morpheme A morpheme that must be attached to other morphemes, e.g., *-ly*, *-ed*, *non-*. Bound morphemes are **prefixes**, **suffixes**, **infixes**, **circumfixes**, and some **roots** such as *cran* in *cranberry*. See **free morpheme**.

bound pronoun A pronoun (or more generally, a **pro-form**) whose antecedent is explicitly mentioned in the discourse. See **unbound**, **free pronoun**.

broadening A semantic change in which the meaning of a word changes over time to become more encompassing, e.g., *dog* once meant a particular breed of *dog*.

Broca, Paul A French neurologist of the nineteenth century who identified a particular area of the left side of the brain as a language center.

Broca's aphasia See **agrammatism**.

Broca's area A front part of the left hemisphere of the brain, damage to which causes **agrammatism** or **Broca's aphasia**. Also called Broca's region.

calligraphy The art of writing or drawing Chinese characters.

case A characteristic of nouns and pronouns, and in some languages articles and adjectives, determined by the function in the sentence, and generally indicated by the morphological form of the word, e.g., *I* is in the nominative case of the first-person singular pronoun in English and functions as a subject; *me* is in the accusative case and functions as an object.

case endings Suffixes on the noun based on its grammatical function, such as *'s* of the English genitive case indicating possession, e.g., Robert*'s* sheepdog.

case theory The study of thematic roles and grammatical case in languages of the world.

cause/causative The thematic role of the noun phrase whose referent is a natural force that is responsible for a change, e.g., *the wind* in *The wind damaged the roof.*

cerebral hemispheres The left and right halves of the brain, joined by the **corpus callosum**.

characters (Chinese) The units of Chinese writing, each of which represents a morpheme or word. See **ideogram**, **ideograph**, **logogram**.

Chicano English (ChE) A dialect of English spoken by some bilingual Mexican Americans in the western and southwestern United States.

child-directed speech (CDS) The special intonationally exaggerated speech that some adults sometimes use to speak with small children, sometimes called **baby talk**. See **motherese**.

circumfix A bound morpheme, parts of which occur in a word both before and after the root, e.g., *ge - - - t* in German *geliebt*, "loved," from the root *lieb*.

classifier A grammatical morpheme that marks the semantic class of a noun, e.g., in Swahili, nouns that refer to human artifacts such as beds and chairs are prefixed with the classifiers *ki* if singular and *vi* if plural; *kiti*, "chair" and *viti*, "chairs."

click A speech sound produced by sucking air into the mouth and forcing it between articulators to produce a sharp sound, e.g., the sound often spelled *tsk*.

clipping The deletion of some part of a longer word to give a shorter word with the same meaning, e.g., *phone* from *telephone*. See **abbreviation**.

closed class A category, generally a **functional category**, that rarely has new words added to it, e.g., prepositions, conjunctions. See **open class**.

coarticulation The transfer of phonetic features to adjoining segments to make them more alike, e.g., vowels become [+ nasal] when followed by consonants that are [+ nasal].

cocktail party effect An informal term that describes the ability to filter out background noise and focus on a particular sound source or on a particular person's speech.

coda One or more phonological segments that follow the **nucleus** of a syllable, e.g., the /st/ in /prist/ *priest*.

code-switching The movement back and forth between two languages or dialects within the same sentence or discourse.

cognates Words in related languages that developed from the same ancestral root, such as English *man* and German *Mann*.

coinage The construction and/or invention of new words that then become part of the lexicon, e.g., *podcast*.

collocation analysis Textual analysis that reveals the extent to which the presence of one word influences the occurrence of nearby words.

comparative linguistics The branch of historical linguistics that explores language change by comparing related languages.

comparative method The technique linguists use to deduce forms in an ancestral language by examining corresponding forms in several of its descendant languages.

comparative reconstruction The deducing of forms in an ancestral language of genetically related languages by application of the **comparative method**.

competence, linguistic The knowledge of a language represented by the mental grammar that accounts for speakers' linguistic ability and creativity. For the most part, linguistic competence is unconscious knowledge.

complement The constituent(s) in a phrase other than the head that complete(s) the meaning of the phrase and which is **C-selected** by the verb. In the verb phrase *found a puppy*, the noun phrase *a puppy* is a complement of the verb *found*.

complementary distribution The situation in which phones never occur in the same phonetic environment, e.g., [p] and [pʰ] in English. See **allophones**.

complementary pair Two **antonyms** related in such a way that the negation of one is the meaning of the other, e.g., *alive* means *not dead*. See **gradable pair**, **relational opposites**.

complementizer (Comp) A syntactic category, also functional category, of words, including *that*, *if*, *whether*, that introduce an embedded sentence, e.g., *his belief that sheepdogs can swim*, or, *I wonder if sheepdogs can swim*. The complementizer has the effect of turning a sentence into a complement.

compositional semantics A theory of meaning that calculates the truth value or meaning of larger units by the application of semantic rules to the truth value or meaning of smaller units.

compound A word composed of two or more words, e.g., *washcloth*, *childproof cap*.

computational linguistics A subfield of linguistics and computer science that is concerned with the computer processing of human language.

computational morphology The programming of computers to analyze the structure of words.

computational phonetics and phonology The programming of computers to analyze the speech signal into phones and phonemes.

computational pragmatics The programming of computers to take context and situation into account when determining the meaning of expressions.

computational semantics The programming of computers to determine the meaning of words, phrases, sentences, and discourse.

computational syntax The programming of computers to analyze the structure of sentences. See **parse**, **bottom-up processing**, **top-down processing**.

concatenative (speech) synthesis The computer production of speech based on assembling prerecorded human pronunciations of basic units such as phones, syllables, morphemes, words, phrases, or sentences.

concordance An alphabetical index of the words in a text that gives the frequency of each word, its location in the text, and its surrounding context.

conditioned sound change Historical phonological change that occurs in specific phonetic contexts, e.g., the voicing of /f/ to [v] when it occurs between vowels.

connectionism Modeling grammars through the use of networks consisting of simple neuron-like units connected in complex ways so that different connections vary in strength, and can be strengthened or weakened through exposure to linguistic data. For example, in phonology there would be stronger connections among /p/,

/t/, and /k/ (the voiceless stops and a natural class) than among /p/, /n/, and /i/. In morphology there would be stronger connections between *play/played* and *dance/danced* than between *play* and *danced*. Semantically, there would be stronger connections between *melody* and *music* than between *melody* and *sheep-dog*. Syntactically there would be stronger connections between *John loves Mary* and *Mary is loved by John* than between *John loves Mary* and *Mary knows John*.

connotative meaning/connotation The evocative or affective meaning associated with a word. Two words or expressions may have the same **denotative meaning** but different connotations, e.g., *president* and *commander-in-chief*.

consonant A speech sound produced with some constriction of the air stream. See **vowel**.

consonantal The phonetic feature that distinguishes the class of obstruents, liquids, and nasals, which are [+ consonantal], from other sounds (vowels and glides), which are [− consonantal].

consonantal alphabet The symbols of a **consonantal writing** system.

consonantal writing A writing system of symbols that represent only consonants; vowels are inferred from context, e.g., Arabic.

constituent A syntactic unit in a **phrase structure tree**, e.g., *the girl* is a noun phrase constituent in the sentence *the boy loves the girl*.

constituent structure The hierarchically arranged syntactic units such as noun phrase and verb phrase that underlie every sentence.

constituent structure tree See **phrase structure tree**.

content words The nouns, verbs, adjectives, and adverbs that constitute the major part of the vocabulary. See **open class**.

context The discourse preceding an utterance together with the real-world knowledge of speakers and listeners. See **linguistic context**, **situational context**.

continuant A speech sound in which the air stream flows continually through the mouth; all speech sounds except stops and affricates.

contour tones Tones in which the pitch glides from one level to another, e.g., from low to high as in a rising tone.

contradiction Describes a sentence that is false by virtue of its meaning alone, irrespective of context, e.g., *Kings are female*. See **analytic**, **tautology**.

contradictory Mutual negative entailment: the truth of one sentence necessarily implies the falseness of another sentence, and vice versa, e.g., *The door is open* and *The door is closed* are contradictory sentences. See **entailment**.

contralateral Refers to stimuli that travel between one side of the body (left/right) and the opposite **cerebral hemisphere** (right/left).

contrast Different sounds contrast when their presence alone distinguishes between otherwise identical forms, e.g., [f] and [v] in *fine* and *vine*, but not [p] and [pʰ] in [spik] and [spʰik] (two variant ways of saying *speak*). See **minimal pair**.

contrasting tones In tone languages, different tones that make different words, e.g., in Nupe, *bá* with a high tone, and *bà* with a low tone mean "be sour" and "count," respectively.

contrastive stress Additional stress placed on a word to highlight it or to clarify the referent of a pronoun, e.g., in *Joe hired Bill and he hired Sam*, with contrastive stress on *he*, it is usually understood that Bill rather than Joe hired Sam.

convention, conventional The agreed-on, although generally arbitrary, relationship between the form and meaning of words.

Cooperative Principle A broad principle within whose scope fall the various **maxims of conversation**. It states that in order to communicate effectively, speakers should agree to be informative and relevant.

coordinate structure A syntactic structure in which two or more constituents of the same syntactic category are joined by a conjunction such as *and* and *or*, e.g., *bread and butter*, *the big dog or the small cat*, *huffing and puffing*.

coreference The relation between two noun phrases that refer to the same entity.

coreferential Describes noun phrases (including pronouns) that refer to the same entity.

coronals The class of sounds articulated by raising the tip or blade of the tongue, including **alveolars** and **palatals**, e.g., [t], [ʃ].

corpus A collection of language data gathered from spoken or written sources used for linguistic research and analysis.

corpus callosum The nerve fibers connecting the right and left **cerebral hemispheres**.

cortex The approximately ten billion neurons that form the outside surface of the brain; also referred to as gray matter.

count nouns Nouns that can be enumerated, e.g., *one potato*, *two potatoes*. See **mass nouns**.

cover symbol A symbol that represents a class of sounds, e.g., C for consonants, V for vowels.

creativity of language, creative aspect of linguistic knowledge Speakers' ability to combine the finite number of linguistic units of their language to produce and understand an infinite range of novel sentences.

creole A language that begins as a **pidgin** and eventually becomes the first language of a speech community through its being learned by children.

critical age hypothesis The theory that states that there is a window of time between early childhood and puberty for learning a first language, and beyond which first language acquisition is almost always incomplete.

critical period The time between early childhood and puberty during which a child can acquire language easily, swiftly, and without external intervention. After this period, the acquisition of the grammar is difficult and, for some individuals, never fully achieved.

C-selection The classifying of verbs and other lexical items in terms of the syntactic category of the complements that they accept (*C* stands for categorial), sometimes called **subcategorization**, e.g., *find* C-selects, or is subcategorized for, a noun phrase complement.

cuneiform A form of writing in which the characters are produced using a wedge-shaped stylus.

data mining Complex methods of retrieving and using information from immense and varied sources of data through the use of advanced statistical tools.

declarative (sentence) A sentence that asserts that a particular situation exists. See **interrogative**.

declension A list of the inflections or cases of nouns, pronouns, adjectives, and determiners in categories such as grammatical relationship, number, and gender.

deep structure See **D-structure**.

definite Describes a noun phrase that refers to a particular object known to the speaker and listener.

deictic/deixis Refers to words or expressions whose reference relies on context and the orientation of the speaker in space and time, e.g., *I*, *yesterday*, *there*, *this cat*.

demonstrative articles, demonstratives Words such as *this*, *that*, *those*, and *these* that function syntactically as articles but are semantically **deictic** because context is needed to determine the referent of the noun phrase in which they occur.

denotative meaning The referential meaning of a word or expression. See **connotative meaning**.

dental A place-of-articulation term for consonants articulated with the tongue against, or nearly against, the front teeth. See **interdental**.

derivation The steps in the application of rules to an underlying form that results in a surface representation, e.g., in deriving a syntactic S-structure from a D-structure, or in deriving a phonetic form from a phonemic form.

derivational morpheme A morpheme added to a stem or root to form a new stem or word, possibly, but not necessarily, resulting in a change in syntactic category, e.g., *-er* added to a verb like *kick* to give the noun *kicker*.

derived structure Any structure resulting from the application of transformational rules.

derived word The form that results from the addition of a derivational morpheme, e.g., *firmly* from *firm + ly*.

descriptive grammar A linguist's description or model of the mental grammar, including the units, structures, and rules. An explicit statement of what speakers know about their language. See **prescriptive grammar**, **teaching grammar**.

determiner (Det) The syntactic category, also functional category, of words and expressions, which when combined with a noun form a noun phrase. Includes the articles *the* and *a*, **demonstratives** such as *this* and *that*, quantifiers such as *each* and *every*, etc.

diacritics Additional markings on written symbols to specify various phonetic properties such as **length**, **tone**, **stress**, **nasalization**; extra marks on a written character that change its usual value, e.g., the tilde [~] drawn over the letter *n* in Spanish represents a palatalized nasal rather than an alveolar nasal.

dialect A variety of a language whose grammar differs in systematic ways from other varieties. Differences may be lexical, phonological, syntactic, and semantic. See **regional dialect**, **social dialect**, **prestige dialect**.

dialect area A geographic area defined by the predominant use of a particular language variety, or a particular characteristic of a language variety, e.g., an area where *bucket* is used rather than *pail*. See **dialect**, **dialect atlas**, **isogloss**.

dialect atlas A book of **dialect maps** showing the areas where specific dialectal characteristics occur in the speech of the region.

dialect leveling Movement toward greater uniformity or decrease in variations among dialects.

dialect map A map showing the areas where specific dialectal characteristics occur in the speech of the region.

dichotic listening Experimental methods for brain research in which subjects hear different auditory signals in the left and right ears.

digraph Two letters used to represent a single sound, e.g., *gh* represents [f] in *enough*.

diphthong Vowel + glide, e.g., [*aj*, *aw*, *ɔj*] as in *bite*, *bout*, *boy*. See **monophthong**.

direct object The grammatical relation of a noun phrase when it appears immediately below the verb phrase (VP) and next to the verb in deep structure; the noun phrase complement of a transitive verb, e.g., *the puppy* in *the boy found the puppy*.

discontinuous morpheme A morpheme with multiple parts that occur in more than one place in a word or sentence, e.g., *ge* and *t* in German *geliebt*, "loved." See **circumfix**.

discourse A linguistic unit that comprises more than one sentence.

discourse analysis The study of broad speech units comprising multiple sentences.

discreteness A fundamental property of human language in which larger linguistic units are perceived to be composed of smaller linguistic units, e.g., *cat* is perceived as the phonemes /k/, /æ/, /t/; *the cat* is perceived as *the* and *cat*.

dissimilation rules Phonological rules that change feature values of segments to make them less similar, e.g., a fricative dissimilation rule: /θ/ is pronounced [t] following another fricative. In English dialects with this rule, *sixth* /sɪks + θ/ is pronounced [sɪkst].

distinctive Describes linguistic elements that contrast, e.g., [f] and [v] are distinctive segments; voice is a distinctive phonetic feature of consonants.

distinctive features Phonetic properties of phonemes that account for their ability to contrast meanings of words, e.g., *voice*, *tense*. Also called **phonemic features**.

ditransitive verb A verb that appears to take two noun-phrase objects, e.g., *give* in *he gave Sally his cat*. Ditransitive verb phrases often have an alternative form with a prepositional phrase in place of the first noun phrase, as in *he gave his cat to Sally*.

dominate In a **phrase structure tree**, when a continuous downward path can be traced from a node labeled A to a node labeled B, then A dominates B.

downdrift The gradual lowering of the absolute pitch of tones during an utterance in a tone language. During downdrift, tones retain their *relative* values to one another.

D-structure Any phrase structure tree generated by the phrase structure rules of a transformational grammar. The basic syntactic structures of the grammar. Also called **deep structure**. See **transformational rule**.

dyslexia A cover term for the various types of reading impairment.

Early Middle English Vowel Shortening A sound change that shortened vowels such as the first *i* in *criminal*. As a result, *criminal* was unaffected by the **Great Vowel Shift**, leading to word pairs such as *crime/criminal*.

ease of articulation The tendency of speakers to adjust their pronunciation to make it easier, or more efficient, to move the articulators. Phonetic and phonological rules are often the result of ease of articulation, e.g., the rule of English that nasalizes vowels when they precede a nasal consonant.

Ebonics An alternative term, first used in 1997, for the various dialects of **African American English**.

embedded sentence A sentence that occurs within a sentence in a phrase structure tree, e.g., *You know that **sheepdogs cannot read***.

emoticon A string of text characters that, when viewed sideways, forms a face or figure expressing a particular emotion, e.g., [8<\ to express "dismay." Frequently used in e-mail.

entailment The relationship between two sentences, where the truth of one infers the truth of the other, e.g., *Corday assassinated Marat* and *Marat is dead*; if the first is true, the second must be true.

entails One sentence entails another if the truth of the first necessarily implies the truth of the second, e.g., *The sun melted the ice* entails *The ice melted* because if the first is true, the second must be true.

epenthesis The insertion of one or more phones in a word, e.g., the insertion of [ə] in *children* to produce [tʃɪlədrən] instead of [tʃɪldrən].

eponym A word taken from a proper name, such as *Hertz* for "unit of frequency."

etymology The history of words; the study of the history of words.

euphemism A word or phrase that replaces a taboo word or is used to avoid reference to certain acts or subjects, e.g., *powder room* for *toilet*.

event/eventive A type of sentence that describes activities such as *John kissed Mary*, as opposed to describing states such as *John knows Mary*. See **state/stative**.

event-related brain potentials (ERP) The electrical signals emitted from different areas of the brain in response to different kinds of stimuli.

experiencer The thematic role of the noun phrase whose referent perceives something, e.g., *Helen* in *Helen heard Robert playing the piano*.

extension The referential part of the meaning of an expression; the referent of a noun phrase. See **reference, referent**.

feature matrix A representation of phonological segments in which the columns represent segments and the rows represent features, each cell being marked with a + or – to designate the presence or absence of the feature for that segment.

feature-changing rules Phonological rules that change feature values of segments, either to make them more similar (See **assimilation rules**) or less similar (See **dissimilation rules**).

feature-spreading rules See **assimilation rules**.

finger spelling In signing, hand gestures that represent letters of the alphabet used to spell words for which there is no sign.

flap A speech sound in which the tongue touches the alveolar ridge and withdraws. It is often an allophone of /t/ and /d/ in words such as *latter* and *ladder*. Also called **tap**.

folk etymology The process whereby the history of a word is derived from nonscientific speculation or false analogy with another word, e.g., *hooker* for "prostitute" is falsely believed to be derived from the name of the U.S. Civil War general Joseph Hooker.

form The phonological or gestural representation of a morpheme or word.

formant In the frequency analysis of speech, a band of frequencies of higher intensity than surrounding frequencies, which appears as a dark line on a **spectrogram**. Individual vowels display different formant patterns.

formant (speech) synthesis The computer production of sound based on the blending of electronic-based acoustic components; no prerecorded human sounds are used.

fossilization A characteristic of second-language learning in which the learner reaches a plateau and seems unable to acquire some property of the L2 grammar.

free morpheme A single morpheme that constitutes a word, e.g., *dog*.

free pronoun A pronoun that refers to some object not explicitly mentioned in the sentence, e.g., *it* in *Everyone saw it*. Also called **unbound**. See **bound**.

free variation Alternative pronunciations of a word in which one sound is substituted for another without changing the word's meaning, e.g., pronunciation of *bottle* as [batəl] or [baʔəl].

fricative A consonant sound produced with so narrow a constriction in the vocal tract as to create sound through friction, e.g., [s], [f].

front vowels Vowel sounds in which the tongue is positioned forward in the mouth, e.g., [i], [æ].

function word A word that does not have clear lexical meaning but has a grammatical function; function words include **conjunctions**, **prepositions**, **articles**, **auxiliaries**, **complementizers**, and **pronouns**. See **closed class**.

functional category One of the categories of function words, including **determiner**, **aux**, **complementizer**, and **preposition**. These categories are not lexical or phrasal categories. See **lexical categories**, **phrasal categories**.

fundamental difference hypothesis Second language acquisition (L2) differs fundamentally from first language acquisition (L1).

fundamental frequency In speech, the rate at which the vocal cords vibrate, symbolized as F_0, called F-zero, perceived by the listener as **pitch**.

gapping The syntactic process of deletion in which subsequent occurrences of a verb are omitted in similar contexts, e.g., *Bill washed the grapes and Mary, the cherries.*

garden path (sentences) Sentences that appear at first blush to be ungrammatical, but with further syntactic processing, turn out to be grammatical, e.g., *The horse raced past the barn fell.*

geminate A sequence of two identical sounds; a long vowel or long consonant denoted either by writing the phonetic symbol twice as in [biiru], [sakki] or by use of a colon-like symbol [biːru], [sakːi].

generic term A word that applies to a whole class, such as *wombat* in *the wombat lives across the seas, among the far Antipodes*. A word that is ordinarily masculine, when used to refer to both sexes, e.g., *mankind* meaning "the human race"; the masculine pronoun when used as a neutral form, as in *Everyone should do **his** duty*.

genetically related Describes two or more languages that developed from a common, earlier language, e.g., French, Italian, and Spanish, which all developed from Latin.

glide A speech sound produced with little or no obstruction of the air stream that is always preceded or followed by a vowel, e.g., /w/ in *we*, /j/ in *you*.

gloss A word in one language given to express the meaning of a word in another language, e.g., "house" is the English gloss for the French word *maison*.

glottal/glottal stop A speech sound produced with constriction at the glottis; when the air is stopped completely at the **glottis** by tightly closed vocal cords, a glottal stop is produced.

glottis The opening between the vocal cords.

goal The thematic role of the noun phrase toward whose referent the action of the verb is directed, e.g., *the theater* in *The kids went to the theater.*

gradable pair Two antonyms related in such a way that more of one is less of the other, e.g., *warm* and *cool*; more warm is less cool, and vice versa. See **complementary pair**, **relational opposites**.

gradual language death The disappearance of a language over a period of several generations, each of which has fewer speakers of the language until finally no speakers remain. See **sudden language death**, **radical language death**, **bottom-to-top language death**.

grammar The mental representation of a speaker's linguistic competence; what a speaker knows about a language, including its phonology, morphology, syntax, semantics, and lexicon. A linguistic description of a speaker's mental grammar.

grammar translation A method of second-language learning in which the student memorizes words and syntactic rules and translates them between the native language and target language.

grammatical, grammaticality Describes a well-formed sequence of words, one conforming to rules of syntax.

grammatical case See **case**.

grammatical categories Traditionally called "parts of speech"; also called **syntactic categories**; expressions of the same grammatical category can generally substitute for one another without loss of grammaticality, e.g., **noun phrase**, **verb phrase**, **adjective**, **auxiliary**.

grammatical morpheme A function word or bound morpheme required by the syntactic rules, e.g., *to* and *s* in *he wants to go*. See **inflectional morpheme**.

grammatical relation Any of several structural positions that a noun phrase may assume in a sentence. See **subject**, **direct object**.

graphemes The symbols of an alphabetic writing system; the letters of an alphabet.

Great Vowel Shift A sound change that took place in English some time between 1400 and 1600 C.E. in which seven long vowel phonemes were changed.

Grimm's Law The description of a phonological change in the sound system of an early ancestor of the Germanic languages formulated by Jakob Grimm.

Hangul An alphabet based on the phonemic principle for writing the Korean language designed in the fifteenth century.

head (of a compound) The rightmost word, e.g., *house* in *doghouse*. It generally indicates the category and general meaning of the compound.

head (of a phrase) The central word of a phrase whose lexical category defines the type of phrase, e.g., the noun *man* is the head of the noun phrase *the man who came to dinner*; the verb *wrote* is the head of the verb phrase *wrote a letter to his mother*; the adjective *red* is the head of the adjective phrase *very bright red*.

hemiplegic An individual (child or adult) with acquired unilateral lesions of the brain who retains both hemispheres (one normal and one diseased).

hemispherectomy The surgical removal of a hemisphere of the brain.

heteronyms Different words spelled the same (i.e., **homographs**) but pronounced differently, e.g., *bass*, meaning either "low tone" [bes] or "a kind of fish" [bæs].

hierarchical structure The groupings and subgroupings of the parts of a sentence into syntactic categories, e.g., *the bird sang* [[[the] [bird]] [sang]]; the groupings and subgroupings of morphemes in a word, e.g., *unlockable* [[un] [[lock][able]]]. Hierarchical structure is generally depicted in a **tree diagram**.

hieroglyphics A pictographic writing system used by the Egyptians around 4000 B.C.E.

hiragana A Japanese syllabary used to write native words of the language, most often together with ideographic characters. See **kanji**.

historical and comparative linguistics The branch of linguistics that deals with how languages change, what kinds of changes occur, and why they occur.

historical linguistics See **historical and comparative linguistics**.

holophrastic The stage of child language acquisition in which one word conveys a complex message similar to that of a phrase or sentence.

homographs Words spelled identically, and possibly pronounced the same, e.g., *bear* meaning "to tolerate," and *bear* the animal; or *lead* the metal and *lead*, what leaders do.

homonyms/homophones Words pronounced, and possibly spelled, the same, e.g., *to*, *too*, *two*; or *bat* the animal, *bat* the stick, and *bat* meaning "to flutter" as in "bat the eyelashes."

homorganic consonants Two sounds produced at the same place of articulation, e.g., [m] and [p]; [t], [d], [n]. See **assimilation rules**.

homorganic nasal rule A phonological assimilation rule that changes the place of articulation feature of a nasal consonant to agree with that of a following consonant, e.g., /n/ becomes [m] when preceding /p/ as in *impossible*.

hypercorrection Deviations from the "norm" thought by speakers to be "more correct," such as saying *between he and she* instead of *between him and her*.

hyponyms Words whose meanings are specific instances of a more general word, e.g., *red*, *white*, and *blue* are hyponyms of the word *color*; *triangle* is a hyponym of *polygon*.

iconic, iconicity A nonarbitrary relationship between form and meaning in which the form bears a resemblance to its meaning, e.g., the male and female symbols on (some) restroom doors.

ideogram, ideograph A character of a word-writing system, often highly stylized, that represents a concept, or the pronunciation of the word representing that concept.

idiolect An individual's way of speaking, reflecting that person's grammar.

idiom/idiomatic phrase An expression whose meaning does not conform to the **principle of compositionality**, that is, may be unrelated to the meaning of its parts, e.g., *kick the bucket* meaning "to die."

ill-formed Describes an ungrammatical or anomalous sequence of words.

illocutionary force The intended effect of a speech act, such as a warning, a promise, a threat, and a bet, e.g., the illocutionary force of *I resign!* is the act of resignation.

imitation A proposed mechanism of child language acquisition, according to which children learn their language by imitating adult speech.

immediately dominate If a node labeled A is directly above a node labeled B in a phrase structure tree, then A immediately dominates B.

implication Some linguists describe presupposition in terms of implication. Thus *John wants more coffee* carries the implication or **entails** that John has already had some coffee. See **entailment**, **presupposition**.

impoverished data Refers to the incomplete, noisy, and unstructured utterances that children hear, including slips of the tongue, false starts, and ungrammatical and incomplete sentences, together with a lack of concrete evidence about abstract grammatical rules and structure. Also referred to as **poverty of the stimulus**.

Indo-European The descriptive name given to the ancestor language of many modern language families, including Germanic, Slavic, and Romance. Also called **Proto-Indo-European**.

infinitive An uninflected form of a verb, e.g., (to) *swim*.

infinitive sentence An embedded sentence that does not have a tense and therefore is a "to" form, e.g., *sheepdogs to be fast readers* in the sentence *He believes sheepdogs to be fast readers.*

infix A bound morpheme that is inserted in the middle of another morpheme.

INFL Abbreviates "inflection," a term sometimes used in place of **Aux**; the head of a **sentence**.

inflectional morpheme A bound grammatical morpheme that is affixed to a word according to rules of syntax, e.g., third-person singular verbal suffix -*s*.

information retrieval The process of using a computer to search a database for items on a particular topic. See **data mining**.

innateness hypothesis The theory that the human species is genetically equipped with a **Universal Grammar**, which provides the basic design for all human languages.

instrument The thematic role of the noun phrase whose referent is the means by which an action is performed, e.g., *a paper clip* in *Houdini picked the lock with a paper clip*.

intension The inherent, nonreferential part of the meaning of an expression, also called **sense**. See **sense, extension**.

intensity The magnitude of an acoustic signal, which is perceived as loudness.

interdental A sound produced by inserting the tip of the tongue between the upper and lower teeth, e.g., the initial sounds of *thought* and *those*.

interlanguage grammars The intermediate grammars that second-language learners create on their way to acquiring the (more or less) complete grammar of the target language.

internal borrowing See **analogic change**.

International Phonetic Alphabet (IPA) The phonetic alphabet designed by the International Phonetic Association to be used to represent the sounds found in all human languages.

International Phonetic Association (IPA) The organization founded in 1888 to further phonetic research and develop the International Phonetic Alphabet.

interrogative (sentence) A sentence that questions whether a particular situation exists. See **declarative**.

intonation The pitch contour of a phrase or sentence.

intransitive verb A verb that must not have (does not **C-select** for) a direct object complement, e.g., *sleep*.

IP Inflection Phrase. A term sometimes used in place of *Sentence*. A phrasal category whose head is **INFL**.

ipsilateral Refers to stimuli that travel between one side of the body (left/right) and the same **cerebral hemisphere** (left/right). See **contralateral**.

isogloss A geographic boundary that separates areas with dialect differences, e.g., a line on a map on one side of which most people say *faucet* and on the other side of which most people say *spigot*.

jargon Special words peculiar to the members of a profession or group, e.g., *glottis* for phoneticians. See **argot**. Also, the nonsense words sometimes used by Wernicke aphasics.

jargon aphasia Form of aphasia in which phonemes are substituted, resulting in nonsense words; often produced by people who have severe **Wernicke's aphasia**.

kana The characters of either of the two Japanese syllabaries, **katakana** and **hiragana**.

kanji The Japanese term for the Chinese characters used in Japanese writing.

katakana A Japanese syllabary generally used for writing loan words and to achieve the effect of italics.

L2 acquisition See **second language acquisition**.

labial A sound articulated at the lips, e.g., [b], [f].

labiodental A sound produced by touching the bottom lip to the upper teeth, e.g., [v].

labio-velar A sound articulated by simultaneously raising the back of the tongue toward the velum and rounding the lips. The *w* of English is a labio-velar glide.

larynx The structure of muscles and cartilage in the throat that contains the vocal cords and **glottis**; often called the "voice box."

Late Closure Principle A psycholinguistic principle of language comprehension that states: Attach incoming material to the phrase that was most recently processed, e.g., *he said that he slept yesterday* associates *yesterday* with *he slept* rather than with *he said*.

lateral A sound produced with air flowing past one or both sides of the tongue, e.g., [l].

lateralization, lateralized Term used to refer to cognitive functions localized to one or the other side of the brain.

lax vowel A vowel produced with relatively less tension in the vocal cords and little tendency to diphthongize, e.g., [ʊ] in *put*, [pʊt]. Most lax vowels do not occur at the ends of syllables, that is [bʊ] is not a possible English word. See **tense/lax vowel**.

length A prosodic feature referring to the duration of a segment. Two sounds may contrast in length, e.g., in Japanese the first vowel is [+ long] in /biːru/ "beer" but [− long], therefore short, in /biru/ "building."

level tones Relatively stable (nongliding) pitch on syllables of tone languages. Also called **register tones**.

lexical access The process of searching the mental lexicon for a phonological string to determine if it is an actual word.

lexical ambiguity Multiple meanings of sentences due to words that have multiple meanings, e.g., *He blew up the pictures of his ex-girlfriend.*

lexical category A general term for the word-level syntactic categories of noun, verb, adjective, and adverb. These are the categories of content words like *man*, *run*, *large*, and *rapidly*, as opposed to functional category words such as *the* and *and*. See **functional categories**, **phrasal categories**, **open class**.

lexical decision Task of subjects in psycholinguistic experiments who on presentation of a spoken or printed stimulus must decide whether it is a word or not.

lexical gap Possible but nonoccurring words; forms that obey the **phonotactic rules** of a language yet have no meaning, e.g., *blick* in English.

lexical paraphrases Sentences that have the same meaning due to synonyms, e.g., *She lost her purse* and *She lost her handbag*.

lexical semantics The subfield of semantics concerned with the meanings of words and the meaning relationships among words.

lexicographer One who edits or works on a dictionary.

lexicography The editing or making of a dictionary.

lexicon The component of the grammar containing speakers' knowledge about morphemes and words; a speaker's mental dictionary.

lexifier language The dominant language of a pidgin (and creole) that provides the basis for the majority of the lexical items in the language.

lingua franca A language common to speakers of diverse languages that can be used for communication and commerce, e.g., English is the lingua franca of international airline pilots.

linguistic competence See **competence, linguistic**.

linguistic context The discourse that precedes a phrase or sentence that helps clarify meaning.

linguistic determinism The strongest form of the **Sapir-Whorf hypothesis**, which holds that the language we speak establishes how we perceive and think about the world.

linguistic performance See **performance, linguistic**.

linguistic relativism A weaker form of the **Sapir-Whorf hypothesis**, which holds that different languages encode different categories, and that speakers of different languages therefore think about the world in different ways. For example, speakers of languages that are poor in their number of color words will be less sensitive to gradations of color.

linguistic sign Sounds or gestures, typically morphemes in spoken languages and signs in sign languages, that have a form bound to a meaning in a single unit, e.g., *dog* is a linguistic sign whose form is its pronunciation [dag] and whose meaning is *Canis familiaris* (or however we define "dog").

linguistic theory A theory of the principles that characterize all human languages; the "laws of human language"; **Universal Grammar**.

liquids A class of consonants including /l/ and /r/ and their variants that share vowel-like acoustic properties and may function as syllabic nuclei.

loan translations Compound words or expressions whose parts are translated literally into the borrowing language, e.g., *marriage of convenience* from French *mariage de convenance*.

loan word Word in one language whose origins are in another language, e.g., in Japanese *besiboru*, "baseball," is a loan word from English. See **borrowing**.

localization The hypothesis that different areas of the brain are responsible for distinct cognitive systems. See **lateralization**.

location The thematic role of the noun phrase whose referent is the place where the action of the verb occurs, e.g., *Oslo* in *It snows in Oslo*.

logograms The symbols of a **word-writing** or **logographic writing** system.

logographic writing See **word writing**.

machine translation See **automatic machine translation**.

magnetic resonance imaging (MRI) A technique to investigate the molecular structures in human organs including the brain, which may be used to identify sites of brain lesions.

main verb The verb that functions as the head in the verb phrase, e.g., *save* in *Dagny will always save money for travel*. See **head of a phrase**.

manner of articulation The way the airstream is obstructed as it travels through the vocal tract. Stop, nasal, affricate, and fricative are some manners of articulation. See **place of articulation**.

marked In a gradable pair of antonyms, the word that is not used in questions of degree, e.g., *low* is the marked member of the pair *high/low* because we ordinarily ask *How high is the mountain?* not **How low is the mountain?*; in a masculine/feminine pair, the word that contains a derivational morpheme, usually the feminine word, e.g., *princess* is marked, whereas *prince* is unmarked. See **unmarked**.

mass nouns Nouns that cannot ordinarily be enumerated, e.g., *milk, water*; **two milks* is ungrammatical except when interpreted to mean "two kinds of milk," "two containers of milk," and so on. See **count nouns**.

maxim of manner A conversational convention that a speaker's discourse should be brief and orderly, and should avoid ambiguity and obscurity.

maxim of quality A conversational convention that a speaker should not lie or make unsupported claims.

maxim of quantity A conversational convention that a speaker's contribution to the discourse should be as informative as is required, neither more nor less.

maxim of relevance A conversational convention that a speaker's contribution to a discourse should always have a bearing on, and a connection with, the matter under discussion.

maxims of conversation Conversational conventions such as the **maxim of quantity** that people appear to obey to give coherence to discourse.

mean length of utterances (MLU) The average number of words or morphemes in a child's utterance. It is a more accurate measure of the acquisition stage of language than chronological age.

meaning The conceptual or semantic aspect of a sign or utterance that permits us to comprehend the message being conveyed. Expressions in language generally have both form—pronunciation or gesture—and meaning. See **extension**, **intension**, **sense**, **reference**.

mental grammar The internalized grammar that a descriptive grammar attempts to model. See **linguistic competence**.

metalinguistic awareness A speaker's conscious awareness *about* language and the use of language, as opposed to linguistic *knowledge*, which is largely unconscious. This book is very much about metalinguistic awareness.

metaphor Nonliteral, suggestive meaning in which an expression that designates one thing is used implicitly to mean something else, e.g., *The night has a thousand eyes*, to mean "One may be unknowingly observed at night."

metathesis The phonological process that reorders segments, often by transposing two sequential sounds, e.g., the pronunciation of *ask* /æsk/ in some English dialects as [æks].

metonym, metonymy A word substituted for another word or expression with which it is closely associated, e.g., *gridiron* to refer to the game of American football.

mimetic Similar to imitating, acting out, or miming.

Minimal Attachment Principle The principle that in comprehending language, listeners create the simplest structure consistent with the grammar, e.g., *the horse raced past the barn* is interpreted as a complete sentence rather than a noun phrase containing a relative clause, as if it were *the horse* (that was) *raced past the barn*.

minimal pair (or set) Two (or more) words that are identical except for one phoneme that occurs in the same position in each word, e.g., *pain* /pen/, *bane* /ben/, *main* /men/.

modal An auxiliary verb other than *be*, *have*, and *do*, such as *can*, *could*, *will*, *would*, and *must*.

modularity The organization of the brain and mind into distinct, independent, and autonomous parts that interact with each other.

monogenetic theory of language origin The belief that all languages originated from a single language. See **Nostratic**.

monomorphemic word A word that consists of one morpheme.

monophthong Simple vowel, e.g., *ɛ* in *bɛd*. See **diphthong**.

monosyllabic Having one syllable, e.g., *boy*, *through*.

morpheme Smallest unit of linguistic meaning or function, e.g., *sheepdogs* contains three morphemes, *sheep*, *dog*, and the function morpheme for plural, *s*.

morphological parser A process, often a computer program, that uses rules of word formation to decompose words into their component morphemes.

morphological rules Rules for combining morphemes to form stems and words.

morphology The study of the structure of words; the component of the grammar that includes the rules of word formation.

morphophonemic orthography A writing system, such as that for English, in which morphological knowledge is needed to read correctly, e.g., in *please/pleasant* the *ea* represents [i]/[ɛ].

morphophonemic rules Rules that specify the pronunciation of morphemes; a morpheme may have more than one pronunciation determined by such rules, e.g., the plural morpheme /z/ in English is regularly pronounced [s], [z], or [əz].

motherese See **child-directed speech** (**CDS**).

naming task An experimental technique that measures the response time between seeing a printed word and saying that word aloud.

narrowing A semantic change in which the meaning of a word changes in time to become less encompassing, e.g., *deer* once meant "animal."

nasal (nasalized) sound Speech sound produced with an open nasal passage (lowered velum), permitting air to pass through the nose as well as the mouth, e.g., /m/. See **oral sound**.

nasal cavity The passageways between the throat and the nose through which air passes during speech if the velum is open (lowered). See **oral cavity**.

natural class A class of sounds characterized by a phonetic property or feature that pertains to all members of the set, e.g., the class of stops. A natural class may be defined with a smaller feature set than that of any individual member of the class.

negative polarity item (NPI) An expression that is grammatical in the presence of negation, but ungrammatical in simple affirmative sentences, e.g., *James hasn't got a red cent* but **James has a red cent*; *give a hoot*, *pot to piss in*, *any*.

Neo-Grammarians A group of nineteenth-century linguists who claimed that sound shifts (i.e., changes in phonological systems) took place without exceptions.

neurolinguistics The branch of linguistics concerned with the brain mechanisms that underlie the acquisition and use of human language; the study of the neurobiology of language.

neutralization Phonological processes or rules that obliterate the contrast between two phonemes in certain environments, e.g., in some dialects of English /t/ and /d/ are both pronounced as voiced flaps between vowels, as in *writer* and *rider*, thus neutralizing the voicing distinction so that the two words sound alike.

node A labeled branch point in a phrase structure tree; part of the graphical depiction of a transition network represented as a circle, pairs of which are connected by arcs. See **arc**, **phrase structure tree**, **transition network**.

noncontinuant A sound in which air is blocked momentarily in the oral cavity as it passes through the vocal tract. See **stops**, **affricates**.

nondistinctive features Phonetic features of phones that are predictable by rule, e.g., aspiration in English.

nonphonemic features See **nondistinctive features**.

nonredundant A phonetic feature that is distinctive, e.g., *stop*, *voice*, but not *aspiration* in English.

nonsense word A permissible phonological form without meaning, e.g., *slithy*.

Nostratic A hypothetical language that is postulated as the first human language.

noun (N) The syntactic category, also lexical category, of words that can function as the head of a noun phrase, such as *book*, *Jean*, *sincerity*. In many languages nouns have grammatical alternations for number, case, and gender and occur with determiners.

noun phrase (NP) The syntactic category, also phrasal category, of expressions containing some form of a noun or pronoun as its head, and which functions as the subject or as various objects in a sentence.

nucleus That part of a syllable that has the greatest acoustic energy; the vowel portion of a syllable, e.g., /i/ in /mit/ *meet*.

obstruents The class of sounds consisting of nonnasal stops, fricatives, and affricates. See **sonorants**.

onomatopoeia/onomatopoeic Refers to words whose pronunciations suggest their meaning, e.g., *meow*, *buzz*.

onset One or more phonemes that precede the syllable **nucleus**, e.g., /pr/ in /prist/ *priest*.

open class The class of lexical content words; a category of words that commonly adds new words, e.g., nouns, verbs.

Optimality Theory The hypothesis that a universal set of ranked phonological constraints exists, where the higher the constraint is ranked, the more influence it exerts on the language, e.g., in English, one constraint is the following: Obstruent sequences may not differ with respect to their voice feature at the end of a word.

oral cavity The mouth area through which air passes during the production of speech. See **nasal cavity**.

oral sound A non-nasal speech sound produced by raising the velum to close the nasal passage so that air can escape only through the mouth. See **nasal sound**.

orthography The written form of a language; spelling.

overgeneralization Children's treatment of irregular verbs and nouns as if they were regular, e.g., *bringed*, *goed*, *foots*, *mouses*, for *brought*, *went*, *feet*, *mice*. This shows that the child has acquired the regular rules but has not yet learned that there are exceptions.

palatal A sound produced by raising the front part of the tongue to the palate.

palate The bony section of the roof of the mouth behind the **alveolar ridge**.

paradigm A set of forms derived from a single root morpheme, e.g., *give*, *gives*, *given*, *gave*, *giving*; or *woman*, *women*, *woman's*, *women's*.

paradox A sentence to which it is impossible to ascribe a truth value, e.g., *the barber shaves himself*, in the context of a village in which it is true that the barber shaves everyone who does not shave himself, and shaves no person who does shave himself.

parallel processing The ability of a computer to carry out several tasks simultaneously as a result of the presence of multiple central processors.

parameters The small set of alternatives for a particular phenomenon made available by Universal Grammar. For example, Universal Grammar specifies that a phrase must have a head and possibly complements; a parameter states whether the complement(s) precedes or follows the head.

paraphrases Sentences with the same truth conditions; sentences with the same meaning, except possibly for minor differences in emphasis, e.g., *He ran up a big bill* and *He ran a big bill up*. See **synonymy**.

parse The act of determining the grammaticality of sequences of words according to rules of syntax, and assigning a linguistic structure to the grammatical ones.

parser A computer program that determines the grammaticality of sequences of words according to whatever rules of syntax are stored in the computer's memory, and assigns a linguistic structure to the grammatical ones.

participle The form of a verb that occurs after the auxiliary verbs *be* and *have*, e.g., *kissing* in *John is kissing Mary* is a present participle; *kissed* in *John has kissed many girls* is a past participle; *kissed* in *Mary was kissed by John* is a passive participle.

passive sentence A sentence in which the verbal complex contains a form of *to be* followed by a verb in its participle form, e.g., *The girl was kissed by the boy*; *The robbers must not have been seen*. In a passive sentence, the direct object of a transitive verb in D-structure functions as the subject in S-structure. See **active sentence**.

performance, linguistic The *use* of linguistic competence in the production and comprehension of language; behavior as distinguished from linguistic knowledge, e.g., linguistic competence permits one million word sentences; linguistic performance prevents this from happening.

performative sentence A sentence containing a performative verb used to accomplish some act. Performative sentences are affirmative and declarative, and are in first-person, present tense, e.g., *I now pronounce you husband and wife*, when spoken by a justice of the peace in the appropriate situation is an act of marrying.

performative verb A verb, certain usages of which comprise a **speech act**, e.g., *resign* when the sentence *I resign!* is interpreted as an act of resignation.

person deixis The use of terms to refer to persons whose reference relies entirely on context, e.g., pronouns such as *I*, *he*, *you* and expressions such as *this child*. See **deictic**, **time deixis**, **place deixis**, **demonstrative articles**.

petroglyph A drawing on rock made by prehistoric people.

pharynx The tube or cavity in the vocal tract above the glottis through which the air passes during speech production.

phone A phonetic realization of a **phoneme**.

phoneme A contrastive phonological segment whose phonetic realizations are predictable by rule.

phonemic features Phonetic properties of phonemes that account for their ability to contrast meanings of words, e.g., *voice*, *tense*. Also called **distinctive features**.

phonemic principle The principle that underlies alphabetic writing systems in which one symbol typically represents one phoneme.

phonemic representation The phonological representation of words and sentences prior to the application of phonological rules.

phonetic alphabet Alphabetic symbols used to represent the phonetic segments of speech in which there is a one-to-one relationship between each symbol and each speech sound.

phonetic features Phonetic properties of segments (e.g., voice, nasal, alveolar) that distinguish one segment from another.

phonetic representation The representation of words and sentences after the application of phonological rules; symbolic transcription of the pronunciation of words and sentences.

phonetic similarity Refers to sounds that share most phonetic features.

phonetics The study of linguistic speech sounds, how they are produced (**articulatory phonetics**), how they are perceived (**auditory** or perceptual **phonetics**), and their physical aspects (**acoustic phonetics**).

phonographic symbol A symbol in a writing system that stands for the sounds of a word.

phonological rules Rules that apply to phonemic representations to derive phonetic representations or pronunciation.

phonology The sound system of a language; the component of a grammar that includes the inventory of sounds (phonetic and phonemic units) and rules for their combination and pronunciation; the study of the sound systems of all languages.

phonotactics/phonotactic constraints Rules stating permissible strings of phonemes, e.g., a word-initial nasal consonant may be followed only by a vowel (in English). See **possible word**, **nonsense word**, **accidental gaps**.

phrasal category The class of syntactic categories that occur on the left side of phrase structure rules, and are therefore composed of other categories, including other phrasal categories, e.g., noun phrase. See **lexical categories**, **functional categories**.

phrasal semantics See **sentential semantics**.

phrase structure rules Principles of grammar that specify the constituency of syntactic categories and of phrase structure trees, e.g., VP → V NP.

phrase structure tree A tree diagram with syntactic categories at each node that reveals both the linear and hierarchical structure of phrases and sentences.

phrenology A pseudoscience, the practice of which is determining personality traits and intellectual ability by examination of the bumps on the skull. Its contribution to neurolinguistics is that its methods were highly suggestive of the modular theory of brain structure.

pictogram A form of writing in which the symbols resemble the objects represented; a nonarbitrary form of writing.

pidgin A simple but rule-governed language developed for communication among speakers of mutually unintelligible languages, often based on one of those languages called the **lexifier language**.

Pinyin An alphabetic writing system for Mandarin Chinese using a Western-style alphabet to represent individual sounds.

pitch The **fundamental frequency** of sound perceived by the listener.

pitch contour The intonation of a sentence.

place deixis The use of terms to refer to places whose reference relies entirely on context, e.g., *here*, *there*, *behind*, *next door*. See **deictic**, **time deixis**, **person deixis**, **demonstrative articles**.

place of articulation The part of the vocal tract at which constriction occurs during the production of consonants. See **manner of articulation**.

plosives Oral, or non-nasal, stop consonants, so called because the air that is stopped explodes with the release of the closure.

polyglot A person who speaks several languages.

polymorphemic word A word that consists of more than one morpheme.

polysemous/polysemy Describes a single word with several closely related but slightly different meanings, e.g., *face*, meaning "face of a person," "face of a clock," "face of a building."

positron-emission tomography (PET) Method to detect changes in brain activities and relate these changes to localized brain damage and cognitive tasks.

possessor The thematic role of the noun phrase to whose referent something belongs, e.g., *the dog* in *The dog's tail wagged furiously*.

possible word A string of sounds that obeys the **phonotactic constraints** of the language but has no meaning, e.g., *gimble*. Also called a **nonsense word**.

poverty of the stimulus See **impoverished data**.

pragmatics The study of how context and situation affect meaning.

predictable feature A nondistinctive, noncontrastive, redundant phonetic feature, e.g., aspiration in English voiceless stops, or nasalization in English vowels.

prefix An **affix** that is attached to the beginning of a morpheme or stem, e.g., *in-* in *inoperable*.

preposition (P) The syntactic category, also functional category, that heads a prepositional phrase, e.g., *at, in, on, up*.

prepositional object The grammatical relation of the noun phrase that occurs immediately below a **prepositional phrase** (**PP**) in D-structure.

prepositional phrase (PP) The syntactic category, also phrasal category, consisting of a prepositional head and a noun phrase complement, e.g., *father of the bride*.

prescriptive grammar Rules of grammar brought about by grammarians' attempts to legislate what speakers' grammatical rules should be, rather than what they are. See **descriptive grammar**, **teaching grammar**.

prestige dialect The dialect usually spoken by people in positions of power, and the one deemed correct by prescriptive grammarians, e.g., RP (*received pronunciation*) (British) English, the dialect spoken by the English royal family.

presupposition Implicit assumptions about the world required to make an utterance meaningful or appropriate, e.g., "some tea has already been taken" is a presupposition of *Take some more tea!*

primes The basic formal units of sign languages that correspond to phonological elements of spoken language.

priming An experimental procedure that measures the response time from hearing to accessing a particular word as a function of whether the participant has heard a related word previously.

Principle of Compositionality A principle of semantic interpretation that states that the meaning of a word, phrase, or sentence depends both on the meaning of its components (morphemes, words, phrases) and how they are combined structurally.

productive Refers to morphological rules that can be used freely and apply to all forms to create new words, e.g., the addition to an adjective of *-ish* meaning "having somewhat of the quality," such as *newish, tallish, incredible-ish*.

pro-form A word that replaces another word or expression found elsewhere in discourse, or understood from the situational context. Pronouns are the best known pro-forms, but words like *did* may function as "pro-verb phrases" as in *John washed three sheepdogs and Mary did too*.

proper name A word or words that refer to a person, place, or other entity with a unique reference known to the speaker and listener. Usually capitalized in writing, e.g., Nina Hyams, New York, Atlantic Ocean.

prosodic feature The duration (**length**), **pitch**, or loudness of speech sounds.

Proto-Germanic The name given by linguists to the language that was an ancestor of English, German, and other Germanic languages.

Proto-Indo-European (PIE) See **Indo-European**.

protolanguage The first identifiable language from which genetically related languages developed.

psycholinguistics The branch of linguistics concerned with **linguistic performance**, language acquisition, and speech production and comprehension.

radical language death The disappearance of a language when all speakers of the language cease to speak the language. See **sudden language death**, **gradual language death**, **bottom-to-top language death**.

rebus principle In writing, the use of a **pictogram** for its phonetic value, e.g., using a picture of a bee to represent the verb *be* or the sound [b].

recursive rule A **phrase structure rule** that repeats its own category on its right side, e.g., VP → VP PP, hence permitting phrase structures of potentially unlimited length, corresponding to speakers' **linguistic competence**.

reduced vowel A vowel that is unstressed and generally pronounced as schwa [ə] in English.

redundant Describes a nondistinctive, nonphonemic feature that is predictable from other feature values of the segment, e.g., [+ voice] is redundant for any [+ nasal] phoneme in English because all nasals are voiced.

reduplication A morphological process that repeats or copies all or part of a word to produce a new word, e.g., *wishy-washy*, *teensy-weensy*, *hurly-burly*.

reference That part of the meaning of a noun phrase that associates it with some entity. That part of the meaning of a declarative sentence that associates it with a **truth value**, either true or false. Also called **extension**. See **referent**, **sense**.

referent The entity designated by an expression, e.g., the referent of *John* in *John knows Sue* is the actual person named John; the referent of *Raleigh is the capital of California* is the truth value *false*. Also called **extension**.

reflexive pronoun A pronoun ending with -*self* that generally requires a noun-phrase antecedent within the same S, e.g., *myself*, *herself*, *ourselves*, *itself*.

regional dialect A dialect spoken in a specific geographic area that may arise from, and is reinforced by, that area's integrity. For example, a Boston dialect is maintained because large numbers of Bostonians and their descendants remain in the Boston area. See **social dialect**.

register A stylistic variant of a language appropriate to a particular social setting. Also called **style**.

register tones Level tones; high, mid, or low tones.

regular sound correspondence The occurrence of different sounds in the same position of the same word in different languages or dialects, with this parallel holding for a significant number of words, e.g., [aj] in non-Southern American English corresponds to [aː] in Southern American English. Also found between newer and older forms of the same language.

relational opposites A pair of **antonyms** in which one describes a relationship between two objects and the other describes the same relationship when the two objects are reversed, e.g., *parent/child*, *teacher/pupil*; John is the parent of Susie describes the same relationship as Susie is the child of John. See **gradable pair**, **complementary pair**.

retroflex sound A sound produced by curling the tip of the tongue back behind the alveolar ridge, e.g., the pronunciation of /r/ by many speakers of English.

retronym An expression that would once have been redundant, but which societal or technological changes have made nonredundant, e.g., *silent movie*, which was redundant before the advent of the "talkies."

rime The **nucleus + coda** of a syllable, e.g., the /en/ of /ren/ *rain*.

root The morpheme that remains when all affixes are stripped from a complex word, e.g., *system* from *un + system + atic + ally*.

rounded vowel A vowel sound produced with pursed lips, e.g., [o].

rules of syntax Principles of grammar that account for the grammaticality of sentences, their hierarchical structure, their word order, whether there is structural ambiguity, etc. See **phrase structure rules**, **transformational rules**.

SAE See **Standard American English**.

Sapir-Whorf hypothesis The proposition that the structure of a language influences how its speakers perceive the world around them. It is often presented in its weak form, **linguistic relativism**, and its strong form, **linguistic determinism**.

savant An individual who shows special abilities in one cognitive area while being deficient in others. Linguistic savants have extraordinary language abilities but are deficient in general intelligence.

second language acquisition The acquisition of another language or languages after first language acquisition is under way or completed. Also **L2 acquisition**.

segment (1) An individual sound that occurs in a language; (2) the act of dividing utterances into sounds, morphemes, words, and phrases.

semantic features Conceptual elements by which a person understands the meanings of words and sentences, e.g., "female" is a semantic feature of the nouns *girl* and *filly*; "cause" is a semantic feature of the verbs *darken* and *kill*.

semantic network A network of **arcs** and **nodes** used to represent semantic information about sentences.

semantic priming The effect of being able to recognize a word (e.g., *doctor*) more rapidly after exposure to a semantically similar word (e.g., *nurse*) than after exposure to a semantically more distant word. The word *nurse* primes the word *doctor*.

semantic properties See **semantic features**.

semantic rules Principles for determining the meaning of larger units like sentences from the meaning of smaller units like noun phrases and verb phrases.

semantics The study of the linguistic meaning of morphemes, words, phrases, and sentences.

sense The inherent part of an expression's meaning that, together with context, determines its referent. Also called **intension**. For example, knowing the sense or intension of a noun phrase such as *the president of the United States in 2006* allows one to determine that George W. Bush is the referent. See **intension**, **reference**.

sentence (S) A syntactic category of expressions consisting minimally of a **noun phrase (NP)** followed by a **verb phrase (VP)** in D-structure. Also called a **TP (tense phrase)**. The head of S is the category **Aux**.

sentential semantics The subfield of semantics concerned with the meaning of syntactic units larger than the word.

separate systems hypothesis The bilingual child builds a distinct lexicon and grammar for each language being acquired.

shadowing task An experiment in which subjects are asked to repeat what they hear as rapidly as possible as it is being spoken. During the task, subjects often unconsciously correct "errors" in the input.

sibilants The class of sounds that includes affricates, and alveolar and palatal fricatives, characterized acoustically by an abundance of high frequencies perceived as "hissing," e.g., [s].

sign A single gesture (possibly with complex meaning) in the sign languages used by the deaf.

sign languages The languages used by deaf people in which linguistic units such as morphemes and words as well as grammatical relations are formed by manual and other body movements.

sisters In a phrase structure tree, two categories that are directly under the same node, e.g., V and the direct object NP are sisters inside the verb phrase.

situational context Knowledge of who is speaking, who is listening, what objects are being discussed, and general facts about the world we live in, used to aid in the interpretation of meaning.

slang Words and phrases used in casual speech, often invented and spread by close-knit social or age groups, and fast-changing.

slip of the tongue An involuntary deviation of an intended utterance. See **spooner-ism**. Also called **speech error**.

sluicing The syntactic process in which material following a *wh* word is deleted when it is identical to previous material, e.g., *John is talking with* is deleted from the second clause in *John is talking with someone but nobody knows who* _____.

social dialect A dialect spoken by members of a group delineated by socioeconomic class, racial background, place of origin, or gender, and perpetuated by the integrity of the social class. See **regional dialects**.

sociolinguistic variable A linguistic phenomenon such as double negation whose occurrence varies according to the social context of the speaker.

sonorants The class of sounds that includes vowels, glides, liquids, and nasals; nonobstruents. See **obstruents**.

sound shift Historical phonological change.

sound symbolism The notion that certain sound combinations occur in semantically similar words, e.g., *gl* in *gleam*, *glisten*, *glitter*, which all relate to vision.

sound writing A term sometimes used to mean a writing system in which one sound is represented by one letter. Sound-writing systems do not employ the phonemic principle and are similar to phonetic transcriptions.

source The thematic role of the noun phrase whose referent is the place from which an action originates, e.g., *Mars* in *Mr. Wells just arrived from Mars*.

source language In automatic machine translation, the language being translated. See **target language**, **automatic machine translation**.

specific language impairment (SLI) Difficulty in acquiring language faced by certain children with no other cognitive deficits.

specifier The category of the left sister of X' in **x-bar theory**, e.g., a **determiner** in an NP or an **adverb** in a VP. It is a modifier of the head and is often optional.

spectrogram A visual representation of speech decomposed into component frequencies, with time on the *x* axis, frequency on the *y* axis, and intensity portrayed on a gray scale—the darker, the more intense. Also called **voiceprint**.

speech act The action or intent that a speaker accomplishes when using language in context, the meaning of which is inferred by hearers, e.g., *There is a bear behind you* may be intended as a warning in certain contexts, or may in other contexts merely be a statement of fact. See **illocutionary force**.

speech error An inadvertent deviation from an intended utterance that often results in ungrammaticality, nonsense words, anomaly, etc. See **slip of the tongue**, **spoonerism**.

speech recognition In computer processing, the ability to analyze speech sounds into phones, phonemes, morphemes, and words.

speech synthesis An electronic process that produces speech either from acoustically simulated sounds or from prerecorded units. See **formant synthesis, concatenative synthesis**.

speech understanding Computer processing for interpreting speech, one part of which is **speech recognition**.

spelling pronunciation Pronouncing a word as it is spelled, irrespective of its actual pronunciation by native speakers, e.g., pronouncing *Wednesday* as "wed-ness-day."

split brain The result of an operation for epilepsy in which the **corpus callosum** is severed, thus separating the brain into its two hemispheres; split-brain patients are studied to determine the role of each hemisphere in cognitive and language processing.

spoonerism A speech error in which phonemic segments are reversed or exchanged, e.g., *you have hissed my mystery lecture* for the intended *you have missed my history lecture*; named after the Reverend William Archibald Spooner, a nineteenth-century Oxford University professor.

S-selection The classifying of verbs and other lexical items in terms of the semantic category of the head and complements that they accept, e.g., *find* S-selects for an animate subject and a concrete NP complement.

S-structure The structure that results from applying transformational rules to a D-structure. It is syntactically closest to actual utterances. Also called **surface structure**. See **transformational rule**.

standard The dialect (regional or social) considered to be the norm.

Standard American English (SAE) An idealized dialect of English that some prescriptive grammarians consider the proper form of English.

states/statives A type of sentence that describes states of being such as *Mary likes oysters*, as opposed to describing events such as *Mary ate oysters*. See **events/eventives**.

stem The base to which one or more affixes are attached to create a more complex form that may be another stem or a word. See **root, affix**.

stops [– Continuant] sounds in which the airflow is briefly but completely stopped in the oral cavity, e.g., /p, n, g/.

stress, stressed syllable A syllable with relatively greater length, loudness, and/or higher pitch than other syllables in a word, and therefore perceived as prominent. Also called **accent**.

structural ambiguity The phenomenon in which the same sequence of words has two or more meanings that is accounted for by different phrase structure analyses, e.g., *He saw a boy with a telescope*.

structure dependent (1) A principle of Universal Grammar that states that the application of **transformational rules** is determined by phrase structure properties, as opposed to structureless sequences of words or specific sentences; (2) the way children construct rules using their knowledge of syntactic structure irrespective of the specific words in the structure or their meaning.

style A situation dialect, e.g., formal speech, casual speech; also called **register**.

subcategorization See **C-selection**.

subject The grammatical relation of a noun phrase to a S(entence) when it appears immediately below that S in a phrase structure tree, e.g., *the zebra* in *The zebra has stripes*.

subject-verb agreement The addition of an inflectional morpheme to the main verb depending on a property of the noun phrase subject, such as number or gender. In English, it is the addition of *s* to a verb when the subject is third-person singular present-tense, e.g., *A greyhound runs fast* versus *Greyhounds run fast*.

sudden language death The disappearance of a language when all speakers of the language die or are killed in a short time period. See **radical language death**, **gradual language death**, **bottom-to-top language death**.

suffix An **affix** that is attached to the end of a morpheme or stem, e.g., *-er* in *Lew is taller than Bill*.

summarization The computer scanning of a text and condensation to its most salient points.

suppletive forms A term used to refer to inflected morphemes in which the regular rules do not apply, e.g., *went* as the past tense of *go*.

suprasegmentals **Prosodic features**, e.g., length, tone.

surface structure See **S-structure**.

syllabary The symbols of a syllabic writing system.

syllabic A phonetic feature of those sounds that may constitute the nucleus of syllables; all vowels are syllabic, and liquids and nasals may be syllabic in such words as *towel, button, bottom*.

syllabic writing A writing system in which each syllable in the language is represented by its own symbol, e.g., **hiragana** in Japanese.

syllable A phonological unit composed of an **onset**, **nucleus**, and **coda**, e.g., *elevator* has four syllables: *el e va tor*; *man* has one syllable.

synonyms Words with the same or nearly the same meaning, e.g., *pail* and *bucket*.

synonymy A meaning relation in which sentences have the same truth values in all situations, e.g., *the boss put off the meeting*; *the boss put the meeting off*; *the boss postponed the meeting*. See **paraphrase**.

syntactic category/class See **grammatical category**.

syntax The rules of sentence formation; the component of the mental grammar that represents speakers' knowledge of the structure of phrases and sentences.

T (Tense) A term sometimes used in place of *Aux*. The syntactic category that is the head of **TP** or *Sentence*.

taboo Words or activities that are considered inappropriate for "polite society," e.g., *cunt, prick, fuck* for vagina, penis, and sexual intercourse, respectively.

tap A speech sound in which the tongue quickly touches the alveolar ridge, as in some British pronunciations of /r/. Also called **flap**.

target language In automatic machine translation, the language into which the source language is translated. See **source language**, **automatic machine translation**.

tautology A sentence that is true in all situations; a sentence true from the meaning of its words alone; e.g., *kings are not female*. Also called **analytic**.

teaching grammar A set of language rules written to help speakers learn a foreign language or a different dialect of their language. See **descriptive grammar**, **prescriptive grammar**.

telegraphic speech Utterances of children that may omit **grammatical morphemes** and/or **function words**, e.g., *He go out* instead of *He is going out*.

telegraphic stage The period of child language acquisition that follows the two-word stage and consists primarily of **telegraphic speech**.

tense/lax Features that divide vowels into two classes. Tense vowels are generally longer in duration and higher in tongue position and pitch than the corresponding lax vowels, e.g., in English [i, e, u, o] are tense vowels and carry the feature [+ tense], whereas the corresponding [ɪ, ɛ, ʊ, ɔ] are their lax counterparts and carry the feature [– tense]. See **lax vowels**.

text-to-speech A computer program that converts written text into the basic units of a speech synthesizer, such as phones for **formant synthesizers**, or **diphones**, **disyllables**, etc. for **concatenative synthesizers**.

thematic role The semantic relationship between the verb and the noun phrases of a sentence, such as **agent, theme, location, instrument, goal, source**.

theme The thematic role of the noun phrase whose referent undergoes the action of the verb, e.g., *Martha* in *George hugged Martha*.

time deixis The use of terms to refer to time whose reference relies entirely on context, e.g., *now, then, tomorrow, next month*. See **deictic, deixis, demonstrative articles, person deixis, place deixis**.

tip of the tongue (TOT) phenomenon The difficulty encountered from time to time in retrieving a particular word or expression from the mental lexicon. Anomic aphasics suffer from an extreme form of this problem. See **anomia**.

tone The contrastive pitch of syllables in **tone languages**. Two words may be identical except for such differences in pitch, e.g., in Thai [naa] with falling pitch means "face," but with a rising pitch means "thick." See **register tones, contour tones**.

tone language A language in which the tone or pitch on a syllable is phonemic, so that words with identical segments but different tones are different words, e.g., Mandarin Chinese, Thai. See **tone**.

top-down processing Expectation-driven analysis of linguistic input that begins with the assumption that a large syntactic unit such as a sentence is present, and then analyzes it into successively smaller constituents (e.g., phrases, words, morphemes), which are ultimately compared with the sensory or acoustic data to validate the analysis. If the analysis is not validated, the procedure backs up to the previously validated point and then resumes. See **bottom-up processing, backtracking**.

topicalization A transformation that moves a syntactic element to the front of a sentence, e.g., deriving *Dogs I love very much* from *I love dogs very much*.

TP Tense Phrase. A term sometimes used in place of *Sentence*. A phrasal category whose head is **Aux**.

transcription, phonemic The phonemic representation of speech sounds using phonetic symbols, ignoring phonetic details that are predictable by rule, usually given between slashes, e.g., /pæn/, /spæn/ for *pan, span* as opposed to the phonetic representation [pʰæn], [spæn].

transcription, phonetic The representation of speech sounds using phonetic symbols between square brackets. They may reflect nondistinctive predictable features such as aspiration and nasality, e.g., [pʰat] for *pot* and [mæn] for *man*.

transfer of grammatical rules The application of rules from one's first language to a second language that one is attempting to acquire. The "accent" that second-language learners have is a result of the transfer of first language phonetic and phonological rules.

transformational rule, transformation A syntactic rule that applies to an underlying phrase structure tree of a sentence (either D-structure or an intermediate structure already affected by a transformation) and derives a new structure by moving or inserting elements, e.g., the transformational rules of *wh* movement and *do* insertion relate the deep structure sentence *John saw who* to the surface structure *Who did John see*.

transformationally induced ambiguity This occurs when different D-structures are mapped into the same S-structure by one or more transformations, e.g., the ambiguous *George loves Laura more than Dick* may be transformationally derived from the D-structures *George loves Laura more than Dick <u>loves Laura</u>*, or *George loves Laura more than <u>he loves</u> Dick*, with the underlined words being deleted under identity by a transformation in either case.

transition network A graphical representation that uses nodes connected by labeled arcs to depict syntactic and semantic relationships of grammar. See **node, arc**.

transitive verb A verb that C-selects an obligatory noun-phrase complement, e.g., *find*.

tree diagram A graphical representation of the linear and hierarchical structure of a phrase or sentence. A **phrase structure tree**.

trill A speech sound in which part of the tongue vibrates against part of the roof of the mouth, e.g., the /r/ in Spanish *perro* ("dog") is articulated by vibrating the tongue tip behind the alveolar ridge; the /r/ in French *rouge* ("red") may be articulated by vibrations at the uvula.

truth conditions The circumstances that must be known to determine whether a sentence is true, and therefore part of the meaning, or **sense**, of declarative sentences.

truth value TRUE or FALSE; used to describe the truth of declarative sentences in context. The **reference** of a declarative sentence in **truth-conditional semantics**.

truth-conditional semantics A theory of meaning that takes the semantic knowledge of knowing when sentences are true and false as basic.

unaspirated Phonetically voiceless stops in which the vocal cords begin vibrating immediately upon release of the closure, e.g., [p] in *spot*. See **aspirated**.

unbound A pronoun or pro-form whose reference is determined from context rather than linguistic discourse. See **free pronoun, bound pronoun**.

unconditioned sound change Historical phonological change that occurs in all phonetic contexts, e.g., the **Great Vowel Shift** of English in which long vowels were modified wherever they occurred in a word.

ungrammatical Describes structures that fail to conform to the rules of grammar.

uninterpretable Describes an utterance whose meaning cannot be determined because of nonsense words, e.g., *All mimsy were the borogoves*.

unitary system hypothesis A bilingual child initially constructs only one lexicon and one grammar for both (or all) languages being acquired.

Universal Grammar (UG) The innate principles and properties that pertain to the grammars of all human languages.

unmarked The term used to refer to that member of a gradable pair of antonyms used in questions of degree, e.g., *high* is the unmarked member of high/low; in a masculine/feminine pair, the word that does not contain a derivational morpheme, usually the masculine word, e.g., *prince* is unmarked, whereas *princess* is marked. See **marked**.

uvula The fleshy appendage hanging down from the end of the **velum**, or soft palate.

uvular A sound produced by raising the back of the tongue to the **uvula**.

velar A sound produced by raising the back of the tongue to the soft palate, or **velum**.

velum The soft palate; the part of the roof of the mouth behind the hard palate.

verb (V) The syntactic category, also lexical category, of words that can be the head of a verb phrase. Verbs denote actions, sensations, and states, e.g., *climb, hear, understand.*

verb phrase (VP) The syntactic category of expressions that contains a verb as its head along with its complements such as noun phrases and prepositional phrases, e.g., *gave the book to the child.*

verbal particle A word identical in form to a preposition which, when paired with a verb, has a particular meaning. A particle, as opposed to a preposition, is characterized syntactically by its ability to occur next to the verb, or transposed to the right, e.g., *out,* in *spit out* as in *he spit out his words,* or *he spit his words out.* Compare with: *He ran out the door* versus **he ran the door out,* where *out* is a preposition.

Verner's Law The description of a conditioned phonological change in the sound system of certain Indo-European languages wherein voiceless fricatives were changed when the preceding vowel was unstressed. It was formulated by Karl Verner as an explanation to some of the exceptions to Grimm's Law. See **Grimm's Law**.

vocal tract The oral and nasal cavities, together with the vocal cords, glottis, and pharynx, all of which may be involved in the production of speech sounds.

vocalic The phonetic feature that distinguishes vowels and liquids, which are [+ vocalic], from other sounds (obstruents, glides, nasals), which are [– vocalic].

voiced sound A speech sound produced with vibrating vocal cords.

voiceless sound A speech sound produced with open, nonvibrating vocal cords.

voiceprint A common term for a **spectrogram**.

vowel A sound produced without significant constriction of the air flowing through the **oral cavity**.

well-formed Describes a grammatical sequence of words, one conforming to rules of syntax. See **grammatical**, **ill-formed**.

Wernicke, Carl Neurologist who showed that damage to specific parts of the left cerebral hemisphere causes specific types of language disorders.

Wernicke's aphasia The type of aphasia resulting from damage to Wernicke's area.

Wernicke's area The back (posterior) part of the left brain that if damaged causes a specific type of aphasia. Also called Wernicke's region.

wh questions Interrogative sentences beginning with one or more of the words *who(m), what, where, when,* and *how,* and their equivalents in languages that do not have *wh* words, e.g., *Who do you like?*

word writing A system of writing in which each character represents a word or morpheme of the language, e.g., Chinese. See **ideographic**, **logographic**.

x-bar theory A universal schema specifying that the internal organization of all phrasal categories (i.e., NP, PP, VP, TP(=S), AdjP, AdvP) can be broken down into three levels, e.g., NP, N', and N.

yes-no question An interrogative sentence that inquires as to whether a certain situation holds (is true), e.g., *Is the boy asleep?*

Index